Lecture Notes in Computer Science

Lecture Notes in Artificial Intelligence   13926

Founding Editor

Jörg Siekmann

Series Editors

Randy Goebel, *University of Alberta, Edmonton, Canada*
Wolfgang Wahlster, *DFKI, Berlin, Germany*
Zhi-Hua Zhou, *Nanjing University, Nanjing, China*

The series Lecture Notes in Artificial Intelligence (LNAI) was established in 1988 as a topical subseries of LNCS devoted to artificial intelligence.

The series publishes state-of-the-art research results at a high level. As with the LNCS mother series, the mission of the series is to serve the international R & D community by providing an invaluable service, mainly focused on the publication of conference and workshop proceedings and postproceedings.

Hamido Fujita · Yinglin Wang · Yanghua Xiao · Ali Moonis

Editors

Advances and Trends in Artificial Intelligence

Theory and Applications

36th International Conference
on Industrial, Engineering and Other Applications
of Applied Intelligent Systems, IEA/AIE 2023
Shanghai, China, July 19–22, 2023
Proceedings, Part II

Springer

Editors
Hamido Fujita (iD)
Universiti Teknologi Malaysia
Kuala Lumpur, Malaysia

Yanghua Xiao
Fudan University
Shanghai, China

Yinglin Wang
Shanghai University of Finance
and Economics
Shanghai, China

Ali Moonis
Texas State University
San Marcos, TX, USA

ISSN 0302-9743   ISSN 1611-3349 (electronic)
Lecture Notes in Artificial Intelligence
ISBN 978-3-031-36821-9   ISBN 978-3-031-36822-6 (eBook)
https://doi.org/10.1007/978-3-031-36822-6

LNCS Sublibrary: SL7 – Artificial Intelligence

This Springer imprint is published by the registered company Springer Nature Switzerland AG
The registered company address is: Gewerbestrasse 11, 6330 Cham, Switzerland

Preface

In the last few years, significant progress has been made in computing infrastructures, deep learning, and big foundation models, catalyzing the rapid advancement of artificial intelligence. Computing infrastructures have witnessed remarkable improvements, with the popularity of cloud computing and graphical processing units providing researchers and practitioners with immense computational resources to train and deploy complex AI models. Deep learning enables machines to automatically learn intricate patterns and representations from vast amounts of data. Additionally, big foundation models, such as transformer architectures, have emerged as building blocks for natural language processing and computer vision, empowering AI systems with enhanced understanding and decision-making capabilities. These developments have accelerated the development of more effective intelligent systems to solve real-world complex problems. Moreover, innovative applications of artificial intelligence are continually emerging.

This volume contains the proceedings of the 36th edition of the International Conference on Industrial, Engineering, and other Applications of Applied Intelligent Systems (IEA/AIE 2023), which was held on July 19–22, 2023, in Shanghai, China. IEA/AIE is a yearly conference that focuses on applications of applied intelligent systems to solve real-life problems in all areas including business and finance, science, engineering, industry, cyberspace, bioinformatics, automation, robotics, medicine and biomedicine, and human-machine interactions. IEA/AIE 2023 was organized in cooperation with the ACM Special Interest Group on Artificial Intelligence (SIGAI). This year, 129 submissions were received. Each paper was evaluated using double- blind peer review by at least three reviewers from an international Program Committee consisting of 174 members from 25 countries. Based on the evaluation, a total of 50 papers were selected as full papers and 20 as short papers, which are presented in the two volumes of this book. The acceptance rate was 54%. We would like to thank all the reviewers for the time spent on writing detailed and constructive comments for the authors, and to the latter for the proposal of many high-quality papers.

In the program of IEA/AIE 2023, four special sessions were organized: Collective Intelligence in Social Media (CISM 2023), Intelligent Knowledge Engineering in Decision Making Systems (IKEDMS 2023), Intelligent Systems and e-Applications (iSeA 2023) and Causal Inference and Machine Learning (CIML 2023). In addition, two keynote talks were given by two distinguished researchers, one by Michael Sheng from Macquarie University (Australia) and the other by Cewu Lu from Shanghai Jiaotong University (China). We would like to thank everyone who has contributed to the success of this year's edition of IEA/AIE, that is the authors, reviewers, keynote speakers, Program Committee members and organizers. We would like thank all the sponsors and institutions that have provided strong support for the conference, including Association for the Advancement of Artificial Intelligence (AAAI), Association for Computing Machinery (ACM), Shanghai Computer Society, i-SOMET Incorporated Association, Springer and the Conference Management Toolkit. We are particularly grateful to the organizers of this year's event, including Shanghai University of Finance and Economics, Fudan University and Shanghai Business School. Their support was crucial for the success of this year's conference.

May 2023   Hamido Fujita
                                                  Yinglin Wang
                                                  Yanghua Xiao
                                                  Ali Moonis

Organization

Honorary Chair

Tao Wu   Shanghai University of Medicine and Health Sciences, China

General Chairs

Hamido Fujita   Universiti Teknologi Malaysia, Kuala Lumpur, Malaysia

Ali Moonis   Texas State University, USA

Program Committee Chairs

Yinglin Wang   Shanghai University of Finance and Economics, China

Yanghua Xiao   Fudan University, China

Organizing Chairs

Jun Sasaki   i-SOMET Inc., Japan

Duoqian Miao   Tongji University, China

Liang Zhou   Shanghai University of Medicine and Health Sciences, China

Xing Wu   Shanghai University, China

Bo Huang   Shanghai University of Engineering Science, China

Special Session Chairs

Ali Selamat   Universiti Teknologi Malaysia, Malaysia

Ngoc Thanh Nguyen   Wroclaw University of Technology, Poland

Xiaodong Yue   Shanghai University, China

| Xin Xu | Wuhan University of Science and Technology, China |
| Yufei Chen | Tongji University, China |

Program Committee

Alban Grastien	Australian National University, Australia
Alberto Cano	Virginia Commonwealth University, USA
Andreas Speck	Kiel University, Germany
Andrew Tzer-Yeu Chen	University of Auckland, New Zealand
Arkadiusz Liber	Wroclaw University of Science and Technology, Poland
Ayahiko Niimi	Future University Hakodate, Japan
Azri Azmi	Universiti Teknologi Malaysia, Malaysia
Bilel Marzouki	National School of Computer Science, Tunisia
Bin Zhou	National University of Defense Technology, China
Bing Liu	Harbin Institute of Technology, China
Binh Nguyen	University of Science, VNUHCM, Vietnam
Bo Huang	Shanghai University of Engineering Science, China
Bo Xu	Donghua University, China
Chao Shi	Shanghai University of Finance and Economics, China
Chao Tong	Beihang University, China
Chen Chen	Huawei HK, China
Chenkai Guo	Nankai University, China
Chenxu Wang	Xi'an Jiaotong University, China
Claudio Tomazzoli	University of Verona, Italy
Danyang Chen	Guangxi University, China
Dongbo Li	Harbin Institute of Technology, China
Dongdong Zhao	Lanzhou University, China
Dosam Hwang	Yeungnam University, South Korea
Du Nguyen	Nong Lam University, Vietnam
Duc Nguyen	Vietnam Maritime University, Vietnam
Dung Hoang	HCMC University of Technology and Education, Vietnam
Erlei Zhang	Northwest A&F University, China
Erping Zhao	Xizang Minzu University, China
Fan Liu	Hohai University, China
Fei Wang	Xi'an Jiaotong University, China

Francisco Javier Cabrerizo	University of Granada, Spain
Frederick Maier	University of Georgia, USA
Gang Pan	Tianjin University, China
Gautram Srivastava	Brandon University, Canada
Guanghui Zhu	Nanjing University, China
Guoqing Chao	Harbin Institue of Technology at Weihai, China
Hafiza Ayesha Hoor Chaudhry	University of Turin, Italy
Hai Tran	Ho Chi Minh City University of Pedagogy, Vietnam
Han Ding	Xi'an Jiaotong University, China
Hao Sun	Central China Normal University, China
Hao Zhang	Harbin Institute of Technology, China
Haopeng Chen	Shanghai Jiao Tong University, China
Hau Pham	Quang Binh University, Vietnam
Heeryon Cho	Chung-Ang University, South Korea
Hien Nguyen	University of Information Technology, VNU-HCM, Vietnam
Hongming Cai	Shanghai Jiao Tong University, China
Hongping Gan	Northwestern Polytechnical University, China
Hongwei Feng	Fudan University, China
Hua Huang	Guizhou University, China
Huafeng Li	Kunming University of Science and Technology, China
Huiyan Wang	Nanjing University, China
Iman Dehzangi	Rutgers University, USA
Jerry Chun-Wei Lin	Western Norway University of Applied Sciences, Norway
Jia Wei	South China University of Technology, China
Jianming Zhang	Changsha University of Science and Technology, China
Jianqiang Huang	Qinghai University, China
Jiapeng Xiu	Beijing University of Posts and Telecommunications, China
Jiaqing Liang	Fudan University, China
Jing Huo	Nanjing University, China
Jingping Liu	East China University of Science and Technology, China
Jinsong Bao	Donghua University, China
Jixiang Guo	Sichuan University, China
Jukka Ruohonen	University of Turku, Finland
Jun Zhou	East China Normal University, China
Junwei Zhou	Wuhan University of Technology, China
Jyrki Nummenmaa	Tampere University, Finland

Kejia Chen	Nanjing University of Posts and Telecommunications, China
Krishna Reddy P.	International Institute of Information Technology, Hyderabad, India
Lei Huang	Ocean University of China, China
Liang Hu	Tongji University, China
Liang Li	Tianjin University, China
Liang Tao	Hong Kong Metropolitan University, China
Liang Wang	Nanjing University, China
Liangyu Chen	East China Normal University, China
Li-Fang Zhou	Chongqing University of Posts and Telecommunications, China
Liming Zhang	University of Macau, China
Lingyan Ran	Northwestern Polytechnical University, China
Lingyun Song	Northwestern Polytechnical University, China
Lizong Zhang	University of Electronic Science and Technology of China, China
M. Saqib Nawaz	Shenzhen University, China
Marcin Pietranik	Wroclaw University of Science and Technology, Poland
Masaki Kurematsu	Iwate Prefectural University, Japan
Ming Dong	Central China Normal University, China
Mingxi Zhang	University of Shanghai for Science and Technology, China
Min-Ling Zhang	Southeast University, China
Miroslav Hudec	University of Economics in Bratislava, Slovakia
Miroslav Velev	Aries Design Automation, LLC, USA
Mohammad Rashedur Rahman	North South University, Bangladesh
Moulay A. Akhloufi	Université de Moncton, Canada
Mourad Nouioua	Mohamed El Bachir El Ibrahimi University of Bordj Bou Arréridj, Algeria
Nannan Wu	Tianjin University, China
Ngoc-Thanh Nguyen	Wroclaw University of Technology, Poland
Ning Xu	Southeast University, China
Nurulhuda Zainuddin	Universiti Teknologi Malaysia, Malaysia
Pengpeng Zhao	Soochow University, China
Phi Le Nguyen	Hanoi University of Science and Technology, Vietnam
Pingpeng Yuan	Huazhong University of Science & Technology, China
Qian Huang	Hohai University, China
Qian Jiang	Yunnan University, China
Qidong Liu	Zhengzhou University, China

Qingsong Guo	University of Helsinki, Finland
Qiuzhen Lin	Shenzhen University, China
Qiyang Zhao	Beihang University, China
Senyue Zhang	Shenyang Aerospace University, China
Sergei Gorlatch	Münster University, Germany
Shangce Gao	University of Toyama, Japan
Sheng Fang	Shandong University of Science and Technology, China
Shengdong Du	Southwest Jiaotong University, China
Stefania Tomasiello	University of Tartu, Estonia
Tai Dinh	Kyoto College of Graduate Studies for Informatics, Japan
Takeru Yokoi	Tokyo Metropolitan College of Industrial Technology, Japan
Tao Lian	Taiyuan University of Technology, China
Tao Shen	Kunming University of Science and Technology, China
Tao Wang	Northwestern Polytechnical University, China
Tat-Bao-Thien Nguyen	Thuyloi University, Vietnam
Tauheed Khan Mohd	Augustana College, USA
Teeradaj Racharak	Japan Advanced Institute of Science and Technology, Japan
Thi Huyen Trang Phan	Yeungnam University, South Korea
Thomas Lacombe	University of Auckland, New Zealand
Tianxing Wu	Southeast University, China
Tieyun Qian	Wuhan University, China
Ting Liu	Northwestern Polytechnical University, China
Tong Liu	Shandong University of Science and Technology, China
Uday Rage	University of Aizu, Japan
Wai Khuen Cheng	Universiti Tunku Abdul Rahman, Malaysia
Wang Yunlan	Northwestern Polytechnical University, China
Wanyuan Wang	Southeast Univerity, China
Wanyun Cui	Shanghai University of Finance and Economics, China
Wei Ke	Xi'an Jiaotong University, China
Wei Wang	Wuhan University of Science and Technology, China
Wei Zhang	Harbin Institute of Technology, China
Weiguo Zheng	Fudan University, China
Weihao Zheng	Lanzhou University, China
Weixin Jiang	Northwestern University, USA
Wu Yirui	Hohai University, China

Xiao Wang	Shanghai University of Finance and Economics, China
Xiaofang Xia	Xidian University, China
Xiaofeng Ding	Huazhong University of Science and Technology, China
Xiaojun Zhou	Central South University, China
Xiaolin Han	Northwestern Polytechnical University, China
Xiaoxia Zhang	Chongqing University of Posts and Telecommunications, China
Xiaoyan Jiang	Shanghai University of Engineering Science, China
Xiaozhi Du	Xi'an Jiaotong University, China
Xin Jin	Yunnan University, China
Xin Xu	Wuhan University of Science and Technology, China
Xing Wu	Shanghai University, China
Xingpeng Zhang	Southwest Petroleum University, China
Xinshan Zhu	Tianjin University, China
Xizi Chen	Huazhong Agricultural University, China
Xue Rui	China Academy of Railway Sciences, China
Yang Li	East China Normal University, China
Yang Zou	Hohai University, China
Yanyan Xu	Shanghai Jiao Tong University, China
Yasser Mohammed	Assiut University, Egypt
Yong Wang	Ocean University of China, China
Yonghong Song	Xi'an Jiaotong University, China
Youcef Djenouri	University of Southern Denmark, Denmark
Youshan Zhang	Yeshiva University, USA
Yu Liu	Huazhong University of Science and Technology, China
Yufei Chen	Tongji University, China
Yu-Jie Xiong	Shanghai University of Engineering Science, China
Yun Chen	Shanghai University of Finance and Economics, China
Yun Liu	Southwest University, China
Yunhai Wang	Shandong University, China
Yupeng Hu	Hunan University, China
Yutaka Watanobe	University of Aizu, Japan
Yuwei Peng	Wuhan University, China
Zaki Brahmi	University of Sousse, Tunisia
Zalán Bodó	Babeş-Bolyai University, Romania

Keynote Speech

Smart IoT Sensing for Aging Well: Research Activities and Future Directions

Michael Sheng

School of Computing, Faculty of Science and Engineering, Macquarie University, Sydney, Australia
michael.sheng@mq.edu.au

Abstract. Worldwide, the population is aging due to increasing life expectancy and decreasing fertility. The significant growth in older population presents many challenges to health and aged care services. Over the past two decades, the Internet of Things (IoT) has gained significant momentum and is widely regarded as an important technology to change the world in the coming decade. Indeed, IoT will play a critical role to improve productivity, operational effectiveness, decision making, and to identify new business service models for social and economic opportunities. Indeed, with the development of low-cost, unobtrusive IoT sensors, along with data analytics and artificial intelligence (AI) technologies, there is now a significant opportunity to improve the wellbeing and quality of life particularly of our older population. In this talk, we will overview some related research projects and also discuss several research directions.

Biography: Michael Sheng is a full Professor and Head of School of Computing at Macquarie University, Sydney, Australia. Before moving to Macquarie University, he spent 10 years at School of Computer Science, the University of Adelaide. Michael Sheng's research interests include the Internet of Things (IoT), service computing, big data analytics, machine learning, and Web technologies. He is ranked by Microsoft Academic as one of the Most Impactful Authors in Services Computing (ranked Top 5 All Time) and in Web of Things (ranked Top 20 All Time). Michael Sheng is the recipient of AMiner Most Influential Scholar in IoT (2018), ARC (Australian Research Council) Future Fellowship (2014), Chris Wallace Award for Outstanding Research Contribution (2012), and Microsoft Research Fellowship (2003). He is the Vice Chair of the Executive Committee of the IEEE Technical Community on Services Computing

(IEEE TCSVC), the Associate Director of Macquarie University Smart Green Cities Research Center, and a member of the ACS (Australian Computer Society) Technical Advisory Board on IoT.

Behavior Understanding and Embodied Intelligence

Cewu Lu

Department of Computer Science and Engineering, Shanghai Jiao Tong University,
Shanghai, China
lu-cw@cs.sjtu.edu.cn

Abstract. This talk discusses the problem of behavior understanding of intelligent agents. From the perspective of machine cognition, how to make the machine understand the behavior? We introduce the work of human behavior knowledge engine and behavior semantic unification under Poincaré space. From the perspective of neurocognition, what is the inner relationship between machine semantic understanding and brain neurocognition? We introduce how to explain the intrinsic relationship between visual behavior understanding and brain nerves, and establish a stable mapping model. From the perspective of embodied cognition, how to make the robot have the first-person behavior ability? We introduce the proposed PIE (perception-imagination-execution) scheme, in which the representative work grassNet reaches the human level for the first time in grasping unknown objects.

Biography: Cewu Lu is a professor of Shanghai Jiao Tong University. In 2016, he was selected under the National "1000 Youth Talents Plan". In 2018, he was selected as one of 35 Innovators Under 35 (MIT TR35) by MIT Technology Review. In 2019, he was awarded Qiu Shi Outstanding Young Scholar. In 2020, he was awarded the Special Prize of Shanghai Science and Technology Progress Award (ranked third). In 2021, he won the title of Highly Cited Scholar in China. In 2022, he was awarded one of the best papers in IROS (6/3579). he, as the corresponding author or the first author, has published 100 papers in high-level journals and conferences. He has served as reviewer for Science main issue, Nature sub-journal, Cell sub-journal and other journals, area chair of NeurIPS, CVPR, ICCV, ECCV, IROS, ICRA. His research interests fall mainly in Computer Vision and Robot Learning.

Contents – Part II

Optimization

Prediction

Reinforcement Learning

Security

Various Applications

Contents – Part I

Information Fusion

Knowledge Graph and Link Prediction

Machine Learning Theory

Pattern Recognition

Industrial Applications

LIME: Long-Term Forecasting Model for Desalination Membrane Fouling to Estimate the Remaining Useful Life of Membrane

Sohaila Eltanbouly[1]([⊠]), Abdelkarim Erradi[1], Ashraf Tantawy[2],
Ahmed Ben Said[1], Khaled Shaban[1], and Hazim Qiblawey[3]

[1] Computer Science and Engineering Department, College of Engineering,
Qatar University, Doha, Qatar
{se1403101,erradi,abensaid,khaled.shaban}@qu.edu.qa
[2] School of Computer Science and Informatics, De Montfort University, Leicester, UK
ashraf.tantavy@dmu.ac.uk
[3] Chemical Engineering Department, College of Engineering, Qatar University,
Doha, Qatar
hazim@qu.edu.qa

Abstract. Membrane fouling is one of the major problems in desalination processes as it can cause a severe drop in the quality and quantity of the permeate water. This paper presents a data-driven approach for long-term forecasting of fouling behavior in membrane-based desalination processes. The proposed **Long-term forecastIng ModEl** (LIME) consists of two intertwined machine learning models trained separately by historical operating conditions of ultrafiltration for pretreatment of reverse osmosis seawater where transmembrane pressure is used as a fouling indicator. The first model predicts the increase in fouling due to filtration. This output is fed to the second model to predict the fouling reduction due to membrane cleaning. In turn, this output is used as the initial fouling condition for predicting the next filtration cycle. The forecasted fouling is used to estimate the membrane's remaining useful life (RUL), which ends when cleaning no longer reduces the fouling below a safety threshold. Evaluation results show that the model can predict the membrane fouling for 1400 cycles with an R-squared score of 0.8. Moreover, the RUL is estimated for various thresholds with an average percentage error of 7%.

Keywords: Membrane fouling · Desalination · Machine Learning

1 Introduction

With the scarcity of natural potable water and the steady increase in world population, there has been a growing demand for the development of water purification technologies to fulfill the global need for high-quality drinking water.

© The Author(s), under exclusive license to Springer Nature Switzerland AG 2023
H. Fujita et al. (Eds.): IEA/AIE 2023, LNAI 13926, pp. 3–14, 2023.
https://doi.org/10.1007/978-3-031-36822-6_1

In this regard, tremendous improvements have occurred in desalination methods, especially in membrane-based desalination processes that account for 65% of the water treatment industry in the world [8]. One of the major problems in membrane-based desalination processes is membrane fouling because it can degrade the performance of the process in terms of the permeate water quality. Membrane fouling refers to the accumulation of contaminants on the membrane pores or surface that restricts the water flow.

Several mathematical models have been proposed in the literature for fouling in different membrane processes [14, 16]. These models provide an understanding of the membrane fouling phenomenon during operation and help optimize and control the processes. However, mathematical models require extensive knowledge about the underlying processes. Data-driven approaches based on recently advanced Artificial Intelligence (AI) and Machine Learning (ML) techniques have been used to identify, predict and optimize membrane fouling propensity. The main advantages of such techniques are their generalization ability and high accuracy. Several studies have been conducted to quantify the membrane condition within a short time period. For example, in [12], several ANN models are built with different combinations of features to determine the most relevant features for the transmembrane pressure (TMP) prediction. Oishi, et al. [11] predicted the TMP for effective scheduling of chemical cleaning using the partial least square regression. In [4], the multilayer perceptron (MLP) and M5P tree models were trained to predict the relative feed pressure and the relative differential pressure for a full-scale Reverse Osmosis (RO) plant. In [3], the particle swarm optimization (PSO) algorithm was used to improve the performance of a wavelet neural network (WNN) for the prediction of membrane flux in membrane bioreactors. Zhou, et al. [17] proposed A data-driven model using several Neural Networks models with the Alopex-based evolutionary algorithm and AdaBoost ensemble learning for fouling prediction in an ultrafiltration (UF) process.

The short-term prediction of membrane fouling helps in the decision-making of membrane cleaning routines such as backwash and CIP. However, the gradual buildup of foulants can reach a critical level causing severe degradation of the permeate quality [6]. At the stage when the cleaning procedure cannot restore the membrane to an acceptable condition, membrane replacement has to take place. The remaining useful life (RUL) estimation for the membranes is important to determine the optimal times to clean or replace them. RUL estimation refers to the estimation of the time to failure [15] and is concerned with prognostic maintenance and health state monitoring of components of industrial processes.

Different techniques have been adopted for fouling prediction for membrane-based desalination processes. However, most of the work focused on fouling prediction for the immediate future or a short forecasting period. Membrane fouling depends on various factors that change over time and the age of the membrane. Thus, long-term fouling prediction and RUL estimation are needed for planning and scheduling the backwash, chemical cleaning, and replacement. In turn, this will ensure that the quality of the produced water does not deteriorate and that the water demand is satisfied. This paper aims to develop a data-driven framework to predict long-term fouling behavior based on the operating conditions and the operating history of the membrane. The proposed framework consists of two ML models for predicting the increasing curve of TMP as a fouling indicator during filtration and the TMP plummet point due to regular cleaning, e.g., backwash. The novelty of the work is that the proposed models can be used recursively to predict the membrane's long-term behavior while being able to adjust the process operating variables. The full-time horizon prediction helps in determining the RUL of the membrane to decide the optimal time for membrane replacement. The contribution of this paper can be summarized as follow:

1. Feature engineering for extracting new features from the process variables that summarize the operating history of the membrane.
2. A Long-term forecastIng ModEl (LIME) composed of two intertwined ML models to predict the increasing curve of the TMP during filtration and the TMP plummet point after membrane cleaning.
3. Estimation of membrane Remaining Useful Life using different thresholds.

The rest of the paper is organized as follows: A detailed description of our proposed approach is provided in Sect. 2. Section 3 presents the experimental setup, evaluation, and analysis of results. Finally, Sect. 4 concludes the paper.

2   Methodology

The membrane-based desalination processes operate under two operation cycles, filtration and cleaning. In the filtration cycle, the plant is operated to produce the required permeate flux. After that, the cleaning cycle is triggered using either a preset periodic interval or a threshold for a fouling indicator, such as an upper limit for TMP or a lower limit for permeate flux [13]. The maintenance or replacement of the membrane should occur when the cleaning fails to restore the membrane to an acceptable condition. Figure 1 shows the dynamic process of the two operating cycles with an upper limit threshold of a fouling indicator.

Fig. 1. The high-level operation dynamics of desalination plants

In this study, a data-driven framework is developed to estimate the RUL of membranes in desalination to aid in the decision-making of membrane maintenance and replacement. In the first step, feature engineering techniques are used to summarize the history of the membrane operation. These techniques extract temporal and statistical features from the TMP time series. Then, the Random Forest (RF) algorithm is used to select the most relevant features for prediction, including the engineered features and the plant's operating conditions, such as flow rates and pressure. After that, the selected features are used to train two ML models for long-term fouling prediction. The fouling is measured using TMP, which is a fouling indicator for constant-flux processes. The first model predicts the increasing curve of the TMP during the filtration cycle. This model predicts the TMP one time step ahead at each step, taking the previous TMP value as input. To enable long-term prediction and RUL estimation, an autoregressive model is used to iteratively feed the output of the prediction model back to itself until the end of the filtration duration. Then, the second model predicts the TMP decrease after backwash, which also represents the initial TMP value for the next filtration cycle. This model takes as input the last TMP value from the previous filtration cycle. In the last step, the two models are connected to build a **L**ong-term forecast**I**ng **M**od**E**l (LIME). LIME takes as input the state of the membrane at any point in time and runs recursively to forecast the fouling of the membrane over its RUL. Figure 2 illustrates the workflow of LIME.

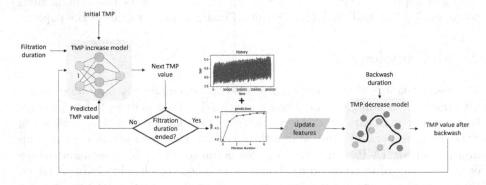

Fig. 2. The Long-Term Fouling Prediction Model Architecture

2.1   Feature Engineering and Selection

To estimate the RUL of the membrane, the prediction models have to get insights from the entire operating history of the membrane to capture the membrane degradation behavior. However, supplying the time series as input to the prediction model will introduce computational overhead since the input will have a variable length. Feature engineering has the advantages of increasing the predictive power and reducing the complexity of the model. In this work, the engineered features summarize the operating history of the membrane into a set of features that describe the current state of the membrane. The engineered features are extracted using time-series feature extraction techniques.

To illustrate the feature engineering process, assuming $Y = \{y_0, y_1, \ldots, y_L\}$ is the TMP time-series of length L. Y is divided into n cycles, where each cycle c_i

constitutes a filtration cycle c_{f_i} followed by a backwash cycle c_{b_i}. An expanding window starting from $t = 0$ to $t = t_{f_i}$ is considered for extracting the features, where t_{f_i} represents the ending time of the c_{f_i} filtration cycle. Equations 1 and 2 show how any engineered feature P is extracted for the c_{f_i} and c_{b_i}.

$$P(c_{f_i}) = f(y_0, y_1, \ldots, y_{t_{f_{i-1}}}) \tag{1}$$

$$P(c_{b_i}) = f(y_0, y_1, \ldots, y_{t_{f_i}}) \tag{2}$$

where f represents the function applied to extract the feature. Some examples of time-series features are standard deviation, the area under the curve, frequency, slope, and entropy. After extracting the features, the data can be represented by $D = \{d_1, d_2, \ldots, d_n\}$ where D has a tabular format such that each record d_i contains m features.

For feature selection, the RF ML algorithm is utilized to select the features with the most predictive power. RF algorithm has an inherent property for computing feature importance by measuring how much each feature contributes to the decision. RF is a supervised ML algorithm that uses an ensemble learning method for classification and regression [2]. It combines several decision trees using the bagging ensemble learning technique. This technique allows the individual trees in the forest to be constructed using different random samples from the dataset. The final output of the RF is computed as the average of the individual trees' outputs. The importance of each feature is measured by computing how much the usage of the feature reduces the impurity across all the trees.

2.2 TMP Increase Model

The AutoRegressive TMP increase model ($ARTMP+$) predicts the increasing curve of the TMP for a specific filtration cycle. To illustrate the workflow of $ARTMP+$, let $D = \{d_1, d_2, \ldots, d_n\}$ be the input samples after feature engineering, where n refer to the number of cycles in the dataset. Each record d_i contains m features that can be categorized into: operating condition features $OCF = \{f_0, f_1, \ldots, f_j\}$, time-series features $TSF = \{f_{j+1}, f_{j+2}, \ldots, f_{m-2}\}$, and varying features $V = \{TMP_i[t], T_i[t]\}$. The feature sets OCF and TSF contain $m - 2$ features that remain constant for the prediction within the same cycle. The features in OCF include the initial operating conditions of the cycle, while TSF contains time-series features that summarize the operation history of the membrane using Eq. 1. The features in V include $TMP[t]$, the fouling indicator, and $T[t]$, the cycle time where $t = \{1, \ldots, k\}$ and k = cycle duration. For the prediction of each cycle, the $ARTMP+$ model takes the three inputs: the feature sets OCF_i and TSF_{i-1}, $TMP_i[t = 0]$, and an integer k representing the cycle duration. At each iteration, the output of $ARTMP+$ is $TMP_i[t + 1]$, which will be fed back to the model as input in the next iteration. The feature $T_i[t]$ is initialized internally by the prediction model to zero and incremented by one each iteration to represent the elapsed time since the current cycle has started. The model will output a varying length sequence depending on the value of k. The output of $ARTMP+$ can be represented by $O_i = \{TMP_i[t = 1], TMP_i[t = 2], \ldots, TMP_i[t = k]\}$. Figure 3(a) illustrates the workflow of the $ARTMP+$ model.

2.3 TMP Decrease Model

The Backwash TMP decrease model ($BWTMP-$) predicts the reduction in the TMP given a specific backwash duration. For the backwash cycle i, the inputs will be the features sets OCF_i and TSF_i, backwash duration $BW-Dur_i$, and the last TMP value of the filtration cycle $TMP_i[t = k]$. The output of $BWTMP-$ represents the lowest point the TMP reaches after the backwash. This output is used as the initial TMP value for the next filtration cycle, represented by $TMP_{i+1}[t = 0]$. Figure 3(b) shows the architecture of $BWTMP-$.

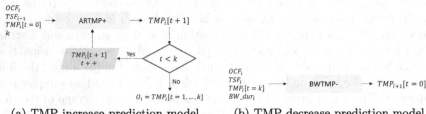

(a) TMP increase prediction model   (b) TMP decrease prediction model

Fig. 3. TMP prediction models. TSF: Time Series Features, k: Filtration cycle duration, i: cycle index, O: Output

2.4   LIME: Long-Term Forecasting Model for Membrane Fouling

LIME combines the $BWTMP-$ and $ARTMP+$ models for the prediction of the fouling behavior of the membrane over its RUL. The two models are intertwined such that their outputs are used as inputs to each other. First, $ARTMP+$ predicts the TMP values of the filtration cycle i based on the input filtration duration. Once the cycle duration is ended, the time-series features TSF_i will be updated, taking into consideration the k predicted values combined with the TMP time series of the full operating history. Then, the updated TSF_i features and the last predicted TMP value $TMP_i[t = k]$ will be used as input to $BWTMP-$ to predict the TMP falling point due to the backwash. This value is then used as the initial TMP value $TMP_{i+1}[t = 0]$ for the next filtration cycle by $ARTMP+$. The OCF are updated at the start of each filtration cycle representing the operating points of the process at the start of the cycle. LIME is used for online prediction, which runs recursively for the number of specified cycles. Figure 2 shows the prediction model workflow.

For estimating the RUL of the membrane, a safety threshold that should not be exceeded must be known. This safety threshold refers to the fouling condition that should not be exceeded after cleaning. In this work, the RUL is determined when the safety threshold is exceeded for three consecutive backwash cycles. Equation 3 shows how the RUL is determined for the safety threshold th, where t_i is the time at the prediction of $TMP_i[0]$ and t_c is the current time.

$$RUL = t_i - t_c$$
$$\textbf{\textit{if}}\ TMP_{i-2}[0]\ \&\ TMP_{i-1}[0]\ \&\ TMP_i[0] > th \tag{3}$$

3   Case Study

3.1   Dataset

The authors in [7] proposed an integrated seawater UF-RO pilot plant where UF is used for the pre-treatment of RO feedwater. The plant utilizes direct integration between the UF and RO, where the UF filtrate is directly fed into the RO pressure pump. The objective of the UF control system is to ensure that the required UF filtrate flow is provided to the RO system. As a result of this study, a dataset [5] was produced containing data collected under various field studies with different operating conditions and water quality. The dataset contains the information for the UF operation for the pre-treatment of RO feedwater. The collection period lasted for 422 days, in which short-term and long-term operational periods were considered. The dataset was used in a data-driven modeling approach to describe the performance of the UF-RO system [17].

Two data cleaning steps are applied to the raw data to prepare the dataset for feature engineering. First, the moving average (MA) smoothing technique is used to minimize the noise. Moreover, the dataset contains unevenly spaced data points across the files. Thus, a fixed sampling rate was used to unify the timestep across all the data files. We choose a sampling rate of 2 min. After the preprocessing steps and filtering out the outliers, the processed dataset contained 70193 samples and 8824 cycles.

3.2   Feature Engineering and Selection

For the time-series features, the Time Series Feature Extraction Library (TSFEL) is used [1] to extract features in the temporal, statistical, and spectral domains. The total number of features is 72, categorized into 23 for the operating condition features (OCF) and 49 for time-series features (TSF).

Two RF models are trained to find the feature importance. For training the RF model for feature selection, we set the parameter for the maximum feature to 5. This parameter determines the number of random features to be considered when looking at the best split for each node in the trees. Setting the maximum feature to a small value allows each tree in the forest to explore different features. The final feature sets include all the features with a score greater than 0.01. Figure 4 shows the importance of the selected features. Table 1 presents the selected features for the two models.

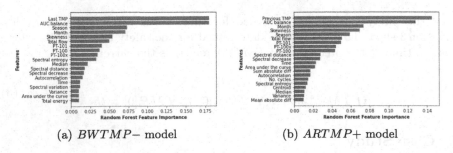

(a) $BWTMP-$ model   (b) $ARTMP+$ model

Fig. 4. The random forest feature importance of the selected features

3.3   Evaluation Results

To evaluate the performance of the proposed approach, three evaluation metrics for regression problems are used, which are Mean Square Error (MSE), Mean Absolute Error (MAE), and R-squared (R^2).

Prediction of TMP. Different ML algorithms have been used for implementing the $BWTMP-$ model. The algorithms are Linear Regression (LR), RF, XGBoost, Radial Basis Function (RBF) kernel Support Vector Machine (SVM), and Feedforward Neural Network (FNN). The FNN is built with the scaled exponential linear unit (SELU) activation function that provides self-normalization for FNN, which makes it suitable for tabular data [9]. Table 2 shows the evaluation metrics for the 5 algorithms. The RF attained the lowest scores in all the metrics, followed by LR and XGBoost. The SVM and FNN models achieved close results, with SVM taking the lead with differences of 0.01, 0.02, and 0.03 in MSE, MAE, and R^2. Therefore, the SVM model is considered in the subsequent steps.

For the $ARTMP+$ model, 3 neural networks are tested. The first one is a two-layer FNN with ReLU activation. The network produces a varying length output corresponding to the filtration duration. For each step, the inputs are the initial operating conditions, the time-series features, the current time of the cycle, and the previous TMP. The two other networks contain one FNN layer and an RNN layer with Long short-term memory (LSTM) or Gated Recurrent Unit (GRU) cells. For these networks, the operating conditions and the time-series features are passed once to the FNN layer, while the LSTM and GRU process the varying inputs (i.e., time and the TMP). Then for each step, the outputs of the two layers are concatenated and passed to a fully connected layer to produce the output. The RNNs can learn the long-term dependencies of the TMP sequence. Table 2 shows the evaluation results for the 3 networks. The network with the LSTM showed better R^2 performance by 0.1 and 0.06 compared to the FNN and GRU. Thus, the LSTM network is chosen as the final model for the $ARTMP+$.

Long-Term Fouling Prediction. After training and evaluating the two models separately, LIME is evaluated by integrating the two models to work recursively. Initially, LIME takes the time series features from the first sample in the

Table 1. The selected operating conditions features and the time-series features that summarize the history of the membrane

Feature	Description	Model
PT-100	MF Trans-filter Pressure	BWTMP−, ARTMP+
PT-101	UF Inlet Filtration Pressure	BWTMP−, ARTMP+
PT-100x	MF Inlet Pressure	BWTMP−, ARTMP+
Total flow	The total flow rate of the 3 membranes	BWTMP−, ARTMP+
Time	Timestamp	BWTMP−, ARTMP+
Month	The month when the data is collected	BWTMP−, ARTMP+
Season	The season when the data is collected	ARTMP+
Last TMP	The last TMP value of the previous filtration cycle	BWTMP−
# Cycles	The total number of cycles	ARTMP+
Initial TMP	The initial TMP value of the current filtration cycles	ARTMP+
Spectral decrease	The amount of decreasing of the spectra amplitude	BWTMP−, ARTMP+
Spectral distance	The distance of the cumulative sum of the FFT elements to the respective linear regression	BWTMP−, ARTMP+
Spectral entropy	The peakiness of the spectrum based on Fourier transform	BWTMP−, ARTMP+
Spectral variation	The amount of variation of the spectrum along time	BWTMP−
Median	The middle value of the time-series	BWTMP−, ARTMP+
Skewness	A statistical measure of the asymmetry of the probability distribution	BWTMP−, ARTMP+
Variance	The spread between numbers in the time-series	BWTMP−, ARTMP+
Area under the curve	The definite integral between the limits of the starting and ending points of the time-series	BWTMP−, ARTMP+
Autocorrelation	The degree of similarity between the time-series signal and a lagged version of itself	BWTMP−, ARTMP+
Total energy	The area under the squared signal	BWTMP−
Centroid	The value of the center point in the time-series	ARTMP+
Mean absolute difference	The mean value of the absolute difference between every two consecutive points	ARTMP+
Sum absolute difference	The summation of the absolute difference between every two consecutive points	ARTMP+
AUC balance	The cumulative sum of the difference between the area under the curve of every two consecutive cycles for a fixed cycle duration	BWTMP−, ARTMP+

Table 2. The evaluation metrics of $BWTMP-$, $ARTMP+$, and LIME

Model	Algorithm	Metric		
		MSE	MAE	R2
BWTMP	LR	0.03	0.14	0.78
	RF	0.04	0.15	0.71
	XGBoost	0.03	0.13	0.81
	FNN	0.02	0.10	0.87
	SVM	**0.01**	**0.09**	**0.90**
ARTMP	FNN	0.09	0.22	0.66
	GRU	0.08	0.21	0.70
	LSTM	**0.06**	**0.16**	**0.76**
LIME	SVM+LSTM	0.07	0.19	0.80

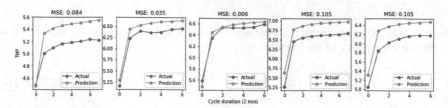

Fig. 5. Actual values vs. prediction. The first point in each cycle is predicted from the $BWTMP-$ model, while the rest are predicted by the $ARTMP+$ model

testing data. Then for each iteration, the prediction of $BWTMP-$ is fed to the input of $ARTMP+$. After that, the TMP values resulting from the $BWTMP-$ and $ARTMP+$ models are combined to calculate the time-series features for the next iteration, and the last TMP value predicted from $ARTMP+$ is used as input to $BWTMP-$ in the next iteration. The operating condition features are taken from the dataset. Table 2 shows the evaluation results for LIME using the best-performed models for the $BWTMP-$ and $ARTMP+$. Figure 5 shows some samples from the test data for the prediction of LIME. The long-time prediction of the membrane fouling is shown in Fig. 6. The figures show the starting and ending TMP values of all the cycles in the testing data. The figures show that the model captured the overall increasing trend of TMP over time.

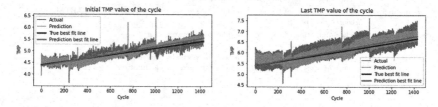

Fig. 6. The prediction of 1400 cycles using LIME. The left figure shows the $BWTMP-$ predictions. The right figure shows the $ARTMP+$ last TMP values.

3.4   RUL Estimation

The RUL is calculated by the difference between the current time and the failure time. Equation 4 is used to calculate the $\%Error$ on the estimated RUL, where $ActRUL$ is the true value and $\widehat{RUL}$ is the predicted value.

$$\%Error = \frac{ActRUL - \widehat{RUL}}{ActRUL} * 100 \tag{4}$$

There is a lack of desalination datasets that run the membrane near the failure point. Thus, to test the applicability of LIME in estimating the RUL of the membrane, we tested our model with different assumed safety thresholds. For the threshold, we considered different quantiles of the TMP values. Since the failure time of the membrane is considered as the time when the cleaning cannot restore the membrane condition, we consider only the TMP values after the backwash for the threshold calculations. A total of 6 thresholds are chosen, ranging from 0.6 to 0.85 quantile. Usually, the RUL is estimated as the difference between the current time and the first time the failure occurs. However, because of the variations in the backwash efficiency, we consider the failure point of the membrane as the time when the membrane condition cannot be restored for 3 consecutive cycles. Table 3 shows the actual and estimated RUL for the different thresholds and the percentage errors. The lowest error is achieved with the first threshold value, which is expected because the error accumulates over time. It is worth mentioning that, in all cases, the estimated RUL is underestimated, which means that the RUL is predicted earlier than the actual RUL. Early prediction is generally more acceptable than late prediction for the RUL estimation problems [10]. The average percentage error achieved by our model is 7%.

Table 3. The true and estimated RUL with the different thresholds.

	0.6 q	0.65 q	0.7 q	0.75 q	0.8 q	0.85 q
True RUL (hours)	229	246	250	313	362	369
Prediction RUL (hours)	228	228	246	259	321	352
%Error	**0.7%**	**7.4%**	**1.8%**	**17.3%**	**11.2%**	**4.6%**

4   Conclusion

In this paper, we addressed the problem of RUL estimation of membranes in desalination by developing a long-term fouling prediction model using ML techniques. The proposed model works recursively such that at any point in time, given the current state of the membrane captured by a set of features, the long-term behavior can be predicted. The model has the ability to output variable-length sequences depending on the filtration duration. This model provides great potential to be used for determining the suitable time for cleaning and RUL estimation. Since the predictions are conducted in cycles, the cleaning time can be determined based on a safety threshold for the maximum allowed TMP. Furthermore, it can also be used for estimating the RUL to avoid system failure and plan the membrane replacement. The main limitation of this work is the lack of datasets for desalination plants. To the best of our knowledge, the used dataset is the only available dataset that captures membrane degradation. In future work, other ML techniques will be investigated to enhance the performance of the prediction model. Furthermore, correlation analysis will be conducted to analyze the relationships between the input features and the fouling behavior.

Acknowledgment. This publication was made possible by Qatar University High Impact grant [QUHI-CENG-21/22-2] from Qatar University. The statements made herein are solely the responsibility of the authors.

References

1. Barandas, M., et al.: TSFEL: time series feature extraction library. SoftwareX **11**, 100456 (2020)
2. Breiman, L.: Random forests. Mach. Learn. **45**(1), 5–32 (2001)
3. Cai, G., Li, C.: Application of improved wavelet neural network in MBR flux prediction. In: Proceedings of the 16th IEEE/ACIS International Conference on Computer and Information Science, ICIS 2017, pp. 359–363. Institute of Electrical and Electronics Engineers Inc. (2017)
4. Choi, Y., Lee, Y., Shin, K., Park, Y., Lee, S.: Analysis of long-term performance of full-scale reverse osmosis desalination plant using artificial neural network and tree model. J. Environ. Eng. **25**(5), 763–770 (2020)
5. Cohen, Y., Zhou, Y., Khan, B., Gu, H.: Dryad Data - UF pre-treatment of seawater RO feedwater - performance data (2021)
6. Fane, T.: Irreversible fouling. In: Drioli, E., Giorno, L. (eds.) Encyclopedia of Membranes, pp. 1–2. Springer, Heidelberg (2015). https://doi.org/10.1007/978-3-642-40872-4_328-1
7. Gao, L.X̄., Rahardianto, A., Gu, H., Christofides, P.D., Cohen, Y.: Novel design and operational control of integrated ultrafiltration - reverse osmosis system with RO concentrate backwash. Desalination **382**, 43–52 (2016)
8. Jawad, J., Hawari, A.H., Javaid Zaidi, S.: Artificial neural network modeling of wastewater treatment and desalination using membrane processes: a review. Chem. Eng. J. **419**, 129540 (2021)
9. Klambauer, G., Unterthiner, T., Mayr, A., Hochreiter, S.: Self-normalizing neural networks. In: Proceedings of the 31st International Conference on Neural Information Processing Systems, pp. 972–981 (2017)
10. Nectoux, P., et al.: PRONOSTIA: an experimental platform for bearings accelerated degradation tests. In: IEEE International Conference on Prognostics and Health Management, PHM 2012, Colorado, USA, pp. 1–8 (2012)
11. Oishi, H., Kaneko, H., Funatsu, K.: Adaptive model and model selection for long-term transmembrane pressure prediction in membrane bioreactors. J. Memb. Sci. **494**, 86–91 (2015)
12. Schmitt, F., Banu, R., Yeom, I.T., Do, K.U.: Development of artificial neural networks to predict membrane fouling in an anoxic-aerobic membrane bioreactor treating domestic wastewater. Biochem. Eng. J. **133**, 47–58 (2018)
13. Zhang, B., et al.: Backwash sequence optimization of a pilot-scale ultrafiltration membrane system using data-driven modeling for parameter forecasting. J. Memb. Sci. **612**, 118464 (2020)
14. Zhang, W., Liang, W., Huang, G., Wei, J., Ding, L., Jaffrin, M.Y.: Studies of membrane fouling mechanisms involved in the micellar-enhanced ultrafiltration using blocking models. RSC Adv. **5**(60), 48484–48491 (2015)
15. Zhao, Z., Wu, J., Li, T., Sun, C., Yan, R., Chen, X.: Challenges and opportunities of AI-enabled monitoring, diagnosis & prognosis: a review. Chin. J. Mech. Eng. **34**(1), 1–29 (2021)
16. Zheng, Y., Zhang, W., Tang, B., Ding, J., Zheng, Y., Zhang, Z.: Membrane fouling mechanism of biofilm-membrane bioreactor (BF-MBR): pore blocking model and membrane cleaning. Bioresour. Technol. **250**, 398–405 (2018)
17. Zhou, Y., Khan, B., Gu, H., Christofides, P.D., Cohen, Y.: Modeling UF fouling and backwash in seawater RO feedwater treatment using neural networks with evolutionary algorithm and Bayesian binary classification. Desalination **513**, 115129 (2021)

Value Stream Repair Using Graph Structure Learning

Marco Wrzalik[1]([✉]), Julian Eversheim[1], Johannes Villmow[1], Adrian Ulges[1], Dirk Krechel[1], Sven Spieckermann[2], and Robert Forstner[2]

[1] RheinMain University of Applied Sciences, Wiesbaden, Germany
{marco.wrzalik,julian.eversheim,johannes.villmow,adrian.ulges,
dirk.krechel}@hs-rm.de
[2] SimPlan AG, Hanau, Germany
{sven.spieckermann,robert.forstner}@simplan.de

Abstract. Value streams are attributed graphs used for modeling and simulating production processes. We suggest a machine learning-based approach to identify and repair modeling errors in value streams, specifically incorrect edges or product annotations. Our approach recasts graph attribution as a link prediction problem and uses graph-based features describing the local constellation in the value stream, such as the classes of successor and predecessor nodes or the product consistency in the material flow. By wrapping our model – which suggests single repair steps – into a beam search process, we can derive entire repair sequences. An expert study shows that for all 16 constellations tested, our model suggests the right changes to repair typical errors. Furthermore, our experiments based on five simultaneous random edge corruptions on a set of 70 value streams achieves an average precision up to 96.4%.

Keywords: Value Stream Mapping · Graph-Based Machine Learning · Assistive Technologies

1 Introduction

Value stream modelling and simulation are well established approaches to assess engineering and production processes [6]. The methodology itself dates back to 1999 and was initially described by Rother and Shook [5]. It allows experts to model production processes in the form of attributed graphs, which include actions on an aggregated functionality level, such as stock, processes, process times etc.

While value streams are still sometimes sketched on paper, it is getting much more common for experts to use digital tools such as SimVSM[1] or eVSM[2]. These allow users to model value streams in a drag&drop fashion, to visualize the resulting graph, to quickly alternate through multiple variants of a value stream, and - in case of SimVSM - to analyze these variants' productivity and robustness through simulation.

---

[1] https://www.simvsm.de/en/.
[2] https://www.evsm.com/.

© The Author(s), under exclusive license to Springer Nature Switzerland AG 2023
H. Fujita et al. (Eds.): IEA/AIE 2023, LNAI 13926, pp. 15–32, 2023.
https://doi.org/10.1007/978-3-031-36822-6_2

However, an important challenge with these tools is that modeling value streams may be *error-prone*. Value streams in practice may consist of hundreds of typed nodes, edges and attributes, and users – particularly if not familiar with the particular tool at hand – tend to easily mislabel or forget certain items. Similar to bugs in software code, pinpointing those mistakes from a value stream's simulated behavior can be extremely challenging.

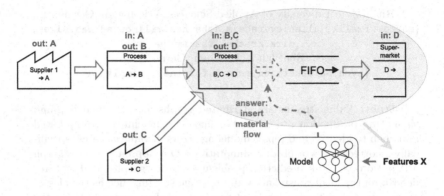

Fig. 1. Repairing a (strongly simplified) value stream: Our model inspects edges and product annotations (red) using features describing the local constellation in the graph (yellow). The result are plausibility score confirming the existing value stream or suggesting local changes. (Color figure online)

The objective of the work presented in this paper is to support users with debugging their value streams. We assume a value stream to be given that is complete in general but may contain some mistakes, e.g. missing edges or incorrect product labels. We propose a machine learning model that suggests actions to repair the value stream (e.g. inserting a certain edge). A simplified illustration is given in Fig. 1: An edge between two nodes (Process and FIFO) is missing. The system observes that the subsequent supermarket node (right) requires Product D, that the process node delivers product D, and suggests to insert the missing edge. Since situations in practice are more complex and multiple options for fixing a value stream may appear viable, defining hand-crafted rules is infeasible. Instead, we suggest rule learning using a decision tree-based approach, which exploits graph-based features describing the local constellation in the value stream, ranging from simple statistics over node and edge types to consistency of the product flow. We have integrated our model into SimVSM such that users can get suggestions for repairing their value streams, which they can accept or reject. Research on value stream modelling and simulation often considers the extension of content and scope of value streams, e.g. by integrating aspects of sustainability or by improving data quality (see Uriarte et al.'s [8] comprehensive survey). However, a combination of value stream mapping and machine learning is not amongst current research topics.

Obviously, machine learning research offers a variety of methods for link prediction and node classification in graphs, which could be transfered to value streams, e.g. using graph neural networks [4] or embedding-based link prediction models for knowledge graphs [10]. We are only of two prior works on graph modification in industrial material-flow networks: Vernickel et al. [9] train a gradient boosting model based on production system data (which include data from the past to the present) to determine parameters of existing network elements. Becker and Funke [1] proposed to use graph embedding models such as Node2Vec or DeepWalk to predict future changes in material flow networks to adapt manufacturing processes to flexible demands. Neither of these works addresses the repair of modeling errors.

Overall, our contributions are the following:

1. To our knowledge, we suggest the first machine learning approach towards value stream repair, which infers modifications to the value stream graph from a variety of local features. Internally, we recast node attribution as link prediction by adding virtual nodes and edges to the graph.
2. Per se, our model suggests single repair steps to be accepted/rejected by the user. However, we also wrap our model into a beam search process, which facilitates a complete multi-step repair of a value stream.
3. We show in simulation experiments that our model is able to repair up to 5 edge corruptions in value streams with a precision of 96.4% among the first five suggestions. In an expert study, we demonstrate our model's practical applicability and outline open challenges.

2   Foundations: Modeling Value Streams

Figure 2 gives an impression of the frontend of the value stream modelling app SimVSM. Besides the main menu (far left, marked with (1)) for switching between projects and value streams, the so-called "toolbox" (2) shows the elements made available to users to build a value stream. These elements comprise icons for different aggregated functionalities like processing, transporting and storing of products (a selection of possible elements is also shown in Fig. 3). The largest part of the screen is taken up by the modelling surface, on which the user creates the value stream using the elements from the toolbox (3). In order to set up a coherent model, a value stream analyst needs to create a graph starting with one or more supplier nodes (sources) leading to one or more customer nodes (sinks). The most common nodes between suppliers and customers are processes (representing one or more manufacturing or logistic operations) and different kind of buffers to store material between processes. Along with other, more specialized node types such as rework or kanban, there are a significant number of different node types that need to be considered. For example, in SimVSM there are 18 different node types that a user can choose from to model a value stream. Between these nodes, four different types of edges can create directed connections: *materialFlow, informationFlow, kanban* and *rework*.

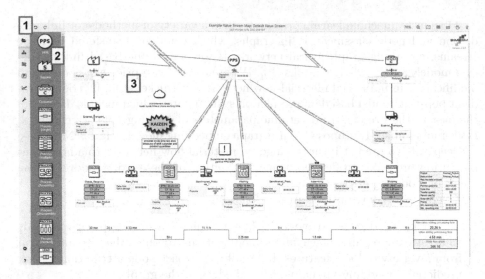

Fig. 2. Sample value stream modelled in SimVSM (with (1) menu, (2) toolbox and (3) modelling area)

In general, due to a multi-product related value stream mapping (VSM) approach, every process expects one or more products from preceding (upstream) nodes and hands on one or more products to succeeding nodes. A product expected by a node has to be provided by at least one of the upstream nodes. Within a process node, it is also possible to have product transitions from an incoming product to an outgoing product which leads to the possibility of complex product structures within a value stream.

With the differentiation of above mentioned edge types, another important feature is the modelling of edges to indicate the order flow between nodes: customers trigger orders for part demands in certain intervals. These orders must be forwarded to e.g., a production planning system (PPS) as central information hub. To indicate this flow, a customer is connected to the PPS via an information flow edge. From the PPS, the orders can be forwarded again through information flow edges to process nodes which are placed in a node sequence after passive storages, e.g. simple inventories or supermarkets.

Finally, software tools also allow users to simulate value streams, thereby dynamically computing logistical key performance indicators such as stock levels in the buffer nodes, throughput time of products and parts and produced volume per day, week, or month. However, in order to simulate a value stream it needs to be free of inconsistencies such as missing or wrong edges or incomplete or incorrect products, which we will discuss in the next section.

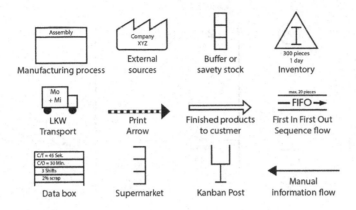

Fig. 3. Icons used in value stream mapping [5].

2.1 Errors in Value Stream Simulations

Software tools such as SimVSM are connected to rule-based simulation implementations, but not every possible value stream graph is allowed as model input for a simulation job. To simulate correctly, value streams must satisfy a variety of specific constraints. For users not strongly familiar with the domain or the specific software at hand, it can be challenging to produce a correct model. We give three examples for this in the following (see Fig. 4), (1) regarding product transitions and (2), (3) regarding the information flow in the model:

Example (2) highlights a process which follows a passive storage but is not information or order flow controlled. Passive storages have no active simulation logic to push parts to their successor, but are rather designed for succeeding process nodes to retrieve parts based on orders. These orders are modeled by an information flow edge from the PPS to the process node, which is missing in the depicted constellation.

Example (3) indicates a direct material flow in which a process is a direct successor of a FIFO (transport) object. With this direct material flow push, the process cannot decide which parts to produce, it has to take in the parts in the sequence in which they are moved from the FIFO predecessor, since this predecessor is actively pushing its parts to succeeding nodes. The depicted information flow edge from the PPS to Node "Process_4" therefore has to be removed.

Besides correct information flow edges, the simulation system also requires correct product transitions between direct node successors. If these product annotations to the nodes are incomplete, the material flow of parts cannot be calculated in the simulation. In Example (1), two passive inventories are providing in total three products to be merged at a succeeding assembly station into a single product. If the assembly station has a flawed product definition which would miss one of the incoming base products, it would lead to an invalid product transition between the inventories and the succeeding assembly station.

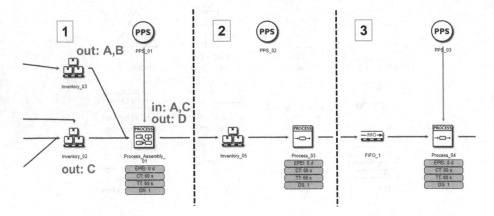

Fig. 4. Three Examples of typical errors in value stream ((1) product inconsistencies, (2), (3) information flow edges).

3   Approach

With our approach, we address situations such as the ones described in the last section, in which all nodes (processes) have already been mapped out by the modeler, but some connections and/or attributes are either wrong or missing (see Sect. 2.1 for examples). We address two general types of errors:

- **incorrect edges:** These include forgotten edges, edges in the wrong direction, and edges that are invalid or do not make sense in the current state of the value stream map.
- **incorrect products:** We also address faulty product attributions of nodes, i.e. incorrectly specified products or products that have been forgotten to be assigned to nodes.

3.1   Formalization and Preprocessing

We model value streams as directed heterogeneous graphs [7] $\mathcal{G} = (V, E, \mathcal{T}^V, \mathcal{T}^E, t^v, t^e, P, t^i, t^o)$, where V is a finite set of nodes and $E \subseteq V \times V$ a set of directed edges. $\mathcal{T}^V$ denotes a set of node types (such as *assembly* or *storage*) and $\mathcal{T}^E$ a set of edge types (such as *material flow* or *information flow*). The function $t^v : V \to \mathcal{T}^V$ assigns a node type to each node, the function $t_e : E \to \mathcal{T}^E$ an edge type to each edge. We denote the set of all products in the value stream with P. Note that – unlike $\mathcal{T}^E$ and $\mathcal{T}^V$ – P varies between value streams, depending on the particular business domain. Finally, each node is assigned a set of incoming products and a set of outgoing products by two functions $t^i, t^o : V \to \mathcal{P}(P)$.

Preprocessing: We would like to address both the above errors – incorrect edges and incorrect products – with the same type of model. To do so, we deviate from the usual notion of products as attributes of nodes, and transform value stream graphs in a preprocessing step: (1) For each product $p \in P$, we add an additional node of type *product* to the value stream graph, obtaining an extended node set $V' := V \cup P$. (2) We add edges labeled with *in-product* and *out-product* from *regular nodes*[3] v to the new product nodes p, indicating if a product p is specified as an outgoing or incoming product for v. Figure 5 illustrates this transformation. The preprocessing allows us handle the repair of faulty edges as well as faulty product annotations as link prediction problems.

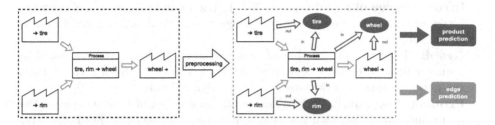

Fig. 5. Overview of our approach: A preprocessing step maps product attributes to additional virtual edges and nodes. Product edges (red) and regular edges (blue) are predicted with two different models (right). (Color figure online)

3.2   Feature Engineering

Our goal is to predict if – and if yes, of which type – an edge is present between two nodes. To do so, our model inspects the local constellation of the graph $\mathcal{G}$ in the surrounding of the two nodes. Thereby, different features may be interesting for predicting product edges than "regular" edges. This is why we introduce two feature sets, denotes as *edge features* and *product features* in the following.

The following **edge features** are used to predict links between node pairs $(u, v) \in V \times V$:

- **Node u class** $(|\mathcal{T}^V|)$:[4] One-hot encoded class of node u. This feature is also used for the product prediction model.
- **Node v class** $(|\mathcal{T}^V|)$: The same, for node v.
- **Edge-type validity** $(|\mathcal{T}^E|)$: Value stream mapping uses syntactic rules to specify that only nodes of certain types can be connected with each other (for example, a *materialFlow* edge from a customer to a process is not allowed). This feature indicates, based on the classes of u and v, whether an edge of type x is allowed.
- **Positional offset (2):** As outlined in Sect. 2, all regular nodes are placed on a canvas by the user. The spatial proximity of nodes on the canvas is a strong indicator of relatedness (for example, subsequent steps of a production line are often placed as horizontal neighbors). Therefore, we include the X and Y position offsets from node u to v. Both values are standardized globally over all samples.

---

[3] With *regular nodes* we refer to all non-product nodes.
[4] Feature lengths are given in parenthesis.

- **Node u successor classes** ($|\mathcal{T}^V|$): Classes of direct successors of u, excluding v if present. If no successor is present, a repair action is likely needed. Multiple occurrences of the same class have no effect.
- **Node v predecessor classes** ($|\mathcal{T}^V|$): Classes of direct predecessors of v excluding u if present. Similar to the above feature, having no predecessor indicates that a repair action is probably required.
- **Node u predecessor classes** ($|\mathcal{T}^V|$): Classes of direct predecessors of u.
- **Node v successor classes** ($|\mathcal{T}^V|$): Classes of direct successors of v.
- **In/out degree of u and v** ($2 \cdot 2 \cdot |\mathcal{T}^E|$): The in and out degrees of u and v, listed separately for each edge type. Edges from u to v and vice versa, if any, are excluded.
- **Graph distance** (1): Number of hops in the graph from u to v, clipped to a maximum of 5 to limit computational cost. If an edge from u to v exists, the graph distance is calculated as if this edge did not.
- **Product-flow validity** (1): Whether an out product of node u is one of the in products of v. Note that nodes of some types, such as the FIFO-Lane, have no product attributes, or the products assignments might still be missing. In this case we perform a look-back/look-forward until we find the first node with an assigned product.

Separate from suggestions for edges, we define a second set of features for **repairing products**. These features are applied to node pairs (u, p), where u is a "regular" node and p a product node:

- **Node u class** ($|\mathcal{T}^V|$): Since node p will always be of type *product*, only the one-hot encoded class of node u is utilized as a feature.
- **Node u position** (2): X and Y position of this node, globally standardized over all training value streams.
- **Product Position** (2): Products have no actual position on the canvas. However, since most products are transformed into other products, it is common that a product only appears in nodes of a certain area. If p is currently used by any nodes, this feature contains the mean of the X and Y positions of these nodes, globally standardized.
- **Product has supplier/customer** (2): Whether the product p is delivered by a supplier or is delivered to a customer.
- **Product is transformed** (1): Whether product p is transformed from other product(s). In theory, if a product is neither delivered by a supplier nor created throughout the value stream there must be an error with this product somewhere.
- **Successors supplied** (1): In case any of u's successors require p as an in product, whether p is already delivered from another node than u.
- **Predecessors fetched** (1): This flag indicates if a product delivered to Node u is not yet consumed. It is true iff. any of the direct predecessors of u produce p as an out product and p is not delivered to another node than u.

3.3   Model

Since a value stream map is a heterogeneous graph (having different edge classes), we handle the link prediction problem as a single class classification problem: Given a pair of nodes (u, v), we predict the probability distribution over the available edge types. These edge types include NONE for node pairs that should not have an edge from u to v. We use this pipeline both for edge prediction and product prediction, but use different input features and output classes:

Edge Prediction: This submodel decides whether to add an edge between two regular nodes u and v. We capture the local situation in both nodes' surrounding with the features outlined in Sect. 3.2, namely feature set B, concatenated to a feature vector $\mathbf{x}^E(u, v, \mathcal{G})$, which is fed to a random forest classifier ϕ^E [2]. The output classes are $\mathcal{T}^E \cup \{NONE\}$. The final output $\phi^E(\mathbf{x}^E(u, v, \mathcal{G}), c)$ estimates the probability that an edge of Type c between the two nodes should be drawn.

Product Prediction: This submodel decides whether to add an edge from a regular node u to a product node p. We follow the same approach, using all features described in Sect. 3.2, concatenated to a feature vector $\mathbf{x}^P(u, p, \mathcal{G})$. This vector is fed to another random forest classifier ϕ^P with output classes IN-PRODUCT, OUT-PRODUCT, and NONE.

3.4   Training and Inference

We train the model in a supervised fashion, assuming a set of correct value streams to be given. We preprocess these value streams (Sect. 3.1). From all preprocessed value streams, we select two subsets of their node pairs for training our two submodels:

- All pairs of regular nodes $(u, v) \in V \times V$ are collected in a training set for the edge prediction model ϕ^E.
- All pairs of regular nodes and product nodes $(v, p) \in V \times P$ form the training set for the product prediction model ϕ^P.

The ground truth labels for both classifiers are derived from the presence of respective edges in the training value streams. Note that we also collect unconnected node pairs, and label them with NONE.

Inference: We apply our model to make suggestions how to fix a broken test value stream $\mathcal{G}$. To do so, we preprocess the value stream and apply the edge model to $V \times V$ and the product model to $V \times P$. If the model's top-scored edge type for a node pair equals the true edge type in $\mathcal{G}$, our model simply confirms the constellation in the value stream, and no change is applied. Otherwise, the model makes a *repair suggestion* for said node pair. We rank all those node pairs with repair suggestions by their score. Thereby, we merge suggestions by both models into a joint ranked list of recommendations.

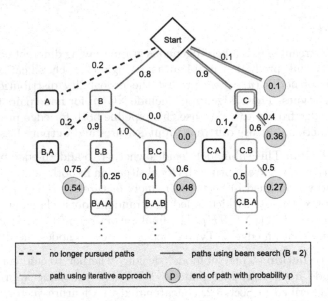

Fig. 6. An illustration of beam search and the iterative approach. Confidences of the model's suggestions are noted on the edges. Each node (except the root) represents a suggestion. The total accumulated confidence of a path is noted at the ends of the paths. In this example, beam search follows the best two ($B = 2$) paths, finding more promising paths ($p = 0.54$, $p = 0.48$) than its competitor ($p = 0.36$).

3.5   Multi-step Repair

So far, the above link prediction can be applied to make single repair suggestions in the graph (e.g., suggesting to add a certain edge or product). These changes can then be confirmed by the user one by one. An interesting question, however, is if the model is able to suggest a multi-step repair that corrects a graph with K corruptions without additional input by an expert. This enables a fully auto-mated repair of a corrupted value stream, making troubleshooting more efficient and convenient. To do so, three strategies are described in the following:

Ad hoc: This strategy simply picks the K highest-scored changes and applies all of them to the value stream.

Iterative: A more promising approach is to apply the K changes one by one: In each round only the highest-scored repair action is applied to the value stream, after which new predictions are generated. Note that this allows the model to adapt to changes made in early repair rounds. This approach corresponds to a real-life scenario in which an expert accepts one repair suggestion before request-ing the next set of suggestions.

Beam Search: This approach is an extension of the iterative strategy. How-ever, not only the best, but the best B suggestions of the model are considered. We obtain a tree of repair suggestions, from which the B most promising paths are selected at each level. The score of a path is defined as the product of the probabilities of the path's individual suggestions. In each level of the tree, the B highest-scored paths are expanded. An illustration is given in Fig. 6. The expectation of this strategy is that paths are found, which have a higher path probability, although these achieve lower confidences in the early suggestions. In the illustration, the iterative (orange) strategy finds a path with overall probability $p = 0.36$, while beam search (blue) finds two different paths with probabilities of $p = 0.48$ and $p = 0.54$. As in the iterative approach, the tree is explored down to level K.

An additional challenge is that K – the number of errors to repair – is unknown in a real-life-scenario. Correspondingly, all strategies must include a way to stop the repair process:

Ad hoc and **iterative** both stop when the model offers no more repair suggestions.

Beam Search: As mentioned, the path probability is the product of its individual suggestions. We additionally consider the probability of a path ending by taking the counter probability of the highest-scored suggestion in the next level of the tree (see Fig. 6). Thus, the end of the B most promising paths can be calculated in each level. The path with the highest probability (including the path's end) found in the tree is used. Additionally, we prevent loops in which repair suggestions cancel one another, and we stop whenever the tree reaches a certain depth (e.g. $depth_{max} = 10$).

4 Experiments

We have conducted two types of experiments: First, we conduct a simulation in which we measure how well our model fixes *randomly sampled* errors in value streams (Sects. 4.1–4.4). Second, the model is integrated into the value stream modeling software SimVSM and an expert evaluation is conducted, in which typical error cases are evaluated and the limitations of the model are explored (Sect. 4.5).

4.1 Dataset and Protocol

For training and evaluation we use a set of 70 value streams. Many of them are variations of small-scale examples that were created for tutoring purposes (note that real-world value streams contain trade secrets and are thus confidential). The value streams contain 17.3 nodes and 15.7 products on average. We train the random forest classifiers ϕ^E and ϕ^p for the prediction of edges and product annotations respectively. We employ the random forest implementation of *sklearn* [3] (which we found to outperform an MLP, gradient boosting and an RBF-SVM in previous tests). We use a forest of 100 decision trees, and refrain to the default parameters otherwise.

As stated in Sect. 3.4, we use all combinations of regular nodes $(V \times V)$ for the edge model (which makes 31,340 samples, of which 1,821 are associated with an edge) and all combinations of regular nodes and products $(V \times P)$ for the product model (27,181 samples, of which 3,851 represent an existing product relation).

For evaluation of our model(s) we employ a Leave-One-Out (LOO) testing protocol. For each value stream, we train our model with the remaining value streams and run N tests, in which K random corruptions are applied to the value stream, which are described in Sect. 4.2 in detail. Our model is then asked to predict repair actions reversing the corruptions using either of the strategies outlined in Sect. 3.5.

In addition to the LOO evaluation, we also test on a larger real-world value stream created by a German automotive OEM. With 72 nodes, 11 product and 93 edges it is much bigger than the average value stream in our training set. When testing this value stream, we conduct N with each K corruptions, just as done for the LOO evaluation. In both the LOO evaluation and the real-world value stream testing, we perform $N = 100$ tests with $K = 5$ corruptions per value stream, if not otherwise specified.

To measure our model's quality, we evaluate truncated lists of ranked repair suggestions with a maximum length of 10. However, the lists can be shorter than 10 suggestions if no further predictions can be made that differ from the current state of the value stream. As one of our main evaluation metric we use precision. Depending on the number of errors K we incorporate per corrupted value stream, we calculate precision only on the K first elements. For example, if we employ 5 errors per test instance, we measure precision among the top 5 suggestions. We refer to this as $P@5$. We also report the mean average precision (mAP) on the whole ranking with up to 10 repair suggestions.

4.2   Automated Value Stream Corruption

We automatically corrupt value streams to evaluate the repair suggestion of our models. For the evaluation of the **edge model** ϕ^E, the following corruptions are made on edges between regular nodes:

- **Remove random edge:** We randomly sample one present edge between regular nodes and remove it. We consider this one of the main errors in real life scenarios, thus the corresponding corruption function has a sampling weight of 60%.
- **Add random edge:** We randomly sample a node pair (u, v) that has no edge assigned from u to v, and insert an edge whose type is randomly sampled from the real-life distribution.
- **Switch random edge:** We sample a present edge between regular nodes (u, v), remove it, and re-insert the oppositely directed edge (v, u). In our system this counts as two corruptions (one removal and one insert) and can therefore only be applied when at least two more corruptions should be applied to the value stream at hand. The sampling weight amounts 20%.

When testing the predictions from our **product model** ϕ^p, we apply the following corruptions on a value stream:

- **Remove random product relation:** We randomly sample one existing product annotation and delete it. We give this corruption function a sampling weight of 50%.
- **Add random product relation:** We randomly sample all combinations of regular nodes and products that do not already have a product annotation, and add product p either as in-products or as out-products. The sampling weight of this corruption type is 50%.

We also test the combination of edge and product corruptions while fusing the suggestions of both models. In this case we simply use all corruption functions and effectively halve the sampling weights.

4.3   Suggesting Single Repair Actions

Applying only one repair action at a time and request new suggestions based on the partly repaired value stream (*iterative repair*) is expected to be advantageous over attempting to repair all errors at once (*ad hoc repair*). While the most obvious repair actions can be done first, which have a relatively high chance of being correct, the remaining errors tend to become easier to detect. As shown in Fig. 7, based on our LOO evaluation protocol, *P@1* (the chance that the first repair action is correct) is highest for 4 errors or more. Applying the first repair action may then make detecting the remaining errors easier, which is also illustrated in Fig. 7. This is due to the fact that some features rely on an intact material flow and complete product annotations. Consequently, the iterative approach improves the quality of repair suggestion lists. However, the iterative approach rather simulates the behavior of our model when used by an expert rather than being an actual approach used in the SimVSM application. Therefore, we argue, the iterative repair strategy represent the quality of our model better than the ad hoc repair.

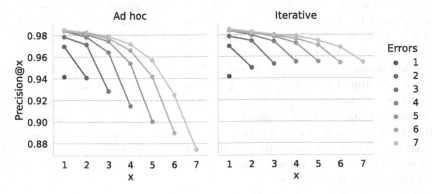

Fig. 7. Precision measures with various cut-offs from LOO evaluation runs with different numbers of errors using *ad hoc* (left) and *iterative* repair (right).

Table 1. Edge model feature ablation using LOO evaluation (left) and repeated testing on a real-world value stream

Features (accum.)	LOO Evaluation		Test Value Stream	
	P@5	*mAP*	*P@5*	*mAP*
Node u, v Classes	31.2	29.0	22.0	19.2
+ Node Pos Delta	85.9	87.4	25.0	16.1
+ Node u Success	89.5	90.8	57.0	46.4
+ Node v Predecess	94.4	94.9	82.2	82.8
+ Edge Validity (A)	**95.6**	**96.1**	83.6	85.1
+ Product Consistency	92.4	92.5	88.2	87.9
+ Graph Distance	92.6	92.7	87.6	87.3
+ Node Degrees	90.4	89.7	95.4	94.8
+ Node u Predecess	90.7	90.1	**97.2**	**96.5**
+ Node v Success. (B)	90.4	89.9	96.2	95.8

In the following we discuss the impact of individual features of the edge model and the product model using the iterative approach. Table 1 displays repair quality measurements of the edge repair model in terms of *P@5* and *mAP* for different sets of features. Each row adds another feature from Sect. 3.2. As this ablation was created, if a feature impaired suggestion quality on the LOO evaluation, this feature has been set aside for later re-evaluation. With this procedure we come to feature set A. All remaining features (lower half in Table 1) are then added in no specific order and form (together with A) the feature set B. Interestingly, as some of the features degrade the suggestion quality on the LOO evaluation, they often improve suggestion quality on the real-world test value stream. Here, using feature set B performs much better than A, while A performs better on the LOO evaluation. With a precision of 96.2% on the test value stream, the edge repair suggestions are highly accurate. Specialized on the test value stream, we could find the ideal feature set for a even higher accuracy. However, this would resemble to optimizing on a test sample and the ideal set of features might be different when using another real world value stream. Hence, we use feature set B for all future experiments in this work, although another subset of features could achieve even better results.

Table 2 shows a similar ablation study for the features of the product model. Since all individual features improved LOO evaluation performance, a distinction in feature sets it not necessary. Compared with the edge repair model, however, the accuracy is much lower. A problem that occurs on this value stream is that even if the value stream was not corrupted, our model makes false positive repair suggestions. This increases repair difficulty, since the desired repair actions for a corrupted version of this value stream must have a higher confidence than those of the false positive predictions.

Table 2. Product model feature ablation using LOO evaluation (left) and repeated testing on a real-world value stream

Features (accum.)	LOO Evaluation		Test Value Stream	
	P@5	*mAP*	*P@5*	*mAP*
Product used before/after	34.5	28.8	41.8	29.9
+ Node u Class	42.7	38.0	49.8	37.2
+ p has Supplier/Customer	46.7	43.2	58.0	49.7
+ p is Transformed	46.7	43.5	59.8	51.3
+ u/p Position	73.7	71.5	60.0	58.0
+ Predecessors Supplied	73.9	71.9	63.0	61.1
+ Successors Fetched	**75.1**	**72.7**	**69.2**	**69.0**

4.4 Multi-step Repair Using Beam Search

In Sect. 3.5 we introduced three methods to implement a fully automated repair of a corrupted value stream. These strategies are targeted at reconstructing a faulty graph by finding the exact K correct fixes in a value stream, where K is an unknown variable. To address this, we consider the so-called *reconstruction rate* as a quality measure, which measures the percentage in which a strategy could successfully reconstruct graphs (including a correct repair stop). Table 3 shows the results. In the evaluation, each value stream was manipulated with $K = 5$ errors. The value streams were then repaired using the different strategies:

Table 3. Comparison of multi-step repair strategy using LOO evaluation (left) and repeated testing on a real-world value stream

Repair Strategy	LOO Evaluation			Test Value Stream		
	P@5	*mAP*	*r%*	*P@5*	*mAP*	*r%*
Edges						
Ad hoc	80.3	84.1	3.5	85.6	90.8	3.0
Iterative	90.4	**89.9**	62.4	96.2	**95.8**	88.0
Beam Search	**90.8**	**89.9**	**69.7**	**96.4**	**95.8**	**89.0**
Products						
Ad hoc	67.9	69.7	0.9	65.2	71.0	0.0
Iterative	**75.1**	**72.7**	26.0	**69.2**	**69.0**	0.0
Beam Search	74.6	71.7	**37.0**	65.4	64.2	**12.0**
Edges & Products						
Ad hoc	69.3	73.7	0.5	69.0	74.8	0.0
Iterative	**80.4**	**80.2**	31.3	**77.2**	**76.3**	0.0
Beam Search	78.9	77.8	**45.9**	70.2	68.6	**18.0**

Ad hoc: Performs worst out of all strategies. Since ad hoc considers only the initial state of the value stream, it lacks information about the dependencies of the previous suggested repairs. For the metric $P@5$, ad hoc comes close to the results of its competitors, but falls off in *reconstruction rate*, which is an indication of its naive stopping criterion engaging too late. In return, ad hoc achieves a constant time complexity.

Iterative: This strategy was most successful on the $P@5$ and mAP metrics in combination with feature set A, but often suffers from severe drops in reconstruction rate since it tends to suggest too many repair steps.

Beam Search: The *reconstruction rate* indicates that beam search is by far the best strategy when it comes to entirely repairing a given graph, performing best both in the LOO evaluation and on the test value stream. We observed that it often found shorter ($<K$) paths due to our termination criterion, which negatively effects the precision ($P@5$ and mAP).

In general, we observe that product prediction is much more challenging than edge prediction. This can be explained by its inherent ambiguities: For example, if we corrupt the graph in Fig. 1 by removing the out products B and C in the corresponding two nodes, we cannot recover the information *which* input node produced which product.

4.5   Practice Test

A practice test was conducted in cooperation with SimPlan, the provider and developer of the software SimVSM. In a pilot implementation phase, the AI model was integrated within the user interface functionalities of the software. With modelling or importing value stream models into the software, the user was able to trigger the AI model and obtain a ranked list of correction proposals for invalid or missing edges or for invalid or missing product annotations to nodes. As depicted in Fig. 8, these proposals are directly integrated into the modelling area of the GUI, including a visual illustration of possible changes. By accepting or denying adjustments, proposals can selectively be included into the modelling area of the value stream. Note that edge and product proposals are placed in separate tabs, since users may focus on these aspects in different phases of their modeling.

To practically test the model, additional value streams were used which are not included in the training data. For this, SimPlan combined and anonymized value streams and model constellations provided by a German automotive OEM from their applied use cases. To these values streams, the most reported modelling errors from the OEM were reproduced manually. Besides this user feedback, SimPlan also included the knowledge which constellations lead to certain errors on a SimVSM test server for new users.

Section 2.1 already outlined exemplary invalid model constellations in this test data set. Correlating to these exemplary invalid model constellations, Fig. 8 depicts the model's correction suggestions for constellations (2) and (3) in Fig. 4:

(2) The AI model detected that a process after a storage has to be order or information controlled. This leads to a proposal of including an information flow edge from the PPS to "Process_3", which is correct.
(3) The AI model recognizes the material flow constellation with a FIFO object connection which renders the information flow input from the PPS to "Process_4" invalid, the process has to take in parts in the sequence the preceding FIFO object is delivering. Correspondingly, our model provided a correct proposal for removal of the edge between the PPS and the "Process_4".

Besides the material flow connectors, the model was also able to detect the incorrect product transitions between nodes and suggested as first step to include a missing in product within the product definition of the assembly station. By accepting the mentioned proposals, the value stream was afterwards structurally correct and able to be simulated.

Additionally to the above exemplary practical tests, 13 further (structural) tests were successfully conducted where the AI model was able to propose correct suggestions for fixing the graph.

In the error case of missing material flow edges in a node line with equal product transitions, there were (besides correct suggestions with high probabilities) sporadically and locally ambiguous and partly unnecessary edge suggestions with lower probabilities. After the user accepted the most probable suggestions, these were omitted and the simulation capability of the graph was maintained.

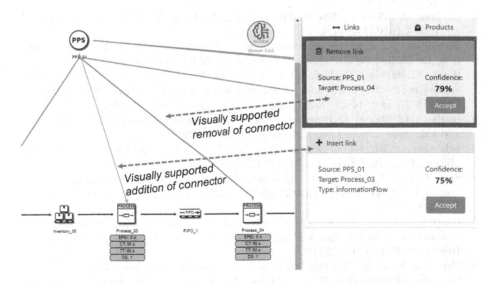

Fig. 8. Example suggestions from the practice test (right).

5   Conclusion

We have suggested the first known approach towards repairing modeling errors in value streams. By utilizing domain-specific graph-based features, our model displays high accuracy when it comes to suggesting single repair steps even with a limited training set of 70 value streams. Via beam search, the model can – to some extent – derive entire repair sequences.

In the future, we plan to increase robustness (especially for product predictions) by generating a larger training set through augmentation and thus bootstrapping a graph neural network approach. Also, integrating dynamic aspects of simulation (such as stock and queue levels) might improve the model's ability to pinpoint modeling errors. Finally, while our current model addresses only links and product annotations for existing nodes, we are working on an extension that suggests new nodes to be added to the graph.

Acknowledgements. This work was supported by the Federal State of Hesse (Research Program "Distral", project "AI-Mod", project ID 493 20_0051_2A).

References

1. Becker, T., Funke, T.: Machine learning methods for prediction of changes in material flow networks. Procedia CIRP **93**, 485–490 (2020). https://doi.org/10.1016/j.procir.2020.04.030
2. Breiman, L.: Random forests. Mach. Learn. **45**(1), 5–32 (2001). https://doi.org/10.1023/A:1010933404324
3. Pedregosa, F., et al.: Scikit-learn: machine learning in python. J. Mach. Learn. Res. **12**, 2825–2830 (2011). https://doi.org/10.5555/1953048.2078195
4. Rossi, A., Barbosa, D., Firmani, D., Matinata, A., Merialdo, P.: Knowledge graph embedding for link prediction: a comparative analysis. ACM Trans. Knowl. Discov. Data **15**(2), 14:1–14:49 (2021). https://doi.org/10.1145/3424672
5. Rother, M., Shook, J.: Learning to See: Value Stream Mapping to Create Value and Eliminate Muda. Lean Enterprise Institute (1999)
6. Schönemann, M., Kurle, D., Herrmann, C., Thiede, S.: Multi-product EVSM simulation. Procedia CIRP **41**, 334–339 (2016)
7. Sun, Y., Han, J.: Mining heterogeneous information networks: a structural analysis approach. SIGKDD Explor. **14**(2), 20–28 (2012). https://doi.org/10.1145/2481244.2481248
8. Uriarte, A.G., Ng, A.H.C., Moris, M.U.: Bringing together lean and simulation: a comprehensive review. Int. J. Prod. Res. **58**(1), 87–117 (2020). https://doi.org/10.1080/00207543.2019.1643512
9. Vernickel, K., et al.: Machine-learning-based approach for parameterizing material flow simulation models. Procedia CIRP **93**, 407–412 (2020). https://doi.org/10.1016/j.procir.2020.04.018
10. Wu, Z., Pan, S., Chen, F., Long, G., Zhang, C., Yu, P.S.: A comprehensive survey on graph neural networks (2021). https://doi.org/10.1109/TNNLS.2020.2978386

Which Components to Blame?
Integrating Diagnosis into Monitoring
of Technical Systems

Franz Wotawa[✉]

Institute for Software Technology, Graz University of Technology,
Inffeldgasse 16b/2, 8010 Graz, Austria
wotawa@ist.tugraz.at

Abstract. System monitoring is essential for detecting failures during
operation and ensuring reliability. A monitoring system obtains observations and checks their consistency concerning requirements formalized
as properties. However, finding property violations does not necessarily
mean finding the causes. In this paper, we contribute to the latter and
suggest introducing model-based diagnosis for root cause identification.
We do this by adding information regarding the source of observations.
Furthermore, we suggest implementing properties using ordinary programming languages from which we can obtain a formal model directly.
Finally, we explain the process of integrating diagnosis into monitoring
and show its value using a case study from the automotive domain.

Keywords: System monitoring · Model-based diagnosis · Explaining
deviations

1   Introduction

Monitoring is a function for observing the system's state and signals over time
to determine its health. In technical systems like cars, it is of interest to find
failures during operation and raise warnings and errors that trigger maintenance
activities (see, e.g., [11]), like bringing a car to a workshop for repair. As such,
monitoring (and in particular, condition monitoring) can be seen as part of prognosis and health management (PHM) and is also considered in several standards,
like [6,7], and [8]. Condition monitoring is becoming more and more relevant for
automotive applications where knowing that a component conducts degraded
behavior allows for actions to be taken in advance to avoid failures occurring
during runtime.

In this paper, we extend previous work on monitoring [16], where the focus
was on the foundations of hierarchical monitoring systems. Hierarchical monitoring systems capture faults at different levels of the system hierarchy and allow
easier integration of knowledge. Instead of sending all signal and state values to a
centralized monitoring system, monitoring components that correspond to a specific level of the hierarchy handle local cases and submit errors to the next level

© The Author(s), under exclusive license to Springer Nature Switzerland AG 2023
H. Fujita et al. (Eds.): IEA/AIE 2023, LNAI 13926, pp. 33–44, 2023.
https://doi.org/10.1007/978-3-031-36822-6_3

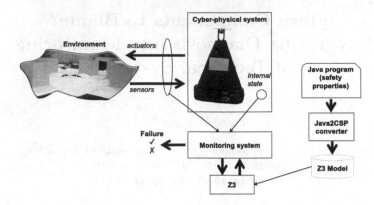

Fig. 1. The system architecture of a diagnosis-enhanced monitoring system comprising a constraint solver for monitoring and diagnosis.

of the hierarchy. Moreover, cases requiring knowledge from different sub-levels can be more easily solved at the first level in the hierarchy, where all information is available. In [16], the authors introduced the foundations of hierarchical monitoring, defining the monitoring task as a consistency-checking procedure considering signals and states, i.e., observations, and monitoring properties, i.e., formalized knowledge that must be true always. Such properties might check for safety requirements or invariant knowledge during operation.

The extension of hierarchical monitoring we will discuss in this paper is the introduction of diagnostic capabilities for monitoring to identify and localize the reason behind a property violation. The underlying idea is to use given information to indicate which signal or state information leads to an inconsistency. Given that observed signals or states can be mapped to corresponding components, we can identify the components to be considered for future maintenance activities. We utilize a model-based approach [9,10,12,13,15] for diagnosis. Model-based diagnosis (MBD) takes observations and a formal system model (i.e., the formalized properties) for localizing faults directly, not requiring specific model transformations or machine learning. Hence, MBD seems to be well adapted for the particular purpose.

In Fig. 1, we depict the architecture of our monitoring system comprising a cyber-physical system from which we obtain signals and internal states and the monitoring system that is coupled with a constraint solver (in our case Z3 [2]) for checking the system's properties. The properties are expected to be formalized in a simplified Java-like programming language. We use the Java2CSP tool [14] to convert these programs into an SMT-LIB form Z3 can operate on. The reason for using an ordinary program instead of SMT-LIB relies on the fact that most engineers know programming languages similar to Java but not necessarily specific forms like SMT-LIB or logic in sufficient detail. Hence, the expectation is to devise an approach for monitoring that does not require a lot of professional training.

We structure this paper as follows. First, we introduce the basic foundations capturing hierarchical monitoring and diagnosis based on models. Afterward, we outline diagnosis-enhanced monitoring and discuss a concrete use case from the automotive domain. For the use case, we describe the formalization of properties using a Java-like programming language, the use of the Java2CSP tool for conversion, and Z3 for computing diagnosis. Furthermore, we outline further research required and finally conclude the paper.

2   Basic Foundations

This section briefly discusses the monitoring system concepts and model-based diagnosis. We start with *monitoring* outlining the ideas and concepts introduced in a previous article [16]. In this work, the authors suggest and advertise the use of hierarchical monitoring to represent different system levels naturally in the monitoring system. Such a representation allows the distribution of available knowledge about invariants and other properties more easily at the relevant locations of a system. For example, we might have an invariant for a particular subcomponent that might be violated, which does not influence the overall behavior in a form requiring to stop operation. Or we might have a situation where there are no errors at a lower level of the hierarchy but an invariant violation at a higher level.

The concept of hierarchical monitoring is based on hierarchically connected components where each component stores its predecessors, the one successor, and a set of constraints to be checked during operation. Note that a monitoring component might not correspond to a physical component of a system. During operation, a behavior is observed and checked. Formally, for each monitoring component C we check whether $constr(C) \cup behav(C)$ is inconsistent or not, where $constr(C)$ is the set of constraints, and $behav(C)$ the set of monitored signals of a component C. In case of inconsistency, a monitoring system raises an error. In the case of a hierarchy, all components of the hierarchy check the behavior. Hence, monitoring can be seen as checking the consistencies of observations considering given properties to detect failures during the operation of a system.

In contrast to monitoring, where the focus is on fault detection, the objective is to find the causes of detected failures in diagnosis. In this paper, we rely on model-based diagnosis (MBD), which Reiter [12] formalized. Most recently, Kaufmann and Wotawa [15] introduced and discussed the use of recent theorem provers concepts, i.e., Answer Set Programming (ASP) (see, for example, [3]) for computing diagnoses for given systems. Other work using SMT solvers like Z3 includes [4]. MBD has also been used in the context of system control, e.g., [1].

The idea behind MBD is to utilize models of systems directly for computing root causes. In the terminology of MBD, a root cause is a set of components the system is composed of that, if assumed to be faulty, remove any inconsistency between the modeled behavior and the given observations. Formally, a diagnosis problem is stated as a tuple $(SD, COMP, OBS)$, where SD is a formal model,

$COMP$ is a set of components, and OBS is a formal sentence specifying the observations. A solution to the diagnosis problem, i.e., a diagnosis we define as follows:

Definition 1 (Diagnosis). *Given a diagnosis problem* $(SD, COMP, OBS)$. *A set* $\Delta \subseteq COMP$ *of components is a diagnosis if and only if* $SD \cup OBS \cup \{ab(C)|C \in \Delta\} \cup \{\neg ab(C)|C \in COMP \setminus \Delta\}$ *is consistent.*

It is worth mentioning that this definition assumes a predicate ab having the semantics *"abnormal"* for components. Hence, if $ab(C)$ is true, the component C is assumed to behave wrong. It is obvious that when assuming that all components in $COMP$ are faulty, the condition is always fulfilled. Hence, in practice, we rely on minimal diagnosis (or parsimonious diagnosis), considered sets of components where non of its real subset is a diagnosis.

Given the discussions on monitoring and diagnosis, it is straightforward to bring together monitoring and diagnosis from a formal point of view. In monitoring, we have constraints representing properties that are checked against the observed behavior. In diagnosis, we have a system model where certain components have attached ab predicates and observations. We search for components that, when assumed to behave wrongly, no longer lead to inconsistencies between the observed and the expected behavior. The latter is derived from the model.

However, properties are only partially describing the system's behavior. Hence, the question remains to what extent properties can be used together with observations to gain meaningful diagnoses. In the next section, we discuss this issue with other more technical challenges and illustrate the approach using a small example.

3   Diagnosis-Enhanced Monitoring

The idea behind diagnosis-enhanced monitoring is to use properties, e.g., safety properties stating that no bad things will happen, and to map them to a formal model, which we utilize for identifying the causes of misbehavior. We assume that a cause of misbehavior must correspond to an observed value. Hence, it is possible to find the component that causes the observed value when tracing back from observations to their origin. On the other hand, if a fault is masked, we may not obtain any observation that contradicts a property. In this case, we cannot find the fault and, therefore, also not localize it.

In the following, we discuss introducing diagnosis-enhanced monitoring given a system S and a set of signals SIG from S we want to monitor. We assume any means for obtaining values at given points in time t for each signal. In addition, we assume to have properties P that refer to the signals. The monitoring system checks these properties at each point in time. Note that if a property requires considering previous values for a particular signal, we introduce new signals for storing these values. Hence, the property checks can be considered stateless.

To blame certain parts of a system responsible for a wrong value, we must map signals to the components from which they originate. For this purpose, we assume a function $\Gamma : SIG \mapsto COMP$ mapping signals to components from $COMP$. For example, a signal T_{BAT} indicating the temperature of a battery corresponds to the battery, i.e., $\Gamma(T_{BAT}) = BAT$. Hence, we introduce a rule stating that if the battery is not abnormal, it will deliver the correct value v. We represent such a rule as an implication of the form: $\neg ab(BAT) \rightarrow T_{BAT} = v$ stating that the signal has a concrete value v. The value can be assumed to be available when monitoring the system at a time t. We can now use such a rule and a property for computing diagnoses. We illustrate the diagnosis computation considering a property stating that the battery's temperature should always be between 20 and 30 °C. Formally, we write this property as follows: $(T_{BAT} > 20) \wedge (T_{BAT} < 30)$[1].

For example, let us assume that we observe a value of 19 °C, which is unexpected. The system description SD for the corresponding diagnosis problem is: $(\neg ab(BAT) \rightarrow T_{BAT} = v) \wedge (T_{BAT} > 20) \wedge (T_{BAT} < 30)$.

The observations $OBS = \{T_{BAT} = 19\}$. When assuming $ab(BAT)$ to be false, we derive $T_{BAT} = 19$, which contradicts $T_{BAT} > 20$. Hence, the assumption that the battery works correctly cannot be true. When assuming $ab(BAT)$ to be true via stating $\Delta = \{BAT\}$, no contradiction can be derived, and $\{BAT\}$ must be a diagnosis.

In summary, *diagnosis-enhanced monitoring* requires identifying the components of the system responsible for observed signals. For each of these signals S, we add a rule $\neg ab(\Gamma(S)) \rightarrow S = v_S$ to the system description. The observations are the current values v_S for all signals. We can apply the concept of diagnosis-enhanced monitoring for hierarchical monitoring. We only need to add the diagnosis part to each monitoring component considering only properties used in this component.

For *implementing diagnosis-enhanced monitoring*, we suggest using an ordinary programming language for specifying properties. The rationale behind this is to make formulating properties as easy as possible. However, using logic or even equations directly often burdens engineers who are often not educated in formal logic, especially when they do not have a computer science background. Hence, we want to develop a framework for representing monitored signals and properties in a Java-like programming language.

First, the representation should declare a variable sig_S for all signals $S \in SIG$ using the data type of S. We can represent this declaration in the form of an assignment, where the value to be assigned is the currently observed value v, i.e., DT sig_S = v; where DT represents the data type of S.

Second, we introduce an error variable error_p for each property p. Initially, this variable is set to false when declared. Finally, we add a condition of the form if $\neg p$ { error_p = true; } where $\neg p$ is a representation of the negated form of

---

[1] In ordinary MBD, we would directly write this property on the right side of the implication $\neg ab(AB) \rightarrow$ .... In monitoring, however, we may have different signals originating from a component and different properties to be fulfilled. The coding of the described knowledge allows for separating the originator of signal values from stated properties.

p in the programming language. Note that we might compute at least parts of the property before calling the condition.

We can develop a program that checks the given properties using the described framework. For example, the program representing the battery example would look like this:

```
1.  public class Test {
2.      public void check_property () {
3.          int sig_BAT = 19;
4.          boolean error_1 = false;
5.          if (sig_BAT < 20) {
6.                  error_1 = true;
7.          }
8.          if (sig_BAT > 30) {
9.                  error_1 = true;
10.         } } }
```

Note that in this example, we present the property regarding the expected temperature range separately. We immediately see that the program would return error_1 to be true, indicating a violation. But how can we compute the reason behind it? The answer is using Java2CSP [14], which converts Java-like programs into a formal constraint representation a constraint-solver like Z3 [2] can read. In the following, we explain how we can use the output of Java2CSP for our purpose.

Consider our battery example again. Java2CSP would generate the following SMT-LIB representation where we shortened the declaration part:

```
(declare-const ab_0 Bool)
...
(declare-const error_1_4 Bool)
(assert (or ab_0 (= sig_BAT_1 19)))
(assert (or ab_1 (= error_1_1 false)))
(assert (or ab_2 (= temp_0_0 (< sig_BAT_1 20))))
(assert (or ab_3 (= error_1_2 true)))
(assert (= error_1_3 (ite temp_0_0 error_1_2 error_1_1)))
(assert (or ab_4 (= temp_1_0 (> sig_BAT_1 30))))
(assert (or ab_5 (= error_1_4 true)))
(assert (= error_1_5 (ite temp_1_0 error_1_4 error_1_3)))
(assert (= error_1_5 false))
```

What we see is that ab_0 is responsible for sig_BAT. Hence, only this abnormal value should be set either to true or false. The other abnormality assumptions can be set to false. This can be done using the following statement (assert (= ab_i false)) for all $i \neq 0$ in our case. Note that we may have more than one ab_i that we need to consider for diagnosis. To run Z3, we also need to add (check-sat) at the end so that we know whether the assumptions regarding the abnormals lead to a contradiction, i.e., unsatisfiability, or not.

When using a diagnosis algorithm like hitting set computation (see [5,12]) and Z3 as theorem prover, we would get the following result: ab_0 must be true, and consequently BAT must be the corresponding diagnosis.

Note that the required changes in the STM-LIB file can be done automatically. Moreover, we can easily couple Z3 with any diagnosis algorithm for computing all minimal diagnoses. The following section discusses a more sophisticated use case showing that diagnosis-enhanced monitoring can generate solutions considering different monitored observations.

4   Automotive Use Case

We concretize the initially described use case from [16]. In their article, the authors motivated the hierarchical monitoring device using an example comprising a car's velocity measures from different sources at different conceptual levels inside a car. These measures include the rotation velocity from the wheels v_W, a velocity estimate from the motor control v_M considering the engine speed and the current gear, and the GPS data v_G. If all sensors are accurate enough, someone would expect the velocity measures to be within a certain boundary b. Formally, and to be precise, we would check the condition: $(|v_G - v_M| \leq b) \wedge (|v_G - v_W| \leq b) \wedge (|v_M - v_W| \leq b)$.

This condition shall always hold when operating the car and can, therefore, be considered an invariant we want to check as part of the monitoring activity. Note that in practice, the sensors' boundaries may differ because of knowing specific inaccuracies. However, we use a simplified example to show the provided capabilities of diagnosis-enhanced monitoring for presentation purposes.

In the following, we describe how the invariant can be represented in a procedure language, how it is represented as a set of constraints, and how this representation allows for computing the component to be blamed.

For representing a velocity measure, we have to use the corresponding signal in the car. For monitoring, we assume this information is available using a communication channel like a CAN bus or any other onboard network. In the following program, we assume that a signal <sig> is represented as a variable sig_<sig>. Hence, for our example, we assume the following mapping between the mathematical representation of a velocity and the program variable: for v_M sig_vmot, for v_W sig_vwhe, and v_G sig_vgps. For the boundary b, we use the variable boundary.

Figure 2 depicts the source code. In lines 4 to 6, the variables, which correspond to velocity signals, are defined and get their values. For the first part of the use case, we set the velocity values as given, where we see that the measured speed at the wheels deviates more than expected. Note that in the final implementation, the values will not be given in the program but added to the

```
1. public class Test {
2.     public void check_property () {
3.             // Set the input values for the check
4.             int sig_vgps = 103;
5.             int sig_vwhe = 109;
6.             int sig_vmot = 102;
7.
8.             // Initialize the checking procedure
9.             boolean error_1 = false;
10.            boolean error_2 = false;
11.            boolean error_3 = false;
12.
13.            // Compute the differences between signal values
14.            // and provide absolute values
15.            int diff_1 = sig_vwhe - sig_vgps;
16.            int diff_2 = sig_vwhe - sig_vmot;
17.            int diff_3 = sig_vgps - sig_vmot;
18.            int boundary = 5;
19.            if (diff_1 < 0) {
20.                    diff_1 = (-1)*diff_1; }
21.            if (diff_2 < 0) {
22.                    diff_2 = (-1)*diff_2; }
23.            if (diff_3 < 0) {
24.                    diff_3 = (-1)*diff_3; }
25.
26.            // Check the poperties
27.            if (diff_1 > boundary) {
28.                    error_1 = true;
29.            }
30.            if (diff_2 > boundary) {
31.                    error_2 = true;
32.            }
33.            if (diff_3 > boundary) {
34.                    error_3 = true;
35.            } } }
```

Fig. 2. The Java-like program representing the velocity invariant checking

constraint representation before calling the constraint solver for checking consistency and computing diagnoses. In lines 9–11, we initialize variables corresponding to specific errors, i.e., violations of specific parts of a property or a single property. Lines 14 to 24 compute the absolute values of the differences between the velocities. The property check is in lines 27 to 35, where we do a separate check for each part of the property. It is worth noting that we decided to check the parts differently to allow stating that all parts must be true separately.

```
(declare-const ab_8 Bool)
(declare-const diff_3_1 Int)
....
(declare-const ab_1 Bool)
(assert (or ab_0 (= sig_vgps_1 103)))
(assert (or ab_1 (= sig_vwhe_1 109)))
(assert (or ab_2 (= sig_vmot_1 102)))
(assert (or ab_3 (= error_1_1 false)))
(assert (or ab_4 (= error_2_1 false)))
(assert (or ab_5 (= error_3_1 false)))
(assert (or ab_6 (= diff_1_1 (- sig_vwhe_1 sig_vgps_1))))
(assert (or ab_7 (= diff_2_1 (- sig_vwhe_1 sig_vmot_1))))
(assert (or ab_8 (= diff_3_1 (- sig_vgps_1 sig_vmot_1))))
(assert (or ab_9 (= boundary_1 5)))
(assert (or ab_10 (= temp_0_0 (< diff_1_1 0))))
(assert (or ab_11 (= diff_1_2 (* (- 0 1) diff_1_1))))
(assert (= diff_1_3 (ite temp_0_0 diff_1_2 diff_1_1)))
(assert (or ab_12 (= temp_1_0 (< diff_2_1 0))))
(assert (or ab_13 (= diff_2_2 (* (- 0 1) diff_2_1))))
(assert (= diff_2_3 (ite temp_1_0 diff_2_2 diff_2_1)))
(assert (or ab_14 (= temp_2_0 (< diff_3_1 0))))
(assert (or ab_15 (= diff_3_2 (* (- 0 1) diff_3_1))))
(assert (= diff_3_3 (ite temp_2_0 diff_3_2 diff_3_1)))
(assert (or ab_16 (= temp_3_0 (> diff_1_3 boundary_1))))
(assert (or ab_17 (= error_1_2 true)))
(assert (= error_1_3 (ite temp_3_0 error_1_2 error_1_1)))
(assert (or ab_18 (= temp_4_0 (> diff_2_3 boundary_1))))
(assert (or ab_19 (= error_2_2 true)))
(assert (= error_2_3 (ite temp_4_0 error_2_2 error_2_1)))
(assert (or ab_20 (= temp_5_0 (> diff_3_3 boundary_1))))
(assert (or ab_21 (= error_3_2 true)))
(assert (= error_3_3 (ite temp_5_0 error_3_2 error_3_1)))
(assert (= error_1_3 false))
(assert (= error_2_3 false))
(assert (= error_3_3 false))
```

Fig. 3. The SMT-LIB representation of the Java-like program from Fig. 2.

We pass this program to the Java2CSP tool, which delivers an SMT-LIB representation, which we depict partially in Fig. 3. In this figure, we removed most of the variable declarations at the beginning and focused on the **assert** commands used to specify the constraints that represent the program. For diagnosis, we add the assumptions regarding the correctness/incorrectness of statements. In particular, we set all ab_i where $i > 2$ to false using **assert** and let the remaining ab vary for computing the diagnoses. We do this as described in the previous section. For varying the values for ab_0, ab_1, ab_2, we start by setting them all to false and then one after the other to true, obtaining the outcome depicted in Table 1.

Table 1. Runtime satisfiability check for the *ab* predicates used in the SMT-LIB presentation of Fig. 3 for the relevant signals.

ab_0	ab_1	ab_2	satisfiable	total time [sec]
false	false	false	no	0.02
true	false	false	no	0.02
false	true	false	yes	0.03
false	false	true	no	0.01

In this table, the time in seconds is reported by Z3 Version 4.8.10 - 64 bit using the -st option. We conducted the experiments using a MacBook Pro Apple M1, 16 GB RAM, running under Ventura 13.1. From the table, we see only one consistent behavior when setting ab_1 to true. The ab_1 variable belongs to sig_vwhe. Knowing that this variable belongs to the velocity measured from the wheel's rotation, we can conclude that the sensor used there is no longer reliable. Moreover, the total time for making all checks was less than 0.1 s. Note also that the whole process can be automated using one of the existing diagnosis algorithms.

To show that the given observations from monitoring influence the diagnoses, let us assume a slightly different value of sig_vwhe. Change line 5 to int sig_vwhe = 108;. In this case, we receive two diagnoses: ab_1 and ab_2, which corresponds to signals sig_vwhe and sig_mot. We cannot distinguish whether the wheel velocity sensor or the motor controller has given us back a value that is out of range. This is because the value of sig_vwhe is outside the boundary when compared with sig_vmot but both of these signals are within the boundary of the GPS value from sig_vgps. In practice, we can use this information and trust this value, not the others.

In summary, this use case allows drawing the following conclusions. First, the diagnosis computation is (at least for smaller systems) reasonable. When considering single faults only, we have a polynomial increase in runtime. Moreover, the approach allows for explaining property violations, which may also be used in a smart control system to improve the decision-making process, i.e., ignoring some sensor values for reasoning.

5   Conclusions

In this paper, we showed how monitoring based on properties could be enhanced using model-based diagnosis. Monitoring is observing signals and states of a system and checking whether they still fulfill the requirements over time. The requirements are captured formally in properties. However, when we detect a property violation, we cannot necessarily state its reason. In the presented approach, we suggested formulating properties using ordinary programming languages from which we can extract constraints. The constraints can be used for diagnosis when introducing specific variables allowing us to state the correctness of observed values. We rely on previous research introducing the Java2CSP tool for the proposed conversion. In the paper, we explain the required modification of the resulting constraints, which can be automated.

In addition, we introduced a case study from the automotive domain showing that the discussed approach delivers valuable results within a feasible amount of time. Moreover, we saw that changes in observations influence the outcome of diagnoses. Hence, the proposed diagnosis-enhanced monitoring approach is flexible and adapts to the observed situation. Furthermore, the results of the diagnosis systems can use to improve decision-making. For example, if one of two sensors might deliver wrong results, but a third one seems healthy, we would rely only on the third one for making decisions. Hence, we could improve reliability when using the proposed method.

In future research, we want to implement the whole method, including the framework for representing properties and automating changes of the Java2CSP output required for our purposes. In addition, we want to carry out more extensive case studies and investigate the diagnosis capabilities of Z3 when considering examples with more constraints and signals to be observed.

Acknowledgements. ArchitectECA2030 receives funding within the Electronic Components and Systems For European Leadership Joint Undertaking (ESCEL JU) in collaboration with the European Union's Horizon2020 Framework Programme and National Authorities, under grant agreement number 877539. All ArchitectECA2030 related communication reflects only the author's view and the Agency and the Commission are not responsible for any use that may be made of the information it contains. The work was partially funded by the Austrian Federal Ministry of Climate Action, Environment, Energy, Mobility, Innovation and Technology (BMK) under the program "ICT of the Future" project 877587.

References

1. Cordier, M.O., et al.: AI and automatic control approaches of model-based diagnosis: links and underlying hypotheses. IFAC Proc. Volumes **33**(11), 279–284 (2000). https://doi.org/10.1016/S1474-6670(17)37373-1. 4th IFAC Symposium on Fault Detection, Supervision and Safety for Technical Processes 2000 (SAFEPROCESS 2000), Budapest, Hungary, 14–16 June 2000
2. de Moura, L., Bjørner, N.: Z3: an efficient SMT solver. In: Ramakrishnan, C.R., Rehof, J. (eds.) TACAS 2008. LNCS, vol. 4963, pp. 337–340. Springer, Heidelberg (2008). https://doi.org/10.1007/978-3-540-78800-3_24
3. Eiter, T., Ianni, G., Krennwallner, T.: Answer set programming: a primer. In: Tessaris, S., et al. (eds.) Reasoning Web 2009. LNCS, vol. 5689, pp. 40–110. Springer, Heidelberg (2009). https://doi.org/10.1007/978-3-642-03754-2_2
4. Grastien, A.: Diagnosis of hybrid systems with SMT: opportunities and challenges. In: Proceedings of the Twenty-First European Conference on Artificial Intelligence, ECAI 2014, pp. 405–410. IOS Press (2014)
5. Greiner, R., Smith, B.A., Wilkerson, R.W.: A correction to the algorithm in Reiter's theory of diagnosis. Artif. Intell. **41**(1), 79–88 (1989)
6. ISO17359: Condition monitoring and diagnostics of machines? General guidelines (2018)

7. ISO18129: Condition monitoring and diagnostics of machines? Approaches for performance diagnosis (2015)
8. ISO20958: Condition monitoring and diagnostics of machine systems? Electrical signature analysis of three-phase induction motors (2013)
9. Kaufmann, D., Nica, I., Wotawa, F.: Intelligent agents diagnostics - enhancing cyber-physical systems with self-diagnostic capabilities. Adv. Intell. Syst. 2000218 (2021). https://doi.org/10.1002/aisy.202000218
10. de Kleer, J., Williams, B.C.: Diagnosing multiple faults. Artif. Intell. **32**(1), 97–130 (1987)
11. Pecht, M., Wang, W.: Economic analysis of canary-based prognostics and health management. IEEE Trans. Ind. Electron. **7**(58), 3077–3089 (2011)
12. Reiter, R.: A theory of diagnosis from first principles. Artif. Intell. **32**(1), 57–95 (1987)
13. Wotawa, F.: Using model-based reasoning for self-adaptive control of smart battery systems. In: Sayed-Mouchaweh, M. (ed.) Artificial Intelligence Techniques for a Scalable Energy Transition, pp. 279–310. Springer, Cham (2020). https://doi.org/10.1007/978-3-030-42726-9_11
14. Wotawa, F., Dumitru, V.A.: The Java2CSP debugging tool utilizing constraint solving and model-based diagnosis principles. In: Fujita, H., Fournier-Viger, P., Ali, M., Wang, Y. (eds.) IEA/AIE 2022. LNCS, vol. 13343, pp. 543–554. Springer, Heidelberg (2022). https://doi.org/10.1007/978-3-031-08530-7_46
15. Wotawa, F., Kaufmann, D.: Model-based reasoning using answer set programming. Appl. Intell. **52**(15), 16993–17011 (2022)
16. Wotawa, F., Lewitschnig, H.: Monitoring hierarchical systems for safety assurance. In: Camacho, D., Rosaci, D., Sarné, G.M.L., Versaci, M. (eds.) IDC 2021. SCI, vol. 1026, pp. 331–340. Springer, Heidelberg (2021). https://doi.org/10.1007/978-3-030-96627-0_30

A Comprehensive Analysis on Associative Classification in Building Maintenance Datasets

Joel Mba Kouhoue[1,2]([✉]), Jerry Lonlac[1], Alexis Lesage[2], Arnaud Doniec[1], and Stéphane Lecoeuche[1]

[1] IMT Nord Europe, Institut Mines-Télécom, University of Lille,
Center for Digital Systems, Lille, France
`joel.mba-kouhoue@imt-nord-europe.fr`
[2] Intent Technologies, Lille, France

Abstract. Several works have been conducted to promote a standard for exchanging building data. However, during the operation and maintenance phase of a building, there is still no emerging standard. Existing solutions continue to require manual tasks to match and share data and information among various actors such as owners, service providers, and occupants. This process becomes tedious due to the large volume of exchanged data, hence there is a need to find other ways of matching and identifying association rules between data of different views. In this paper we propose a new associative classification approach that integrates multi-criteria analysis at the association rule ranking level, and some application for data matching and system interoperability. We conducted experiments on both real building maintenance data sets and some UCI Machine Learning data sets, and the results show that our approach achieves good precision/accuracy and produces a less complex classifier that is easily exploitable by business experts.

Keywords: Association rule · Associative classification · Rule ranking · Multi-criteria decision making · Smart building

1 Introduction

Several works have been conducted to promote a standard for exchanging building data. One of the most common solutions is based on Building Information Modeling (BIM), which is primarily focused on building design and not widely adopted during the operation and maintenance phase of buildings. We also have the works of the buildingSMART Linked Data Working Group (LDWG) and the W3C Linked Building Data Community Group (W3C LBD CG) [3], which aim for standardization of the representation and exchange of building data over the web [17]. However, the ontologies developed by these organizations mainly focus on the static data of buildings and do not consider the dynamics of operations around the buildings. To address these issues, *Intent Technologies* [2] has

H. Fujita et al. (Eds.): IEA/AIE 2023, LNAI 13926, pp. 45–58, 2023.
https://doi.org/10.1007/978-3-031-36822-6_4

developed a Software as a Service (SaaS) digital platform to ensure the interoperability of different systems and facilitate the sharing of building maintenance data. However, this solution requires a significant amount of configuration and manual data matching from one system to another, which becomes tedious due to the large volume of exchanged data.

The goal of this research is to speed up the process of data sharing between real estate stakeholders, such as maintenance service providers and property managers, by developing a rule-based association classifier that can map data from different systems. The challenge is to propose approaches that allow to automatically discover from different data views, rules of the form $X \rightarrow Y$ matching the subset of values X of a view V1 with the conclusion Y of a view V2. For this, we consider different Associative Classification (AC) techniques [18] to build effective multi-class classifiers for the challenge of building maintenance data matching. These AC techniques combine association rule mining [5] and classification to yield highly interpretable and accurate classifiers. Essentially, the output of an AC algorithm is a set of if-then rules, which are easy to understand and interpret for experts. The rules, called Class Association Rules (CARs), represent the correlations among different attributes and the class attribute simultaneously.

Our expected contributions in this research work are:

- Build an accurate and understandable associative classifier model, adapted to unbalanced data and with integrates expert knowledge.
- Improve the process of sharing building maintenance data.

There is a variety of AC algorithms that take different approaches for generating and selecting rules (classifier building) [18]. However, to achieve our goals we propose a new method based on TOPSIS (Technique for Order Preference by Similarity to Ideal Solution) [21] method for the ranking of association rules and which allows us to inject expert knowledge into our models. We conducted our experiments on 3 building maintenance data sets produced by the company Intent. In order to generalize our approach, we also conducted experiments on 5 other data sets from the UCI Machine Learning Repository [4]. We then compared the experimental results with 6 well-known rule-based classification algorithms, based on the accuracy, precision and the number of rules contained in each classifier.

The rest of the paper is organized as follows: Sect. 2 provides background information that is useful for understanding this work. Section 3 presents related works and describes the problem that this paper aims to solve. Our methodology is presented in Sect. 4, followed by experimental evaluations in Sect. 5, and an application example in Sect. 6. Finally, Sect. 7 presents our conclusions and future plans.

2   Common Background

Let $\mathcal{I} = \{x_1, x_2, ..., x_m\}$ be a set of elements called items. A set $X \subseteq \mathcal{I}$ is called an *itemset*. Let $\mathcal{T} = \{t_1, t_2, ..., t_n\}$ be another set of elements called transaction identifiers *(tids)*. A set $T \subseteq \mathcal{T}$ is called a *tidset*. Let $\mathbf{D}$ be a binary relation on the set of tids and items, i.e. $\mathbf{D} \subseteq \mathcal{T} \times \mathcal{I}$. Thus, $(t, x) \in \mathbf{D}$ if the transaction t contains the item x. Let $\mathbf{f} : 2^{\mathcal{T}} \rightarrow 2^{\mathcal{I}}$ be a function defined as follows: $\mathbf{f}(T) = \{x \mid \forall t \in T, (t, x) \in \mathbf{D}\}$ i.e., $\mathbf{f}(T)$ is the set of items that are common to all the transactions in the tidset T. Let $\mathbf{g} : 2^{\mathcal{I}} \rightarrow 2^{\mathcal{T}}$ be a function defined as follows: $\mathbf{g}(X) = \{t \mid \forall x \in X, (t, x) \in \mathbf{D}\}$ i.e., $\mathbf{g}(X)$ is the set of tids that contain all the items in the itemset X.

The *support* of an itemset X, denoted *sup(X)*, is the number of transactions that contain X, i.e., $sup(X) = |\mathbf{g}(X)|$.

An itemset X is said to be *frequent* if $sup(X) \geq minsup$, where $minsup$ is a user-defined threshold. The problem of mining all frequent itemsets can be described as follows: determine all subsets $X \subseteq \mathcal{I}$ such that $sup(X) \geq minsup$.

An *association rule* (AR) is an expression of the form $X \rightarrow Y$, where X and Y are itemsets and $X \cap Y = \emptyset$. X is called antecedent and Y is called consequent of the rule. The support of an association rule $X \rightarrow Y$ is the number of transactions that contain the itemset $X \cup Y : sup(X \rightarrow Y) = sup(X \cup Y)$. The confidence of an association rule $X \rightarrow Y$ measures its predictive accuracy and is given by $conf(X \rightarrow Y) = sup(X \cup Y)/sup(X)$. A rule is considered a strong rule if $conf(X \rightarrow Y) \geq minconf$, where $minconf$ is a user-defined threshold. However, it is sometimes useful to extract co-occurrences between a set of items and a specific target attribute of interest. These rules are known as *class association rules* (CARs).

Associative classification (AC) is a special case of association rule discovery in which only the class attribute is considered in the rule's right-hand side (consequent) [18]. For example, in a rule such as $X \rightarrow Y$, Y must be a class attribute. One of the main advantages of using a classification based on association rules over classic classification approaches is that the output of an AC algorithm is represented in simple if-then rules, which makes it easy for the end-user to understand and interpret it.

3 Related Work and Problem Definition

In this section, we present some existing associative classification approaches, and the common limitations of theses algorithms.

3.1 Associative Classification Algorithms

Among the methods used for associative classification, CBA (Classification Based on Association, [14]) is the first proposed algorithm. CBA uses the Apriori algorithm for the generation of association rules that satisfy predefined support and confidence thresholds. For the prediction phase, CBA uses a heuristic algorithm described as follows: for each learning case, the rule with the highest confidence among the rules covering it is stored [6]. The stored rules are ranked in decreasing order by confidence and the selection of the rule depends on which one covers a new case with the highest confidence. CBA2 [15] is an improved version of CBA which addresses the problem of unbalanced classes by using *multiple class minsups* in rule generation (i.e. each class is assigned a different minsup), rather than using only a single minsup as in CBA.

To improve the efficiency of the Apriori candidate generation step, CMAR (Classification based on Multiple Association Rules) [20] and L3 [7] AC methods use approaches based on the Frequent Pattern (FP)- growth method [11] to discover rules, and store these rules in a prefix tree data structure known as a CR-tree. Algorithms that use the CR-tree consider the common attribute values contained in the rules, which use less storage if compared with CBA. In addition, rules can be retrieved efficiently as CR-tree indices rules [18]. Recently, [8] proposed several variations of these associative classification algorithms that take into account data consisting of several features of different types.

3.2   Problem Definition

In general, we observe that associative classification algorithms typically follow the steps shown in Fig. 1. However, one of the most common limitations of these algorithms is incorrect predictions in the case of class imbalance. These algorithms require the user to set a minimum rule support threshold, which negatively impacts the classifier's performance. To overcome this problem, it is recommended to run these algorithms with a low support threshold to avoid neglecting the minority classes. However, when the classes are highly unbalanced, even a low support threshold may not produce enough rules for minority classes. Therefore, we need to use an algorithm at the association rules mining phase (step 1) that does not impose a minimum input support. Another problem is the underutilization of business knowledge at the association rule ranking level (step 3). Current association rule ranking methods only use objective criteria such as support and confidence, neglecting subjective or qualitative knowledge. In the following section, we propose a new associative classification methodology that is adapted to the context and addresses the limitations of existing approaches.

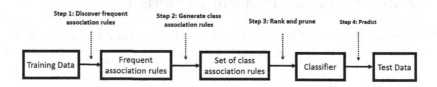

Fig. 1. Associative classification steps

4   Proposed Methodology

To address these limitations, we propose a new associative classification methodology called CARRT (Classification based on Association Rule Ranking with Topsis method). At the association rules discovery step, we use TopKClass-Rules algorithm proposed by [10] for discovering the top-k class association rules appearing in a transaction database. At the ranking stage, we develop a new ranking association rules algorithm based on the TOPSIS (Technique for Order Preference by Similarity to Ideal Solution) [21] method, which is a multi-criteria decision making technique which has the advantage of taking into account both objective criteria (support, confidence, etc.) and the subjective knowledge held by domain experts. The classifier is then built by taking only the best rules leading to each class. Finally, for the evaluation of our classifier (prediction stage) we developed a two-step prediction algorithm: First, for each case to be predicted, we search in the classifier the list of candidate rules (rules whose bodies match the testing example), then we use a voting strategy to choose the predicted class rule. More details about these variations are given in the next three sections.

4.1 Rules Discovery Strategy

For the rule generator stage, CARRT uses TopKClassRules [1] which is an algorithm for discovering the top-k class association rules appearing in a transaction database. It is a variation of the TopKRules [10] consists in finding association rules with a consequent containing a single item chosen from a set of items allowed by the user. However, it is really useful for our application case since the user is only interested in the rules containing specific elements in the consequence part. In addition, TopKClassRules is particularly useful in the context of associative classification mining [18] because it does not take as input the minimum support threshold, which allows us to obtain the rules of classes weakly represented in the data. In practice, it is important to choose a large number k in order to be sure that the rules obtained are sufficiently representative and that there is no loss of information. However, given the high number of these extracted rules, it is important to filter these rules in a more optimal way (taking into account the domain experts' knowledge) in order to keep only the most important rules in our classifier.

4.2 Ranking Rules Based on TOPSIS Method

TOPSIS is a method for ranking a set of alternatives based on a set of favorable or unfavorable criteria. This method is part of the techniques used in the field of MADM (Multiple Attribute Decision Making) [13]. In the following we propose an adaptation by using the following decision criteria: support, confidence and the size of the rules (which represents the number of elements contained in the antecedent of the rule). The principle consists in determining for each rule a score between 0 and 1 based on the Euclidean distances between each rule and the best rule, and Euclidean distances between each rule and the worst rule. In this section, we will present the different steps of our association rule ranking method based on the TOPSIS method.

For each criterion we will assign a weight that reflects the importance of the criterion in our final choice and also refers to subjective knowledge. Note here that several strategies for assigning weights to criteria, among which the manual assignment of weights and the use of entropy [9]. After having tested these different strategies we have chosen to use the entropy, which allows to have the best result.

Step 1 (Decision matrix): The first step in our ranking process is to build the decision matrix $(x_{ij})_{m*n}$ that consisting of m rules and n criteria, with the intersection of each rule and criterion given as x_{ij}. Note here that a decision criterion can be either positive or negative signal. In our case, the support and the confidence represent positive criteria (to be maximized) while the size of the rule is a negative criterion (to be minimized). Since these criteria are of different scales, they have to be normalized.

Step 2 (Decision matrix Normalization): In this step we normalize the matrix $(x_{ij})_{m*n}$ to form the matrix $R = (r_{ij})_{m*n}$. For this we chose a Euclidean normalization because the metrics which will be calculated in the following are based on the Euclidean distance, which guarantees consistent results.

$$r_{ij} = \frac{x_{ij}}{\sqrt{\sum_{k=1}^{m} x_{kj}^2}}, \ i = 1, 2, ..., m, \ j = 1, 2, ..., n \tag{1}$$

Step 3 (Weighting of the normalized decision matrix): Criteria weights reflect the decision makers' subjective preference as well as the objective characteristics of the criteria themselves. In this step, all entries of the normalized matrix are multiplied by the weight associated with each criterion. We thus obtain the weighted decision matrix $(t_{ij})_{m*n}$.

$$t_{ij} = r_{ij} \cdot w_j, \ i = 1, 2, ..., m, \ j = 1, 2, ..., n \tag{2}$$

Step 4 (Evaluation of the ideal rules): The ideal favorable and unfavorable rules represent respectively the best association rule (AR_b) and the worst association rule (AR_w) which are both virtual rules (they are just benchmarks for comparing the distances of all our rules).

$$AR_b = \{\langle min(t_{ij} \,|\, i = 1, 2, ..., m) \,|\, j \in J_- \rangle, \langle max(t_{ij} \,|\, i = 1, 2, ..., m) \,|\, j \in J_+ \rangle\} \tag{3}$$

$$AR_w = \{\langle max(t_{ij} \,|\, i = 1, 2, ..., m) \,|\, j \in J_- \rangle, \langle min(t_{ij} \,|\, i = 1, 2, ..., m) \,|\, j \in J_+ \rangle\} \tag{4}$$

where, $J_+ = \{j = 1, 2, ..., n\} \,|\, j$ associated with the criteria having a positive impact, and $J_- = \{j = 1, 2, ..., n\} \,|\, j$ associated with the criteria having a negative impact.

Step 5 (Euclidean distances between the rules): In this step we compute for each rule i its deviation from both the ideal favorable rule (AR_b) and the ideal unfavorable rule (AR_w) using the following formulas.

$$d_{i_{BR}} = \sqrt{\sum_{j=1}^{n} (t_{ij} - t_{bj})^2}, \ i = 1, 2, ..., m, \tag{5}$$

$$d_{iWR} = \sqrt{\sum_{j=1}^{n}(t_{ij} - t_{wj})^2}, \ i = 1, 2, ..., m. \tag{6}$$

where d_{iBR} and d_{iWR} are Euclidean distances from the target rule i to the best and worst rules, respectively.

Step 6 (Proximity rate and ranking): In this last step we calculate the similarity to the worst condition, by using the following formula:

$$s_{iw} = d_{iWR} / (d_{iWR} + d_{iBR}), \ 0 \leq s_{iw} \leq 1, \ i = 1, 2, ..., m. \tag{7}$$

$$s_{iw} = \begin{cases} 1 \text{ if and only if the target rule has the best condition;} \\ 0 \text{ if and only if the target rule has the worst condition.} \end{cases}$$

Finally, we can rank our association rules according to $s_{iw}(i = 1, 2, ..., m)$ and choose the best rules for each class label in order to build our classifier.

4.3 Prediction

After building our classifier, we evaluate its performance through predictions on the test data sets. For this we propose Algorithm 1 which is an extension of the prediction algorithm proposed in [16]. It takes as input the classifier and the test data and returns the predicted values. For each sample of the test data set, we search inside the classifier the list of *candidate rules* (lines 5–9). A candidate rule represents a rule whose antecedent part is contained in the set of attribute values or itemsets of the current individual. After obtaining a set of candidate rules, a voting strategy is used which consists in counting the number of occurrences of each class (conclusion part of the rule) to determine which one will be chosen as the predicted class value (line 11). If there is no candidate rule for a given individual, then the algorithm returns the majority class value of the classifier (line 13). Otherwise we return the majority class value of the set of candidate rules (line 16). However, if we have several majority class values in the set of candidate rules, we return the class of the maximum score rule (line 19).

5 Experimental Evaluation

The data used for our experiments consist of eight data sets from two data sources. Table 1 shows the characteristics of these data sets. The first three data sets represent the elevator maintenance data produced by the company Intent Technologies on the perimeter of some elevator service providers and their customers (real estate owners or property managers). We also tested our model on five real-life data sets taken from the UCI Machine Learning Repository [4]. We evaluate our framework by comparing it with six well-known classification methods (ACAC [12], ADT [19], CBA [14], CBA2 [15], CMAR [20], L3 [7]), using the accuracy and precision metrics. The benefit of using precision is that it allows us to better take into account the possible bad results on the minority classes [6].

Algorithm 1. Prediction process of CARRT

Input: $Test\,Dataset\,D, Classifier\,C$
Output: $Predictions\,P$
1: $P \leftarrow \emptyset$
2: $CandidateRules\,CR$
3: **for all** $Individual\,i \in D$ **do**
4:     $CR \leftarrow \emptyset$
5:     **for all** $Rule\,r \in C$ **do**
6:         **if** $Antecedent(r) \subset Itemset(i)$ **then** $CR.add(r)$;
7:     **for all** $Rule\,r \in CR$ **do**
8:         $class\_count[r.class] + +$;
9:         **if** $max(class\_count) = 0$ **then** $predicted\_class \leftarrow majority\_classifier$;
10:        **if** $max(class\_count) = 1$ **then** $predicted\_class \leftarrow max\_index(class\_count)$;
11:        **if** $max(class\_count) > 1$ **then** $predicted\_class \leftarrow max\_score\_rule$;
12:    $i.class \leftarrow predicted\_class$;
13:    $P.add(i)$;
14: **return** P;

Table 1. Description of data sets(1)

Data set	# of Attributes	# of Classes	# of Records
Intent_1	7	5	797
Intent_2	5	5	765
Intent_3	6	4	453
breast-cancer	9	2	286
car	6	4	11728
hayes	4	3	132
tictactoe	9	2	958
nursery	8	5	12960

CARRT was run with default parameter minimum confidence = 60%. For the ranking phase, we use the algorithm proposed in Sect. 4.2 considering as input criteria the support, the confidence and the size of the rules (number of elements contained in the antecedent). Since we wish to maximize the support and the confidence, we assign positive signals (MAX) to these two criteria, while the size of the rules that we wish to minimize is considered as a negative signal (MIN).

We use 70% of the data for building our classifier (training data) and 30% for the evaluation of the classifier performance (test data). The results of our proposed method (CARRT) on the precision are shown in Fig. 2, where we vary the precision according to the number of rules in the classifier. At each iteration, we take the k best rules leading to each class. We observe that on the "Intent_3" data set, the precision curve is almost constant, which means that we only need

Table 2. Description of data sets(2)

Data set	Class	# of Records	Highly_unbalanced
Intent_1	asc-troubleshooting	250	Yes
	asc-serious-fact	47	
	asc-user-blocked	250	
	asc-monthly-visit	250	
	asc-semi-annual-visit	1	
Intent_2	elevator-annual-verification-visit	117	Yes
	elevator-monthly-visit	250	
	semi-annual-cable-inspection	250	
	elevator-troubleshooting	250	
	emergency-repair-extrication	48	
Intent_3	elevator-annual-verification-visit	30	Yes
	elevator-monthly-visit	214	
	emergency-repair-extrication	23	
	troubleshooting	250	
breast-cancer	no-recurrence-events	201	No
	recurrence-events	85	
car	acc	384	Yes
	good	69	
	unacc	1210	
	vgood	65	
hayes	one	51	No
	three	30	
	two	51	
tictactoe	negative	332	No
	positive	626	
nursery	not_recom	4320	Yes
	priority	4266	
	recommend	2	
	spec_prior	4044	
	very_recom	328	

the first best rule leading to each class to have a good precision score. For the "Intent_2" data set, we observe that the maximum precision value is reached after the third iteration (the 3 best rules leading to each class). In general, we observe that our model (CARRT) produces good results with classifiers made of very few rules, which is not the same case with most existing associative classification algorithms.

The comparison between our method and some classification algorithms on accuracy and precision are respectively shown in Table 3 and 4. For the accuracy, we observed that our framework achieves the best results on business data ("Intent_1", "Intent_2" and "Intent_3"). The particularity of these data is that

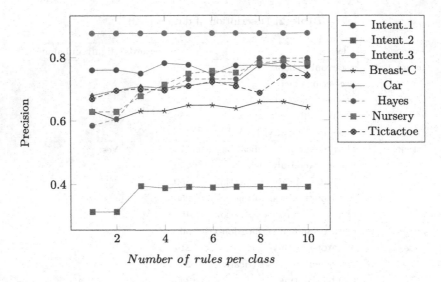

Fig. 2. CARRT Precision results

they are really unbalanced, as we can see in Table 2 (which contains for each data set, the set of classes and the number of records for each class label). For the precision, our proposed method achieves better results on the "Intent_1", "Intent_3", "car" and "nursery" data sets, which are all unbalanced. An average precision of 72%, slightly higher than all other algorithms. Even if the CBA and CBA2 algorithms are better on the "tictactoe" data set. In general, CARRT is well adapted in the case of highly unbalanced data.

Table 3. The comparison between our method and some classification algorithms on accuracy.

Data set	ACAC	ADT	CBA	CBA2	CMAR	L3	CARRT
Intent_1	0.75	0.71	0.79	0.78	0.75	0.79	**0.79**
Intent_2	0.25	0.26	0.55	0.54	0.28	0.29	**0.61**
Intent_3	0.87	0.90	**0.93**	**0.93**	0.88	**0.93**	**0.93**
breast-c	0.62	0.69	0.65	0.65	0.17	**0.72**	0.65
car	0.69	0.69	0.90	**0.94**	0.79	0.84	0.70
hayes	0.32	0.65	0.75	0.75	0.50	**0.77**	0.75
tictactoe	0.12	0.12	**0.78**	**0.78**	0.15	0.39	0.74
nursery	0.33	**0.94**	0.92	0.96	0.85	0.92	0.82
Mean	0.49	0.62	0.78	**0.79**	0.54	0.70	0.74

Table 5 shows the number of rules for each classifier. The idea is to have classifiers with good precision and as few rules as possible. For the data sets

Table 4. The comparison between our method and some classification algorithms on precision.

Data set	ACAC	ADT	CBA	CBA2	CMAR	L3	CARRT
Intent_1	0.56	0.74	0.60	0.72	0.57	0.60	**0.78**
Intent_2	0.24	0.05	**0.41**	0.40	0.35	0.33	0.39
Intent_3	0.68	0.71	0.71	0.71	0.44	0.71	**0.87**
breast-c	0.53	0.34	0.53	0.53	0.64	**0.66**	0.65
car	0.17	0.17	0.42	0.85	0.36	0.65	**0.78**
hayes	0.6	**0.89**	0.79	0.79	0.65	0.81	0.79
tictactoe	0.32	0.32	1	1	0.75	0.99	0.74
nursery	0.20	0.73	0.55	0.72	0.52	0.55	**0.78**
Mean	0.41	0.49	0.62	0.71	0.53	0.66	**0.72**

"Intent_1" and "Intent_2", our method produced classifiers with the minimum number of rules. In general, our method produces the best ratio of model precision/accuracy per number of classifier rules. In some applications, these results are particularly interesting because it allows business experts to better understand and exploit the classifier, since it contains very few rules.

Table 5. The number of classification rules generated by the classifiers.

Data set	ACAC	ADT	CBA	CBA2	CMAR	L3	CARRT
Intent_1	17	59	49	82	91	326	**16**
Intent_2	15	14	22	26	33	114	**6**
Intent_3	30	7	**3**	5	61	621	4

In the next section, we will present an application of our associative classification approach for elevator maintenance data matching.

6 Application

In this section we present an application example of our framework for matching building maintenance data in the context of the company Intent Technology. In fact, Intent has built a digital platform for sharing data between the main actors of the real estate profession. However, several configuration operations are done first to ensure the interoperability of the data. These setting operations are done manually, which is very complicated given the large volume of data exchanged.

The CARRT method allows to automate this matching process by building a simple and compact classifier made of relevant business rules. Table 6 represents the classifier produced from the "Intent_3" data set (which consists of the operation history of a given service provider on the perimeter of its customer). The operation history (interventions performed by the service provider) are considered as input and the goal is to determine the association rules allowing to predict the corresponding category at the customer or property manager system level.

The first rule in indicates that if the resolution process of an anomaly is between 4 and 16 h, then it is an annual verification visit, which corresponds to the customer category "elevator_annual_verification_visit", while the second and third rules indicate that if the criticality level of a failure (or intervention) is 5 or 1 then it is respectively an urgent repair or a simple repair. The last rule indicates that if the requested event (event materializing a request for intervention from a customer to his service provider) is false, then it is necessarily a monthly visit intervention planned in advance.

Table 6. Final classifiers with our method

Classifier	Rules
Intent_3	$processingDuration =]4 - 16] \rightarrow elevator\_annual\_verification\_visit$
	$criticalLevel = 5 \rightarrow customerCategory = emergency\_repair\_extrication$
	$criticalLevel = 1 \rightarrow customerCategory = troubleshooting$
	$requested = False \rightarrow customerCategory = elevator\_monthly\_visit$

We notice that the classifier produced by our method contains very few rules and has low complexity, in the form of if-then conditions. Therefore, the results are more explainable and understandable by human experts. Returning to our targeted application, this means that business experts can be assisted when they have to match data manually.

7   Conclusion

In this paper, we proposed a new associative classification approach which uses multi-criteria decision analysis at the association rule ranking stage, and some application for building maintenance data matching. We conducted our experiments on three building maintenance data sets and five UCI Machine Learning data sets and compare results to some efficient associative classification algorithms. Results show that our proposal obtains a low-complexity classifier with the least number of rules while keeping a good prediction score compared to some existing data matching approaches. This makes our classifier easily exploitable by business experts in charge of the data matching process. It is the main advantage of associative classification models which are fairly explanatory models compared to classical models which are black box models. The results also show that our framework achieves good accuracy and precision on the building maintenance data sets (which are highly unbalanced), and fairly good results on the other data sets.

Future work can build upon this paper in two directions concerning algorithms and data sets. Regarding algorithmic future work, one direction could be to explore novel algorithms and enhancements that may perform better on building maintenance data classifications. Another direction could be to extend the proposed association rule ranking algorithm by considering other ranking criteria such as Lift, Conviction, and the Loevinger measure, which can take into account the class distribution. Concerning data sets, in addition to elevator maintenance data, we plan to investigate data related to the maintenance of heating equipment, ventilation, multiservices, and other data sources that can be useful for matching building maintenance data.

References

1. Example: Mining the Top-K Class Association Rules (rules with a fixed consequent) (SPMF - Java). https://www.philippe-fournier-viger.com/spmf/TopKClassAssociationRules.php
2. The leading platform for building and city services. https://intent.tech/
3. Linked Building Data Community Group. https://www.w3.org/community/lbd/
4. UCI Machine Learning Repository. http://archive.ics.uci.edu/ml/index.php
5. Agrawal, R., Srikant, R.: Fast algorithms for mining association rules in large databases. In: VLDB, pp. 487–499 (1994)
6. Bahri, E., Lallich, S.: Proposition d'une méthode de classification associative adaptative. Revue des Nouvelles Technologies de l'Information EGC, RNTI-E-19, pp. 501–512 (2010)
7. Baralis, E., Garza, P.: A lazy approach to pruning classification rules. In: ICDM, pp. 35–42 (2002)
8. Dam, K.H.T., Given-Wilson, T., Legay, A., Veroneze, R.: Packer classification based on association rule mining. Appl. Soft Comput. **127**, 109373 (2022)
9. Dehdasht, G., Ferwati, M.S., Zin, R.M., Abidin, N.Z.: A hybrid approach using entropy and TOPSIS to select key drivers for a successful and sustainable lean construction implementation. PLOS ONE **15**(2) (2020)
10. Fournier-Viger, P., Wu, C.-W., Tseng, V.S.: Mining top-k association rules. In: Kosseim, L., Inkpen, D. (eds.) AI 2012. LNCS (LNAI), vol. 7310, pp. 61–73. Springer, Heidelberg (2012). https://doi.org/10.1007/978-3-642-30353-1_6
11. Han, J., Pei, J., Yin, Y.: Mining frequent patterns without candidate generation. ACM SIGMOD Rec. **29**(2), 1–12 (2000)
12. Huang, Z., Zhou, Z., He, T., Wang, X.: ACAC: associative classification based on all-confidence. In: ICGC, pp. 289–293 (2011)
13. Hwang, C.L., Yoon, K.: Methods for multiple attribute decision making. In: Hwang, C.-L., Yoon, K. (eds.) Multiple Attribute Decision Making. LNE, vol. 186, pp. 58–191. Springer, Heidelberg (1981). https://doi.org/10.1007/978-3-642-48318-9_3
14. Liu, B., Hsu, W., Ma, Y.: Integrating classification and association rule mining. In: KDD, p. 80–86 (1998)
15. Liu, B., Ma, Y., Wong, C.-K.: Classification using association rules: weaknesses and enhancements. In: Grossman, R.L., Kamath, C., Kegelmeyer, P., Kumar, V., Namburu, R.R. (eds.) Data Mining for Scientific and Engineering Applications. MC, vol. 2, pp. 591–605. Springer, Boston (2001). https://doi.org/10.1007/978-1-4615-1733-7_30

16. Mattiev, J., Kavsek, B.: Coverage-based classification using association rule mining. Appl. Sci. **10**(20), 7013 (2020)
17. Petrova, E.A.: AI for BIM-based sustainable building design: integrating knowledge discovery and semantic data modelling for evidence-based design decision support (2019)
18. Thabtah, F.: A review of associative classification mining. Knowl. Eng. Rev. **22**(1), 37–65 (2007)
19. Wang, K., Zhou, S., He, Y.: Growing decision trees on support-less association rules. In: ACM SIGKDD, pp. 265–269 (2000)
20. Li, W., Han, J., Pei, J.: CMAR: accurate and efficient classification based on multiple class-association rules. In: ICDM, pp. 369–376 (2001)
21. Zulqarnain, R., Saeed, M., Ahmad, N., Dayan, F., Ahmad, B.: Application of TOPSIS method for decision making. Int. J. Sci. Res. Math. Stat. Sci. **7**(2) (2020)

Deep Learning Based Solution for Appliance Operational State Detection and Power Estimation in Non-intrusive Load Monitoring

Mohammad Kaosain Akbar$^{(\boxtimes)}$ [ID], Manar Amayri [ID], and Nizar Bouguila [ID]

Concordia Institute for Information Systems Engineering, Concordia University, Montreal, Canada
mo_kbar@live.concordia.ca, {manar.amayri, nizar.bouguila}@concordia.ca

Abstract. This paper introduces a novel NILM algorithm that utilizes deep learning Temporal Convolutional Networks (TCN) for the regression and classification NILM tasks. The deep TCN layers in the proposed architecture allow the extraction of complex patterns in the data and can estimate the power consumption and the operational state of individual appliances. The proposed algorithm is evaluated using real-world household power usage data. The results show the effectiveness of the proposed method in detecting the appliance states and estimating individual appliance loads when compared to a benchmarking approach.

Keywords: Non-Intrusive Load Monitoring (NILM) · Temporal Convolutional Network · Regression · Classification

1 Introduction

Non-intrusive load monitoring (NILM), termed as Energy Disaggregation, is considered as a technique that analyzes the total power consumption readings obtained from the main meter of a household or commercial unit to estimate energy consumption and detect the operational states of individual appliances. This method does not require any smart meters to be attached to any appliance, reducing maintenance costs, and decreasing intrusion into users' properties. Based on the output, a NILM task can be categorized into either a classification or regression problem. When each appliance's operational state (ON/OFF) is extracted from the given aggregated load, this NILM problem is referred to as the NILM classification problem. On the other hand, the NILM problem, where the consumption made by the individual appliance is deduced from the aggregated signal, is viewed as a NILM regression problem [1].

Various deep learning based NILM techniques were proposed which either predicts the operational states or the energy consumed by individual appliances with only a handful of research that explores NILM deep learning techniques which performs regression and classification NILM task at the same time. However, majority of these approaches

H. Fujita et al. (Eds.): IEA/AIE 2023, LNAI 13926, pp. 59–65, 2023.
https://doi.org/10.1007/978-3-031-36822-6_5

used different stacked Deep Neural Network layers [2–5] which requires sufficient computational memory and often faces vanishing gradient problem. In order to mitigate these challenges, a novel NILM deep learning technique based on Temporal Convolutional Network (TCN) architecture is proposed in this article that simultaneously performs both NILM regression and classification task. The main idea of this proposed model is to disaggregate the total load into fine-grained and accurate consumption values and the operational states (either ON or OFF) of individual appliances.

2 NILM Problem Formulation

Consider a residential or commercial unit with total of A appliances. For time t period, each appliance a consume power p_t, and are in the operational state s_t that denotes On/Off (i.e. s_t is either 0 or 1). Then the aggregate power P_t is represented by

$$P_t = \sum_{a=1}^{A} s_t^{(a)} p_t^{(a)} + \epsilon_t$$

where, ϵ_t is the noise term. The purpose of the proposed NILM technique in this article is to breakdown the aggregate power P_t into power $p_t^{(a)}$ consumed and operational state $s_t^{(a)}$ for each appliance a simultaneously at time timestep t.

3 Description of Temporal Convolutional Network (TCN)

TCN is an improved version of one-dimensional convolutional neural network. The advantage of TCN lies in the integration of causal convolution, dilated convolution, and skip connection into the network structure. The motivation behind using causal convolution is to ensure that the output of time step t will not use future information and will only be obtained based on convolution operations at $t - 1$ and previous time steps. Dilated convolution allows the input of convolution to have interval sampling, and the sampling interval is determined by the dilation rate d. Therefore, this allows TCN to use fewer layers and obtain a large receptive field. For a one-dimensional time, series input $X = (x_0, x_1, x_2, \ldots, x_t, \ldots, x_T)$ and a filter $f : \{0, 1, 2, 3, \ldots, n - 1\}$, the dilated convolution operation $H(\cdot)$ of the sequence element T is defined as follows:

$$H(T) = (X *_d f)(T) = \sum_{i=0}^{n-1} f(i) \cdot x_{T-d \cdot i}$$

where n denotes the filter size, d represents the dilation factor and $T - d \cdot i$ accounts for the direction of the past. Increasing the filter size n and dilated factor d, the TCN can expand the receptive field, allows an output at the top layer to receive a wider range of input information. Moreover, parallelly processing the same filter in each layer improves computation efficiency of the whole model. Skip connection is directly connecting the feature map of the lower layer to the upper layer and 1×1 convolution ensures the addition of the same shape of feature maps. Skip connection helps to avoid the disappearance of the gradient when there is an increase in the number of network layers to strengthen the stability of the network. Thus, it can be said that TCN uses causal convolution and dilated convolution as standard convolutional layers. Using batch normalization and spatial dropout to each layer helps to regularize the network. Figure 1(a), shows two such layers with skip connection of 1×1 convolution that are encapsulated into a residual module. The deep TCN network is formed by stacking multiple number of these residual modules. Components of each residual block is shown in Fig. 1(b).

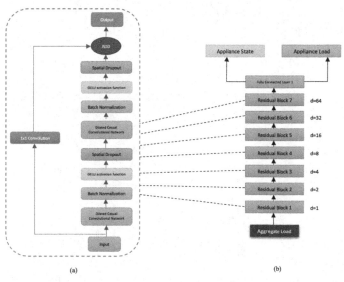

Fig. 1. (a) Residual Block of the proposed TCN NILM model. (b) The architecture of the proposed TCN NILM model

4 Dataset Description and Preparation

For training and evaluating the proposed model, a publicly accessible NILM dataset called REFIT [6] is used. Five appliances, namely Fridge-Freezer (F), Washing machine (WM), Dishwasher (DW), Microwave (MW) and Kettle (K) are selected to perform the NILM regression and classification task using the proposed technique. Two houses – house 3 and house 11 were selected. The consumption record of these two houses were down sampled to 60 s. The missing values were filled up using linear interpolation. After down sampling the records, house 3 had a total of 885095 instances and house 11 had 564697 instances. Consumption data of each house is used to separately train and evaluate the proposed model, i.e., the proposed model is trained and tested twice. 80% of the data from house 3 was split for training and remaining 20% for testing. Similar train-test split was done for house 11. The operational states of the appliances are derived from the consumption values of appliance by using the Middle Point Thresholding technique (MPT) [2]. Once the threshold values for each appliance is obtained, for each instance if the consumption of an appliance for a house is equal or greater than the respective threshold value then that appliance is set to ON state (value 1 is assigned), otherwise the appliance is set to OFF state (value 0 is assigned). Table 1 presents the threshold values of five appliances from house 3 and 11 (Fig. 2).

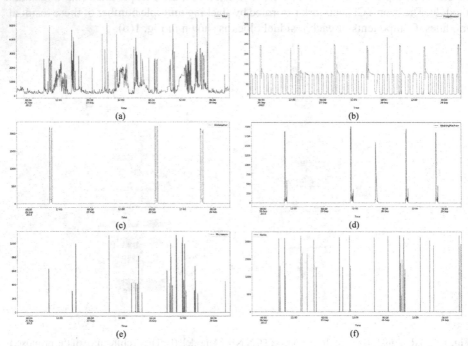

Fig. 2. Aggregated power load along with consumption value of five appliances for 48 h of House 3 data. (a) represents the aggregate power load, (b) consumption value of fridge-freezer, (c) dishwasher, (d) washing machine, (e) microwave and (f) kettle.

Table 1. Threshold values of the five different appliances of house 3 and 11. If the consumption value of an appliance is equal or greater than their respective threshold value, then that appliance is considered as ON otherwise it is OFF.

House Number	F	WM	DW	MW	K
House 3	50	892	1042	554	801
House 11	41	1000	1098	436	782

5 Result and Discussion

The Receptive field of TCN network should be large for the output of the respective network to receive wider range of input information. Increasing the number of hidden layers to achieve large TCN receptive field will increase the overall computational complexity. Therefore, it is important to choose the right filter size and dilation factor to increase the size of the TCN receptive field. For the proposed approach, the filter size is set to 3 and dilation factor for each residual block is set to 2^i where i is the residual block number. There are seven TCN residual blocks with each block having 128 filters for hidden layers. The final layer is a fully connected layer from which the final appliance states and power consumption are obtained. The spatial dropout rate is set to 0.2.

After the proposed model was trained and evaluated twice by data of house 3 and 11 separately, the regression task of the model was evaluated using MAE score and the classification task was evaluated using F1-score. The performance of the proposed model was also compared to the performance of the method proposed in [2] where a model comprised of CNN and LSTM architecture was used to obtain the appliance state and power consumption from the aggregated load signal. The benchmarking model is trained with the same set of data (house 3 and 11 of Refit dataset) which is used towards the training of the proposed model.

From Table 2 it is observed that the MAE scores based on the regression task of proposed TCN model for estimating power consumed by all five appliances of house 3 dataset is significantly better than the benchmarking LSTM-CNN model. The model scored an average MAE score of 14.35 for all the five appliances with overall MAE score of 15.36. The washing machine had the lowest MAE score of 8.67. The benchmarking method had an average MAE score of 18.17, with overall score of 25.67 for house 3. In terms of model trained and tested by house 11, similar observation is made where again the proposed TCN model outperformed the benchmarking approach in terms of MAE score for all the five appliances. The average MAE score of all the appliances for proposed model is 15.44 while the benchmarking method had MAE score of 18.86. Overall, the MAE score of the proposed model was 16.42 which is better than the benchmarking MAE score of 27.28 (Table 3).

Table 2. MAE score comparison between the proposed TCN model and the LSTM-CNN model

	Model	F	WM	DW	MW	K	Overall Score	Average Score
MAE score for House 3	TCN [proposed]	**10.95**	**8.76**	**15.97**	**14.43**	**21.68**	**15.36**	**14.35**
	LSTM-CNN	17.66	11.90	17.42	18.56	25.35	25.67	18.17
MAE score for House 11	TCN [proposed]	**8.41**	**10.38**	**18.52**	**12.93**	**26.78**	**16.42**	**15.44**
	LSTM-CNN	9.88	11.67	22.60	15.32	31.46	27.28	18.86

Table 3. F1-score comparison between the proposed TCN model and the LSTM-CNN model

	Model	F	WM	DW	MW	K	Overall Score	Average Score
F1-score for House 3	TCN [proposed]	**0.92**	**0.95**	**0.95**	**0.97**	**0.98**	**0.97**	**0.96**
	LSTM-CNN	0.83	0.91	0.94	0.88	0.92	0.91	0.89
F1-score for House 11	TCN [proposed]	**0.94**	**0.97**	**0.98**	**0.98**	**0.96**	**0.97**	**0.97**
	LSTM-CNN	0.88	0.92	0.89	0.93	0.95	0.90	0.92

For the classification NILM task, the proposed model again outperformed the benchmarking method in F1-score for classifying appliance operational state. For house 3, the average F1-score of the proposed model for all five appliance is 0.96 which is significantly higher than the average score of the benchmark LSTM-CNN model which is 0.89. Kettle had the highest F1-score of 0.98. Likewise for house 11 data, similar performance of the proposed model was observed where the TCN model outperformed the LSTM-CNN benchmark model for classifying appliance states. The proposed model had an overall score of 0.97 with an average 0.97 F1-score for all five appliances. Meanwhile the benchmark method overall scored 0.90 with average F1-score of 0.92 for all five appliances. The main reason of superiority of TCN model over LSTM-CNN model is for the option of having large receptive field which allows output to receive more input information, which makes the proposed model significantly better for the NILM regression and classification task.

6 Conclusion and Future Scope

This paper presented a novel NILM approach which combined classification and regression to predict power consumption along with on/off state of five different appliances of two houses in Refit dataset. The proposed model used TCN architecture to perform the NILM regression and classification task. The proposed approach was shown to have high accuracy when tested against the performance of the benchmarking technique which was comprised of LSTM-CNN architectures. In Future, semi-supervised learning approach that performs both regression and classification NILM task could be explored. It is important to mention that such simultaneous strategy of solving NILM regression and classification task performed by the proposed approach in this article will provide better understanding of load usage patterns, enabling residential and commercial buildings to support the smart grid.

References

1. Azizi, E., Beheshti, M.T., Bolouki, S.: A novel event-based non-intrusive load monitoring algorithm. arXiv preprint arXiv:2009.02656 (2020)

2. Precioso, D., Gómez-Ullate, D.: NILM as a regression versus classification problem: the importance of thresholding. arXiv preprint arXiv:2010.16050 (2020)
3. Saraswat, G., Lundstrom, B., Salapaka, M.V.: Scalable hybrid classification-regression solution for high-frequency nonintrusive load monitoring. arXiv preprint arXiv:2208.10638 (2022)
4. Naderian, S.: A novel hybrid deep learning approach for non-intrusive load monitoring of residential appliance based on long short term memory and convolutional neural networks. arXiv preprint arXiv:2104.07809 (2021)
5. Faustine, A., Pereira, L., Bousbiat, H., Kulkarni, S.: UNet-NILM: a deep neural network for multi-tasks appliances state detection and power estimation in NILM. In: Proceedings of the 5th International Workshop on Non-Intrusive Load Monitoring, pp. 84–88 (2020)
6. Murray, D., Stankovic, L., Stankovic, V.: An electrical load measurements dataset of United Kingdom households from a two-year longitudinal study. Sci. Data 4(1), 1–12 (2017)

Sentiment Analysis of Mobile Apps Using BERT

Wajhee Ullah[✉], Zheying Zhang, and Kostas Stefanidis

Tampere University, Tampere, Finland
{wajhee.ullah,zheying.zhang,konstantinos.stefanidis}@tuni.fi

Abstract. In this paper, we focus on identifying issues in mobile app updates that adversely impact the opinion in user reviews by analyzing the sentiment of the reviews. We use sentiment analysis using BERT to evaluate the performance of mobile apps and the sentiment distribution of reviews for identifying the cause of sentiment shifts. Using our method, developers can correctly locate the period of specific sentiment and review the sentences and keywords used in reviews to identify the problems and complaints in recent updates. An increase in negative sentiments after any major update can help identify the exact issue causing the problem. Our experimental analysis shows the effectiveness of the proposed method in recognizing issues and identifying any potential problematic updates.

Keywords: Sentiment Classification · BERT · Mobile Apps

1 Introduction

The rapid development of distributed computing has enabled the analysis of vast amounts of data and the prediction of customer preferences and demands. Understanding customers' emotional inclinations towards the application that they use daily has become increasingly important [9–11,17]. User reviews and ratings are critical factors in app selection, with studies indicating that users typically download apps based on these factors [7]. The reviews also help developers gain insight into user sentiment about applications and help to make decisions in rolling out updates to address issues or introduce new features. Sentiment analysis, a technique that extracts opinions from text, is a very powerful tool for finding out the emotions hidden behind the review and feedback.

In this work, we focus on identifying issues in mobile app updates that adversely impact the opinion in user reviews by analyzing the sentiment of user reviews. We classify the app reviews into three categories: positive, negative, and neutral, and use this distinction to identify the problematic mobile app updates based on the number of negative reviews in a certain period. This approach allows developers to be aware of user opinions on app updates and guides them proactively to address the most important issues early.

To perform sentiment analysis, we utilize the BERT model, namely the Bidirectional Encoder Representation from Transformers [4]. BERT is a deep learning

H. Fujita et al. (Eds.): IEA/AIE 2023, LNAI 13926, pp. 66–78, 2023.
https://doi.org/10.1007/978-3-031-36822-6_6

model where weights bctween elements are dynamically determined depending on their relationship. It uses an encoder to read text input and a decoder to provide predictions. The transformer, which is the attention mechanism that learns contextual relationships between words in a text, is integral to the model. The encoder processes a series of tokens to produce an output transformed into vectors and used for sentiment analysis. The paper's approach is essential because negative reviews can significantly impact the success of a mobile app. Therefore, it is crucial to identify any issues that lead to negative sentiment and address them promptly. The proposed method is effective in recognizing issues and identifying any potentially problematic updates. By leveraging the approach, developers can improve their mobile apps, enhance user experience, and increase user satisfaction.

2   Related Work

Sentiment analysis research has been extensively reported in the literature. Many studies applied lexicon-based approaches to extracting words that express positive or negative feelings in the text and analyzing the overall opinion by aggregating the sentiment score of these words. This approach uses a given lexical database or corpus-based lexicons tailored to specific domains, and each word is labeled as positive, negative, or neutral sentiments along with polarity. For example, [3] retrieved adjectives in the Amazon and CNET datasets and analyze the sentiment of reviews based on the positive or negative polarity of adjectives, using WordNet[1]. [5] investigated different techniques for calculating prior polarity scores based on SentiWordNet. [12] presents a Lexicon-based approach that considers positive, comparative, and superlative comparisons. This dictionary-based technique matches words inside phrases to determine their polarity by matching emotional lexis with both positive and negative terms. It uses a combination of lexicon heuristics and a pre-trained model to analyze text and provide sentiment scores. It also takes into account the intensity of sentiment. Vader [8] also provides a compound score which is a normalized, weighted composite score. This score is computed by summing the valence scores of each word in the lexicon, adjusted according to the rules, and then normalized. When information is scarce, this lexicon could provide useful polarity alternatives to machine learning methodologies, and it is imperative to consider other workable possibilities.

In addition to the traditional lexicon-based methods, machine learning approaches are widely used for studies on sentiment analysis. [15] investigated pre-processing techniques for sentiment analysis of Twitter datasets using four machine learning algorithms. [2] uses *Bidirectional Encoder Representations from Transformers* (BERT) to analyze emotions. Four machine learning algorithms are utilized to compare with the BERT. Overall, experiments have shown that BERT surpasses machine learning approaches with socially constructed baselines for emotional analysis. For TextCNN, accuracy slightly increases than other machine learning techniques. Although the differences are not large, SVM gives

---

[1] https://wordnet.princeton.edu/.

better results when compared to Naive Bayes and *k-Nearest Neighbors algorithm* (k-NN) in terms of relative performance. [6] conducted a comparative analysis of four commonly used algorithms, and they are Naive Bayes, Max Entropy, Boosted Trees, and Random Forest Algorithms. This study reported that, although requiring a lot of training time, the Random Forest classifier has good accuracy and performance, is easy to comprehend, and consistently produces incremental results over time. The NB classifier uses less memory and takes less time to train. Max Entropy is a worthy alternative if less training time is the highest priority. On average, when considering different aspects, the best-performing classifier is the boosted Tress. Additionally, [14] proposed a hybrid approach by combining rule-based classification, supervised learning, and machine learning into a new combined method, and tested it on movie reviews, product reviews, and MySpace comments.

The feature extraction methods employed in the emotional analysis had undergone a fair amount of adjustment [13]. The Stanford parser is used to parse movie reviews. Four feature extraction strategies are applied for feature extraction across many corpora. This approach is called the *Intrinsic Extrinsic Domain Relevance Approach* (IEDR), it is not industry-specific in its design, and when compared to other methodologies utilized for sentiment classification and analysis, it suggests feature extraction for performance improvements. A proportional examination of emotional location using *Support Vector Machine* (SVM) and Naive Bayes techniques was conducted in [1]. The best accuracy is obtained when utilizing Naive Bayes with the synthetic word method and linear SVM. An evaluation study on movies shows that dramatic film genres distinguish out for their greater authenticity when compared to other film genres. Using a graph, the authors also display the polarity of certain words.

3   The BERT Model

BERT is an open-source machine learning framework for natural language processing. It targets grasping the meaning of uncertain words in a phrase or sentence by building meaning from adjacent information. Originally, it was trained using 2500M words from English Wikipedia and 800M words from the BooksCorpus Dataset. BERT can operate across both directions while simultaneously reading, i.e., can understand the text from both left to right or right to left. Using this bidirectional capacity, BERT is pre-trained on two different but related natural language processing tasks. In turn, *Masked Language Model* (MLM) conceals some percentage of the input tokens at random to predict the original vocabulary of the concealed word based only on its context. The model enables pre-trained deep bidirectional representations. The *Next Sentence Prediction* (NSP) task trains a model that understands sentence relationships.

The main purpose of almost any natural language processing method is to understand human language. For achieving this, traditional models are usually trained using a large pool of exact data. BERT, on the other hand, is trained with just an unstructured simple text collection. Despite its use in real-world scenarios, it continues to acquire knowledge unattended from sequences of words. The pre-processing serves as any knowledge ground.

BERT's model architecture is a multi-layer bidirectional Transformer encoder. This transformer is the model component that enables BERT to detect background and uncertainty. It is achieved by the transformer by assessing each phrase and comparing it to every other part of a phrase. Examining the related letters assists BERT in grasping the full background of the word, helping it to better comprehend the searcher's intent.

In contrast to the traditional word embedding strategy, older systems might convert each singular phrase into such a directional quantity that conveyed nothing but one fragment regarding the definition of words. Such embedding models demand a large amount of labeled data. While they succeed at several broad natural language processing tasks, they fail to demonstrate effectiveness, due to the fact that every word is in one way or another linked to a definition.

BERT takes into account the use of MLM to prevent the required word from *seeing itself* and acquiring a limited interpretation irrespective of its surroundings. As a result, BERT only considers camouflaged text by looking at the preface. In this framework, texts are based on their conditions rather than by being identified upon some static approach.

This note is of great importance since words frequently alter meaning as a phrase progresses. Each new word adds to the overall significance of the term targeted by natural language processing mechanisms. The more words in each piece of writing, the less evident the term in focus becomes. By reading two-way communications, taking into consideration the impact of all other words in the sentence on the target word, and minimizing the movement that causes words to have a specific connotation as a sentence progresses, BERT gives enhanced meaning.

Prediction of Next Phrase. During the BERT training process, the system is given a series of inputs and is asked to do some calculations and guess whether the next input of the series is the next word of the given data. Half of the values are in the form of pairs in which the next value is the next sentence of the original input value. The remaining 50% of the total are arbitrary words from the corpus. It is expected that the randomized text is distinct from the first sentence. To assist the model in distinguishing between the two phrases during training, the data is handled as follows before reaching the model:

- A token appears at the start of the first sentence, and a token appears just at the end of every text. Token embeddings are a way to represent words or other discrete units of text as dense vectors of real numbers.
- Each token receives a sentence embedding. Sentences with a range of 2, extracted features are essentially equivalent to token word embeddings.
- A positional embedding is assigned to each token to signify its location in the paragraph. Transformer describes the idea and execution of directional embedding.

To predict if the second sentence is connected to the first, the following procedure is carried out:

– The Transformer model goes through the whole input sequence.
– The [CLS] token output is transformed into a 2 * 1 shaped vector using a basic classification layer (learned matrices of weights and biases).
– The probability of something being the next sequence is predicted by Soft-Max.

In the BERT model, MLM and NSP are trained concurrently with the goal of minimizing the combined loss function of the two approaches. The data for this classification job must be split into two parts: test sample and training batch. The learning is required to train the classifier, and the second sample is used to evaluate the classifier's performance.

The sentiment classifier is built on top of the BERT model. we took advantage of BERT's ability to encode and understand the contextual relationships between words in a sentence. To adapt BERT for sentiment classification, we fine-tuned the pre-trained model on a labeled dataset of reviews and their corresponding sentiment labels. During the training process, the weights of the BERT model are updated on the basis of input data for sentiment classification which allow the model to learn the sentiments.

4   Experimental Setting

In this section, we study how to identify the abnormal days and the mobile app updates that adversely affect the sentiments of user reviews.

Dataset. The dataset contains user reviews from five social media mobile apps, collected using google-play-scraper[2]. The reviews for each app are from September 1, 2016, to August 31, 2017. Altogether, the dataset contains 202,870 reviews for IMO, 122,622 reviews for Hangouts, 1,654,360 reviews for Messenger, 153,128 reviews for Skype, and 1,660,145 reviews for Whatsapp.

Pre-processing. During the pre-processing phase, non-English reviews are filtered out. We eliminate non-English reviews with Langdetect[3], a handy language detection program for Python.

Mobile app reviews are usually short compared to the reviews on other platforms but still, the multiple sentences in a single review could affect the sentiment and mean [3]. The next step in pre-processing is to separate the multiple sentences in a single review into individual sentences. For this purpose, sentence tokenizers are used to split the text or whole reviews into individual sentences. We have used the *Natural Language Toolkit* (NLTK) python package to split the reviews into sentences. NLTK is a leading platform for building Python programs to work with human language data.

Table 1 shows the statistics for the datasets. Imo and Hangout contain fewer reviews compared to Messenger and WhatsApp which have over 1M reviews. Reviews are classified into positive, negative, or neutral based on their rating score, where a review containing a rating score of 4 or 5 is classified as Positive,

---

[2] https://github.com/JoMingyu/google-play-scraper.
[3] https://pypi.org/project/langdetect/.

Table 1. Apps Reviews Statistics

App Name	Reviews	English Reviews	Sentences	Updates
Imo	202,870	86,194	100,838	84
Hangouts	122,622	68,535	101,704	43
Messenger	1,654,360	886,643	1,185,368	105
Skype	153,128	105,875	189,995	76
Whatsapp	1,660,145	851,662	1,098,583	49

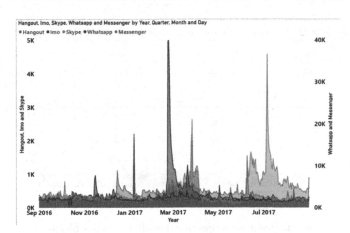

Fig. 1. Frequency of Apps Reviews over Time

a review containing a rating score of 3 is classified as Neutral, and a review with a rating score 1 or 2 is categorized as Negative. Together with the reviews, the number of updates of each mobile app in the given period is also shown in the table. Also, Fig. 1 shows the frequency of all app reviews over the period of time. Finally, we classify the dataset into training and validation sets. The training set consists of 85% of the original dataset, while the validation set contains the remaining 15%.

Training. For training, the learning rate, the weight of the network with respect to the loss gradient descent, is 0.001. It determines how fast or slow we will move toward the optimal weights. The dropout for the training model is set at 0.5. The dropout layer prevents the overfitting of the model by ignoring some neurons during the training phase. We used Adam as our optimizer, CategoricalCrossentropy as our loss function, and SparseCategoricalAccuracy as our accuracy metric. The training model is trained for 10 epochs.

5   Evaluation

5.1   Identify Abnormal Days

In this section, we analyze the sentiment of the users' reviews of 5 apps, from 1 September 2016 to 31 August 2017. The abnormal distribution of some specific

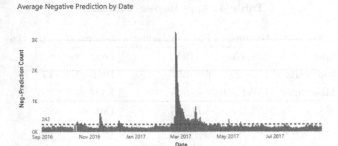

Fig. 2. Predicted Negative Trends by days - Whatsapp

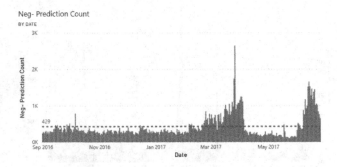

Fig. 3. Predicted Negative Trends by days - Skype

days helps to identify the days with most probably some problem in the app. The distribution of negative reviews of individual apps and analysis are shown below.

Whatsapp. Based on the obtained results, the count of negative value trended up and resulting in a 21.19% increase between Thursday, September 1, 2016, and Thursday, August 31, 2017. Also from the predicted values, the negative value started trending down on Wednesday, March 29, 2017, falling by 41.53% (130) in 5.07 months. It can also be concluded from Fig. 2 that the count of negative values jumped from 251 to 1,007 during its steepest incline between Monday, February 20, 2017, and Tuesday, February 28, 2017.

Skype. The trends obtained from the predicted values in Fig. 3 show that the average negative prediction trended up, resulting in a 217.84% increase between Thursday, September 1, 2016, and Sunday, June 25, 2017, while the average negative prediction started trending down on Saturday, June 10, 2017, falling by 34.70% (407) in 15 days. It is also evident from the results that the average negative prediction jumped from 368 to 755 during its steepest incline between Wednesday, June 7, 2017, and Friday, June 9, 2017.

Hangout. Figure 4 shows the average negative prediction trended down, resulting in a 62.96% decrease between Thursday, September 1, 2016, and Thurs-

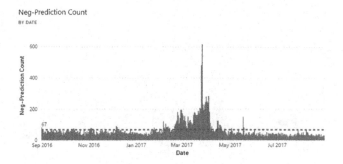

Fig. 4. Predicted Negative Trends by days - Hangout

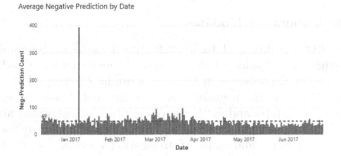

Fig. 5. Predicted Negative Trends by days - Imo

day, August 31, 2017. It can also be concluded that average negative prediction started trending down on Sunday, April 23, 2017, falling by 46.43% (26) in 4.27 months while negative prediction gained during its steepest incline between Thursday, March 30, 2017, and Sunday, April 30, 2017.

Imo. Figure 5 shows the average negative prediction trended down, resulting in a 16.00% decrease between Thursday, September 1, 2016, and Thursday, August 31 2017 also average negative prediction started trending down on Tuesday, January 10, 2017, falling by 4.55% in 7.70 months. It is also evident that the average negative prediction jumped from 38 to 47 during its steepest incline between Tuesday, January 3, 2017, and Monday, January 9, 2017.

Messenger. Figure 6 shows that the average negative prediction trended down, resulting in a 1.57% decrease between Monday, December 12, 2016, and Sunday, June 25 2017 also the average negative prediction started trending down on Monday, June 12, 2017, falling by 0.30% in 12 days. It is also shown from the results that the average negative prediction jumped from 977 to 1,066 during its steepest incline between Monday, June 5, 2017, and Sunday, June 11, 2017.

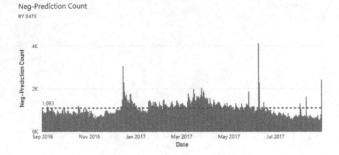

Fig. 6. Predicted Negative Trends by days - Messenger

5.2   Identify Abnormal Updates

The results obtained are used to identify the days with abnormal negative reviews. Further investigation of the negative reviews and the trends helps to identify the potential abnormal updates. The update history of the apps and their relationship with the negative review count could help to identify the adverse impact of updates and further exploring the reviews would also provide the reasons for the issue which could help the developers to identify the potential problems in app-updates and cause of application's low rating. We have manually analyzed the reviews about the days that have an abnormal amount of negative reviews predicted by the algorithm. Reviews on those specific days provide insight into potential issues in the apps which are further discussed below.

Whatsapp. Based on the results of analyzing the number of negative reviews on WhatsApp and the update history of the app, we found that the update on February 22, 2017 overlaps with the dates when the number of negative reviews increases the most. The update introduced the story feature that enables users to share status messages in the form of a GIF, video, or an image[4]. The results of sentiment analysis show the number of negative reviews jumped from 251 to 1007, which is the steepest incline in negative reviews between February 20, 2017, to February 28, 2017. This could be argued that the update may have been responsible for the sudden increase in negative reviews and be identified as a problematic update, which can be confirmed by looking at the example reviews in Table 2. The newly added story feature and the change to the location of the contacts tab are not appreciated by many users.

Imo. From the predicted results for the Imo application, we looked into the duration from January 03, 2017, to January 09, 2017, and investigate further the reasons that cause the increased negative reviews. The previous update from the negative spike update between January 03 2017 to January 09 2017 was on December 21, 2016 (9.8.000000004201 (1248)) so we can conclude that the

---

[4] https://www.businesstoday.in/technology/news/story/whatsapp-changes-everything-with-its-new-status-feature-71508-2017-02-21.

Table 2. WhatsApp Negative reviews after new update

Date	Review	Rating
22/02/2017	"New update is so bad, deleted the photo or video story update, its not Instagram or line apps, as long as I know, whats app is only chatting apps"	1
22/02/2017	how to stop new status updates, I don't want to see people status"	1
23/02/2017	"I am looking forward to yhe new update where there is a separate status and story tab for both of them"	1

Table 3. Imo reviews after increased negative review count

Date	Review	Rating
07/01/2017	"Something happened to where I had to reinstall the app and after that I am not able to verify my number on it to reinstall"	2
07/01/2017	"My imo acount not working properly even I uninstall app and installed again not but it doesn't working and take a long time for verification code after that it shut down automatically"	2
08/01/2017	"Update versions is not good. . ."	2

previous update was not the cause for increased negative reviews. But analyzing the reviews of this duration it could be concluded that failure in some app functionality and abnormal closing of the app is the main issue users were facing in this duration (Table 3).

Skype. According to the results of the skype application, in Early, June 2017 there is an abnormal no. of negative reviews from users. Review analysis from these dates could help us to identify the problem. Skype had an update at the start of June 2017[5] and the negative reviews trended upwards since the start of June 2017. The negative reviews mostly state the issue faced after the app update. Some users were worried about the new UI introduced in the application while some reviews are due to technical issues in the application like not being able to send a file etc.

Hangouts. From the results of the Hangouts application, we have a negative review increase at the end of February 2017 and the beginning of March 2017. Further study of the reviews helps us to identify the reasons. Hangouts had an update on February 27, 2017[6] and the negative reviews trended upwards after

---

[5] https://www.greenbot.com/microsoft-completely-revamps-skype-new-ui-snapchat-like-stories/.

[6] https://www.apkmirror.com/apk/google-inc/hangouts/hangouts-17-0-148298972-release/hangouts-17-0-148298972-17-android-apk-download/.

Table 4. Skype reviews after increased negative review count

Date	Review	Rating
08/06/2017	"If these kinda updates continue then doom's day is not far away skype"	1
08/06/2017	"Cannot send file on new version ?!?!?!?!"	1
04/06/2017	"Terrible new UI treating me like I have reading difficulties, displaying everything very big and feels very sticky"	2

Table 5. Hangouts reviews after increased negative review count

Date	Review	Rating
03/03/2017	"Really wish Google had better quality control and a better vision for its products."	1
03/03/2017	"Its a great app and u should download it but plz fix the bugs it wasnt working when i was chating with my friend and we couldnt video call because it say on going call when we hung up"	1
02/03/2017	"Why y'all forcing me to update my shit I'm good with the old version"	1

Table 6. Messenger reviews after increased negative review count

Date	Review	Rating
11/03/2017	"Would be fine if it wasn't draining my battery"	2
11/02/2017	"It takes extremely long to send an image which I never had a problem in the past"	1
11/03/2017	"Should be fast and photo uploading new ways should be introduced"	2

then and in the start of March 2017. The negative reviews mostly stated the issue about the forcefully close and crash of the application while using.

Messenger. According to the results of the Messenger application, in Dec 2016 there is a sudden increase in the number of negative reviews from users. Further review analysis from these dates could help us to identify the problem. Messenger has an update on 15 December 201 and 8 March 2017[7] and we see the negative reviews increased after that. The reviews mention a problem with the battery drain which could be an ongoing issue with the application but the problem with the photo uploading that takes much longer could be the issue that has been coming with the update (Tables 4, 5 and 6).

---

[7] https://www.apkmirror.com/apk/facebook-2/messenger/messenger-100-0-0-29-61-release/.

6   Conclusion

This paper presents a sentiment analysis of reviews for five different mobile apps using BERT. Sentiment analysis is an effective method to evaluate the performance of applications, and the sentiment distribution of reviews is particularly useful for identifying the cause of sentiment shifts. Developers can use this method to correctly identify the period of specific sentiment and further review the sentences and keywords used in reviews to identify the problems and complaints in recent updates. An increase in negative sentiments after any major update can help identify the exact issue causing the problem. This method presented in the paper aims to help developers stay informed about any major issues that cause low ratings in user reviews and identify any potential update that adversely impacts the sentiment of reviews. The results demonstrate the effectiveness of the proposed method in recognizing issues and identifying any potential problematic updates.

Acknowledgement. This work is based on the Master Thesis "Sentiment Analysis of Mobile Apps Using BERT" [16], appearing at the digital library of the Tampere University. We thank the Tampere University for supporting this research.

References

1. Alnashwan, R., O'Riordan, A., Sorensen, H., Hoare, C.: Improving sentiment analysis through ensemble learning of meta-level features. In: KDWeb (2016)
2. Cao, Y., Sun, Z., Li, L., Mo, W.: A study of sentiment analysis algorithms for agricultural product reviews based on improved BERT model. Symmetry **14**(8), 1604 (2022)
3. Cui, H., Mittal, V.O., Datar, M.: Comparative experiments on sentiment classification for online product reviews. In: Proceedings, The Twenty-First National Conference on Artificial Intelligence and the Eighteenth Innovative Applications of Artificial Intelligence Conference (2006)
4. Devlin, J., Chang, M., Lee, K., Toutanova, K.: BERT: pre-training of deep bidirectional transformers for language understanding. In: NAACL-HLT (2019)
5. Guerini, M., Gatti, L., Turchi, M.: Sentiment analysis: how to derive prior polarities from sentiwordnet. In: EMNLP (2013)
6. Gupte, A., Joshi, S., Gadgul, P., Kadam, A.: Comparative study of classification algorithms used in sentiment analysis. IJCSIT **5**(5), 6261–6264 (2014)
7. Harman, M., Jia, Y., Zhang, Y.: App store mining and analysis: MSR for app stores. In: MSR (2012)
8. Hutto, C.J., Gilbert, E.: VADER: a parsimonious rule-based model for sentiment analysis of social media text. In: ICWSM. The AAAI Press (2014)
9. Li, X., Zhang, B., Zhang, Z., Stefanidis, K.: A sentiment-statistical approach for identifying problematic mobile app updates based on user reviews. Inf. **11**(3), 152 (2020)
10. Li, X., Zhang, Z., Stefanidis, K.: Mobile app evolution analysis based on user reviews. In: SoMeT. Frontiers in Artificial Intelligence and Applications (2018)
11. Li, X., Zhang, Z., Stefanidis, K.: A data-driven approach for video game playability analysis based on players' reviews. Inf. **12**(3), 129 (2021)

12. Mandal, S., Gupta, S.: A novel dictionary-based classification algorithm for opinion mining. In: ICRCICN (2016)
13. Pasarate, S., Shedge, R.: Comparative study of feature extraction techniques used in sentiment analysis. In: ICICCS-INBUSH (2016)
14. Prabowo, R., Thelwall, M.: Sentiment analysis: a combined approach. J. Informetr. **3**(2), 143–157 (2009)
15. Symeonidis, S., Effrosynidis, D., Arampatzis, A.: A comparative evaluation of pre-processing techniques and their interactions for twitter sentiment analysis. Expert Syst. Appl. **110**, 298–310 (2018)
16. Ullah, W.: Sentiment analysis of mobile apps using BERT. Master of Science Thesis, Faculty of Information Technology and Communication Sciences, Tampere University, Finland (2023)
17. Zhang, L., Hua, K., Wang, H., Qian, G., Zhang, L.: Sentiment analysis on reviews of mobile users. In: MobiSPC (2014)

Heterogeneous Ensemble for Classifying Electrical Load Reduction in South Africa

Solomon Oluwole Akinola[✉], Qing-Guo Wang, Peter Olukanmi, and Tshilidzi Mawala

Institute for Intelligent Systems, University of Johannesburg, Johannesburg, South Africa
oluwolea@uj.ac.za

Abstract. Electricity outages in South Africa have become a growing concern for businesses and individuals. Despite improvements in supply, planned outages are becoming regular and manual load reduction is an ever-increasing concern for utility electricity agencies. This study presents a heterogeneous ensemble technique for classifying manual load reduction based on the contributing features of electricity generation sources and demand. Classical Random Forest (RF), Sparse Partial Least Squares (SPLS), and Averaged Neural Network (AvNNet) machine learning techniques were used as benchmarks. Three ensemble approaches were explored. Our results showed that the weighted average technique outperforms every other technique investigated. This is true for Precision 65.40%, F1 score 78.52%, Balanced Accuracy 97.15%, Kappa 76.53%, and Confusion Matrix. The only exception is Recall 98.24%, slightly outperformed by the majority voting 98.81%. It correctly classified 89.3% and 6.9% for Eskom no-load reduction (normal) and load reduction (anomaly), respectively. 3.7% and 0.1% accounted for the type-I and type-II errors, respectively.

Keywords: load reduction · heterogeneous ensemble · neural network

1 Introduction

Globally, the electricity demand is an existential requirement. The generation, transmission, and distribution of electricity require continuous monitoring to avoid the collapse of the electricity grid infrastructure and maintain a regular supply. The advent of the Fourth Industrial Revolution (4IR) [1] through artificial intelligence [2] has paved the way for modern cyber-physical systems with sophisticated sensory equipment to collect multivariate historical electricity grid system datasets. A significant problem with an electricity grid system is the effect of load reduction from insufficient generation sources, seasonal peak demand, breakdowns, and extraneous factors [3]. These anomalies can significantly reduce production time and income and negatively impact a nation's economy [4]. Predictive unplanned load reduction is critical for the electricity demand, supply, and planned maintenance indicators. Predicting potential load reduction is a crucial decision for the electric utility sector. As a result, the underlying features (indicators) in the existing demand and supply data can provide critical computational intelligence for achieving reliable classification tasks in load reduction.

© The Author(s), under exclusive license to Springer Nature Switzerland AG 2023
H. Fujita et al. (Eds.): IEA/AIE 2023, LNAI 13926, pp. 79–89, 2023.
https://doi.org/10.1007/978-3-031-36822-6_7

Since 2007, load reduction in South Africa has developed into an occasionally observed dilemma [3]. When electricity consumption increases, it must be met with a sufficient supply, which results in economic benefits [4]. Eskom's long-serving coal power plants are almost four decades old [4]. The consequence is unplanned maintenance leading to load reduction, as the electricity plant system is unpredictable, thus jeopardising the electricity supply and undermining South Africa's economic growth potential.

Machine learning (ML) techniques perform exceptionally well in classification and regression experiments. In electric power outage investigations, addressing related tasks with the prime merits of 4IR ability and computational intelligence is evolving. Forecasting [2, 3, 5], demand-supply mismatch [4, 6], and electricity consumption aggregates [7] have been explored for electric power systems. The challenge is associated with modelling techniques for the complexities of the electric grid system features.

We considered manual load reduction (MLR)-related outages as a classification task because they are related to consumer electric power demand and Eskom electric power supply sources to preserve the electric power grid stability and avoid overload. We used the hourly contracted demand and electric power generation sources to classify possible load reductions from the MLR indicators. The applied approach is based on proven techniques using heterogeneous ensemble predictors. The heterogeneous ensemble technique combines base predictors to aggregate dataset results [8]. The ensemble model aggregates several heterogeneous models and improves the overall accuracy of the results. Simple averaging (EA), majority voting (MV), and weighted average (WA) were ensemble combined with tree-based models for various independent optimisations. In equivalent experiments, WA was applied to classification and regression tasks in disease prediction [9–12], image defect detection [8], and image classification tasks [13, 14].

The remainder of this paper is organised as follows. Section 2 presents Eskom electric power generation and consumption data, models, evaluations, and workflow. Section 3 estimates the model parameters using a model simulation and discusses the findings. Finally, conclusions are presented in Sect. 4.

2   Materials and Method

2.1   Eskom Electric Power Generation and Consumption Data

Eskom is a South African company responsible for generating, transmitting, distributing, and selling electricity, expanding power stations, and distributing electric power infrastructure. The MLR indicator is an extreme measure to avoid expensive breakdowns and ensure regular maintenance. The Eskom data portal provides much-needed support to harmonise the national grid demand and supply hourly data indicators available on Eskom shareable website: https://www.eskom.co.za/dataportal.

A considerable amount of hourly data was collected from Eskom. Our experiment focused on the sources and demand of electric power generation in South Africa. Table 1 presents the hourly Eskom electricity sources. Thermal power constituted 81.75% of the generation, indicating Eskom's reliance.

Table 1. Eskom Electricity power sources

S/N	Eskom Electricity Source	Description
1	International imports	Electric power supply from neighbouring countries to South Africa
2	Thermal power	Electric power generated by coalfired power stations
3	Nuclear power	Electric power generated by nuclear power stations
4	Eskom gas	Electric power generated by the gas turbine
5	Eskom OCGT	Electric power generated from an open-cycle gas turbine (the primary resource is diesel)
6	Hydrowater	Electric power generated by hydropower stations
7	Pumped water	Electric power generated from pumped-storage power stations
8	Wind	Electric power generated by the wind
9	CSP	Electric power generated from solar power units
10	Other RE sources	Electric power generated from plants (small hydro, biomass, landfill gas, etc.)
11	Manual Load Reduction (MLR)	MLR represent the hourly outage from guided load reduction

2.2 Data Collection

Table 2 and Fig. 1 show four years of hourly electricity load data from April 1, 2018. Over 43,824 hourly observations were reduced from incomplete entries to 38,240. The proportion of Eskom no-load reduction (normal) was significantly higher than that of Eskom load reduction (anomaly). The no-load reduction (normal) was 89.4%, and the load reduction (anomaly) was 10.6%. Imbalanced data is shared in real-world data classification tasks.

Table 2. Eskom MLR Data Distribution

	Normal	Anomaly
Observations	34509 (89.31%)	4193 (10.68%)
Train	25910 (89.32%)	3070 (10.67%)
Test	10348 (89.28%)	1242 (10.71%)

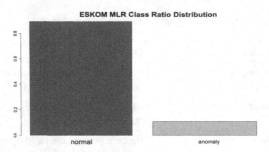

Fig. 1. Class count for Eskom load reduction (anomaly) and no-load reduction (normal).

RSA Contracted Demand. Hourly average demand from all Eskom electric power suppliers.

2.3 Machine Learning Techniques

Random Forest (RF). RF is a well-known learning algorithm that performs well in categorisation and regression tasks. RF merges comparatively uncorrelated decision tree predictors. A voting phase is initiated with the majority vote class as the final predictor [10].

Sparse Partial Least Squares (SPLS). SPLS is an adaptation of the partial least squares (PLS) technique, which allows both sparse feature selection and dimension reduction of correlated features. SPLS incorporates LASSO [15] penalisation in feature selection for predictor and outcome features. We applied SPLS based on the merits of dimensional reduction in classification tasks.

Averaged Neural Networks (AvNNet). In Ripley [16] demonstrated that multiple averaging neural networks produce improved results for test data. The AvNNet model results were converted into class labels for classification. The tunable parameter for AvNNet is a random seed. The random-seed method yielded reproducible results. Input and output observations in non-deterministic models require random seeds for reproducibility and benchmark results [17].

Ensemble. Predictors are a set of associated predictions obtained using multiple ML techniques. The results from these combinations were superior to those obtained using independent classical techniques [18]. Simple averaging (EA), majority voting (MV), and weighted average (WA) ensembles improve model accuracy in experimental evaluations for classification and regression problems [10, 19]. The WA technique was implemented to achieve superior generalisation performance in the classification task.

2.4 Performance Evaluation

True Positive (*TP*). *TP* represents the number of MLR correctly classified as load reductions (anomalies).

True Negative (*TN*). *TN* represents the number of MLR correctly classified as no-load reduction and denotes normal.

False Positive (*FP*). *FP* represents the number of misclassified MLR as an anomaly, but is normal. *FP* is described as a type-I error.

False Negative (*FN*). *FN* represents the number of MLR misclassified as normal. FN is described as a type-II error.

Balanced Accuracy (*A_B*). This is the ratio of *TP* rate (sensitivity/S_{TP}) and *TN* rate (specificity/S_{TN}).

$$A_B = \frac{S_{TP} + S_{TN}}{2} \tag{1}$$

Precision (*P_r*).   This represents the correctly classified anomaly (*TP*) ratio to the total MLR predicted to have an anomaly (*TP* + *FP*).

$$P_r = \frac{TP}{TP + FP} \tag{2}$$

Recall (*R_e*). This is the ratio of correctly classified anomalies (*TP*) to the total number of MLR with an actual anomaly. The recall is described equally as sensitivity.

$$R_e = \frac{TP}{TP + FN} \tag{3}$$

F1 Score (*F_1*). This is also described as the F Measure, which is the ratio between precision and recall.

$$F_1 = \frac{2 * P_r * R_e}{P_r + R_e} \tag{4}$$

Cohen's Kappa (Kappa). Cohen's kappa (Kappa) is the ratio of the difference between the correct anomaly and the normal classifier from the expected prediction based only on random guessing. In a Kappa score, a numerical rating close to the statistical value of 1 is in good agreement [20].

Confusion Matrix. The Confusion Matrix, also known as the error matrix, describes the performance of a classification model on a set of test data.

2.5 Model Workflow

As shown in Fig. 2, the workflow incorporates an ensemble model using classical ML techniques. In the first stage, features excluding class-label observations were transformed using normalisation techniques. Class label observations were created using

Eskom MLR data. Two classes were generated no-load reduction (normal) and Eskom load reduction (anomaly). The features and labels were split into training and holdout sets, respectively. The classical RF [10], SPLS, and AvNNet [16] techniques were trained using the training set, and the models were evaluated on the holdout set. A weighted average combination of conventional methods (RF, SPLS, and AvNNet) was implemented using heterogeneous EA, MV, and WA. The performances of all models on the holdout set were compared using Precision, recall, F1 score, kappa, and confusion matrices.

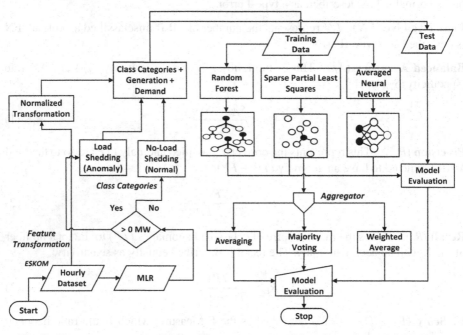

Fig. 2. Heterogeneous ensemble workflow process describing stages for implementation.

RStudio with the caret package [21] was used to design and construct models. The caret package is a library suite used for workflow implementation. Tuneable parameters for RF, SPLS, AvNNet, EA, MV, and WA are summarised. The RF model is configured with the mtry parameter because it is considered to have a noticeable impact. The mtry is the number collected for sampling in every split time run. The optimal mtry was six with five-fold cross-validation using an accuracy metric. The AvNNet is a decay function; the hidden layer is set to one with a size argument by default. In SPLS, ten hidden components and a 90% thresholding parameter were the optimal configurations. EA is described as calculating the average of model predictions with the highest percentage. MV chooses the forecasts with the most votes to be selected. In WA, weights are determined by the model's significance before prediction.

3 Results and Discussion

3.1 Results

The experimental results demonstrate that the WA was the highest among all the models presented in the performance evaluation. To further investigate the capability of the classical ensemble and ML models with Eskom load-shedding data, Fig. 3(a) to Fig. 3(f) illustrate the test results from the confusion matrices for RF, AvNNet, SPLS, EA, MV, and WA. The Eskom MLR shedding data categories were distributed for load reduction (anomaly) and no-load reduction (normal).

From the RF model Confusion Matrix in Fig. 3(a) and Table 3, no-load reduction (normal) accounted for 89.1% of the normalised count overall, and load reduction (anomaly) accounted for 6.5% of the normalised counts. At the same time, 4% and 0.3% accounted for the RF model FP and FN, respectively. In each Confusion Matrix tile, the percentage at the column bottom and row right (sum $\sum$ rotated 90°) accounted for the column sum and row sum ratios. The performance for the RF model Precision (61.78%), Recall (95.90%), F1 score (75.15%), Balanced Accuracy (95.78%), and Kappa (72.90%) yields a lower score in comparison with the model benchmark and ranks fourth-best. In the AvNNet model Confusion Matrix is shown in Fig. 3(b) and Table 3, no-load reduction (normal) accounted for 88.9% of the normalised count overall, and load reduction (anomaly) accounted for 6.8% of the normalised counts. 4.8% and 0.5% accounted for FP and FN, respectively. The AvNNet Precision was 64.52%, Recall 92.96%, F1 score 76.17%, Balanced Accuracy 94.45%, and Kappa 73.90% compared to the model benchmark ranks lowest. In the SPLS model Confusion Matrix is shown in Fig. 3(c) and Table 3, no-load reduction (normal) accounted for 89.3% of the normalised count overall, and load reduction (anomaly) accounted for 4.3% of the normalised counts. FP and FN accounted for 6.2% and 0.1% of cases, respectively. The SPLS model score for Precision was 54.90%, Recall 97.22%, F1 score 57.73%, Balanced Accuracy 95.34%, and Kappa 54.90% was ranked second most diminutive.

In the EA model Confusion Matrix in Fig. 3(d) and Table 3, no-load reduction (normal) accounted for 89.3% of the normalised count overall, and load reduction (anomaly) accounted for 6.8% of the normalised counts. 3.8% and 0.1% accounted for FP and FN, respectively. The performance for the EA model Precision was 63.93%, Recall 98.20%, F1 score 77.44%, Balanced Accuracy 97.05%, and Kappa 75.39% ranks second best in comparison to the model benchmark. In the MV model Confusion Matrix in Fig. 3(e) and Table 3, no-load reduction (normal) accounted for 89.3% of the normalised count overall, and load reduction (anomaly) accounted for 6% of the normalised counts. FP and FN accounted for 4.6% and 0.1%, respectively. The performance for Precision was 56.70%, Recall 98.81%, F1 score 72.05%, Balanced Accuracy 96.96%, and Kappa 69.71% in the MV model and third-best when compared to the model benchmark. In the WA model Confusion Matrix in Fig. 3(f) and Table 3, no-load reduction (normal) accounted for 89.3% of the normalised count overall, and load reduction (anomaly) accounted for 6.9% of the normalised counts. 3.7% and 0.1% accounted for FP and FN, respectively. The performance for Precision was 65.40%, Recall 98.24%, F1 score 78.52%, Balanced Accuracy 97.15%, and Kappa 76.53% outperforming every other technique investigated and ranking as the benchmark. The only exception is in the WA model Recall score ranked highest.

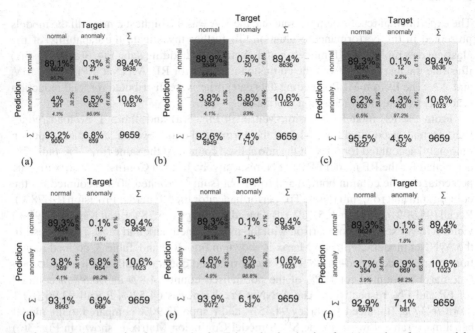

Fig. 3. Confusion Matrix of test results for Eskom load reduction for (a) random forest model, (b) averaged neural network model, (c) sparse partial least model, (d) average ensemble model, (e) ensemble majority voting (%), and (f) weighted average ensemble (%).

3.2 Discussion

Further comparison, in terms of execution time for model fitting, indicates 224.35 s, 30.89 s, and 254.37 s for RF, SPLS, and AvNNet, respectively. The elapsed time for SPLS was the shortest owing to the limited parameters. The difference between the RF and AvNNet models was 30.02 s, much longer than that of the SPLS model. It was also noted that no-load reduction (normal) accounted for over 90% of the evaluation score of the models. This was expected because load reduction (anomaly) accounted for ~10% of the overall MLR class label. Approximately 3% accounted for the margin of error for the no-load reduction (normal) and load reduction (anomaly) cases. SPLS, MV, WA, and EA had the lowest misclassification type-II error score of 0.1%, followed by the RF score of 0.3%. The AvNNet model exhibited the highest FN rate (0.5%). In the FP classification, WA, AvNNet, EA, RF and MV were 3.7%, 3.8%, 3.8%, 4.0%, and 4.6%, respectively, while SPLS had the highest FP of 6.2%. Type-I errors in all models were higher than Type-II errors.

In the balanced accuracy results, there was variation in AvNNet, showing the least accuracy, the marginal difference for AvNNet, and a negligible difference in RF and

SPLS. MV had the highest accuracy but was below EA as the second best. In the F1 score results, WA again had the highest score, with AvNNet as the third best behind EA and SPLS, which was the least. The Kappa results correspond with the F1 score but with lower percentage scores. The recall result variation corresponds with the balanced accuracy scores, except with MV as best over WA. It can be deduced that combined ensemble models offer improved results compared to classical methods. The bar plot in Fig. 4 compares model results for the Eskom MLR classification task aligns with the presented investigation.

Table 3. Performance Comparison Among Different Evaluation Metrices on Eskom Load Reduction Data

Experiments	Balanced Accuracy	F1 Score	Kappa	Precision	Recall
Random Forest	95.78%	75.15%	72.90%	61.78%	95.90%
Averaged Neural Network	94.45%	76.17%	73.90%	64.52%	92.96%
Sparse Partial Least Squares	95.34%	57.73%	54.90%	41.06%	97.22%
Averaging	97.05%	77.44%	75.39%	63.93%	98.20%
Majority Voting	96.96%	72.05%	69.71%	56.70%	**98.81%**
Weighted Average	**97.15%**	**78.52%**	**76.53%**	**65.40%**	98.24%

This paper focused on improving the Eskom electricity demand and supply classification for hourly data with imbalanced no-load reduction (normal) and load reduction (anomaly) classes. The WA results show the effectiveness of classification tasks and provide evidence that the WA with RF, SPLS, and AvNNet discovered feature significance from Eskom hourly electricity demand and supply MLR data. In 2022 alone, South Africa will have an estimated cumulative electricity loss of over 6,993,651 watts from MLR. Over 95% of the electricity consumed in South Africa is locally produced [20], and consumer perceptions of insufficient electricity supply impede electricity use [4]. Despite recommendations to ease the negative effect of load reduction, the infrastructural organisation is prominent among the rest [21].

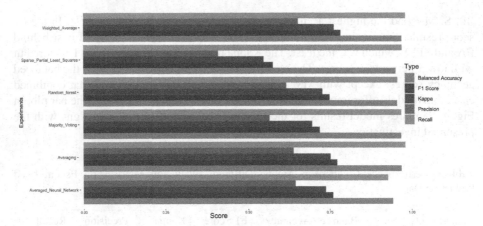

Fig. 4. Comparison of model results for Eskom load reduction classification task.

4   Conclusion

In the present article, we primarily pursued a heterogeneous ensemble classification task for the Eskom electricity demand and supply for the MLR. The initial results showed that the WA technique was superior in performance for MLR no-load reduction (normal) and load reduction (anomaly) classification tasks. This experiment supported a model pool with rooted feature traits in the classical model. Thus, ensemble ML techniques can efficiently classify hourly Eskom MLR no-load reduction (normal) and load reduction (anomaly) in South Africa. Advanced ensemble models will be considered with deep learning parameterisation in future experiments.

Acknowledgement. The authors would like to thank Eskom, South Africa for providing electricity demand, generation sources and load reduction dataset.

References

1. Kademeteme, E., Twinomurinzi, H.: The ineffectiveness of technology adoption models in the 4IR era: a case of SMEs in South Africa. In: 2019 Open Innovations Conference, OI 2019, pp. 252–261 (2019). https://doi.org/10.1109/OI.2019.8908220
2. Motepe, S., Hasan, A.N., Twala, B., Stopforth, R., Alajarmeh, N.: South African power distribution network load forecasting using hybrid ai techniques: ANFIS and OP-ELM. In: Proceedings 2019 International Aegean Conference on Electrical Machines and Power Electronics, ACEMP 2019 and 2019 International Conference on Optimization of Electrical and Electronic Equipment, OPTIM 2019, pp. 557–562 (2019). https://doi.org/10.1109/ACEMP-OPTIM44294.2019.9007218
3. Motepe, S., Hasan, A.N., Shongwe, T.: Forecasting the total South African unplanned capability loss factor using an ensemble of deep learning techniques. Energies (Basel). **15** (2022). https://doi.org/10.3390/en15072546

4. Mabugu, T., Inglesi-lotz, R.: The effect of mismatched supply and demand of electricity on economic growth in South Africa. Energy Sour. Part B: Econ. Plann. Policy 1–18 (2022). https://doi.org/10.1080/15567249.2022.2038731
5. Shettar, S.N., Kinger, R., Tharun Kumar, S.I., Preetham, N.V.R., Ramya, K.: Blackout prediction in smart grids using machine learning. In: Proceedings of the 2nd International Conference on Artificial Intelligence and Smart Energy, ICAIS 2022, pp. 210–214 (2022). https://doi.org/10.1109/ICAIS53314.2022.9742882
6. Rahnamay-naeini, M., Wang, Z., Mammoli, A., Hayat, M.M.: A probabilistic model for the dynamics of cascading failures and blackouts in power grids, pp. 1–8 (2012)
7. Worship, N., David, O.: Munich personal RePEc archive electricity consumption and population growth in South Africa: a panel approach (2022)
8. Ali, M., Bosse, T., Hindriks, K. V, Hoogendoorn, M., Jonker, C.M., Treur, J.: Recent Trends in Applied Artificial Intelligence. Springer, Heidelberg (2013). https://doi.org/10.1007/978-3-642-38577-3
9. Cawood, P., van Zyl, T.L.: Feature-weighted stacking for nonseasonal time series forecasts: a case study of the COVID-19 epidemic curves. In: 2021 8th International Conference on Soft Computing and Machine Intelligence, ISCMI 2021, pp. 53–59 (2021). https://doi.org/10.1109/ISCMI53840.2021.9654809
10. Syed, A.H., Khan, T., Hassan, A., Alromema, N.A., Binsawad, M., Alsayed, A.O.: An ensemble-learning based application to predict the earlier stages of Alzheimer's disease (AD). IEEE Access 8, 222126–222143 (2020). https://doi.org/10.1109/ACCESS.2020.3043715
11. Mahendran, N., et al.: Sensor-assisted weighted average ensemble model for detecting major depressive disorder. Sens. (Switz.) 19 (2019). https://doi.org/10.3390/s19224822
12. Shashvat, K., Basu, R., Bhondekar, A.P., Kaur, A.: A weighted ensemble model for prediction of infectious diseases. Curr. Pharm. Biotechnol. 20, 674–678 (2019)
13. Wang, H., Yu, Y., Cai, Y., Chen, X., Chen, L., Li, Y.: Soft-weighted-average ensemble vehicle detection method based on single-stage and two-stage deep learning models. IEEE Trans. Intell. Veh. 6, 100–109 (2021). https://doi.org/10.1109/TIV.2020.3010832
14. Aloysius, N., Geetha, M.: A scale space model of weighted average CNN ensemble for ASL fingerspelling recognition. Int. J. Comput. Sci. Eng. 22, 154–161 (2020)
15. Tibshirani, R.: Regression Shrinkage and Selection via the Lasso. J. R. Stat. Soc. Ser. B (Methodol.) 58, 267–288 (1995)
16. Ripley, B.D.: Pattern Recognition and Neural Networks. Cambridge University Press, Cambridge (2007)
17. Dutta, S., Arunachalam, A., Misailovic, S.: To seed or not to seed? An empirical analysis of usage of seeds for testing in machine learning projects. In: 2022 IEEE Conference on Software Testing, Verification and Validation (ICST), pp. 151–161. IEEE (2022). https://doi.org/10.1109/ICST53961.2022.00026
18. Clemen, R.T.: Combining forecasts: a review and annotated bibliography. Int. J. Forecast. 5, 559–583 (1989). https://doi.org/10.1016/0169-2070(89)90012-5
19. Pruengkarn, R., Fung, C.C., Wong, K.W.: Using misclassification data to improve classification performance. In: ECTI-CON 2015 - 2015 12th International Conference on Electrical Engineering/Electronics, Computer, Telecommunications and Information Technology (2015). https://doi.org/10.1109/ECTICon.2015.7206950
20. Viera, A.J., Garrett, J.M.: Understanding interobserver agreement: the kappa statistic. Fam. Med. 37, 360–363 (2005)
21. Kuhn, M.: Building predictive models in R using the caret package. J. Stat. Softw. 28, 1–26 (2008). https://doi.org/10.18637/jss.v028.i05

Natural Language Processing

Named Entity Recognition for Nepali Using BERT Based Models

Bishal Debb Pande, Aman Shakya[✉], Sanjeeb Prasad Panday,
and Basanta Joshi

Pulchowk Campus, Institute of Engineering, Tribhuvan University, Lalitpur, Nepal
075mscsk005.bishal@pcampus.edu.np,
{aman.shakya,sanjeeb,basanta}@ioe.edu.np

Abstract. Named Entity Recognition (NER) is one of the vital task for many Natural Language Processing (NLP) tasks. In recent times, transformer architecture-based models have become very popular for NLP tasks including NER achieving state-of-the-art results. The Bidirectional Encoder Representations from Transformers (BERT) model especially has been found to be very good for NER tasks. However, in Nepali limited work has been done using these models with existing works mostly using more traditional techniques. In this work, we show that by using a combination of preprocessing techniques and better-initialized BERT models, we can improve the performance of the NER system in Nepali. We show a significant improvement in results using the multilingual RoBERTa model. Using this, we were able to achieve a 6% overall improvement in the f1 score in EverestNER Dataset. In terms of the fields, we have achieved an increase of up to 22% in the f1 score for the Event entity which has the lowest support.

Keywords: NER · BERT · RoBERTa · mBERT · xlm-r

1 Introduction

Named Entity Recognition (NER) is the process of identifying and categorizing words into pre-defined categories such as a person, organization, date, etc. called named entities. Named Entity Recognition is widely used for tasks such as information extraction from unstructured documents, sentiment analysis, topic detection, text summarizing, machine translation, question answering, and many more. Due to this, they have been thoroughly studied in large resource languages and significant progress has been.

However, in Nepali very limited work has been done in NER. Nepali being a low-resource language poses a significant challenge for any work to be carried out in this domain. In addition to this, the language itself presents different challenges. A few of the major ones are:

1. Context dependent: Same words can be used in different context giving different entity to them e.g. त्रिभुवन शाह <PER>, त्रिभुवन जयन्ती <EVENT>, त्रिभुवन अन्तर्राष्ट्रिय एयरपोर्ट <LOC>, त्रिभुवन विश्वविद्यालय <ORG>

2. Variation in spelling: In Nepali, words can have different accepted correct form used in almost equal frequency. Especially with names, people can use different variation of the word e.g. त्रिभूवन, त्रीभुवन, त्रीभूबन

3. Lack of capitalization: In languages like English, proper nouns are capitalized making it one of the heuristics that can be utilized to identify such entities. However in Nepali, capitalization is not present making it harder to identify the entities.

4. Lack of fixed text order: Nepali is relatively a free word order language where in it follows a subject-object-verb structure. Due to this, word order can be changed but the underlying meaning can be the same e.g. "पोखरा घुम्न जाँदा रामले माचेपुच्छ्रे हिमाल देख्यो" vs "रामले पोखरा घुम्न जाँदा माचेपुच्छ्रे हिमाल देख्यो".

5. Agglutinative nature of words: Two or more words can get combined to form a new words.

6. Loan words: Words that have been inherited from different languages make NER task difficult. Since they are not part of vocabulary and do not have a fixed way of writing, same word might be represented differently by different group of people.

Our notable contributions in this paper include the analysis of different BERT-based models and the effect of using different preprocessing schemes on the performance of the NER system.

2 Literature Review

The Sixth Message Understanding Conference in 1996 [7] coined the term Named Entity Recognition (NER). The first system for entity recognition based on rule and heuristic was built in 1999 by Rau [19] which could recognize company entity. Since then NER has been primarily studied for rich resource languages [12]. Early NER systems were rule-based systems that used handcrafted rules for identifying the named entities. These were followed by supervised machine learning techniques like Hidden Markov Model, Decision Tree, Support Vector Machine (SVM) [8], Conditional Random Fields (CRF) [11], etc. mostly based upon the handcrafted features. Hybrid approaches using a combination of machine learning methods along with rule-based approaches were also explored.

Most modern NER systems depend on word embeddings. Word embedding is the method by which the textual data are converted into a format such that they can be used by a machine learning system. Word2Vec [14], Glove [18] and Fasttext [2] present different approaches to get word embeddings that are created by understanding the underlying relation between words in an unsupervised manner. These have been used in conjunction with architectures such as Recurrent Neural Network (RNN), Long Short Term Memory (LSTM), and Convolutional Neural Networks (CNN) for language understanding. One of the disadvantages of these models for generating word embedding is that they are not able to understand the context in which the word is being used. The rise of transformer architecture [22] has been significant in the field of NLP. The BERT model [5] has been popular lately due to its ability to understand the context of words.

In Nepali, various works have been carried out relating to Named Entity Recognition. Dey et al. [6] have used hybrid methods using the Hidden Markov model and pos tags combined for NER. Bam and Shahi [1] utilized a support vector machine and gazetteer list for NER. They generated features based on the location of the word, word length, and the presence of digits/ other characters. Gazetteer lists were also prepared and the presence of text in the specific list was used as a feature. One vs Rest classification was used to evaluate the performance of each of the models. Transliteration was used to create the Gazetteer list. Maharjan et al. [13] have calculated the named entity recognition using multinomial Bayes, Logistic regression, and support vector machines. They have utilized their internal dataset for this. The dataset consists of four entities Person, Location, Organization, and Miscellaneous. The Miscellaneous tag consists of tagging for entities such as number, measure, time, and designation. The tagging has been done in the CoNLL-2003 IOB format. They utilized a 5 fold cross-validation method to evaluate the performance of their model.

Singh et al. [21] have utilized multiple neural architectures like BiLSTM, BiLSTM+CNN, BiLSTM+CRF, BiLSTM+CNN+CRF, and Stanford CRF model using the Fasttext word embedding for NER. They utilized a 5-fold cross-validation method to evaluate the performance of their model. In addition, they also released their dataset which is the first publicly available dataset for Nepali NER. The dataset is created using news articles from 2015 to 2016. The dataset consists of three entities location, person, and organization. The annotation is done in the standard CoNLL-2003 IO format. The paper however does not describe in detail the process of annotation.

Niraula et al. [17] have utilized the BERT model as well as BLSTM-CRF models. Their results show that the multilingual BERT model can also give good results for the Nepali Language. They have also released their dataset EverestNER which is the largest Nepali NER dataset at the moment and is around four times larger than the preceding ones. It is created using 1000 news articles from setopati.com from 2019 among which 4 were dropped for large size. The articles were broken down into sentences and then NER tags were assigned to the sentences. Only articles that had at least one of the entities were selected. This dataset contains five entities Person, Location, Organization, Date, and Event. In addition to this, they have also released the annotation guideline used for the annotation of the label. The guideline is based on the Finish News corpus for the Named Entity Recognition paper from 2020 [20]. During the annotation, first, the annotators were kept together and made to annotate the same documents before annotating independently. They have also revealed that the inter-rater agreement was 0.74. The dataset is divided into train and test split in the ratio of 85:15. Instead of splitting at the sentence level, the splitting is done at the article level to avoid the same article being present in both train and test split.

3   Methodology

3.1   Dataset Collection

To train a NER system, labeled dataset is vital. For this work, we have carried forward the work mostly using the EverestNER dataset [17]. It consists of a NER dataset tagged in BIO format. The dataset for NER has five entities tagged in it: Person (PER), Organization (ORG), Location (LOC), Date (DATE), and Event (EVENT). It is the largest NER dataset available for Nepali. The tagging has been done in the BIO scheme. In this scheme, the text within the entities is classified as the target entity and any other text is classified as other. Being a dataset created using news articles, it has a good variety in different type of entities that are present in the dataset. The distribution of the dataset is shown in Table 1.

Table 1. Statistics about Everest NER dataset

Dataset	Articles	Sentences	LOC	ORG	PER	EVENT	DATE
Train	847	13848	5148	4756	7707	312	3394
Test	149	1950	809	715	1115	59	572
Total	996	15798	5957	5471	8822	371	3966

One of the major challenges with the dataset is the complexity of entities. The same words can be tagged as different entities depending on context. So giving class predictions based on words alone would not give a good result. Table 2 shows the distribution of unique words and repeated words per entity.

Table 2. Total unique words vs total repeated word

entity	repeated	total_unique	percent
O	17707	19853	89.19
DATE	264	561	47.06
EVENT	72	291	24.74
LOC	958	1531	62.57
ORG	949	2172	43.69
PER	2490	3160	78.80

3.2   Preprocessing

In this step, we convert the data to the format required by the BERT model for training. If the effect of any preprocessing step (stop word removal, stemming, text normalization) is being analyzed, corresponding pre-processing is also carried out on the dataset. After this, the text is passed to the tokenizer which is specific to the model being used. After this, the alignment of the entity label is carried out. During this, only the first token of a word is assigned a B tag. If the first word is split into two or more tokens, the first will be assigned the B tag while the other will be assigned the I tag. After this, padding is done to make all the input the same length.

3.3 Training

The training for the BERT model is done in two steps: pre-training and fine-tuning. In the pre-training step the model understands the working of the language while in the fine-tuning step, the model is trained for the specific language task. For this work, we have utilized different pre-trained models that had been trained on either corpus containing Nepali or for a language similar to Nepali and carried out fine-tuning for the model. Fine-tuning is done for token classification where each token present in a text is classified into one of the required classes using backpropagation. The general model for this is shown in Fig. 1.

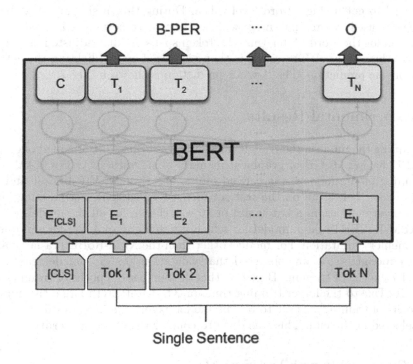

Fig. 1. BERT fine-tuning for NER [5]

3.4   Performance Analysis

The performance analysis of Named Entity Recognition system is carried out based on the comparison between the prediction made by the model to the ground truth which is generally annotated by a human. Based on these the precision (p), recall (r), and F1-score (f1) are calculated. To account for sequence, seqeval [16] package is utilized.

3.5   Prediction

The input for the prediction pipeline is a paragraph of text. The text is then tokenized based on sentences. This is done to avoid the token limit of the trained model. In addition to this, any text normalization/ pre-processing required is also done in this step. Since the dataset used utilizes suffixes separation while creating the dataset, suffixes are separated. In the next step, the text is passed through the model's tokenizer to get tokens that are passed through to the model.

After passing the tokenized input through the model, we get the prediction at the token level. The input needs to be merged to get the prediction back to the word level. The first step for this is to combine the prediction of each token in a word to get a single word-level token. During this, a simple voting-based strategy is used where the entity which is the most occurring is used as the prediction for the word. After this, the token spans are also adjusted as per the word on the new level. The result is then visualized by highlighting the entities based on the prediction. The flow for prediction is shown in Fig. 2.

4   Experimental Results

For training the models, the Kaggle notebook was utilized. It provided one Tesla T4 GPU having 16 GB of graphical memory along with 13 GB of RAM. The fine-tuning of the models was carried out in the EverestNER dataset and the results preset below are on the test set of the EverestNER. For training, after initial experimentation, a batch size of 16 was chosen for all the models except the XLM-RoBERTa-large model for which a batch size of 4 was chosen due to GPU memory limitation. For models other than the XLM-RoBERTa-large after initial experiments, it was observed that validation loss did not decrease after around 7 epochs of training. Based on this the number of epochs of training was set to 10. Due to the larger training time for XLM-RoBERTa-large, the number of epochs of training was set to 5. The model having the lowest evaluation loss was selected in the end. This was done to counter the effect of overfitting.

4.1   Experiments with Different Models

At the start, training was done using different models to see how the performance would be. For this, publicly available models from the huggingface hub were utilized.

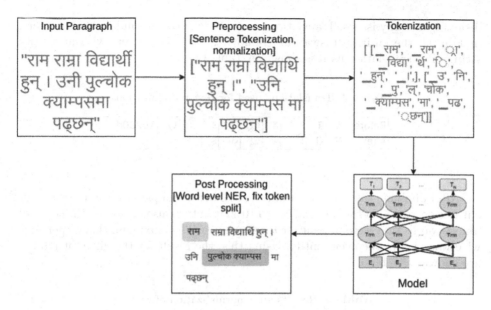

Fig. 2. Prediction Pipeline using XLM-RoBERTa model

Starting with the multilingual models, the multilingual bert cased (bbmc) [5], multilingual bert uncased (bbmu) [5], XLM RoBERTa base (xlm-R) [3], XLM RoBERTa large (xlm-R Lg) [3], and the indic-bert [9] models were considered. In addition to this, models that had been pre-trained on Nepali corpus were also taken. For this models namely Shushant/nepaliBERT (nepbert), nowalab/nepali-bert-npvec1 (nepvec1) [10] were used. The result of the different models is shown in Table 3. Based on the initial results, three models: XLM RoBERTa, XLM RoBERTa large, and Sushant/nepaliBERT were selected.

Table 3. Overall result of different models

Model Metrics	bbmu	xlm-R	xlm-R Lg	NepBERT	nepvec1	indic-bert	bbmc
p	0.87	0.88	0.90	0.86	0.67	0.79	0.83
r	0.86	0.91	0.91	0.87	0.69	0.76	0.85
f1	0.86	0.89	0.91	0.87	0.68	0.78	0.84

4.2 Experiments with Text Normalization

Text normalization was carried out to see if it would help improve the performance. The main reasoning was to see if this would help tackle impact due to spelling mistakes/variations in spelling. Further since while speaking these subtle differences cannot be known, the thought was that the context would help to disambiguate any issues. Translations were made between similar set characters, making all the entities 'raswa' and removing a few characters with an empty string. The translation used is shown in Table 4.

Table 4. Translations used for text normalization

Before	श	ष	◌ौ	ब	◌ृ	ऋ	ई	◌ँ	◌ं	\u200d
After	स	स	िो	व	◌ु	उ	इ			

After applying the normalization, the number of unique words in the different entities decreased in the range of 5% to 10%. It in turn also decreased the count of unique words that were present for those entities. The maximum change percentwise was seen in the event entity. Using this, the result for the different models are shown in Table 5.

Table 5. Results after normalization of text

Model	NepBERT			xlm-R			xlm-R Lg			bbmu		
Field	p	r	f1	p	r	f1	p	r	f1	p	r	f1
DATE	0.91	0.92	0.91	0.90	0.92	0.91	0.93	0.91	0.92	0.91	0.88	0.90
EVENT	0.60	0.59	0.60	0.40	0.58	0.48	0.59	0.75	0.66	0.44	0.44	0.44
LOC	0.86	0.91	0.88	0.84	0.85	0.84	0.89	0.89	0.89	0.81	0.80	0.81
ORG	0.82	0.81	0.82	0.79	0.88	0.83	0.88	0.88	0.88	0.81	0.84	0.82
PER	0.86	0.88	0.87	0.90	0.90	0.90	0.93	0.91	0.92	0.87	0.87	0.87
Overall	0.86	0.87	0.86	0.85	0.88	0.86	0.90	0.90	0.90	0.84	0.84	0.84

4.3   Experiments with Text Correction

Text correction was carried out using the most common form of the word from the training corpus. For this, we see the occurrence of all words having the same normalized form and use the one with the highest count. In case the word is not present in the training corpus, it is used as is. One limitation might be that since the corpus size is small it might not account for the actual distribution of words. Comparing the results with that of text normalization, the overall result seems to be better when using the text correction method. For the event entity, however, the scores were a bit low. This might be because of the low support for these words. The results using this technique are shown in Table 6.

4.4   Experiments with Weighted Loss

During the experimentation, the weighted loss function was also utilized to see the performance difference by using it. For this, the weight for each of the classes

Table 6. Result after text correction

Model	NepaliBert			xlm-R			xlm-R Lg			bbmu		
Field	p	r	f1	p	r	f1	p	r	f1	p	r	f1
Date	0.91	0.90	0.90	0.92	0.91	0.91	0.93	0.92	0.92	0.91	0.91	0.91
Event	0.53	0.64	0.58	0.54	0.71	0.61	0.53	0.69	0.60	0.41	0.47	0.44
LOC	0.87	0.90	0.88	0.89	0.87	0.88	0.91	0.88	0.89	0.84	0.83	0.84
ORG	0.82	0.85	0.83	0.87	0.89	0.88	0.90	0.91	0.90	0.84	0.86	0.85
PER	0.88	0.90	0.89	0.94	0.93	0.93	0.95	0.93	0.94	0.89	0.88	0.89
Overall	0.86	0.88	0.87	0.90	0.90	0.90	0.91	0.90	0.91	0.86	0.86	0.86

was determined using the method mentioned in [4]. Using this approach, the extraction for the minority class (Event) was improved. However, the performance of other entities was reduced. The results are shown in Table 7.

Table 7. Results using weighted loss function

Model	NepBERT			xlm-R			xlm-R Lg			bbmu		
Field	p	r	f1	p	r	f1	p	r	f1	p	r	f1
DATE	0.81	0.89	0.85	0.83	0.90	0.86	0.88	0.91	0.90	0.79	0.88	0.83
EVENT	0.31	0.58	0.40	0.48	0.78	0.59	0.52	0.76	0.62	0.33	0.51	0.40
LOC	0.81	0.90	0.86	0.87	0.90	0.88	0.88	0.90	0.89	0.78	0.86	0.82
ORG	0.69	0.85	0.76	0.80	0.91	0.85	0.86	0.90	0.88	0.76	0.86	0.81
PER	0.80	0.91	0.85	0.91	0.94	0.92	0.91	0.92	0.92	0.84	0.87	0.86
Overall	0.77	0.89	0.82	0.85	0.91	0.88	0.88	0.91	0.89	0.79	0.86	0.82

4.5   Other Experiments

Experiments with Combined Dataset: The training was also carried out by combining other datasets. For this, the OurNepali dataset [6] and the Hindi NER dataset [15] were used. Since they had different entities to the Everest-NER dataset, the common entities were chosen i.e. the person, organization, and location entities. However, the result was not better than only using the EverestNER dataset by itself. There were also a few issues noted where in two datasets had different annotation guidelines which also made using the combined dataset directly an issue.

Stemming: Stemming was carried out to see if it could help improve the performance. However due to lack of good stemming algorithm for Nepali, the results were not good compared to others.

Stop Word Removal: Stop words usually do not carry significant meaning so removing such entities should not affect the result. However, for the date category, many stop words were part of the entity so it was not useful. Further, other entities also had a few stop words present within them.

4.6   Result

Based upon the experiments it was seen that the multilingual roberta models were giving better result. The result of the xlm-R-lg model using different scheme is compared with the performance of the Everest NER paper in Table 8. Similarly, Fig. 3 shows the result of the model on different news articles.

Table 8. Comparison of xlm-R-lg model with baseline EverestNER result

Model	EverestNER			Text correction			weighted			normalized		
Field	p	r	f1	p	r	f1	p	r	f1	p	r	f1
DATE	0.91	0.91	0.91	0.93	**0.92**	**0.93**	0.88	0.91	0.90	**0.93**	0.91	0.92
EVENT	0.46	0.42	0.44	0.53	0.69	0.60	0.52	**0.76**	0.62	**0.59**	0.75	**0.66**
LOC	0.85	0.80	0.82	**0.91**	0.88	**0.89**	0.88	**0.90**	0.89	0.89	0.89	**0.89**
ORG	0.85	0.83	0.84	**0.90**	**0.91**	**0.91**	0.86	0.90	0.88	0.88	0.88	0.88
PER	0.90	0.85	0.88	**0.95**	**0.93**	**0.94**	0.91	0.92	0.92	0.93	0.91	0.92
Overall	0.87	0.84	0.85	**0.91**	**0.90**	**0.91**	0.88	0.91	0.89	0.90	0.90	0.90

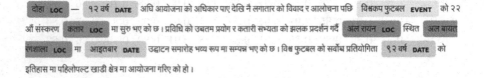

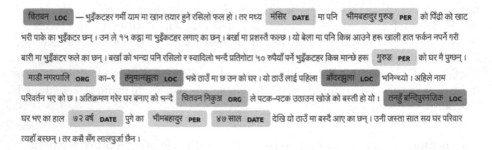

Fig. 3. NER system result on different news articles using the xlm-R model

5 Conclusion and Future Works

Based on the results, it can be seen that a combination of preprocessing and better model weights can improve the performance of NER for Nepali. The xlm-roberta large model gave better performance than other models but at the same time, a lot smaller model trained on Nepali corpus also gave respectable results.

Due to limitation of computing resources and time not all models could be evaluated so analysis of other state of the art models can be carried out. For further improvements, different techniques for better weight initialization can be carried out. Also use of modified BERT models which can better understand the context might also be useful. We have used a simple text correction strategy in this work but using a spelling correction system might help improve performance. Another point of improvement could be in the dataset itself by increasing the size to contain data from different points in time. One point to account for while creating a dataset might be to have compatible annotation guideline with existing works so that datasets can be used in combination and not just one or the other. This is especially necessary due to the limited dataset available for Nepali. In addition to this, tasks relating to entity linking can also be a good follow-up to this work.

Acknowledgment. We would like to thank Dr. Nobal Niraula for his time in helping us understand the Everest NER dataset and various approaches their team had carried forward during their experimentation.

References

1. Bam, S., Shahi, T.: Named entity recognition for Nepali text using support vector machines. Intell. Inf. Manage. **06**, 21–29 (2014). https://doi.org/10.4236/iim.2014. 62004
2. Bojanowski, P., Grave, E., Joulin, A., Mikolov, T.: Enriching word vectors with subword information (2016)
3. Conneau, A., et al.: Unsupervised cross-lingual representation learning at scale (2019). https://doi.org/10.48550/ARXIV.1911.02116, https://arxiv.org/abs/1911. 02116
4. Cui, Y., Jia, M., Lin, T., Song, Y., Belongie, S.J.: Class-balanced loss based on effective number of samples. CoRR abs/1901.05555 (2019). http://arxiv.org/abs/ 1901.05555
5. Devlin, J., Chang, M.W., Lee, K., Toutanova, K.: BERT: pre-training of deep bidirectional transformers for language understanding (2019)
6. Dey, A., Prukayastha, B.: Named entity recognition using gazetteer method and n-gram technique for an inflectional language: a hybrid approach. Int. J. Comput. Appl. **84**, 31–35 (2013). https://doi.org/10.5120/14607-2859
7. Grishman, R., Sundheim, B.: Message understanding conference-6: a brief history. In: Proceedings of the 16th Conference on Computational Linguistics, COLING 1996, vol. 1, pp. 466–471. Association for Computational Linguistics, USA (1996). https://doi.org/10.3115/992628.992709

8. Hearst, M., Dumais, S., Osuna, E., Platt, J., Scholkopf, B.: Support vector machines. IEEE Intell. Syst. Appl. **13**(4), 18–28 (1998). https://doi.org/10.1109/5254.708428
9. Kakwani, D., et al.: IndicNLPSuite: monolingual corpora, evaluation benchmarks and pre-trained multilingual language models for Indian languages. In: Findings of EMNLP (2020)
10. Koirala, P., Niraula, N.B.: NPVec1: word embeddings for Nepali - construction and evaluation. In: Proceedings of the 6th Workshop on Representation Learning for NLP (RepL4NLP-2021), pp. 174–184. Association for Computational Linguistics, Online (2021). https://doi.org/10.18653/v1/2021.repl4nlp-1.18, https://aclanthology.org/2021.repl4nlp-1.18
11. Lafferty, J.D., McCallum, A., Pereira, F.C.N.: Conditional random fields: probabilistic models for segmenting and labeling sequence data. In: Proceedings of the Eighteenth International Conference on Machine Learning, ICML 2001, pp. 282–289. Morgan Kaufmann Publishers Inc., San Francisco (2001)
12. Li, J., Sun, A., Han, J., Li, C.: A survey on deep learning for named entity recognition. IEEE Trans. Knowl. Data Eng. **34**(1), 50–70 (2020)
13. Maharjan, G., Bal, B.K., Regmi, S.: Named entity recognition (NER) for Nepali. In: Kravets, A.G., Groumpos, P.P., Shcherbakov, M., Kultsova, M. (eds.) CIT&DS 2019. CCIS, vol. 1084, pp. 71–80. Springer, Cham (2019). https://doi.org/10.1007/978-3-030-29750-3_6
14. Mikolov, T., Chen, K., Corrado, G., Dean, J.: Efficient estimation of word representations in vector space (2013)
15. Murthy, R., Bhattacharjee, P., Sharnagat, R., Khatri, J., Kanojia, D., Bhattacharyya, P.: HiNER: a large Hindi named entity recognition dataset (2022). https://doi.org/10.48550/ARXIV.2204.13743, https://arxiv.org/abs/2204.13743
16. Nakayama, H.: SeqEval: a python framework for sequence labeling evaluation (2018). https://github.com/chakki-works/seqeval
17. Niraula, N., Chapagain, J.: Named entity recognition for Nepali: data sets and algorithms. In: The International FLAIRS Conference Proceedings, vol. 35 (2022). https://doi.org/10.32473/flairs.v35i.130725
18. Pennington, J., Socher, R., Manning, C.: GloVe: global vectors for word representation. In: Proceedings of the 2014 Conference on Empirical Methods in Natural Language Processing (EMNLP), pp. 1532–1543. Association for Computational Linguistics, Doha (2014). https://doi.org/10.3115/v1/D14-1162, https://www.aclweb.org/anthology/D14-1162
19. Rau, L.F.: Extracting company names from text. In: 1991 Proceedings of the Seventh IEEE Conference on Artificial Intelligence Application, vol. i, pp. 29–32 (1991)
20. Ruokolainen, T., Kauppinen, P., Silfverberg, M., Lindén, K.: A finnish news corpus for named entity recognition. Lang. Resour. Eval. **54**(1), 247–272 (2019). https://doi.org/10.1007/s10579-019-09471-7
21. Singh, O.M., Padia, A., Joshi, A.: Named entity recognition for Nepali language. In: 2019 IEEE 5th International Conference on Collaboration and Internet Computing (CIC), pp. 184–190 (2019). https://doi.org/10.1109/CIC48465.2019.00031
22. Vaswani, A., et al.: Attention is all you need (2017)

Role Understanding for Spoken Dialogue System Based on Relevance Ranking

Xin Huang[1,4(✉)], Huilin Song[2], and Mingming Lu[3]

[1] School of Software, Jiangxi Normal University, Nanchang 330031, China
xinhuang@jxnu.edu.cn
[2] School of International Economics and Trade, Jiangxi University of Finance and Economics,
Nanchang 330013, China
[3] School of Electronic Information Engineering, Tongji University, Shanghai 201804, China
[4] Jiangxi Provincial Engineering Research Center of Blockchain Data Security and Governance,
Nanchang 330031, China

Abstract. Recognizing different roles in spoken dialogue is a challenging task that significantly impacts the quality of tailored and personalized responses. However, current research fails to address the crucial role of identifying roles while matching questions in dialogue. To tackle this issue, we have proposed a relevance ranking method that effectively distinguishes between different roles in dialogue. Our approach involves creating a set of candidate passages that include different roles, and then comparing their semantic similarity with the dialogue to determine the correct role. Our experimental results on the Multiparty-Dialog-RC dataset demonstrate that our proposed method improves performance by 3.52%.

Keywords: Spoken Dialogue · Relevance Ranking · Role Understanding · Deep Learning

1 Introduction

Deep learning-based automatic dialogue systems have gained widespread attention in recent years [1–4]. In several research fields, spoken dialogue exhibits a unique structure with different linguistic phenomena. Normally, a spoken conversation involves two or more speakers, each with their own expressive style. During the conversation, speakers share their thoughts on a particular topic or concept, using either single or multiple sentences to convey their meaning. As a result, the information in spoken dialogue can seem dispersed, requiring the integration of several sentences or speeches to provide a comprehensive understanding of certain concepts. Conversely, in written text, a single sentence may suffice. Moreover, oral dialogue comprehension requires identifying the relationship between the speaker and the content. If this aspect is not achieved, anaphora resolution becomes impossible, which can lead to misunderstandings, and negatively impact the overall conversation. Roles in spoken dialogue pose a particular challenge, including identifying different roles, comprehending what each role is saying, and generating tailored and personalized responses for each role.

© The Author(s), under exclusive license to Springer Nature Switzerland AG 2023
H. Fujita et al. (Eds.): IEA/AIE 2023, LNAI 13926, pp. 105–116, 2023.
https://doi.org/10.1007/978-3-031-36822-6_9

The researchers presented the Friend-sQA dataset for Extractive Reading Comprehension [5], which comprises spoken conversations as the primary body, and the Molweni dataset [6] for interactive question-and-answer that takes account of the context. Regarding models, Chen et al. [7] presented an Entity-Centric model, which relies on manually extracted features and traditional machine learning, and a bi-directional LSTM [8] model based on self-attention. Trischler et al. [9] proposed the EpiReader model that combines a reasoner and extractor and can encode documents and questions using both CNN and RNN. Dhingra et al. [10] proposed a Gated-Attention model that factors in the interaction of document and problem multiplication. Cui et al. [11] introduced the attention-over-attention model to compute document-to-problem Attention and problem-to-document Attention, respectively. Despite the fact that the previously mentioned models all share one common feature, which is to match directly the problem and the dialogue, employing them for role-understanding tasks is unsuitable because they neglect the importance of roles in matching and fail to capture role disparities.

The format of the role comprehension task resembles that of cloze-style reading comprehension, whereby each sample comprises three parts: conversation, question, and answer. Each conversation corresponds to a passage, a summary of the primary content or a paraphrase of a detail from the conversation. The roles include the conversation speaker and the names mentioned in the conversation. Hence, the objective of the role comprehension task is to choose the right role completion question from the conversation. To strengthen the significance of roles in semantic matching between dialogue and questions, we propose a method to replace the sample role set. This involves replacing the placeholders in questions with all possible answer roles one by one, thereby transforming a single question into a set of candidate passages. To measure the differences between the various roles, we propose a relevance ranking method based on candidate passages with different roles. Initially, we compute the semantic similarity between the candidate passages and conversations, and then select the roles corresponding to the top candidate passages as predicted answers by the model. The contributions of this paper are:

1. We introduce a relevance ranking method for identifying differences between all roles in the dialogue. We accomplish this by constructing a set of candidate passages containing various roles and comparing their semantic similarity with the conversation to identify the correct roles.
2. We propose two models, ESIM-rank, and IMN-rank, for evaluating which dialogue processing method and text matching method are more effective for character understanding.
3. We conducted an experiment using the Multiparty-Dialog-RC dataset and demonstrate that both correlation ranking models surpass the previous optimal results, with IMN-rank being superior to ESIM-rank.

2 Related Work

To improve dialogue matching, relevance ranking can be used to change the matching object from a question to a candidate passage, which involves task reformulation [12]. In multi-task learning, a binary classification task is often defined as a pairwise ranking task in literature [13]. Experimental results demonstrate that task reformulation leads to higher accuracy in ranking compared to classification, indicating that this approach can benefit model performance. Additionally, in literature [14], sentence pair modeling tasks such as text semantic similarity, text paraphrase recognition, natural language reasoning, and question answering are compared among five different models to evaluate their performance.

The role understanding task is challenging because it requires distinguishing between different roles and establishing clear relationships between them and the conversation context. Most existing models utilize dialogue and question matching to identify the replaced role. For instance, Ma et al. [15] proposed the CNN + LSTM + UA + DA model, which utilizes both convolutional neural networks and recurrent neural networks to extract rich matching features. Utterance-level Attention and Dialog-level Attention are used to match words in dialogue sentences and questions, as well as individual words in a single dialogue sentence and a question. This approach captures relevant relationship representations from different perspectives, and integrates the representations to determine the role with the highest probability from the set of roles in the sample as the answer to the question. The model demonstrated an accuracy of 72.42% on the MultiParty-Dialog-RC test set, surpassing the benchmark BiLSTM model [7] by 1.21%, particularly in long dialogues.

Subsequently, Hu et al. [16] found that the CNN + LSTM + UA + DA model could not simultaneously capture the global information at a distance (the viewpoint held by someone in the whole conversation) and the local information within the sentence (the detailed facts of a statement's reaction). To solve these problems, they proposed the DeepDial model, which maintains word-level information and conversational structure information at the same time to realize synchronous capture of local information and global information without missing any matching signals. The DeepDial model creatively uses the two-way LSTM output of the middle word of the statement as the statement vector when capturing the conversation representation. Further, Hu et al. use Transformer [17] to replace the two-way LSTM coded conversation representation and obtain a new DeepDial+ model. The accuracy of DeepDial and DeepDial+ reached 79.61% and 83.18% on the Multiparty-Dialog-RC test set, far exceeding the 72.42% achieved by CNN + LSTM + UA + DA. Comparing only the DeepDial and DeepDial+ models, it can be found that Transformer has stronger encoding capability than two-way LSTM, and the information does not degrade with sequence length.

In summary, prior research focused solely on the semantic matching relationship between the conversation and question, overlooking the significance of role centrality in matching. As a result, these models can be applied to any candidate answer set, rather than being limited to task-specific conversation roles. Furthermore, these models do not account for differences between the various roles, and may overlook individuals who provide answers that do not align with the conversation or deviate from its content despite having the assigned role.

3 Method

3.1 Task Definition

For a given dataset $\mathcal{D}$, each sample can be thought of as a triplet (c, q, a) consisting of conversations, questions, and answers. Among them, the conversation is composed of K statement u_k, namely $c = \{u_k\}_{k=1}^{K}$, each statement by the L_{u_k} word $w_{k,i}$, namely $u_k = \{w_{k,i}\}_{i=1}^{L_{u_k}}$. Thus, the total number of words in the conversation is $L_c = \sum_{k=1}^{K} L_{u_k}$. The problem consists of L_q words w_j, i.e. $q = \{w_j\}_{j=1}^{L_q}$, with the special placeholder @*placeholder*. Record the role set composed of all N roles e_n appearing in each sample conversation as $\mathbb{E} = \{e_1, ..., e_N\}$, then the correct answer corresponds to the placeholder $\alpha \in \mathbb{E}$.

The goal of the task is to learn a model $f(c, q)$ from dataset $\mathcal{D}$. For any conversation and question pair (c, q), f predicts the probability of each role in $\mathcal{D}$, and selects the one with the highest probability as the answer. Instead of directly inputting (c, q) into the model, the relevance ranking method first replaces the placeholder @*placeholder* in the problem with each role e_n in $\mathcal{D}$ to obtain a one-to-one mapping of candidate passage d_n to the role e_n. (c, d_n) is then input into the model to obtain a relevance score $g_n \in \mathbb{R}$ for each candidate passage and the conversation. Finally, the N relevance scores are sorted, and the role corresponding to the candidate passage with the highest ranking is the predicted answer $\hat{a}$:

$$\hat{a} = e_{n^*} \tag{1}$$

$$n^* = argmax_n g_n, n = 1, \dots N \tag{2}$$

At this point, the model is:

$$f(c, q) = \frac{\exp(g_n)}{\sum_{n'=1}^{N} \exp(g_{n'})} \tag{3}$$

3.2 Overall Framework

Figure 1 illustrates the overall framework, which accepts two inputs: the conversation c and the candidate passage set $\{d_n\}_{n=1}^{N}$. The conversation (c) is paired with any candidate passage d_n, and a text-matching module is utilized to derive the correlation score g_n between the two. These scores $\{g_n\}_{n=1}^{N}$ are subsequently aggregated to predict the answer $\hat{a}$.

3.3 ESIM-Based Relevance Ranking Model: ESIM-Rank

The input of the module is two sequences, the candidate passages d_n and the conversation sequence c after "concatenating" [18–20] the word w_i and the statement u_k. The concatenated conversation sequence c_{concat} is as follows:

$$c_{concat} = \{w_{1,1}, \dots, w_{1,L_{u_1}}, <\text{eou}>, w_{2,1}, \dots, w_{2,L_{u_2}}, <\text{eou}>, \dots\} \tag{4}$$

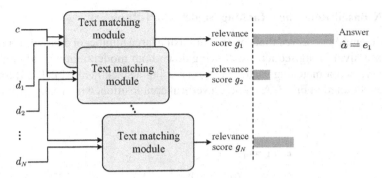

Fig. 1. Role understanding framework based on relevance ranking

$<eou>$ is a special symbol added at the end of each statement to mark the end of the statement and distinguish the two statements before and after. According to Formula 4, the length of c_{concat} is $L_c + K$, L_c is the sum of the length of each statement in the dialogue, and K is the number of $<eou>$.

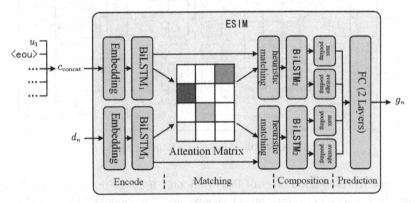

Fig. 2. ESIM-based Relevance Ranking Model

Figure 2 illustrates the process of computing the relevance score g_n between the conversation sequence c_{concat} and the candidate's passages d_n by the ESIM-rank model. The yellow box part in Fig. 2 is the ESIM text matching module.

c_{concat} first converts each word into a vector of size d_e via a word embedding module with vocabulary size $|V|$. Next, the context representation of the word is encoded by the BiLSTM$_1$ with the size of $d_{\vec{h}}$ in the hidden layer, and then the aligned representation of the word is obtained by the bidirectional attention mechanism. Heuristic matching is performed using the above two representations to output a local matching vector of conversation sequences and candidate passages. Finally, the local matching vector at the word level is transformed into the global matching vector at the sentence level by another BiLSTM$_2$ with a hidden layer size of $d_{\vec{h}}$ and the maximum and average pooling. The relevance score can be calculated by combining the global matching vectors obtained from four pools and inputting them into the two-layer fully connected network.

3.4 IMN-Based Relevance Ranking Model: IMN-Rank

We experimentally observed that concatenation of a large number of dialogue rounds can lead to excessively long sequences, slowing down both model training and prediction. Thus, we created a matching model IMN-rank using a stack method [21–23] for comparison, as depicted in Fig. 3. A stack is a vertical composition, which can be formalized as follows:

$$c_{\text{stack}} = [\ \vdots\ ] = [\ \begin{matrix} u_1 \\ \vdots \\ u_K \end{matrix} \quad \begin{matrix} w_{1,1} & \cdots & w_{1,L_{u_1}} \\ & \ddots & \vdots \\ w_{K,1} & & w_{K,L_{u_K}} \end{matrix}\ ] \tag{5}$$

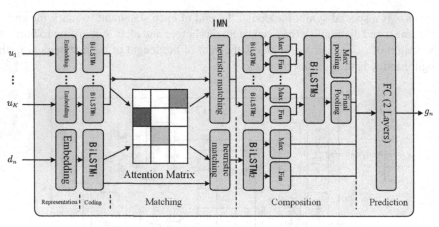

Fig. 3. IMN-based Relevance Ranking Model

The word representation layer of IMN-rank only uses the pre-trained GloVe word embedment; The sentence coding layer has only one bidirectional LSTM, namely $L = 1$, and the attention composition in AHRE is removed. IMN-rank computes the relevance score g_n between conversation c and candidate passages d_n as follows:

Firstly, in each conversation sentence and candidate passages sequence, each word is converted into a vector of size d_e and a context representation of size $2\,d_{\tilde{h}}$ by bidirectional LSTM of the word representation layer and the sentence encoding layer, respectively.

Next, the matching layer uses a bidirectional attention mechanism and a heuristic matching algorithm to transform the context representation of the word into a local matching vector. The conversation sentence performs concatenation and segmentation in the input and output matching layer and participates in matching layer operation in the form of sequence. In the composition layer, the local matching vector of the dialogue is aggregated into the global matching vector of the dialogue by two sets of bidirectional LSTM and pooling operations, while the global matching vector of the candidate description is aggregated by only one set of bidirectional LSTM and pooling operations. Thus, the maximum and last global matching vector of the conversation and the maximum and last global matching vector of the candidate passages can be obtained.

Finally, the above four global matching vectors are concatenated and input into the two-layer fully connected network of the last prediction layer to obtain the relevance score g_n of c and d_n.

3.5 Optimization

For a given conversation, question, and answer triple $(c, q, a) \in D$, the candidate passage set d_n generated by the role set E contains one positive sample and $N - 1$ negative sample of the correct answer a. The relevance score of the positive sample $N_n = 1$ is denoted as g_{n+}, and correspondingly $a = e_{n+}$. Therefore, the objective function $\mathcal{L}$ during learning model $f(c, q)$ is the negative logarithmic likelihood of minimizing the positive sample:

$$\mathcal{L} = -\frac{1}{|\mathcal{D}|} \sum_{(c,q,a) \in \mathcal{D}} f(a = e_{n+} | c, q) \tag{6}$$

$$f(a = e_{n+} | c, q) = \frac{exp(g_{n+})}{\sum_{n'=1}^{N} exp(g_{n'})} \tag{7}$$

where, $|\mathcal{D}|$ is the number of training samples.

4 Experiment

4.1 Dataset

The data set Multiparty-Dialog-RC comes from the American drama "Friends", which includes a total of 1681 conversations. Each conversation consists of 5–25 sentences and involves 2–16 roles. The roles in each conversation are anonymously replaced with the entity ids from @ent00 to @ent15 in order of appearance. The same role is identified by the same entity ID in a single dialogue, and the same role may be identified by different entity ids between different conversations. This anonymous substitution method can avoid overfitting the model on a single role. The total number of samples is 13487, and the training set, verification set, and test set are divided in a ratio of 8:1:1.

4.2 Details

For convenient experimental results contrast, keep only in the glossary structure glove.6B.100d existing in the word, there is no unified replacement in the word $<unk>$, plus a markup statement at the end of the $<eou>$ and the role entity ID @ent00 ~ @ent15, the ultimate vocabulary size $|V| = 11527$. Glove.6B.100d was also used to initialize the word embedding matrix E with the word vector dimension $d_e = 100$. Matrix E is kept updated during training. The hidden layer size of bidirectional LSTM $d_{\tilde{h}} = 100$.

The Adam [24] optimizer was used for training, and the initial learning rate was 0.001. The size of the mini-batch in the ESIM-rank model is 3, and that in the IMN-rank model is 16. Dropout [25] with a probability of 0.3 is used for the input and intermediate hidden layers of the last 2 layers of the fully connected network. In addition, the variational dropout [26] is used to input the bidirectional LSTM at each layer of the network, also with a probability of 0.3. The maximum training iteration is 150 rounds. The training result with the highest accuracy on the verification set is selected as the optimal model to calculate the accuracy of the test set.

4.3 Baseline

In addition to the previously mentioned models, CNN + LSTM + UA + DA and Deep-Dial/DeepDial+, we also include several other models for comparison. These include Majority, a rule-based model, Entity-Centric, a traditional feature-based classifier, and Entity-Centric, a feature-based classifier. Additionally, we selected two deep neural networks that incorporate attention mechanisms - Bi-LSTM [7] and Attentive Reader [27].

5 Results and Analysis

Table 1 displays the accuracy of our two proposed models alongside other models on both the validation and test sets. The accuracy scores of Majority, EntityCentric, Bi-LSTM, and CNN + LSTM + UA + DA are obtained from previous literature [15], while those of AttentiveReader and CNN + LSTM + UA + DA** are obtained from previous literature [16].

To conduct a comparative study of subsequent models, we re-implement the CNN + LSTM + UA + DA model, referred to as CNN + LSTM + UA + DA*, with two changes from the original implementation. Firstly, we utilize the same CNN network for all dialog statements, unlike the original implementation that constructs a CNN network for each dialog statement. Secondly, we modify the similarity calculation between sentence word vector $w_{k,i}$ and question word vector w_j in UA, changing it from $1/(1 + \|w_{k,i} - w_j\|)$.

Table 1. Results of the role understanding experiment

Models	Training	Test
Majority	28.61	30.08
Entity Centric	52.28	47.36
Bi-LSTM	72.24	71.21
Attentive Reader	75.24	72.35
CNN + LSTM + UA + DA*	72.05	72.06
CNN + LSTM + UA + DA	72.21	72.42
CNN + LSTM + UA + DA **	77.53	76.72
DeepDial	78.65	79.61
DeepDial+	81.77	83.18
ESIM-rank	84.88	84.48
IMN-rank	85.99	86.70

As shown in Table 2, the accuracy scores of our two relevance ranking models outperform the previous optimal model DeepDial+ by an improvement percentage ranging from 1.30% to 4.22%. Relative to the CNN + LSTM + UA + DA model, the relevance ranking model yields a more considerable improvement, with the accuracy scores on the validation and test sets increasing by more than 12%. The IMN-rank model that uses the "stack" conversation processing method performs better than the ESIM-rank model that uses the "concatenate" dialog processing method. This indicates that stacking the conversation statements is more efficient in obtaining conversation representation and calculating the similarity between texts. Compared to concatenation, which only captures information at the sentence level, stacking captures information at both the sentence and conversation levels, thereby obtaining more abundant and diverse information. Consequently, stacking performs better than concatenation (Fig. 4).

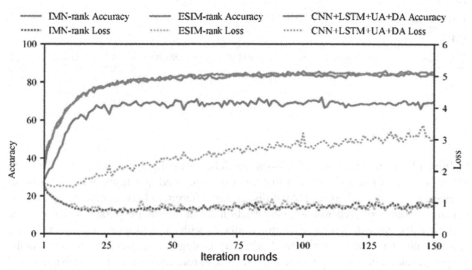

Fig. 4. Curves of accuracy and loss values for Multiparty-Dialog-RC validation set

To exclude the influence of model network structure on the results and show that the performance improvement is due to the construction of candidate passages by relevance ranking thinking, and to calculate the semantic similarity between candidate passages and dialogues, we directly use the original dialogue and problem pairs (c, q) to train ESIM and IMN models (the output layer needs to be transformed into a multi-classification model), and the results are shown in Table 2. The accuracy of ESIM and IMN models is much lower than that of Esim-Rank and IMN-Rank and is inferior to that of CNN + LSTM + UA + DA models. The text-matching model directly applied to the original dialogue and question pairs (c, q) cannot achieve role understanding.

The possible reason is that the @*placeholder* in the problem damages the semantic integrity of the problem. When the @*placeholder* is directly matched between the problem and the conversation, the similarity between the problem and the related content in the conversation is weakened, resulting in the advantages of ESIM and IMN models in text matching. By constructing candidate passages, the semantic integrity of the problem is destroyed, and the original question and conversation matching task is transformed into a candidate passage and conversation matching task. If the candidate passage contains the correct answer role, its similarity to the conversation will be high; otherwise, the similarity will go to 0. Therefore, the relevance ranking method proposed by us can greatly improve the understanding ability of the roles in the conversation. The key to its success lies in this change of thinking.

Table 2. Non-rank model results compared with rank

Models	Validation		Test	
	Accuracy	Δ	Accuracy	Δ
ESIM	68.05	-	68.00	-
ESIM-rank	84.88	16.83	84.48	16.48
IMN	67.90	-	65.26	-
IMN-rank	85.99	180.09	86.70	21.44

6 Conclusion

In light of the inadequacies of existing models, particularly the failure to recognize the central importance of roles in matching dialogue and questions, we offer a novel relevance ranking method capable of discerning differences between all roles in a conversation. The proposed method constructs a set of candidate passages that contain various roles, compares their semantic similarity with the dialogue, and ascertains the correct role. Our experiments on the Multiparty-Dialog-RC dataset demonstrate that the proposed relevance ranking method is superior in role understanding, robustness, and generalization performance.

Acknowledgement. This study was supported by the National Natural Science Foundation of China (No. 62262029), the Natural Science Foundation of Jiangxi Province (No. 20212BAB202016), the Science and Technology Research Project of Jiangxi Provincial Department of Education (No. GJJ200318 and GJJ210520).

References

1. Ni, J., Young, T., Pandelea, V., et al.: Recent advances in deep learning based dialogue systems: a systematic survey. Artif. Intell. Rev. 1–101 (2022)
2. Firdaus, M., Ekbal, A., Cambria, E.: Multitask learning for multilingual intent detection and slot filling in dialogue systems. Inf. Fusion **91**, 299–315 (2023)
3. Liu, Q., Geng, X., Wang, Y., et al.: Disentangled retrieval and reasoning for implicit question answering. IEEE Trans. Neural Netw. Learn. Syst. (2022)
4. Wang, W., Zhang, Z., Guo, J., et al.: Task-oriented dialogue system as natural language generation. In: Proceedings of the 45th International ACM SIGIR Conference on Research and Development in Information Retrieval, pp. 2698–2703 (2022)

5. Yang, Z., Choi, J.D.: FriendsQA: open-domain question answering on TV show transcripts. In: Proceedings of the 20th Annual SIGdial Meeting on Discourse and Dialogue, pp. 188–197 (2019)
6. Li, J., Liu, M., Kan, M.Y., et al.: Molweni: a challenge multiparty dialogues-based machine reading comprehension dataset with discourse structure. In: Proceedings of the 28th International Conference on Computational Linguistics, pp. 2642–2652 (2020)
7. Chen, D., Bolton, J., Manning, C.D.: A thorough examination of the CNN/daily mail reading comprehension task. In: Proceedings of the 54th Annual Meeting of the Association for Computational Linguistics (Volume 1: Long Papers), pp. 2358–2367 (2016)
8. Graves, A.: Long short-term memory. In: Supervised Sequence Labelling with Recurrent Neural Networks, vol. 385, pp. 37–45. Springer, Heidelberg (2012). https://doi.org/10.1007/978-3-642-24797-2_4
9. Trischler, A., Ye, Z., Yuan, X., et al.: Natural language comprehension with the EpiReader. In: Proceedings of the 2016 Conference on Empirical Methods in Natural Language Processing, pp. 128–137 (2016)
10. Dhingra, B., Liu, H., Yang, Z., et al.: Gated-attention readers for text comprehension. In: Proceedings of the 55th Annual Meeting of the Association for Computational Linguistics (Volume 1: Long Papers), pp. 1832–1846 (2017)
11. Cui, Y., Chen, Z., Wei, S., et al.: Attention-over-attention neural networks for reading comprehension. In: Proceedings of the 55th Annual Meeting of the Association for Computational Linguistics (Volume 1: Long Papers), pp. 593–602 (2017)
12. McCann, B., Keskar, N.S., Xiong, C., et al.: The natural language decathlon: multitask learning as question answering. arXiv preprint arXiv:1806.08730 (2018)
13. Liu, X., He, P., Chen, W., et al.: Multi-task deep neural networks for natural language understanding. In: Proceedings of the 57th Annual Meeting of the Association for Computational Linguistics, pp. 4487–4496 (2019)
14. Mikolov, T., Chen, K., Corrado, G., et al.: Efficient estimation of word representations in vector space. arXiv preprint arXiv:1301.3781 (2013)
15. Ma, K., Jurczyk, T., Choi, J.D.: Challenging reading comprehension on daily conversation: passage completion on multiparty dialog. In: Proceedings of the 2018 Conference of the North American Chapter of the Association for Computational Linguistics: Human Language Technologies (Volume 1: Long Papers), vol. 1, pp. 2039–2048 (2018)
16. Hu, N., Zhou, J., Wan, X.: DeepDial: passage completion on dialogs. In: Asia-Pacific Web (APWeb) and Web-Age Information Management (WAIM) Joint International Conference on Web and Big Data, pp. 141–155 (2019)
17. Vaswani, A., Shazeer, N., Parmar, N., et al.: Attention is all you need. In: Advances in Neural Information Processing Systems, pp. 5998–6008 (2017)
18. Lowe, R., Pow, N., Serban, I.V., et al.: The Ubuntu dialogue corpus: a large dataset for research in unstructured multi-turn dialogue systems. In: Proceedings of the 16th Annual Meeting of the Special Interest Group on Discourse and Dialogue, pp. 285–294 (2015)
19. Lowe, R., Pow, N., Serban, I.V., et al.: Training end-to-end dialogue systems with the Ubuntu dialogue corpus. Dialog. Discourse 8(1), 31–65 (2017)
20. Rudolf, K., Martin, S., Jan, K.: Improved deep learning baselines for Ubuntu corpus dialogs. Comput. Sci. (2015)
21. Wu, Y., Wu, W., Xing, C., et al.: Sequential matching network: a new architecture for multi-turn response selection in retrieval-based chatbots. In: Proceedings of the 55th Annual Meeting of the Association for Computational Linguistics (Volume 1: Long Papers), pp. 496–505 (2017)
22. Zhou, X., Li, L., Dong, D., et al.: Multi-turn response selection for chatbots with deep attention matching network. In: Proceedings of the 56th Annual Meeting of the Association for Computational Linguistics (Volume 1: Long Papers), pp. 1118–1127 (2018)

23. Serban, I., Sordoni, A., Lowe, R., et al.: A hierarchical latent variable encoder-decoder model for generating dialogues. In: Proceedings of the AAAI Conference on Artificial Intelligence, vol. 31, no. 1 (2017)

24. Kingma, D.P., Ba, J.: Adam: a method for stochastic optimization. arXiv preprint arXiv:1412. 6980 (2014)

25. Srivastava, N., Hinton, G., Krizhevsky, A., et al.: Dropout: a simple way to prevent neural networks from overfitting. J. Mach. Learn. Res. **15**(1), 1929–1958 (2014)

26. Kingma, D.P., Salimans, T., Welling, M.: Variational dropout and the local reparameterization trick. In: Advances in Neural Information Processing Systems, p. 28 (2015)

27. Hermann, K.M., Kocisky, T., Grefenstette, E., et al.: Teaching machines to read and comprehend. In: Advances in Neural Information Processing Systems, p. 28

Intent Understanding for Automatic Question Answering in Network Technology Communities Based on Multi-task Learning

Xin Huang[1,4](✉), Huilin Song[2,4], and Mingming Lu[3,4]

[1] School of Software, Jiangxi Normal University, Nanchang 330031, China
xinhuang@jxnu.edu.cn
[2] School of International Economics and Trade, Jiangxi University of Finance and Economics,
Nanchang 330013, China
[3] School of Electronic Information Engineering, Tongji University, Shanghai 201804, China
[4] Jiangxi Provincial Engineering Research Center of Blockchain Data Security and Governance,
Nanchang 330031, China

Abstract. In the realm of automatic question-answering (Q&A) for technical communities, accurately perceiving and predicting user intent is a crucial step towards improving Q&A system performance by integrating user intention with answer reasoning processes. We conducted research into intent understanding at the sentence level, aiming to clarify the function of each sentence in technical Q&A communities and improve the system's response accuracy. To address the shortcomings of existing research, which typically ignores information such as speaker type and sentence position, we propose a multi-task learning framework to effectively utilize this information for sentence representation learning. By doing so, the model can acquire richer interactive question-answer language features, thereby enhancing the performance of intent label classification. Within this framework, we present two models: BA-multi and CCR-multi. Our validation experiments on the MSDialog-Intent dataset demonstrate that the multi-task learning model significantly outperforms both the baseline and feature extension models, achieving state-of-the-art performance.

Keywords: Deep Learning · Natural Language Processing · Multi-task Learning · Intent Understanding

1 Introduction

As a form of social media platform, technical Q&A communities focus on providing an open and free knowledge exchange platform for technical professionals. With a clear communication theme and appeal, it is an important channel for users to ask questions, seek information, and share knowledge. Technical community Q&A differs from traditional one-question-one-answer formats, incorporating more information such as conversation context and background, which is diverse and complex. This poses challenges to understanding user input and reasoning answers. Unlike typical input-limited

H. Fujita et al. (Eds.): IEA/AIE 2023, LNAI 13926, pp. 117–129, 2023.
https://doi.org/10.1007/978-3-031-36822-6_10

questions, user input in technical community Q&A can include additional sentences that provide details and feedback on the feasibility of the answer. Thus, understanding the intent of each sentence in the dialogue is essential.

Current research focuses on understanding the contextual information of question and answer sentences; however, it overlooks auxiliary information outside the sentence, such as speaker type and sentence position. The speakers in technical Q&A communities can be divided into two types: users and agents. The sentence position can be represented either as the turn's absolute position or the relative position based on the segment, such as the beginning, middle or end. We therefore propose a multi-task learning framework for intent understanding in technical Q&A communities which utilizes auxiliary information, such as speaker type and sentence location, to improve the performance of intent label classification. The framework includes three tasks, one main task for intent label classification, and two auxiliary tasks focusing on speaker category and sentence position category. In contrast to other multi-task learning approaches that aim to improve the performance of all tasks [1–4], our proposed multi-task learning framework focuses solely on improving the performance of the main task while ignoring training results of auxiliary tasks.

Based on the multi-task learning framework, we introduced the BA-multi and CCR-multi sub-modules to compare different sentence encoding methods. Our experimental results indicate that the multi-task learning system can effectively leverage auxiliary information and improve the performance of intent label classification through complete model training. Compared to directly adding auxiliary information as a feature to the model, multi-task learning boasts superior advantages and yields better results. Our comprehensive analysis and comparison of various auxiliary tasks highlights their significance, the strengths and limitations of multi-task learning under diverse conditions, and the impact of auxiliary information on intention comprehension.

2   Related Work

In a Q&A system, a good intention understanding model can reduce the annotation samples required for training [5]. Traditional intention understanding models are mostly based on maximum entropy [6], hidden Markov model [7], Deep Confidence Network [8], Conditional Random Field [9], Support Vector Machine [10], and other technologies. These models use different features, including lexical features, syntactic features, and so on. In particular, contextual characteristics are heavily considered. For example, in the hidden Markov model used by Venkataraman [11], the hidden state is the intention label, which generates an observable sequence of words. The observation probability is obtained by the language model based on intent-specific words, and the transition probability among intent-specific labels is given by the N-gram language model based on intent-label. Dielmann et al. [12] and Quarteroni et al. [13] use deep confidence networks for sequence decoding and examine generative and conditional modeling methods. As a powerful sequence annotation method, the conditional random field has been widely used for the intent classification of integrated context information [14, 15]. Barahona et al. [16] used different Settings in support vector machine classifiers to capture contextual information, such as n-grams and intent predictive values.

With the rise of deep learning, intention understanding models based on CNN, RNN [17], or a mixture of the two [18] have become the mainstream of research. Currently, two models, CNN-Context-Rep [19] and CRNN [5], are proposed by researchers based on MSDialog-Intent datasets to identify the Intent of statements in multiple rounds of dialogue. In terms of network structure, CNN-Context-Rep only uses CNN [20] network learning intention representation, while CRNN comprehensively utilizes CNN, RNN, Highway [21] connection, and dynamic k max-pooling [22]. In addition, the common feature of the two models is the focus on the fusion of contextual information. CNN-context-rep uses a sliding window of size 3 to consider the Context of each statement before and after, while CRNN uses RNN to collect the Context of the entire conversation.

Although contextual information occupies an important position in the current study of intention understanding, there is a lack of attention to auxiliary information beyond the content of the sentence. There is a strong correlation between auxiliary information and intention, and effective use of auxiliary information can improve the ability to understand the intention.

3 Method

3.1 Formalization

In the dialogue of the technical Q&A community, each sentence can have one or more intent labels, so this paper defines intent understanding as a multi-label classification task. Specifically, for the t-th sentence u_t of the dialogue, it consists of n words, that is, $u_t = \{w_i\}_{i=1}^{n}$. y_t is the intent label corresponding to the sentence, which is a subset of the label set $\mathbb{L} = \{l_1, \ldots, l_c\}$, namely $y_t \subset \mathbb{L}$. Among them, c is the total number of labels and $c = 12$ in this paper. Formally, $y_t = \{y_t^1, \ldots, y_t^c\}$, where $y_t^1 = \{1, 0\}$ $(1 \leq j \leq c)$ indicates whether the label l_j exists or not in y_t, 1 means existence, 0 means do not exist. The speaker type corresponds to the sentences u_t is a_t, and the position is p_t. According to the previous description, $a_t \in \{\text{User}, \text{Agent}\}, p_t \in \{1, \ldots, m\}$, where m is the number of segments of the position. The calculation method of p_t is as follows:

$$p_t = \lceil \frac{t}{T} \times m \rceil \tag{1}$$

where T is the number of dialogue rounds, $1 \leq t \leq T$. For the three tasks proposed in this paper, such as intent label classification, speaker classification, and sentences position classification, the input is the sentence u_t, and the output is y_t, a_t, and p_t.[1] If the data sets are composed of samples (u_t, y_t), (u_t, a_t) and (u_t, p_t) are denoted as $\mathcal{D}_1$, $\mathcal{D}_2$, and $\mathcal{D}_3$, respectively, the goal of intent understanding based on multi-task learning is to learn from these three data sets A model $g(u_t)$: For any sentence u_t, g can predict the probability of each intent label and select all the intent labels with a probability greater than 0.5 as the intent label corresponding to the sentence.

---

[1] We tried various thresholds in the range of 0.3 to 0.7, and found that each index was the best at 0.5.

3.2 Multi-task Learning Model

Multi-task learning can use the information contained in related tasks to improve the generalization ability of the model. We design two related auxiliary tasks to allow the model to learn the speaker type information and sentences position information contained therein, to improve the sentence representation ability of the model. The model structure is shown in Fig. 1. It is mainly divided into left and right parts. The left part is the word representation layer and sentence coding layer shared by all tasks, and the right part is the MLP (Multi-Layer Perceptron, MLP) specific to each task and the corresponding *Sigmoid* or *Softmax* output. Where the word representation layer converts each word w_i into a vector x_i, and the sentence coding layer is used to generate a sentence vector z.

Specifically, the word representation layer is vector concatenated of pre-trained GloVe word embedding, self-trained Word2Vec word embedding, and CNN-based word embedding. The output of the word representation layer x_i:

$$x_i = [x_i^{GloVe}; x_i^{Word2Vec}; x_i^{char}] \tag{2}$$

where [;] represents vector concatenation. We implemented and compared the effects of two different sentence coding methods on the model. One is a BiLSTM network combined with a self-attention mechanism: BiLSTM-Attn; The other is CNN-Context-Rep proposed in [32]. In this paper, the model that uses the BiLSTM-Attn sentence coding layer for multi-task learning is called BA-multi, and the model that uses the CNN-Context-Rep sentence coding layer is called CCR-multi.

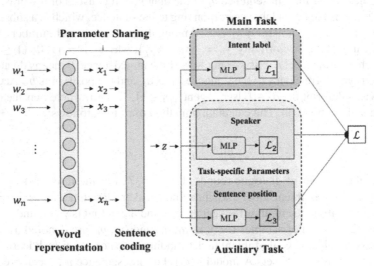

Fig. 1. Multi-task learning model

3.3 BiLSTM-Attn Coding Layer

BiLSTM has proven to be very effective in context modeling, so we use it to obtain the context representation h_i of words:

$$h_i = \text{BiLSTM}(X, i) \tag{3}$$

where $X = \{x_i\}_{i=1}^n$. The weight α_i of each word is normalized by the dot product of h_i and the parameter w to be trained.

$$e_i = w^T h_i \tag{4}$$

$$\alpha_i = \frac{\exp(e_i)}{\sum_{i'=1}^n \exp(e_{i'})} \tag{5}$$

Finally, multiply the context representation of each word with the weight to obtain the sentence vector z:

$$z = \sum_{i=1}^n \alpha_i h_i \tag{6}$$

Although the BiLSTM-Attn network structure is simple but compared with the complex CNN-Context-Rep, the performance gap is not big. Especially after adding multi-task learning, the gap between the two is smaller.

3.4 CNN-Context-Rep Coding Layer

For the sentence coding layer CCR-multi, its input contains three sentences: u_t, the previous sentence u_{t-1} and the next sentence u_{t+1}. To make u_0 and u_{t+1} not null, we add the special word $<eou>$ at the end of each sentence, so $u_0 = u_{t+1} = \{<eou>\}$. For each sentence, CCR-Multi encodes the respective sentences vectors using a separate multi-layer CNN network and then concatenates the three vectors back and forth as the output of the sentence coding layer. For the word vector dimension d_e, the CNN network first applies a convolution kernel of size f to the word vector matrix, and each word vector in the range from i to $i + f - 1$ will be converted into a feature c_i:

$$c_i = \max(0, w^T x_{i:i+f-1} + b) \tag{7}$$

where $w \in \mathbb{R}^{d_f} (d_f = f \cdot d_e)$ is the parameter to be trained. Aggregating these features, a feature map $c = \{c_1, \ldots, c_{n-f+1}\}$ can be generated. The more convolution kernels, the more feature maps are generated, and the more abundant language features are extracted. The convolution operation is followed by maximum pooling, which reduces the f' features into one $\widehat{c_i}$ by picking the maximum value:

$$\widehat{c_i} = \max c_{i:i+f'-1} \tag{8}$$

where f' is the core size of the maximum pooling. After max pooling, dropout is used for regularization. Repeat the above operation twice, and use the global maximum pooling for the last maximum pooling:

$$\hat{c} = \max c \tag{9}$$

Thus, the word vector matrix is converted into a vector with the same size as the number of convolution kernels. After going through a fully connected network, the sentence vector of the sentence is obtained. The sentence vectors of the sentences u_{t-1}, u_t and u_{t+1} are z_{t-1}, z_t and z_{t+1} respectively, and the output z of the CNN-Context-Rep sentence coding layer is:

$$z = [z_{t-1}; z_t; z_{t+1}] \tag{10}$$

Correspondingly, for a single training sample, the loss of the three tasks are calculated as follows:

$$\mathcal{L}_1(u_t, y_t) = -\sum_{j=1}^{c} y_t^i log\hat{y_j} + (1 - y_t^i)log(1 - \hat{y_j}) \tag{11}$$

$$\mathcal{L}_2(u_t, a_t) = -[a_t log\hat{a} + (1 - a_t)log(1 - \hat{a}) \tag{12}$$

$$\mathcal{L}_3(u_t, p_t) = -\sum_{k=1}^{m} p_t^k log\hat{p_k} \tag{13}$$

Thus, the loss function $\mathcal{L}$ of multi-tasking learning is:

$$\mathcal{L} = \sum_{(u_t,y_t)\in\mathcal{D}_1} \mathcal{L}_1(u_t, y_t) + \lambda_2 \sum_{(u_t,a_t)\in\mathcal{D}_2} \mathcal{L}_2(u_t, a_t) + \lambda_3 \sum_{(u_t,p_t)\in\mathcal{D}_3} \mathcal{L}_3(u_t, p_t) \tag{14}$$

4   Experiment

4.1   Dataset

In this paper, two data sets are selected for multi-tasking learning. In addition to the MSDialog-Intent dataset mentioned above, the MSDialog-Complete is also used to construct training samples for two auxiliary tasks. MSDialog-Intent selects a part of the dialogue in MSDialog-Complete for sentence-level intent labeling. The selection conditions are: (1) The number of dialogue rounds must be between 3 and 10; (2) There are 2 to 4 speakers; (3) Has the correct answer; (4) belongs to the four categories of Windows, Office, Bing, and Skype. Compared with MSDialog-Intent, MSDialog-Complete only has fewer intent labels, but it has more dialogue data, which can provide a large number of speaker classification samples and sentences position classification samples for the experiment.

4.2 Details

Because some sentences are long, we truncate the end of the sentences and limit the length of all sentences to no more than 800 words. The word representation layer is composed of three word vectors: (1) The pre-trained GloVe chooses the glove.840B.300d version; (2) The self-trained Word2Vec is obtained by training all sentences in the MSDialog-Complete data set, with a size of 100 dimensions; (3) The word embedding based on CNN is 128-dimensional. Specifically, each word is first converted into a 16-dimensional word vector, and then 128 convolution kernels of size 3 are used for encoding, and the activation function is ReLU.

4.3 Metrics

Multi-label classification tasks often use label-based accuracy Acc, micro-precision P, micro-recall R, and micro-F1 $F1$ as evaluation metrics, and we also follow it. Among them, Acc and $F1$ are the main evaluation metrics. They are calculated as follows:

$$TP_t = y_t \cap \widehat{y_t} \tag{15}$$

$$Acc = \frac{1}{N} \sum_{t=1}^{N} \frac{TP_t}{|y_t \cup \widehat{y_t}|} \tag{16}$$

$$P = \frac{\sum_{t=1}^{N} TP_t}{\sum_{t=1}^{N} |\widehat{y_t}|} \tag{17}$$

$$R = \frac{\sum_{t=1}^{N} TP_t}{\sum_{t=1}^{N} |y_t|} \tag{18}$$

$$F1 = \frac{2 \times P \times R}{P + R} \tag{19}$$

where, $|\cdot|$ denotes the number of set elements, $\widehat{y_t}$ denotes the intent label of the predicted sentence u_t, and N denotes the total number of test samples. Acc is measured from an individual perspective, while P, R, and $F1$ are used to evaluate the prediction results of all sentences from an overall perspective.

4.4 Baseline

The network containing only the main task is taken as the baseline structure, and the two different sentence coding layers correspond to the two baseline models BiLSTM-Attn and CNN-Context-Rep respectively. To compare other auxiliary information fusion methods, we extend the baseline model and add the auxiliary information directly as features to obtain two feature extension models BiLSTM-Attn-fea and CNN-Context-Rep-fea. Specifically, concatenate the two features a_i and p_i with the sentence vector z, and then input the MLP network of each task. The new sentence vector z^+ after concatenation is:

$$z^+ = [z; a_i; p_i] \tag{20}$$

4.5 Main Result

Table 1 shows the experimental results of the two multi-task learning models and comparison methods we proposed. The values of CNN-Context-Rep are directly intercepted from [19]. It should be noted that the results of our reproduced CNN-Context-Rep are much lower than the results published in [19] (Acc: 63.68, F1: 66.69). After the word vector is changed into the three word vectors used in this paper, the two are relatively close, as shown in CNN-Context-Rep* in the table. In the comparison below, the results of CNN-context-rep* will be used to replace the results of the original.

Tabel 1. Intention to Understand Experimental Results

Models	*Acc*	*P*	*R*	*F1*
BiLSTM-Attn	65.89	75.17	62.37	68.17
BiLSTM-Attn-fea	67.20	76.88	63.37	69.54
BA-multi	**69.63**	**77.37**	**66.91**	**71.76**
CNN-Context-Rep	68.85	78.83	65.16	71.34
CNN-Context-Rep *	67.75	77.09	64.52	70.25
CNN-Context-Rep-fea	69.26	78.37	65.16	71.16
CCR-multi	**69.83**	**79.48**	**66.27**	**72.28**

* Reproduce

It can be seen from Table 4 that in all metrics, the two multitasking learning models surpass the comparison model and achieve the current optimal results. Among them, from BiLSTM-Attn to BA-multi, *Acc/F1* has increased by 3.74/3.59, and the effect is the most obvious. From CNN-Context-Rep to CCR-multi, *Acc/F1* has increased by 2.08/2.03, followed by the effect. It can be seen that the introduction of auxiliary tasks allows the model to learn better sentence representations from information such as speaker types and sentences positions, and improves the performance of intent label classification.

From the model of the same network structure, the multi-task learning model (*-multi) is better than the baseline model (BiLSTM-Attn/CNN-Context-Rep) which does not contain auxiliary information. The feature extension model (*-fea), which adds auxiliary information directly as features, is somewhere in between. It shows that auxiliary information can indeed improve the performance of intent label classification, and the use of auxiliary information based on multi-task learning is better than the feature expansion method. Because multi-task learning can use more data to learn language features related to the main task and strengthen the ability of the model to capture the main task information.

Comparing the different sentence coding methods, CNN-Context-Rep, which contains context information of the first and last sentences, is generally better than BiLSTM-Attn, which only has the current sentence, indicating that context information plays an important role in the classification of sentence intention labels. However, with the addition of auxiliary information, the gap between the two has narrowed. From 1.86 *Acc*/2.08

$F1$ of the baseline model to 0.2 Acc/0.52 $F1$ of the multi-task learning model, it shows that auxiliary information can make up for the lack of contextual information. In addition, the close results between BA-MULTI and CCR-MULTI indicate that simple network architecture can have performance comparable to complex network architecture.

5 Analysis and Discussion

5.1 Parameter Tuning

The number of segments in the position of the sentence $m = 4$, and the weight of the loss function for the two auxiliary tasks $\lambda_2 = 0.1$ and $\lambda_3 = 0.2$. The basis is that the model performs best on the validation set when these values are taken. The verification set results for different values of these parameters are presented below to support the above setting. We compared the number of different sentences position segments from 2 to 6, and the results are shown in Table 2. With the increase of the number of segments, the two models showed a trend of first increase and then decrease in the main indexes ACC and F1, and reached the optimal value when $m = 4$.

We use the grid search strategy to find the loss function weights λ_2 and λ_3 of speaker classification task and sentences position classification task that makes the results of verification set optimal between 0.1 and 0.3. As shown in Table 3 and Table 4, the loss function weights λ_2 and λ_3 do not show an obvious rule, but as the value increases continuously, The two main indexes showed a downward trend, and the optimal values were obtained when $\lambda_2 = 0.1$ and $\lambda_3 = 0.2$.

Table 2. Validation Set Results of Segmentation Numbers for Different Sentences Positions

Models	Metrics	2	3	4	5	6
BA-multi	Acc	66.27	67.45	**67.84**	66.81	65.76
	F1	68.10	69.19	**69.65**	68.62	67.55
CCR-multi	Acc	67.55	68.34	**68.70**	67.82	66.89
	F1	69.36	70.50	**70.53**	69.75	68.52

Table 3. Validation Set Results of BA-multi Model under Different Auxiliary Task Weights

(a) Acc				(b) F1			
λ_3	λ_2			λ_3	λ_2		
	0.1	0.2	0.3		0.1	0.2	0.3
0.1	66.91	67.69	67.66	0.1	68.67	69.31	69.01
0.2	**67.84**	66.83	66.45	0.2	**69.65**	68.72	67.91
0.3	66.34	67.29	67.55	0.3	68.26	69.36	69.21

Table 4. Validation Set Results of CCR-multi Model under Different Auxiliary Task Weights

(a) Acc				(b) F1			
λ_3	λ_2			λ_3	λ_2		
	0.1	0.2	0.3		0.1	0.2	0.3
0.1	67.11	67.51	67.92	0.1	69.53	69.19	69.77
0.2	**68.70**	68.46	66.75	0.2	**70.53**	70.19	68.66
0.3	67.05	67.58	66.48	0.3	69.07	69.26	68.96

5.2 Ablation Experiment

To compare the importance of the two auxiliary tasks, we designed an ablation experiment that removes one auxiliary task. The results are shown in Table 5. After BA-multi removes the sentence's position classification, the performance drops more, indicating that the sentence's position information is more important than the speaker type information. However, the result of CCR-multi is just the opposite. After removing the speaker type classification, the performance has declined severely, and the indicators are even lower than the baseline model CNN-Context-Rep. But when it is combined with speaker information, it complements each other and can further improve the performance of the model. Based on this, we have the following conclusion: the two auxiliary tasks are indispensable, and their combination can jointly improve the expressiveness of the intent label classification task.

Table 5. Results of Ablation Experiments

Models	Acc	P	R	F1
BA-multi	69.63	77.37	66.91	71.76
- Speaker type	67.19	75.46	64.60	69.61
- Sentences position	65.98	74.63	63.40	68.56
CCR-multi	69.83	79.48	66.27	72.28
- Speaker type	66.82	77.52	62.29	69.08
- Sentences position	69.67	79.40	65.63	71.86

5.3 Compare by Number of Sentence Labels

Intent label classification is a multi-label classification task, so this section attempts to analyze the performance of multi-task learning on sentences with multiple labels. In the MSDialog-Inten test set, the maximum number of labels per sentence is 3. Most sentences have only one label. 25.67% of sentences have two labels, and less than 2% of sentences have three labels. Then we summarized the experimental results according to the number of labels, as shown in Table 6. In the table, BA-multi comprehensively exceeds BiLSTM-Attn, indicating that the multi-task learning model has a good effect on all kinds of tag numbers.

Table 6. Experimental Results of Different Sentence Labels

Numbers	Proportion (%)	Acc		F1	
		BiLSTM-Attn	BA-multi	BiLSTM-Attn	BA-multi
1	72.37	73.65	**77.54**	73.37	**77.13**
2	25.67	45.85	**48.96**	59.61	**62.55**
3	1.96	42.11	**48.25**	57.83	**65.12**

5.4 Compare by Q&A Rounds

Section 5.1 mentions that dialogue in MSDialog-Intent has a maximum of 10 sentences, so we summarize the experimental results of BiLSTM-Attn and BA-multi according to dialogue rounds 1–10, as shown in Fig. 2. In the figure, BA-multi is better than BiLSTM-Attn or equal to BiLSTM-Attn in all rounds. Especially for round 1, the improvement of both indicators is about 8%. Between rounds 4–7, the lifting effect is also obvious.

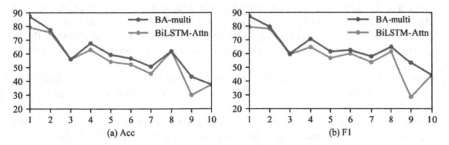

Fig. 2. Experimental Results of Different Dialogue Rounds

6 Conclusion

This paper is centered on the sentence-level classification of intention labels in technical Q&A communities. To enhance the performance of intention label classification, we propose a multi-task learning framework that enables the effective utilization of such information for sentence representation learning, thereby enabling the model to extract richer features of Q&A language. The framework includes two sub-modules, BA-multi and CCR-multi. Using the MSdialog-Intent dataset for validation experiments, we demonstrate that the multi-task learning model significantly outperforms the baseline model and the feature extension model, thus achieving the optimal results. Ultimately, through thorough comparative analysis, we demonstrate the effectiveness of multi-task learning.

Acknowledgement. This study was supported by the National Natural Science Foundation of China (No. 62262029), the Natural Science Foundation of Jiangxi Province (No. 20212BAB202016), the Science and Technology Research Project of Jiangxi Provincial Department of Education (No. GJJ200318 and GJJ210520).

References

1. Liu, X., He, P., Chen, W., et al.: Multi-task deep neural networks for natural language understanding. In: Proceedings of the 57th Annual Meeting of the Association for Computational Linguistics, pp. 4487–4496 (2019)
2. Deng, Y., Xie, Y., Li, Y., et al.: Multi-task learning with multi-view attention for answer selection and knowledge base question answering. In: Proceedings of the AAAI Conference on Artificial Intelligence, vol. 33, pp. 6318–6325 (2019)
3. Trinh, T., Dai, A., Luong, T., et al.: Learning longer-term dependencies in RNNs with auxiliary losses. In: International Conference on Machine Learning, pp. 4965–4974 (2018)
4. Kacupaj, E., Plepi, J., Singh, K., et al.: Conversational question answering over knowledge graphs with transformer and graph attention networks. arXiv preprint arXiv:2104.01569 (2021)
5. Yu, Y., Peng, S., Yang, G.H.: Modeling long-range context for concurrent dialogue acts recognition. In: Proceedings of the 28th ACM International Conference on Information and Knowledge Management, pp. 2277–2280 (2019)
6. Ang, J., Liu, Y., Shriberg, E.: Automatic dialog act segmentation and classification in multi-party meetings. In: Proceedings of the IEEE International Conference on Acoustics, Speech, and Signal Processing (ICASSP 2005), vol. 1 (2005)
7. Surendran, D., Levow, G.A.: Dialog act tagging with support vector machines and hidden Markov models. In: Ninth International Conference on Spoken Language Processing (2006)
8. Ji, G., Bilmes, J.: Dialog act tagging using graphical models. In: Proceedings of the IEEE International Conference on Acoustics, Speech, and Signal Processing (ICASSP 2005), vol. 1 (2005)
9. Kim, S.N., Cavedon, L., Baldwin, T.: Classifying dialogue acts in one-on-one live chats. In: Proceedings of the 2010 Conference on Empirical Methods in Natural Language Processing, pp. 862–871 (2010)
10. Fernandez, R., Picard, R.W.: Dialog act classification from prosodic features using support vector machines. In: International Conference on Speech Prosody 2002 (2002)
11. Venkataraman, A., Ferrer, L., Stolcke, A., et al.: Training a prosody-based dialog act tagger from unlabeled data. In: Proceedings of the 2003 IEEE International Conference on Acoustics, Speech, and Signal Processing (ICASSP 2003), vol. 1 (2003)
12. Dielmann, A., Renals, S.: Recognition of dialogue acts in multiparty meetings using a switching DBN. IEEE Trans. Audio Speech Lang. Process. **16**(7), 1303–1314 (2008)
13. Quarteroni, S., Ivanov, A.V., Riccardi, G.: Simultaneous dialog act segmentation and classification from human-human spoken conversations. In: 2011 IEEE International Conference on Acoustics, Speech and Signal Processing (ICASSP), pp. 5596–5599 (2011)
14. Chen, L., Di Eugenio, B.: Multimodality and dialogue act classification in the RoboHelper project. In: Proceedings of the SIGDIAL 2013 Conference, pp. 183–192 (2013)
15. Ribeiro, E., Ribeiro, R., de Matos, D.M.: The influence of context on dialogue act recognition. arXiv preprint arXiv:1506.00839 (2015)
16. Barahona, L.M.R., Gasic, M., Mrki, N., et al.: Exploiting sentence and context representations in deep neural models for spoken language understanding. In: Proceedings of COLING 2016, the 26th International Conference on Computational Linguistics: Technical Papers, pp. 258–267 (2016)

17. Khanpour, H., Guntakandla, N., Nielsen, R.: Dialogue act classification in domain-independent conversations using a deep recurrent neural network. In: Proceedings of COLING 2016, the 26th International Conference on Computational Linguistics: Technical Papers, pp. 2012–2021 (2016)
18. Liu, Y., Han, K., Tan, Z., et al.: Using context information for dialog act classification in DNN framework. In: Proceedings of the 2017 Conference on Empirical Methods in Natural Language Processing, pp. 2170–2178 (2017)
19. Qu, C., Yang, L., Croft, W.B., et al.: User intent prediction in information-seeking conversations. In: Proceedings of the 2019 Conference on Human Information Interaction and Retrieval, pp. 25–33 (2019)
20. Kim, Y.: Convolutional neural networks for sentence classification. In: Proceedings of the 2014 Conference on Empirical Methods in Natural Language Processing (EMNLP), pp. 1746–1751 (2014)
21. Srivastava, R.K., Greff, K., Schmidhuber, J.: Highway networks. arXiv preprint arXiv:1505.00387 (2015)
22. Liu, J., Chang, W.C., Wu, Y., et al.: Deep learning for extreme multi-label text classification. In: Proceedings of the 40th International ACM SIGIR Conference on Research and Development in Information Retrieval, pp. 115–124 (2017)

Matching Intentions for Discourse Parsing in Multi-party Dialogues

Tiezheng Mao[1], Jialing Fu[2], Osamu Yoshie[1(✉)], Yimin Fu[3], and Zhuyun Li[1]

[1] Graduate School of Information, Production and Systems, Waseda University, Shinjuku City, Japan
yoshie@waseda.jp
[2] Guangdong University of Finance and Economics, Guangzhou, China
[3] International Campus, Zhejiang University, Hangzhou, China

Abstract. Discourse parsing in multi-party dialogues is a fundamental task in dialogue systems, which involves identifying relations between elementary discourse units (EDUs), where an EDU is an utterance in a dialogue. Despite the variety of approaches that have been proposed to enhance context information in utterances, detecting related utterances that share only a few common words remains a challenging task. This paper proposes a novel insight that utilizing intention matching can significantly improve the modeling of utterance relations. Specifically, the intention of a speaker's utterance represents a high-level abstraction of the utterance semantics, including the dialogue context and speaker context. In our model, a graph neural networks is utilized to encode each utterance's intention, then the graph contrastive learning is used to study the match between utterances and intentions. Furthermore, we design three layers of intention to capture the meaning of utterances at different granularities. We conduct extensive experiments on two standard benchmark datasets, and the results show that our proposed model achieves state-of-the-art performance compared to current approaches, including the GPT-3.5 model.

Keywords: Multi-party dialogue · Intention · Graph neural networks

1 Introduction

The discourse parsing on multi-party dialogues is a hot direction. There are many multi-party dialogues in daily life. With the help of discourse parsing in multi-party dialogues, the dialogues can be well organized and easier to comprehend. In multi-party dialogue discourse parsing, the model needs to find the related utterances and classify the utterance relation into the correct category. An example is in Fig. 1. Each utterance is an elementary discourse unit(EDU); there are discourse dependency links between the EDUs, and each link can be classified into categories, such as QAQ, and QAP [1].

There has been many works on traditional monologue discourse parsing but only a few works on multi-party dialogue. Compared with traditional tasks,

H. Fujita et al. (Eds.): IEA/AIE 2023, LNAI 13926, pp. 130–140, 2023.
https://doi.org/10.1007/978-3-031-36822-6_11

discourse parsing on multi-dialogue is more challenging. Many utterances cannot express their intact meanings only by raw text, and the context needs to be considered to comprehend them. To enhance the utterance's context, some works manage to use the dialogue historical information [26] or improve the dialogue dataset [19]; some other works introduce the speakers' interaction graph [18,32] or utterance interaction graph [29]. However, it is difficult for current methods to detect the related utterances which only have few common words. The problem will be more severe when dialogue contains more than two speakers, which is very common in the experiment dataset or in real life.

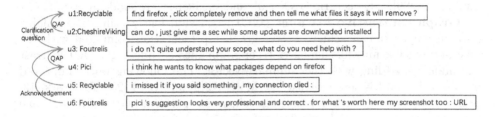

Fig. 1. A example of discourse parsing on multi-party dialogue.

We find an insight that the utterance relation is bound up with the match of utterance intentions. It is because the intention is a higher-level abstraction of the utterance meaning, which includes the semantics, the context and the motivation of speaker. Introducing the utterance intentions can guide the model to train in a more generalized way. We have proposed the intention contrastive learning model, which involves the intentions information to detect the utterance relations. Firstly, a graph neural network (GNN) on text is used to represent intentions, which can record the semantics structurally. Then, a graph contrastive learning (GCL) is adopted to make the different intentions distinguishable, because in the discourse parsing task the relation between intentions is preferred than the explicit representation of intention. Moreover, the multi-level intentions are designed to capture the utterance meaning from different granularities. There are three levels of utterance intention; the utterance-level intention intends to represent its semantics; the dialogue-level intention considers the context of dialogue, such as the historic response between utterances; the speaker-level intention manages to model the cross-dialogue interest of the speaker, such as the communication between speakers and the historic utterance. Our contributions are as follows:

1. Our model use intention to help with modeling the utterance relation. It has the benefit of detecting the related utterances with few common words, which frequently occurs in complex multi-party dialogue.
2. We propose a proper way to represent intention. Three intention levels are defined and a graph constrastive learning method is adopted to study each intention layer.
3. The extentive experiments and analysis on datasets STAC [2] and Molweni [17] show the effectiveness of our model.

2   Related Work

Discourse parsing is a fundamental work in NLP, which can automatically parse the semantics relations in discourse. The traditional discourse parsing include RST-style [21] and PDTB-style [22], which are not suitable for the multi-party dialogue. The early works of discourse parsing on multi-party dialogue mainly by using the handcraft features, including MST [1] and ILP [24]. Recent years deep neural network has been introduced into the direction. The popular works including deep sequential neural network [26], multi-task of combining with tasks like reading comprehension [31] and pronoun recovery [31], domain integration [29], edge centric GNN [29], and speaker-aware modeling [18,32].

Graph contrastive learning (GCL) can sufficiently utilize the unlabel data in graph. It can achieve better graph representation compared with the unsupervised learning like node2vec [7] or graph auto-encoders [15]. DGI contrast the node embedding with the summary vector. The following works improved by importing multi-view contrast like MVGRL [9] and GMI [23]. The work [13] scale the contrast granularity to subgraph, which perform better with less time consumption. In our work, we find the intention information very effective for discoursing parsing on multi-party dialogues. To the best of our knowledge, our work is the first to introduce the intention in discourse parsing. We model the utterance intention with graph neural networks as well as graph contrastive learning so as to involve the speaker context and dialogue context.

3   Task Definition

Follow the works [18,29,32], the input of our task is the multiparty dialogue D and $D = u_1, u_2, ..., u_N$, u_i is the ith utterance in the dialogue. Here we regard each utterance as an EDU. Each $u_i = p_i, c_i$, where p_i indicates the speaker and c_i is the content. We intend to predict all relations $(u_i, u_j, l_{ji}) \| i > j$ between utterance pairs. The (u_i, u_j, l_{ji}) indicates the discourse link of relation typel_{ji} from u_j to u_i.

4   Model

The framework of our model is as Fig. 2. The section Subgraphs of different intention levels (Sect. 4.1) will output a series of subgraphs representation, and the different types of subgraphs indicate the different intention levels. The section Subgraph contrastive learning (Sect. 4.2) will find the utterance relations by augmenting the subgraph data and training with the graph contrastive loss and the supervised training loss.

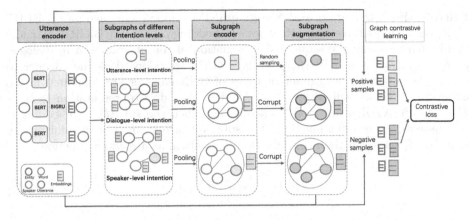

Fig. 2. Overview of our model. From left to right, firstly, each utterance is encoded by pre-trained language model BERT [5] and BIGRU [4]. Then the subgraphs are sampled to represent the different intention levels, and then each subgraph is encoded by GNN models. At last, we augment the subgraphs and do graph contrastive learning.

4.1 Subgraphs of Different Intention Levels

We propose three layers of intention to cover most situations of multi-party dialogue: 1) utterance-level intention based on text semantics, 2) dialogue-level intention based on historical utterances, and 3) speaker-level intention based on speaker interests. Text encoders are input to the pre-trained language model BERT [5] to obtain embeddings $\mu_i = BERT(u_i)$. The graph model is used to represent the complex dialogue-level and speaker-level intentions.

Build Dialogue Subgraph: In the dialogue-level intention, the entity node ϵ is by formulating utterance u's words as 1-gram/2-gram phrases, and looking up the phrases by WordNet and Wikipedia API TagMe [6]. The utterance-utterance edge e_{uu} are connecting related utterances in the dialogue, with the text embedding similarity as edge weight w_{uu}^e. The utterance-entity edge $e_{u\epsilon}$ are connecting utterance and its entity words with the text embedding similarity as the edge weight $w_{u\epsilon}^e$.

Build Speaker Subgraph: In the speaker-level intention, the representation of speaker node sp is by averaging the speaker's historical utterance embeddings. The edge weight between speakers is the normalized count of connections and the edge weight between the speaker and the utterance is always 1.0. In addition, we use the personalized pagerank algorithm on the whole training dialogue dataset [12] to find the important nodes to a speaker. With the $\overline{A}$ as column-normalized adjacency matrix, I as the identity matrix and α as a hyper parameter, the impact score matrix S is the Eq. 1, its top k nodes are extracted to build the edges with speaker i.

$$S = \alpha \cdot (I - (1 - \alpha) \cdot \overline{A}) \tag{1}$$

Encode the Utterance and Subgraph: Pre-trained language model BERT [5] is used to model a certain utterance's embedding μ_i, and the BiGRU [4] model is adopted to study the sequential information of the utterances h in dialogue as $h_1, h_2, ..., h_n = BiGRU(\mu_1, \mu_2, ...\mu_n)$. GNN are adopted as the encoder to model the subgraphs and different types of GNN encoder are compared in the experiment. To the subgraph $g_i = (X_i, A_i)$, its node's representation is H_i is $H_i = GNN(X_i, A_i)$. after GNN encoder and then the subgraph embedding is calculated via a readout function. The subgraph size is small in the multi-party dialogue dataset and the mean function is practical as a readout function.

$$R(H) = \sigma(\frac{1}{N'} \sum_{i=1}^{N'} h_i), \tag{2}$$

where $\sigma(x) = 1/(1 + exp(-x))$, N' is the count of nodes in the subgraph H.

4.2   Subgraph Contrastive Learning

In Sect. 4.1, we use graphs to represent the different intention levels, and then the *subgraph contrastive learning* is adopted to model relations between intentions and between utterances. Existing intention methods such as key sentence mining [3] and LDA topic model [11] are ineffective in multi-party dialogues due to the complexity of intention's multi-level nature and the diversity of the dialogue corpus. Our model emphasizes on intention relations instead of modeling intention explicitly, which solve the problem effectively. We use graph contrastive learning to bring the intentions of related utterances closer and those of unrelated utterances further apart. We first augment subgraphs and labeled data for better training examples, and then use a contrastive loss for self-supervised learning and a cross-entropy loss to learn from labeled data.

Augmentation of Positive Samples: To an utterance u_i, firstly we get the directly positive samples: its labeled related utteranceu_j, the dialogue subgraph representation and the speaker subgraph representation of both u_i and u_j. Then we further augment the positive samples: If nodes count is bigger threshold N_{sub}, drop the node with probability of its reciprocal multiplied by 10 times its degree; If both nodes connected by an edge are not leaf nodes, drop the edge with probability β [30]. This way the generalization of the model can be improved.

Augmentation of Negative Samples: To the utterance u_i, firstly we get the random sample, including random sample utterances in the train set and randomly sample the dialogue subgraph and speaker subgraph from other dialogue. Then we propose the feature shuffle to get more negative sample, which is keeping the subgraph's adjacent matrix fixed and shuffling the feature row [28].

Contrastive Loss: Because the dialogue subgraph has the characters of cross-utterance and the speaker subgraph has the characters of cross-dialogue, it will lead to the intersection nodes between different subgraphs. The margin triplet loss [25] is a good choice under the circumstance. The contrastive loss of dialogue-level intention is as follows:

$$L_D = \frac{1}{N} \sum_{i=1}^{N} (-max(\sigma(h_i, s_i^d) - \sigma(h_i, \widehat{s_i^d}) + \varepsilon), 0), \tag{3}$$

where h_i is the embedding of utterance u_i, which is the anchor in loss, it composes the positive pair with dialogue subgraph embedding $s_i^d = R(H_{d_i})$ and composes the negative pair with dialogue subgraph embedding $\widehat{s_i^d}$. N indicates the number of training samples. The L_U and L_S is constructed from the same way. Then we can get the three contrastive loss L_U,L_S and L_D for the utterance-level intention, the speaker-level intention and the dialogue level intention respectively, and L_{con} is the total contrastive loss.

$$L_{con} = L_D + L_U + L_S, \tag{4}$$

The labels of the link prediction task and relation classification task are used to compose the cross entropy loss [29]. The P_{lp} and P_{rel} are the our model's prediction probability to the link prediction task and relation classification task respectively. It is calculated by concatenating the embedding h_i and h_j, feeding in to different feed-forward layers, and normalizing with softmax function.

$$P_{lp} = softmax(W_{lp}(concat(h_i, h_j))), \tag{5}$$
$$P_{rel} = softmax(W_{rel}(concat(h_i, h_j))), \tag{6}$$

Then the cross entropy loss of link prediction L_{lp} and relation classification L_{rel} is as follows.

$$L_{lp} = -\sum_{i=1}^{\|d\|} log P_{lp}(x_i^* \| \overline{\mathbf{R}}_{i,<i})), \tag{7}$$

$$L_{rel} = -\sum_{i=1}^{\|d\|} log P_{rel}(l_{ji}^* \| \overline{\mathbf{R}}_{i,j,x_j=x_i^*}), \tag{8}$$

where $\|d\|$ is the count of utterances pairs in dataset, x_i^* and l_{ji}^* represent utterance u_i's gold parent and its relation with gold parent. The $\overline{\mathbf{R}}_{i,<i}$ indicates the utterance ahead of u_i.

5   Experiments

We manage to address the following questions in the experiments.

- **Q1:** Whether our model outperforms the current method?
- **Q2:** How to adapt the GPT-3.5 model to the discourse parsing task? Can our model outperform the GPT-3.5 model?
- **Q3:** How does each module of the our model contribute to the performance?
- **Q4:** How do the hyperparameters affect the performance of our model?

5.1   Experiment Setup

1. **Experimental Dataset:** We evaluate on dataset STAC [2] and Molweni [17]. STAC data is collected from an online game trading corpus with 1173 annotated dialogues, while Molweni is collected from Ubuntu dialogue corpus [20] and contains 10000 annotated dialogues. We follow [26] to preprocess the two data sets.
2. **Evaluation:** We use the micro F1 score of standard <u>Link</u> and <u>Link&Rel</u> metrics [18,26]. The <u>Link</u> metrics evaluate the link prediction performance while the <u>Link&Rel</u> metrics add the evaluation on discourse relations.
3. **Implementation Details:** Our work is implemented in PyTorch. All models are run with V100 GPU. The PLM model is BERT-base[1]. The model's parameters are opitmized by Adam algorithm [14] with an initial learning rate of 0.01 and update parameters with a batch size of 10. The hidden dimension is set to 768. The dropout rate on Molweni is 0.4 and the dropout rate for STAC is 0.2. The learning rate on Molweni and STAC is 5e-3 and 5e-4 respectively. The $\alpha = 0.8$ and $\beta = 0.2$.

5.2   Baseline

We compare our model with several current works to answer the question **Q1**. MST [1] model adopts the handcrafted feature. The work [26] proposes Deep+MST by introducing GloVE embeddings to MST. The work ILP [24] proposes a linear programming-based method, and the Deep+ILP introduces Glove word embeddings to ILP. DeepSequential [26] uses a deep neural network to learn the structured presentation with the help of speaker information. Multi(DP+MRC) [10] proposes a multi-task framework for discourse parsing and reading comprehension tasks together. The DiscoProReco [31] introduces the modeling of pronoun recovery to help discourse parsing. The DomainIntegration [19] introduces multi datasets for the domain integration to improve the result. The SSA [29] uses edge-centric GNN to model the dialogue. The SSP-BERT + SCIJE [32] introduces a Speaker-Context Joint Representation for modeling the speaker's interaction with utterance. The HG-MDP [18] uses a heterogeneous graph neural network to encode the speakers and utterances in dialogue graphs. We also propose several different GNN encode to make the comparison, including Ours+GraphSage [8], Ours+GAT [27], Ours+GCN [16], all GNN encoders is set to 2 layers.

Moreover, to answer **Q2**, we conducted a comparative analysis with the widely-used GPT-3.5 model, denoted as $text - davinci - 003$, which boasts approximately 175 billion parameters[2]. To evaluate the efficacy of our approach, we devised several prompts and utilized it to perform on discourse parsing tasks. An example of our prompts is: Find all the response relation between the following utterances. Only output all the utterance index pair and their relations

---

[1] https://huggingface.co/bert-base-uncased.
[2] https://platform.openai.com/docs/model-index-for-researchers.

in a line. The relations include Background,Continuation,Correction,Contrast, Result,Elaboration, Narration, Conditional· · ·. For example: utter 0:apt-get i doubt my apt thing is bad though, i just installed ubuntu today. Utter 1: now you're inside your sources.list (the file that apt uses to find servers). Output: (2 to 1 Comment).

Because the instability of the generative model, we run each sample 5 times and select the best answer of model. Due to resource constraints, we randomly selected 100 instances from the test dataset, with a maximum token count of 2048 and a temperature of 0.2.

Table 1. Main result

Method	STAC		Molweni	
	Link	Link&Rel	Link	Link&Rel
MST [1]	68.8	50.4	–	–
ILP [24]	68.6	52.1	–	–
Deep+MST [26]	69.6	52.1	69.3	49.9
Deep+ILP [26]	69.0	53.1	67.0	48.4
DeepSequential [26]	73.2	55.7	78.1	54.8
Multi(DP+MRC) [10]	–	–	75.9	56.2
DomainIntegration [19]	**75.3**	57.1	79.5	55.7
DiscoProReco [31]	74.1	57.0	–	–
SSA [29]	73.8	55.1	81.4	56.9
HG-MDP [18]	72.0	55.6	81.5	58.5
SSP-BERT+SCIJE [32]	73.0	**57.4**	83.7	59.4
GPT-3.5(text-davinci-003)[a]	38.2	–	43.9	–
Ours-GraphSage	73.8	56.5	85.5	**60.8**
Ours-GAT	73.5	56.6	**85.8**	60.7

[a] https://platform.openai.com/docs/model-index-for-researchers

5.3 Overall Performance

Analyzing the main results in Table 1 to answer **Q1** and **Q2**, we have several valuable findings. Our final model is Ours+GAT. Compared with the SOTA on dataset Molweni, our Link score has an increase of +2.1%, and the Link&Rel score has an increase of +1.3%. The gain in performance mainly comes from the high-level intention matching, which is the speaker-level and dialogue-level intention. Some utterance pairs have no apparent relevance in text or near context, and need to be judged with the help of more abstract intentions. Ours can model these instances better. The DomainIntegration [19] performs the SOTA in the STAC dataset and our model has a decrease of -1.8% on the Link score and a decrease of −0.5% on the Link&Rel score. Manually inspecting the cases, we find that the STAC's utterances also need the intention modeling to find their relations. However, our model can not model the intention well because the dataset is too small with 1173 samples and there is not enough samples to build the high-level intentions. The DomainIntergration proposes a finetune across multi dialogue dataset, which benefit the model's generalization and perform well on small dataset like STAC.

Referring to GPT-3.5 model, it doesn't performance well on the task discourse parsing. This is because there exists a gap between the task of discourse parsing and the training process employed by the GPT-3.5 model. The GPT-3.5 model did not record enough knowledge pertaining to this task during the pre-training phase. In the few-shot learning, the prompts is to excavate the knowledge that the model has learned, so it is difficult for to detect the utterance relations without knowledge. However, it should be noted that the GPT-3.5 model still performs significantly better than random.

5.4   Ablation Study

To answer the question **Q3**, an ablation study is proposed on Molwin dataset and the result is in Table 2. The performance drop most when removing speaker-level intention(-4.4% on Link&Rel and -2.9% on Link) or dialogue-level intention(-1.7% on Link&Rel and -1.5% on Link). It shows the significance of the intention match in our model. Comparing the two intention modules, we find that the w/o speaker-level intention performs even worse because the speaker-level intention reveals more distinguishable information in matching than the dialogue-level intention. Then removing the augmentation of the graph in contrasive learning (Sect. 4.2) makes -1.1% on Link and -1.2%, which shows that only the raw labeled data cannot let the model learn sufficiently.

Table 2. Ablation study

Model settings	Link	Link&Rel
Ours-GAT	85.8	60.7
w/o speaker-level intention	82.9	56.3
w/o dialogue-level intention	84.1	59.2
w/o graph augmentation	84.7	59.5

5.5   Further Analyses on the Important Parameters

This section manages to answer the question **Q4**.

1. The **ratio of positive samples and negative samples** will affect the performance a lot. We find that the best ratio is 1:2 and the lower ratio performs better than the higher one, which indicates that the model relies heavily on the negative samples.

2. The **number of GAT layers** is an import parameter. The two-layer GAT performs best. With the increase of the layer's number, the over-smoothing problem occurs. It indicates that the utterance labels change rapidly in multi-turns and make the nodes in the subgraph irrelevant from the neighbors in a few hops.

6   Conclusion

This work introduces the intention matching model for the discourse parsing on multi-party dialogues. Particularly, it designs utterance-level, dialogue-level and speaker-level intention. The dialogue-level and speaker-level intentions use GNN to encode the complex structure information. Then the graph contrastive learning is adopted to study a distinguishable representation of the intentions and utterances. The experiment shows that our model outperforms current methods. In the future, we plan to continuously refine model by enhancing its generalization for the more complicated forum dialogue dataset.

References

1. Afantenos, S., Kow, E., Asher, N., Perret, J.: Discourse parsing for multi-party chat dialogues. In: Proceedings of EMNLP (2015)
2. Asher, N., Hunter, J., Morey, M., Farah, B., Afantenos, S.: Discourse structure and dialogue acts in multiparty dialogue: the STAC corpus. In: Proceedings of LREC (2016)
3. Cao, B., Ma, K., Liu, Y., Xu, Y., Zhu, L.: Intention classification in multiturn dialogue systems with key sentences mining. Comput. Intell. **37**(2), 758–773 (2021)
4. Cho, K., et al.: Learning phrase representations using RNN encoder-decoder for statistical machine translation. arXiv preprint arXiv:1406.1078 (2014)
5. Devlin, J., Chang, M.W., Lee, K., Toutanova, K.: BERT: pre-training of deep bidirectional transformers for language understanding. arXiv preprint arXiv:1810.04805 (2018)
6. Ferragina, P., Scaiella, U.: TAGME: on-the-fly annotation of short text fragments (by Wikipedia entities). In: Proceedings of the 19th ACM Conference on Information and Knowledge Management, CIKM 2010, 26–30 October 2010, Toronto, Ontario, Canada (2010)
7. Grover, A., Leskovec, J.: node2vec: scalable feature learning for networks. In: Proceedings of KDD (2016)
8. Hamilton, W.L., Ying, Z., Leskovec, J.: Inductive representation learning on large graphs. In: Proceedings of NeurIPS (2017)
9. Hassani, K., Ahmadi, A.H.K.: Contrastive multi-view representation learning on graphs. In: Proceedings of ICML (2020)
10. He, Y., Zhang, Z., Zhao, H.: Multi-tasking dialogue comprehension with discourse parsing. In: Proceedings of the 35th Pacific Asia Conference on Language, Information and Computation (2021)
11. Hoffman, M.D., Blei, D.M., Bach, F.R.: Online learning for latent Dirichlet allocation. In: Proceedings of NeurIPS (2010)

12. Jeh, G., Widom, J.: Scaling personalized web search. In: Proceedings of WWW (2003)
13. Jiao, Y., Xiong, Y., Zhang, J., Zhang, Y., Zhang, T., Zhu, Y.: Sub-graph contrast for scalable self-supervised graph representation learning. In: Proceedings of ICDM (2020)
14. Kingma, D.P., Ba, J.: Adam: a method for stochastic optimization. In: Proceedings of ICLR (2015)
15. Kipf, T.N., Welling, M.: Variational graph auto-encoders. ArXiv preprint (2016)
16. Kipf, T.N., Welling, M.: Semi-supervised classification with graph convolutional networks. In: Proceedings of ICLR (2017)
17. Li, J., et al.: Molweni: a challenge multiparty dialogues-based machine reading comprehension dataset with discourse structure. In: Proceedings of COLING (2020)
18. Li, J., Liu, M., Wang, Y., Zhang, D., Qin, B.: A speaker-aware multiparty dialogue discourse parser with heterogeneous graph neural network. Cogn. Syst. Res. (2023)
19. Liu, Z., Chen, N.: Improving multi-party dialogue discourse parsing via domain integration. In: Proceedings of the 2nd Workshop on Computational Approaches to Discourse (2021)
20. Lowe, R., Pow, N., Serban, I., Pineau, J.: The Ubuntu dialogue corpus: a large dataset for research in unstructured multi-turn dialogue systems. In: Proceedings of the 16th Annual Meeting of the Special Interest Group on Discourse and Dialogue (2015)
21. Mann, W.C., Thompson, S.A.: Rhetorical structure theory: toward a functional theory of text organization. Text-interdisc. J. Study Discour. (1988)
22. Miltsakaki, E., Prasad, R., Joshi, A., Webber, B.: The Penn discourse treebank. In: Proceedings of LREC (2004)
23. Peng, Z., et al.: Graph representation learning via graphical mutual information maximization. In: Proceedings of WWW (2020)
24. Perret, J., Afantenos, S., Asher, N., Morey, M.: Integer linear programming for discourse parsing. In: Proceedings of NAACL (2016)
25. Schroff, F., Kalenichenko, D., Philbin, J.: FaceNet: a unified embedding for face recognition and clustering. In: Proceedings of CVPR (2015)
26. Shi, Z., Huang, M.: A deep sequential model for discourse parsing on multi-party dialogues. In: Proceedings of AAAI (2019)
27. Velickovic, P., Cucurull, G., Casanova, A., Romero, A., Liò, P., Bengio, Y.: Graph attention networks. In: Proceedings of ICLR (2018)
28. Velickovic, P., Fedus, W., Hamilton, W.L., Liò, P., Bengio, Y., Hjelm, R.D.: Deep graph infomax. In: Proceedings of ICLR (2019)
29. Wang, A., et al.: A structure self-aware model for discourse parsing on multi-party dialogues. In: Proceedings of IJCAI (2021)
30. Wu, J., et al.: Self-supervised graph learning for recommendation. In: Proceedings of SIGIR (2021)
31. Yang, J., et al.: A joint model for dropped pronoun recovery and conversational discourse parsing in Chinese conversational speech. In: Proceedings of ACL (2021)
32. Yu, N., Fu, G., Zhang, M.: Speaker-aware discourse parsing on multi-party dialogues. In: Proceedings of COLING (2022)

Natural Language Modeling
with the Tsetlin Machine

Saeed Rahimi Gorji$^{(\boxtimes)}$ (iD), Ole-Christoffer Granmo (iD), and Morten Goodwin (iD)

Centre for Artificial Intelligence Research, University of Agder, Grimstad, Norway
{saeed.r.gorji,ole.granmo,morten.goodwin}@uia.no

Abstract. The Tsetlin Machine, a recently developed supervised learning algorithm with interpretability prospect, has been used in tackling challenging problems in classification, regression, and convolution in its short presence and obtained competitive results in terms of accuracy and computational resources. In the present work, we build a statistical language model based on the Tsetlin machine, which predicts the next most likely character in a partially given word. Moreover, with an online application in mind, we train and evaluate our model as a (one-pass) streaming algorithm emphasizing adaptability and customizability. Furthermore, we provide empirical evidence that our model exhibits comparable performance regarding learning speed and accuracy to a similar model based on multi-layer perceptrons.

Keywords: Tsetlin Machine · Statistical Language Model · Streaming Algorithm

1 Introduction

Predictive systems for natural language have been around since 1980s, and in the past few decades, faster computers have helped more theoretical models turn into reality. One of the prominent directions in the field concerns the development of assistive technologies for language [4]. In particular, computers' ability to learn certain patterns from data resulted in computational models aiming toward various tasks for understanding and generating natural language [2].

Writing assistant systems, as one of the most important classes of assistive tools, aim to predict the next item in a piece of text. Depending on the design and application of such a system, the item predicted may refer to letters, words, or phrases which are likely to follow the current input text. These predictions are based on an underlying language model which has been developed during training [1,16].

A language model, or more specifically, a statistical language model, aims to describe the relation among the building blocks through probability distributions. This is possible due to the presence of statistical structures and frequent

Funding supporting this work was partially provided by Norges Forskningsråd (Human-Chatbot Interaction Design project, grant number 270940).

occurrences of certain items together in natural language. These items can be phonemes, syllables, letters, words, or even larger language constructs. Language models have many applications in different areas of NLP-information content and prediction [12,13], enhancing error correction [8,15] and text recognition [6,9] to name a few. As the models get more sophisticated, a collection of such items from a given sample text or speech may be considered, which is referred to as an n-gram [14]. Training a language model comes down to building a probability distribution on the presence of n-grams, among other techniques, to predict or conclude additional information from the model. Accordingly, an n-gram model assumes that the probability of an item being the next one in a sequence depends on the previous $(n-1)$-items and uses an $(n-1)$-order Markov model to make a prediction. This class of Markov models was first introduced by Claude Shannon [11], among other ideas.

Paper Contributions. In the present work, we utilize the TM as an assistive tool in NLP applications. Considering the scope and complications of such a task, we limit ourselves to a simpler problem of predicting the next letter in a partially given word [7]. In this problem, the Tsetlin machine uses a (tokenized) text stream as the input (presented as individual words) to build a statistical model representing the underlying word structure. After ample training, such a model could predict the most likely candidate for the next letter in the given partial word. We train and evaluate our model on a text stream in an online and one-pass manner. Furthermore, we compare our results with similar systems based on multi-layer perceptron as benchmarks, providing empirical evidence on the suitability of the TM for such a task.

2   The Tsetlin Machine

A TM takes a vector $X = (x_1, \ldots, x_o)$ of Boolean features as input to be classified into one of two classes, $y = 0$ or $y = 1$. Together with their negated counterparts, $\bar{x}_k = \neg x_k = 1 - x_k$, the features form a literal set $L = \{x_1, \ldots, x_o, \bar{x}_1, \ldots, \bar{x}_o\}$.

A TM pattern is formulated as a conjunctive clause C_j (Eq. 1), formed by ANDing a subset $L_j \subseteq L$ of the literal set:

$$C_j(X) = \bigwedge_{l \in L_j} l = \prod_{l \in L_j} l.$$

$$(1)$$

The number of clauses employed is a user-set parameter n. Half the clauses are assigned positive polarity, and the other half negative. The clause outputs are combined into a classification decision through summation and thresholding using the unit step function $u(v) = 1$ **if** $v \geq 0$ **else** 0, and classification is performed based on a majority vote, with the positive clauses voting for $y = 1$ and the negative for $y = 0$ (Eq. 2). The classifier $\hat{y} = u(x_1 \bar{x}_2 + \bar{x}_1 x_2 - x_1 x_2 - \bar{x}_1 \bar{x}_2)$, e.g., captures the XOR-relation (illustrated in Fig. 1).

$$\hat{y} = u\left(\sum_{j=1}^{n/2} C_j^+(X) - \sum_{j=1}^{n/2} C_j^-(X)\right).$$

$$(2)$$

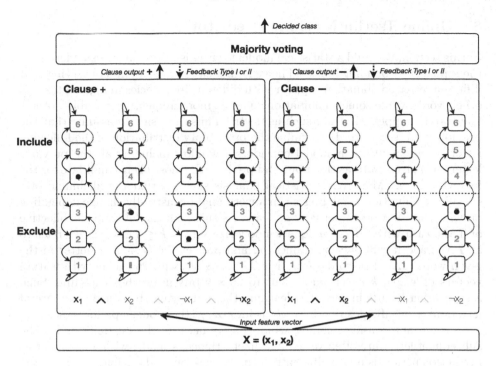

Fig. 1. The TM architecture. Each clause is constructed using Tsetlin Automata (TA), which learn to include or exclude their corresponding literals. The number of clauses is chosen beforehand. Here, only one positive and one negative clause are shown.

A clause j is composed by a Tsetlin Automata (TA) team, one TA per literal l_k in L. The TA for literal l_k has a state $a_{j,k}$ deciding the inclusion of l_k in clause j. Learning which literals to include is based on two reinforcement types, Type I and Type II. Type I feedback produces frequent patterns, while Type II feedback increases the discrimination power of the patterns [5].

TMs learn on-line, processing one training example $(\mathbf{X}, y)$ at a time and update clauses as shown in Fig. 1. Here, resource allocation dynamics ensure that clauses distribute themselves across the frequent patterns rather than missing some and over-concentrating on others. That is, for any input $\mathbf{X}$, the probability of reinforcing a clause gradually drops to zero as the voting sum v approaches a user-set target T for $y = 1$ (and $-T$ for $y = 0$).

If a clause is not reinforced, it does not give feedback to its TAs, and these are thus left unchanged. In the extreme, when the voting sum v equals or exceeds the target T (the TM has successfully recognized the input $\mathbf{X}$), no clauses are reinforced. They are then free to learn new patterns, naturally balancing the pattern representation resources [5].

3   Online Tsetlin Machine Predictor

In this section, we build a statistical model for English vocabulary using letters in the alphabet as building blocks. The general idea revolves around observing that different letter combinations appear with different frequencies in a given text. In other words, while some combinations may be more frequent, e.g., "able", others may rarely happen, if at all, such as "swtr". Thus, it is safe to assume that the previous letters in a word determine the probability distribution of the following letter. Consequently, our model considers a window including all the previous letters in a given word as the input and predicts the most likely candidate for the following letter. Moreover, statistical analysis suggests that the likelihood of a specific combination being present in a word might drastically change depending on where in the word it actually appears. As such, our model trains a collective of TMs, each with a fixed unique window size k $(3 \leq k \leq 7)$, which we refer to as TM_k, and it will only be trained on and predict the $(k+1)$-th letter in the given words. In other words, TM_k is a TM classifier with 26 classes with feature vectors of length k letter, equivalent to $26 \times k$ bits in one-hot encoding. Such a separation results in each TM learning the underlying statistical structure of letters at a specific position in a word, improving the model's performance.

We did not consider smaller window sizes because the possibilities for the subsequent letter are often varied and likely. Hence, a model with a single-letter prediction performs poorly. In contrast, in the case of windows longer than 7, the possibilities are usually from the same family (inflected or derived forms). However, as the window length increases, the number of occurrences drops drastically, which may disrupt or delay training for the corresponding TM(s).

Note that many frequent and equal-sized letter combinations may only differ in the last letter, especially the ones with fewer letters. Thus, reaching a prediction error rate of 0% (100% accuracy) may not be possible with only one predicted letter as the output. Instead, the objective is to predict the most likely candidate for the next letter, which may sometimes result in wrong predictions.

Considering the application side, namely predicting the next anticipated letter in a partially given word, training the model as a streaming or one-pass algorithm seems the most appropriate [10]. Thus, assuming adequate training data, we use it as a data stream to train and evaluate our model. For small datasets with low word frequencies, however, it is conceivable that a single pass on the dataset may not provide sufficient training for the model. In such cases, multiple passes or epochs may be needed to offer ample training.

A well-trained and accurate model may be deemed outdated in a new context or style of input. That is because, despite converging to the underlying statistical characteristics of the training data, as the input changes context or evolves into a new style, its vocabulary and statistics change and may not be aligned with that of the model. Consequently, a static model needs frequent updates to address such issues. On the other hand, learning in an online manner offers adaptivity and customizability, making the model more versatile in the face of new input. Furthermore, adaptive models propound the idea of transfer learning and using pre-training models, which can adapt to a new context or style expeditiously.

Notwithstanding the limitation on the scope and variety of our results, we argue that learning the statistical structure of words is highly transferable. In contrast to learning phrases and sentences, which have a broad context and almost infinite scope, words are remarkably limited, and a pre-trained model could easily adapt and be used in a new environment.

4   Consecutive Prediction

In the previous section, we built several classifiers that predict the most likely next letter in a partially given word. As a natural next step, we can combine those classifiers to make consecutive predictions and predict the most likely word(s) given the first few letters. To that end, after training each classifier individually, we will use the output of each TM as the input for the next one.

Although such a setup benefits from the collective prediction abilities of several TMs, their dependencies compound the effect of inaccurate predictions. To address this issue, we generalize the model where instead of predicting the most likely letter, each TM outputs multiple letters with the highest likelihoods. In turn, the next TM makes its prediction(s) based on each output. Consequently, instead of one final word, the team builds a prediction tree resulting in multiple candidates for the

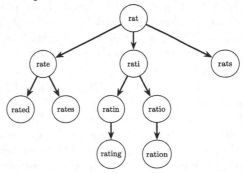

Fig. 2. A tree structure example for consecutive predictions of the partial word "rat"

final word. More preciously, the prediction tree is characterized by a root node representing the initial input, e.g., the first three letters of the input word, and a branching factor b as the maximum number of children for internal (non-leaf) nodes in the tree. As such, at each internal node in the tree, the relevant TM from the team predicts the b most likely candidates for the next letter and extends its input by each predicted character for their corresponding child node. Finally, when all TMs made their predictions, the process is deemed successful if and only if the actual word is present somewhere in the prediction tree. Figure 2 depicts an example of such a prediction tree for the input *rat*. Considering the exponential growth of the prediction tree, we only used $b = 1$, 2, and 3 as the branching factors resulting in unary, binary, and ternary trees, respectively (Fig. 13, 14, and 15).

5   Empirical Results and Analysis

We evaluated our model on the *NIPS full papers* (NIPS) and *KOS blog entries* (KOS) datasets[1]. NIPS contains around two million words collected from 1500

---

[1] https://archive.ics.uci.edu/ml/datasets/bag+of+words.

NIPS articles, comprising over 12000 unique words. On the other hand, KOS features around half a million words and 7000 unique words [3]. Considering the size and nature of these datasets, we treated each as a stream of words from a stream of documents in batches of 10000 words. For each batch, we first measured the models' prediction accuracy before training them on that batch. Thus, the models only train on each word in the dataset once (single-pass).

For each model, we trained a team of five Tsetlin machine classifiers with 1000 clauses, corresponding to window sizes of 3 to 7. Moreover, we chose the threshold value of 20 empirically to accommodate the complexity of the patterns, and we tuned the specificity parameter s of each TM individually for the best performance. Furthermore, as benchmarks in terms of learning speed and accuracy, we trained several teams of (fully connected feed-forward) multi-layer perceptron (MLP) with different configurations in the same manner. As expected, as the size of these MLPs grows, their error rate drops, and considering the size of the problems, we used $MLP - 2 \times 20$ and $MLP - 3 \times 10$ as our benchmark, where $MLP - k \times n$ indicates an MLP with k hidden layers each consisting of n nodes with the learning rate tuned from the range of 0.0005 to 0.02 for the best performance.

Figure 3, 4, 5, 6, 7, 8, 9, 10, 11 and 12 compare the performance of our model and the benchmark MLPs ($MLP - 2 \times 20$ and $MLP - 3 \times 10$). Figures suggest that for both TM- and MLP-based models, the learning happens rather quickly, and they converge to their final error rate within the first few batches of words. Moreover, a certain amount of error remains throughout the learning and after convergence which relates to the variety of potential letters following a letter combination. Furthermore, the figures suggest an inverse relationship between the final error and the window size, consistent with longer letter combinations demonstrating less variety.

Our results for the two datasets, NIPS: Fig. 3, 4, 5, 6 and 7; KOS: Fig. 8, 9, 10, 11 and 12, suggest that when there is adequate data available, the TM shows comparable performance to the benchmarks. In contrast, the TM falls behind when the data gets scarce, e.g., longer windows in the KOS dataset, which only have a few batches.

As described in Sect. 4, we integrate the TMs to predict words. Like the previous experiments, the model only performs one pass on the data and will be evaluated on the next batch before training. Moreover, instead of evaluating each TM individually, we build a prediction tree and check whether the correct word is present somewhere in the tree. In other words, a prediction tree is successful if all the TMs have the correct letter among their predictions. We only used the NIPS dataset for this part, but considering its significant size, we broke it down into three equal parts, which we refer to as NIPS-A, NIPS-B, and NIPS-C, and we treated them as independent datasets.

Figure 13, 14, and 15, compare the performance of the prediction trees built by the TM and the best benchmark MLP. Each chart includes three sets of results corresponding to three branching factors, $b = 1$, 2, and 3. The charts indicate

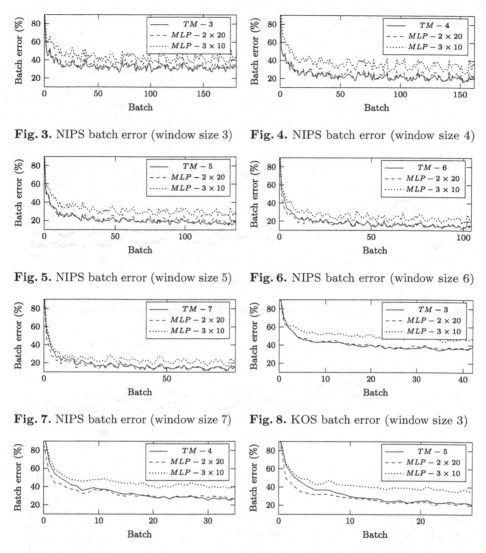

Fig. 3. NIPS batch error (window size 3)   **Fig. 4.** NIPS batch error (window size 4)

Fig. 5. NIPS batch error (window size 5)   **Fig. 6.** NIPS batch error (window size 6)

Fig. 7. NIPS batch error (window size 7)   **Fig. 8.** KOS batch error (window size 3)

Fig. 9. KOS batch error (window size 4)   **Fig. 10.** KOS batch error (window size 5)

that although the MLP-based model learns slightly faster than the TM-based model in the first few batches, both models produce similar results afterward.

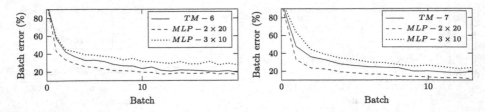

Fig. 11. KOS batch error (window size 6)   **Fig. 12.** KOS batch error (window size 7)

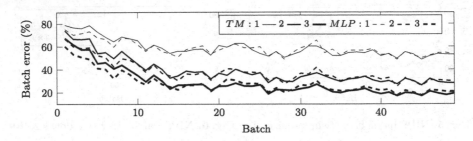

Fig. 13. NIPS-A batch error for prediction tree with branching factor of 1, 2 and 3

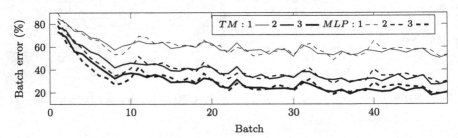

Fig. 14. NIPS-B batch error for prediction tree with branching factor of 1, 2 and 3

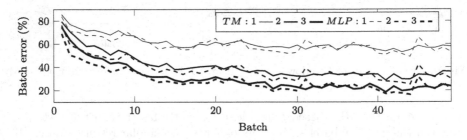

Fig. 15. NIPS-C batch error for prediction tree with branching factor of 1, 2 and 3

6   Conclusion and Future Work

In this work, we aimed to develop a statistical language model for English vocabulary using the TM. To that end, we trained a team of TM classifiers to predict the most likely candidates for the next letter in a partially given word. Moreover, we combined the classifiers' predictions to predict the most likely words. Finally, we discussed and compared the results with similar models based on MLP as our benchmarks and argued that our TM-based model exhibits comparable performance to the benchmarks.

A potentially promising future work relates to using other types of data from other disciplines which may have underlying statistical structures and patterns, such as computational biology (e.g., protein sequencing and DNA sequencing [17]).

References

1. Brown, P.F., Della Pietra, V.J., Desouza, P.V., Lai, J.C., Mercer, R.L.: Class-based n-gram models of natural language. Comput. Linguist. **18**(4), 467–480 (1992)
2. Chowdhary, K.R.: Natural language processing. In: Chowdhary, K.R. (ed.) Fundamentals of Artificial Intelligence, pp. 603–649. Springer, New Delhi (2020). https://doi.org/10.1007/978-81-322-3972-7_19
3. Dua, D., Graff, C.: UCI machine learning repository (2017). https://archive.ics.uci.edu/ml
4. Ghayoomi, M., Momtazi, S.: An overview on the existing language models for prediction systems as writing assistant tools. In: 2009 IEEE International Conference on Systems, Man and Cybernetics, pp. 5083–5087 (2009). https://doi.org/10.1109/ICSMC.2009.5346027
5. Granmo, O.C.: The Tsetlin machine - a game theoretic bandit driven approach to optimal pattern recognition with propositional logic. arXiv preprint arXiv:1804.01508 (2018). Unpublished
6. Hanson, A.R., Riseman, E.M., Fisher, E.: Context in word recognition. Pattern Recogn. **8**(1), 35–45 (1976)
7. Martin, J.: Word prediction technology: what it is and how it works. https://www.understood.org/articles/en/word-prediction-technology-what-it-is-and-how-it-works
8. Morris, R., Cherry, L.L.: Computer detection of typographical errors. IEEE Trans. Prof. Commun. **1**, 54–56 (1975)
9. Neuhoff, D.: The Viterbi algorithm as an aid in text recognition (corresp.). IEEE Trans. Inf. Theory **21**(2), 222–226 (1975)
10. Schweikardt, N.: One-pass algorithm. In: Liu, L., Özsu, M.T. (eds.) Encyclopedia of Database Systems, pp. 1948–1949. Springer, Boston (2009). https://doi.org/10.1007/978-0-387-39940-9_253
11. Shannon, C.E.: A mathematical theory of communication. Bell Syst. Tech. J. **27**(3), 379–423 (1948)
12. Shannon, C.E.: Prediction and entropy of printed English. Bell Syst. Tech. J. **30**(1), 50–64 (1951)
13. Smith, F.: The use of featural dependencies across letters in the visual identification of words. J. Verbal Learn. Verbal Behav. **8**(2), 215–218 (1969)
14. Suen, C.Y.: n-gram statistics for natural language understanding and text processing. IEEE Trans. Pattern Anal. Mach. Intell. **PAMI-1**(2), 164–172 (1979). https://doi.org/10.1109/TPAMI.1979.4766902
15. Ullmann, J.R.: A binary n-gram technique for automatic correction of substitution, deletion, insertion and reversal errors in words. Comput. J. **20**(2), 141–147 (1977)

16. Wu, C.P., Hsu, L.S., Tan, C.L.: A survey on statistical approaches to natural language processing. Citeseer (1992)
17. Yang, A., Zhang, W., Wang, J., Yang, K., Han, Y., Zhang, L.: Review on the application of machine learning algorithms in the sequence data mining of DNA. Front. Bioeng. Biotechnol. **8**, 1032 (2020). https://doi.org/10.3389/fbioe.2020.01032

Optimization

Path Inference Based on Voronoi Graph

Xin Xu[✉]

Science and Technology on Information System Engineering Laboratory,
Nanjing 210023, China
xinxu_nriee@sina.com

Abstract. Traditional path planning approach is generally focused on finding a single one shortest path given the temporal or spatial constraints. However, the strategy of single-one optimal path is unable to adapt to various situations in real applications. For example, in the scenarios of vehicle patrolling and search&rescue, the comprehensiveness of coverage is much more important. Rather than finding a single one optimal shortest path as the traditional path planning does, our path inference approach aims at inferring all the possible paths which satisfy the specified temporal and spatial constraints. Path inference is able to provide more valuable insights for internet routing, migration pattern study, urban construction and adversary profiling. In this work, we propose a novel path inference algorithm based on Voronoi graph. We model the 2D geospatial topology with Voronoi cells according to the spatial constraint, represent the adjacency relationships of Voronoi cells with an adjacency matrix and infer all the possible paths in the derived Voronoi graph satisfying the user-specified temporal and spatial constraints. Experimental results indicate that our path inference algorithm based on Voronoi graph is able to perform more delicately and efficiently than the traditional path planning approach in term of both space partition and path inference.

Keywords: Path planning · Path inference · Voronoi graph

1 Introduction

Path inference generally infers all the possible paths starting from a specified source position and arriving at a specified destination position which satisfy certain temporal and spatial constraints. Path inference is closely related with but significantly different from the traditional path planning approach.

Traditional path planning task is devoted to identifying a single one optimal shortest path given the specified constraints [1]. Comparatively, path inference is able to reveal a more complete picture for decision making as the shortest path would probably not always be the best one for the task. For example, in the scenarios of vehicle patrolling and search&rescue, the comprehensiveness of path coverage is much more important for fulfillment. In internet routing, discovering various potential paths between autonomous systems (ASes) is essential for understanding the behaviors of Internet routing system and underlying Internet

© The Author(s), under exclusive license to Springer Nature Switzerland AG 2023
H. Fujita et al. (Eds.): IEA/AIE 2023, LNAI 13926, pp. 153–158, 2023.
https://doi.org/10.1007/978-3-031-36822-6_13

services. In zoology, a rich set of migratory paths helps zoologists uncover animal migration patterns. In urban construction, the different ways of traveling routes of people provides useful clues for urban planning.

In this paper, we have brought forward a flexible Voronoi graph construction scheme to accommodate various task requirements, a novel concept of Voronoi diameter path for acurate path length estimation and an efficient depth-first exploration algorithm for path inference. Experimental results indicated the effectiveness and efficiency of our algorithm.

2 Related Work

Our path inference algorithm based on Voronoi graphs is closely related with the traditional path planning methods. Path planning, also referred to as motion planning, usually judges the optimality of paths by travelling time and distance. The optimal path is usually the shortest and fastest one. A variety of different strategies have been adopted for path planning, including artificial potential field, weighted graph, heuristic searching, dynamic programming and reinforcement learning.

The potential field method [2,3] generally assigns a value calculated via an artificial potential function to every point in the space. In that way, it simulates the reaction of a vehicle to the potential field as it navigates towards the minimum potential. It is assumed that the potential field is continuous and differentiable. However, there exists a problem of local minima trap for the potential field method. The Floyd-Warshall method [4,5] uses pre-defined discretized cells to solve the "all pairs shortest path (APSP) problem" through a weighted graph. This technique is mainly used for offline path planning and unsuitable for dynamic path discovery [6]. The genetic algorithm [7], greedy heuristic and Multi-Step Look-Ahead Policy (MSLAP) algorithms all utilize the heuristic searching strategy for path planning. Though an optimal solution is not guaranteed, these algorithms are able to reach a sub-optimal solution with less computation time. Both Dijkstra's algorithm and Bellman-Ford algorithm [8] utilize the dynamic programming (DP) strategy. These DP algorithms calculate the distance to the goal from all the points based on the pre-computed distances in a dynamic way. Reinforcement learning is another popular strategy for path planning, which has a long-term versus a short-term trade-off. Simulations and iterative reinforcement are generally applied together to speed up the learning process.

Instead of discovering a single one optimal path as path planning, our path inference method based on Voronoi graph explores all the possible paths satisfying the specified constraints. Though the purposes of two tasks are quite different, the underlying path exploration strategies could be shared.

3 Method

Our path inference algorithm based on Voronoi graph is composed of three major steps: Voronoi graph construction, Voronoi graph representation and depth-first path exploration.

3.1   Voronoi Graph Construction

Our Voronoi graph construction scheme is capable of partitioning the spatial topology flexibly to separate restricted and normal areas. In mathematics, a Voronoi graph is a partition of a plane into a set of Voronoi cells, each represented by a Voronoi seed. The data points in the Voronoi cell are closer to its Voronoi seed than any of the remaining seeds. During the space partiton, we assume the shape of restricted area is approximately a circle and customize a regular polygon-shaped Voronoi cell for the restricted area.

Mathematically, assume there is a circle-shaped restricted area on a 2D plane with center O and radius R as highlighted in red in Fig. 1. And assume one seed is located at point O, k seeds are evenly-distributed along the circumference of circle C' centered at O with radius $2R$ and other seeds are located outside circle C'. Then, the circle-shaped restricted area denoted as circle C must be covered by the Voronoi cell represented by the seed at O.

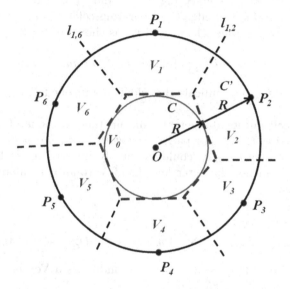

Fig. 1. Voronoi graph construction for circle-shaped restricted area.

For example, Fig. 1 illustrates an example of Voronoi graph construction for a circle-shaped restricted area highlighted in red. When $k = 6$, six points, denoted as P_1-P_6 are picked up on circle C' located at point O. The constructed Voronoi graph is composed of seven Voronoi cells, denoted as $V_0 - V_6$ represented by seeds O and P_1-P_6 respectively. The Voronoi cell V_0 represented by seed O is highlighted in blue dotted lines. It has covered the circle-shaped restricted area.

3.2   Voronoi Graph Representation

We describe the spatial and topology information of Voronoi graph in term of cell adjacency relationships, anchor cell diameters and inter-cell shortest paths. In this way, the potential paths satisfying the temporal and spatial constraint could be inferred effectively and efficiently.

The adjacency relationships between Voronoi cells are represented with a list of adjacency arrays, denoted as L. Each element of list L is an adjacency array Arr_i for Voronoi cell v_i, indicating its neighboring cells, as shown in Eq. 1:

$$Arr_i = \{v_j \in v_i.neighborhood\}. \tag{1}$$

For any Voronoi cell v_k corresponding to a restricted area, we assume it has no neighboring cells and thus the adjacency arry is empty, $Arr_k = \emptyset$.

Next, we calculate the inter-cell *anchor diameter length* for each Voronoi cell v_j across a pair of its adjacent cells $v_i - v_k$, denoted as $AncD_{i,k}^j$. The anchor diameter length of cell v_j connecting cell v_i and v_k is defined as the distance between the middle point of edge $l_{i,j}$ separating cells v_i and v_j and the middle point of edge $l_{j,k}$ separating cells v_j and v_k, as shown in Eq. 2:

$$AncD_{i,k}^j = ||l_{i,j}.mid - l_{j,k}.mid||, \tag{2}$$

where $l_{i,j}.mid$ and $l_{j,k}.mid$ indicate the middle points of edges $l_{i,j}$ and $l_{j,k}$ respectively.

These inter-cell anchor diameters build up the backbone of inferred paths, which are referred as the anchor paths. The *shortest anchor path length* between a pair a Voronoi cells $v_u - v_q$ could be simply inferred as well, which is the minimum sum of anchor diameter lengths of Voronoi cells along the path, as indicated in Eq. 3:

$$ShortestAPLen(v_u, v_q)$$
$$= Min_{P=v_u \prec v_{t_1} \prec v_{t_2} \prec \ldots \prec v_{t_m} \prec v_q} \sum (AncD_{u,t_2}^{t_1} + AncD_{t_1,t_3}^{t_2} + \ldots + AncD_{t_{m-1},q}^{t_m}), \tag{3}$$

where $P = v_u \prec v_{t_1} \prec v_{t_2} \prec \ldots \prec v_{t_m} \prec v_q$ indicates a Voronoi cell path from cell v_u towards v_q, $p_{start} \in v_{t_0}$ and $p_{end} \in v_{t_m}$.

3.3   Depth-First Path Exploration Based on Voronoi Graph

Each potential path could be mapped to a *diameter path* composed of a starting point p_S, an ending point p_E and a sequence of traversed Voronoi cells $v_{t_0} \prec v_{t_1} \prec v_{t_2} \prec \ldots \prec v_{t_m}$, where $p_S \in v_{t_0}$ and $p_E \in v_{t_m}$. To provide a refined estimation of diameter path length across the sequence of Voronoi cells, we further define the concept of minimum anchor diameter length as the minimum sum of distance from the starting point p_S to the middle point of edge l_{t_0,t_1}, shortest anchor diameter path length between cells v_S and v_E and distance from the middle point of edge l_{t_{m-1},t_m} to the ending point p_E, as illustrated in Eq. 4:

$$ShortestAncDPLen(p_S, p_E)$$

$$= Min_{P=v_{t_0} \prec v_{t_1} \prec v_{t_2} \prec ... \prec v_{t_m}} \sum (dist(p_S, l_{v_{t_0}, v_{t_1}}.mid)$$

$$+ ShortestAPLen(v_{t_0}, v_{t_m}) + dist(l_{v_{t_{m-1}}, v_{t_m}}.mid, p_E)) \tag{4}$$

Based on the shortest anchor diameter path length, the potential paths w.r.t. the spatial constraint could be modelled with threshold δ_{max} such that $ShortestAncDPLen(p_S, p_E) \leq \delta_{max}$. We carry out a depth-first exploration of potential diameter paths and output the set of discovered anchor diameter paths satisfying threshold δ_{max}.

4   Experimental Results

We evaluated the performance of our path inference algorithm based on Voronoi graph under the scenario of search&rescue (SAR) at sea. The experiments were performed on iMac with Core i5CPU, 8 GB memory and 1 TB hard disk.

Assume the area with high survival probability in the two-dimensional space was highlighted as a gray square in Fig. 2. We compared our path inference algorithm based on Voronoi graph against the grid-based path planning algorithm in space partition and path discovery.

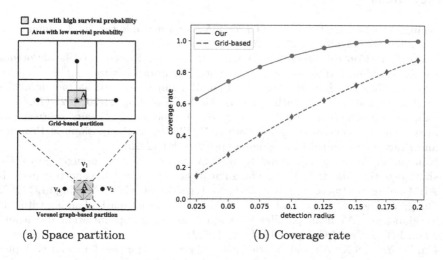

(a) Space partition   (b) Coverage rate

Fig. 2. Comparison of space partition reasonability and coverage rate.

For the space partition, the traditional grid-based path planning algorithm partitioned the space into six grids of equal sizes, while our path inference algorithm partitioned the space into five Voronoi cells, where the area with higher survival probability was represented by one Voronoi cell particularly (Fig. 2(a)).

As can be seen, our path inference algorithm was able to partition the space according to the priority. For the path discovery, the number of inferred paths from the grid-based partition was only three while that of our algorithm was six as shown in Fig. 2(a). Comparatively, our inferred paths were more delicate than those of the grid-based algorithm. In addition, our inferred paths had a significantly higher coverage rate for the area with higher survival probability as well, as illustrated in Fig. 2(b).

In summary, our path inference algorithm based on Voronoi graph was more adaptive to the search&rescue task than the traditional grid-based path planning approach.

5   Conclusion

In this work, we have proposed a novel path inference approach based on Voronoi graph, enabling a flexible modelling of two-dimensional geospatial topology, an adaptive representation of spatial information and a comprehensive inference of potential paths. Experimental results indicate that our method is efficient and scalable as well as effective in both space partition and path inference when compared against the traditional path planning algorithm. We will evaluate its performance under more scenarios in our future work.

References

1. Zhang, T., Chai, L.: Path planning for UAVs and multiple targets. Command Inf. Syst. Technol. **11**(06), 32–36 (2020)
2. Gevargiz, P.: Control and Path Planning of Multi-Agent Systems: Artificial Potential Field Algorithm. California State University, Northridge (2019)
3. Fan, X., Guo, Y., Liu, H., Wei, B., Lyu, W.: Improved artificial potential field method applied for AUV path planning. Math. Probl. Eng. **2020**, 1–21 (2020)
4. Sao, P., Kannan, R., Gera, P., Vuduc, R.: A supernodal all-pairs shortest path algorithm. In: Proceedings of the 25th ACM SIGPLAN Symposium on Principles and Practice of Parallel Programming, pp. 250–261 (2020)
5. Kannan, V., Appasamy, S., Kandasamy, G.: Comparative study of fuzzy Floyd Warshall algorithm and the fuzzy rectangular algorithm to find the shortest path. In: AIP Conference Proceedings, vol. 2516, no. 1, p. 200029. AIP Publishing LLC (2022)
6. Gong, Y., Chen, K., Niu, T., Liu, Y.: Grid-based coverage path planning with NFZ avoidance for UAV using parallel self-adaptive ant colony optimization algorithm in cloud IoT. J. Cloud Comput. **11**(1), 29 (2022)
7. Hu, Y., Yang, S.X.: A novel knowledge-based genetic algorithm for robot path planning in complex environments. arXiv preprint arXiv:2209.01482 (2022)
8. Polak, A.: Bellman-Ford is optimal for shortest hop-bounded paths. arXiv preprint arXiv:2211.07325 (2022)

Study on Branch-and-Price for Solving Single-Machine Total Weight Tardiness Scheduling Problem

Zaichang Hai and Xingye Dong[(✉)]

School of Computer and IT, Beijing Jiaotong University, Beijing 100044, China
{20120356,xydong}@bjtu.edu.cn

Abstract. Single-machine total weighted tardiness scheduling problem (SMTWTSP) is a classic problem in the field of production scheduling, which is a NP-Hard problem. The branch-and-price based on a time-indexed formulation is used to solve it accurately. The influence that different column selection strategies of column generation have on the rate of algorithm convergence is studied. Two column selection strategies are proposed, which improved the efficiency of solving linear relaxation solutions compared with the classical column selection strategy. The precedence theorems are added to the process of branch-and-price to reduce the search space. The 40-job instances provided by OR-Library are solved successfully. And the time of working out each instance is increased by 1000 s on average. It is proved that changing the strategy of column selection can significantly improve the efficiency of branch-and-price, and the precedence theorems can reduce the search space of SMTWTSP through the results of this experiment.

Keywords: Time-Indexed Formulation · Branch-and-Price · Single-Machine · Column Generation · Strategy of Column Selection Strategy · Precedence Theorem

1 Introduction

In the production activities of enterprises, the production scheduling problem is the key to the efficiency of production activities, and the single machine is the basis of many production scheduling models. This paper focuses on SMTWTSP. The problem has been studied extensively since the 1980s and is proved NP-Hard by Lawler [1] and Lenstra [2].

SMTWTSP considered in this paper asks to determine an optimal sequence of n jobs in set $N = (1, ..., n)$, which are processed without interruption (i.e., idle time is not permitted) on a single machine. Each job j becomes available at time 0, and requires an integer processing time p_j, due time d_j and weight w_j. The cost is $w_j T_j$, where $T_j = max(0, d_j - C_j)$, if the j-th job is completed at time C_j. All jobs are processed in time interval $[0, t_{max}]$, where $t_{max} = \sum_{j \in N} p_j$. This problem can be noted as $1 || \sum wT$ [3].

H. Fujita et al. (Eds.): IEA/AIE 2023, LNAI 13926, pp. 159–170, 2023.
https://doi.org/10.1007/978-3-031-36822-6_14

Potts and Wassenhove [4] presented a new branch-and-bound algorithm for the SMTWTSP and obtained lower bounds using a Lagrangian relaxation approach, they solved problems with up to 50 jobs; Abdul-Razaq and Potts [5] mapped the state-space onto a smaller state-space, thereby giving a lower bound, and presented a dynamic programming formulation; Abdul-Razaq et al. [6] studied two dynamic programming algorithms and four branch-and-bound algorithms; Sousa and Wolsey [7] studied the single-machine scheduling problem based on the time label model and the 20/30 scale instance; Ibaraki and Nakamura [8] put forward the Successive Sublimation Dynamic Programming (SSDP) method to reduce the dynamic programming state of management and solved it on 30-job instances; Akker et al. [9] used the branch-and-price method based on column generation algorithm to solve he SMTWTSP, and adopted Dantzig-Wolfe decomposition to speed up the convergence rate of algorithm; Bigras et al. [10] proposed a decomposition method to accelerate the convergence rate of column generation algorithm; Tanaka et al. [11] improved the SSDP method, which optimally solved 300-job instances of the total weighted tardiness problem and the total weighted earliness-tardiness problem.

Column generation algorithm is a method proposed by Dantzig and Wolfe [12] in 1960 for solving large-scale linear programming problems, which belongs to simplex method. As the column generation algorithm is considered, the classical column selection strategy which always chooses the column with the maximum reduced cost and adds it to the master problem is a prior method to SMSTWTSP. However, the shortcoming of this method is slow convergence rate caused by column selection. The final aim to solve the problem is to optimize the objective by adding new columns and the less, the better. This paper studies the effect of different column selection strategies on the convergence rate of the algorithm and proposes two column selection strategies. At the same time, two precedence theorems is added in the branch process to reduce the search space algorithm. In the end, it is verified that these column selection strategies in this paper are better than the classical strategy through solving the 40-job instances provided by OR-Library.

2   Time-Indexed Formulations

In various production problems involving sequencing and scheduling, (i, t) is used as the index of decision variables which are based on a decomposition of the time horizon H into T periods. The description of applying the time-indexed formulation to SMTWTSP is as follows [9]:

$$min \sum c_{jt} x_{jt} \tag{1}$$

$$s.t. \sum_{j=1}^{N} \sum_{s=t}^{min(t+p_j-1,t_{max})} x_{js} = 1, t = 1, 2, \ldots, t_{max} \tag{2}$$

$$\sum_{t=p_j}^{t_{max}} x_{jt} = 1, j = 1, 2, \ldots, N \qquad (3)$$

$$x_{jt} \in \{0, 1\}, j = 1, 2, \ldots, N; t = 1, 2, \ldots, t_{max} \qquad (4)$$

The assignment constraints (2) state that each job has to be started exactly once, and the capacity constraints (3) state that the machine can handle at most one job during any time period. Where $c_{jt} = w_{jt}T_{jt}$ indicates the weighted tardiness of job j starting at t and the binary variable x_{jt} for each job $j(j = 1, 2, \ldots, N)$ and time period $t(t = 1, \ldots, T - p_j + 1)$ indicates whether job j starts in period $t(x_{jt} = 1)$ or not $(x_{jt} = 0)$. The notation $t_{max} = \sum_{j=1}^{N} p_j$ represents the makespan of the last job. Since the machine has no idle time, the makespan of the last job is the sum of the processing time of all the jobs.

For SMTWTSP of size N, variables size of time-indexed formulation is $N \sum_{j=1}^{N} p_j$. It is hard to solve the linear programming problem directly. Therefore, the column generation algorithm is introduced to construct the main problem as a restricted master problem with limited variables.

2.1 The Restricted Master Problem

The Original feasible solution is worked out by the Earliest Due Date (EDD) and Weighted Shortest Processing Time (WSPT) [3], and the restricted master problem contains only N variables, with the objective as (5):

$$min \quad c_{1t_1}x_{1t_1} + c_{2t_2}x_{2t_2} + \cdots + c_{Nt_N}x_{Nt_N} \qquad (5)$$

wherein, each column represents the processing scheme of a job, with the same constraints as (2), (3) and (4).

The purpose of the RMP is to provide dual variables: To be transferred to the sub-problem, and to control our stopping criterion [13]. Since the decision variable in the restricted main problem is a binary variable, according to the optimization theory, when solving the problem by using the column generation algorithm, relaxation operation is required for the decision variables, and the discrete decision variable is a continuous variable. The constraints are shown as (6):

$$0 \leq x_{jt} \leq 1, j = 1, 2, \ldots, N; t = 1, 2, \ldots, t_{max} \qquad (6)$$

That is the relaxation restricted master problem.

2.2 Pricing Subproblem

The role of the pricing subproblem is to provide a column that prices out profitably or to prove that the columns which can improve RMP don't exist [13], which is also the core idea of column generation algorithm. For the j-th job, if the processing time is t, the corresponding pricing subproblem is as (7):

$$z_{jt} = F_j + \sum_{s=t}^{t+p_j} f_s - T_{jt} \qquad (7)$$

where z_{jt} indicates the reduced cost of the pricing subproblem of job j starting at t, F_j implies the dual variate of constraint (2) and f_s implies the dual variate of constraint (3). According to optimization theory and the definition of pricing subproblem (6), only columns with reduced cost greater than 0 can optimize objective (1). Therefore, after solving the pricing subproblem, the columns with the reduced cost greater than 0 are added to RMP, and the objective function value of RMP is reduced through continuous iteration, until the column with the reduced cost greater than 0 cannot be obtained, the linear relaxation solution of the restricted master problem is obtained. The column generation algorithm is finished, and the algorithm flow chart is shown in Fig. 1. The detailed steps of the column generation algorithm are described as follows:

Step 1: Constructing the RMP from the initial solution which can be obtained by EDD and WSPT;

Step 2: Solving the pricing subproblem according to the dual information of RMP to obtain a new column;

Step 3: Add the columns whose reduced cost is greater than zero into RMP, and repeat Step2;

Step 4: Otherwise, the algorithm stops. And the answer is the optimal solution of the relaxation restricted master problem.

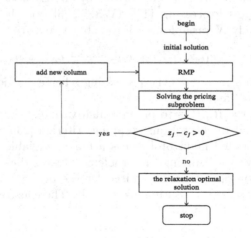

Fig. 1. Flow chart of column generation

Due to many columns with reduced cost greater than zero in step 3, how to formulate a reasonable strategy and select an appropriate column from a large number of columns to add to RMP are the main focus of this paper.

2.3 Description of Branch-and-Price

Because the result obtained by column generation is not necessarily an integer solution, the Integer programming is solved by branch-and-price which needs to combine column generation and branch-and-bound. The specific steps are as Fig. 2. There were pseudo unsolvable problems because of not all columns included in RMP when RMP can not be solved. Relaxation variables were introduced into RMP to solve pseudo unsolvable problems. RMP was changed as (8)–(11).

$$min c_{1t_1} x_{1t_1} + c_{2t_2} x_{2t_2} + \cdots + c_{Nt_N} x_{Nt_N} + \sum M y_j \qquad (8)$$

$$s.t. \sum_{j=1}^{N} \sum_{s=t}^{min(t+p_j-1,t_{max})} x_{js} = 1, t = 1, 2, \ldots, t_{max} \qquad (9)$$

$$\sum_{t=p_j}^{t_{max}} x_{jt} = 1 + y_j, j = 1, 2, \ldots, N \qquad (10)$$

$$0 \le x_{jt} \le 1, 0 \le y_j \le 1, j = 1, 2, \ldots, N; t = 1, 2, \ldots, t_{max} \qquad (11)$$

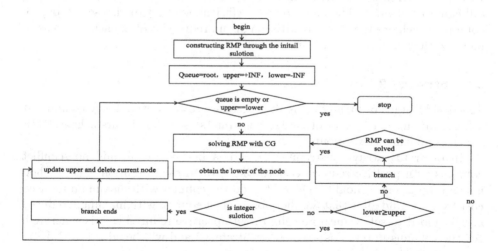

Fig. 2. Flow chart of branch-and-price

3 Column Selection Strategies

On condition that adding different columns can affect the convergence of the objective, and it is hard to work out RMP if there are too many columns, two aspects should be considered during this process:

(1) After adding appropriate columns, the objective function should be optimized as much as possible.
(2) The fewer columns are added, the better.

Three column selection strategies are discussed below. The strategies proposed in this paper were named as Strategy 1 and Strategy 2, respectively.

3.1   Classic Strategy

At present, the prior column selection strategy is to add only one column with the largest number of reduced cost to RMP in each iteration. That's because it is expected to have the best optimization effect on the objective function. However, this strategy increase the number of iterations of the column generation algorithm.

3.2   Strategy 1

In order to decrease the number of iterations of the column generation algorithm, more than one column is added to the RMP each iteration. Adding all columns with positive reduced cost to RMP leads to a lager scale of RMP, making it difficult to work out. Therefore, it is an efficient method to choose a group of columns which are the columns with maximum reduced cost of each job so as to increase the speed of column generation.

3.3   Strategy 2

The disadvantage of Strategy 1 is that there are some contradictory columns at each iteration, which can not satisfy constraints (s). That incurs a huge RMP which is difficult to work out.

In order to satisfy constraints (3), it is a better way to add non-conflict columns with positive reduced cost to the RMP in each iteration. The method is: The top priority should be given to add the column with maximum reduced cost to set X, and after that another non-conflict column with maximum reduced cost is added to set X until no column with positive reduced cost is generated. All the columns in set X is selected for Strategy2 and will be added to RMP in the next iteration.

The Strategy 2 is based on greedy strategy. This strategy can accelerate the iteration speed of column generation algorithm by adding multiple columns in each iteration, and avoid the conflicts between new columns that lead to a bigger RMP.

3.4   Experimental Comparison

Three strategies were tested on the first ten problems provided by OR-Library with 40 jobs. The results are shown in Table 1. The meaning of each column in Table 1 is as follows:

(1) col: the number of columns generated when obtaining linear relaxation solutions.
(2) time: the time in seconds taken to obtain a linear relaxation solution for RMP.
(3) ite: the number of iterations of column generation when RMP was figured out.

The classic column selection strategy has the largest number of iterations, since each iteration produces at most one column, the final number of columns is the smallest. Since the most columns are added to RMP in each iteration in Strategy 1, the minimum number of iterations is obtained. But the speed of the algorithm is limited by lager scale of RMP. The convergence speed of Strategy 2 is the fastest. The number of columns generated by the algorithm is more than that of the classical strategy, but it is much less than that of Strategy 1, and the number of iterations of Strategy 2 is the least.

As shown in Table 1, since many columns are added each iteration, the number of iterations of column generation drops, and algorithm efficiency is improved. As for the convergence, it is significant to take the influence of contradictory columns into consideration.

Table 1. The Results of compared experiment for linear relaxation solution of RMP

Problem	classic strategy			Strategy 1			Strategy 2		
	col	ite	time	col	ite	time	col	ite	time
wt40.1	3319	257	3320	9147	81	229	911	1	51
wt40.2	3624	327	3625	9650	73	294	4370	36	201
wt40.3	3039	212	3040	9039	23	202	2482	21	157
wt40.4	3476	298	3477	11393	100	251	4078	32	184
wt40.5	3334	283	3335	9779	37	293	4232	37	211
wt40.6	4610	465	4611	11529	109	331	5127	48	282
wt40.7	4607	496	4608	11690	114	338	5590	60	343
wt40.8	4177	445	4178	11674	106	315	4794	41	276
wt40.9	5387	735	5388	13203	71	388	5946	71	334
wt40.10	5606	757	5607	15410	196	376	6345	81	335
avg	4117.9	427.5	4118.9	11251.4	112	301.7	4487.5	43	237.4

4   Precedence Theorems

The precedence theorems are methods to judge whether there is a sequence better than the current scheduling sequence in a particular case. Therefore, the use of the precedence theorems in branch-and-bound can effectively reduce the search space and improve the efficiency of algorithm. Emmons [14] proposed three precedence theorems for the priority relationship between job pairs in single-machine total tardiness problem. Kanet [15] further extended the precedence theorems to the SMTWT. Kanet aimed to find the pair(j, k) satisfying $j \prec k$ from jobs, but this can not be applied to the partly fixed sequence. Therefore, aimed at partly fixed sequences obtained in branch-and-bound, two precedence theorems are proposed based on swap and insertion strategies, respectively. The symbol definition involved in the precedence theorems are shown in Table 2.

Table 2. Symbol definition and description

symbol	description
S	Original scheduling sequence
S'	New sequence obtained after changing the positions of jobs in S
Δ	Difference of total weighted tardiness between S and S', $\Delta = T' - T$
$J(K)$	Difference of total weighted tardiness between S and S', $\Delta = T' - T$
$U(K)$	The set of jobs left without jobs in K
$C(K)$	Makespan of the last job in K
$K|u$	New sequence obtained by scheduling job u after K
$\sum(K|u)$	The sequence of all jobs staring with $K|u$
$wT(S)$	The total weighted tardiness of S

According to the swap tactic, if the operation swapping the pair(i, k) of jobs in S can optimize the objective, current node doesn't need to be branched, which can reduce the searching scope.

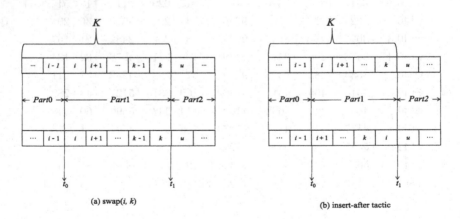

(a) swap(i, k) (b) insert-after tactic

Fig. 3. Change the scheduling order of (i, k) according to different rules

Theorem 1. $\exists i, [i] \in J(K)$, $\Delta_T = (p_k - P_i) \sum_{j=i+1}^{k-1} w_j + t_0(w_k - w_i) + t_1(w_i - w_k) + w_k p_k - w_i p_i \leq 0$, $\sum(k|u)$ *is not optimal.*

Proof. As shown in Fig. 3(a), the whole scheduling sequence is divided into three parts: Part 0, Part 1, and Part 2. The original scheduling sequence is marked as S, and the new scheduling sequence after the exchange of job i and job k is marked as S'. The total weighted tardiness of Part 0, Part 1, and Part 2 are calculated respectively.

The total weighted tardiness of S is equal to S' in Part 0 and Part 2. The distinction between S and S' is in Part 1. Therefore, it is necessary to prove that the total weighted tardiness of S in Part 1 is greater than that of S' in Part 1 under the assumed condition.

$$(w_j T_j)' - w_j T_j = w_j((C'_j - d_j) - (C_j - d_j)) = w_j(p_k - p_i); j \in [i+1, k-1] \quad (12)$$

$$(wT)' - wT = \sum_{j=i+1}^{k-1} w_j(p_k - p_i) + w_k T'_k + w_i T'_i - w_i T_i - w_k T_k \quad (13)$$

$$(wT)' - wT = (p_k - p_i)\sum_{j=i+1}^{k-1} w_j + t_0(w_k - w_i) + t_1(w_i - w_k) + w_k p_k - w_i p_i \leq 0 \quad (14)$$

In conclusion, $wT(S') \leq wT(S)$ □

In addition to swapping job pairs, it is possible to change the scheduling sequence by insert-after tactic. According to the insert-after tactic, if the operation inserting job i after job k can optimize the objective of S, current node doesn't need to be branched, which can reduce the searching scope.

Theorem 2. $\exists i, [i] \in J(K), \Delta_T = w_i \sum_{j=i+1}^{k} p_j - p_i \sum_{j=i}^{k} w_j \leq 0, \sum(k|u)$ is not optimal.

Proof. As shown in Fig. 3(b) the whole scheduling sequence is divided into three parts: Part 0, Part 1, and Part 2. The original scheduling sequence is marked as S, and the new scheduling sequence after the exchange of job i and job k is marked as S'. The total weighted tardiness of Part 0, Part 1, and Part 2 are calculated respectively.

The total weighted tardiness of S is equal to S' in Part 0 and Part 2. The distinction between S and S' is in Part 1. Therefore, it is necessary to prove that the total weighted tardiness of S in Part 1 is greater than that of S' in Part 1 under the assumed condition.

$$(w_j T_j)' - w_j T_j = -w_j p_i; j \in [i+1, k] \quad (15)$$

$$w_i T'_i - w_i T_i = w_i\left(\sum_{j=i+1}^{k} p_j - p_i\right) \quad (16)$$

$$(wT)' - wT = w_i \sum_{j=i+1}^{k} p_j - p_j \sum_{j=i}^{k} w_j \leq 0 \quad (17)$$

In conclusion, $wT(S') \leq wT(S)$ □

The precedence theorems are used as pruning strategy in branch-and-bound to reduce search space. In order to test the efficiency of the precedence theorems, the experiment is conducted with/without precedence theorems during the branch-and-price process. All of the 125 problems provided by OR-Library with 40 jobs are worked out through the experiment and the average and maximum of the experiment is calculated. The experimental results are shown in Table 3.

Table 3. The Results of solving SMTWTSP with/without precedence

		without precedence theorems		with precedence theorems	
		avg	max	avg	max
	classic strategy	9031.3	21092	8129	20280
col	Strategy 1	18389.7	40892	15121.94	40210
	Strategy 2	9561	23957	9332.14	23671
	classic strategy	1439.89	4546	1327.34	4423
time	Strategy 1	392.8	2682	361.9	2267
	Strategy 2	307.4	2364	280.7	2288

According to Table 3, after adding the precedence theorems, the final columns generated by the algorithm reduce, indicating that the search space reduced. Moreover, the running time of the algorithm falls slightly. The efficiency of the algorithm is improved. The experimental results verify the effectiveness of the precedence theorems.

5   Experimental Results

The linear relaxation solution of the problem was obtained by directly using the column generation algorithm. When solving the integer programming problem, the column generation algorithm needed to be embedded in the branch-and-bound algorithm. At the same time, the precedence theorems were used to cut when branching. Table 4 shows the experimental results of using the branch pricing algorithm with the precedence theorems to solve the SMTWT problem, and compares three different column selection strategies. The problems used in Table 4 are 40-job instances provided by OR-Library. The CPLEX was used to solve the linear programs of RMP.

According to Table 4, the classic strategy can provide the least columns, but there are too many iterations of column generation when solving the lower bound of node, resulting in slow speed. The number of iterations of the algorithm drops significantly in Strategy 1. However, conflict columns are added into RMP, causing far lager scale of RMP, which makes it even harder to figure out final LP. Not only does iteration times reduce but also avoids conflict columns in Strategy 2, bringing out the quickest speed.

Table 4. The Results of solving SMTWTSP with different strategy

Problem	classic strategy			Strategy 1			Strategy 2		
	col	ite	time	col	ite	time	col	ite	time
wt40.1	4384	4355	342	18448	802	373	397	189	35
wt40.6	10582	10602	1738	17763	922	366	10311	1092	469
wt40.11	9355	1345	1648	17480	1010	404	10061	896	409
wt40.16	10595	10589	2021	16861	953	552	11323	877	315
wt40.21	7962	7939	865	16295	884	251	10582	683	151
wt40.26	57	20	0	9447	280	66	59	14	0
wt40.31	10606	10605	2183	18720	972	492	11861	1308	618
wt40.36	10672	10719	1855	18138	1214	407	11015	1138	304
wt40.41	9921	9903	1854	16034	959	351	11173	863	215
wt40.46	6104	6077	507	12994	720	128	7433	465	65
wt40.51	40	2	0	40	2	0	40	2	0
wt40.56	8107	8115	982	16265	700	210	7836	708	157
wt40.61	9552	9548	1298	16455	1311	397	11100	999	185
wt40.66	9401	9385	1311	17575	1076	512	11015	794	249
wt40.71	7434	7404	754	15551	752	198	8964	494	101
wt40.76	40	2	0	40	2	0	40	2	0
wt40.81	6316	6289	589	14375	736	145	7174	569	109
wt40.86	10120	10122	1574	16813	1227	474	11541	1143	292
wt40.91	10332	10323	1819	17247	1157	343	11091	869	210
wt40.96	9861	9849	1988	17464	910	475	10552	677	210
wt40.101	40	2	0	40	2	0	40	2	0
wt40.106	40	2	0	40	2	0	40	2	0
wt40.111	9473	9453	1243	18078	1220	443	11204	881	253
wt40.116	8753	8745	1099	16842	1130	280	10569	767	173
wt40.121	10076	10061	1736	19128	1148	461	12750	838	292
avg	7192.92	6858.24	1096.24	13925.32	803.64	293.12	7926.84	650.88	192.48
max	10672	10719	2183	19128	1311	552	12750	1308	1618

6 Conclusions and Extensions

This paper casts light on the impact of different column selection strategies
on the convergence speed of the column generation algorithm, and adds precedence theorems to the branch-and-price algorithm to speed up the algorithm.
An improved column selection strategy is that multiple columns that meet the
constraint conditions should be added into RMP during each iteration of the
column generation algorithm, which contributes to reduce iteration times of the
algorithm, and avoids too large linear programming problems, bringing out convenient relaxation solution of RMP. In the future, focus should be put on the
influence of different columns having on the objective in theory. Assuming that
the useless columns are deleted during the process of algorithm, it is potential
to accelerate the speed of algorithm.

References

1. Lawler, E.L.: A "pseudopolynomial" algorithm for sequencing jobs to minimize total tardiness. Ann. Discrete Math. **1**(08), 331–342 (1977)
2. Lenstra, J.K., Rinnooy Kan, A.H.G., Brucker, P.: Complexity of machine scheduling problems. Ann. Discrete Math. **1**(4), 343–362 (1977)
3. Pinedo, M.L.: Scheduling Theory, Algorithms, and Systems, 5th edn. Springer, Cham (2016). https://doi.org/10.1007/978-3-319-26580-3
4. Potts, C.N., Wassenhove, L.N.V.: A branch and bound algorithm for the total weighted tardiness problem. Oper. Res. **33**(2), 363–377 (1985)
5. Abdul-Razaq, T.S., Potts, C.N.: Dynamic programming state-space relaxation for single-machine scheduling. Oper. Res. Soc. **39**, 141–152 (1988)
6. Abdul-Razaq, T.S., Potts, C.N., Van Wassenhove, L.N.: A survey of algorithms for the single machine total weighted tardiness scheduling problem. Discret. Appl. Math. **26**(2), 235–253 (1990)
7. Sousa, J.P., Wolsey, L.A.: A time indexed formulation of non-preemptive single machine scheduling problems. Math. Program. **54**, 353–367 (1992)
8. Ibaraki, T., Nakamura, Y.: A dynamic programming method for single machine scheduling. Eur. J. Oper. Res. **76**(1), 72–82 (1994)
9. van den Akker, J.M., Hurkens, C.A.J., Savelsbergh, M.W.P.: Time-indexed formulations for machine scheduling problems: column generation. INFORMS J. Comput. **12**(2), 111–124 (2000)
10. Bigras, L.P., Gamache, M., Savard, G.: Time-indexed formulations and the total weighted tardiness problem. INFORMS J. Comput. **20**(1), 133–142 (2008)
11. Tanaka, S., Fujikuma, S., Araki, M.: An exact algorithm for single-machine scheduling without machine idle time. J. Sched. **12**, 575–593 (2009)
12. Dantzig, G.B., Wolfe, P.: Decomposition principle for linear programs. Oper. Res. **8**(1), 101–111 (1960)
13. Ford, L.R., Jr., Fulkerson, D.R.: A suggested computation for maximal multicommodity network flows. Manage. Sci. **5**(1), 97–101 (1958)
14. Emmons, H.: One-machine sequencing to minimize certain functions of job tardiness. Oper. Res. **17**(4), 701–715 (1969)
15. Kanet, J.J.: New precedence theorems for one-machine weighted tardiness. Math. Oper. Res. **32**(3), 579–588 (2007)

Improved Differential Evolutionary Algorithm Based on Adaptive Scaling Factor

Chen Zhang[1] , Haotian Li[1] , Yifei Yang[1] , Baohang Zhang[1] ,
Huisheng Zhu[2] , and Shangce Gao[1]($\boxtimes$)

[1] Faculty of Engineering, University of Toyama, Toyama 930-8555, Japan
gaosc@eng.u-toyama.ac.jp
[2] School of Physics and Information Engineering, Jiangsu Second Normal University,
Nanjing, China

Abstract. The differential evolution algorithm is a meta-heuristic algorithm with the advantages of a simple structure, few control parameters, and robustness. However, in the face of different problems, if the factor F controlling the difference amplification is fixed, it will be difficult for the algorithm to adapt to complex and changeable problems. In order to enable the differential evolution algorithm to deal with many problems with the optimal F parameter, this paper proposes a differential evolution algorithm with Adaptive Scaling Factor. The algorithm continuously explores the optimal F parameters for the current problem while ensuring that it does not converge prematurely, which eventually leads to an improvement in the search efficiency of the algorithm.

Keywords: Meta-heuristic Algorithm · Differential Evolution Algorithm · Adaptive Scaling Factor

1 Introduction

In recent years, optimization problems have faced more and more challenges, and meta-heuristic algorithms (MHAs) are increasingly attracting the attention of scholars due to their excellent performance in dealing with single versus multi-objective optimization, discrete versus continuous optimization, and a host of other problems inspired by natural and physical phenomena [1–4].

The differential evolution algorithm (DE) [5] proposed by Storn and Price is a typical meta-heuristic algorithm. It is mainly designed for solving numerical optimization problems, and it is noteworthy that the DE algorithm has shown strong competitiveness in many fields despite its relatively simple structure and the very small number of control parameters [6]. Nevertheless, DE still faces some challenges in solving complex and variable problems [7], such as parameter setting problems, slow convergence, high-dimensional problems, and some nonlinear problems.

© The Author(s), under exclusive license to Springer Nature Switzerland AG 2023
H. Fujita et al. (Eds.): IEA/AIE 2023, LNAI 13926, pp. 171–176, 2023.
https://doi.org/10.1007/978-3-031-36822-6_15

In this paper, we propose an improvement to the differential evolution algorithm at the level of control parameters [8]. In the original differential evolution algorithm, the F parameter is typically set to a fixed value between 0 and 2. However, due to the varying scales of different problems, using a fixed F parameter can make it difficult for DE to perform optimally when dealing with complex and diverse problems [9]. Therefore, when applying DE to complex real-world problems, it is crucial to choose appropriate F parameters that can vary according to the problem's complexity [10].

In order to tackle the aforementioned issues, this paper introduces a new amplitude parameter that controls the selection of the differential amplification factor F. Under this mechanism, the range of the F parameter is no longer limited to positive numbers, and the direction of the differential variance is controlled by the positive or negative of the F parameter. Experimental results show that the adaptive F parameters not only enhance the algorithm's search capability but also reduce the complexity of parameter settings, but also improve the convergence speed and robustness of the algorithm.

2   Proposed FED Algorithm

2.1   Motivation

The basic differential evolution algorithm can be roughly divided into two parts [11]. The first link is called variation, as shown in Eq. 1, and G is used to distinguish between parents and offspring. This is the process by which two random individual vectors $x_{r1,G}$ and $x_{r3,G}$ in the population are subtracted and multiplied by F plus a random individual vector $x_{r1,G}$ to obtain the vector $v_{i,G+1}$. The second link is the crossover, which uses CR as a reference to decide whether the element at the corresponding position in the vector $u_{i,G+1}$ is from $v_{i,G+1}$ or $x_{i,G}$.

$$v_{i,G+1} = x_{r1,G} + F\left(x_{r2,G} - x_{r3,G}\right) \tag{1}$$

2.2   Description of FDE

The FDE introduces an automatic retrieval mechanism for the optimal value of the F parameter based on the DE, with the help of which the parameter F is debugged several times to finally ensure that the adaptation value of the vector v_i in this cycle can be better than the adaptation value of the underlying vector x_{r1}, by this method, the adaptation value of v_i can be made to gradually approximate the optimal solution as the parameter F is continuously debugged, and then by a step of crossover variation. If this mechanism is used, the crossover constant CR should be set to a larger value. In this experiment, CR was set to 0.9.

Here, a debugging magnitude constant, α is first introduced, as shown in Eq. 2. The k in the formula is a positive integer. α controls the magnitude of the parameter F change, the larger α is the lower the computational cost and

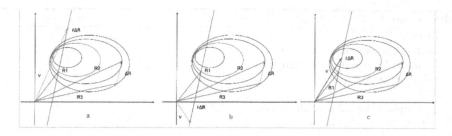

Fig. 1. Mechanism diagram of FDE.

the lower the probability of finding the optimal vector v_i. The lower the value of *alpha*, the higher the computational cost and the likelihood of finding the optimal vector v_i. In this experiment, *alpha* is set to 0.1.

$$\alpha = \frac{F}{k}, k \in N^* \tag{2}$$

In each debugging cycle, if the adaptation value of vector v_i is larger than the adaptation value of the base vector x_{r1}, the F parameter will go through a cycle of: reverse → add debug magnitude constant → reverse → subtract debug magnitude constant → reverse, and the adaptation value of vector v_i and vector v_i will be recalculated after each debugging until the adaptation value of vector v_i is smaller than the adaptation value of vector x_{r1}.

As shown in Fig. 1, the distribution of population adaptation values is nested in circles, and the closer to the inner circle, the lower the adaptation value. The red circle represents the adaptation distribution of vector x_{r1}. Throughout the debugging cycle, the F parameter keeps reversing and shrinking, while the vector $F\Delta R$ keeps reversing and shrinking, which eventually makes the vector v_i keep changing, and the endpoints of the vector v_i can be connected as the red solid line in the figure. The vector v_i cannot be found in one debugging cycle when and only when the red solid line is tangent to the red circle making the vector v_i better adapted than the vector x_{r1}. In summary, this mechanism ensures that the adaptation value of vector v_i is not higher than the adaptation value of vector x_{r1} after each debugging cycle.

The mechanism can also be represented by Eq. 3 and Eq. 4, with β being the amplitude constant α coefficient. i represents the number of times the vector v_i is computed.

$$F_a = \begin{cases} -F_a - \beta \cdot \alpha, & i \in \{4n - 2, 4n - 1\} \\ F_a + \beta \cdot \alpha, & i \in \{4n, 4n + 1\}, n \in N^* \end{cases} \tag{3}$$

$$\beta = \begin{cases} \frac{i-1}{2}, & i \in 2n + 1 \\ \frac{i-2}{2}, & i \in 2n \end{cases} \tag{4}$$

Finally, the vector v_i can be expressed by:

$$v_{i,G+1} = x_{r1,G} + F_a (x_{r2,G} - x_{r3,G}) \tag{5}$$

Algorithm 1. The main procedure of FDE

Require:

1: Calling the operation of the DE
   Evaluate best and fbest from DE;
2: **while** $f_v > f_{x_{r1}}$ **do**
3:     $F = -F$;
4:     compute the value of the vector v_i;
5:     Calculating the fitness of v_i;
6:     **while** $f_v > f_{x_{r1}}$ **do**
7:         **if** $F < 0$ **then**
8:             $F = F + \alpha$;
9:         **end if**
10:        **if** $F > 0$ **then**
11:            $F = F - \alpha$;
12:        **end if**
13:        compute the value of the vector v_i;
14:        Calculating the fitness of v_i;
15:    **end while**
16: **end while**
17: return the best fitness value

---

3   Experiment Result

The purpose of this experiment is to evaluate the performance of the FDE algorithm using the IEEE CEC2017 benchmark set. In addition, the experiment compares the performance of FDE with other algorithms. The results in Table 1 and Fig. 2 show that the performance of the DE algorithm is significantly improved after the introduction of the mechanism described in this paper, proving the success of borrowing this mechanism. The four algorithms, CWFS, MDBSO, LES, and MGSA, are recently proposed and improved meta-heuristics that represent the latest developments in the field.

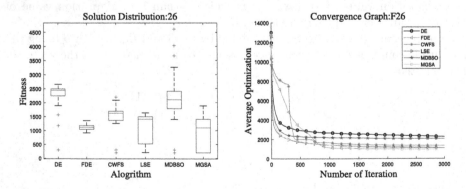

Fig. 2. Convergence graphs and Box-and-whisker diagrams comparison between FDE and other meta-heuristic algorithms in F26. (Color figure online)

Table 1. Comparison results of FDE with other algorithms

	FDE	DE	CWFS	MDBSO	LES	MGSA
W/T/L	-/-/-	16/4/10	27/1/2	28/1/1	28/1/1	18/4/8

3.1 Criteria for Performance Evaluation

The following is a description of the evaluation of the algorithm's performance:

W/T/L: W represents the number of functions where FDE significantly outperforms the other five algorithms; the number of functions where FDE performs similarly to the other five algorithms is denoted by T; and L represents the number of functions where FDE's performance is significantly worse. Table 1 shows the experimental results of the IEEE CEC2017 function set, where 16/4/10, 27/1/2, 29/0/1, 28/1/1, and 17/5/8 represent the number of winning, tying, and losing functions of the FDE algorithm after comparing DE, CWFS, MDBSO, LSE, and MGSA.

Box-and-whisker: The red line in the box plot in Fig. 2 represents the median, while the blue upper and lower edges represent the maximum and minimum values, and the red "+" symbols represent outliers. In addition, the length of the box represents the stability of the algorithm's performance, the shorter the box, the more stable the algorithm's performance. The box plot in Fig. 2 shows that the FDE is more stable in terms of adaptability and stability.

Convergence curve: In the convergence plot shown in Fig. 2, the average error is denoted by y and the number of descending generations is denoted by x. It can be observed from the plot that the convergence efficiency of the FDE algorithm is better than the other five algorithms.

4 Conclusion

In this study, a cycle of successive debugging F parameters is added to the original differential evolution algorithm to ensure that the vector v_i after each differential change is better than the base vector x_{r1}. With the improvement of this mechanism, the performance of the algorithm is improved by this improvement, and the algorithm will find the optimal target more efficiently. In summary, the FDE algorithm is an algorithm with good improvement in performance. However, after several experiments, we found that the experimental results of FDE on simple problems are not satisfactory. In our future work, we will focus on enhancing and refining the algorithm for better performance, and the following is an overview of the next work to be carried out: 1) Find the reason why FDE does not perform as well as DE on simple problems. 2) Explore the possibility of adaptive CR parameters. 3) Study the relationship between the amplitude constant α and the population relationship between density.

Acknowledgment. This research was partially supported by the Japan Society for the Promotion of Science (JSPS) KAKENHI under Grant JP22H03643, Japan Science and Technology Agency (JST) Support for Pioneering Research Initiated by the Next Generation (SPRING) under Grant JPMJSP2145, JST through the Establishment of University Fellowships towards the Creation of Science Technology Innovation under Grant JPMJFS2115, the National Natural Science Foundation of China grants 61802274, and Jiangsu Province Engineering Research Center of Basic Education Big Data Application.

References

1. Yang, H., et al.: An intelligent metaphor-free spatial information sampling algorithm for balancing exploitation and exploration. Knowl.-Based Syst. **250**, 109081 (2022)
2. Li, X., Yang, H., Li, J., Wang, Y., Gao, S.: A novel distributed gravitational search algorithm with multi-layered information interaction. IEEE Access **9**, 166552–166565 (2021)
3. Dokeroglu, T., Sevinc, E., Kucukyilmaz, T., Cosar, A.: A survey on new generation metaheuristic algorithms. Comput. Ind. Eng. **137**, 106040 (2019)
4. Gao, S., Zhou, M., Wang, Y., Cheng, J., Yachi, H., Wang, J.: Dendritic neuron model with effective learning algorithms for classification, approximation, and prediction. IEEE Trans. Neural Netw. Learn. Syst. **30**(2), 601–614 (2019)
5. Storn, R., Price, K.: Differential evolution-a simple and efficient heuristic for global optimization over continuous spaces. J. Global Optim. **11**(4), 341–359 (1997)
6. Tanabe, R., Fukunaga, A.: Success-history based parameter adaptation for differential evolution. In: 2013 IEEE Congress on Evolutionary Computation, pp. 71–78. IEEE (2013)
7. Gao, S., Yu, Y., Wang, Y., Wang, J., Cheng, J., Zhou, M.: Chaotic local search-based differential evolution algorithms for optimization. IEEE Trans. Syst. Man Cybern. Syst. **51**(6), 3954–3967 (2021)
8. Yang, H., Tao, S., Zhang, Z., Cai, Z., Gao, S.: Spatial information sampling: another feedback mechanism of realising adaptive parameter control in meta-heuristic algorithms. Int. J. Bio-Inspired Comput. **19**(1), 48–58 (2022)
9. Zhang, J., Sanderson, A.C.: JADE: adaptive differential evolution with optional external archive. IEEE Trans. Evol. Comput. **13**(5), 945–958 (2009)
10. Lei, Z., Gao, S., Gupta, S., Cheng, J., Yang, G.: An aggregative learning gravitational search algorithm with self-adaptive gravitational constants. Expert Syst. Appl. **152**, 113396 (2020)
11. Pant, M., Zaheer, H., Garcia-Hernandez, L., Abraham, A.: Differential evolution: a review of more than two decades of research. Eng. Appl. Artif. Intell. **90**, 103479 (2020)

Dealing with New User Problem Using Content-Based Deep Matrix Factorization

Nguyen Thai-Nghe, Nguyen Thi Kim Xuyen, An Cong Tran, and Tran Thanh Dien[✉]

Can Tho University, Can Tho, Vietnam
{ntnghe,thanhdien}@ctu.edu.vn

Abstract. Recommender systems (RS) are very necessary and important in digital life. Especially, the RS can support users to select appropriate products/items in online systems such as shopping, entertainment, education and other domains. However, techniques in RS are facing with new user problem which means that the RS has no history data to learn and recommend for the users who have not rated the items. This work proposes an approach which is called Content-Based Deep Matrix Factorization (CBDMF) for RS, especially for the new user problem. In this approach, the item information (e.g., item descriptions and other item meta-data) is pre-processed and converted to Term Frequency-Inverse Document Frequency (TF-IDF) vector, then, this vector is integrated with the user and item latent factor vectors before inputting to a deep neuron networks for predictions. We provide architecture of the CBDMF as well as evaluated on several scenarios of new user problems. Experimental results on published Movie and Book data sets show that the CBDMF can work well for recommendations in case of new user problem.

Keywords: New user problem · Cold-start problem · Deep matrix factorization · Recommender systems · TF-IDF

1 Introduction

Recommender systems (RS) are very necessary and important in digital life. Especially, the RS can support users to select appropriate products/items in online systems such as shopping, entertainment, education and other domains. The RS is a kind of information filtering system which uses machine learning algorithms to predict the users' preferences then providing recommendations to the users. Basically, the RS is based on history behavior/actions of the users to suggest the items that the users may like or interest.

In the RS, we usually collect the user-item-rating matrix data as presented in Fig. 1. Let denote X as that matrix, u as a user, i as an item, and r as a rating of the user on an item. The main purpose of RS is to predict the empty ratings in this matrix X, which means that the users have not seen/rated the items. After

H. Fujita et al. (Eds.): IEA/AIE 2023, LNAI 13926, pp. 177–188, 2023.
https://doi.org/10.1007/978-3-031-36822-6_16

prediction, the items with the highest prediction scores (e.g., TOP-5 items) are recommended to the users. However, techniques in RS are facing with new user problem (or cold-start problem) which means that the RS has no history data to learn and recommend for the new users, as presented in the last row of Fig. 1.

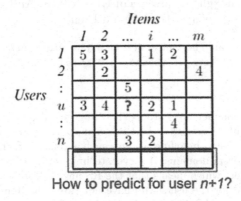

How to predict for user *n+1*?

Fig. 1. The last row is presented for a case of new user problem in RS

Based on Deep Matrix Factorization methods [1–4], this work proposes an approach which is called Content-Based Deep Matrix Factorization (CBDMF) for RS, especially for the new user problem. In this approach, the item information is pre-processed and converted to Term Frequency-Inverse Document Frequency (TF-IDF) vector, then, this vector is integrated with the user and item latent factor vectors before inputting to a deep neuron networks for prediction. The advantage of this approach is that it can combine the item information to the model in case of the new users who have no rating data. Moreover, the CBDMF replaces the DOT product in the standard matrix factorization with a deep neuron network for a better non-linear combination, thus, getting better prediction results.

This paper is organized as follows: A short review of related works is presented in Sect. 2. In Sect. 3, we present the state-of-the-art method in recommender system. Section 4 presents our architecture, including deep factorization matrix methods to develop workflow processes. Experimental results are introduced in Sect. 5. Finally, Sect. 6 concludes the paper with an outlook on future research.

2   Related Work

There are several works in dealing with new user problem (cold-start problem) in RS. The author in [5] presented a classification that divides the relevant studies addressing the new user cold-start problem into three major groups and summarize their advantages and disadvantages in a tabular format and several algorithms are described. The work in [6] have proposed using a semantic-based approach to tackle the cold-start problem in recommender systems. With this approach, they create a semantic model to retrieve past similarity data given a new user. Experimental results show that the proposed approach works well for the cold-start problem. The authors in [7] have proposed a set of methodologies for the automatic generation of stereotypes to address the cold-start problem. Their approach can improve recommendation quality under a variety of metrics and can reduce the dimension of the recommendation models.

The work in [8] presents a social network-based recommender system for new products or services. They used indirect relations between friends and "friends' friends" as well as sentinel friends to improve the recommendation accuracy. Another study of [9] reviewed the research trends linking recommendation systems' advanced technical aspects. The authors systematized the trend in recommendation system models, the technologies used in recommendation systems, and the business fields of the recommendation systems. It also showed that the filtering models of the recommendation systems using techniques such as text mining, KNN, clustering, matrix factorization, and neural network were used for a long period. However, applying neural network technology to a recommendation system has recently increased. In addition, several studies that aim to improve the performance of recommendation systems are actively conducted and expanded. Other works can be found in [4, 9, 10, 13].

This work proposes an approach which is called Content-Based Deep Matrix Factorization (CBDMF) for RS, especially for the new user problem. The proposed approach combines the rating data and the TF-IDF of the items to create the inputs for a deep neuron network.

3   Matrix Factorization for Recommendation

One state-of-the-art method in RS is the Matrix Factorization (MF) [9, 11, 12].

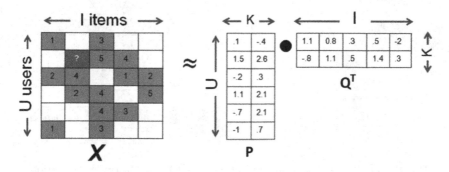

Fig. 2. Matrix factorization method for recommendation systems

The MF decomposes a matrix X (each row of X is a user, each column is an item, and each element is a rating of the user on that item, respectively) to two small matrices P and Q such that we can reconstruct X from these two P and Q matrices, as presented in Fig. 2 and Eq. (1).

$$X \approx PQ^T \tag{1}$$

where $P \in \mathbb{R}^{|U| \times K}$; $Q \in \mathbb{R}^{|I| \times K}$; K is number of latent factors, $K <<$ $|U|, K << |I|$. The latent factors P and Q can be obtained from optimizing the objective function as the following (Eq. (2)):

$$\mathcal{O}^{MF} = \sum_{(u,i) \in \mathcal{D}^{train}} \left(r_{ui} - \sum_{k=1}^{K} p_{uk} q_{ik} \right)^2 + \lambda(||P||_F^2 + ||Q||_F^2) \tag{2}$$

$\lambda \in (0..1)$ is a regularization and $|| \cdot ||_F$ is the Frobenius norm. One benefit of the MF approach is its flexibility in dealing with various data aspects. Details of these methods are described in [11,12].

4   Proposed Approach

The main idea of the MF model is that it decomposes the big matrix into two smaller ones. Then, each element of the big matrix is approximated from the two smaller matrices using a DOT product, as presented on the left side of Fig. 3. The DOT product runs very fast, thus, it can work well for larger data sets. However, it is a linear combination between two latent factors of the user and the item.

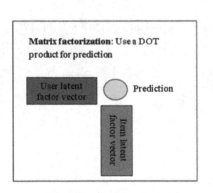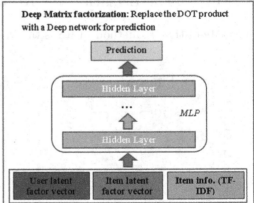

Fig. 3. Matrix Factorization vs Content-Based Deep Matrix Factorization

To tackle this linear combination, in our previous work [1], the deep matrix factorization (DMF) replaces the DOT product by deep neuron networks for a better non-linear combination. However, the DMF and other techniques in RS

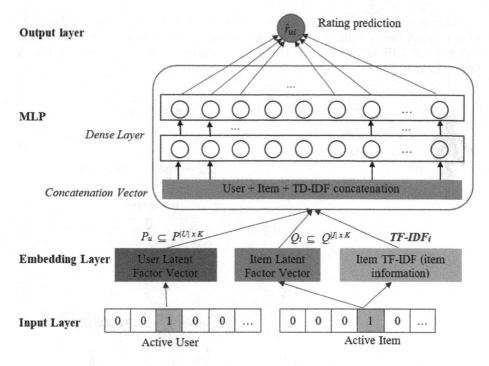

Fig. 4. Content-Based Deep Matrix Factorization (CBDMF)

are facing with the new user problem which means that the RS has no history data to learn, thus, the user and item latent factors can not be updated precisely.

This study proposes and approach which combines item information with the user and item latent factors to the DMF, as presented on the right side of Fig. 3 to tackle the new user problem. In this approach, the item information is pre-processed and converted to TF-IDF vector, then, this vector is integrated with user and item latent factor vectors before inputting to a deep neuron network.

The architecture of the proposed CBDMF is described in detail in Fig. 4. The proposed model has four layers. First, an input layer represents the current user/item; second, an embedding layer for reducing the user and item features' dimensions (the user and item latent factors). These two vectors are concatenated with a TF-IDF which contains information of the current item (e.g., item descriptions, item meta-data, etc.); Third, the DOT product is replaced by a deep neuron network for a better non-linear combination. Fourth, two embedding features are concatenated as the Multilayer Perceptron (MLP) layer input. Finally, an output layer for the prediction score. In this model, the MLP and the latent factors are trained simultaneously. The MLP can be set up by adding more hidden layers or changing the number of neurons depending on different datasets/domains. In this study, the number of nodes/neurons is selected using a hyper-parameter search [1,2].

The system architecture is described in detail in Fig. 5. In case of the new user login to the system, since it has no history rating data to learn, the system will use TF-IDF information of the item concatenated with the user and item latent factors.

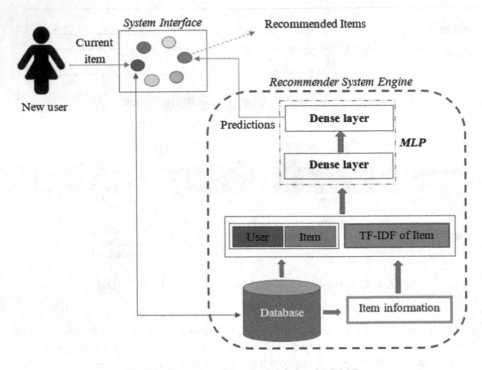

Fig. 5. System architecture of the CBDMF

5   Evaluation

5.1   Data Sets

Movie Dataset: This dataset is extracted from the Netflix system[1]. This dataset has 470,758 users, 4499 movies, and 24,058,263 ratings. The ratings are on a five star (from 1 to 5). However, this dataset only has the title attribute (text column) which can be extracted for calculating the TF-IDF. We have combine this dataset with another dataset[2] to get more meta-data (e.g., overview of the movie and original title).

---

[1] https://www.kaggle.com/datasets/netflix-inc/netflix-prize-data.
[2] https://www.kaggle.com/datasets/rounakbanik/the-movies-dataset.

Book Dataset: This dataset contains a Tag Genome[3] generated for a set of books along with book-tag ratings. For calculating TF-IDF, we have used the title and review columns. After pre-processed, this dataset has 350,332 users, 9,374 books, and 5,152,656 ratings (from 1 to 5).

5.2   Evaluation Metrics

The root means squared error (RMSE) is used to evaluate the models. They are calculated by Eq. (3)

$$\sqrt{\frac{1}{n}\sum_{i=1}^{n}(r_{ui} - \hat{r}_{ui})^2} \qquad (3)$$

where r_{ui} is the true value, $\hat{r}_{ui}$ is the predicted value, and n is the number of samples in the test set.

5.3   Train/Test Splits for New User Problem

In the experiments, the data sets were splited into 70% for training and 30% for testing. For testing new user problem, we create 3 scenarios which includes 10%, 20%, and 30% of new users, respectively.

5.4   Hyper-Parameter Settings

To find suitable hyper-parameters for each dataset, we have performed the hyper-parameter search to look for the best epochs, number of neurons, number of hidden layers of the MLP, and number of latent factors of the matrix factorization model. Based on previous work [2], on these datasets, we found that the MLP with 128 neurons is the best one. The numbers of latent factors of the matrix factorization and the CBDMF are 40 and 10, respectively. The numbers of epochs for the matrix factorization and the CBDMF are 30 and 2, respectively. Detailed analysis of these hyper-parameters can be found in [2]. In this work, the Adam optimizer is used. The matrix factorization uses standard DOT product. We have used the TensorFlow, Keras and Sklearn libraries for implementations.

5.5   Experimental Results

In the first scenario, we have performed the evaluation using 10% new users in the test set, as presented in Fig. 6. These results show that without dealing with new user problem, the standard matrix factorization has more errors in predictions than the proposed CBDMF on both datasets.

---

[3] https://grouplens.org/datasets/book-genome/.

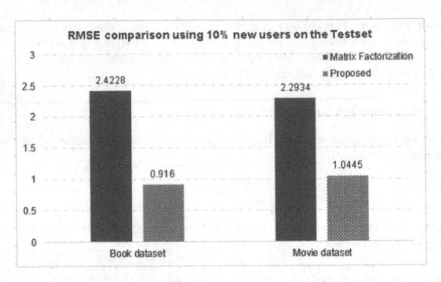

Fig. 6. RMSE on 10% new users of the test set

In the second and the third scenarios, we have performed the evaluation using 20% and 30% new users in the test set, respectively. The RMSE comparisons are presented in Figs. 7 and 8. Please note that, in the third scenario, all users in the test set are new. Results show that the proposed CBDMF can improve the prediction results significantly.

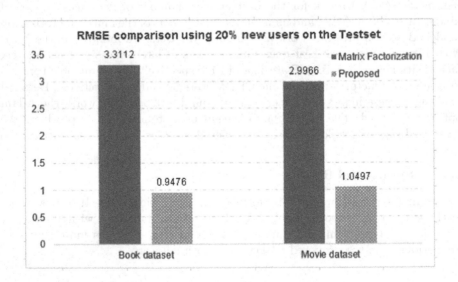

Fig. 7. RMSE on 20% new users of the test set

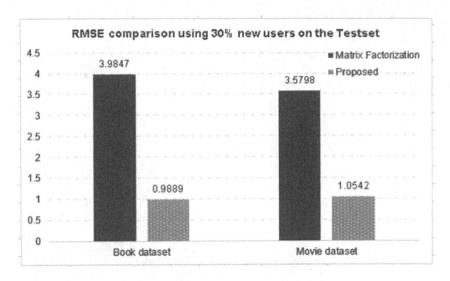

Fig. 8. RMSE on 30% new users of the test set

Figure 9 presents the relationship between the prediction errors (RMSE) and the percentage of new users on both datasets. Clearly, these results show that when the percentage of new users increase, the prediction errors also increase. However, the results of dealing with the new user problem by using CBDMF are still better than the original matrix factorization.

We also investigate the loss during training and validation phases as presented in Fig. 10 (using Book dataset, the Movie dataset also has similar results). These results show that both the methods are not overfitting. However, in case of all new users in the test set, the standard matrix factorization could not work well since it has no data to learn while the CBDMF show good results.

The advantage of the proposed CBDMF is that it replaces a linear combination in the standard matrix factorization with a non-linear one (a deep neuron networks) thus it get better results. Moreover, by concatenating the TF-IDF (information of the items) can help the model dealing with new user problem since in that case, the user and item latent factors can not precisely be updated during training phase. Another the advantage of these factorization models is their dimensionality reduction feature. For example, the user/item collaborative filtering methods (using K-nearest neighbors) can not run on large data sets due to an out of memory on PC computers [2].

In contrast, the CBDMF spent more times on training phase compared to the standard matrix factorization, for example, the CBDMF need more than 2 h for training on the Movie dataset while the matrix factorization needs only 10 min. However, this is not problem for the real systems since we can schedule for continuous training and updating the models.

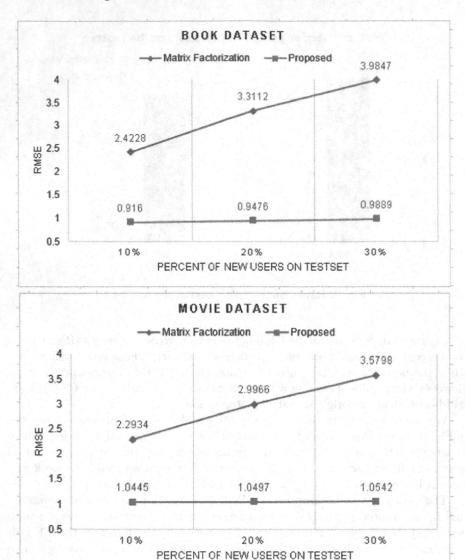

Fig. 9. Impact of % new users on prediction errors

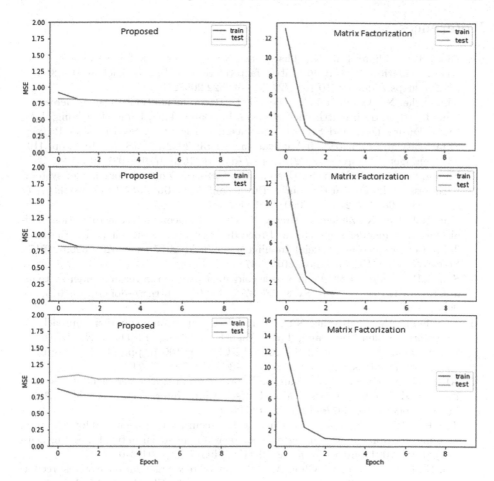

Fig. 10. Loss during train and test phase - Book dataset

6 Conclusion

This work proposes an approach which is called Content-Based Deep Matrix Factorization (CBDMF) for RS, especially for the new user problem. In this approach, the item information is pre-processed and converted to Term Frequency - Inverse Document Frequency (TF-IDF) vector, then, this vector is integrated with user and item latent factor vectors before inputting to a deep neuron networks. We provide a detailed architecture of the CBDMF as well as evaluated on several scenarios of new user problems. Experimental results on published data sets show that the CBDMF can work well for recommendations in case of new user problem.

In future work, we can integrate both the user and item information into the DMF. This combination could provide more information for the model to learn, thus, it would have better recommendation results. Moreover, comparison with other methods in new user problem will also be done in the future.

References

1. Dien, T.T., Thanh-Hai, N., Thai-Nghe, N.: An approach for learning resource recommendation using deep matrix factorization. J. Inf. Technol. **6**(4), 381–398 (2022). https://doi.org/10.1080/24751839.2022.2058250
2. Thai-Nghe, N., Thanh-Hai, N., Dien, T.T.: Recommendations in e-commerce systems based on deep matrix factorization. In: Dang, T.K., Küng, J., Chung, T.M. (eds.) Future Data and Security Engineering. Big Data, Security and Privacy, Smart City and Industry 4.0 Applications (FDSE 2022). CCIS, vol. 1688, pp. 419–431. Springer, Singapore (2022). https://doi.org/10.1007/978-981-19-8069-5_28
3. Zhang, F., Song, J., Peng, S.: Deep matrix factorization for recommender systems with missing data not at random. J. Phys: Conf. Ser. **1060**, 012001 (2018). https://doi.org/10.1088/1742-6596/1060/1/012001
4. Xue, H.J., Dai, X., Zhang, J., Huang, S., Chen, J.: Deep matrix factorization models for recommender systems. In: Proceedings of the Twenty-Sixth International Joint Conference on Artificial Intelligence (IJCAI 2017), pp. 3203–3209 (2017). https://doi.org/10.24963/ijcai.2017/447
5. Son, L.H.: Dealing with the new user cold-start problem in recommender systems: a comparative review. Inf. Syst. **58**, 87–104 (2016). https://doi.org/10.1016/j.is.2014.10.001
6. Thanh-Tai, H., Thai-Nghe, N.: A semantic-based recommendation approach for cold-start problem. In: Dang, T.K., Wagner, R., Küng, J., Thoai, N., Takizawa, M., Neuhold, E.J. (eds.) FDSE 2017. LNCS, vol. 10646, pp. 433–443. Springer, Cham (2017). https://doi.org/10.1007/978-3-319-70004-5_31
7. AlRossais, N., Kudenko, D., Yuan, T.: Improving cold-start recommendations using item-based stereotypes. User Model. User-Adap. Inter. **31**(5), 867–905 (2021). https://doi.org/10.1007/s11257-021-09293-9
8. Tey, F.J., Wu, T.-Y., Lin, C.-L., Chen, J.-L.: Accuracy improvements for cold-start recommendation problem using indirect relations in social networks. J. Big Data **8**(1), 1–18 (2021). https://doi.org/10.1186/s40537-021-00484-0
9. Ko, H., Lee, S., Park, Y., Choi, A.: A survey of recommendation systems: recommendation models, techniques and application fields. Electronics **11**, 141 (2022). https://doi.org/10.3390/electronics11010141
10. De Handschutter, P., Gillis, N., Siebert, X.: A survey on deep matrix factorizations. Comput. Sci. Rev. **42**, 100423 (2021). https://doi.org/10.1016/j.cosrev.2021.100423
11. Koren, Y., Bell, R., Volinsky, C.: Matrix factorization techniques for recommender systems. Computer **42**, 30–37 (2009)
12. Thai-Nghe, N., Schmidt-Thieme, L.: Factorization forecasting approach for user modeling. J. Comput. Sci. Cybern. **31**(2), 133–148 (2015)
13. Abdullah, N.A., Rasheed, R.A., Nasir, M.H.N.M., Rahman, M.M.: Eliciting auxiliary information for cold start user recommendation: a survey. Appl. Sci. **11**(20), 9608 (2021). https://doi.org/10.3390/app11209608

Scheduling Algorithm Based on Load-Aware Queue Partitioning in Heterogeneous Multi-core Systems

Kai Hong$^{(\boxtimes)}$, Junjie Zhong, Linqi Chen, Chengguang Wang, and Lei Wang$^{(\boxtimes)}$

University of Electronic Science and Technology of China, Chengdu, China
1764498528@qq.com, 3408768095@qq.com

Abstract. There are inefficient global scheduling parallelism and local scheduling parallelism prone to processor starvation in current scheduling algorithms. Regarding this issue, this paper proposed a load-aware queue partitioning scheduling strategy by first allocating the queues according to the number of processor cores, calculating the load factor to specify the load queue capacity, and it assigned the awaiting nodes to the appropriate perceptual queues through the precursor nodes and the communication computation overhead. At the same time, real-time computation of the load factor could effectively prevent the processor from being starved for a long time. Experimental comparison with two classical algorithms shows that there is a certain improvement in both performance metrics of scheduling length and task speedup ratio.

Keywords: Load-aware · Scheduling algorithm · Perceptual queue · Heterogeneous multi-core

1 Introduction

With the rapid development of social media technology and the widespread popularity of Internet applications, native computing systems have begun to withstand the test of the traffic era, and the surge in the number of users has also forced related industries to face the challenge of rapid iteration. At the same time, more and more bandwidth pressures have prompted the transformation of stand-alone computing resources into large-scale cluster computing resources, such as cloud computers and supercomputers [1]. In the process of task computing, cluster servers process applications in parallel through data sharing and task blocking, and the scheduling problem is one of the key issues to improve the parallel efficiency of processors, especially in a large-scale heterogeneous cluster environment [2]. The task scheduling strategy is an important factor affecting the performance of computing resources.

1.1 Relevant Reviews

The task scheduling problem belongs to the multi-field interdisciplinary problem in the field of mathematical optimization, high-performance computing, etc. It involves

H. Fujita et al. (Eds.): IEA/AIE 2023, LNAI 13926, pp. 189–200, 2023.
https://doi.org/10.1007/978-3-031-36822-6_17

both mathematical combinatorial optimization and high-performance computing parallel processing [3]. At the same time, the task model is becoming more and more complex as the demand continues to grow, and efficient computing power promotes the gradual heterogeneity and asymmetry of the computing system [4]. With the increasing task base size and the trend of highly sophisticated processing devices, balancing the gap between complex task models and efficient heterogeneous computing resources has become the main responsibility of scheduling strategies. During the scheduling process, the scheduling strategy needs to take into account the priority order of task elements and the consumption of computing resources. The scheduling strategy first performs model element scheduling based on whether the dependency conditions are met between the application model characteristics (including model element priority level, model element calculation cost, and model element transmission cost) and calculation model characteristics (including the number of calculation elements and the availability time of calculation elements) [5]. Combined allocation, according to the scheduling efficiency and then determine whether the combined allocation is the optimal scheduling scheme [6]. An efficient scheduling strategy can not only effectively organize heterogeneous computing capabilities, but also fully improve the execution efficiency of the task model.

Scheduling problems proven by relevant scholars to be NP problems [7]; that is, the optimal solution cannot be found in polynomial time, and the optimal solution of the scheduling scale can only be approached continuously through an approximate optimal algorithm. For scheduling problems in heterogeneous environments, domestic and foreign scholars have proposed many approximate algorithms. Task scheduling algorithms in a heterogeneous cluster environment can be mainly divided into list-based scheduling algorithms, random search-based scheduling algorithms, clustering scheduling algorithms, and replication-based scheduling algorithms [8]. Literature [9] proposes the HEFT algorithm and the CPOP algorithm with low implementation complexity. The two algorithms determine the order of tasks according to the average computing cost of tasks when prioritizing tasks, without considering the performance differences of processors in heterogeneous environments. And does not consider the communication overhead of subsequent tasks. Literature [10] proposes an optimal scheduling algorithm based on the iterative optimization mechanism, by iteratively calculating the earliest completion time of all subsequent tasks on the processor and selecting the processor with the smallest completion time. Literature [11] proposes a new table scheduling algorithm based on the HEFT algorithm. This algorithm calculates the maximum communication overhead between the earliest task completion time and its exit task, and assigns tasks based on the minimum value of the product of the two. Literature [12] proposes a two-stage multi-task scheduling algorithm. In the first stage of the algorithm, the initial optimal solution is generated through the dynamic critical path algorithm, and then the optimal solution is continuously searched on the basis of the optimal solution through the dynamic state transfer method. Literature [13] proposes a parallel-aware scheduling algorithm, which determines the priority level of the task through the longest path value of the task and the exit task. When allocating processor cores, the correlation degree and the earliest executable time of the task are considered, and the best matching evaluation is set. Function. Literature [5] proposes a priority queue division algorithm, which establishes relevant priority queues through the number of entry nodes, and assigns tasks to the processor with the earliest completion time and the smallest completion time in the processor selection phase.

1.2 Problem Descriptions

The list-based scheduling method has been widely studied because of its low algorithm complexity, and most of the list-based scheduling research determines the priority level of tasks and computing resources according to the greedy strategy; the global scheduling method is used for combinatorial optimization, and the proposed scheduling strategy is parallel low efficiency. Some local scheduling methods, such as priority queue scheduling, do not consider the difference in processor computing performance and are not robust to single-entry task scheduling.

1.3 Contributions

This paper proposes a queue partition scheduling strategy based on load perception in a heterogeneous environment. By establishing a perception queue, the parallel efficiency of task allocation is improved, and the robustness of the algorithm to task graphs with different topologies is enhanced; the introduction of load factors can effectively avoid processing device starvation. Finally, the algorithm is compared with HEFT (Heterogeneous Earliest-Finish-Time Algorithm) algorithm and PQDSA (Priority Queue Dividing Scheduling Algorithm) algorithm to further illustrate the effectiveness of the algorithm.

1.4 Paper Structure

The first chapter of this paper expounds the background knowledge of the research content and the relevant research progress at home and abroad, and leads to the next research content. The second chapter mainly describes the application model, calculation model and specific related scheduling methods. The third chapter mainly introduces the algorithms proposed by the author, including task priority selection algorithm and processor core queue selection algorithm. The fourth chapter compares the algorithm proposed in this paper with the algorithm to be compared and draws the experimental conclusion. Finally, it summarizes the research process of the full text and clarifies the research plan for the next step.

2 Background Information

2.1 Task Model

Scheduling problems in heterogeneous multi-core systems first require mathematical modeling of the task to be solved. The task model is described using a DAG graph, that is $G = \{V, E, C, W\}$, the task model is described by a quadruple, where, $V = \{v_i | i = 1, 2, 3..., n\}$ represents the task set in the task graph to be solved, v_i represents the task numbered in the task set, and $n = |V|$ represents the number of task sets. $E = \{(v_i, v_j) | 1 \leq i \leq n, 1 \leq j \leq n\}$ indicates that there is an association relationship between any two task nodes in the task set, namely there is a directed edge relationship between task node and task node. $C = \{c_{ij} | 1 \leq i \leq n, 1 \leq j \leq n\}$ represents the communication overhead of any two associated tasks in the task set, where c_{ij} represents the communication overhead between task i and task j, task i is the predecessor task j, and task j is the successor task i. $W = \{w_{ij} | 1 \leq i \leq n, 1 \leq j \leq m\}$ indicates the computing overhead of the task i on the processor core P_j, and m is the total number of processor cores. The priority level of the task node in each DAG graph is higher than that of all its successor nodes. Only when all the predecessor parent nodes of the node are scheduled, the successor node can be scheduled. In the task graph shown in Fig. 1, $v_1 - v_{10}$ represents 10 task nodes in the task graph.

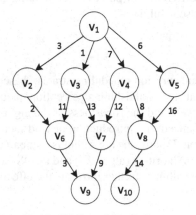

Fig. 1. DAG model task diagram

2.2 Scheduling Model

After the overall task set is modeled through the DAG graph, the associated tasks need to be assigned to the corresponding processor core queues according to the algorithm steps. Due to the differences in the computing capabilities of different types of processor cores in a heterogeneous environment, when assigning tasks to specific queues, it is necessary to further consider the problem of long-term starvation of processor cores. On the premise of satisfying the load balance, the task is scheduled to the processor core queue with the earliest completion time and the smallest time.

2.3 Scheduling Method

According to the number of queues maintained in the task set scheduling process, the scheduling methods can be divided into global scheduling and local scheduling. Global scheduling means that there is only one global queue in the scheduling process. For example, the HEFT algorithm sorts tasks with different priorities into the queue according to specific rules. For processors, low-priority tasks need to wait for high-priority tasks to be allocated before they can be allocated. The sequential dequeuing mechanism of the global scheduling is obviously not conducive to the parallelism between mining tasks, and the global scheduling does not consider the communication overhead between the processor cores scheduled by the tasks and the processor cores scheduled by the predecessor tasks. Local scheduling is to establish different numbers of local queues according to specific rules, tasks enter the ready queue according to the algorithm steps, and tasks in different queues select the same or different processor cores for calculation. In the processor selection phase, each task in the local ready queue is scheduled to the processor core with the least overhead.

3 LAQPSA Algorithm

3.1 Parameter Definition

Facing the shortcomings of global scheduling and local scheduling in heterogeneous multi-core systems, the algorithm proposed in this paper can improve the potential parallelism of tasks in the scheduling process, and the introduction of load factor as an indicator of dispatch queue can effectively improve processor utilization. The load-aware queue division scheduling algorithm is mainly divided into two steps: the task priority division phase and the processor queue allocation phase. The task priority division considers four factors: maximum priority level of the predecessor node, maximum task calculation overhead, communication overhead of the predecessor node and communication overhead of the follow-up node to determine the task value, and minimize the inaccurate task priority caused by the difference in the computing power of the processor core. In the processor queue selection stage, under the premise of satisfying the real-time load factor, tasks are assigned to the core queue with the smallest sum of computing overhead and communication overhead (Table 1).

Table 1. Parameter descriptions tables.

Symbol	Definition
ζ_0	Initial load factor
Q	Queue load capacity
Pr_{ecount}	The number of task
ζ_{max}	Maximum component
ζ_{min}	Minimum component
EST	Start time of earliest task
EFT	Finish time of earliest task
$Avail$	Available time
η	Load threshold
σ	Fluctuation value

3.2 Task Prioritization Algorithm

In order to improve the robustness of perceptual queues to single-entry task sets, in the task prioritization stage, firstly, a corresponding number of perceptual queues (Q_m) are established according to the number of processor cores. Secondly, calculate the initial load factor of the processor core. The initial factor is the ratio of the number of tasks processed by each processor core per unit time, and the computing power of the cores in the same processor is approximately the same. The load factor is a parameter for real-time performance of the perceived queue load. By repeatedly calculating the load factor in each scheduling process, the starvation state of the processor core can be avoided, thereby improving the utilization rate of heterogeneous processors. When calculating the priority level of each node ($Level(v_i)$, i = 1,2,...n), considering the difference in computing performance of heterogeneous processors and the impact of communication overhead on priority ranking, the node priority is determined by the maximum predecessor node priority level, the maximum computing overhead of the node and the maximum communication overhead of the front- and rear-drivers are jointly determined. For an entry task without a predecessor node, the node priority level is determined by the maximum computing overhead and the maximum communication overhead of the rear-driver. The calculation formula of the initial load factor of the processor core is shown in formula (1):

$$\zeta_0 = Q_1 : Q_2 : \dots : Q_j, j \leq m \tag{1}$$

Q_j is the number of tasks in the processor core j perception queue.

The queue load threshold can be calculated according to the initial load factor, and the calculation formula is shown in formula (2):

$$\eta = \max(Q_i) - \min(Q_j) \tag{2}$$

Q_i and Q_j are respectively the queue with the largest initial load factor capacity and the queue with the smallest initial load factor capacity. The priority level calculation of the task starts from the entry node, and the calculation formula is shown in (3):

$$Level(V_i) = \max_{V_j \in dads(V_i)} \{Level(V_j) + C_{ji}\} + \\ \max_{V_k \in sons(V_i)} C_{ik} + \max\{W(i,p)\}\} \tag{3}$$

In the priority calculation formula, C_{ji} is the communication overhead between the predecessor node V_j and the node V_i, C_{ik} is the communication overhead between the task node V_i and the successor node V_k, and $W(i,p)$ is the computing overhead of the task V_i on the processor p. For an entry task node without a predecessor node, its priority calculation is shown in formula (4):

$$Level(V_{entry}) = \max_{V_k \in sons(V_{entry})} C_k + \\ \max\{W(entry,p)\}\} \tag{4}$$

Among them, C_k is the communication overhead between the entry node V_{entry} and the successor node V_k, and $W(entry, p)$ is the computation overhead of the entry node on the processor p.

In the prioritization stage, after comprehensively considering the impact of various factors on task priority, the task priority is comprehensively evaluated from the three aspects of predecessor task node priority, processor performance difference, and communication overhead, so that it is more in line with heterogeneous performance. Partition features in a symmetrical environment.

3.3 Processor Queue Selection Algorithm

The task prioritization algorithm integrates three aspects to prioritize the tasks, which greatly reduces the influence of the difference in processor calculation and the communication overhead of the predecessor and the rear driver on the division results. At the same time, the prioritization stage takes into account the topology of the overall task and the relationship between tasks. The order of tasks at the same level may be out of order. Tasks must wait for the completion of task division at the previous level before they can be prioritized. In the processor core queue selection phase, tasks are assigned to appropriate processor core queues according to task priority levels, and tasks entering the processor core queue are scheduled to run on the corresponding processor cores of the queue in turn, that is, tasks entering the processor core queue are on the processing core calculation. Agreed tasks are assigned to the processor core queue in order of priority. During the process of enqueueing tasks, the task start time (*EST*), task end time (*EFT*), processor core available time (*Avail*) and scheduling fluctuation values σ are shown in formula (5)–(8) as shown:

$$\sigma(i) = \zeta_{max} - \zeta_{min} \tag{5}$$

$$EST(v_i) = \max\{Avail(j), \max_{v_k \in dads(v_i)} EFT(v_k)\} \\ + \lambda C_{ki} \tag{6}$$

$$EFT(v_i) = EST(v_i) + W(i, j) \tag{7}$$

$$Avail(j) = EFT(v_i) \tag{8}$$

In the queue selection algorithm, the tasks waiting to enter the corresponding queue are called waiting tasks. The selection of the queue number is mainly determined by the four parameters of the current scheduling fluctuation value (σ), the earliest task start time (*EST*), the earliest task end time (*EFT*) and the processor core available time (*Avail*). The main process is as follows:

First, getting ζ_{max} and ζ_{min} after the last scheduling before entering the queue. Calculate the scheduling fluctuation value of the current scheduling, and compare the initial load factor load threshold η with the scheduling fluctuation value σ.

Case 1: If the fluctuation value σ is less than η, at this time, as defined by the above formula (6) and formula (7), the waiting task is scheduled to the processor core queue with the earliest end time and the smallest end time; there is a precursor node of the waiting task in the target queue, $\lambda = 0$; If there is no predecessor node waiting for the task in the target queue, then $\lambda = 1$. At the same time, as formula (7) describes to update the available time of the processor core, the value of the queue capacity Q of the target processor core increases automatically.

Case 2: If the fluctuation value σ is not less than η, the waiting task is scheduled to the corresponding ζ_{min} processor core queue; if the corresponding ζ_{min} processor core queue exists and is not unique, the waiting task is assigned to the processor core with the earliest end time and the smallest time. When the target queue also has a waiting task precursor node, $\lambda = 0$; if there is no waiting task precursor node in the target queue, then $\lambda = 1$. Finally, update the processor core available time and update capacity value Q of the target processor core.

4 Experiment and Analysis

4.1 Experiment Environment

In order to verify the validity and efficiency of the LAQPSA algorithm, the algorithms proposed in this paper are all implemented in C/C++ language. The experimental hardware environment is Intel Core i7-9700 CPU, NVIDIA GeForce RTX 2070 GPU, and 16 GB DDR4 main memory. The software environment is Ubantu 20.04.3 LTS, g++ 9.3.0. In this paper, DAG graphs with different numbers of tasks are randomly generated as the experimental task set, and the two parameters of schedule length (Schedule Length, SL) and task acceleration ratio (Speedup Ratio, SR) are used as evaluation indicators. Finally, the experimental comparison with the HEFT algorithm and the PQDSA algorithm is carried out. The expressions of scheduling length SL and speedup ratio SR are as follows:

$$SL = \min\{EFT(v_{exit})\} \tag{9}$$

$$SR = \frac{\min_{p_j \in P}\{T_{exit}\}}{SL} \tag{10}$$

Among them, $EFT(v_{exit})$ represents the earliest end time of the exit task node in the task graph, the smaller the SL value of the scheduling result, the better the scheduling efficiency of the algorithm. The speedup ratio indicates the ratio of the earliest end time of the task executed on a single processor core to the scheduling length, and T_{exit} indicates the end time of the exit task. The larger the SR value generated by the scheduling algorithm, the more efficient the algorithm scheduling performance.

4.2 Results Analysis

The experiment uses a DAG task graph consisting of 10, 20, 30, and 40 task nodes, and a DAG graph with the same number of nodes to carry out simulation experiments under the conditions of 2, 4, 8, and 12 processor core queues, and compares the results proposed in this paper. The difference between the algorithm and the HEFT algorithm and PQDSA algorithm in the performance index scheduling length and speedup ratio. In order to ensure the objectivity of the experiment, multiple DAG graphs with the same number of tasks are randomly generated during the simulation experiment, that is, under the constraints of different number of tasks and different number of processor cores, several groups of experiments are carried out for the two performance indicators of scheduling length and scheduling speedup ratio. For comparison, the results of multiple experiments under the same conditions were averaged.

As shown in Fig. 2, the number of task nodes, and 10 DAG graphs with different topological structures, are randomly generated under the same number of tasks; a total of 40 different experiments are carried out to compare the differences of the three algorithms in the scheduling length index. The number of processor core queues is 4 in the simulation experiment of DAG diagram with different number of tasks. The experimental results show that the LAQPSA algorithm has a minimum increase of 6.5% and a maximum increase of 32.3% in the scheduling length index compared with the HEFT algorithm under the condition of different task numbers. Compared with the PQDSA algorithm, the LAQPSA algorithm has a minimum increase of 6.2% and a maximum increase of 18.5% in the scheduling length index under the condition of different task numbers.

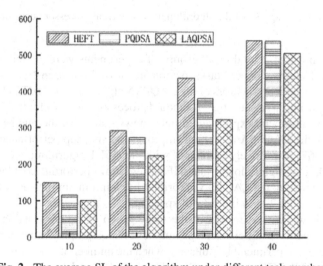

Fig. 2. The average SL of the algorithm under different task numbers

Figure 3 shows the processor queue. A total of 40 different experiments were carried out under the same constraint conditions to compare the differences in scheduling length performance between the LAQPSA algorithm, the HEFT algorithm, and the PQDSA algorithm. The number of DAG graph tasks under different processor queue numbers is 20. From the experimental results in the figure, it can be concluded that the LAQPSA algorithm has a minimum increase of 5.8% and a maximum increase of 37.2% compared with the HEFT algorithm under different processing core queue numbers. Compared with the PQDSA algorithm, the number of processing core queues has a minimum increase of 9%, and a maximum increase of 17.5%.

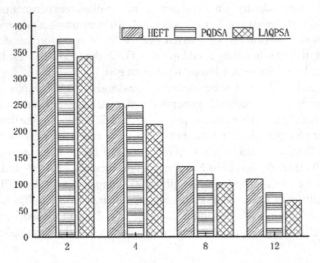

Fig. 3. The average SL of the algorithm under different processor queue numbers

As shown in Fig. 4, a total of 40 groups of experiments were carried out under the conditions of different number of tasks to compare the differences in the average speedup ratio of the performance indicators of the LAQPSA algorithm, the HEFT algorithm, and the PQDSA algorithm. The number of standard processor cores is 4 for the DAG diagram of different task numbers; experimental data shows that when the number of nodes is 10, 20, and 30, the LAQPSA algorithm improves the speedup performance by 37.1%, 22.6%, and 27.6% respectively compared with the HEFT algorithm; when the number of nodes is 40, it is slightly lower than HEFT algorithm performance. Compared with the PQDSA algorithm, the LAQPSA algorithm has a minimum increase of 4.5% and a maximum increase of 22.6% in terms of speedup.

Figure 5 shows the test results of the same group of experiments under different processor core queue conditions, and the number of DAG graphs with different numbers of cores is 20. The experimental results are: when the number of queues is 2, the average speedup ratios of HEFT algorithm, PQDSA algorithm and LAQPSA algorithm are: 1.5491, 1.3872, 1.5241 respectively, and the speedup ratio performance of LAQPSA algorithm is slightly lower than HEFT algorithm, slightly higher than PQDSA algorithm. As the number of queues gradually increases, the speedup index of LAQPSA algorithm is obviously better than the other two algorithms. Among them, the LAQPSA algorithm has a minimum increase of 9.8% and a maximum increase of 47.7% compared with the HEFT algorithm; the LAQPSA algorithm has a minimum increase of 15.8% and a maximum increase of 21.2% compared with the PQDSA algorithm.

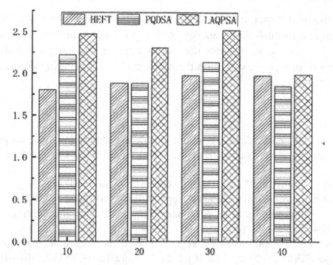

Fig. 4. The average speedup of the algorithm under different number of tasks

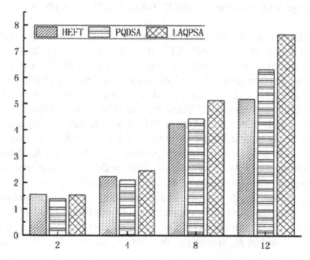

Fig. 5. The average speedup ratio of the algorithm under different processor queue numbers

5   Conclusions

In the traffic era, powerful computing systems are urgently needed to provide computing power support, and the scheduling problem is a key issue in the field of high-performance computing and the improvement of the computing power of computing systems. The algorithm proposed in this paper is oriented to heterogeneous multi-core computing systems, fully considering the asymmetric characteristics of processor cores in heterogeneous systems and the inherent shortcomings of the two scheduling methods. Both the HEFT algorithm and the PQDSA algorithm have certain improvements in performance indicators. In the next step, the author will study high-efficiency heterogeneous environment scheduling algorithms under energy consumption constraints in large-scale cluster computing systems, so as to improve the load balancing efficiency of cluster machines and achieve lower power consumption through excellent scheduling algorithms.

References

1. Lan, W., Longxin, Z., Junfeng, M., et al.: Scheduling algorithms based on priority queue division in heterogeneous computing environments. Small Micro Comput. Syst. **41**(02), 303–309 (2020)
2. Qingyan, M., Jingjing, W.: Task scheduling optimization in cloud computing based on hybrid firefly genetic algorithm. Microcomput. Appl. **37**(05), 158–160+164 (2021)
3. Khan, M.A.: Scheduling for heterogeneous systems using constrained critical paths. Parallel Comput. **38**(4–5), 175–193 (2012)
4. Khan, M.A.: Task scheduling for heterogeneous systems using an incremental approach. J. Supercomput. **73**(5), 1905–1928 (2016). https://doi.org/10.1007/s11227-016-1894-5
5. Fortnow, L.: The status of the P versus NP problem. Commun. ACM **52**(9), 78–86 (2009)
6. Topcuoglu, H., Hariri, S., Wu, M.Y.: Performance-effective and low-complexity task scheduling for heterogeneous computing. IEEE Trans. Parallel Distrib. Syst. **13**(3), 260–274 (2002)
7. Ma, M., Sakellariou, R.: Code-size-aware scheduling of synchronous dataflow graphs on multicore systems. ACM Trans. Embed. Comput. Syst. **20**(3), 1–24 (2021)
8. Xing, Z.J.: Research on task scheduling strategy of CPU-GPU heterogeneous computing platform for high performance. Beijing University of Technology (2020)
9. Huang, T.W., Lin, D.L., Lin, C.X., et al.: Taskflow: a lightweight parallel and heterogeneous task graph computing system. IEEE Trans. Parallel Distrib. Syst. **33**(6), 1303–1320 (2021)
10. Bittencourt, L.F., Sakellariou, R., Madeira, E.R.: Dag scheduling using a lookahead variant of the heterogeneous earliest finish time algorithm. In: 2010 18th Euromicro Conference on Parallel, Distributed and Network-Based Processing, pp. 27–34. IEEE (2010)
11. Yunyang, L., Chuan, Z., Qi, W.: A new table scheduling algorithm in heterogeneous distributed computing environment. Comput. Eng. **44**(08), 43–47 (2018)
12. Maoxing, Z., Degang, X., Zhifang, S., et al.: Research on two-stage multi-task scheduling algorithm for heterogeneous multi-core platforms. Control Eng. **25**(12), 2140–2146 (2018)
13. Qiuling, L., Xiangli, Z., Hongmei, Z., et al.: A parallel aware scheduling algorithm for associated tasks based on multi-core processors. Comput. Eng. **47**(07), 212–217 (2021)

Solving Job-Shop Scheduling Problem via Deep Reinforcement Learning with Attention Model

Zijun Liao, Jinbiao Chen, and Zizhen Zhang[✉]

Sun Yat-sen University, Guangzhou, China
zhangzzh7@mail.sysu.edu.cn

Abstract. The job-shop scheduling problem (JSP), as an NP-hard problem, is widely applied in real-world production scheduling problems, such as assembly plants, chemical production, and semiconductor production. Although some deep reinforcement learning (DRL) methods for scheduling problems are recently developed, these methods are limited to tackling various-size problems. For this purpose, we propose a DRL method with an attention model to solve JSP. We formulate JSP as a Markovian decision process and design a size-agnostic policy network based on an attention model. Experimental results show that our method can automatically produce a dispatching scheme for various-size JSP without any expert knowledge, which surpasses traditional priority dispatching rules and the state-of-the-art DRL method.

Keywords: Job-shop scheduling problem · Deep reinforcement learning · Attention model

1 Introduction

In today's era of intelligent manufacturing, smart scheduling plays a key role in automation and intelligence, which can help factories achieve high efficiency and high profit. The job-shop scheduling problem (JSP) is closely related to many industrial scenarios, such as assembly plants [1], chemical production [2], and semiconductor manufacturing [3]. It is a classic NP-hard problem in operations research and computational intelligence fields [4]. JSP contains several machines and jobs. Each job requires several operations with predefined processing routes. A scheduling scheme is composed of the processing order of the jobs on each machine. The goal of JSP is to seek an optimal scheduling scheme to minimize the makespan, i.e., the completion time of all jobs. Due to the high complexity of JSP, exact and meta-heuristic methods are time-consuming. Hence, priority dispatching rules (PDRs) are more popular in practice, since they spend short solving time. Recently, some deep reinforcement learning (DRL) methods are proposed to rapidly produce a scheduling scheme, but their performance still needs to be improved.

The exact algorithms for solving JSP include mathematical programming and branch-and-bound algorithms [5], etc. Although these methods can find the

H. Fujita et al. (Eds.): IEA/AIE 2023, LNAI 13926, pp. 201–212, 2023.
https://doi.org/10.1007/978-3-031-36822-6_18

optimal solution, they can only solve small-scale problems due to dimensional explosion. Meta-heuristic algorithms, such as the genetic algorithm [6], search for near optimal solutions in the solution space by an iterative improvement manner. However, this iterative search process is still time-consuming. To quickly solve the JSP, researchers manually design various PDRs [7] to engender scheduling orders of jobs. However, PDRs are still limited to achieve better results due to the reliance on manual design. To address this problem, more and more researchers have recently tried to use learning-based approaches to solve JSP.

There are a lot of works applying DRL to solve JSP. [8] cast JSP as a distributed optimization problem to solve complex JSP in manufacturing. Zhang et al. [9] used DRL with graph isomorphic networks to compute the priority of each operation from the optimized sparse distinguish graph and obtained the scheduling policy. Park et al. [10] also used a similar idea and evaluate the stability of this method. Liao et al. [11] used hierarchical reinforcement learning to learn the policies. Zhao et al. [12] calculated the priority of the operations using Transformer and Pointer Network. Yang, Shanggen [13] attempted representation learning on disjunctive graphs using graph attention networks. Chen et al. [14] used a parallel-computing encoder and a recurrent-computing decoder to generate the scheduling scheme.

Many researchers also use DRL to solve scheduling problems in various scenarios. Waschneck et al. [15] used DQN in a scheduling system of semiconductor production and proposed a pre-training and then fine-tuning approach to migrate the model to a new scenario. Cao et al. [16] used Q-learning and a surrogate model to optimize the parameters of the cuckoo search, and then used the cuckoo search to solve the scheduling problem in semiconductor production. Kuhnle et al. [17] used DRL to deal with the automated order scheduling problem in a simulated production system. Kuhnle et al. [18] conducted extensive experiments in two real semiconductor production environments and proposed a DRL-based adaptive production control system. Zhang et al. [19] proposed an experience-sharing DQN approach integrating the experiences of different agents to solve the truck scheduling problem in a highly dynamic mining environment. Li et al. [20] treated the scheduling sequence as a natural language and proposed an end-to-end graph attention model to solve the open shop scheduling problem.

In summary, some of the existing DRL methods have been studied on the JSP. However, most DRL methods can not be generalized to JSP with various sizes. The model proposed by [9] has the size-generalization ability, but its performance needs to be further improved.

The contributions of this work are presented as follows. We propose a DRL method with an attention model to solve JSP. We formulate the scheduling process as a Markovian decision process (MDP). The policy is parameterized by the attention model, which could extract state information and compute the scheduling priority of operations. Our proposed model has desirable generalization capability across different problem sizes. Moreover, our proposed method outperforms the state-of-the-art DRL method and traditional PDRs.

2   Problem Statements

JSP consists of a job set $\mathcal{J}$ and a machine set $\mathcal{M}$. The problem size is denoted as $n \times m$, where $n = |\mathcal{J}|$ and $m = |\mathcal{M}|$. Each job J_i ($1 \leq i \leq n$) in the job set consists of m operations. The j-th ($1 \leq j \leq m$) operation O_{ij} of job J_i needs to be processed on the specified machine $M_{ij} \in \mathcal{M}$ with processing time $P_{ij} \in \mathbb{N}$. J_i needs to be processed in sequence $O_{i1} \rightarrow O_{i2} \rightarrow \cdots \rightarrow O_{i(m-1)} \rightarrow O_{im}$, where $O_{ij} \rightarrow O_{i(j+1)}$ indicates that the operation $O_{i(j+1)}$ can only start processing when the operation O_{ij} is completed. Only one operation can be processed on a machine M_k ($1 \leq k \leq m$) at the same time, so a schedule is made up of the processing order of the operations on each machine. Each machine is used for only one operation of each job. An example is given in Fig. 1, showing the impact of different scheduling sequences.

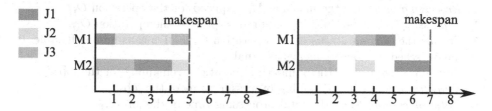

Fig. 1. Two examples of different solutions on a 3×2 JSP instance. The scheduling sequence in left is J1-J3-J2-J1-J3-J2, and in right is J2-J3-J3-J2-J1-J1.

When an operation O_{ij} is assigned to machine M_{ij} at time T, its start time is noted as $S_{ij} = T$, and completion time is noted as $C_{ij} = S_{ij} + P_{ij}$. Therefore the earliest start time of the next operation $O_{i(j+1)}$ is C_{ij} and the earliest completion time is $C_{ij} + P_{i(j+1)}$. Define the makespan as $C_{\max} = \max_{i,j} C_{ij}$. Our goal is to minimize the makespan. It is a common indicator for scheduling, which means that all jobs can be completed in a shorter time.

3   Methodology

3.1   Markovian Decision Process

The core principle of DRL is the Markovian decision process, in which the next state s_{t+1} of the environment is only related to the current state s_t. MDP can be represented by a tuple as $(\mathcal{S}, \mathcal{A}, P, R, \gamma)$, where the set $\mathcal{S}$ is the state space and the set $\mathcal{A}$ is the action space. When an agent selects an action $a \in \mathcal{A}$ under the state $s \in \mathcal{S}$, the environment is transferred to the state s' with a probability according to the state transfer function $P : \mathcal{S} \times \mathcal{A} \times \mathcal{S} \rightarrow [0, 1]$ and feeds a reward signal r to the agent based on the reward function $R : \mathcal{S} \times \mathcal{A} \times \mathcal{S} \rightarrow \mathbb{R}$. The agent aims to maximize the discounted cumulative reward $r + \gamma^1 r' + \gamma^2 r'' + \cdots$, where γ is the discount factor.

For JSP, the decision-making time T is not continuous. An operation O_{ij} is assignable when the precursor operation $O_{i(j-1)}$ is completed and the required machine M_{ij} is idle. The agent only makes a decision when assignable operations exist. When the agent selects O_{ij} at step t and there are still assignable operations after that, the current moment T remains unchanged. Otherwise, the decision step $t + 1$ is transferred to the moment $T + x$ once there are any assignable operations. For JSP, the MDP can be designed as follows.

State. We define the state $s_t \in \mathbb{R}^{(n \times m) \times 9}$ as a feature matrix. The feature matrix consists of the feature vectors $f_{ij} \in \mathbb{R}^9$ of the operations stacked in order, containing the following nine pieces of attributes:

1. *Job number*: the number i of the job J_i to which the operation O_{ij} belongs.
2. *Operation number*: the number j of the operation O_{ij} in the job J_i.
3. *Processing machine*: the machine M_k required for the operation O_{ij}.
4. *Processing time*: the time P_{ij} required to process the operation O_{ij}.
5. *Status*: the current status of the operation O_{ij}, -1 means non-assignable, 0 means scheduled, and 1 means assignable.
6. *Operation remaining*: the number of operations remaining for the job J_i.
7. *Work remaining*: the remaining processing time of the job J_i.
8. *Total processing time*: the total processing time of the job J_i.
9. *Arrival time*: the arrival time of operation O_{ij}, i.e., the completion time of the precursor operation $O_{i(j-1)}$. In particular, the arrival time of the first operation O_{i0} is 0.

Transition. When the agent selects action $a_t = O_{ij}$ in state s_t, the *status* attribute of operation O_{ij} will change from assignable to scheduled, the *arrival time* of $O_{i(j+1)}$ will change to C_{ij}, and the *operation remaining* of all operations under job J_i minus one. Note that all assignable operations originally required machine M_{ij} will become non-assignable. Once an operation $O_{i'j'}$ is completed after time x, the *status* of operation $O_{i'(j'+1)}$ and the operations requiring machine $M_{i'j'}$ will probably change from non-assignable to assignable. In addition, the *work remaining* of all operations is reduced by x.

Action. We mask the non-assignable operations to narrow down the choices of the agents, so the action a_t is one of the assignable operations. An operation is assignable only if its precursor operation $O_{i(j-1)}$ is completed and the required machine M_{ij} is idle. At each decision step, all non-assignable operations are masked.

Reward. Since makespan can only be obtained after all operations are completed, so we use expected makespan $\hat{C}_{\max}^t$ as a temporary alternative to makespan $C_{\max}$. Define the expected completion time of operation O_{ij} as follows,

$$\hat{C}_{ij}^t = \begin{cases} C_{ij}, & \text{if } O_{ij} \text{ is scheduled at decision step } t \\ \hat{C}_{i(j-1)}^t + P_{ij}, & \text{other} \end{cases} \tag{1}$$

Based on $\hat{C}_{ij}^t$, define the expected makespan decision step t as $\hat{C}_{\max}^t = \max_{i,j} \hat{C}_{ij}^t$. Define the reward function as the expected makespan difference as follows,

$$R(s_t, a_t) = \hat{C}_{\max}^t - \hat{C}_{\max}^{t+1}. \tag{2}$$

The calculation of the expected makespan assumes that the adjacent operations are always seamless, but the real situation is that the adjacent operations cannot always be processed seamlessly, so the expected makespan is a lower bound of the makespan, i.e., $\hat{C}_{\max}^t \leq C_{\max}$. After each selection of an action a_t, it is an approximation to the real situation, therefore $\hat{C}_{\max}^t \leq \hat{C}_{\max}^{t+1}$, and $R(s_t, a_t) \leq 0$. When all operations are completed, there are $\hat{C}_{\max}^t = C_{\max}$. Note that maximizing the cumulative reward implies minimizing the makespan.

Policy. A policy network $\pi_{\theta_p}(a_t|s_t)$ will calculate the priority of each operation and select the operation based on the priority, where θ_p is the actor network parameter.

3.2   Attention Model

The proposed attention model, composed of an encoder and a decoder, can handle instances of arbitrary size, as shown in Fig. 2. At each decision step, the encoder produces the operation embeddings, and the decoder computes a probability vector to select an operation. The decision process is iteratively repeated until all the operations are scheduled.

Encoder. The encoder consists of a feed-forward (FF) layer and a l self-attention layers [21]. The FF layer increases the dimensionality of the feature vector before the self-attention layers, which helps to increase the expressiveness of the network. Then the self-attention layers analyze the important operations by calculating attention weights. Since assignable operations are unordered, it is not necessary to use positional encoding. Finally, the encoder obtains the embedding $h_{ij} \in \mathbb{R}^d$ as follows,

$$h_{\mathcal{J}} = \text{AM}_{\theta_a}(\text{FF}_{\theta_e}(f_{\mathcal{J}})), \tag{3}$$

where $f_{\mathcal{J}} = (f_{11}, f_{12}, \ldots, f_{nm})$ and $h_{\mathcal{J}} = (h_{11}, h_{12}, \ldots, h_{nm})$. θ_e and θ_a are the network parameters of FF layer and self-attention layers, respectively.

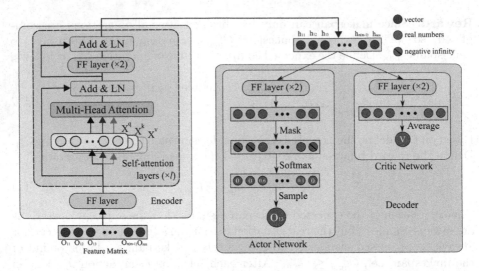

Fig. 2. The architecture of the attention model.

Self-Attention. The self-attention layer is mainly composed of multi-head attention, FF layers, layer normalization (LN), and residual connections (Add). For the input feature matrix $X = (x_1, x_2, \ldots, x_n) \in \mathbb{R}^{n \times d}$, the query vector x_i^q, key vector x_i^k and value vector x_i^v of each feature vector x_i are first computed separately using three linear projections $W^q, W^k, W^v \in \mathbb{R}^{d \times d}$. Then the query matrix $X^q = (x_1^q, x_2^q, \ldots, x_n^q) \in \mathbb{R}^{n \times d}$ with the transpose of key matrix $(X^q)^T = (x_1^q, x_2^q, \ldots, x_n^q)^T \in \mathbb{R}^{d \times n}$ are matrix multiplied and divided by $\sqrt{d}$, and then input to softmax to get the attention weight $X^a \in \mathbb{R}^{n \times n}$. Finally, the attention weight X^a is matrix multiplied with the value matrix $X^q = (x_1^v, x_2^v, \ldots, x_n^v) \in \mathbb{R}^{n \times d}$. On this basis, the multi-head attention is calculated as follows,

$$\text{MultiHead}(X) = \text{Concat}(head_1, head_2, \ldots, head_H),$$
$$\text{where } head_i = \text{softmax}\left(\frac{(X \cdot W_i^q) \cdot (X \cdot W_i^k)^T}{\sqrt{d}}\right) \cdot (X \cdot W_i^v). \tag{4}$$

After multi-head attention, the embeddings are successively computed by Add & LN, FF, and Add & LN layers.

Decoder. The decoder consists of a actor network $\pi_{\theta_p}(h_{\mathcal{J}})$ and a critic network $v_{\theta_v}(h_{\mathcal{J}})$. The actor network consists of two FF layers and a *softmax* activation layer. The actor network uses $h_{ij} \in \mathbb{R}^d$ to calculate the priority $p_{ij} \in \mathbb{R}$ of O_{ij}. When calculating the priority of each operation, the non-assignable operations are masked, and the *softmax* activation layer converts the priority to the corresponding probability. In this way, the selection probabilities of all assignable operations are obtained. The critic network also consists of two FF layers that use h_{ij} to calculate the value of the corresponding operation $v_{ij} \in \mathbb{R}$, and the value of the current state $\bar{v} = \frac{1}{n \times m} \sum_{i,j}^{n,m} v_{ij}$. Finally, the calculation of the actor network and the critic network can be defined as follows,

$$\pi_{\theta_p}(h_{\mathcal{J}}) = \text{softmax}(\text{mask}(\text{FF}_{\theta_p^2}(\text{FF}_{\theta_p^1}(h_{\mathcal{J}})))), \tag{5}$$

$$v_{\theta_v}(h_{\mathcal{J}}) = \text{average}(\text{FF}_{\theta_v^2}(\text{FF}_{\theta_v^1}(h_{\mathcal{J}}))). \tag{6}$$

3.3 Training Algorithm

We use proximal policy optimization (PPO) [22] to train the network. The pseudo-code of PPO for JSP is shown in Algorithm 1. In the training phase, we use softmax to convert the priority into a probability distribution and sample the operations to be assigned. In the test phase, we remove the softmax layer and greedily select the operation with the highest priority for scheduling.

Algorithm 1. The PPO-based training method

1: Initialize $Buffer$ with batch size B
2: Initialize PPO network with random weights $\theta = \theta_a, \theta_p, \theta_v$
3: Initialize old PPO network with weights $\theta_{old} = \theta$
4: **for** episode = 1, 2, ... **do**
5:     Reset JSP environment with the size $n \times m$
6:     Get the JSP environment initial state s_0
7:     **for** t=0, 1, 2, ... **do**
8:         Sample action a_t from policy $\pi_{\theta_p}(a|s_t)$
9:         Get reward r_t and next state s_{t+1} from environment for action a_t
10:        Store (s_t, a_t, r_t) to $Buffer$
11:        **if** length of buffer $\geq B$ **then**
12:            Sync old model $\theta_{old} = \theta$
13:            **for** iteration=1, 2, ..., K **do**
14:                Compute advantage estimates $\hat{A}_t$ with discount factor γ
15:                Compute the loss L of PPO-Clip objective with prune ϵ
16:                Perform a gradient descent step with respect to the parameter θ
17:            **end for**
18:            Clear the buffer
19:        **end if**
20:        Go to next step $s_t = s_{t+1}, t = t + 1$
21:    **end for**
22: **end for**

---

4   Experiments

4.1   Experiment Setup

The experiments are all conducted on an NVIDIA GeForce GTX 1080 Ti GPU. The optimizer is Adam [23], with a learning rate of 0.0001 initially and decaying to 0.9 of the current learning rate every 400 episodes. The hyperparameters required for the PPO algorithm are shown in Table 1. In the encoder, d is equal to 32, l is equal to 3, the hidden layer dimension is 32, and the head number of multi-head attention is set to 4. In the decoder, the input dimension is $d = 32$, the hidden layer dimension is $d/2 = 16$, and the output dimension is 1.

In the training phase, random instances with a specific size are generated on the fly, e.g., PPO10×5 indicates that the agent is trained only on 10×5 generated instances. Each generated instance complies with the Taillard specification[1] The processing times of each operation in the generated instances satisfy a uniform distribution $P_{ij} \sim U(5, 20)$ and the processing machines are randomly arranged. In the training phase, we sample the actions from the distribution, while in the testing phase, we greedily select the operation with maximum priority p_{ij}. We test both on generated instances and on the well-known public benchmark OR-Library [24].

The state-of-the-art DRL method proposed by Zhang et al. [9] and traditional PDRs are chosen as baselines. These PDRs include FIFO (first in first out) where the first operation to arrive has the highest priority, LOR (least operation remaining) where the job with the least remaining operations has the highest priority, SPT (shortest processing time) where the operation with the shortest processing time has the highest priority, STPT (shortest total processing time) where the job with the shortest total processing time has the highest priority, and LWKR (least work remaining) where the job with the longest remaining processing time has the highest priority.

Table 1. Hyperparameters for PPO.

Hyperparameters	Value
training episodes	1000
discount factor γ	0.99
batch size B	32
prune ϵ	0.2
update steps K	20

4.2   Results on Generated Instances

We train on generated instances at the sizes of 10×5, 10×10, 20×10, and 20×20. We then test them on 100 randomly generated instances of each size. The results are shown in Table 2. PPO 20×10 achieves a lower makespan for all test sizes. This shows that the model trained on the size 20×10 is far more powerful.

---

[1] http://jobshop.jjvh.nl/explanation.php#taillard_def.

Table 2. Average makespan on generated instance.

Size	PPO10 × 5	PPO10 × 10	PPO20 × 10	PPO20 × 20
10 × 5	166.03	163.18	**159.07**	167.98
10 × 10	229.21	229.73	**221.72**	242.83
20 × 10	346.45	349.42	**336.34**	374.3
20 × 20	475.87	466.54	**454.56**	510.98
50 × 10	712.82	719.35	**688.59**	751.99

We believe that the learning difficulty is not consistent with different sizes. This is impacted by many factors, such as the amount of data and the length of episodes. The combined effect of these factors overlaps, resulting in easier training for good models at certain scales. In our experiments, 20 × 10 is the most suitable size for training, and the knowledge learned by the agent can be generalized to the instances of other scales.

Table 3. Average makespan on generated instance.

Size	FIFO	LOR	SPT	STPT	LWKR	PPO
10 × 5	162.98	184.72	170.01	178.67	184.5	**159.07**
10 × 10	227.3	254.41	229.64	253.29	252.62	**221.72**
20 × 10	340.1	392.92	348.53	388.36	392.54	**336.34**
20 × 20	462.85	526.38	475.15	530.53	534.41	**454.56**
50 × 10	693.84	794.17	724.16	771.13	799.35	**688.59**

We also compare our method (PPO 20 × 10) with other baselines on generated instances for each scale. The results are shown in Table 3. We can find that the proposed method consistently outperforms the baseline PDRs on all sizes. This result shows that our method is able to extract knowledge and works well on smaller or larger sizes. Our method can achieve better results than manual designed PDRs, which demonstrates that our method can automatically use more effective problem characteristics.

4.3   Results on Benchmark Instances

We then test them on the public well-known Taillard 's benchmark [25] which contains 8 sizes and 10 instances per size. The experimental results are shown in Table 4 and Table 5. TA 15 × 15 indicates the 15 × 15 instances in Taillard's benchmark. LB is the currently available lower bound[2].

---

[2] http://jobshop.jjvh.nl/index.php.

Table 4. Average makespan and the gap with LB on Taillard's benchmark.

Instances		PPO10×5	PPO10×10	PPO20×10	PPO20×20	LB
TA 15×15	makespan	1529.6	1569.5	**1514.4**	1687	1228.9
	gap	24.5%	27.7%	**23.2%**	37.3%	-
TA 20×15	makespan	1830.5	1815	**1689.2**	1950	1362.9
	gap	34.3%	33.2%	**23.9%**	43.1%	-
TA 20×20	makespan	2190.3	2166.5	**1978.3**	2271.8	1586.1
	gap	38.1%	36.6%	**24.7%**	43.2%	-
TA 30×15	makespan	2386	2410.2	**2275.5**	2499.5	1787
	gap	33.5%	34.9%	**27.3%**	39.9%	-
TA 30×20	makespan	2622.3	2650.4	**2538**	2845	1898.4
	gap	38.1%	39.6%	**33.7%**	49.9%	-
TA 50×15	makespan	**3290.4**	3400.1	3316.3	3624.6	2773.8
	gap	**18.6%**	22.6%	19.6%	30.7%	-
TA 50×20	makespan	3571.5	3660.5	**3494**	3950.9	2843.9
	gap	25.6%	28.7%	**22.9%**	38.9%	-
TA 100×20	makespan	**5976.1**	6173.1	6056.8	6546.8	5365.7
	gap	**11.4%**	15.0%	12.9%	22.0%	-

Table 5. Average makespan and the gap with LB on Taillard's benchmark.

Instances		FIFO	LOR	SPT	STPT	LWKR	Zhang et al. [9]	PPO	LB
TA 15 × 15	makespan	1522.8	1732.8	1546.1	1735	1814.7	1547.4	**1514.4**	1228.9
	gap	23.9%	41.0%	25.8%	41.2%	47.7%	25.9%	**23.2%**	-
TA 20 × 15	makespan	1793.3	2067.8	1813.5	1958.4	2007.2	1774.7	**1689.2**	1362.9
	gap	31.6%	51.7%	33.1%	43.7%	47.3%	30.2%	**23.9%**	-
TA 20 × 20	makespan	2059.9	2269.6	2067	2416.8	2388.3	2128.1	**1978.3**	1586.1
	gap	29.9%	43.1%	30.3%	52.4%	50.6%	34.2%	**24.7%**	-
TA 30 × 15	makespan	2347.7	2781.3	2419.3	2684.5	2679.3	2378.8	**2275.5**	1787
	gap	31.4%	55.6%	35.4%	50.2%	49.9%	33.1%	**27.3%**	-
TA 30 × 20	makespan	2553.5	3056.2	2619.1	3016.6	3098.9	2603.9	**2538**	1898.4
	gap	34.5%	61.0%	38.0%	58.9%	63.2%	37.2%	**33.7%**	-
TA 50 × 15	makespan	3346.4	3761.1	3441	3729.3	3838.7	3393.8	**3316.3**	2773.8
	gap	20.6%	35.6%	24.1%	34.4%	38.4%	22.4%	**19.6%**	-
TA 50 × 20	makespan	3525	4081.5	3570.8	3987.4	4167	3593.9	**3494**	2843.9
	gap	23.9%	43.5%	25.6%	40.2%	46.5%	26.4%	**22.9%**	-
TA 100 × 20	makespan	6095	6986.8	6139	6718.2	6916.1	6097.6	**6056.8**	5365.7
	gap	13.6%	30.2%	14.4%	25.2%	28.9%	13.6%	**12.9%**	-

In Table 4, PPO 20 × 10 also has the best overall performance, achieving the best results in almost all instances. The comparisons among our method (PPO 20 × 10), the state-of-the-art DRL method, and conventional PDRs are shown in Table 5. Even on the public benchmark with the unseen distribution, our method still achieves better performance than PDRs and the state-of-the-art DRL method. This fully illustrates the strong generalization capability of our method, which is important in practice.

5   Conclusion

In this paper, we propose a DRL method with an attention model to solve JSP. We formulate JSP as MDP and design an attention model to extract valid information from the states. Our method outperforms conventional PDRs and the state-of-the-art DRL method. Besides, our proposed model also has good generalization ability across various problem sizes.

In the future, we will propose better deep models and training algorithms for larger-scale problems. In addition, our proposed method can be extended to scheduling problems with more complex and practical constraints.

References

1. Wang, H., et al.: Adaptive scheduling for assembly job shop with uncertain assembly times based on dual q-learning. Int. J. Prod. Res. **59**(19), 5867–5883 (2021)
2. Hubbs, C.D., et al.: A deep reinforcement learning approach for chemical production scheduling. Comput. Chem. Eng. **141**, 106982 (2020)
3. Gupta, A.K., Sivakumar, A.I.: Job shop scheduling techniques in semiconductor manufacturing. Int. J. Adv. Manuf. Technol. **27**(11), 1163–1169 (2006)
4. Garey, M.R., Johnson, D.S., Sethi, R.: The complexity of flowshop and jobshop scheduling. Math. Oper. Res. **1**(2), 117–129 (1976)
5. Manne, A.S.: On the job-shop scheduling problem. Oper. Res. **8**(2), 219–223 (1960)
6. Gonçalves, J.F., Magalhães Mendes, J.J., Resende, M.G.: A hybrid genetic algorithm for the job shop scheduling problem. Eur. J. Oper. Res. **167**(1), 77–95 (2005)
7. Haupt, R.: A survey of priority rule-based scheduling. Oper. Res. Spektrum **11**(1), 3–16 (1989)
8. Hameed, M.S.A., Schwung, A.: Reinforcement learning on job shop scheduling problems using graph networks. arXiv preprint arXiv:2009.03836 (2020)
9. Zhang, C., et al.: Learning to dispatch for job shop scheduling via deep reinforcement learning. In: Advances in Neural Information Processing Systems, vol. 33, pp. 1621–1632 (2020)
10. Park, J., et al.: Learning to schedule job-shop problems: representation and policy learning using graph neural network and reinforcement learning. Int. J. Prod. Res. **59**(11), 3360–3377 (2021)
11. Liao, Z., et al.: Learning to schedule job-shop problems via hierarchical reinforcement learning. In: In 2022 IEEE International Conference on Systems, Man, and Cybernetics (SMC), pp. 3222–3227. IEEE (2022)
12. Zhao, L., et al.: An end-to-end deep reinforcement learning approach for job shop scheduling. In: 2022 IEEE 25th International Conference on Computer Supported Cooperative Work in Design (CSCWD), pp. 841–846, 2022. https://doi.org/10.1109/CSCWD54268.2022.9776116

13. Yang, S.: Using attention mechanism to solve job shop scheduling problem. In: 2022 2nd International Conference on Consumer Electronics and Computer Engineering (ICCECE), pp. 59–62, 2022. https://doi.org/10.1109/ICCECE54139.2022.9712705

14. Chen, R., Li, W., Yang, H.: A deep reinforcement learning framework based on an attention mechanism and disjunctive graph embedding for the job-shop scheduling problem. IEEE Trans. Ind. Inform. **19**(2), 1322–1331 (2023). https://doi.org/10.1109/TII.2022.3167380

15. Waschneck, B., et al.: Deep reinforcement learning for semiconductor production scheduling. In: 2018 29th annual SEMI Advanced Semiconductor Manufacturing Conference (ASMC), pp. 301–306. IEEE (2018)

16. Cao, Z., et al.: Scheduling semiconductor testing facility by using cuckoo search algorithm with reinforcement learning and surrogate modeling. IEEE Trans. Autom. Sci. Eng. **16**(2), 825–837 (2018)

17. Kuhnle, A., Röhrig, N., Lanza, G.: Autonomous order dispatching in the semiconductor industry using reinforcement learning. Procedia CIRP **79**, 391–396 (2019)

18. Kuhnle, A., et al.: Designing an adaptive production control system using reinforcement learning. J. Intell. Manuf. **32**(3), 855–876 (2021)

19. Zhang, C., et al.: Dynamic dispatching for large-scale heterogeneous fleet via multi-agent deep reinforcement learning. In: 2020 IEEE International Conference on Big Data (Big Data), pp. 1436–1441. IEEE (2020)

20. Li, J., et al.: Solving open shop scheduling problem via graph attention neural network. In: 2020 IEEE 32nd International Conference on Tools with Artificial Intelligence (ICTAI), pp. 277–284. IEEE (2020)

21. Vaswani, A., et al.: Attention is all you need. In: Advances in Neural Information Processing Systems, vol. 30 (2017)

22. Schulman, J., et al.: Proximal policy optimization algorithms. arXiv preprint arXiv:1707.06347 (2017)

23. Kingma, D.P., Ba, J.: Adam: a method for stochastic optimization. arXiv preprint arXiv:1412.6980 (2014)

24. Beasley, J.E.: Or-library: distributing test problems by electronic mail. J. Oper. Res. Soc. **41**(11), 1069–1072 (1990)

25. Taillard, E.: Benchmarks for basic scheduling problems. Eur. J. Oper. Res. **64**(2), 278–285 (1993)

Prediction

Time Series Forecasting Model Based on Domain Adaptation and Shared Attention

Yuan Li[1,2], Jingwei Li[1,2], Chengbao Liu[1,2], and Jie Tan[1,2(✉)]

[1] Institute of Automation, Chinese Academy of Sciences, Beijing 100190, China
tan.jie@tom.com
[2] School of Artificial Intelligence, University of Chinese Academy of Sciences,
Beijing 100049, China

Abstract. Time series forecasting is an essential problem involving many fields. Recently, with the development of big data technology, deep learning methods have been widely studied and achieved promising performance in time series forecasting tasks. But there is a limited number of time series or observations per time series. In this case, a time series forecasting model, which is based on domain adaptation and shared attention (DA-SA), is proposed in this study. First, we employ Transformer architecture as the basic framework of our model. Then, we specially design a selectively shared attention module to transfer valuable information from the data-rich domain to the data-poor domain by inducing domain-invariant latent features (queries and keys) and retraining domain-specific features (values). Besides, convolutional neural network is introduced to incorporate local context into the self-attention mechanism and captures the short-term dependencies of data. Finally, adversarial training is utilized to enhance the robustness of the model and improve prediction accuracy. The practicality and effectiveness of DA-SA for time series forecasting are verified on real-world datasets.

Keywords: Time series forecasting · Domain adaptation · Shared attention · Adversarial training

1 Introduction

Time series forecasting is essential in many fields, such as industry, energy consumption estimation, and electric load forecasting. It has a wide range of application values in our daily life and industrial production. For example, we can make proper delivery and distribution plans for the microgrid can improve energy efficiency. In addition, predicting the operating status of equipment during production can avoid accidents.

Supported by the National Nature Science Foundation of China under Grant 62003344 and the National Key Research and Development Program of China under Grant 2022YFB3304602.

Over the years, many studies have been conducted to build reliable and accurate time series forecasting models. Traditional methods, such as autoregressive (AR) [1], AutoRegressive Integrated Moving Average (ARIMA) [7], and exponential smoothing, work well when the time series is stationary or has a systematic trend or seasonality. For complex systems, machine learning methods can better fit the data at each moment and achieve better prediction performance. But for modern large-scale systems, they are undesirable, partly because they do not capture the deep internal characteristics of the data well.

In recent years, similar to other fields with forecasting tasks, time series forecasting tasks have benefited from the development of deep neural networks, including convolutional neural network (CNN) and recurrent neural network (RNN), showing encouraging signs on more complex large-scale systems [11,16,18,21,24]. However, these CNN-based and RNN-based methods suffer from limitations in learning long-term dependencies on the data. For real-world applications, it is significant to make long-sequence time-series forecasting. In particular, Transformer-based methods show promising performance on these tasks [9,22,23,25]. This attention mechanism of the Transformer can directly attend to any significant events that occur despite the distance, which helps to capture the long-term repeating patterns.

Although these deep learning models are good at capturing complex temporal dynamics and features from large amounts of historical data, the data in real systems are limited and noisy [3,4,10]. As a result, collecting enough valuable data for training a reliable prediction model is difficult and unrealistic. Fortunately, transfer learning provides a promising way to solve this problem and is considered a cut-in point to improve the prediction performance of deep models [19]. Introducing information from another related dataset (called source domain) can help the current task (target domain) make predictions. However, directly generalizing a deep neural network trained on one specific domain to another does not perform well due to the difference in data distribution between the two domains.

Domain adaptation (DA) techniques show promising capabilities to mitigate the harmful effect of domain shift by aligning features extracted across source and target domains [6,13,14]. Currently, domain adaptation methods have been designed for image data, and minimal work has focused on adaptation approaches for time series data, which may be because prediction is usually more complex than classification [12]. The classifiers in these methods utilize the source domain data to learn domain-invariant features and complete the mapping between labels in the latent space [5,20]. Therefore, the classifier can learn the cross-domain common information between domains and be applied to the target domain.

There are two challenges in current Transformer-based methods for time series forecasting. First, due to the characteristics of time series data, the evolution pattern of time series data includes periodicity and locality. Current Transformer-based methods can capture the long-term dependence between data but are insensitive to the local context. Second, extracting domain-invariant information through domain adaptation from time-series data is still challenging. Because most domain adaptation methods are designed for image classification tasks, the output space in prediction tasks is generally not fixed across domains. As a result, the output values are heavily dependent on specific domains. Therefore, we must develop better models to capture long-term and short-term dependencies and design better domain adaptive methods for time series prediction models.

To tackle the challenges mentioned above, we propose a time series forecasting model based on domain adaptation and shared attention (DA-SA). First, we introduce a domain adaptation strategy to learn domain-invariant information from other related datasets and design a shared attention module. This module extracts domain-invariant and domain-specific features and then combines them into prediction to model domain-related attributes, to adequately approximate the respective domains' data distribution. Then, we employ convolution operation to the Transformer model to better learn the short-term dependencies of time series data, which solves the problem that the Transformer model is insensitive to the local context. Finally, we employ adversarial training on the model to help better capture the long-term dependencies of time series. By adding a discriminator to model the data distribution, we learn a better representation of data and improve the prediction accuracy from the global perspective. The main contributions of our paper are as follows:

1. We propose a novel time series forecasting method based on domain adaptation and shared attention (DA-SA). Our work provides an end-to-end framework for multilevel prediction tasks and improves accuracy and computational efficiency compared to prior work. Experiments on real-world datasets show the effectiveness of our model.
2. We design a shared attention module as the domain adaptation strategy, which correctly selects domain-invariant and domain-specific features to make multi-horizon forecasts for source and target domains, effectively enhancing the datasets.
3. We add a convolution operation before the attention block. By using causal convolutions to produce queries and keys, the model becomes more aware of local context information and improves its prediction accuracy.
4. We employ adversarial training to shape the distribution of the output by back-propagation. Ablation studies show the discriminator of model can make better performance than other potential variants.

2   Methodology

2.1   Problem Definition

In this paper, we focus on the time series prediction problem. Only a few data are available, but enough data can be provided from other relevant sources. In this time series forecasting problem, given T past observations and all future input covariates, we aim to make τ multi-horizon future predictions at time T through model F:

$$z_{i,T+1}, \ldots, z_{i,T+\tau} = F\left(z_{i,1}, \ldots, z_{i,T}; \xi_{i,1}, \ldots, \xi_{i,T+\tau}\right) \tag{1}$$

In this section, we elaborate on the overall architecture of the time series forecasting method based on domain adaptation and shared attention (DA-SA). Figure 1 illustrates an overview of the proposed architecture.

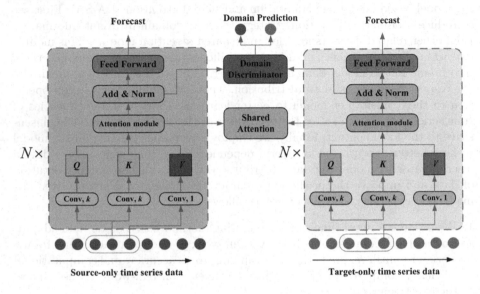

Fig. 1. An architectural overview of DA-SA.

The main composition of our proposed method is the encoder-only Transformer model. DA-SA consists of two novel blocks: the shared attention module and the domain discriminator. Both domains share the shared attention module for adaptation. The domain discriminator is used for adversarial training to improve forecasting performance from a global perspective.

2.2 Shared Attention

The shared attention module is designed to transfer knowledge captured from a source domain with sufficient data to the target domain with unlabeled or insufficiently labeled data for prediction tasks. Considering the characteristic of time series forecasting tasks, this method keeps the encoder blocks privately owned by the respective domain and shares domain-invariant features by shared attention module. We introduce the convolution layer before the attention module to take advantage of CNN's good at acquiring local dependencies from data.

CNNs are traditionally designed for image recognition and are good at catching local dependencies from data. Therefore, we introduce the idea of convolution into our proposed model. The bottom of Fig. 1 shows a diagram of this block. The implementation details are: First, we feed the time series data into a causal convolutional layer, which turns it into queries (**Q**) and keys (**K**). Then the generated domain-invariant queries (**Q**) and keys (**K**) are fed into the shared attention module.

In detail, we then project **Q** and **K** into d-dimensional vector via a position-wise MLP:

$$(\mathbf{q}_t, \mathbf{k}_t) = \text{MLP}\left(\mathbf{Q}, \mathbf{K}; \boldsymbol{\theta}_s\right). \tag{2}$$

As a result, an attention score $\aleph$ is computed after the normalized alignment through a positive semi-definite kernel function $\mathcal{K}(\cdot, \cdot)$:

$$\alpha\left(\mathbf{q}_t, \mathbf{k}_{t'}\right) = \frac{\mathcal{K}\left(\mathbf{q}_t, \mathbf{k}_{t'}\right)}{\sum_{t' \in \mathcal{N}(t)} \mathcal{K}\left(\mathbf{q}_t, \mathbf{k}_{t'}\right)}. \tag{3}$$

2.3 Adversarial Training

In order to solve the time series forecasting problem studied in this paper, this paper casts the problem in terms of finding a suitable forecasting model F on a data space time series datasets. In this domain adaptation problem, we have sample-rich source data $\mathcal{D}_S$ and sample-limited target data $\mathcal{D}_T$. We aim at making a more accurate predicting results on the target domain T. Inspired by the idea of GAN, we use adversarial training to improve the forecasting performance from a global perspective.

Our method aims to maximize the probability of assigning the correct label to both ground truth and prediction values. The loss of the neural network is:

$$\min_{G_S, G_T} \max_D \mathcal{L}_\text{b}\left(\mathcal{D}_S; G_S\right) + \mathcal{L}_\text{b}\left(\mathcal{D}_T; G_T\right) - \lambda \mathcal{L}_\text{d}\left(\mathcal{D}_S, \mathcal{D}_T; D, G_S, G_T\right), \tag{4}$$

where G_S and G_T denote encoder-only Transformer block that estimate prediction values in each domain, respectively; D denotes a discriminator that aims to recognize which domain the sample comes from. Besides, $\mathcal{L}_\text{b}$ denotes the loss of the agent prediction network, which contains the basic cross-entropy loss and the Kullback-Leibler (KL) divergence to align the predicted distribution:

$$\mathcal{L}_\text{b}(\mathcal{D}; G) = \sum_{i=1}^{N} \left(\frac{1}{\tau} \sum_{t=T+1}^{T+\tau} l\left(z_{i,t}, \hat{z}_{i,t}\right)\right) + D_{KL}\left(Z_\text{true}(z) \parallel \hat{Z}_\text{pred}(z)\right). \tag{5}$$

The domain classification error $\mathcal{L}_\text{d}$ denotes the cross-entropy loss in the latent spaces as follows:

$$\mathcal{L}_\text{d} = -\frac{1}{N_d} \sum_{n=1}^{N_d} z_n \log\left(z_n\right) + (1 - d_n) \log(1 - \hat{z}_n). \tag{6}$$

The minimax objective Eq. 4 is optimized via adversarial training alternately. We detail the training procedure in the following Sect. 3.

3   Experiments

In this section, we evaluate our proposed method DA-SA on real-world datasets for time-series prediction and compare our approach to current state-of-the-art methods.

3.1   Datasets

The method proposed in this paper belongs to the domain adaptive method, so it needs to be compared with related methods. One of the requirements for selecting a dataset to test domain fitness is that the dataset contains an attribute for splitting the data into domains. These attributes can include different data collection days or different generation processes (e.g., different users in the case of electricity forecasting). Our chosen multivariate time series dataset contains a participant identifier, and we use this feature to segment the data into multiple domains. Thus, our adaptation problems consist of the realistic use-case adapting a model from one or more participants' data to another participant's data.

Air Quality Prediction Dataset[1]. The air quality prediction dataset contains air quality data, meteorological data, weather forecast data, etc. This dataset covers 4 major cities in China: Beijing (B), Tianjin (T), Guangzhou (G) and Shenzhen (S). We use air quality data and weather data to predict PM2.5.

In-Hospital Mortality Prediction Dataset[2]. It contains health-related data on more than 40,000 patients admitted to the intensive care units of Israeli medical centers between 2001 and 2012. We select 12 time series (such as heart rate, temperature, systolic blood pressure, etc.) from 35637 records. In addition, we grouped patients by age to test the effect of preconditioning. (Group1: 20–45, Group2: 46–65, Group3: 66–85, Group4: >85).

3.2   Experimental Setup

Training Details. All our experiments are training and testing on a single GeForce RTX 3080 10 GB GPU. And all the methods are performed in PyTorch library [15] three times. In these experiments, all parameters of networks are updated by back-propagation with ADAM [8] optimizer. The batch size is set to 32. To comprehensively evaluate the performance of our proposed prediction method, we employ the root mean square error (RMSE) as the performance metric:

$$\text{RMSE} = \sqrt{\sum_{j=1}^{n} \frac{(\hat{y}_j - y_j)^2}{n}}, \tag{7}$$

where $\hat{y}_j$ and y_j are the prediction value and ground truth, respectively, and n represents the total time step.

---

[1] https://www.microsoft.com/en-us/research/project/urban-air/.
[2] https://mimic.physionet.org/gettingstarted/demo/.

Table 1. RMSE on air quality prediction.

$\mathcal{D}_T$	$\mathcal{D}_S$	DeepAR	Autoformer	R-DANN	SASA	Our proposed method
T	B	43.67	40.82	39.93	34.26	**33.94**
	G			40.98	33.84	**33.82**
	S			46.16	40.91	**40.20**
B	T	59.14	56.36	52.72	48.15	**46.56**
	G			55.65	54.14	**53.32**
	S			66.47	56.80	**55.72**
G	B	19.76	18.99	18.00	16.40	**16.20**
	T			18.47	15.41	**14.92**
	S			15.18	14.23	**14.10**
S	B	13.82	13.80	13.82	13.49	**13.28**
	T			13.78	13.46	**13.22**
	G			13.79	13.38	**12.95**

Table 2. RMSE on in-hospital mortality prediction.

$\mathcal{D}_T$	$\mathcal{D}_S$	DeepAR	Autoformer	R-DANN	SASA	Our proposed method
1	2	33.52	30.82	29.93	30.33	**23.75**
	3			30.86	31.84	**26.83**
	4			32.16	30.91	**29.25**
2	1	49.03	46.36	42.72	41.15	**40.56**
	3			45.65	44.14	**37.56**
	4			48.47	46.8	**35.72**
3	1	19.30	18.99	18.00	16.39	**16.27**
	2			17.67	15.41	**14.92**
	4			17.18	16.78	**15.43**
4	1	45.61	38.83	35.82	34.49	**33.28**
	2			36.78	35.46	**33.22**
	3			36.79	36.77	**32.76**

3.3 Comparison with State-of-the-Art Methods

To illustrate the effectiveness and superiority of the proposed method, it is compared with four typical time series forecasting methods, which contain single-domain and cross-domain baselines. The traditional single-domain models trained only on the target domain data include:

- **DeepAR** [18]. A methodology based on training an auto-regressive recurrent network model on a large number of related time series, which can estimate the probability distribution of results.

– **Autoformer.** Autoformer [22] is a Transformer-based method that specially designed for long sequence time-series forecasting.

The cross-domain models trained on both source and target domain include:

– **R-DANN.** R-DANN [2] is a representative of the unsupervised method. It is a straightforward solution for sequence domain adaptation.
– **SASA.** SASA [17] is a metric-based domain adaptation method, which is extended from regression task to multi-horizon time series forecasting.

We conduct multi-dimensional experiments on two representative datasets that are widely used in forecasting literature: the air quality prediction dataset and the in-hospital mortality prediction dataset. For a fair comparison, each method was performed three times and averaged as the performance evaluation results shown in Table 1 and Table 2. The best results are highlighted in boldface. From all the results of RMSE, we can draw the following conclusions.

(1) DeepAR is the most popular and effective RNN-based method for time series forecasting. However, this method performs worse than other methods in Tables due to the issue of gradient vanishing and exploding, which makes the model lack the ability to learn long-term dependencies.
(2) Autoformer is a variant of Transformer models. It performs better than DeepAR in all cases maybe due to the fact that Transformer architecture can access any part of the historical data regardless of distance. But Autoformer gets worse results than other methods with domain adaptation strategy.
(3) R-DANN is a typical representation of the domain adaptation model for sequence prediction. Therefore, directly applying DANN to time series forecasting performs better than single-domain methods. Lack of sufficient theory and careful design makes R-DANN's prediction accuracy lower than SASA's, probably because the feature extraction ability of RNN is poor than the LSTM variant.
(4) SASA is an LSTM-based method with domain adaptation strategy and sparse associative structure. It performs worse than our proposed model in all experiments, indicating that our proposed method's transfer learning works well, effectively capturing domain invariant features and transferring valuable knowledge to the new network.

Through the above analysis, the superiority of our method can be highlighted. Thanks to the powerful feature extraction and domain transfer ability, the performance of our proposed method is better than that of the other four methods.

3.4   Ablation Study

We conduct additional experiments on air quality datasets with ablation consideration to verify the validity of each component.

Table 3. RMSE results of ablation studies of DA-SA variants on three adaptation tasks on air quality prediction datasets.

$\mathcal{D}_T$	$\mathcal{D}_S$	no-share	all-share	no-adv	our proposed method
T	B	34.93	32.25	33.34	**33.94**
	G	36.98	34.21	34.25	**33.82**
	S	46.16	40.91	42.15	**40.20**
B	T	47.72	47.67	47.89	**46.56**
	G	55.65	54.36	56.74	**53.32**
	S	60.27	57.43	58.44	**55.72**
G	B	19.43	16.96	16.99	**16.20**
	T	18.47	16.47	16.32	**14.92**
	S	15.18	14.23	15.65	**14.10**
S	B	14.82	13.49	14.21	**13.28**
	T	13.78	13.36	13.45	**13.22**
	G	13.78	13.38	12.98	**12.95**

To examine the effectiveness of each module, ablation studies are performed by sequentially tuning key components. Table 3 shows the RMSE results of DA-SA over its variants on the target domain on three adaptation tasks. From the results, we noted that the sharing attention mechanism (*all-share*) in DA-SA results in performance gains over not sharing (*no-share*). Besides, our design choice of the values to be domain specific for domain-dependent forecasts rather than shared has the largest positive impact on the performance. Finally, compared with the non-adversarial variant (*no-adv*), DA-SA improves the effectiveness of domain adaptation by introducing a domain discriminator.

4   Conclusion and Future Work

This paper proposes a domain adaption based approach for time series forecasting. This method can solve the problem of data scarcity and can be adaptively used for prediction in other fields. This model identifies the difference between the prediction task and common domain adaptation scenarios and proposes a shared attention module. This module can selectively transfer valuable information from the source domain to the target domain. Our predictor combines the advantages of CNN and Transformer to capture both short-term context and long-term dependencies. Besides, by using adversarial training, we can better learn long-term repeating patterns and improve forecasting model performance from a global perspective. Experiments on real datasets demonstrate that our model outperforms state-of-the-art single-domain predictors and domain adaptation baselines. Furthermore, extensive ablation studies further demonstrate our unique design's effectiveness.

For future work, we plan to extend our work at both theoretical and applied levels. On the one hand, we need further to study related theories about domain-invariant features in attention models. On the other hand, we plan to experiment with more datasets and develop the model as a platform.

Acknowledgements. This work was supported in part by the National Nature Science Foundation of China under Grant 62003344 and the National Key Research and Development Program of China under Grant 2022YFB3304602.

References

1. Box, G.E., Jenkins, G.M., Bacon, D.W.: Models for forecasting seasonal and non-seasonal time series. Technical report, WISCONSIN UNIV MADISON DEPT OF STATISTICS (1967)
2. da Costa, P.R.D.O., Akçay, A., Zhang, Y., Kaymak, U.: Remaining useful lifetime prediction via deep domain adaptation. Reliab. Eng. Syst. Saf. **195**, 106682 (2020)
3. Guo, H., Pasunuru, R., Bansal, M.: Multi-source domain adaptation for text classification via distancenet-bandits. In: Proceedings of the AAAI Conference on Artificial Intelligence, vol. 34, pp. 7830–7838 (2020)
4. Gururangan, S., et al.: Don't stop pretraining: adapt language models to domains and tasks. arXiv preprint arXiv:2004.10964 (2020)
5. Hu, H., Tang, M.J., Bai, C.: Datsing: data augmented time series forecasting with adversarial domain adaptation. In: Proceedings of the 29th ACM International Conference on Information & Knowledge Management, pp. 2061–2064. ACM, Virtual Event Ireland (2020)
6. Hoffman, J., et al.: CyCADA: cycle-consistent adversarial domain adaptation. In: International Conference on Machine Learning, pp. 1989–1998. PMLR (2018)
7. Kalpakis, K., Gada, D., Puttagunta, V.: Distance measures for effective clustering of ARIMA time-series. In: Proceedings 2001 IEEE International Conference on Data Mining, pp. 273–280. IEEE (2001)
8. Kingma, D.P., Ba, J.: Adam: a method for stochastic optimization. arXiv preprint arXiv:1412.6980 (2014)
9. Li, S., et al.: Enhancing the locality and breaking the memory bottleneck of transformer on time series forecasting. Adv. Neural Inf. Process. Syst. **32** (2019)
10. Li, Y., Wang, H., Li, J., Tan, J.: A 2D long short-term memory fusion networks for bearing remaining useful life prediction. IEEE Sens. J. **22**, 21806–21815 (2022)
11. Lim, B., Zohren, S., Roberts, S.: Recurrent neural filters: learning independent Bayesian filtering steps for time series prediction. In: 2020 International Joint Conference on Neural Networks (IJCNN), pp. 1–8. IEEE (2020)
12. Wang, M., Deng, W.: Deep visual domain adaptation: a survey. Neurocomputing **312**, 135–153 (2018)
13. Long, M., Cao, Z., Wang, J., Jordan, M.I.: Conditional adversarial domain adaptation. In: Advances in Neural Information Processing Systems, vol. 31. Curran Associates, Inc. (2018)
14. Motiian, S., Jones, Q., Iranmanesh, S., Doretto, G.: Few-shot adversarial domain adaptation. Adv. Neural Inf. Process. Syst. **30** (2017)
15. Paszke, A., et al.: PyTorch: an imperative style, high-performance deep learning library. Adv. Neural Inf. Process. Syst. **32** (2019)

16. Rangapuram, S.S., Seeger, M.W., Gasthaus, J., Stella, L., Wang, Y., Januschowski, T.: Deep state space models for time series forecasting. Adv. Neural. Inf. Process. Syst. **31**, 7785–7794 (2018)
17. Cai, R., et al.: Time series domain adaptation via sparse associative structure alignment. In: Proceedings of the AAAI Conference on Artificial Intelligence, vol. 35, no. 8, pp. 6859–6867 (2021)
18. Salinas, D., Flunkert, V., Gasthaus, J., Januschowski, T.: DeepAR: probabilistic forecasting with autoregressive recurrent networks. Int. J. Forecast. **36**(3), 1181–1191 (2020)
19. Wang, H., Bai, X., Tan, J., Yang, J.: Deep prototypical networks based domain adaptation for fault diagnosis. J. Intell. Manuf. **33**(4), 973–983 (2020). https://doi.org/10.1007/s10845-020-01709-4
20. Wang, H., Bai, X., Wang, S., Tan, J., Liu, C.: Generalization on unseen domains via model-agnostic learning for intelligent fault diagnosis. IEEE Trans. Instrum. Meas. **71**, 1–11 (2022)
21. Wang, Y., Smola, A., Maddix, D., Gasthaus, J., Foster, D., Januschowski, T.: Deep factors for forecasting. In: International Conference on Machine Learning, pp. 6607–6617. PMLR (2019)
22. Wu, H., Xu, J., Wang, J., Long, M.: AutoFormer: decomposition transformers with auto-correlation for long-term series forecasting. Adv. Neural. Inf. Process. Syst. **34**, 22419–22430 (2021)
23. Wu, S., Xiao, X., Ding, Q., Zhao, P., Wei, Y., Huang, J.: Adversarial sparse transformer for time series forecasting. Adv. Neural. Inf. Process. Syst. **33**, 17105–17115 (2020)
24. Young, T., Hazarika, D., Poria, S., Cambria, E.: Recent trends in deep learning based natural language processing. IEEE Comput. Intell. Mag. **13**(3), 55–75 (2018)
25. Zhou, H., et al.: Informer: beyond efficient transformer for long sequence time-series forecasting. In: Proceedings of the AAAI Conference on Artificial Intelligence, vol. 35, pp. 11106–11115 (2021)

TSPRocket: A Fast and Efficient Method for Predicting Astronomical Seeing

Cheng-Qin Zhang and Wei-Jian Ni(✉) [ID]

College of Computer Science and Engineering, Shandong University of Science and Technology, Qingdao 266510, China
`niwj@foxmail.com`

Abstract. When using large optical telescopes, astronomical seeing prediction is an essential and challenging work. It can provide observation tips for optical telescopes and help astronomical observers to arrange observation tasks reasonably. The traditional method of seeing prediction mainly uses meteorological models to capture atmospheric turbulence patterns and then implement seeing prediction through data analysis. In recent years, data-driven methods have made good progress in seeing prediction research. This paper proposes a new data-driven seeing prediction method called TSPRocket (**T**ime **S**eries **P**rediction **R**and**O**m **C**onvolutional **KE**rnel **T**ransform), which uses a large number of convolution kernels to transform time series data, and then the transformed features are used to train a simple linear predictor. Because there is no need to calculate gradient when performing convolution calculation, TSPRocket is much more efficient than existing methods. In order to facilitate the research, we collected the observation data of a large astronomical telescope, and then carried out necessary data preprocessing. The experimental results show that our TSPRocket has higher accuracy and speed than baseline models.

Keywords: TSPRocket · Seeing prediction · Astronomical telescope · Time series prediction · Convolution

1 Introduction

Improving the observation quality of optical telescopes has always been the most concerned issue of astronomers and observers. Astronomical seeing is one of the indicators to quantify the clarity of the image displayed by optical telescopes. Accurate and fast seeing prediction can help experts better adjust the optical telescope to collect higher-quality observation data. This paper provides a new data-driven seeing prediction method, using a non-training convolution architecture to transform seeing data, and feeding the transformed features to a simple linear predictor.

The work is supported by Shandong Provincial Natural Science Foundation (No. ZR2022MF319), National Natural Science Foundation of China (No. U1931207), and the Taishan Scholars Program of Shandong Province (TS20190936).

Modern optical telescopes pursue larger apertures to obtain higher image sensitivity and resolution [25]. However, when the aperture of the mirror is large enough to exceed the coherence length of the atmosphere, the turbulence in the atmosphere, such as rolling clouds and smoke from the chimney, can easily affect the observation range and final resolution of the telescope [5].

Astronomical seeing is an important parameter to describe the image clarity of the telescope display, which mainly depends on the degree of atmospheric turbulence phenomenon. Astronomical seeing prediction uses historical seeing data and historical meteorological data to predict future seeing. Accurate seeing prediction can help astronomers plan observation periods and improve the performance of adaptive optical systems [1]. In this study, the seeing prediction task can be formulated as a multiple time series prediction task. Because of the complexity of feature engineering of multivariate sequences, deep learning has been the dominant technique for time series prediction. However, deep learning models tend to have higher computational complexity despite of improved accuracy.

Rocket (RandOm Convolutional KErnel Transform) is newly proposed time series classification method. It uses a large number of random convolution kernels to transform the time series and then uses the transformed features to train a simple linear classifier. Rocket can achieve the most advanced classification accuracy and is much faster than most existing time series classification methods because it does not need to calculate the gradient during the convolution calculation [8]. Inspired by Rocket, we propose a new efficient time series prediction called TSPRocket. In the convolution transformation part, we design new convolution mechanism and use the pooling operator with local positive value proportion to capture the sequential relationship in the time series. In addition, the smoothing of the sequence will be beneficial to the prediction of astronomical seeing, so we also made an additional transformation of the first-order difference of the original sequence. Because there are a large number of temperature features of the same type in the seeing data, such as the temperature data captured by a temperature sensor with uniform distribution under a large mirror, we performed a grouping feature difference operation on the temperature data before used for convolution transformations. In the model training part, a LightGBM regression model is trained with these transformed features.

This study's contributions can be summarized as follows:

- A new time series prediction method called TSPRocket is proposed, which is faster and more accurate than traditional time series prediction models on the astronomical seeing prediction task;
- A new causal convolution mechanism including variable stride convolution is proposed. It can help TSPRocket capture long-term and short-term correlations in time series;
- The feasibility and advantages of TSPRocket in astronomical seeing prediction are studied. The results show that TSPRocket can achieve the highest seeing prediction accuracy and is much faster than other methods.

2   Literature Review

2.1   Seeing Prediction

Since the late 1990s, large professional observatories such as Mauna kea Meteorological Centre and the European Southern Observatory have provided atmospheric seeing forecasting services based on numerical models from mesoscale regions and real-time satellite imagery [10]. MKWC uses the Global Forecast System (GFS) and Weather Research and Forecasting Model (WRF) [22] to predict future turbulence conditions and seeing [6]. Herve Trinquet and Jean Vernin [24] proposed a new model AXP to minimize the locally observed 1km thick difference in seeing by using meteorological quantities (P, T) at low vertical resolution, 50 m boundary layer, and 100 m free atmosphere. Giordano et al. [11] added a scheme called site learning to the existing meteorological model, focusing on the importance of using local measurements to improve the predictive turbulence model.

In recent years, many researchers have begun to use data-driven methods to study astronomical seeing prediction. Kornilov [16] used the Autoregressive Integrated Moving Average (ARIMA) model to predict atmospheric optical turbulence on the Shatdzhatmaz Mountain, which can be used to predict image features of direct astronomical observations. Milli et al. [18] used a variety of machine learning frameworks to predict optical turbulence in near real-time. Cherubini [7] proposes a novel machine learning method that first uses logistic regression classification to classify whether the night is available for observation and then predicts mean turbulence at ground level and in the free atmosphere if the weather data is available. Ni et al. [19] systematically studied the application of different architectural methods in seeing prediction. It is found that the Transformer, based on deep learning, has reached the most advanced accuracy, and the idea of combining XGBoost with a deep learning model can also achieve high accuracy.

2.2   Multivariate Time Series Analysis

Deep Learning Based Methods. This section introduces state-of-the-art time series analysis models with different architectures. Recurrent Neural Network (RNN) [12] has achieved great success in natural language processing. As a sequence-to-sequence model, it is often used in time series prediction tasks [17,21]. Due to the problem of gradient explosion and disappearance, traditional RNN variants are limited in processing long-term dependence on sequence data [4,15]. To solve this problem, Long Short-Term Memory (LSTM) [13] introduces the unit state of storing long-term information and solves the limitation of RNN's inability to extract long-term sequence dependence by improving the network's gradient flow.

Initially, Convolutional Neural Networks are mainly used for feature extraction of image data. Its advantage lies in the invariance of the extracted data's local spatial dimension and the low calculation complexity due to the convolution kernel's shared parameters. Therefore, the convolution kernel can capture many time series features, such as shape, frequency, and variance. Recently, many effective CNN-based time series classification methods, such as ResNet and Inception-Time, were proposed [12]. Researchers designed a multi-layer causal convolution such that CNN can be applied to time series prediction better [20]. Based on the multi-layer convolutional layer structure, the receptive field of each node in each convolutional layer is a window ahead of its time node, which ensures that only the past information is used in each prediction. The hollow convolution method was proposed to expand the causal convolution network's receptive field of historical information [3].

Attention-based neural networks [2] also improves the long-term dependent learning of sequence-to-sequence models. It abandons the traditional CNN and RNN structures, and the entire network structure is wholly composed of the attention mechanism. For example, Transformer has achieved the most advanced performance on sequence data. However, as the sequence grows longer, the complexity of Transformer will show a quadratic growth. In recent years, the academic community has been working on improvements of Transformer. Nikita Kitaev et al. [14] proposed Locality Sensitive Hashing Attention. The attention scores with similar keys are divided into the same bucket, the author approximated the final attention score and reduced the complexity from $O(n^2)$ to $O(nlogn)$. Haoyi Zhou et al. [26] proposed a ProbSpare self-attention mechanism to reduce the complexity of the attention module, i.e., the sparsity between query and key is measured by using Kullback-Leibler Divergence and only the dominant query is selected for calculation. The complexity drops from $O(n^2)$ to $O(nlogn)$. At the same time, the parallel generative decoder mechanism is also added to improve the reasoning speed and avoid cumulative errors.

Rocket Series. The Rocket series consists of Rocket [9], MiniRocket [9], and MultiRocket [23], designed initially for the time series classification task. The basic principle is to use large amounts of convolution kernels for dimensional transformation and then train a simple linear classifier for prediction. The Rocket series achieve state-of-the-art accuracy and speed in time series classification tasks. Rocket uses 10,000 random convolution kernels to transform the input time series (without computing the gradient) and then uses PPV (the proportion of positive value) and maximum global pooling to compute two features from each convolutional output, resulting in 20,000 features that are then used to train a linear classifier. The randomness is reflected in the length, weight, deviation, dilation, and padding of the convolution kernel. In Rocket, dilation and PPV are key to achieving state-of-the-art accuracy, and convolution transformations without calculating gradients are key to fast training. The MiniRocket ups to 75 times faster than the Rocket on large data sets. Unlike Rocket, MiniRocket uses a small fixed kernel set (with different bias and bloat combinations) and only calculates PPV features. Since MiniRocket has the same accuracy as Rocket and is faster, it is recommended as the default variant of Rocket. The MultiRocket is an improvement on the Rocket and MiniRocket. By extending the feature set generated by the transformation, the accuracy of MultiRocket is significantly improved. However, some additional computing costs are also incurred, and the speed is about ten times slower than that of MiniRocket.

3 Preliminary

3.1 Problem Definition

The astronomical seeing prediction task is formulated as a multivariate time series prediction problem, the input is obtained by using a fixed-size sliding window on the time series data. The window size is l_x, i.e., the length of each input sequence is l_x. The input is $X^t = \{x_1^t, \ldots, x_{l_x}^t \mid x_i^t \in \mathbf{R}^{d_x}, 1 \leq i \leq l_x\}$ at time t, and the output is $Y^t = \{y_1^t, \ldots, y_{l_y}^t \mid y_i^t \in \mathbf{R}^{d_y}, 1 \leq i \leq l_y\}$. In the astronomical seeing prediction task, we adopt single-step prediction from multivariate to univariate, i.e., $l_x > 1$, $d_x > 1$, $l_y = 1$, $d_y = 1$.

3.2 Dataset

The dataset used in this study is derived from monitoring data from a large optics observatory in China. The monitoring information includes the condition of the large telescope within the observatory and the local meteorological conditions. The dataset contains an illustrative data set showing the location of the large telescope mirror and the temperature sensors near the mirror, and a tabular data set of telescope monitoring data, including temperature data in the telescope, seeing data at the focal plane, local atmospheric seeing data, and meteorological information.

Position Data of the Mirror and Temperature Sensor Near the Mirror. The detector in the position description data only refers to the temperature sensor, and the collected data are all temperature data. The telescope mainly comprises mirror A, mirror B, focal plane, and buildings supporting them. There are 196 temperature monitors, which can be roughly divided into 6 groups according to the detection range. The grouping descriptions are shown in the Table 1.

Table 1. Position data of the mirror and temperature sensor near the mirror.

	Group	Sensors number	Example
1	Mirror A	24	A sensor under mirror A
2	Mirror A Building	66	A sensor under the truss of mirror A
3	Focal plane	3	A sensor under focal plane
4	Focal plane Building	17	A sensor under the truss of focal plane
5	Mirror B	35	A sensor under mirror B
6	Mirror B Building	51	A sensor under the truss of mirror B

Telescope Monitoring Data. The monitoring data spans from 2020-09-01 02:12:30 to 2020-11-05 04:38:00, with a sampling interval of 30 s, a total of 25731 samples, 207 useful features, one target value, and one timestamp record. To facilitate the study, we named this tabular data SeeingData_30s, and the fields are introduced as shown in Table 2.

Table 2. SeeingData_30s Data set field description. "[target]" indicates the target to be predicted. "(3)" indicates that there are three features of the same type, e.g., there are three atmospheric temperature values from monitors at different locations.

	Field	Range	Unit	Example
1	Timestamp	–	–	2020-09-01 02:13:00
2	Total seeing [target]	[0, 5]	Arc second	2.88
3	Site seeing	[0, 5]	Arc second	1.50
4	Air temperature (3)	[−15, 35]	$°C$	18.72
5	Relative humidity (2)	[10, 100]	–	71.42
6	Air pressure	[890, 950]	mb	909.34
7	Wind speed	[0, 20]	m/s	2.83
8	Wind direction	[0, 205]	F	121.26
9	Dew point	[0, 15]	$°C$	13.45
10	Rain probability	[0, 100]	%	0.16
11	Interior temperature (196)	[−15, 35]	$°C$	11.98

4 Methods

This section describes the details of the proposed TSPRocket architecture. The TSPRocket architecture can be divided into three parts from input to output: differential processing, convolution transformation, and downstream predictor.

4.1 Differential Processing of Monitoring Data

The original time series data SeeingDataset_30s was called as the base time series X. The temperature data T in the base time series is first processed by grouping feature difference to get the temperature difference data T' which is merged into X to get a new time series data set X'. Then, first-order difference processing of the time series X' gives a first-order difference sequence X''. The convolution kernel set is applied to the time series X' and the first difference series X''.

Grouping Feature Difference for Temperature Data. Due to the influence of indoor and outdoor temperature difference and equipment heat capacity, the temperature transfer of the mirror is not uniform, resulting in air turbulence near the mirror, and the reduction of observation quality. According to the location data in Table 1, the temperature features in SeeingData_30s are grouped, and the intra-group temperature difference features are obtained by comparing the intra-group features in pairs. At the same time, after each group of temperatures is averaged, the inter-group temperature difference features are obtained by comparing the intra-group features in pairs, and the two are incorporated into SeeingData_30s.

First-Order Difference. In the time series prediction task, the higher the stationarity of historical series data, the easier it is to predict. Data with high stationarity can be obtained by differential processing in the direction of the time axis. In addition, first-order differences also have practical implications for meteorological data. For example, the temperature difference data indicates warming or cooling over some time. Given a continuous time series $X = [x_1, x_2, \ldots, x_L \mid x_i \in \mathbb{R}^{d_x}, 1 \leq i \leq L]$, its first-order difference is obtained by

$$X' = [x_i - x_{i-1} \mid \forall i \in \{2, \ldots, L\}] \tag{1}$$

4.2 Convolution Transformation

Kernels. This section describes the convolution kernel used by TSPRocket. TSPRocket uses a one-dimensional convolution kernel for sliding dot product operations on multivariate time series. In time series classification task, convolution computation can well represent the sequence pattern and allow for highly optimized transformation, thus producing high accuracy in downstream tasks. However, in the time series prediction task, the standard convolution calculation cannot capture the long-term and short-term relationship between the predicted target and the historical data, as well as the periodicity of the time series. Thus in TSPRocket, we make the following improvements to the convolution kernel. The length, weight, bias, dilation, and padding of the TSPRocket kernels are shown below:

- **Length and weight:** TSPRocket's kernel length is 9, and the weight range is limited to $\{-1, 0, 1\}$ to capture the difference between different variables and points in time. In this way, there will be $3^9 = 19683$ different kernels. According to MiniRocket, the kernel set should be as small as possible to improve computing efficiency [9]. To ensure that the kernel function is only sensitive to the relative size of the input value (i.e., $X * W = (X \pm c) * W$, where $*$ denotes convolution computation), the sum of the nine weight values should be 0, and -1 and 1 should have the same number. For example, $W = [-1, 1, 0, 0, 0, 0, 0, 0, 0]$. There are 72 different cores in total. Since the kernel set contains both W and $-W$, and $-W$ can be calculated by W, the actual size of the kernel set is only 36.
- **Variable stride:** The variable step size is used to convolve input data to capture the relationship between the prediction target and historical data. In

the calculation of convolution, the time point of the predicted target value is taken as the starting point to step backward. After each convolution calculation, the step size is increased by one, and the initial step size is 1.

- **Dilation:** To capture the periodicity of the sequence, a dilation set is assigned to each kernel. The scope of dilation value is $D = \{\lfloor 2^0 \rfloor, ..., \lfloor 2^{max} \rfloor\}$, where the index of uniform distribution is between 0 and $max = log_2 \frac{(l_{input}-1)}{(l_{kernel}-1)}$. Here, $\lfloor \cdot \rfloor$ means rounding down, l_{input} is the length of the input sequence samples, and l_{kernel} convolution kernel size, so the maximum size of the expanded convolution kernel does not exceed the length of the input sequence.

- **Bias:** The bias value is extracted from the convolutional output. For a randomly selected training sample, given a convolution kernel, its output $W_d * X$ is calculated, and then its quantile $[0.25, 0.5, 0.75]$ is taken as the optional value of bias. The random selection of training samples is the only part of the whole kernel transformation process with randomness.

- **Padding:** Padding was not used for the time series prediction in this study.

Reference sequence and temperature difference feature sequence share a kernel set. Since the sequence length of the first-order difference sequence is one point shorter than that of the reference sequence, the dilation used in the reference sequence and temperature difference feature sequence is different from that used in the first-order difference sequence, and the kernel set used also slightly different. Besides, the length and weight of the two types of sequences are the same.

Pooling. The output is obtained using convolution calculation on the base sequence, first-order difference sequence, and temperature difference characteristic sequence. TSPRocket will perform the local positive proportional (LPPV) pooling operation on each convolution kernel output $Z = [z_1, ...z_n]$. To calculate LPPV, the sequence Z is sliced isometrically, and the number of slices f needs to be set manually ($f = 3$, by defaults). Then the proportion of positive values is calculated for each sequence slice.

The formula for calculating the local proportion of positive values is as follows. If the number of output features of each convolution kernel after LPPV is set to f, then the feature is:

$$LPPV_f(Z) = [ppv_1, ..., ppv_i, ..., ppv_f] \tag{2}$$

where $ppv_i = ppv([z_{(i-1)\sigma+1}, ..., z_{i\sigma}])$, $ppv_f = ppv([z_{(f-1)\sigma+1}, ..., z_n])$, $i \in \{1, ..., f\}$, $\sigma = \lfloor \frac{n}{f} \rfloor$, $\lfloor . \rfloor$ represents rounding down, and the calculation formula of ppv is:

$$ppv([z_p, ..., z_q]) = \frac{1}{q-p+1} \sum_{i=p}^{q} [z_i > 0] \tag{3}$$

where $1 \le p \le q \le n$, n represents the number of convolution output values. ppv is bounded between 0 and 1.

4.3 Predictor

After the above transformation, the time series features are used to train the downstream predictor. By default, TSPRocket uses nearly 50000 features (49998 to be exact. i.e., 8333 kernels and two sequences are used to represent the features, and the number of LPPV features is set to 3) as the input of the downstream predictor. Due to a large number of features after transformation, few downstream predictors are available. According to the experiment of Dempster et al., the downstream predictors can be simple, and simple ridge regression models and tree models are enough. The downstream predictor of this study uses the LightGBM regression model based on a tree structure. The reasons are **1)** the tree model is highly interpretable and can better capture information for many feature data; and **2)** the LightGBM model is the model that make better tradeoff between the speed and effect among many tree models, and its speed is seven times that of Xgboost.

5   Experiments

This chapter describes the evaluation results of TSPRocket. The purpose of the experiment is as follows:

1. To evaluate the accuracy and time of TSPRocket and existing time series prediction models in the astronomical seeing prediction task. The selected baseline model is representative of each time series prediction genre.
2. To study the impact of the number of features of TSPRocket in terms of accuracy and training time so as to select the optimal solution.
3. To study the selection of the number of LPPV operator features of TSPRocket, detailed to the number of cores and LPPV features.

5.1   Comparing with Current State-of-the-Art

We selected 8 baseline methods as baseline methods, which can be broadly classified into four categories. They are baselines based on statistical learning methods, including ARIMA and Prophet, baselines based on machine learning, XGBoost and LightGBM, and baselines based on deep learning, including LSTM, DeepAR, TCN, Transformer.

Precision. The evaluation indicators are MAE, MSE, RMSE, and MAPE, all in the range of $[0, +\infty)$, with smaller values indicating that the predicted value is closer to the actual value. We used Bayesian Optimization to tune the model parameters, and the best experimental results were selected for each model, as shown in Table 3. The experimental results show that the TSPRocket (50k) achieves the best results, followed by the deep learning method, which is generally better than the machine learning method. The results get worse when the number of transformed features of TSPRocket drops to 20k.

Table 3. The effect of different prediction models on the SeeingData_30s. "TSPRocket (50k)" represents 50000 features after TSPRocket transformation.

	models	mae	mse	rmse	mape
Statistical learning	ARIMA	0.1348	0.0451	0.2124	0.7299
	Prophet	0.1614	0.0510	0.2258	0.7385
Machine learning	LightGBM	0.1417	0.0385	0.1789	0.0360
	XGBoost	0.1422	0.0375	0.1937	0.0409
Deep learning	LSTM	0.1398	0.0398	0.1997	0.0393
	DeepAR	0.1458	0.0382	0.1796	0.0383
	TCN	0.1292	0.0311	0.1766	0.0370
	Transformer	0.1213	0.0289	0.1701	0.0346
TSPRocket	TSPRocket (50k)	**0.1125**	**0.0252**	**0.1587**	**0.0322**
	TSPRocket (20k)	0.1636	0.0483	0.2199	0.0470

Training Time. We recorded the training time of each model, as shown in Fig. 1. The CPU used for model training and testing is Intel i7-8750H @ 2.2 GHZ, and the memory is 16 GB. The deep learning model is trained and tested on a single Nvidia GeForce GTX 1060 6 GB GPU. The experimental results show that the training time of LightGBM based on machine learning method is the shortest, followed by TSPRocket, and the training time of deep learning method is the longest. Among the TSPRocket, it can be seen that the TSPRocket with 20K takes the least time to train, followed by the TSPRocket with 50K.

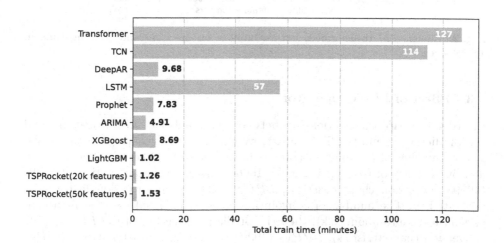

Fig. 1. Training time of different models on the SeeingData_30s.

5.2   Relationship Among Prediction Accuracy, Training Time, and Number of Features

We studied the relationship among prediction accuracy, training time consumption, and number of features in TSPRocket. The number of features is evenly selected from 10k to 80k, the precision index is MSE, and the training time consumption unit is seconds. The experimental results on the SeeingData_30s dataset are shown in Fig. 2. It can be seen from the figure that the training time consumption increases monotonously with the number of transformed features. To pursue the model's high speed, we should reduce the number of transformed features while ensuring the prediction accuracy is not poor. Therefore, we select 50k as the number of transformed features by default.

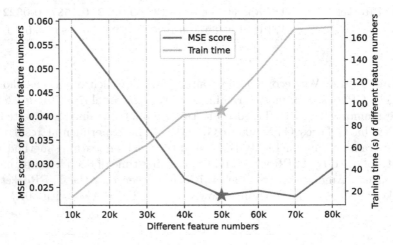

Fig. 2. Influence of transformed feature number on precision and training time in TSPRocket.

5.3   Effect of LPPV Operator

In order to verify the relationship between the number of LPPV features and the prediction accuray of TSPRocket, we designed two groups of experiments: **a.** The number of convolution cores is fixed (set to 8333 cores), then the prediction accuracy of $LPPV_1$ (i.e. PPV, 16666 conversion characteristics), $LPPV_3$ (49998 conversion characteristics), $LPPV_5$ (83330 transformation features) is evaluated; **b.** The number of convolution cores is not fixed (set the final conversion feature to about 50k), then the prediction accuracy of the $LPPV_1$ (50k conversion characteristics), $LPPV_3$ (49998 conversion characteristics), $LPPV_5$ (50k transformation features) and is evaluated. The evaluation index is MSE, and the experimental results are shown in the Table 4. It can be seen that when the final effect is mainly determined by the number of converted features, it has little to do with number of kernels.

Table 4. Effect of combination of different pooling operators.

	$LPPV_1$	$LPPV_3$	$LPPV_5$
Fixed number kernels	0.0545	0.0252	0.0302
Varying number kernels	0.0252	0.0252	0.0252

6   Conclusion

In this study, we proposed a new model TSPRocket to predict the astronomical seeing at the focal plane of the telescope. It can be better applied to multivariate time series problems than statistical and machine learning methods. Compared with deep learning methods, it is faster and more accurate. The conversion kernel function of TSPRocket projects the features of the original data to high dimensions and then uses the linear model for better time series prediction. The advantage is that only random and fixed convolution calculation is required, and then the converted features are used to train the downstream predictor, significantly improving the training speed.

References

1. Amico, P., Campbell, R.D., Christou, J.C.: Laser operations at the 8–10m class telescopes Gemini, Keck, and the VLT: lessons learned, old and new challenges. In: Observatory Operations: Strategies, Processes, and Systems III, vol. 7737, pp. 62–72 (2010)
2. Bahdanau, D., Cho, K., Bengio, Y.: Neural machine translation by jointly learning to align and translate. In: International Conference on Learning Representations (2015)
3. Bai, S., Kolter, J.Z., Koltun, V.: An empirical evaluation of generic convolutional and recurrent networks for sequence modeling. arXiv preprint arXiv:1803.01271 (2018)
4. Bengio, Y., Simard, P., Frasconi, P.: Learning long-term dependencies with gradient descent is difficult. IEEE Trans. Neural Netw. **5**(2), 157–166 (1994)
5. Businger, S., Cherubini, T.: Seeing clearly: the impact of atmospheric turbulence on the propagation of extraterrestrial radiation (2011)
6. Cherubini, T., Businger, S.: Another look at the refractive index structure function. J. Appl. Meteorol. Climatol. **52**(2), 498–506 (2013)
7. Cherubini, T., Lyman, R., Businger, S.: Forecasting seeing for the Maunakea observatories with machine learning. Mon. Not. R. Astron. Soc. **509**(1), 232–245 (2022)
8. Dempster, A., Petitjean, F., Webb, G.I.: ROCKET: exceptionally fast and accurate time series classification using random convolutional kernels. Data Min. Knowl. Disc. **34**(5), 1454–1495 (2020)
9. Dempster, A., Schmidt, D.F., Webb, G.I.: MiniRocket: a very fast (almost) deterministic transform for time series classification. In: Proceedings of the 27th ACM SIGKDD Conference on Knowledge Discovery & Data Mining, pp. 248–257 (2021)
10. Erasmus, D.A., Sarazin, M.S.: Forecasting precipitable water vapor and cirrus cloud cover for astronomical observatories: satellite image processing guided by

synoptic model dissemination data. In: Remote Sensing of Clouds and the Atmosphere V, vol. 4168, pp. 317–328 (2001)

11. Giordano, C., et al.: Contribution of statistical site learning to improve optical turbulence forecasting. Mon. Not. R. Astron. Soc. **504**(2), 1927–1938 (2021)
12. Goodfellow, I., Bengio, Y., Courville, A.: Deep Learning. MIT Press, Cambridge (2016)
13. Hochreiter, S., Schmidhuber, J.: Long short-term memory. Neural Comput. **9**, 1735–1780 (1997)
14. Kitaev, N., Kaiser, L., Levskaya, A.: Reformer: the efficient transformer. arXiv preprint arXiv:2001.04451 (2020)
15. Kolen, J.F., Kremer, S.C.: Gradient flow in recurrent nets: the difficulty of learning longterm dependencies. In: A Field Guide to Dynamical Recurrent Networks (2011)
16. Kornilov, M.V.: Forecasting seeing and parameters of long-exposure images by means of arima. Exp. Astron. **41**(1), 223–242 (2016)
17. Lim, B., Zohren, S., Roberts, S.: Recurrent neural filters: learning independent Bayesian filtering steps for time series prediction. In: 2020 International Joint Conference on Neural Networks, pp. 1–8 (2020)
18. Milli, J., et al.: Nowcasting the turbulence at the paranal observatory. arXiv preprint arXiv:1910.13767 (2019)
19. Ni, W.J., Shen, Q.L., Zeng, Q.T., Wang, H.Q., Cui, X.Q., Liu, T.: Data-driven seeing prediction for optics telescope: from statistical modeling, machine learning to deep learning techniques. Res. Astron. Astrophys. **22**(12), 125003 (2022)
20. Oord, A.V.D., et al.: WaveNet: a generative model for raw audio. arXiv preprint arXiv:1609.03499 (2016)
21. Salinas, D., Flunkert, V., Gasthaus, J., Januschowski, T.: DeepAR: probabilistic forecasting with autoregressive recurrent networks. Int. J. Forecast. **36**(3), 1181–1191 (2020)
22. Skamarock, W.C., et al.: A description of the advanced research WRF model version 4. Natl. Cent. Atmos. Res.: Boulder CO USA **145**, 145 (2019)
23. Tan, C.W., Dempster, A., Bergmeir, C., Webb, G.I.: MultiRocket: effective summary statistics for convolutional outputs in time series classification. arXiv preprint arXiv:2102.00457 (2021)
24. Trinquet, H., Vernin, J.: A model to forecast seeing and estimate C2N profiles from meteorological data. Publ. Astron. Soc. Pac. **118**(843), 756 (2006)
25. Védrenne, N., et al.: Turbulence effects on bi-directional ground-to-satellite laser communication systems. In: International Conference on Space Optical Systems and Applications, vol. 12 (2012)
26. Zhou, H., et al.: Informer: beyond efficient transformer for long sequence time-series forecasting. In: Proceedings of the AAAI Conference on Artificial Intelligence, vol. 35, pp. 11106–11115 (2021)

Return Forecasting for Cryptocurrency Using Labeled Sequences and Reinforced Seq2Class Model

Youwu Liu[(✉)] and Zijiang Yang

York University, Toronto, ON M3J 1P3, Canada
{jliu99,zyang}@yorku.ca

Abstract. Cryptocurrencies have been experiencing explosive growth in recent years, which attracts not only investors or traders but also researchers. Many models have been proposed for forecasting or predicting cryptocurrencies. In this paper, we propose a labeled sequence data model that preserves sequential pattern information and a Seq2class model to categorize such patterns. To reinforce deep learning with the Seq2class model, we propose a mathematically viable method to expand our training dataset. Initial results from implementing our proposed methods exhibit some promising prospects. If the methods were implemented as a decision support system, investment transactions could be profitable.

Keywords: Seq2Class · Reinforcement Training · Labeled Sequences

1 Introduction

Cryptocurrencies have been experiencing an explosive growth in recent years, which attracts not only traders but also researchers. Their market behavior has been studied from several perspectives. For example, Bitcoin market volatility is studied by Ardia et al. [1] and Zhang et al. [2]. Market risks and returns are studied by Troster et al. [3] and Liu et al. [4]. Social media's impact on crypto market are investigated by Ortu et al. [5] and Poongodi et al. [6].

Researchers also proposed their methods to perform forecast or predictions. Forecasting objects include trading returns [7, 8], returns and volatility [9], intraday-volatility [10], and movement directions and high-frequency trend [11–15]. The random walk theory, a foundation of modern financial economics, claims that market prices are unpredictable. However, cryptocurrency price prediction is still a trending research subject [16–21]. In recent years, various models have been proposed for forecasting or predicting price of cryptocurrencies such as ARIMA [14] and GARCH [1–3] model, random forests [7, 15], SVM [7], MLP [14, 17], CNN [13, 21], RNN [18], LSTM [17], CNN-LSTM [19], and LSTM-GRU [16].

Our review of the literature indicates that all published models process data as one single time series. We consider that there are a couple of drawbacks with the single time series approach. First, when thousands of data points are processed by a predictive

H. Fujita et al. (Eds.): IEA/AIE 2023, LNAI 13926, pp. 239–246, 2023.
https://doi.org/10.1007/978-3-031-36822-6_21

model as a single time series, information contributed by each data point is dramatically decreasing as its timestamp is going more remote to the past. Prices of last quarter (hundred days ago) certainly possess less predictive power for future price actions than last week's prices. This character of data effectively limits the length of a time series that a predictive model can really handle, because increasing the length of the time series does not add much information for future outcomes as the length exceeds the limits. Second, a string of time series data points possesses time related sequential patterns. When time series data is processed as single data points, such sequential pattern information will be lost. In this paper, we propose a labeled sequence data model that preserves sequential pattern information. In order to learn sequential patterns from the data, we propose a Seq2class model that captures and categorizes such patterns.

Many proposed deep learning models are trained using limited amounts of data, which in some cases account for only a few hundred data points. A deep learning model with limited training data can only produces overfitting outcomes. To reinforce deep learning with our proposed Seq2class model, we propose a mathematically viable method to expand our training dataset. This proposed expansion method is suitable to add sufficient data points to a training dataset.

In the remaining of this paper, we will briefly introduce the technique we use. Then we explain our proposed methodology, followed by implementation and discussion. We conclude our paper in the final section.

2 Technique

Recurrent neural network (RNN) can process sequential data, such as time series data. A single unit of RNN is illustrated [22] in Fig. 1. Input x_t receives data at time t.

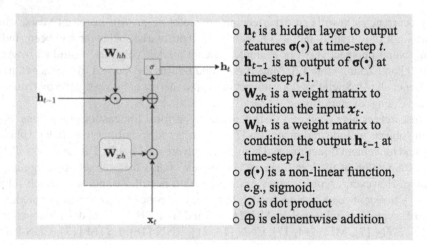

o $\mathbf{h}_t$ is a hidden layer to output features $\sigma(\cdot)$ at time-step t.
o $\mathbf{h}_{t-1}$ is an output of $\sigma(\cdot)$ at time-step t-1.
o $\mathbf{W}_{xh}$ is a weight matrix to condition the input x_t.
o $\mathbf{W}_{hh}$ is a weight matrix to condition the output $\mathbf{h}_{t-1}$ at time-step t-1
o $\sigma(\cdot)$ is a non-linear function, e.g., sigmoid.
o $\odot$ is dot product
o $\oplus$ is elementwise addition

Fig. 1. Recurrent Neural Network Element

When RNN is connected sequentially, hidden state is passed from one element in the sequence to the next, allowing the network to memorize information from previous elements. The hidden neuron is computed $\mathbf{h}_t = \sigma(\mathbf{W}_{hh} \odot \mathbf{h}_{t-1} \odot \mathbf{W}_{xh} \odot x_t)$. If output y_t presents, it is computed as $y_t = softmax(\mathbf{W}_{hy} \odot \mathbf{h}_t)$, where $\mathbf{W}_{hy}$ is weight matrix to condition the output $\mathbf{h}_t$ at time-step t. With RNN elements, we can construct a sequence model to accomplish our forecasting tasks.

3 Proposed Methodology

Our model is constructed upon three foundational assumptions. First, data sequences preserve better pattern information than a single data point. Second, the sequential pattern can be learned by a well-suited neural network model. The last but not least, deep learning requires sufficient data for model training. Our proposed model addresses all three merits in the following sections.

3.1 Labeled Data Sequence Model

Our data model converts time series data from single data points into labeled data sequences. The raw data will be in the form of daily close price of a cryptocurrency or a tradable security asset. As the random walk theory claims that the price of a financial asset is unpredictable, we will not predict price actions of a cryptocurrency. Instead, we are trying to forecast returns of cryptocurrency trading. Therefore, the raw data is transformed into "daily returns" ("returns"). The returns are calculated in logarithmic scale as $r_t = \log\left(\frac{c_t}{c_{t-1}}\right) = \log(c_t) - \log(c_{t-1})$, which is often used for volatile financial assets. There are a couple of advantages to adopt logarithmic returns in the calculations. One of them is that logarithmic returns are symmetric. Another is that logarithmic returns are additive, which makes it simpler to calculate compound returns over the period of study.

With the time series data "returns", labeled sequences are constructed as follows.

r_{t-i}	...	...	r_{t-2}	r_{t-1}	r_t	1/0

Here i represents the length of the short sequences. The label (1/0) of the short sequences indicates positive or negative returns. Label $= \begin{cases} 1, & r_{t+1} > 0 \\ 0, & r_{t+1} \leq 0 \end{cases}$. If the source dataset has n data points and the length of the short sequences is i, then the total number of labeled sequences constructed is $n - i - 1$.

One advantage of the labeled data sequence model is that 'local' temporal patterns are better preserved. One example of such a pattern is the probable return after three or five consecutive positive (negative) returns. Another example is likely the returns after several alternate positive and negative returns. Sequence patterns can be learned by a specially configured neural network.

3.2 Seq2class Model

Our proposed Seq2class model is to classify the data sequences. The input of the model is sequence and the output is classification (prediction). The model is assembled with

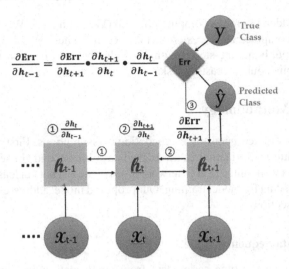

$$\frac{\partial \text{Err}}{\partial h_{t-1}} = \frac{\partial \text{Err}}{\partial h_{t+1}} \cdot \frac{\partial h_{t+1}}{\partial h_t} \cdot \frac{\partial h_t}{\partial h_{t-1}}$$

Fig. 2. Seq2class model

recurrent neural network units presented in the technique section. The number of the units being used in the Seq2class model equals to the length of data sequence constructed. The units are concatenated sequentially as illustrated in Fig. 2.

Training method of the Seq2class model is called the backpropagation through time (BPTT), which utilizes the chain rule of partial derivatives as shown in Fig. 2. Assume that our Seq2class model contains only three hidden units, h_{t+1}, h_t, and h_{t-1}. When an error is generated by comparing the predicted value of the class to the true value of the class, the gradient $\frac{\partial \text{Err}}{\partial h_{t+1}}$ is passed to h_{t+1}, $\frac{\partial h_{t+1}}{\partial h_t}$ is passed to h_t, and $\frac{\partial h_t}{\partial h_{t-1}}$ is passed to h_{t-1}. Thus, the error gradient with respect to h_{t-1} is $\frac{\partial \text{Err}}{\partial h_{t-1}} = \frac{\partial \text{Err}}{\partial h_{t+1}} \cdot \frac{\partial h_{t+1}}{\partial h_t} \cdot \frac{\partial h_t}{\partial h_{t-1}}$ by the chain rule. In general form, the gradient of the loss (Err) function $\mathcal{L}$ with respect to the hidden state at time step t is defined as $\frac{\partial \mathcal{L}(r)}{\partial h_t} = \frac{\partial h_{t+1}}{\partial h_t} \cdots \frac{\partial h_r}{\partial h_{r-1}} \frac{\partial \mathcal{L}(r)}{\partial h_r}$, where $\mathcal{L}(r)$ is the loss value time step r. The BPTT efficiently propagates the error gradient to trainable weight matrices (*Jacobian*) to achieve error minimization (through gradient descent). The propagation of errors to every previous step enables the model to learn the sequential pattern of the input data.

As we can see, the longer the sequence of units in the Seq2class becomes, the more gradient components will be contained in the gradient of the loss function $\mathcal{L}$. Product of large number of gradient components may produce exponentially larger results (exploding gradients) or exponentially closer-to-zero results (vanishing gradients). Either exploding gradients or vanishing gradients will prevent the Seq2class model from effective learning. In order to minimize the risk of vanishing and exploding gradients, we limit the number of units that the Seq2class model contains.

3.3 Reinforcement Training Method

Deep learning requires sufficient training data. More neural network training iterations without adequate data only generates overfitting results. However, available data on one particular asset is often inadequate. To increase the quantity of training data, we expand it to other tradable assets, which hold similar risk profiles.

Here we briefly explain the mathematical viability of our proposed training method. Assume that we have an original dataset $B = \{(X_{B_i}, y_{B_i})\}_{i=1}^{n_B}$. Our training objective is to solve model parameters $\theta_B^* = \arg\min_{\theta_B \in \Theta} \mathbb{E}_{(X,y) \in \mathbb{P}_B(X,Y)}[\mathcal{L}(X, y, \theta_B)]$. To add data, we introduce an expansion dataset $A = \{(X_{A_i}, y_{A_i})\}_{i=1}^{n_A}$, which is similar to the original dataset B. The similarity means that two attributes are the same for both datasets A and B, i.e., the same range of values in feature space and the same values in label space. Thus, the training parameters become $\theta_B^* = \arg\min_{\theta_B \in \Theta} \mathbb{E}_{(X,y) \in \mathbb{P}_A(X,Y)}\left[\frac{P_B(X,y)}{P_A(X,y)} \mathcal{L}(X, y, \theta_B)\right] = \arg\min_{\theta_B \in \Theta} \mathbb{E}_{(X,y) \in \mathbb{P}_A(X,Y)}\left[\frac{P_B(X)}{P_A(X)} \mathcal{L}(X, y, \theta_B)\right]$. Note that because the label space $\{y\}$ for both A and B are equal, y is dropped from $P_A(X, y)$ and $P_B(X, y)$. In the above formula, $\mathbb{E}$ denotes expectation while $P_A(X)$ and $P_B(X)$ are distributions of the datasets A and B respectively. Because A and B have the same range of values, we can approximate $\frac{P_B(X)}{P_A(X)}$ by calculating it with data in A only, i.e., $\frac{P_B(X_i^A)}{P_A(X_i^A)}$, which can be estimated with the kernel embedding of distributions. Plugging the estimated values into θ_B^* formula, we can train the model with any original model's loss function $\mathcal{L}(X, y, \theta_B)$ with the expansion dataset A.

4   Implementation and Discussion

Our experiment of return forecasting, we use Bitcoin's daily close price as raw data, which is publicly available at Yahoo Finance (from September 16, 2014 onwards). 3,119 data points in total are downloaded as our original dataset B. Among the data obtained, the last 59 data points (data for February and March 2023) in the time series sequence are reserved as testing data, which is used to verify the accuracy of the forecasting model. In addition, we use QQQ, a proxy ETF of NASDAQ 100, which is also available at Yahoo Finance to expand our training dataset. Our expanded training dataset is three times larger than the original Bitcoin dataset. The raw data is converted to a labeled data sequence as described in the proposed methodology section. The length of the sequence we adopted is seven, equivalent to a week of Bitcoin trading days. Both datasets are used in the Seq2class model.

There are two types of estimates of forecasting in the research literature, in-sample estimation and out-of-sample estimation. The in-sample estimation is just one type of interpolation computation, hence it should not be considered as forecasting for financial returns. For this reason, we implement only out-of-sample estimates for return forecasting in the testing phase.

Trend prediction is popular among predictive models published. Trend forecasts are actually produced by multi-step estimation. Generally, multi-step estimation is conducted upon estimated values. The longer period it forecast the more estimated values the model has to use. Due to the random walk behavior of the market prices, future price estimations based on historical price data are generally inaccurate and ineffective. The multi-step estimation will magnify estimation errors more strongly due to the cumulative effect. Instead of the trend prediction, we perform only a single-step forecast for directions, either gain or loss, which has its operational values. If the forecast is adequately accurate, it can guide profitable trading transactions over time.

The single-step forecast does not use any estimated values as its input. In our study, we construct the test data sequences with the method described in Sect. 3.1 using reserved February and March (2023) data. We obtain the predicted value (class) for each sequence of data as it is fed into the Seq2class model. By comparing the predicted value (class) with its real value, we can record true or false, which measures the performance of the model. The accuracy of forecasting with Seq2class trained by the original dataset (Bitcoin data only) is 60%. The accuracy with Seq2class trained by the expanded dataset (Bitcoin + QQQ data) is 73% (confusion matrix is omitted to save space). This result, if stable and consistent, is practically valuable for assisting a profitable trading strategy.

In this study, we experiment with a binary classification of data sequences. However, the Bitcoin data can also be modeled as multiclass data sequences if sufficient data was available. For example, four-class data sequences can be labeled as (i) "0" when the loss is greater than 1; (ii) "1" when the loss is less than 1; (iii) "2" when the gain is less than 1; and (iv) "3" when the gain is greater than 1. Our proposed Seq2class model is capable of processing such multiclass data sequences.

In this study, the length of the labeled sequence is seven. It is chosen mainly on the consideration that a longer sequence may lead to difficulty in model training, such as exploding gradients or vanishing gradients. Seven is by no means an optimum number for the length of the labeled sequence. If the model can be improved to accommodate longer sequence without training difficulty, more sequential patterns will be captured and learned to generate better forecasts.

The data used in this study is daily closing prices. Our proposed data model, the labeled sequence, and the Seq2class model can also be applied to trading data with higher frequency, i.e., time series with a span of one minute or five minutes. Forecasting accuracy with higher frequency data may be better for two main reasons. First, there will exist a much larger quantity of data for training the Seq2class model. Second, there will be richer sequential patterns embedded in financial time series with a shorter time span for Seq2class to learn. However, Bitcoin trading data of higher frequency is not available publicly.

5   Conclusion

In this paper, we present a novel idea of preserving sequential patterns for financial time series data, and then propose a neural network model, Seq2class, to capture such sequential patterns for forecasting financial returns. In addition, we propose a mathematically viable method to supplement training dataset that is often inadequate for deep learning.

Initial results from implementing our proposed methods exhibit some promising prospects. If the methods were implemented as a decision support system, investment transactions could be profitable. In spite of such benefit, the idea is juvenile and the methods are immature. They deserve scrutiny and further research.

One area for future research is the further expansion of the training dataset. In this study, the extended dataset based on our proposed method demonstrated better performance in training the Seq2class model. It will be interesting to see if accuracy can be further improved as more training data is added.

References

1. Ardia, D., Bluteau, K., Rüede, M.: Regime changes in bitcoin GARCH volatility dynamics. Financ. Res. Lett. **29**, 266–271 (2019)
2. Zhang, W., Li, Y.: Is idiosyncratic volatility priced in cryptocurrency markets? Res. Int. Bus. Financ. **54**, 101252 (2020)
3. Troster, V., Tiwari, A.K., Shahbaz, M., Macedo, D.N.: Bitcoin returns and risk: a general GARCH and GAS analysis. Financ. Res. Lett. **30**, 187–193 (2019)
4. Liu, Y., Tsyvinski, A.: Risks and returns of cryptocurrency. Rev. Financ. Stud. **34**, 2689–2727 (2021)
5. Ortu, M., Uras, N., et al.: On technical trading and social media indicators for cryptocurrency price classification through deep learning. Expert Syst. Appl. **198**, 116804 (2022)
6. Poongodi, M., Nguyen, T.N., Hamdi, M., Cengiz, K.: Global cryptocurrency trend prediction using social media. Inf. Process. Manag. 58, 102708 (2021)
7. Akyildirim, E., Goncu, A., Sensoy, A.: Prediction of cryptocurrency returns using machine learning. Ann. Oper. Res. **297**, 3–36 (2021)
8. Yae, J., Tian, G.Z.: Out-of-sample forecasting of cryptocurrency returns: a comprehensive comparison of predictors and algorithms. Physica A **598**, 127379 (2022)
9. Balcilara, M., Bouri, E., Guptac, R., Roubaudb, D.: Can volume predict Bitcoin returns and volatility? A quantiles-based approach. Econ. Model. **64**, 74–81 (2017)
10. Tapia, S., Kristjanpoller, W.: Framework based on multiplicative error and residual analysis to forecast bitcoin intraday-volatility. Physica A **589**, 126613 (2022)
11. Alonso-Monsalve, S., Suárez-Cetrulo, A., Cervantes, C.A., Quintana, A.: Convolution on neural networks for high-frequency trend prediction of cryptocurrency exchange rates using technical indicators. Expert Syst. Appl. **149**, 113250 (2020)
12. Lahmiri, S., Bekiros, S.: Deep learning forecasting in cryptocurrency high-frequency trading. Cogn. Comput. **13**(2), 485–487 (2021). https://doi.org/10.1007/s12559-021-09841-w
13. Cavalli, S., Amoretti, M.: CNN-based multivariate data analysis for bitcoin trend prediction. Appl. Soft Comput. J. **101**, 107065 (2021)
14. Ibrahim, A., Kashef, R., Corrigan, L.: Predicting market movement direction for bitcoin: a comparison of time series modeling methods. Comput. Electr. Eng. **89**, 106905 (2021)
15. Basher, S.A., Sadorsky, P.: Forecasting Bitcoin price direction with random forests: how important are interest rates, inflation, and market volatility? Mach. Learn. Appl. **9**, 100355 (2022)
16. Maheshkumar, M., Tanwar, S., Gupta, R., Kumar, N.: A deep learning-based cryptocurrency price prediction scheme for financial institutions. J. Inf. Secur. Appl. **55**, 102583 (2020)
17. Uras, N., Marchesi, L., Marchesi, M., Tonelli, R.: Forecasting Bitcoin closing price series using linear regression and neural networks models. PeerJ Comput. Sci. **6**, e279 (2020)
18. Serrano, W.: The random neural network in price predictions. Neural Comput. Appl. **34**(2), 855–873 (2021). https://doi.org/10.1007/s00521-021-05903-0
19. Livieris, I.E., Kiriakidou, N., Stavroyiannis, S., Pintelas, P.: An advanced CNN-LST modal for cryptocurrency forecasting. Electronics **10**, 287 (2021)
20. Guo, H., Zhang, D., Liu, S., Wang, L., Ding, Y.: Bitcoin price forecasting: a perspective of underlying blockchain transactions. Decis. Support Syst. **151**, 113650 (2021)

21. Zhang, Z., Dai, H., Zhou, J., Mondal, S.K., García, M.M., Wang, H.: Forecasting cryptocurrency price using convolutional neural networks with weighted and attentive memory channels. Expert Syst. Appl. **183**, 115378 (2021)
22. Iosifidis, A., Tefas, A.: Deep Learning for Robot Perception and Cognition, 1st edn. Academic Press, Cambridge (2022). ISBN: 9780323857871

Reinforcement Learning

Improving Generalization in Reinforcement Learning Through Forked Agents

Olivier Moulin[1]([✉]), Vincent Francois-Lavet[1], Paul Elbers[2], and Mark Hoogendoorn[1]

[1] Department of Computer Science, Vrije Universiteit Amsterdam, Amsterdam, The Netherlands
o.moulin@vu.nl
[2] Department of Intensive Care, Amsterdam UMC, Vrije Universiteit Amsterdam, Amsterdam, The Netherlands

Abstract. An eco-system of agents, each having their own policy with limited generalizability, has proven to be a reliable approach to increase generalization across procedurally generated environments. In such an approach, new agents are regularly added to the eco-system when encountering a new environment that is outside of the scope of the eco-system. The speed of adaptation and general effectiveness of the eco-system approach highly depends on the initialization of new agents. In this paper we propose different initialization techniques, inspired from Deep Neural Network initialization and transfer learning, and study their impact.

Keywords: Reinforcement Learning · Generalization · Agents

1 Introduction

Generalization of reinforcement learning (RL) agents to previously unseen environments is a key topic. RL agents have the tendency to overfit the environment on which they have been trained. This problem has been highlighted often in the literature, for example by Cobbe et al. [3] and Packer et al. [10].

The eco-system approach described by Moulin et al. [1] is one of the approaches put forward to improve generalization across environments while maintaining performance on previously seen environments. It is based on an eco-system of agents with the idea that each agent has its own policy with some generalizability, where the combination makes up a highly generalizable system. When a new environment is encountered, existing agents are used, or a new agent is trained when none performs satisfactorily. While the approach is unique in its ability to avoid catastrophic forgetting, it requires a lot of access to the environment to achieve its goal.

In this paper, we aim to improve this approach. Hereby, we focus on initialization procedures for new agents. Better initialization has the potential to reduce the heavy burden of ample accesses to the environments and can additionally

H. Fujita et al. (Eds.): IEA/AIE 2023, LNAI 13926, pp. 249–260, 2023.
https://doi.org/10.1007/978-3-031-36822-6_22

improve generalizability. Drawing inspiration from papers on initialization techniques for Deep Neural networks (e.g. Boulila et al. [19]) and on transfer learning (e.g. Taylor et al. [20]), we consider the following initialization options: (i) initialization with the agent in the pool performing the best on the new environment, (ii) with a random agent chosen from a pool, (iii) with an agent not included in the pool and trained on all past environments that we refer as forked agent (iv) and with default initialization, which matches the setup from Moulin et al. [1]. We evaluate the performance of our contribution in the minigrid environments [12] and compare to existing state-of-the-art methods.

Our contributions are:

- Identifying the impact of different initialization techniques on the speed of learning and usage of resources for newly encountered environments.
- Proposing a new setup improving generalization in reinforcement learning in the context of the eco-system approach.

This paper is organized as follows. Section 2 presents the related work which has inspired the approaches tested in this paper. Section 3 provides an explanation of our approach. Next, Sect. 4 presents the experimental setup used to evaluate the approach. Section 5 presents the results of the experiments. We end with a discussion in Sect. 6.

2 Related Work

We first dive into related work. The way to assess generalization of a given RL system and the usage of procedurally generated environments is inspired by the papers from Cobbe et al. [3,4]. Several papers have focused on improving generalization in the Reinforcement Learning context. In addition to the newly proposed eco-system approach we base our work on, two other main categories can be found. The first category is focused on creating a representation of the environment. This approach helps learning a good policy and reducing at the same time over-fitting (see e.g. Sonar et al. [15]). The second category is focused on adding noise and/or information bottlenecks in the Neural Network. This approach also reduces the risk of over-fitting to the training environment (e.g. Chen [16], Lu et al. [17] and Igl et al. [14]).

Several approaches have been proposed for specialist and generalist agents to improve training. Zhiwei et al. [2] propose to use a set of specialist agents with imitation learning techniques to improve the learning capabilities of a generalist agent when additional training steps on it does not help to improve the accuracy. After leveraging the specialist agents to train the main generalist agent by imitation learning, it resumes the training of the generalist agent by normal accesses to the environment. This approach offers some similarities to our approach by using very specialized agents as well as leveraging the generalizability of one agent being trained on multiple environments, but it also differs from the variant we call the forked agent approach where we use one agent trained on multiple environment (generalist agent) to initialize the agents of the eco-system (specialist agents) and we build the overall generalization by combining the generalizability of all specialist agents in the pool.

Next, several works exist that focus on improved initialization of neural network and/or RL agents. In this paper we show that the initialization of the agents (Neural Network/Policy of the agent) in an eco-system setup has an impact on the performance of the overall system. The ideas for the different initialization techniques presented in this paper have been inspired by a survey paper from Boulila et al. [19] where they list the most used techniques to initialize the weights of a neural network as well as another survey paper done in the area of transfer learning from Taylor et al. [20]. The latter paper gives a good overview of the transfer learning domain. These papers have been used as inspiration and have helped us trigger new ideas on how to improve the initialization of the new agents. These papers are also quite different from our approaches in the fact that they do not relate specifically to Reinforcement Learning or the eco-system setup.

3 Approach

The eco-system approach, taken from Moulin et al. [1], is based on the assumption that each agent trained on an environment is able to generalize a bit, which makes it able to perform properly on a limited number of other environments. The eco-system is composed of multiple agents (a pool of agents). Each agent part of the eco-system is trained as a standard RL agent, but only on one environment (specialist). The generalization improvement is made by gathering the generalization capabilities of the individual agents. In this paper we look at different techniques to improve the overall performance of this approach, thereby focusing on the initialization of new agents. The performance increase is defined as any action which leads to improving how the overall system generalizes to new environments as well as how it reduces the resources needed (number of agents in memory, number of training cycles needed) to accomplish the same or better level of generalization.

3.1 Reinforcement Learning Formulation

Reinforcement Learning is based on the interactions between an agent and its environment over discrete time-steps. The data used to train the agent is gathered directly from the environment at the same time the agent explores it, or at a later time (e.g. when using a replay memory). The environment is formalized as an MDP (Markov Decision Process, as described by Puterman [22]) defined by (i) a state space (composed of all the potential observations from the environment which can be gathered by the agent), called S which can be continuous or not, (ii) an action space, called $A = \{1, \dots, N_A\}$, (iii) a transition function noted $T : S \times A \to \mathbb{P}(S)$, and (iv) the reward function, noted $R : S \times A \times S \to \mathcal{R}$ where $\mathcal{R}$ encompass all the possible rewards in a range $R_{\max} \in \mathbb{R}^+$ ($[0, R_{\max}]$). After initialization of the MDP, noted M, the agent starts in a state sampled from a distribution of initial states, noted $b_0(s)$. At each time step t, the agent selects an action available in the current state of the system, noted $s_t \in S$. The action is selected based on the policy $\pi : S \to \mathbb{P}(A): a_t \sim \pi(s_t, \cdot)$, which moves the agent in a new state noted $s_{t+1} \in S$, and will grant the agent a reward signal noted $r_t \in \mathcal{R}$.

3.2   Proximal Policy Optimization Formulation

Different algorithms can be used to implement the Reinforcement Learning approach, e.g. DDQN ([8, Van Hasselt et al.]), Actor-Critic ([13, Konda et al., 1999]), and PPO ([18, Schulman et al., 2017]). In this paper we choose to focus on the Proximal Policy Optimization (PPO) to match what was done by Moulin et al. [1], as our goal is to show how optimizing the initialization of the agents can increase the overall performance of the approach. The Proximal Policy Optimization (PPO) algorithm (cf. [18, Schulman et al., 2017]) is an improvement of the actor-critic method ([13, Konda et al., 1999]). The parameters, noted w of a given policy $\pi_w(s, a)$ are updated to optimize $A^{\pi_w}(s, a) = Q^{\pi_w}(s, a) - V^{\pi_w}(s)$. The PPO algorithm adds a limit on the policy changes to reduce instability and avoid too much variation after each training step. This results in maximizing the following objective in expectation over $s \sim \rho^{\pi_w}, a \sim \pi_w$:

$$\min \left(r_t(w) A^{\pi_w}(s, a), \mathrm{clip}\big(r_t(w), 1 - \epsilon, 1 + \epsilon\big) A^{\pi_w}(s, a) \right)$$

Where:

- $r_t(w) = \frac{\pi_{w + \triangle w}(s, a)}{\pi_w(s, a)}$,
- ρ^{π_w} being the discounted state distribution defined as
  $\rho^{\pi_w}(s) = \sum_{t=0}^{\infty} \gamma^t Pr\{s_t = s | s_0, \pi_w\}$
- $\epsilon \in \mathbb{R}$ being a hyper-parameter.

The implementation of the PPO algorithm, we are using in this paper, is stable-baselines 3 (cf. [21, OpenAI]).

3.3   Eco-System Algorithm

The ecosystem algorithm, described by Moulin et al. [1] works as follows: each time the eco-system meets a new environment, it will browse its pool of agents and try to find one that can solve the environment (solving means obtaining a reward greater than a given threshold). If no agent from the pool can be found, then a new agent will be created, trained on the new environment and added to the pool. The eco-system will then check whether this new agent can replace an existing agent in the pool, and if it is the case, the old agent from the pool is removed. The generalization of the eco-system is accomplished by all the agents in the pool. We summarized it in Algorithm 1. The non colored part of the algorithm correspond to the original eco-system algorithm. The colored parts are used to highlight the changes made for each initialization technique that we introduce.

3.4   Initialization Techniques

In order to improve the performance of the eco-system, we have focused our work on finding a better way to initialize the agents when they are created, trained and added to the pool.

Algorithm 1. eco-system - learn(M_i)//*updated from Moulin et al. original*

$e^* \leftarrow \emptyset$ #*good enough agent found*

$n \leftarrow 0$ #*loop var.*

while $e^* = \emptyset$ **and** $\bigcup e_{0...n} \neq \mathcal{E}$ **do**

    #*while good policy not found*

    #*and not all agents reviewed*

    $\mathcal{R}_{M_i}^{\pi_{e_n}} = \text{test\_agent}(e_n, M_i)$

    #*Total reward from e_n on M_i*

    if $\mathcal{R}_{M_i}^{\pi_{e_n}} \geq l$ **then** #*if e_n solve M_i*

        $e^* \leftarrow e_n$ #*good enough agent found = e_n*

    else

        $n \leftarrow n + 1$

The following while statement replaces the previous one

$best\_performing \leftarrow 0$ #*loop var.*

$best\_reward \leftarrow 0$ #*loop var.*

while $\bigcup e_{0...n} \neq \mathcal{E}$ **do**

    #*while good policy not found*

    #*and not all agents reviewed*

    $\mathcal{R}_{M_i}^{\pi_{e_n}} = \text{test\_agent}(e_n, M_i)$

    #*Total reward from e_n on M_i*

    if $\mathcal{R}_{M_i}^{\pi_{e_n}} \geq l$ **then** #*if e_n solve M_i*

        $e^* \leftarrow e_n$ #*good enough agent found = e_n*

    else

        $n \leftarrow n + 1$

    if $\mathcal{R}_{M_i}^{\pi_{e_n}} \geq best\_reward$ **then** #*if e_n beats previous best agent*

        $best\_performing \leftarrow n$

        $best\_reward \leftarrow \mathcal{R}_{M_i}^{\pi_{e_n}}$

if $e^* = \emptyset$ **then** #*if e^* not found*

    $e \leftarrow \text{new\_agent}()$

    $e.\text{Neural\_Network} \leftarrow e_{randomly\_chosen}.\text{Neural\_Network}$

    $e.\text{Neural\_Network} \leftarrow e_{best\_performing}.\text{Neural\_Network}$

    $e.\text{Neural\_Network} \leftarrow Main\_Agent.\text{Neural\_Network}$

    while $\mathcal{R}_{M_i}^{\pi_e} \leq l$ **do** #*while e cannot solve M_i*

        $\text{learn-epoch}(e, M_i)$

        $\mathcal{R}_{M_i}^{\pi_e} = \text{test\_agent}(e, M_i)$

    $\mathcal{E} \leftarrow \mathcal{E} + e$ #*add e to the pool*

    $Main\_Agent.\text{Neural\_Network} \leftarrow e.\text{Neural\_Network}$

    #*The following For statement is optional*

    #*Only needed if optimization of the pool is needed*

    for $f \in \mathcal{E}$ **do** #*for all agent f in the pool*

        for $w \in \delta^f$ **do** #*for all env. w solved by f*

            $\mathcal{R}_w^{\pi_{e^*}} = \text{test\_agent}(e^*, w)$

            if $\mathcal{R}_w^{\pi_{e^*}} \geq l$ **then** #*if e can solve w*

                $\delta^e \leftarrow \delta^e + w$ #*add w to e list*

        if $\delta^f \in \delta^e$ **then**

            #*if e can solve all env. of f*

            $\mathcal{E} \leftarrow \mathcal{E} - f$ #*remove f from pool*

    Sort $\mathcal{E}$ by size δ descending order

else

    $\delta^{e^*} \leftarrow \delta^{e^*} + M_i$ #*add M_i to e^* list*

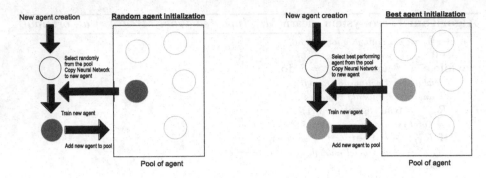

Fig. 1. Random and Best agent initialization techniques

Basic Initialization. This is the initialization introduced with the eco-system approach. The agent is simply created with randomly initialized weights before being trained on the new environment and then added to the pool of agents.

Random Initialization. With this approach (Fig. 1), each time an agent is created, its neural network is copied from another agent randomly chosen from the pool of agents. The new agent initialized this way is then trained on the new environment and added to the pool of agents. The changes in the code are highlighted in Algorithm 1 in purple.

Best Agent Initialization. In the eco-system a new agent is created only if no agent from the pool was able to solve the new environment (reaching the threshold). With this approach (Fig. 1), when testing if an existing agent can solve the new environment, the agent tested which performed the best (while still performing below the desired standard) is stored. When initializing the new agent, the neural network from the best performing agent is used. In case we have multiple agents candidate for the best agent (identical reward), the first one encountered while browsing the pool of agent is selected. The new agent initialized this way is then trained on the new environment and added to the pool of agents. For this initialization approach, we modify the initial algorithm (Algorithm 1) in two places. The changes in the code are highlighted in Algorithm 1 in orange.

Forked Agent Initialization. With this approach (Fig. 2), we create a new agent, called Main Agent outside of the pool of agents. The Neural Network of the Main Agent is used to initialize each new agent created. This is done by creating a fork (or copy) of the Main Agent Neural Network weights and using those weights as initial value for the weights of the Neural Network of the new agent. The new agent is then trained on the specific environment for which it has been created, and added to the pool of agents. The Neural Network of the newly created agent then replaces the Neural Network of the Main Agent. The agent outside of the pool of agents has been trained on all the environments where additional training/agents in the pool are needed. The Main Agent outside of the pool of agents used for initialization of new agents can forget previously learned environment, but it is not an issue as it stays outside of the eco-system and is not used for generalization purpose. The changes in the code are highlighted in Algorithm 1 in green.

4   Experimental Setup

The experimental setup we use in this paper is similar to the one used in the paper from Moulin et al. [1], to clearly highlight the improvements brought by our proposed initialization techniques and setup.

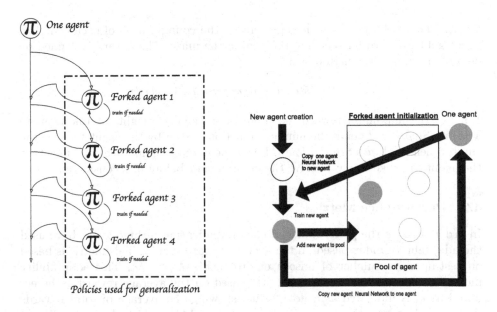

Fig. 2. Forked Agent initialization technique

4.1   Environments

The experiments are conducted on Minigrid with the FourRooms setup (cf. [12, Chevalier-Boisvert et al., 2018]). Minigrid FourRooms (Fig. 3) is a procedurally generated environment, which means in our case that the map, start position, goal position, and obstacles are positioned randomly according to the seed of each level, while the other components of the experiments like reward given to the agents are kept the same. In these environments we use the basic view of Minigrid which returns as state a partially observable view of the environment using a compact encoding, composed of 3 input values per visible grid cell. The total structure returned is a 3D table with $7 \times 7 \times 3$ values. These values are not pixels. The 7×7 area represents the part of the environment visible to the

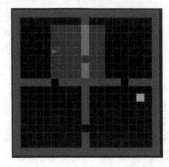

Fig. 3. Minigrid FourRoom and Multiroom environment

agent. The 3 values are a code representing the configuration of each cell. The agent gets a reward for reaching the goal in the maze. The reward is defined by default in Minigrid FourRooms as:

$$1 - 0.9 * (stepsUsed/maxStepsAllowed)$$

1 being the maximum reward, 0.9 being the penalty weight for taking more actions, $StepsUsed$ being the number of actions taken by the agent to solve the environment and $maxStepsAllowed$ being the maximum number of actions that the agent can take to try to solve the environment before it is considered failed.

4.2   Performance Metrics

In order to asses the performance of each initialization technique, we have used the adaptability index based on the average reward metric. This metric is based on testing on a number of unseen environments $M_i \in \mathcal{M}$. This adaptability index (introduced by Moulin et al. [1]) based on the average reward gathered, noted as ζ, is indicated as a float value, showing the average of total rewards $\mathcal{R}$ gathered over all the new environments $M_i \in \mathcal{M}$ on which the approach was tested. It is formalized as follows:

$$\zeta = \frac{\sum_{i=0}^{n} R_{M_i}}{n}$$

The higher the adaptability index based on the average reward metric, the better the system is generalizing to never seen environments. The metrics are calculated periodically after each approach has been presented to 50 additional environments (and completed the associated training if necessary). The number of training steps necessary to solve an initial set of 500 environments has been periodically gathered to assess if one approach allows to reduce the computational requirements. The lower the number of training steps the better the system is performing as it has a direct impact on the computing resources needed. The last performance metric is the number of agents needed to solve the initial set of 500 environments. The lower the number of agents in the pool, the better the system is performing as it means that each agent in the pool generalizes better. The hyper-parameters available are the ones defined by default for stable-baselines 3. The threshold used to indicate that an environment has been solved is a reward of 0.8 which means that any agent gathering more than 0.8 on an environment is considered as having solved the environment (identical to the one used in the paper from Moulin et al. [1]) For all experiments, the performance metrics are gathered after running 5 experiments with each proposed technique.

5   Results

Below we discuss the results we obtained in our experiments. The figures displayed in this section show the average of each indicator as well as the standard error based on the 5 runs.

Adaptability Index Based on Average Reward. We can see in Fig. 4 that the forked agent initialization technique performs better than all other initialization approaches. This performance increase is shown by the average reward gathered at each test step over never seen environments. This approach also starts providing a significant increase early on (after training on 50 environments). This indicates that this approach generalizes better but also faster than the other ones. We also highlight that this approach increases stability too, as shown by the smaller magnitude of the standard error than the other approaches. The random initialization technique performs worse than the basic initialization. The best agent initialization performs similar as the basic initialization.

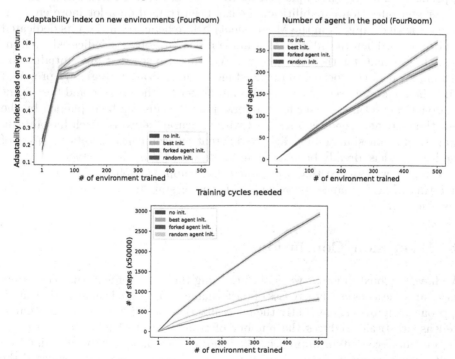

Fig. 4. Initialization techniques results and standard error (shaded area)

Number of Agents in the Pool. The number of agents in the pool (Fig. 4) also reflects the capacity of each agent to cover a wider number of environments on which the eco-system has been trained. In Fig. 4, we can see that the forked agent approach shows a bit higher number of agents in the pool compared to the best agent and the basic initialization approaches. This increase of the number of agents comes from the fact that each agent trained using the forked agent initialization embeds a better generalization to other environments. This means that each agent created this way covers a wider number of environments than with the other initialization techniques. The optimization technique only removes agents from the pool when all environments of an agent can be solved by another agent. The better generalization capabilities in this case makes it more difficult for one agent to fully match all the environments of another agent, leading to some overlap and an increase in the number of agents in the pool. The random initialization technique uses a higher number of agents, but this is only due to the lack of performance of the agents initialized this way. The basic initialization and the best agent initialization again have similar performance.

Number of Training Steps. Reducing the number of training steps without decreasing the overall generalization score has a direct impact on usage of computational resources. The forked agent approach (Fig. 4) is clearly superior when looking at the number of training steps needed to complete the training on 500 environments, being nearly half of what is needed by the best agent and random approaches. This can be explained by the fact that each agent created embeds better generalization capabilities as it has been trained on a lot more environments (as all coming from the Main Agent) before being trained on its dedicated environment. Then the additional training needed to solve its dedicated environment is less than for the other options. We can also see that any initialization techniques performs better than the standard initialization originally proposed with the eco-system setup, around 3 times better for the random and best agent approach and 6 times better for the forked agent. This can be explained by the fact that any new agent is initialized with a Neural Network which has already been trained on similar but slightly different environment, therefore a part of the learning has already been done and is transferred to the new agent.

Overall, we can see that the forked agent approach offers a large increase in terms of performance as well as in terms of stability when comparing the deviation error.

6   Discussion/Conclusion

We have explored different ways of initializing the new agents in the eco-system setup and the associated increases of performance. The forked agent initialization approach improves significantly the generalization capabilities of the solution as well as drastically reduces the number of training cycles needed compared to the original eco-system approach. By using agents that have been trained on multiple environments before joining the pool of policies, we have increased the generalization of each agent used in this new setting. This approach leverages the best of the two worlds, the increased generalizability of an agent which has been trained on multiple environments as well as the stability of the eco-system setting where catastrophic forgetting has been fully eliminated. In order to enhance the performance of both the eco-system as well as the newly proposed forked agent approach, it would be interesting to see if we can find a way to predict which agents are more prone to generalize and focus on these to quickly remove the other ones from the pool. In addition, trying to reduce the number of inferences by predicting if a given agent will offer good performance on a given environment without running it would give a significant performance increase.

Acknowledgements. A preprint version (earlier iteration) of this paper, written by the same authors can be found on arXiv: Moulin et al. [23]).

References

1. Moulin, O., Francois-Lavet, V., Elbers, P., Hoogendoorn, M.: Improving adaptability to new environments and removing catastrophic forgetting in Reinforcement Learning by using an eco-system of agents arXiv preprint arXiv:2204.06550 (2021)
2. Zhiwei, J., Xuanlin, L., Zhan, L., Shuang, L., Yiran, W., Hao, S.: Improving Policy Optimization with Generalist-Specialist Learning arXiv preprint arXiv:2206.12984 (2022)
3. Cobbe, K., Klimov, O., Hesse, C., Kim, T., Schulman, J.: Quantifying generalization in reinforcement learning. In: Proceedings of the 36th International Conference on Machine Learning, in Proceedings of Machine Learning Research, vol. 97, pp. 1282–1289 (2019). https://proceedings.mlr.press/v97/cobbe19a.html
4. Cobbe, K., Hesse, C., Hilton, J., Schulman, J.: Lever- aging procedural generation to benchmark reinforcement learning. In International Conference on Machine Learning, pp. 2048–2056. PMLR, 2020a (2020)
5. Ghosh, D., Singh, A., Rajeswaran, A., Kumar, V., Levine, S.: Divide-and-conquer reinforcement learning (2017). arXiv preprint arXiv:1711.09874 (2017)
6. Justesen, N., Torrado, R.R., Bontrager, P., Khalifa, A., Togelius, J., Risi, S.: Illuminating generalization in deep reinforcement learning through procedural level generation. arXiv preprint arXiv:1806.10729 (2018)
7. Ghiassian, S., Rafiee, B., Lo, Y.L., White, A.: Improving performance in reinforcement learning by breaking generalization in neural networks. arXiv preprint arXiv:2003.07417 (2020)
8. Van Hasselt, H., Guez, A., Silver, D.: Deep reinforcement learning with double q-learning. In: Proceedings of the AAAI Conference on Artificial Intelligence (vol. 30, no. 1) (2016)
9. Nichol, A., Pfau, V., Hesse, C., Klimov, O., Schulman, J.: Gotta learn fast: A new benchmark for generalization in RL. arXiv preprint arXiv:1804.03720 (2018)
10. Packer, C., Gao, K., Kos, J., Krähenbühl, P., Koltun, V., Song, D.: Assessing generalization in deep reinforcement learning. arXiv preprint arXiv:1810.12282 (2018)
11. Raffin, A., et al.: Stable Baselines3 (2019). https://github.com/DLR-RM/stable-baselines3
12. Chevalier-Boisvert, M., Willems, L., Pal, S.: Minimalistic Gridworld Environment for OpenAI Gym (2018). https://github.com/maximecb/gym-minigrid

13. Konda, V., Tsitsiklis, J.: Actor-Critic algorithms. In: Advances in Neural Information Processing Systems, vol. 12. (NIPS 1999) (1999)
14. Igl, M., et al.: Generalization in reinforcement learning with selective noise injection and information bottleneck. arXiv preprint arXiv:1910.12911 (2019)
15. Sonar, A., Pacelli, V., Majumdar, A.: Invariant policy optimization: towards stronger generalization in reinforcement learning. In: Learning for Dynamics and Control, pp. 21–33. PMLR (2021)
16. Chen, J.Z.: Reinforcement Learning Generalization with Surprise Minimization. arXiv preprint arXiv:2004.12399 (2020)
17. Lu, X., Lee, K., Abbeel, P., Tiomkin, S.: Dynamics Generalization via Information Bottleneck in Deep Reinforcement Learning. arXiv preprint arXiv:2008.00614 (2020)
18. Schulman, J., Wolski, F., Dhariwal, P., Radford, A., Klimov, O.: Proximal policy optimization algorithms. arXiv preprint arXiv:1707.06347 (2017)
19. Boulila, W., Driss, M., Alshanqiti, E., Al-Sarem, M., Saeed, F., Krichen, M.: Weight Initialization Techniques for Deep Learning Algorithms in Remote Sensing: Recent Trends and Future Perspectives arXiv:2102.07004 (2021)
20. Taylor, M.E., Stone, P.: Transfer learning for reinforcement learning domains: a survey. J. Mach. Learn. Res. **10**(2009), 1633–1685 (2009)
21. Stable baselines 3. Details on stable baselines 3 PPO implementation. https:// spinningup.openai.com/en/latest/algorithms/ppo.html
22. Puterman, M.L.: Markov Decision Processes: Discrete Stochastic Dynamic Programming. Wiley, Hoboken (2014)
23. Moulin, O., Francois-Lavet, V., Elbers, P., Hoogendoorn, M.: Improving generalization in reinforcement learning through forked agents, previous version of this paper, arXiv preprint, arXiv:2212.06451 (2022)

Accelerating Deep Reinforcement Learning with Fuzzy Logic Rules

Jinxin Zhan[1,2], Xiaodong Yue[1,2(✉)], Zihao Li[1], and Kai Han[1,2]

[1] School of Computer Engineering and Science, Shanghai University,
Shanghai 20444, China
{zjx97420,yswantfly,zihao,hankai}@shu.edu.cn
[2] Artificial Intelligence Institute of Shanghai University, Shanghai, China

Abstract. Most deep reinforcement learning methods focus on the agent's learning performance but ignore the uncertainty in the environment, which would lead to a lot of redundant interaction data and slow learning speed. We propose two novel policy frameworks that extract human knowledge through fuzzy inference systems and incorporate it into deep reinforcement learning to accelerate agent training. We also compared agent learning for two different combinations. Our frameworks allow the agent to choose an action based on a new probability distribution that reduce the negative impact of future events. Thereby helping the agent reduce invalid interaction data and improve learning efficiency. We conduct experiments in multiple game environments, and the result exhibits that our method can effectively reduces training episodes, and achieve a better learning result in the mid-term.

Keywords: Deep reinforcement learning · Fuzzy inference system · Policy framework · Learning efficiency

1 Introduction

Reinforcement learning [15] depicts a way of programming an agent to complete a task by rewarding and punishing it without specific instruction. But reinforcement learning is inherently limited to fairly low-dimensional problems. In tasks with large action and state spaces, reinforcement learning is almost infeasible. With the deep reinforcement learning [10] emerged, reinforcement learning extends from non-parametric methods to achieve low-dimensional pixel-level tasks to end-to-end implementation of high-dimensional video-level tasks. But deep reinforcement learning still has problems. Figure 1 is an implementation of Proximal Policy Optimization (PPO) [14] in the FlappyBird environment. Deep reinforcement learning lacks guidance on the agent's actions at the beginning of

This work was supported by National Natural Science Foundation of China (Serial Nos. 61991410, 61976134, 61991415) and Natural Science Foundation of Shanghai (NO. 21ZR1423900) and Open Project Foundation of Intelligent Information Processing Key Laboratory of Shanxi Province, China (No. CICIP2021001).

H. Fujita et al. (Eds.): IEA/AIE 2023, LNAI 13926, pp. 261–272, 2023.
https://doi.org/10.1007/978-3-031-36822-6_23

training, requires a lot of exploration to form an effective strategy, and only the feedback (reward) of the environment will greatly increase the training time.

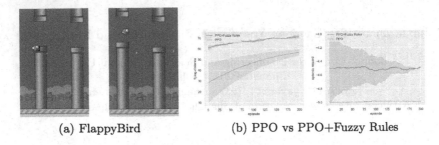

(a) FlappyBird   (b) PPO vs PPO+Fuzzy Rules

Fig. 1. Learn forward policy at FlappyBird environment. Under the premise of training only 200 episodes, the policy that incorporate fuzzy logic rules have longer flying distance and larger episode reward, which means it can pass more obstacles.

To mitigate this problem, incorporating prior knowledge [3] is considered a useful method. There are several ways to incorporate prior knowledge into reinforcement learning methods [1] to enhance performance. The first is imitative learning [6,12,13]. Imitative learning can be learned from trajectories provided by experts. But for non-experts, it is difficult and time-consuming to provide demonstration data to agents. Simple and high-level representation is more suitable for guiding agents in learning unknown scenarios, where the main challenge is how to represent human prior knowledge in high-level representations. The use of natural language [4,5,7] to represent human knowledge is a straightforward idea. In fact, this is a promising technology, but it also has its limitations. The biggest problem is that it needs to be pre-trained. These knowledge that needs to be pre-trained is often imprecise and prone to semantic uncertainty with insufficient trained data and annotation. In contrast to fuzzy logic, which is an excellent tool for dealing with semantic uncertainty.

Fuzzy logic [18] is able to solve complex and ill-defined systems and improve the interpretability of algorithms by processing input data in a flexible way similar to human. It provides theoretical support for the representation of prior knowledge in partially uncertain states while reinforcement learning works better in unknow environments. In this paper, we propose a new prior knowledge representation that integrates fuzzy logic rules into deep reinforcement learning to accelerate training.

The main contributions of this work are:

- A new adaptive rule module is provided to form a simple but effective representation of fuzzy rules and incorporate deep reinforcement learning, which accepts simple, incomplete rule descriptions;
- Our approach does not need to pre-trained, and the model can use the information in fuzzy rules to accelerate training in an end-to-end manner;
- Provides a new idea for agent learning in scenes with sparse rewards.

2   Background

2.1   Deep Reinforcement Learning

In reinforcement learning, the interaction process between agent and environment can be considered as a Markov decision process(MDP). An MDP is defined by the 5-tuple $\langle \mathcal{S}, \mathcal{A}, \mathcal{P}, \mathcal{R}, \gamma \rangle$, where $\mathcal{S}$ is the state space, $\mathcal{A}$ is the action space, $\mathcal{P}$ represents the state transition function, $\mathcal{R}$ is the reward function and γ is the discount factor. At a timestep t, agent obtains a state from the state space $\mathcal{S}$, and then selects an action to execute in the action space $\mathcal{A}$ according to the policy π, which is a mapping from the state space to the action space. Through the reward function $\mathcal{R}$ and state transition function $\mathcal{P}$, the agent receives the reward and transitions to the next state. The goal of the agent is to learn a discounted long-term reward expectation that maximizes each state. The state value function $V_\pi(s)$ is an estimate of the expected future reward when following the policy π, which measures how good each state is:

$$V_\pi(s) = \mathbb{E}_\pi \left[R_t | s_t = s \right], R_t = \sum_{k=0}^{\infty} \gamma^k r_{t+k} \tag{1}$$

2.2   Fuzzy Logic and Fuzzy Inference Systems

The idea of fuzzy logic (FL) was originally proposed by Prof. Lotfi Zadeh [17] and it was presented not as a control methodology, but rather as a way of processing data by allowing partial set membership.

Compared to crisp set, fuzzy logic is based on fuzziness rather than being limited to zero and one gives it the ability to represent and process semantic sentences in natural language. And the fuzzy rule R_i can be represented as:

$$R_i : If \ x_1 \ is \ A_1^h \ And \ x_2 \ is \ A_2^h \ Then \ y \ is \ B \tag{2}$$

where R_i is the ith rule of the rule base, x_j $(j = 1, 2)$ is the observed value of the environment, A_j^h is the hth linguistic value for input i, and $h = \{1, 2, ..., n\}$ where n is the total number of membership functions for input x_j, y is the output variable of fuzzy system and B is the linguistic value for y.

Fuzzy inference system [8] is the process of mapping a given input to an output using fuzzy logic. For a fuzzy set A, where the element x belongs to the set with a value in the [0,1] interval, we can use the fuzzy membership function to describe the degree to which the input variable belongs to the fuzzy set:

$$\mu_A : X \to [0, 1] \tag{3}$$

X is a space defined in specific scenario for membership function.

In fuzzy sets, *Zadeh* defines the basic operation rules of fuzzy sets. For the two fuzzy sets A_1 and A_2, μ_1 and μ_2 are their membership functions respectively. There are two main calculation methods for fuzzy sets: *Union* and *Intersection*.

Union. Assuming a new fuzzy set called U, its membership function called f_U. In *Union* computation, U can be written as $U = A_1 \cup A_2$, whose membership function is related to A_1 and A_2 by:

$$\mu_U(x) = max\,[\mu_{A_1}, \mu_{A_2}] \tag{4}$$

Intersection. Similarly, assuming a new fuzzy set called I, its membership function called μ_I. In *Intersection* computation, I can be written as $I = A_1 \cap A_2$, whose membership function is related to A_1 and A_2 by:

$$\mu_I(x) = min\,[\mu_{A_1}, \mu_{A_2}] \tag{5}$$

In our work, we use multiplication operation to compute the *Intersection*.

3   Deep Reinforcement Learning with Fuzzy Logic Rules

To implement the deep reinforcement learning with fuzzy logic rules, we propose two strategies to incorporate the action preferences of fuzzy rules into the policy networks (i.e., actor networks). The first one is state concate strategy, in which we directly concate the state vector with the action preference vector output by the fuzzy inference system. Figure 3 presents the framework or the state concate strategy. In the second strategy, we utilize an attention mechanism to integrate the fuzzy action preferences with the state vector and present the framework in Fig. 4. Both of the two frameworks support end-to-end model training.

3.1   Action Preference with Adaptive Fuzzy Inference System

Considering the different effects of different fuzzy rules on action choices, we construct an adaptive fuzzy inference system $\psi(s)$ to generate the preferences of actions. A shown in Fig. 2, different from the traditional fuzzy inference system, we set the weight parameter α for the fuzzy membership of each feature of a state. The weight parameters are used to measure and state features for action choice.

The adaptive fuzzy inference system takes the state information of the environment as the input and outputs a vector p of fuzzy preferences of actions. Given a l-dimensional feature vector of a state $s = (s_1, s_2, \ldots, s_l)$, for each fuzzy rule r, we construct a fuzzy set and the corresponding membership function $\mu_{R_r}^i(s_i)$ for the ith feature in the state vector s.

As the Fig. 2 shown, the adaptive network included in the fuzzy system is a multilayer feed-forward network, hyperparameters of the membership functions need to be learned. The first layer of network is responsible for the fuzzification of the state input, for each membership function will get an output of this layer O_i^1 ($i = 1, 2, \cdots, l$). The second layer is a rule strength release layer. In order to

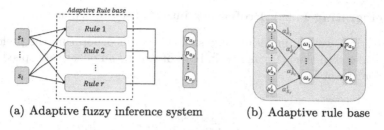

(a) Adaptive fuzzy inference system   (b) Adaptive rule base

Fig. 2. Architecture of adaptive fuzzy inference system.

be able to calculate the gradient, we multiply the membership functions to get the value of min and get the rule strength $\boldsymbol{w}$:

$$w_r = min\{\alpha_r^1 \cdot \mu_r^1(s_1), \ldots, \alpha_r^l \cdot \mu_r^l(s_l)\}, \tag{6}$$

where $\alpha_r^1 \ldots \alpha_r^l$ are the significance weights of the state features. In all tasks, we initialize the values of the weight parameters as 1 and iteratively update the parameters according to the Eq. (16). We set each fuzzy membership function as the following segmented linear function,

$$\mu_r^i(s_i) = \begin{cases} 0 & s_i < \underline{\xi} \\ \omega_i \cdot s_i + \eta_i & \underline{\xi} \le s_i < \overline{\xi} \\ 1 & s_i \ge \overline{\xi}. \end{cases} \tag{7}$$

$\underline{\xi}, \overline{\xi}$ are the thresholds of feature values and the parameters ω_i, η_i can be set based on the domain experience in specific tasks.

In the third layer of the network we normalize the strength of all rules, calculate the credibility of each rule and output $p_{a_j} (j = 1, 2, \cdots, j, \cdots, r)$. It is the decision of each fuzzy rule corresponds to an action a_r, the preference of the action p_{a_j} inferred by the rule can be computed as

$$p_{a_j} = \frac{w_j}{\Sigma_t w_t}(t = 1, 2, \cdots, r), \tag{8}$$

Combining the preferences of all the fuzzy rules, we can obtain the following action preference vector $\boldsymbol{p}$ of the entire fuzzy system.

$$\boldsymbol{p} = \psi_\alpha(\boldsymbol{s}) = [p_{a_1}, \ldots p_{a_k} \ldots, p_{a_{|\mathcal{A}|}}], \tag{9}$$

where $\mathcal{A}$ is the action space, p_{a_k} denotes the preference of the action k. If there are multiple fuzzy rules corresponding to the same action a, we set the preference of the action as the maximum preference produced by the rules, e.g., for two rules r_1 and r_2, if $a = a_{r_1} = a_{r_2}$, $p_a = max\{p_{a_{r_1}}, p_{a_{r_2}}\}$. The high preference indicates that the fuzzy inference system has a strong tendency to choose the action.

3.2 Integrating Fuzzy Preference into Actor Network

In this section, we will introduce two strategies of incorporating the preferences of fuzzy rules into the actor network, both of which can effectively speed up the deep enforcement learning.

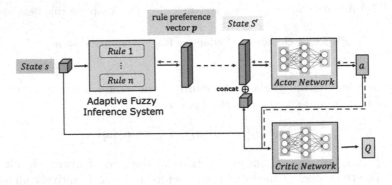

Fig. 3. State concate strategy of incorporating fuzzy preference into actor network.

State Concate Strategy. Figure 3 presents the framework of the state concate strategy, which consists of three modules of adaptive fuzzy inference system, actor network and critic network. The vector of action preference $p = [p_{a_1}, \ldots, p_{a_{|\mathcal{A}|}}]$ produced by the fuzzy system is concated with the state vector s and form the extended state vector as

$$s' = concat\,[s, p]\,. \tag{10}$$

Inputting the extended state vector s' into the action network, the fuzzy preference of actions will influence the final decision of choosing actions.

Attention Strategy. The rule policy vector output by the fuzzy inference system should be different under different states, which means that the mapping relation from states to rule policies is required to be constantly changing. So it may not be sufficient to use a fully connected network to learn this relation only. In order to learn this dynamic and complex relationship, we decided to refer to the attention mechanism [11] to capture it (shown in Fig. 4). The attention mechanism is widely used in deep learning. The attention mechanism can help the agent focus on the features in the state information that have a greater impact on the action. The rule preference vector p obtained at this time can reflect the important part of the state vector s. First we calculate the feature importance value in the state vector at timestep t:

$$Atten(s, p) = Linear(Tanh(Linear(s) + p)) \tag{11}$$

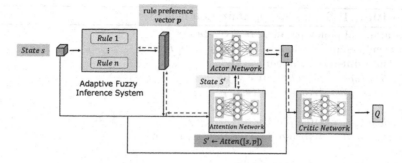

Fig. 4. Attention strategy of incorporating fuzzy preference into actor network.

From this, we can calculate the importance of different features in the state space at timestep t, that is, the weight vector of the feature:

$$\partial = softmax(Atten(\boldsymbol{s}, \boldsymbol{p})) \tag{12}$$

By linearly weighting each element of the state vector and the corresponding weight, we recalculate and obtain a new state vector $\boldsymbol{s}'$:

$$\boldsymbol{s}' = \partial \cdot \boldsymbol{s} \tag{13}$$

The new state $\boldsymbol{s}'$ obtained through the attention mechanism can strengthen the features related to the rules and improve the learning efficiency of the agent.

Policy with Incorporating Rule Preference. Now we can give the representation of the policy with incorporating rule preference $\pi_\theta(a|s,p)$. Under our frameworks, the policy $\pi_\theta(a|s,p)$ can take the form as:

$$\pi_\theta(a|s,p) = Actor(concat(s,p)) \tag{14}$$

$$\pi_\theta(a|s,p) = Actor(softmax(Atten(s,p) \cdot s)) \tag{15}$$

where θ is the parameter of the Actor network, we can further expand p, given $\psi_\alpha(s)$ is the adaptive fuzzy inference system, $p = \psi_\alpha(s)$, then the policy π can be expressed as $\pi_\theta(a|s, \psi_\alpha(s))$, α is the parameter of the fuzzy inference system. In the whole module, p actually can be seen as an output in the middle of the entire policy network, so α can update with stochastic gradient descent of the objective function:

$$\alpha, \theta = \underset{\alpha,\theta}{argmax} \frac{1}{|\mathcal{D}|T} \sum_{\tau \in \mathcal{D}} \sum_{t=0}^{T} min(\frac{\pi_\theta(a_t|s_t, \psi_\alpha(s_t))}{\pi_{\theta_{old}}(a_t|s_t, \psi_\alpha(s_t))} \hat{A}_t,$$
$$clip(\frac{\pi_\theta(a_t|s_t, \psi_\alpha(s_t))}{\pi_{\theta_{old}}(a_t|s_t, \psi_\alpha(s_t))}, 1 - \epsilon, 1 + \epsilon)\hat{A}_t) \tag{16}$$

With the update of α, the fuzzy inference system can adaptively adjust the influence of different rules on agent in the current state.

Algorithm 1: Simulation-optimization heuristic

Data: initial policy parameters θ, α, state s

1 set membership functions μ and fuzzy rules R;

2 p =Fuzzy Inference System $\psi_\alpha(s)$;

3 **if** *policy type = concat* **then**

4 | $\pi_\theta(a|s,p) = Actor(concat(s,p))$;

5 **end**

6 **if** *policy type = attention* **then**

7 | $\pi_\theta(a|s,p) = Actor(softmax(Atten(s,p)) \cdot s)$;

8 **end**

9 **while** *episode < MaxEpisode* **do**

10 | **if** *game over* **then**

11 | | episode $\leftarrow$ episode $+$ 1

12 | **end**

13 | Collect a set of trajectories $\mathcal{D}$ by running policy $\pi_\theta(a|s,p)$ in the environment;

14 | Compute the Generalized Advantage Estimator $\hat{A}_t$;

15 | Update the policy by maximizing objective function:

16 | $\alpha, \theta = \underset{\alpha,\theta}{argmax} \frac{1}{|\mathcal{D}|T} \sum_{\tau \in \mathcal{D}} \sum_{t=0}^{T} min(\frac{\pi_\theta(a_t|s_t,\psi_\alpha^t(s))}{\pi_{\theta_{old}}(a_t|s_t,\psi_\alpha^t(s))} \hat{A}_t(s_t,a_t),$

| $clip(\frac{\pi_\theta(a_t|s_t,\psi_\alpha^t(s))}{\pi_{\theta_{old}}(a_t|s_t,\psi_\alpha^t(s))}, 1 - \epsilon, 1 + \epsilon)\hat{A}_t(s_t,a_t))$

17 **end**

---

4   Experiments

In this section, we will evaluate the above two policy frameworks. In order to compare the effects, we take policy-based method PPO as baseline algorithm and conduct experiments in multiple different types of environments.

4.1   Experimental Setting

We conducted experiments in a total of four tasks, including FlappyBird [16], MountainCarContinuous, CartPole, and LunarLander [2], which included discrete, continuous and reward-sparse environments to illustrate the superior performance of our approach. We also conducted the ablation experiments to illustrate the effect of rules on agent's learning.

The parameters of the experiments are set as follows: for all tasks, our activation function uses *softmax*, we set the discounted factor $\gamma = 0.99$. Adam optimizer [9] is used in our framework with the learning rate of 1.0e$-$4, no delay is set to get the reward, and the advantage function is used. Agent's update timesteps is 128 with batchsize $=$ 128.

the dynamic relationship between the state and the rules in the early epoch, and the reward increases faster than the state concate strategy at first.

We also conducted ablation experiments and shown results in Fig. 7. We set up a comparison experiment using two rules, four rules and baseline under the two policy frameworks. It can be seen that both the attention strategy and the state concate strategy are verified that the optimized fuzzy inference system proposed in this paper can accelerate learning efficiently.

Table 1. The agent's score at different stages of training and the average number of episodes the agent completed the task.

Environment	Method	Start	Median	End	MeanEpisode
FlappyBird	Baseline	−5.00	−5.00	6.88	1024
	Attention strategy	**0.22**	5.42	7.28	**134**
	Concat strategy	−4.20	6.22	7.30	303
CartPole	Baseline	75.95	415.34	440.24	1331.5
	Attention strategy	**308.05**	428.07	468.82	**719**
	Concat strategy	302.68	470.48	477.07	795
LunarLander	Baseline	91.32	116.65	150.47	1339.5
	Attention strategy	**205.31**	196.35	224.79	**541.5**
	Concat strategy	155.07	239.90	261.71	801.5
MountainCar Continuous	Baseline	−171.50	−157.28	−158.26	False
	At tention strategy	**−88.15**	−88.54	−88.60	**114**
	Concat strategy	−89.35	−87.96	−88.88	152

5   Conclusion

In this paper, we propose two policy frameworks to incorporate fuzzy rules as human prior knowledge into deep reinforcement learning algorithms. It will significantly reduce the computational resources required for training and make it possible for deep reinforcement learning to complete tasks in large and complex topological systems. We build a trainable and optimized fuzzy inference system, so that the human prior knowledge can guide the agent better. Both in discrete and continuous environments, we provide a practical end-to-end solution for the implementation of deep reinforcement learning in real tasks.

In the comparison experiment of the two methods, we found that the complex rule fusion method hinders the agent's exploration to some extent in the midterm. When the rules still have an impact on the agent, the rules may collide with the agent's greedy strategy and force the agent to choose actions that are more consistent with the rules. In future work, we consider making the output of the fuzzy inference system uncertain to make the agent's choice of actions more flexible, thus balancing the "exploration and exploitation" problem in the middle of training.

References

1. Arumugam, D., Lee, J.K., Saskin, S., Littman, M.L.: Deep reinforcement learning from policy-dependent human feedback. ArXiv abs/1902.04257 (2019)
2. Brockman, G., et al.: OpenAI gym (2016)
3. Christiano, P.F., Leike, J., Brown, T., Martic, M., Legg, S., Amodei, D.: Deep reinforcement learning from human preferences. In: Guyon, I., et al. (eds.) Advances in Neural Information Processing Systems, vol. 30. Curran Associates, Inc. (2017)
4. Goyal, P., Niekum, S., Mooney, R.: Pixl2r: guiding reinforcement learning using natural language by mapping pixels to rewards. In: Proceedings of the 2020 Conference on Robot Learning. Proceedings of Machine Learning Research, vol. 155, pp. 485–497. PMLR (2021)
5. Goyal, P., Niekum, S., Mooney, R.J.: Using natural language for reward shaping in reinforcement learning. In: Proceedings of the Twenty-Eighth International Joint Conference on Artificial Intelligence, IJCAI-19, pp. 2385–2391. International Joint Conferences on Artificial Intelligence Organization (2019). https://doi.org/10.24963/ijcai.2019/331
6. Ho, J., Ermon, S.: Generative adversarial imitation learning. In: Advances in Neural Information Processing Systems, vol. 29. Curran Associates, Inc. (2016)
7. Jiang, Y., Gu, S.S., Murphy, K.P., Finn, C.: Language as an abstraction for hierarchical deep reinforcement learning. In: Wallach, H., Larochelle, H., Beygelzimer, A., d'Alché-Buc, F., Fox, E., Garnett, R. (eds.) Advances in Neural Information Processing Systems, vol. 32. Curran Associates, Inc. (2019)
8. Jouffe, L.: Fuzzy inference system learning by reinforcement methods. IEEE Trans. Syst. Man Cybern. Part C (Appl. Rev.) 28(3), 338–355 (1998). https://doi.org/10.1109/5326.704563
9. Kingma, D.P., Ba, J.: Adam: A method for stochastic optimization. arXiv preprint arXiv:1412.6980 (2014)
10. Mnih, V., et al.: Playing Atari with deep reinforcement learning. CoRR abs/1312.5602 (2013)
11. Niu, Z., Zhong, G., Yu, H.: A review on the attention mechanism of deep learning. Neurocomputing 452, 48–62 (2021)
12. Pomerleau, D.A.: Efficient training of artificial neural networks for autonomous navigation. Neural Comput. 3(1), 88–97 (1991)
13. Reddy, S., Dragan, A.D., Levine, S.: SQIL: imitation learning via reinforcement learning with sparse rewards. In: International Conference on Learning Representations (2020)
14. Schulman, J., Wolski, F., Dhariwal, P., Radford, A., Klimov, O.: Proximal policy optimization algorithms. CoRR abs/1707.06347 (2017)
15. Sutton, R.S., Barto, A.G.: Reinforcement Learning: An Introduction, 2nd edn. The MIT Press, Cambridge (2018)
16. Tasfi, N.: Pygame learning environment (2016). https://github.com/ntasfi/PyGame-Learning-Environment
17. Zadeh, L.: Fuzzy sets. Inf. Control 8(3), 338–353 (1965). https://doi.org/10.1016/S0019-9958(65)90241-X
18. Zadeh, L.A., Klir, G.J., Yuan, B.: Fuzzy Sets, Fuzzy Logic, and Fuzzy Systems. World Scientific, Singapore (1996). https://doi.org/10.1142/2895

Dynamic Attention Model – A Deep Reinforcement Learning Approach for Container Relocation Problem

Fengwei Liu, Te Ye, and Zizhen Zhang$^{(\boxtimes)}$ (ID)

School of Computer Science and Engineering, Sun Yat-sen University,
Guangzhou, China
`zhangzzh7@mail.sysu.edu.cn`

Abstract. Container Relocation Problem (CRP) is one of the most important and fundamental problems in the terminal's operations. Given a specified layout of the container yard with all the container retrieval priorities, CRP aims to identify an ideal container movement sequence so as to minimize the total number of container rehandling operations. In this paper, we are the first to propose a deep reinforcement learning method to tackle the problem. It adopts a dynamic attention model to respond to the changes of the layout. The long short-term memory and multi-head attention layers are introduced to better extract the features of stacks. We use a policy gradient algorithm with rollout baseline to train the model. The experiments demonstrate that our method can solve the problem effectively compared with other classic approaches. We conclude that the deep reinforcement learning approach has a great potential in solving CRP, as it can find desirable solution without using much expert domain knowledge.

Keywords: Container Relocation Problem · Deep Reinforcement Learning · Attention Model

1 Introduction

With the rapid development of globalization, there has been a constant increase in the volume of international trade. Seaborne transportation has experienced rapid expansion in recent years. The seaport container terminal, which serves as a crucial hub for seaborne transportation, is under increasing demand from carriers, shippers and consignees. As a result, advanced automation techniques, mostly based on intelligent algorithms, have been widely applied in the seaport container terminal.

Container Relocation Problem (CRP), also known as block relocation problem (BRP), is one of the most important and fundamental problems in the terminal's operations. It can be briefly stated as follows. A collection of standard containers is stored in a two-dimensional container yard. The retrieval priorities of these containers are specified in advance. Then what is the optimal handling

H. Fujita et al. (Eds.): IEA/AIE 2023, LNAI 13926, pp. 273–285, 2023.
https://doi.org/10.1007/978-3-031-36822-6_24

operations of retrieving all the containers subject to their priorities? Since a container can only be accessed from the top of a stack, when a *target container* to be retrieved is blocked by other containers on top of it in the same stack, those *blocking containers* must first be relocated to other stacks. Such operation is known as a *rehandle*. The goal of CRP is essentially to minimize the number of rehandling operations (or rehandles).

There are a few variants of CRP which have substantial differences. In this work, we consider a classic version that has the following restrictions. However, we believe that our work can also be generalized to solve other kinds of CRP.

1. Only those containers on the top of the target container can be relocated somewhere.
2. All the containers have distinct retrieval priorities.
3. The height of a stack is bounded by an identical value.

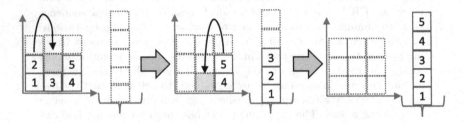

Fig. 1. An example of CRP.

We take Fig. 1 as an example. There are 5 containers in a three-stack yard bay. The container with the smallest label must be retrieved first. The height limitation of each stack is 3. To retrieve target container 1, the blocking container 2 must be moved to an other stack. Note that at this time it is not allowed to move containers in stack 2 or 3 due the first restriction. After container 2 is relocated to the top of the second stack, containers 1, 2 and 3 can be retrieved one by one. Next, container 4 is blocked by container 5. After relocating container 5, all the containers can be retrieved. In sum, the minimum number of rehandles is 2.

CRP is an NP-hard problem [3], it is difficult to find the exact solution in polynomial time. Traditional approaches include iterative algorithms and integer programming formulation handled by solvers like CPLEX. In recent works, some machine learning techniques were proposed to improve the bound calculation in iterative algorithm [27]. To our best knowledge, there is no existing deep reinforcement learning (DRL) method for CRP. We therefore attempt to use a novel end-to-end DRL method to solve the problem. Our experiments show that DRL has a great potential in tackling CRP. In sum, the contributions of this paper can be summarized as follows.

1. We are the first to propose an end-to-end DRL method. We introduce long short-term memory and multi-head attention layers to better extract the feature of stacks. A novel dynamic encoder-decoder architecture is devised to respond to the changes of the layout.
2. We demonstrate that the DRL approach has a great potential in solving different scales of CRP, as it can find desirable solution without using much handcrafted expert domain knowledge.

The remaining of the paper is structured as follows. Section 2 reviews the related literature. Section 3 gives the problem definition of CRP. Section 4 presents the proposed DRL method. Section 5 describes the experimental study and reports the results. Section 6 makes the conclusions.

2   Related Work

2.1   Container Relocation Problem

CRP have been studied for decades. We hereby review some classic approaches in this section. Kim and Hong [10] first introduced CRP and devised a branch-and-bound method, in which they suggested a straightforward lower bound on the overall number of relocations. Caserta et al. [4] used a heuristic influenced by the dynamic programming technique embedded with the corridor method (CM), which places additional constraints on the solution space. Zhu et al. [28] proposed an improved lower limit, denoted as LB3, for CRP with different priorities. They used it to build a distinct-priority iterative deepening A* (IDA*) algorithm for CRP. Tanaka et al. [21] created LB4 and LB4e, which are improvements and extensions of LB3 for CRP with duplicate priorities. They presented an embedded LB4 and LB4e branch-and-bound algorithm within iterative deepening. Zhang et al. [27] made LB4 better for a restricted CRP with different priorities. They acknowledged that computing their lower bound, ELB4, at each node in the branch-and-bound method is not a good idea, because it does not lead to a meaningful improvement over LB4 in proportion to the additional computation. More recently, Tanaka et al. [22] proposed a novel exact algorithm, which is an iterative deepening branch-and-bound (IDBB) algorithm. Until the optimality gap is zero, it iteratively calculates lower and upper bounds by resolving the associated integer programming issues.

CRP can also be handled by state-of-the-art solvers by mathematical programming formulations. BRP-II, a binary formulation, was presented by Caserta et al. [3]. Later, it is enhanced in Zehendner et al. [25] by deleting extraneous variables, tightening some constraints, and using a preprocessing step to modify some variables. The latter two improvements are made in [6] and [25]. Zehendner and Feillet [26] suggested a relocation sequence-based reformulation to allow a column generation method for BRP. Additionally, Galle et al. [7] and da Silva et al. [18] recently presented a few stronger binary formulations. Bacci et al. [1] proposed an IP model along with an exponential number of constraints.

Lu et al. [15] developed a new and strong MIP formulation called BRP-m3, as well as a novel iterative method based on MIP formulation.

For more studies on the variants and classic methods of CRP, readers are encouraged to read [5,8,13,17,20,23].

2.2 Deep Reinforcement Learning for Combinatorial Optimization Problem

Inspired by the great success of DRL in playing games [19], applying DRL on combinatorial optimization problems becomes a hot research area in recent years. For example, to address routing problems, a pointer network-based sequence-to-sequence paradigm [2] was proposed. The multi-head attention method [12] was adopted to enhance the policy network for routing problems, which was inspired by the Transformer architecture designed in Vaswani et al. [24]. To improve the performance, a dynamic attention model with a dynamic encoder-decoder architecture [16] was introduced. It recalculates the embedding after constructing a partial solution. In Li et al. [14], they combined the static and the dynamic embedding to train the attention model.

CRP has some similarities with those well-studied combinatorial optimization problems. However, to our best knowledge, there is no existing DRL method for CRP.

3 Problem Definition

The CRP we study considers a two-dimensional container yard with the width (number of stacks) W and height (number of tiers) H. We use i to indicate the index of stacks from left to right, and use j to indicate the index of tiers from bottom to top. In the initial layout, there are N containers to be retrieved from the yard. Each container has a distinct retrieval order labelled from 1 to N.

The layout of the yard can be represented as a two-dimensional array $X[i,j]$, indicating the label of the container in position (i,j). Specifically, if (i,j) is an empty slot, then $X[i,j] = 0$. For example, the yard layout in Fig. 1 is $[[1,2,0],[3,0,0],[4,5,0]]$. We also view the yard layout from the perspective of stacks, i.e., $X = [x_1, x_2, \ldots, x_W]$, where x_i is an H-dimensional vector with respect to the i-th stack.

In order to retrieve a target container, all the blocking containers on top of it should be moved to other stacks. Note that we consider a restricted version of CRP for simplicity. Only those blocking containers can be operated and no container pre-marshalling is allowed.

After some retrieval and rehandling operations, the yard layout will be changed. The target of CRP is to minimize the total number of rehandles until the final layout is empty.

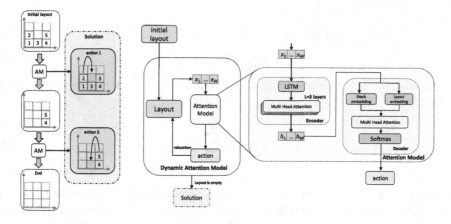

Fig. 2. The Dynamic Attention Model.

4 Proposed Method

In this section, we present the DRL method with the proposed Dynamic Attention Model (DAM), which is designed based on the famous attention model (AM) [12] for routing problems. In traditional AM, the input information is fed into its encoder at the beginning. Then the final solution is directly produced by its decoder without using any intermediate state information. In contrary, our DAM considers dynamic state information. This is because the yard layout will be changed after an operation, and it is better to re-input the new layout into AM to accurately decide the next operation.

4.1 Dynamic Attention Model

Figure 2 shows the overall framework of DAM. It follows the encoder-decoder architecture. The encoder is used to calculate the embeddings of the yard layout. The decoder outputs the action probabilities of a rehandle, i.e., the probabilities of stacks that the blocking container is relocated to. Based on the action probabilities, we can determine a container relocation and obtain a new layout.

Encoder. The inputted layout is represented by $[x_1, x_2, \ldots, x_W]$. Initial stack embeddings $[h_1^0, h_2^0, \ldots, h_W^0]$ are produced by feeding each vector into an LSTM layer, where h_i^0 is a d_h-dimensional tensor ($d_h = 128$ in this work). The design rationale is that a stack is an ordered sequence, so it is natural to apply the recurrent neural network, e.g., LSTM, is to extract its feature.

Next, the hidden embeddings are inputted into $L = 3$ attention layers to produce the final stack embedding $[h_1^L, h_2^L, \ldots, h_W^L]$. Each attention layer consists of two sublayers: a multi-head attention (MHA) sublayer and a fully connected feed-forward (FF) sublayer. Each sublayer involves a batch normalization (BN) and residual connection for better training.

$$\hat{h} = \text{BN}^\ell(h_i^{\ell-1} + \text{MHA}_i^\ell(h_0^{\ell-1}, \dots, h_n^{\ell-1})) \tag{1}$$

$$h_i^\ell = \text{BN}^\ell(\hat{h}_i^\ell + \text{FF}^\ell(\hat{h}_i^\ell)) \tag{2}$$

Finally, the layout embedding $\overline{h}$ is computed by the average of each stack embedding.

$$\overline{h} = \frac{1}{W} \sum_{i=1}^{W} h_i^L \tag{3}$$

Decoder. The decoder outputs the action probabilities according to the stack embedding and layout embedding. Specifically, suppose that a blocking container k in the top of stack i is to be relocated to other stacks. The context embedding h_c is obtained by concatenating the embedding of layout and the i-th stack.

$$h_c = [\overline{h}; h_i^L] \tag{4}$$

The *glimpse* q_g is computed by an MHA layer as follows.

$$q_g = MHA(q, K, V) = softmax(\frac{qK^T}{\sqrt{d_k}})V \tag{5}$$

where q, K and V correspond to the *query, key* and *value*. Specifically, the query $q = W^Q h_c$. The *key* k_i and *value* v_i of i-th stack are computed by the linear projection of stack embedding $k_i = W^K h_i^L$ and $v_i = W^V h_i^L$, respectively. $d_k = \frac{d_h}{M}$ is the query/key dimensionality, where M is the number of heads in MHA ($M = 8$ in this work).

Then, the *compatibility* u_j ($j = 1, 2, \dots, W$) is computed by q_g and k_j as follows.

$$u_j = \begin{cases} -\infty & \text{if stack } j \text{ is masked,} \\ \zeta \cdot tanh(\frac{q_g^T \cdot k_j}{\sqrt{d_k}}) & \text{otherwise.} \end{cases} \tag{6}$$

where ζ is used to clip the result ($\zeta = 10$ in this work). The mask mechanism works as follows. If $j = i$ or $x_{j,H} \neq 0$, u_j is set to $-\infty$. The former condition means that the blocking container in stack i cannot be relocated to the same stack. The latter condition implies that the blocking container cannot be relocated to a *full* stack.

Finally, the probability distribution of selecting stack j is computed by the softmax function.

$$p_j = \frac{e^{u_j}}{\sum_k e^{u_k}}, \quad \forall j = 1, .., W. \tag{7}$$

Algorithm 1. Reinforcement Learning Algorithm for Training DAM.

1: **Input:** training set $\mathcal{X}$, objective function f, batch size B, number of epochs E, batch step S.
2: Initialize θ, $\theta^* \leftarrow \theta$
3: **for** epoch $= 1 \longrightarrow E$ **do**
4:   **for** $step = 1 \longrightarrow S$ **do**
5:     $s_i \leftarrow$ RandomInstance$(\mathcal{X})$, $\forall i \in \{1, ..., B\}$
6:     $l_i^0 \leftarrow s_i$, $\forall i \in \{1, ..., B\}$
7:     $t \leftarrow 0$
8:     **while** layouts $\{l_1^t, ..., l_B^t\}$ are not all empty **do**
9:       $a_i^t \leftarrow$ sampling$(p_\theta(\pi_i^t | l_i^t))$, $\forall i \in \{1, ..., B\}$
10:       $l_i^{t+1} \leftarrow$ operation(l_i^t, a_i^t), $\forall i \in \{1, ..., B\}$
11:       $t \leftarrow t + 1$
12:     **end while**
13:     $b \leftarrow \frac{1}{B} \sum_{i=1}^{B} f(\pi_i)$
14:     $\nabla \mathcal{L} \leftarrow \sum_{i=1}^{B} (f(\pi_i) - b) \nabla_\theta \sum_t \log p_\theta(\pi_i^t | l_i^t)$
15:     $\theta \leftarrow Adam(\theta, \nabla \mathcal{L})$
16:   **end for**
17:   **if** p_θ outperforms p_{θ^*} **then**
18:     $\theta^* \leftarrow \theta$
19:   **end if**
20: **end for**
21: **return** θ^*

4.2 DRL Approach

We use a classic policy gradient DRL method to train DAM [12]. The DAM parameterized by θ learns a stochastic policy $p_\theta(\pi|s)$ to generate the probability distribution of actions for a given instance s. $p_\theta(\pi|s)$ can be computed by the probability chain rule as follows.

$$p_\theta(\pi|s) = \prod_{t=1}^{T} p_\theta(\pi_t | s, \pi_1, ..., \pi_{t-1}) = \prod_{t=1}^{T} p_\theta(\pi_t | l_t), \tag{8}$$

where T corresponds to the time of reaching absorbing goal state (empty layout). l_t is the expected layout at time step t.

In order to train θ to minimize the objective, a standard policy gradient with rollout baseline is adopted. Algorithm 1 shows the whole DRL framework. A batch of B instances is generated to train DAM. For an instance s_i, we use a sampling rollout strategy to determine the next operation a_i^t (line 9), thereby generating the next layout l_i^{t+1} (line 10). When all the instances in a batch are completed, their objective values, i.e., $f(\pi_i)$, $\forall i \in \{1, ..., B\}$, can be obtained as well. We use the mean of batched objective values as a baseline (line 13). Finally, the loss function of DRL is defined in line 14. The network parameters are optimized by Adam optimizer [11] (line 15). The best model θ^* is updated if sampled solutions by θ are better than those by θ^* (lines 17–18).

4.3   Inference Stage

Once the model is well trained, it is leveraged to solve the practical instances. This is known as an *inference* stage. In order to improve the solution quality, we use the sampling rollout strategy several times. In the inference stage for a test instance x, firstly use the greedy rollout strategy on x to produce a solution π_B. Next, a total of U iterations are performed. In each iteration, we use the sampling rollout strategy on the instance x to produce a solution π. The best solution π_B will be updated accordingly.

5   Experiments

In this section, we conduct the computational experiments to evaluate the performance of our method. All the experiments are implemented on a workstation with Intel(R) Xeon(R) CPU E5-2640 v4 at 2.40 GHz and a single GTX1080Ti GPU. The DAM method is implemented using PyTorch. The source code is publicly available.[1]

5.1   Hyperparameters Configurations

Most parameters of DAM follow the settings in [12]. The embedding dimension d_h is set to 128. The number of heads is $M = 8$. The number of MHA layers in the encoder is $L = 3$. The clipping parameter is $\zeta = 10$. The learning rate in Adam optimizer is 10^{-4}. We run 30 epochs to train a model for a particular problem scale. There are 2000 batches in each epoch and the batch size is 128, so there are 256000 randomly generated instances in total. For different problem scales, we randomly generate 1000 instances as the test set to evaluate the model performance.

5.2   Benchmarks and Baselines

We introduce the so-called CM dataset [4] as benchmark data, which is a widely studied dataset[2]. It includes instances with different problem scales. For each problem scale, we use H_0, H, W and N to represent the initial height of a stack, the maximum height of a stack, the width of the yard, and the number of containers, respectively. Note that $H = H_0 + 2$ in this dataset, and $N = H_0 \cdot W$ holds. Finally, each problem scale provides 40 test instances.

The baseline methods include exact methods, heuristic methods and integer programming methods listed as follows.

– KH: It is a branch-and-bound strategy with a mathematical formulation and an efficient heuristic system [10].

---

[1] https://github.com/binarycopycode/CRP_DAM.
[2] https://www.bwl.uni-hamburg.de/en/iwi/forschung/projekte/dataprojekte/brp-instances-caserta-etal-2012.zip.

- ACO: It is an ant colony optimization (ACO) algorithm for CRP proposed by Jovanovic et al. [9].
- IDBB: It is an iterative deepening branch-and-bound (IDBB) algorithm proposed by Tanaka et al. [22]. The source code is available[3].
- BRP-m2: da Silva et al. [18] proposed two new binary formulations of CRP, referred to as BRP-m1 and BRP-m2. We choose BRP-m2 for the comparison, as it is much more efficient than BRP-m1 in their experiments.
- BRP-m3: Lu et al. [15] proposed a new mixed integer programming formulation, and designed a novel MIP-formulation-based iterative procedure with the solver CPLEX.

Table 1. Feasible and optimal solutions found by different methods on CM dataset.

Problem Scale				#Feasible			#Optimal			Time(s)		
H_0	H	W	N	BRP-m2	BRP-m3	DAM	BRP-m2	BRP-m3	DAM	BRP-m2	BRP-m3	DAM
3	5	3	9	40	40	40	40	40	40	1.2	**0.2**	57
3	5	4	12	40	40	40	40	40	38	64.8	**3.5**	90
3	5	5	15	40	40	40	38	40	37	455.2	**46.5**	88
3	5	6	18	35	40	40	25	39	35	1755.2	162.6	**122**
3	5	7	21	30	40	40	17	39	35	2482.6	212.6	**164**
3	5	8	24	14	39	40	3	35	35	3562.3	718.3	**150**
4	6	4	16	31	40	40	25	37	33	1762	515.7	**124**
4	6	5	20	13	35	40	6	21	23	3235	1992.7	**161**
4	6	6	24	6	30	40	2	15	21	3456.7	2480.7	**237**
4	6	7	28	1	14	40	0	7	11	3600	3155.2	**225**
5	7	4	20	8	22	40	3	11	13	3338.7	2697.3	**168**
5	7	5	25	0	8	40	0	2	4	3600	3448	**226**
5	7	6	30	0	0	40	0	0	0	3600	3600	**282**
sum				258	388	**520**	199	**326**	325			

BRP-m2 and BRP-m3 experimental results are copied from [15].

5.3 Results and Analyses

We make comparison among BRP-m2, BRP-m3, KH, ACO, IDBB and our DAM method on the CM dataset. Our solutions are obtained following the procedure in the inference stage.

The results are shown in Table 1 and Table 2. Table 1 presents the number of feasible solutions and optimal solutions that the methods can find on 40 test instances within each problem scale, as well as the total running time. It shows that DAM can always find feasible near-optimal solutions quickly. In contrast, BRP-m2 and BRP-m3 cannot find feasible solutions for some large scale cases. With regard to the number of optimal solutions found, DAM is comparable with BRP-m3, but DAM consumes much less time. The maximum running time is 282 s for handling all the 40 largest scale instances.

---

[3] https://sites.google.com/site/shunjitanaka/brp.

Table 2. Solution results on CM dataset.

Problem Scale				Approximate Method			Exact Method
H_0	H	W	N	KH	ACO	DAM	IDBB
3	5	3	9	7.1	5.00	5.00	5.00
3	5	4	12	10.7	6.18	6.35	6.175
3	5	5	15	14.5	7.02	7.125	7.025
3	5	6	18	18.1	8.40	8.9	8.4
3	5	7	21	20.1	9.28	9.8	9.275
3	5	8	24	16.0	10.65	10.975	10.65
4	6	4	16	16.0	10.20	10.55	10.2
4	6	5	20	23.4	12.95	13.65	12.95
4	6	6	24	26.2	14.02	14.95	14.025
4	6	7	28	32.2	16.12	17.475	16.125
5	7	4	20	23.7	15.42	16.525	15.425
5	7	5	25	37.5	18.95	21.475	18.85
5	7	6	30	45.5	22.15	25.8	22.075

KH results are copied from [4]. ACO results are copied from [9]

Table 3. The impact of the number of sampling times.

Problem Scale				greedy	Number of Sampling Times U					
					80		160		240	
H_0	H	W	N		avg	opt. rate	avg	opt. rate	avg	opt. rate
3	5	3	9	5.662	4.987	88.08%	4.981	87.97%	4.98	87.95%
3	5	4	12	8.095	6.106	75.42%	6.019	74.35%	5.985	73.93%
3	5	5	15	8.982	7.305	81.33%	7.239	80.59%	7.207	80.24%
3	5	6	18	10.74	8.558	79.68%	8.475	78.91%	8.427	78.46%
3	5	7	21	10.691	9.705	90.78%	9.64	90.17%	9.614	89.93%
3	5	8	24	11.587	10.856	93.69%	10.791	93.13%	10.764	92.90%
4	6	4	16	14.645	11.507	78.57%	11.3	77.16%	11.221	76.62%
4	6	5	20	18.244	14.44	79.15%	14.225	77.97%	14.107	77.32%
4	6	6	24	23.157	17.64	76.18%	17.356	74.95%	17.204	74.29%
4	6	7	28	22.155	18.28	82.51%	18.021	81.34%	17.87	80.66%
5	7	4	20	22.38	18.29	81.72%	18.016	80.50%	17.873	79.86%
5	7	5	25	26.597	21.941	82.49%	21.537	80.98%	21.343	80.25%
5	7	6	30	31.567	25.919	82.11%	25.499	80.78%	25.274	80.06%

In Table 2, we summarize the average number of rehandles for different methods. The excellent exact algorithm IDBB can find all the optimal solution. Our DAM method is competitive with other approximate methods. Because DAM is fast and does not need to involve much expert domain knowledge such as heuristic rules, it still has a great potential in several CRP scenarios.

In order to test the impact of the number of sampling rollouts in the inference stage, we randomly generate 1000 instances for each problem scale. Then we test the greedy rollout and the sampling rollouts with $U = 80$, 160 and 240. The average results with optimization rate are reported in Table 3. As we can see, a larger U may generally lead to better results. However, when $U = 240$, the marginal improvement is not very significant.

Table 4. The results of ablation studies.

Problem Scale				AM	DAM-linear	DAM-Conv	DAM
H_0	H	W	N				
3	5	3	9	5.362	4.981	4.983	**4.981**
3	5	4	12	6.509	5.959	**5.938**	5.976
3	5	5	15	8.266	7.192	**7.186**	7.221
3	5	6	18	9.159	8.716	8.581	**8.433**
3	5	7	21	11.612	10.092	10.448	**9.607**
3	5	8	24	11.549	12.091	**10.696**	10.762
4	6	4	16	11.825	11.493	11.213	**11.139**
4	6	5	20	15.308	13.850	14.432	**13.397**
4	6	6	24	18.466	17.526	18.337	**15.669**
4	6	7	28	31.611	21.763	20.606	**17.859**
5	7	4	20	19.469	19.076	18.176	**17.861**
5	7	5	25	24.739	24.211	23.863	**21.325**
5	7	6	30	30.511	26.703	30.412	**25.268**

5.4   Ablation Analyses

In order to exam whether the LSTM and DAM architectures are beneficial in tackling CRP, we further conduct some ablation studies. The following models are tested.

– AM: It is designed by removing the dynamic structure of DAM and following the tradition AM method.
– DAM-linear: It is designed by replacing the LSTM layer with a linear layer.
– DAM-conv: It is designed by replacing the LSTM layer with a convolution layer.

In Table 4, we show the average results on 1000 randomly generated instances for each problem scale. We can find that the dynamic structure has a very significant effect, as AM performs much worse than DAM. In addition, DAM (with LSTM) can outperform DAM with linear/convolution layer for most instances, especially those large scale instances. The ablation studies verify the effectiveness of our approach.

6   Conclusions

In this work, we make the first attempt to apply an end-to-end DRL method for tackling CRP. We design a dynamic encoder-decoder architecture to respond to the changes of yard layout. The LSTM layer and the MHA layer are used to better extract the stack embedding. Our approach can always find feasible and promising solutions efficiently. It is demonstrated that DRL approach has a great potential in solving CRP.

We admit that currently our DRL method is inferior to the state-of-the-art CRP solvers in terms of solution quality. In future, we will try to use more advanced deep neural network and DRL training policy to improve our method. With the rapid development of DRL in combinatorial optimization problems, we believe that more excellent DRL methods can be developed to solve CRP.

Acknowledgements. This work is supported by the Natural Science Foundation of Guangdong Province (No. 2019A1515011169, 2021A1515011301).

References

1. Bacci, T., Mattia, S., Ventura, P.: A branch-and-cut algorithm for the restricted block relocation problem. Eur. J. Oper. Res. **287**(2), 452–459 (2020)
2. Bello, I., Pham, H., Le, Q.V., Norouzi, M., Bengio, S.: Neural combinatorial optimization with reinforcement learning (2017)
3. Caserta, M., Schwarze, S., Voß, S.: A mathematical formulation and complexity considerations for the blocks relocation problem. Eur. J. Oper. Res. **219**(1), 96–104 (2012)
4. Caserta, M., Voß, S., Sniedovich, M.: Applying the corridor method to a blocks relocation problem. OR Spectrum **33**(4), 915–929 (2011)
5. Expósito-Izquierdo, C., Melián-Batista, B., Moreno-Vega, J.M.: A domain-specific knowledge-based heuristic for the blocks relocation problem. Adv. Eng. Inf. **28**(4), 327–343 (2014)
6. Expósito-Izquierdo, C., Melián-Batista, B., Moreno-Vega, J.M.: An exact approach for the blocks relocation problem. Expert Syst. Appl. **42**(17), 6408–6422 (2015). https://doi.org/10.1016/j.eswa.2015.04.021. https://www.sciencedirect.com/science/article/pii/S0957417415002511
7. Galle, V., Barnhart, C., Jaillet, P.: A new binary formulation of the restricted container relocation problem based on a binary encoding of configurations. Eur. J. Oper. Res. **267**(2), 467–477 (2018)
8. Jin, B., Tanaka, S.: An exact algorithm for the unrestricted container relocation problem with new lower bounds and dominance rules. Eur. J. Oper. Res. **304**(2), 494–514 (2022)
9. Jovanovic, R., Tuba, M., Voß, S.: An efficient ant colony optimization algorithm for the blocks relocation problem. Eur. J. Oper. Res. **274**(1), 78–90 (2019)
10. Kim, K.H., Hong, G.P.: A heuristic rule for relocating blocks. Comput. Oper. Res. **33**(4), 940–954 (2006)
11. Kingma, D.P., Ba, J.: Adam: A method for stochastic optimization. arXiv preprint arXiv:1412.6980 (2014)

12. Kool, W., van Hoof, H., Welling, M.: Attention, learn to solve routing problems! In: International Conference on Learning Representations (2018)
13. Ku, D., Arthanari, T.S.: On the abstraction method for the container relocation problem. Comput. Oper. Res. **68**, 110–122 (2016)
14. Li, K., Zhang, T., Wang, R., Wang, Y., Han, Y., Wang, L.: Deep reinforcement learning for combinatorial optimization: covering salesman problems. IEEE Trans. Cybern. **52**(12), 13142–13155 (2021)
15. Lu, C., Zeng, B., Liu, S.: A study on the block relocation problem: lower bound derivations and strong formulations. IEEE Trans. Autom. Sci. Eng. **17**(4), 1829–1853 (2020)
16. Peng, B., Wang, J., Zhang, Z.: A deep reinforcement learning algorithm using dynamic attention model for vehicle routing problems. In: Li, K., Li, W., Wang, H., Liu, Y. (eds.) ISICA 2019. CCIS, vol. 1205, pp. 636–650. Springer, Singapore (2020). https://doi.org/10.1007/978-981-15-5577-0_51
17. Quispe, K.E.Y., Lintzmayer, C.N., Xavier, E.C.: An exact algorithm for the blocks relocation problem with new lower bounds. Comput. Oper. Res. **99**, 206–217 (2018)
18. da Silva, M.D.M., Toulouse, S., Calvo, R.W.: A new effective unified model for solving the pre-marshalling and block relocation problems. Eur. J. Oper. Res. **271**(1), 40–56 (2018)
19. Silver, D., et al.: Mastering the game of go with deep neural networks and tree search. Nature **529**(7587), 484–489 (2016)
20. Tanaka, S., Mizuno, F.: An exact algorithm for the unrestricted block relocation problem. Comput. Oper. Res. **95**, 12–31 (2018)
21. Tanaka, S., Takii, K.: A faster branch-and-bound algorithm for the block relocation problem. IEEE Trans. Autom. Sci. Eng. **1**(13), 181–190 (2016)
22. Tanaka, S., Voß, S.: An exact approach to the restricted block relocation problem based on a new integer programming formulation. Eur. J. Oper. Res. **296**(2), 485–503 (2022)
23. Tricoire, F., Scagnetti, J., Beham, A.: New insights on the block relocation problem. Comput. Oper. Res. **89**, 127–139 (2018)
24. Vaswani, A., et al.: Attention is all you need. In: Advances in Neural Information Processing Systems, vol. 30 (2017)
25. Zehendner, E., Caserta, M., Feillet, D., Schwarze, S., Voß, S.: An improved mathematical formulation for the blocks relocation problem. Eur. J. Oper. Res. **245**(2), 415–422 (2015)
26. Zehendner, E., Feillet, D.: A branch and price approach for the container relocation problem. Int. J. Prod. Res. **52**(24), 7159–7176 (2014)
27. Zhang, C., Guan, H., Yuan, Y., Chen, W., Wu, T.: Machine learning-driven algorithms for the container relocation problem. Trans. Res. Part B: Methodol. **139**, 102–131 (2020)
28. Zhu, W., Qin, H., Lim, A., Zhang, H.: Iterative deepening a* algorithms for the container relocation problem. IEEE Trans. Autom. Sci. Eng. **9**(4), 710–722 (2012)

Deep Determinantal Q-Learning with Role Aware

Kai Han[1], Xiaodong Yue[1,2(✉)], Wei Liu[3], and Jinxin Zhan[1]

[1] School of Computer Engineering and Science, Shanghai University, Shanghai, China
{hankai,yswantfly,jxzhan}@shu.edu.cn
[2] Artificial Intelligence Institute of Shanghai University, Shanghai, China
[3] College of Electronics and Information Engineering, Tongji University,
Shanghai, China

Abstract. Q-DPP is a multi-agent reinforcement learning (MARL) algorithm capable of eliminating the priori structural constraints on the central value function. However, due to the high-dimensional matrix operations with the increasing of the number of agents, Q-DPP shows poor empirical performance in complex environment, such as Starcraft Multi-Agent Challenge (SMAC). To improve the scalability and reduce computational complexity of Q-DPP, we propose a novel Deep Determinantal Q-Learning with Role Aware (RO-DPP). Concretely, we introduce the role concept by learning a role selector and cluster actions based on the impact of agent's actions on the environment and other agents, and thus break down the joint action spaces into reduced role action spaces, which computes the kernel matrix of Q-DPP in a greatly reduced observation-action space. The experiments on micromanagement benchmark of famous game StarCraft II validate the effectiveness of the proposed RO-DPP.

Keywords: Multi-Agent Reinforcement Learning · Deep Q-learning · Determinantal Point Processes

1 Introduction

Multi-agent reinforcement learning (MARL) has great effect for addressing coordination problems in a variety of applications, such as traffic light control [16], multi-player video games [4], resources management [6] and coordination of autonomous vehicles [10]. However, learning executable policies in such complex multi-agent systems is still a very difficult task.

The paradigm of centralized training with decentralized execution (CTDE) [3,5,14] has been created to deal with this issue. Under this paradigm, CTDE

This work was supported by National Natural Science Foundation of China (Serial Nos. 61991410, 61976134, 61991415) and Natural Science Foundation of Shanghai (NO. 21ZR1423900) and Open Project Foundation of Intelligent Information Processing Key Laboratory of Shanxi Province, China (No. CICIP2021001).

H. Fujita et al. (Eds.): IEA/AIE 2023, LNAI 13926, pp. 286–297, 2023.
https://doi.org/10.1007/978-3-031-36822-6_25

trains a central action-value estimator with access to full information of the environment, decomposes the centralized value function into each of agent's utility functions and sets the decentralized policy of agents to maximize the corresponding utility functions. However, it is hard to correctly extract each of agent's individual Q-function from the centralized Q-function and find an executable policy. To address this problem, current methods rely on hypothetical conditions that adopt structural constraints on the factorization of the joint Q-function.

Recently, Q-DPP [17] is proposed to eliminate the need for a priori structural constraints or bespoke neural architectures, where the centralized Q-function can be approximated by RO-DPP. Despite the strong theoretical guarantee of Q-DPP, it has high computational complexity due to the high-dimensional matrix calculation of quality term and diversity feature term of Q-DPP kernels with increasing of the number of agents, which leads a worse performance in complex MARL environments, such as StarCraft Multi-Agent Challenge (SMAC) [11].

To address this limitation, in this paper, we propose a novel Deep Determinantal Q-Learning with Role Aware (RO-DPP), which introduces role concept [15] and decomposes joint action spaces. Concretely, we firstly introduce the role concept by learning a role selector and then cluster actions based on the impact of agent's actions on the environment and other agents, and thus break down the joint action spaces into reduced role action spaces, which computes the kernel matrix of Q-DPP in a greatly reduced observation-action space. In summary, the specific contributions of this paper are:

(1) We propose a novel RO-DPP to improve the scalability and reduce computational complexity of Q-DPP in complex environments with introducing of the role concept.
(2) Our RO-DPP maintains the theoretical benefit of Q-DPP for representing the centralized value function in a natural factorization manner, while significantly improving performance in the famous complex MARL environment, StarCraft Multi-Agent Challenge (SMAC).

2   Preliminary

Determinantal point processes (DPPs) are statistical probabilistic models for modeling sets that focus not only on the quality of the set elements but also on the diversity among the set elements when sampling a subset from a ground set. Therefore, if we combine all agents' observation-action pairs into a ground set in multi-agent reinforcement learning system, it is suited for sampling in the grount set of observation-action pairs using determinantal point process because of the special nature of deterministic point process.

Definition (DPP). A point process $\mathcal{P}$ is a probabilistic estimate that computes the probability of sampling any subset from a ground set $Y = \{1, \ldots, N\}$, which contains 2^y subsets. If any random subset is sampled according to $\mathcal{P}$, we have $A \subseteq Y, P(A \subseteq Y) = \det(K_A)$, then $\mathcal{P}$ can be called a determinantal point process(DPP). K are some positive semidefinite matrix $K \preceq I$ indexed by the elements in Y and all eigenvalues of K are less than or equal to 1. $K_A \equiv [K_{ij}]_{i,j \in A}$ denotes the restriction on the elements of K, where K is indexed by the elements of A. Based on K we can compute the probability of sampling any subset A from Y, we refer to K as the marginal kernel. Then we have $\forall i, j \in Y$,

$$\mathcal{P}(i, j \in Y) = K_{ii}K_{jj} - K_{ij}K_{ji} = \mathcal{P}(i \in Y)\mathcal{P}(j \in Y) - K_{ij}^2. \tag{1}$$

In practice, however, the most common method of determinantal point process construction is not based on the marginal kernel K, but through L-ensembles [1]. The normalization constant for $\mathcal{P}$ follows from the observation that $\sum_{Y' \subseteq Y} \det(L_{A'}) = \det(L + I)$. Therefore, An L-ensemble constructs a determinantal point process through a positive semidefinite matrix L, where the positive semidefinite matrix L is indexed by the elements of Y:

$$\mathcal{P}_L(\mathbf{Y} = Y) = \frac{\det(L_Y)}{\det(L + I)}, \tag{2}$$

where I is the $N \times N$ identity matrix. L_A represents the principal submatrix of the determinantal point process kernel L indexed by elements of A. On the one hand, the diagonal element L_{ii} of the DPP kernel matrix L focuses on the quality of point i. On the other hand, the off-diagonal element $L_{ij} = L_{ji}$ takes into account the diversity between points i and j. Determinantal point process can be constructed in two ways, the marginal kernel K and the L-ensemble, and we can convert the two to each other, for example, we can represent K according to L-ensemble by the following formula:

$$K = \frac{L}{L + I}. \tag{3}$$

Based on both constructions, K and L-ensemble, of the determinantal point process, subsets with higher diversity will be more likely sampled as measured by the corresponding kernel. However, L-ensembles directly model the probabilities of observing each subset of Y when K gives rise to marginal probabilities. However, L is always positive semidefinite, and there exists an upper bound on the eigenvalues of K. Therefore, in our work we choose L-ensembles for the construction of the determinant point process kernel matrix.

3 Deep Determinantal Q-Learning with Role Aware

In this section, we will present a novel value-based MARL framework (RO-DPP), as shown in Fig. 1, it utilizes RO-DPP as general function approximators for the joint Q-functions which apply deep neural networks, and cluster actions based on the impact of agent's actions on the environment and other agents, thus break down the joint action spaces into reduced role action spaces.The following is a description of the problem formulation.

3.1 Problem Formulation

In this paper, we use a fully cooperative multi-agent setting, which can be modeled as a Dec-POMDP [7] consisting of a tuple $M = \langle N, S, A, P, \Omega, O, r, \gamma \rangle$, where $N \equiv \{1, 2, ..., n\}$ is the limited set of n agents and $s \in S$ is the true state of the environment. At every time-step, each agent i receives an observation $o_i \in \Omega$ derived from the observation function $O\{s, i\}$, executes an action $a_i \in A$ and forms a joint action $a \in A^n$, forming the next state s' based on the transition function $P\{s'|s, a\}$. Every agent i learns its individual policy $\pi\{a|\tau_i\}$ that maximizes the global reward based on its local action-observation history $\tau_i \in T \equiv \{\omega \times A\}^*$ and the action-observation histories of all agents form the action-observation space $\tau \in T \equiv T^n$. This eventually leads to a global shared reward $r = R(s, a)$ for all agents. Based on the joint policy π we have a global centralized Q-function: $Q_{tot}^\pi (s, a) = E_{s_{0:\infty}, a_{0:\infty}}[\sum_{t=0}^{\infty} \gamma^t r_t | s_0 = s, a_0 = a, \pi]$, where $\gamma \in [0, 1)$ is a discount factor. Our goal is to find an efficient joint policy $\pi = \langle \pi_1, ..., \pi_n \rangle$ to make global Q value $Q^* = \max_\pi Q^\pi(\tau^t, a^t)$ maximize.

In addition to focusing on the joint value function, we also want to learn a decentralized executable policy for each agent. The paradigm centralized training and decentralized execution (CTDE) [8] combines the advantages of joint action learning [2] and independent learning (IL) [13]. As the number of agent increases, the joint observation-action space will grow exponentially. CTDE solves this problem by centralizing training through a central mixing network and by learning a decentralization policy, where the central mixing network has access to the local observation-action history τ of all agents during training. Moreover, CTDE can be trained to obtain the local action value function of each agent, which are used as input to the central mixing network to compute the global TD loss for centralized training. During execution, the central mixing network of CTDE is removed and only each agent's local history τ_i is used, and each agent acts according to its own local policy learned from its local action value function. Agents are trained centrally and have access to global information, but can only execute based on their own local observation-action histories during execution.

3.2 Samping from RO-DPP

In the beginning, we collect samples including observation-action pairs from RO-DPP. RO-DPP models the ground set of all agents' observation-action pairs: $Y = \{(o_1^1, a_1^1), ..., (o_N^{|O|}, a_N^{|A|})\}$, where the size of the base set is 2. $|Y| = N|O||A|$. RO-DPP, donoted by $\mathcal{P}$, defines a probability measure on $\mathcal{Y} \subseteq Y$. $\mathcal{Y}$ is a random subset based on $\mathcal{P}$ sampling, so that this probability distribution can be expressed as:

$$\mathcal{P}_L(\mathcal{Y} = Y) = \frac{det(L_Y)}{det(L + I)}, \tag{4}$$

where each agent i takes a valid action based on its own observations, and the local observations o_i encode all historical information τ_i for each time step in multi-agent reinforcement learning environment. A valid sample of the RO-DPP must contain one valid observation-action pair of every agent, and the observations in the sampled pair must be consistent with the true observations received by the agents at each time step.

Then we let the rows w_i of a matrix W mutually orthogonal by using Gram-Schmidt [9] process which can orthogonalize a set of vectors. Given a set of linearly independent vectors w_i, it compute $\hat{w}_i := \coprod_{\mathcal{U}_i}(w_i)$ where $\mathcal{U}_i = \text{span}\{w_1, \ldots, w_{i-1}\}$ to output a mutually orthogonal set of vectors $\hat{w}_i$.

Note that we omit the normalizing step of Gram-Schmidt process. As a result, we obtain the determinant by $\det(WW^T) = \prod \|w_i\|^2$. The RO-DPP sampler is built upon the property of volume preservation [12] in Gram-Schmidt. Such that let $\mathcal{U}_i = \text{span}\{w_1, \ldots, w_{i-1}\}$ and $w_i \in R^P$ be the row i of $W \in R^{M \times P}$,then $\prod_{i=1}^{M} \|\coprod_{\mathcal{U}_i}(w_i)\|^2 = \det(WW^T)$.

The sampling process of the RO-DPP study is somewhat simplified by the kernel matrix, in which the rows of kernel matrix are orthogonal to each other. In such scenario, an effective sampler can be defined: from the ground set Y, sample the element $i \in Y$ with $\mathcal{P}(i) \propto \|d_i b_i^T\|^2$, then add i to the output sample $\mathcal{Y}$, and the above steps will be iterated. The probability of computing sample $\mathcal{Y}$ can be written:

$$P(Y) \propto \prod_{i \in Y} \|d_i b_i^T\|^2 = \prod_{i \in Y} \|w_i\|^2 = \det(W_{\mathcal{Y}} W_{\mathcal{Y}}^T) \propto \det(L_{\mathcal{Y}}). \qquad (5)$$

3.3   Decomposing Action Spaces

After collecting samples, we decompose the action space by adopting k-means clustering based on Euclidean distances between agents' action representations, and the policy search spaces can be significantly reduced by restricting the action space. We use K roles, each have a corresponding role action space, and train a predictive model defined below for t_e time-steps.

To decompose action space and let roles focus on actions with similar effects, we learn action denotation based on the impact of actions on the environment and other agents. For details, we measured the impact of the action by adopting induced rewards and changes in agent's observation. Thereby we define an objective for learning action representations. Given the actions of other agents and the observation of the current time-step, we predict the next observation and reward by that objective.

Specifically, we learn an action encoder $f_e(\cdot; \theta_e) : R^{|A|} \to R^d$ which is parameterized by θ_e and maps one-hot actions into a d-dimensional representation. If we have the observation o_i of an agent in this time-step and the one-hot actions $a_{i'}$ of the remaining agent, then the next time-step observation o'_i and the reward r can be predicted based on the representation $z_a = f_e(a; \theta_e)$ of the action a. We can interpret this model as a forward network and will be trained to minimize the loss function, which is defined as follows:

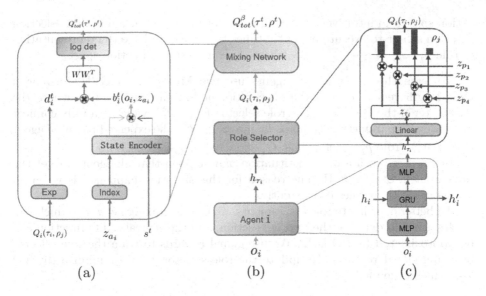

Fig. 1. RO-DPP framework. (a) The centralized mixing network of RO-DPP. (b) The overall architecture of RO-DPP. (c) Every agent's local network and role selector.

$$\mathcal{L}_e(\theta_e, \xi_e) = E_{(o,a,r,o')\sim D}\left[\sum_{i=1}^{N} \|p_o(z_{a_i}, o_i, a'_i) - o'_i\|_2^2\right.$$

$$\left. + \lambda_e \sum_{i=1}^{N}(p_r(z_{a_i}, o_i, a'_i) - r)^2\right]. \tag{6}$$

Note that p_o is a prediction model of the agent's local observation, while p_r is a prediction model for global reward, D is a replay buffer, λ_e is a discount factor, and the loss function is parameterized by ξ_e.

Intuitively, we cluster the action according to their latent representations and set each role's action spaces to contain one of the clusters.

3.4   Specializing Roles

Clustering actions based on the impact of agent's actions on the environment and the remaining agents, and thus break down the joint action spaces into reduced role action spaces, the agents with similar roles can perform a certain function. We coordinate the selection of roles and individual actions by learning a role selector which is shown in Fig. 1(c), it assigns a role for each agent at every c time-steps. After a role is assigned, the agents learn role policies by exploring in corresponding restricted role action spaces.

For the role selector, we take as input the agents' individual history of observation-action pairs, and We take the Q-value of each agent as output which is the input of conventional Q-network. The role selector is based on average representation of available actions, every agent's individual role relates to its role action space and intuitively selecting a role for its' agent, meaning that selecting a action subset to execute in next c time-step. Then we have the representation of role $p_j : z_{\rho_j} = \frac{1}{|A_j|} \sum\limits_{a_k \in A_j} z_{a_k}$, where A_j is its restricted action space.

To learn the role selector, agents use two MLPs and a GRU, forming a fixed-length vector h_τ over the observation-action pair history tau, where the parameter of the GRU is θ. The role selector $f_\beta(h_\tau; \theta_\beta)$, which is a fully connect network with parameters θ_β, maps h_τ into $z_\tau \in R^d$. The expected payoff of agent i selecting a role p_j is defined as: $Q_i^\beta(\tau_i, \rho_j) = z_{\tau_i}^T z_{\rho_j}$.

In practice, such a overkill situation may happen that all agents target the same unit in StarCraft II. The reason for this situation happened is when all agents select their roles concurrently.

To better coordinate role assignments, we use the mixing network, which will be described in detail in the next subsection, and the centralized Q-function can be approximated by RO-DPP. We use global rewards to train the role selector by using global rewards. To update the role selector f_β, we minimize the TD loss which is defined as:

$$L_\beta(\theta_{\tau_\beta}, \theta_\beta, \xi_\beta) = E_D[(\sum_{t'=0}^{c-1} r_{t+t'} + \gamma \max_{\rho'} \overline{Q}_{tot}^\beta(s_{t+c}, \rho') - Q_{tot}^\beta(s_t, \rho_t))^2], \quad (7)$$

where $\rho = \langle \rho_1, \rho_2, \ldots, \rho_n \rangle$ is all agents' joint role, $\overline{Q}_{tot}^\beta$ is the target network.

In details, agents adopt a shared linear layer and a GRU to map a local observation-action history τ to a vector h_τ parameterized by θ_{τ_ρ}. Based on the action denotations z_{a_k} and z_τ, we predict the value of an agent i executing an action a_k as:

$$Q_i(\tau_i, a_k) = z_{\tau_i}^T z_{a_k}. \quad (8)$$

To calculate local value Q_i based on the rewards received by the agents, we reuse the local values as inputs to the centralized network as a way to compute the total value $Q_{tot}(s, a)$. To update role policies, we minimize the TD loss which is defined as:

$$L_\rho(\theta_{\tau_\rho}, \theta_\rho, \xi_\rho) = E_D[(r + \gamma \max_{a'} \overline{Q}_{tot}(s', a') - Q_{tot}(s, a))^2], \quad (9)$$

where $\overline{Q}_{tot}$ is a target network. Moreover, the mixing network used to train the role selector is retained only for the duration of the training process, and they will be removed in the execution.

3.5   Representation of RO-DPP Kernels

We propose a new type of DPP named RO-DPP that the centralized Q-function can be approximated by RO-DPP, which is shown in Fig. 1(a). Given RO-DPP, the representation of centralized value function is defined as:

$$Q^\pi(o, a) := \log \det(L_{Y=\{(o_1, a_1), \ldots, (o_N, a_N)\} \in C(o^t)}), \quad (10)$$

where L_Y represents the sub-matrix of L and the elements of L are indexed by the entries contained in Y. The determinant of kernel matrix determines the Q-value and its elements are indexed by the associated observation-action pairs. RO-DPP relates the relationship between global action and local actions of each agent to a subset sampling process. Our aim is to learn an optimal joint Q-function and maximize Q-value.

But how to represent quality terms and diversity feature terms is still a difficult problem. To address this problem, RO-DPP computes quality terms and diversity feature terms for the sampled subset separately by a deep network. We first embed every discrete action a_i after inputing state s to index the raw diversity feature b_i'. To make full use of this factorization, we encode the direction of the diversity feature vector by a multilayer feedforward network f_d and the norm of the diversity feature vector by another multilayer feedforward network f_n. The neural network f_d outputs a feature vector with same shape as raw diversity feature b_i' to indicate direction, while the neural network f_n outputs a real value to compute the norm. Thereby the decomposition of L can be defined as $L = DB^T BD$ that $B = [b_1, \ldots, b_M]$ and $D = \mathrm{diag}(d_1, \ldots, d_M)$, and the loss function parameterized by D and B is defined by the following equation:

$$L(\theta) = \sum_{j=1}^{E} \|R + \gamma \max_{a'} Q(\tau', a'; \theta^-) - Q^\pi(\tau, a; \theta)\|^2, \qquad (11)$$

where the target parameter θ^- is periodically replicated from θ during the training period. We apply the centralized approach that minimizes the squared temporal difference error $L(\theta)$ in the mini-batch sampling of transition data $\{\langle \tau, a, R, \tau' \rangle\}_{j=1}^{E}$ to find the joint value function parameterized by θ.

Given a observation-action pair, we define quality term D serves for each agent's individual Q-value, such that $\forall (o_i, a_i) \in Y, i = \{1, \ldots, N\}, d_i = \sum_{i=1}^{N} (\frac{1}{2} \exp Q_{I(o_i, a_i)}(o_i, a_i))$, thereby $Q^\pi(o, a)$ is finally defined as:

$$Q^\pi(o, a) = \log \det(\mathcal{W}_Y \mathcal{W}_Y^T) = \log(\mathrm{tr}(D_Y^T D_Y) \det(\mathcal{B}_Y^T B_Y))$$

$$= \sum_{i=1}^{N} Q_{I(o_i, a_i)}(o_i, a_i) + \log \det(B_Y^T B_Y). \qquad (12)$$

Note that only when the associated vectors in B_Y are mutually orthogonal and $\log \det(B_Y^T B_Y) = 0$, the determinant value can reach the maximum. Therefore, RO-DPP takes account into not only the quality of all agents' actions, but also the orthogonality of agents' action from a holistic perspective.

4   Experiments

We choose the StarCraft II micromanagement (SMAC) benchmark [11] as the tested object for its rich environments and high complexity of control. We compare our method with the baseline model Q-DPP [17] which is proposed to eliminate structural constraints and bespoke neural architecture designs and present results.

Performance on StarCraft II. Since the motivation of RO-DPP is to reduce computational complexity and improve scalability by breaking down the joint action spaces. We therefore focus on whether agents with similar roles specializing in corresponding subtasks can improve learning efficiency. StarCraft II consists of a series of scenarios that can be classified as easy, hard, and super hard depending on the difficulty of the map challenge. We tested our approach on two hard maps: $5m\_vs\_6m$ and $8m\_vs\_9m$. In these two maps, the enemy's number is higher than ours, so it is a typical configuration map where there are many enemies and we are outnumbered. The complexity of the environment is greatly increased, and the difficulty of the map scenario is also greatly increased. Our team is at a disadvantage, so all the agents need to work well together to complete this difficult task. We use the default Starcraft settings for the rewards received by the agents.

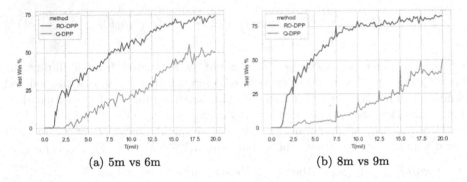

(a) 5m vs 6m   (b) 8m vs 9m

Fig. 2. Performance comparison between RO-DPP and baseline on two hard maps.

As shown in Figure Fig. 2(a), our method produces substantially better results than the baseline Q-DPP on all maps. Especially in the second map, as shown in Fig. 2(b), the performance gap between RO-DPP and the baseline method Q-DPP will further increase as the number of intelligences increases. Q-DPP requires the joint observation-action spaces of all agents to compute the kernel matrix, which will result in higher computational complexity. In contrast, our method reduces the joint observation-action spaces and computes the kernel matrix in the greatly reduced role action spaces. The above results demonstrate the motivation that our method can improve the scalability and reduce the computational complexity of Q-DPP, and by doing so, our method can be applied to larger scale multi-agent system problems.

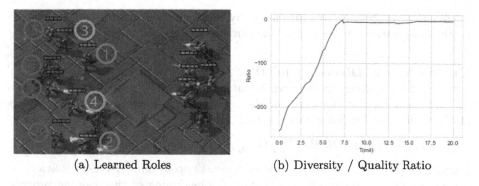

(a) Learned Roles   (b) Diversity / Quality Ratio

Fig. 3. (a): Learned roles on $8m\_vs\_9m$ at a temestep. The green agents have similar roles and the maximum health, while red agents also have similar roles and the lowest health. (b): The ratio of diversity to quality,i.e., $\log \det(\mathcal{B}_Y^T \mathcal{B}_Y) / \sum_{i=1}^{N} Q_{I(o_i, a_i)}(o_i, a_i)$ during training on $8m\_vs\_9m$ map. (Color figure online)

Dynamic Roles. RO-DPP can automatically learn roles and adapt to the dynamic and changing environments, meaning that the every agent' role is not set or stationary. And agents with similar responsibilities have similar roles. Thereby the agents which have similar roles can share parameter of individual local Q-value network and information to accelerate the training speed with the increase of training step. As shown in Fig. 3(a), it is a snapshot in the late stage of the battle on the StarCraft II benchmarks map,i.e., $8m\_vs\_9m$ where 8 marines face 9 enemy marines.

At the beginning of the battle, all of the agents do not have roles and move forward together. But in the middle of the battle, agents learn a policy that all of the agents form a concave arc to maximize the number of agents whose shoot range covers the front line of enemies when our agents meet the enemies and get to the center of the battle field. Although agent's local observation consists of many different parts, including distance, health point, shield point and unit type of allied and enemy forces, etc., RO-DPP obtains the corresponding parts from the local observation separately according to the dynamic changes of the environment. In this stage, RO-DPP learns roles according to agents' relative positions in aims to getting into attacking formation faster.

In the late of the battle, RO-DPP learns roles according to the remaining health points because of agents learn a crucial policy that agents with more health points protect the agents with lower health points. Figure 3(a) shows that the agents with highest health points which have similar roles,i.e., the green agents *1* and *2* stands at the front of the line to draw firepower. And the units with lowest health points stands at the back of the line to fire from a safe distance and avoid firepower,i.e., the red agents *5−8*. With the development of the battle, agents' role also further dynamic change with the change of the health point. Ultimately, RO-DPP receives results that the agents are able to adjust its strategy in time according to the advancement of the phase, and the roles of agents change accordingly, automatically learning effective strategies according to the information of the enemy and our team in the scenarios.

Quality Versus Diversity. RO-DPP focuses on both the quality of agents' actions and the diversity between agents' actions, we are therefore very interested in how the quality term of the agents and the diversity among agents change during the training process. In Fig. 3(b) shows that the ratio of diversity to quality,i.e., $\log \det(\mathcal{B}_Y^T \mathcal{B}_Y) / \sum_{i=1}^{N} Q_{I(o_i,a_i)}(o_i, a_i)$ which reflects how RO-DPP algorithm balances maximizing reward against encouraging diverse behaviors on 8m vs 9m map. We can observe that at the beginning of the training process, agents pay more attention to diversity exploration, because the explorations tend to be rewarded more at the early stage of a task. With the increase of training, the diversity term plays a less important role. Agents pay more attention to acquiring quality for greater global reward when the training stabilizes. Finally we can see that the ratio gradually converges to 0.

5   Conclusion

In this paper, we present RO-DPP, an effective improvement over Q-DPP for cooperative multi-agent reinforcement learning under the paradigm of centralized training with decentralized execution. Our gains mainly come from (i) decomposing joint action spaces according to action effects, (ii) integrating information of action effect into policies, and (iii) introducing role concept and a multi-head mixing network for value transformation. We empirically show how our method improves the performance of Q-DPP in SMAC benchmarks.

References

1. Borodin, A.: Determinantal point processes. arXiv preprint arXiv:0911.1153 (2009)
2. Claus, C., Boutilier, C.: The dynamics of reinforcement learning in cooperative multiagent systems. AAAI/IAAI **1998**(746–752), 2 (1998)
3. Foerster, J., Farquhar, G., Afouras, T., Nardelli, N., Whiteson, S.: Counterfactual multi-agent policy gradients. In: Proceedings of the AAAI Conference on Artificial Intelligence, vol. 32 (2018)
4. Kempka, M., Wydmuch, M., Runc, G., Toczek, J., Jaśkowski, W.: Vizdoom: a doom-based AI research platform for visual reinforcement learning. In: 2016 IEEE Conference on Computational Intelligence and Games (CIG), pp. 1–8. IEEE (2016)
5. Lowe, R., Wu, Y.I., Tamar, A., Harb, J., Pieter Abbeel, O., Mordatch, I.: Multi-agent actor-critic for mixed cooperative-competitive environments. In: Advances in Neural Information Processing Systems, vol. 30 (2017)
6. Mao, H., Alizadeh, M., Menache, I., Kandula, S.: Resource management with deep reinforcement learning. In: Proceedings of the 15th ACM Workshop on Hot Topics in Networks, pp. 50–56 (2016)
7. Oliehoek, F.A., Amato, C.: A Concise Introduction to Decentralized POMDPs. Springer, Cham (2016)

8. Oliehoek, F.A., Spaan, M.T., Vlassis, N.: Optimal and approximate Q-value functions for decentralized POMDPs. J. Artif. Intell. Res. **32**, 289–353 (2008)
9. Olver, P.J., Shakiban, C., Shakiban, C.: Applied Linear Algebra, vol. 1. Springer, Cham (2006)
10. Sallab, A.E.L., Abdou, M., Perot, E., Yogamani, S.: Deep reinforcement learning framework for autonomous driving. Electr. Imaging **2017**(19), 70–76 (2017)
11. Samvelyan, M., et al.: The starcraft multi-agent challenge. arXiv preprint arXiv:1902.04043 (2019)
12. Suetin, P.K., Kostrikin, A.I., Manin, Y.I.: Linear Algebra and Geometry. CRC Press, Cambridge (1989)
13. Tan, M.: Multi-agent reinforcement learning: independent vs. cooperative agents. In: Proceedings of the Tenth International Conference on Machine Learning, pp. 330–337 (1993)
14. Wang, J., Ren, Z., Liu, T., Yu, Y., Zhang, C.: Qplex: duplex dueling multi-agent q-learning. arXiv preprint arXiv:2008.01062 (2020)
15. Wang, T., Dong, H., Lesser, V., Zhang, C.: Roma: multi-agent reinforcement learning with emergent roles. arXiv preprint arXiv:2003.08039 (2020)
16. Wiering, M.A.: Multi-agent reinforcement learning for traffic light control. In: Machine Learning: Proceedings of the Seventeenth International Conference (ICML 2000), pp. 1151–1158 (2000)
17. Yang, Y., et al.: Multi-agent determinantal q-learning. In: International Conference on Machine Learning, pp. 10757–10766. PMLR (2020)

Security

Detection and Classification of Web Application Attacks

Jayanthi Ramamoorthy[✉], Damilola Oladimeji, Laura Garland,
and Qingzhong Liu

Department of Computer Science, Sam Houston State University,
Huntsville, TX 77340, USA
{jxr153,dko011,ljg020,qxl005}@shsu.edu

Abstract. Web applications have become ubiquitous and offer a wide range of services, from content management and e-commerce to social networking. However, these applications are also prime targets for cyber-attacks that exploit a variety of vulnerabilities. With the rise in use of Ubiquitous Web Applications (UWA) which can be accessed globally from various devices, it is imperative to automate the detection and classification of these attacks. In this study, we detect and classify web attacks using several classification machine learning models. We conduct a comparative analysis of the web attack classification results from Decision Trees, Random Forest, Support Vector Classifier (SVC) and K-Nearest Neighbor (KNN) machine learning models, using multiple text feature vectorization techniques such as the context-insensitive TF-IDF vectorizer, the bi-directional context-aware BERT transformer, and a combination of both techniques on the Webserver logs. We find that the Random Forest classifier performs best using BERT transformer for text features captured by the Webserver logs with 99% accuracy and F_1 score for classifying web attacks. We also find that there is no significant gain in the accuracy of transformers over TF-IDF vectorizer for these text features presumably because of the preprocessing techniques we use on the command like syntax. Also, with TF-IDF text vectorization, both SVC and KNN classification models performed better than Random Forest classification model against Webserver logs to detect and classify Web application attacks.

Keywords: Web attack classification · Machine Learning model comparison

1 Introduction

The World Wide Web (www) has facilitated various tasks such as e-commerce, gaming, education, and social networking, leading to a significant increase in website usage over time. Malicious attackers are interested in personal and financial information collected by websites [3]. Websites provide attackers with several attack components such as online apps, web servers, content management

© The Author(s), under exclusive license to Springer Nature Switzerland AG 2023
H. Fujita et al. (Eds.): IEA/AIE 2023, LNAI 13926, pp. 301–312, 2023.
https://doi.org/10.1007/978-3-031-36822-6_26

systems, and source code [26]. Web attacks exploit vulnerabilities to gain unauthorized access, collect sensitive information, insert harmful content, or modify website content. Ubiquitous Web applications (UWA) have increased website vulnerability to various types of attacks. The OWASP (Open Web Application Security Project) published new categories of web application security risks, including Insecure Design, Software and Data Integrity failures, and SSRF (Server-Side request Forgery) in the top 10 web application security risks [13]. Broken Access Control, Cryptographic Failures and Injection attacks, including cross-site scripting (XSS), are the top-ranked categories. XSS is the most common type of website attack, accounting for 40% of cyber attacks in 2019 [14]. It has been used to launch Trojan malware to collect financial information [9]. Other prominent web attacks include phishing, employing unknown or third-party scripts, brute force attacks, man-in-the-middle attacks, Distributed Denial of Service (DDOS), and injection attacks [20]. Figure 1 shows some of the most frequent attacks to which web applications are now susceptible.

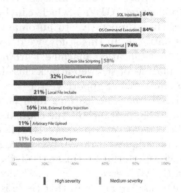

Fig. 1. Most popular web attacks and their impact level [23]

In this paper, we aim to determine the accuracy of various machine learning classification algorithms such as Decision Trees [15], Random Forest [1], SVC [6], and KNN [7] ML models to detect and classify six common categories of web attacks based on the HTTP traffic captured by Webserver logs. We also evaluate the efficacy of using bi-directional, context-aware BERT transformer [2], against TF-IDF (Term Frequency-Inverse Document Frequency) vectorization, to see if there are any significant gains to using transformers for vectorization of command text features like URL, parameter query string etc. We compare the performance of classification models with a combination of BERT for certain text features of the webserver logs, and TF-IDF for others.

This paper is structured as follows: Sect. 2 surveys relevant work, Sect. 3 outlines the methodology, Sect. 4 presents the results and analysis, and Sect. 5 summarizes the conclusion, limitations, and future work.

2   Related Works

In this section, we provide a brief survey of literature on detecting and classifying web attacks using different machine learning algorithms. We discuss the methodologies adopted and the classifiers used, with a focus on the metrics used in these experiments, namely accuracy, precision, and recall.

One study by researchers in [21] investigated reducing false positives and false negatives in web attack scenarios using J48, One Rule, and Naïve Bayes on the CSIC 2010 HTTP dataset. They found that J48 had the best performance at 94.5%. Another study in [22] introduced two additional machine learning algorithms, Random Forest and IBM Watson LGBM, to the same CSIC 2010 HTTP dataset. Among the five models analyzed in this study, the IBM Watson LGBM model performed best with an accuracy of 94.6%.

In [16], the authors used a bag of words natural language processing model to extract features from three datasets containing both benign and malicious code. The Hidden Markov algorithm was used for training and detection, and increasing the number of features extracted using the bag of words resulted in higher accuracy until it plateaued at 96%.

In [5], researchers proposed an intrusion detection system to prevent injection attacks on web services and detect new attack signatures. They used a genetic algorithm with chromosome representations and selection, crossover, and mutation, and found that higher selection and mutation rates resulted in better signature detections. Another study in [24] proposed a method to detect web attacks in real-time using an attack detection framework and implementing hashing on cache log data with a multi-pattern matching algorithm.

In the study [18], BERT model of transformers was used to differentiate between normal and abnormal URLs. BERT was applied during the analysis phase of the experiment, and then CNN was used for classification, resulting in a 96% accuracy. In [12], researchers proposed a novel way of identifying SQL injection attacks using both pattern matching and machine learning for a multi-stage analysis of logs generated during an attack. Their proposed method outperformed both, resulting in an accuracy of 95.4%. Additionally, [17] introduced a new multi-phase model for classifying web attacks using the SR-BH 2020 dataset. They found that the two-phase MultiOutput CatBoost performed best with an accuracy of 88.44%. Multi-phase models also appeared to outperform single-phase models in most performance metrics. Our approach differs from existing literature, since we compare various machine learning classification models using TF-IDF and BERT transformers for vectorization of the text features extracted from the Web server logs to accurately detect and classify web attacks. Section 3 discusses this in more detail.

3   Methodology

In this section, we describe the dataset, feature selection, preprocessing and training with various machine learning classifiers. Figure 2 shows our proposed methodology for this research.

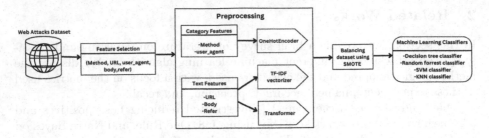

Fig. 2. Proposed Methodology

3.1   Dataset

The dataset consists of malicious HTTP requests that are labeled under six common categories of web attack types. The labelled dataset includes 33,712 malicious web attacks. The webserver log contents such as HTTP method (GET/POST), user agent, URL, refer and body were used for feature selection. Table 1 gives an explanation of the contents that were contained in each column of our dataset.

Table 1. Description of the HTTP requests contents in the Datasets

Column name	Description
Method	When a client sends a request to the server, the HTTP method is logged in the Webserver logs HTTP methods define the action that the server will take with the resource that the client requested Our dataset includes HTTP methods: - GET: Command to retrieve data from the server to the client - POST: Command to send data to the server from the client
User_agent	Information on the application, operating system, and vendor or version of the client requesting a resource. Examples are - Mozilla/5.0 (Windows NT 6.1; Trident/7.0; rv:11.0) - Chrome/73.0.3683/ WorldOfTanks/1.16.1.0 (zh_cn) Identification of the application (chrome, Firefox, etc.) the platform (Windows, Linux, etc.), and the release version.
URL	URL is the address of the unique resource on the web page.
Referer	Records the pages from where the resources are being requested. Contains the address of the page that includes the link.
Body	This is read-only content that contains the request with the body's contents.
label	Web Attack type labeled 0–5

3.2   Feature Selection

We selected the following features to train the model as they are relevant to detection and classification of web attacks: HTTP method, URL, user_agent, body, and refer and identified categorical features and text features.

- Categorical features: Attributes with finite values, such as the HTTP method and user_agent columns are selected as categorical features since the HTTP method column consists of only GET and POST values, and the user_agent column includes a limited selection of browsers used to send requests to the server.
- Text features: The text attributes in this dataset are URL, body, and refer columns.

3.3   Preprocessing Step

In this phase, we determine the preprocessing techniques to use on the features we selected from the dataset. For text features, we evaluate two different vectorization approaches: TF-IDF and BERT transformer. The motivation behind comparing these 2 approaches is to evaluate the relevance of using a context-aware BERT transformer against a command-like syntax of URL, and parameterized query string captured in the Webserver logs. TF-IDF has been widely used for feature extraction from textual data. This method calculates the importance of each term in a document by considering frequency of each term and the frequency of the term with respect to the document. However, it does not take into account the semantic context of the text, unlike BERT transformers. By comparing the performance of these two techniques on webserver logs, we can determine if there is a significant benefit to using BERT for detecting web attacks using webserver logs.

Preprocessing Categorical Features. Categorical features are converted into numerical data using one-hot encoding. This involves replacing the categorical variable with a set of finite values, such as the HTTP "method" column in the dataset with categories "GET" or "POST". One-hot encoding creates a distinct value for each category, resulting in separate values for "GET" and "POST".

Preprocessing Text Features with Term Frequency-Inverse Document Frequency (TF-IDF) Vectorizer. The TF-IDF vectorizer uses the number of occurrences of a specific term in a dataset (term frequency) and an indication of how common that text is in the dataset (document frequency) [11]. Equation 1 shows the formula to get the TF-IDF score, which is calculated by multiplying the term frequency matrix with its inverse document frequency.

$$w_{i,j} = tf_{i,j} \times idf_i \tag{1}$$

where:

$$w_{i,j} = \text{the TF-IDF score for the term i in document j}$$
$$tf_{i,j} = \text{the term frequency for the term i in document j}$$
$$idf_i = \text{the inverse document frequency score for term i}$$

We use SMOTE (Synthetic Minority Oversampling Technique) [4] to oversample minor classes, in order to address the imbalance of different types of attacks in our dataset. We can see the inclusion of this technique in Fig. 3. The preprocessing pipeline for the features extracted from the webserver logs is shown in Fig. 3.

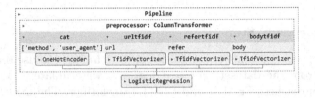

Fig. 3. Preprocessing Pipeline with TF-IDF

Logistic Regression is used as a baseline before training to evaluate the predictive power of input features in the dataset. It helps to establish a performance baseline, and can assist in deciding whether to use advanced algorithms or feature engineering techniques for improved model performance [19]. Equation 1 shows the logistic regression formula.

$$y = \frac{1}{1 + e^{-(\beta 0 + \beta 1 X)}} \tag{2}$$

where:

$$y = \text{the output of the logistic regression function}$$
$$\beta 0 = \text{the slope}$$
$$\beta 1 = \text{the y-intercept}$$
$$X = \text{the independent variable}$$
$$(\beta 0 + \beta 1 X) = \text{is obtained from the equation of a line}$$

The result of using logistic regression on our preprocessed dataset was 97.1% accuracy, which shows that the selected features from the dataset set can be used successfully for prediction. We then combined the preprocessed category features and text features transformed with the TF-IDF dataset and split it into 70% for training, 15% for validation, and 15% for testing.

Preprocessing the Text Features with Transformers. Bidirectional Encoder Representations from Transformers (BERT) models can train on vast volumes of data in a very short period of time, due to effective parallelization techniques [2]. We experiment vectorization of text features with BERT transformer which creates differential weights to determine which words in the text feature selection are the most critical to be processed further. As shown in Fig. 4, the same steps were repeated but we use BERT transformer instead for text feature vectorization. We also ensured to oversample minor classes using SMOTE to handle the data imbalance of the different classes.

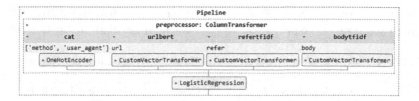

Fig. 4. Preprocessing Pipeline with BERT transformer for text feature vectorization

4   Results and Analysis

In this section, we conduct a comprehensive comparative analysis of the effectiveness of multiple machine learning classifiers for classifying web attacks in webserver logs. Specifically, we evaluate the performance of Decision Trees, Random Forest, SVC, and KNN classification models based on both accuracy and F_1 scores. Also, we compare the results obtained using two different approaches for text feature extraction: TF-IDF vectorizer and BERT transformer.

4.1   Prediction Scores of Machine Learning Classifiers Using TF-IDF for Text Feature Vectorization

With the TF-IDF text feature vectorization approach, Table 3 shows that the precision, recall and F_1 score for Random Forest Classifier performed significantly better with 97% accuracy and F_1 score as compared to the Decision Tree classifier in Table 2 which had an F_1 score of 87%. As seen in Table 4 and Table 5, both SVC classifier and KNN classifier performed the best for each type of web attack, with a weighted average accuracy and F_1 score of 98%. In this approach (TF-IDF), we can see that the best performing classifier algorithms are the SVC and KNN with accuracy and F_1 score of 98%. The least accurate is the Decision Tree, with an accuracy of 87%. The random forest classifier with TF-IDF vectorizer has an F_1 score of 97%.

Table 2. Decision Tree Classifier Report   **Table 3.** Random Forest Classifier Report

Class	Precision	Recall	F_1
0	0.74	0.99	0.85
1	0.96	0.81	0.88
2	0.84	0.84	0.84
3	0.82	0.74	0.78
4	0.93	0.84	0.88
5	0.97	0.98	0.98
accuracy			0.87
macro avg	0.88	0.87	0.87
weighted avg	0.88	0.87	0.87

Class	Precision	Recall	F_1
0	0.96	1.00	0.98
1	0.99	0.95	0.97
2	0.96	0.95	0.96
3	0.96	0.96	0.96
4	0.98	0.96	0.97
5	0.97	1.00	0.98
accuracy			0.97
macro avg	0.97	0.97	0.97
weighted avg	0.97	0.97	0.97

Table 4. SVC Classifier Report   **Table 5.** KNN Classifier Report

Class	Precision	Recall	F_1
0	0.99	1.00	0.99
1	1.00	0.98	0.99
2	0.97	0.98	0.98
3	0.99	0.97	0.98
4	0.97	0.97	0.97
5	0.98	1.00	0.99
accuracy			0.98
macro avg	0.98	0.98	0.98
weighted avg	0.98	0.98	0.98

Class	Precision	Recall	F_1
0	0.97	1.00	0.98
1	0.99	0.96	0.98
2	0.97	0.95	0.96
3	0.97	0.98	0.98
4	0.98	0.97	0.97
5	0.98	1.00	0.99
accuracy			0.98
macro avg	0.98	0.98	0.98
weighted avg	0.98	0.98	0.98

Analysis. SVC (Support Vector Classifiers) and KNN (K-Nearest Neighbor) are non-linear algorithms that can handle complex and non-linear relationships between input features and target labels. Both algorithms rely on distance and boundaries. Using one-hot encoder for categorical features, and scaling facilitates better performance from SVC and KNN as mentioned in [25]. This finding is further supported by the results seen in Fig. 5. a) through d), which show that SVC and KNN had better accuracy and F_1 scores compared to the Random Forest classifier when using TF-IDF vectorization for feature extraction.

4.2   Prediction Scores of Machine Learning Classifiers Using BERT Transformers for Text Feature Vectorization

We conducted additional experiments to evaluate the performance of the same machine learning classifiers when using BERT transformers for text feature vectorization and compared the results with the TF-IDF approach. Tables 6 through 9 show the precision, recall, and F_1 score for the Decision Tree classifier, Random Forest classifier, SVC classifier, and KNN classifier for each type of web attack using the BERT transformer.

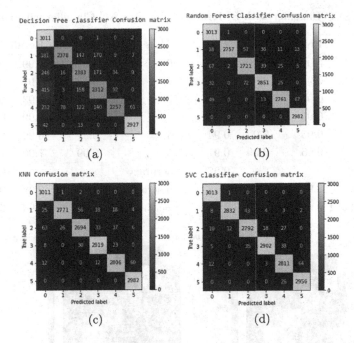

Fig. 5. (a) TF-IDF Decision Tree Confusion matrix (b) TF-IDF Random Forest Confusion matrix (c) TF-IDF KNN confusion matrix (d) TF-IDF SVC Confusion matrix

Table 6. Decision Tree with BERT

Class	Precision	Recall	F_1-score
0	0.89	0.96	0.93
1	0.79	0.89	0.84
2	0.84	0.71	0.77
3	0.70	0.81	0.75
4	0.95	0.74	0.83
5	0.92	0.92	0.92
accuracy			0.84
macro avg	0.85	0.84	0.84
weighted avg	0.85	0.84	0.84

Table 7. Random Forest with BERT

Class	Precision	Recall	F_1
0	0.98	1.00	0.99
1	0.99	0.96	0.98
2	0.98	0.97	0.97
3	0.98	0.99	0.99
4	0.99	0.99	0.99
5	1.00	1.00	1.00
accuracy			0.99
macro avg	0.99	0.99	0.99
weighted avg	0.99	0.99	0.99

The results indicate that the Random Forest classifier is the best-performing model for web attack classification with an overall accuracy of 99%. We also provide the confusion matrices for all classifiers using BERT in Fig. 6 and Fig. 7.

Although it is resource intensive to train all of the text features with BERT, we found that using a combination of BERT and TF-IDF vectorizer performs equally well yielding the same level of accuracy. SVC and KNN classfiers had an accuracy of 97% and 98% respectively as shown in Fig. 6.

Table 8. SVC Classifier with BERT

Class	Precision	Recall	F_1
0	0.99	1.00	0.99
1	0.99	0.97	0.98
2	0.98	0.96	0.97
3	0.95	0.97	0.96
4	0.95	0.92	0.94
5	0.95	0.99	0.97
accuracy			0.97
macro avg	0.97	0.97	0.97
weighted avg	0.97	0.97	0.97

Table 9. KNN Classifier with BERT

Class	Precision	Recall	F_1
0	0.99	0.99	0.99
1	0.98	0.97	0.98
2	0.98	0.93	0.95
3	0.96	0.99	0.98
4	0.97	0.99	0.98
5	0.99	1.00	1.00
accuracy			0.98
macro avg	0.98	0.98	0.98
weighted avg	0.98	0.98	0.98

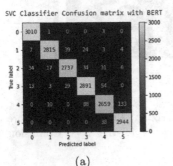
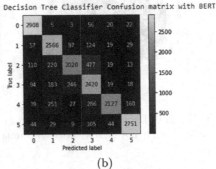

(a)   (b)

Fig. 6. (a) SVC Confusion matrix (F_1 score: 97%) b) Decision Tree Confusion matrix (F_1 score: 84%)

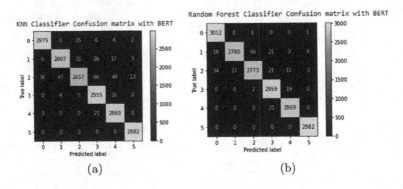

(a)   (b)

Fig. 7. (a) KNN classifier Confusion matrix (F_1 score: 98%) (b)Random Forest classifier Confusion matrix (F_1 score: 99%)

Confusion matrix results for KNN classifier and Random Forest classifier using BERT transformer indicates that the Random Forest classifier had the best overall average accuracy and F_1 score of 99% with the classification of web attacks using this dataset as shown in Fig. 7.

Analysis. Based on the results, the Random Forest classifier outperforms other classifiers when using BERT transformers for text feature vectorization. This can be attributed to the ability of BERT transformers to capture complex relationships between features and labels [8], which can be leveraged by the Random Forest Classifier to make better predictions [10].

5 Conclusion

In this study, we successfully identify and classify the various types of web attacks from webserver logs. Moreover, we compare the performance and results of the various classification models using TF-IDF vectorizer and BERT transformer. Using TF-IDF vectorizer, SVC and KNN classification model had a better F_1 score: 98%. With BERT transformer, Random Forest classifier had a 99% accuracy and F_1 score.

Future works would include evaluating additional categories of web attacks, and comparing various classification machine learning models to web server logs collected from ubiquitous Web application logs, to understand the impact of logs collected from various devices accessing the web application.

References

1. Breiman, L.: Random forests. Mach. Learn. **45**(1), 5–32 (2001)
2. BritneyMuller: Bert 101 - state of the art NLP model explained. https://huggingface.co/blog/bert-101#4-berts-performance-on-common-language-tasks
3. Center, V.S.R.C.I.: 2022 data breach investigations report. https://github.com/vz-risk/dbir/tree/gh-pages/2022
4. Chawla, N.V., Bowyer, K.W., Hall, L.O., Kegelmeyer, W.P.: Smote: synthetic minority over-sampling technique. J. Artif. Intell. Res. **16**, 321–357 (2002)
5. Clincy, V., Shahriar, H.: Web service injection attack detection. In: 2017 12th International Conference for Internet Technology and Secured Transactions (ICITST), pp. 173–178 (2017). https://doi.org/10.23919/ICITST.2017.8356371
6. Cortes, C., Vapnik, V.: Support-vector networks. Mach. Learn. **20**(3), 273–297 (1995)
7. Cover, T.M., Hart, P.E.: Nearest neighbor pattern classification. IEEE Trans. Inf. Theory **13**(1), 21–27 (1967)
8. Devlin, J., Chang, M.W., Lee, K., Toutanova, K.: Bert: Pre-training of deep bidirectional transformers for language understanding. arXiv preprint arXiv:1810.04805 (2019)
9. Gupta, S., Gupta, B.B.: Cross-site scripting (XSS) attacks and defense mechanisms: classification and state-of-the-art. Int. J. Syst. Assur. Eng. Manage. **8**(1), 512–530 (2017)
10. Liaw, A., Wiener, M.: Classification and regression by randomForest. R News **2**(3), 18–22 (2002)
11. Liu, C.z., Sheng, Y.x., Wei, Z.q., Yang, Y.Q.: Research of text classification based on improved TF-IDF algorithm. In: 2018 IEEE International Conference of Intelligent Robotic and Control Engineering (IRCE), pp. 218–222. IEEE (2018)

12. Moh, M., Pininti, S., Doddapaneni, S., Moh, T.S.: Detecting web attacks using multi-stage log analysis. In: 2016 IEEE 6th International Conference on Advanced Computing (IACC), pp. 733–738 (2016). https://doi.org/10.1109/IACC.2016.141
13. OWASP.org: Owasp top ten. https://owasp.org/www-project-top-ten/
14. Profile, T.G.A.V.: The 10 most common website security attacks and how to protect yourself. https://www.tripwire.com/state-of-security/most-common-website-security-attacks-and-how-to-protect-yourself
15. Quinlan, J.R.: C4.5: programs for machine learning. In: Proceedings of the 5th Australian Joint Conference on Artificial Intelligence. Lecture Notes in Computer Science, vol. 717, pp. 424–427. Springer, Cham (1993)
16. Ren, X., Hu, Y., Kuang, W., Souleymanou, M.B.: A web attack detection technology based on bag of words and hidden Markov model. In: 2018 IEEE 15th International Conference on Mobile Ad Hoc and Sensor Systems (MASS), pp. 526–531 (2018). https://doi.org/10.1109/MASS.2018.00081
17. Riera, T.S., Higuera, J.R.B., Higuera, J.B., Herraiz, J.J.M., Montalvo, J.A.S.: A new multi-label dataset for web attacks CAPEC classification using machine learning techniques. Comput. Secur. **120**, 102788 (2022). https://doi.org/10.1016/j.cose.2022.102788, https://www.sciencedirect.com/science/article/pii/S0167404822001833
18. Seyyar, Y.E., Yavuz, A.G., Ünver, H.M.: Detection of web attacks using the BERT model. In: 2022 30th Signal Processing and Communications Applications Conference (SIU), pp. 1–4 (2022). https://doi.org/10.1109/SIU55565.2022.9864721
19. Shah, S., Bhatnagar, D.: Feature selection using logistic regression and support vector machine. Int. J. Eng. Res. Appl. **5**(10), 29–33 (2015)
20. Sharma, C., Jain, S.: Analysis and classification of SQL injection vulnerabilities and attacks on web applications. In: 2014 International Conference on Advances in Engineering & Technology Research (ICAETR-2014), pp. 1–6. IEEE (2014)
21. Sharma, S., Zavarsky, P., Butakov, S.: Machine learning based intrusion detection system for web-based attacks. In: 2020 IEEE 6th Intl Conference on Big Data Security on Cloud (BigDataSecurity), IEEE Intl Conference on High Performance and Smart Computing, (HPSC) and IEEE Intl Conference on Intelligent Data and Security (IDS), pp. 227–230 (2020). https://doi.org/10.1109/BigDataSecurity-HPSC-IDS49724.2020.00048
22. Conde Camillo da Silva, R., Oliveira Camargo, M.P., Sanches Quessada, M., Claiton Lopes, A., Diassala Monteiro Ernesto, J., Pontara da Costa, K.A.: An intrusion detection system for web-based attacks using IBM Watson. IEEE Latin Am. Trans. **20**(2), 191–197 (2022). https://doi.org/10.1109/TLA.2022.9661457
23. Technologies, P.: Web application attack trends (2020). https://www.ptsecurity.com/ww-en/analytics/web-application-attack-trends-2017/
24. Tian, J.W., Zhu, H.Y., Li, X., Tian, Z.: Real-time online detection method for web attack based on flow data analysis. In: 2018 IEEE 9th International Conference on Software Engineering and Service Science (ICSESS), pp. 991–994 (2018). https://doi.org/10.1109/ICSESS.2018.8663848
25. Zhang, Y., Gudmundsson, M., Leiringer, R.: A comparative study of supervised machine learning algorithms for credit scoring purposes. J. Credit Risk **13**(1), 1–32 (2017)
26. Zuech, R., Hancock, J., Khoshgoftaar, T.M.: Detecting web attacks using random undersampling and ensemble learners. J. Big Data **8**(1), 1–20 (2021). https://doi.org/10.1186/s40537-021-00460-8

A False Data Injection Attack
on Data-Driven Strategies in Smart Grid
Using GAN

Smruti P. Dash$^{(\boxtimes)}$ ⓘ and Kedar V. Khandeparkar

Department of Computer Science and Engineering, Indian Institute of Technology
Dharwad, Dharwad, India
{202011002,kedark}@iitdh.ac.in
https://iitdh.ac.in/

Abstract. The smart grid is a critical cyber-physical infrastructure; attackers may exploit vulnerabilities to launch cyber attacks. The smart grid control system relies heavily on the communication infrastructure among sensors, actuators, and control systems, making it vulnerable to cyber-attacks. We propose a method for injecting a false data injection attack (FDIA) into the smart grid using generative adversarial networks (GAN). A sample of disturbance vectors generated using deep temporal convolutional GAN (DTCGAN) is superimposed on the original phasor measurement unit (PMU) measurements to generate compromised data. The performance results show a significant impact of the developed attack on data-driven methods for grid monitoring. Specifically, we demonstrated the attack on a transient stability application.

Keywords: FDIA: False Data Injection Attack · GAN: Generative Adversarial Network · PMU: Phasor Measurement Units

1 Introduction

The increased population and widespread use of electronic gadgets have resulted in increased consumption, making conventional power systems inadequate to meet demands. Thus, the next-generation smart grid aims to provide a reliable and uninterrupted power supply by integrating more renewable and advanced *information and communication technology* (ICT). The ICT in smart grids typically comprises measurement devices such as PMUs and backbone fiber-optic communication networks. The data packets from PMUs deployed across the grid are GPS synchronized and communicated to control centers at a high resolution (30 to 120 packets per second). The ICT network in large power grids is complex and vulnerable to threats from cyber attacks. The incidents of cyber attacks in the recent past corroborate the urgency to look for the cyber security of the smart grid. In all these attacks, the intruder aimed to compromise the ICT's confidentiality by targeting the communication equipment or protocol. Typical

ⓒ The Author(s), under exclusive license to Springer Nature Switzerland AG 2023
H. Fujita et al. (Eds.): IEA/AIE 2023, LNAI 13926, pp. 313–324, 2023.
https://doi.org/10.1007/978-3-031-36822-6_27

communication system attacks include *denial of service* (DoS) attack [24], replay attacks [1], and FDIA [4].

To maintain the security of ICT-enabled smart grids, *machine learning* (ML) based methods are actively used to process large datasets efficiently. Though these methods can deal with the uncertain events created by attackers, they are vulnerable to adversarial examples [3]. Existing research has proved that *neural networks* (NN) operate on high dimensional data while learning the mapping between input and output [3,18]. Hence, those succeed in the research community because of their ability to learn uninterpretable solutions. The smart grids are the host for attacks for economic benefits or affecting the operation of the grids. The adversarial examples can be designed as part of FDIA to significantly impact the NN and ML models because of the inherent uncertainty of their prediction strategy. Adding subtle perturbation to the input data to generate the adversarial samples has been used to mislead different types of neural network models on different datasets in [18]. So, the research on adversarial samples has become a demanding topic. The research community has proposed various methods for adversarial sample generation and corresponding defense techniques. A similar application of adversarial samples has been performed on the power system datasets in [11,15,21] using GAN to generate adversarial samples.

This paper proposes an FDIA strategy that deceptively injects data into the existing stream of PMU time series using a DTCGAN. Unlike other attacks, such as DoS, which disrupt data availability, the proposed attack aims to misguide the system by intertwining original data with the attack data generated using DTCGAN. Moreover, the attack data follows the distribution of known events, and the traceability of the attack becomes a challenge. The proposed approach is validated on the simulated dataset of the IEEE-14 bus system. A summary of the key contributions of this paper is given below:

1. We propose an advanced GAN architecture, namely, DTCGAN. The architecture uses deep learning models that capture the temporal relation of the time series data.
2. The proposed DTCGAN loss function is integrated with a constraint on the amplitude of the time series data. It ensures that the attack data generated by the model follows the range of original signals.
3. We use a clustering-based unsupervised attack detection method to detect the injected attack. Our experiment shows the inability of the method to detect the injected attack.
4. Subsequently, to verify the impact, the attack is used to disturb the frequency prediction strategy. Here we use an LSTM-based prediction model to predict the frequency of the grid. The experiment shows a sufficient violation in the prediction due to the injected attack.

The rest of the paper is organized as follows: Sect. 2 summarizes the related work. Section 3 describes the attack method with the architecture and training procedure of the GAN for generating the attack vector. Section 4 presents the experimental studies and the result of the attack method. Finally, Sect. 5 concludes the work and enlightens the future scopes of the work.

2   Related Works

In the past few decades, many researchers have applied data-driven algorithms for different power system issues, such as transient stability management in [10,20] and state estimation in [13]. The commonly used data-driven techniques includes *deep belief networks* (DBN) [22], *stacked autoencoder* (SAE) [20], *convolutional neural networks* (CNN) [19], and *long-short term memory* (LSTM) network [7]. Moreover, these algorithms lessen the time complexity of the operations done. Different type of deep neural networks has been performed more accurately in state and topology estimation even with some errors in the modeling and measurements [5,13]. A framework analyzing the attack strategies by adversaries and the confidence of profitable attacks is proposed in [12].

Many researchers have been engrossed in imposing attacks against power system control strategies, assuming that the attacker can obtain all the information. Moreover, some recent research focused on imposing cyber-attacks against the data-driven strategies employed for security purposes without accessing all information about the power system. The attack in [16] has been performed using the *differential evolution* (DE) algorithm to generate the attack vector. The DE algorithm is one of the heuristic optimization algorithms. Specifically, they manipulated one pixel of an image to get the adversarial image that could fool the *deep neural network* (DNN) based classifier. However, this approach does not consider the similarity between normal data and the generated attack vector, which is crucial in the case of the power system. Moreover, the calculation speed of this algorithm decreases with population growth. PMUs in smart grids usually transmit a large number of measurements per second. In [21], the authors proposed a GAN-based strategy to generate the attack vector to impose an FDIA. Implementing this strategy on the New England IEEE-39 bus system significantly impacted the data-driven model for *critical clearing time* (CCT) prediction results. In 2022, Liu et al. [11] proposed another GAN-based strategy to generate the attack vectors considering an improved GAN that can generate minimal disturbance in the power grid and disturb the CCT prediction.

To deceive the data-driven strategies of the power system, we need to consider the problems such as: (1) The attack method needs to be easily applicable in real time. (2) The attacker can not obtain all information from the power system. (3) The attack vector has to deceive bad data detection of the power system, impacting normal operation. Though the previous works have focused on the latter two problems, they ignore the time-dependency of the measurements for real-time application during the generation of the attack data. In comparison, we account for the time dependency of the measurements from PMU that is obvious in real time. We use temporal convolution in our model for generating time-series data.

3   Our Approach

This section discusses the steps we follow to model the FDIA. Moreover, we introduce the DTCGAN architecture for time-series generation. We model the attack in 5 steps: (1) We chose a random window of existing event signals. (2) Train the DTCGAN on random window measurements to generate attack data. Here, we perform statistical tests to show that real and generated time series share common key statistical properties. (3) We inject the generated attack vector at any point in the real time-series, using interpolation to smoothen the change of values in the signals. (4) We implement *dynamic time warping* (DTW)-based time-series clustering to detect the injected attack. It is difficult to distinguish the generated and real time-series from the clustering results. A significantly small set of attack samples is detected as anomalies. (5) Trained LSTM-based neural network to predict frequency to verify the attack's impact. Figure 1 illustrates the detailed attack modeling procedure.

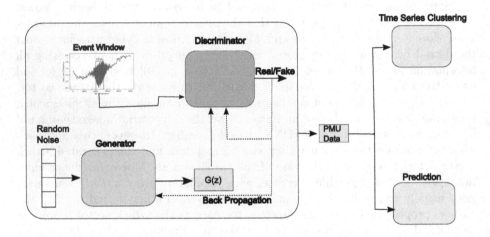

Fig. 1. Data Processing Flow

3.1   GAN-Based Attack Method

We use a GAN to generate the attack vector to achieve an expected impact of the attack and impose a minimized disturbance. In order to process the time-series signals from PMUs in the smart grids, the RNNs are popular high-level neural networks used in recent research. The RNN variants, including LSTM and *gated recurrent units* (GRU), have enhanced performance in learning the temporal dynamics with internal memory mechanisms. However, it is difficult to train these variants correctly; in practice, LSTM requires more memory and time. Hence, to make the training easy and time effective, we use the temporal convolution [9] that can learn the temporal relation across a much longer time sequence. A *temporal convolutional network* (TCN) is a framework that utilizes casual convolutions and dilations to capture sequential data with its temporal dependency. We use the batch normalization layer to speed up the training and discourage the overfitting issue. We introduce DTCGAN with its detailed architecture in the following subsection.

3.2 Deep Temporal Convolutional GAN (DTCGAN)

Here, we formally describe the architecture of DTCGAN. The generator and discriminator of DTCGAN are two CNNs with temporal convolutional filters. The generator comprises 14 layers, including a reshape layer and *three* 1D-transpose convolutional layers, followed by batch-normalization, rectified linear unit (ReLU) layer, and noise injection layer. The discriminator comprises 12 layers, including the input layer, 3 temporal convolutional layers, followed by batch-normalization and ReLU layers, the flattening layer, and the output layer. We use the stochastic gradient optimizer and the binary cross entropy loss for training the discriminator. Figure 2 presents the detailed architecture of the DTCGAN model. During the process of attack vector generation, the loss function of GAN is the most usual cross-entropy loss function as expressed in Eq. 1.

$$L_{GAN} = \mathbb{E}_x \log D(x) + \mathbb{E}_x \log(1 - D(G(x))) \tag{1}$$

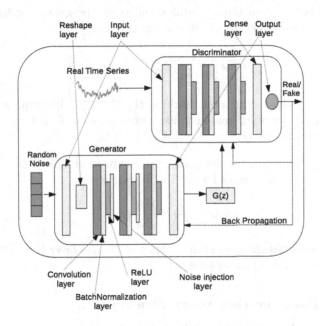

Fig. 2. Deep Temporal Convolutional GAN

To confine the magnitude of the disturbance, we assimilate the amplitude loss function in the GAN loss function as in Eq. 2.

$$L_{amp} = \mathbb{E}_x[min(\|G(x)\|, c)] \tag{2}$$

where c is the maximum allowable amplitude. Hence, the loss function during the training of DTCGAN can be expressed by Eq. 3.

$$L = L_{GAN} + \alpha L_{amp} \tag{3}$$

where α represents the proportion of loss function integrated into the final objective function, it is chosen empirically during the training of GAN.

3.3   Training Procedure

For number of iterations:

1. Sample a random batch of m samples $x^1, x^2, \cdots, x^m$ from the real PMU dataset.
2. Sample a batch of m noise samples $z^1, z^2, \cdots, z^m$.
3. Train the discriminator to update its parameters by ascending its stochastic gradient:

$$\nabla_{\theta_d} \frac{1}{m} \sum_{i=1}^{m} [\log D(x^i) + \log(1 - D(G(z^i)))] \tag{4}$$

4. Repeat steps $1, 2,$ and 3 for k times. We use $k = 5$.
5. Sample a batch of m noise samples and train the generator to update the parameters by descending its stochastic gradient:

$$\nabla_{\theta_d} \frac{1}{m} \sum_{i=1}^{m} [\log(1 - D(G(z^i)))] \tag{5}$$

- Stop training the GAN upon reaching the Nash equilibrium, where the discriminator accuracy for real and fake data gets close to 0.5.
- Generate the attack vectors $X_a = X + X_d$.

The back-propagation of the network can be expressed as in Eq. 6. The gradient of the loss function is obtained from the output layer.

$$\nabla L = \frac{\delta L}{\delta z_l} = \frac{\delta L}{\delta a_l} \odot \sigma(z_l) \tag{6}$$

Where l is the output layer, a_l is the output of the last layer l, $z_l = \theta_w^l a_{(l-1)} + \theta_b^l$, σ is the activation function of layer l.

3.4   False Data Injection Attack Strategy

Let us consider $X \in R^n$, where n is the number of features in the input data. Let (x_i, y_i) be the pair of input feature data and output corresponding to the input feature. The machine learning-based prediction models learn a function f from the feature space X to output space Y. The attackers here target to manipulate the input vector x_i to generate a disturbance vector x_d to get the constructed input vector $x_a = x_i + x_d$. The constructed input vector x_a can lead to a large deviation in the prediction of model f, as $f(x_a) = y + h$. However, the constructed input should be much closer to the original input. Mathematically, we can represent the FDIA as in Eq. 7.

$$F_{(i,j)} = D_{(i,j)} + f_{(i,j)} \tag{7}$$

Here, $D_{(i,j)}$ is the (i,j)th entry of real data, and $f_{(i,j)}$ is the same of false data injected by an attacker. The amalgamation of the injected data with the real data produces the attacked data, $F_{(i,j)}$.

We aim to tamper with a small duration of PMU data to generate an adversarial sample. The DTCGAN takes the sample as input and generates approximately equal measurements that we impose as attack data into the real PMU data. Throughout the training of our GAN network, we aim to optimize our model to obtain significantly similar attack data that can pass bad data detection of the power system and put an expected impact on the data-driven strategies.

3.5   Impact Analysis of FDIA

The cyber-attacks are also known as cyber anomalies in smart grids. There are different groups of techniques for detecting anomalies in time series [2, 23]. We adopt unsupervised time series clustering to detect the injected FDIA on the smart grid. We explain the clustering approach in the following subsection. Further, we assess the impact of the attack on data-driven approaches using the prediction of frequency in the grid. We train an LSTM-based neural network for the prediction of future frequency values in the grid. We explain the prediction method in the subsequent subsection.

Time Series Clustering: The k-means algorithm is a popular clustering algorithm that divides the samples of a dataset into k clusters minimizing the distance of each sample within each cluster. Each data point is an ordered sequence in the case of time series. The Euclidean distance fails to capture the shape of the sequence. Hence, the DTW distance metric helps to measure the similarity between two temporal sequences [14]. The observations that form dense and well-formed clusters are considered normal data; those that do not fall close to the centroids to form a well-formed cluster are detected as anomalies in the data [2].

Prediction of Frequency: Frequency is a central observable in any power system. Reliable frequency forecasting can facilitate necessary control actions improving the power system stability [8]. The deviation in the prediction of frequency implies an imbalance between the power generation and demand, thus hints at the presence of some external disturbance based on which the control actions can be taken. Here, 5 seconds of real PMU data is used to train an LSTM-based NN model for forecasting the next 5 seconds frequency. We predict the frequency of the next 5 minutes on attacked as well as real data. The *mean square error* (MSE) as in Eq. 8 is used as the loss function to measure the prediction accuracy. A sufficient deviation of the predicted value from the real value indicates the injected attack's efficacy in disturbing the grid's normal operation. In the presence of the attack, the control system will encounter the wrong frequency value and thus will respond incorrectly. As a result, the stability of the grid will be affected.

$$M_{loss} = \frac{1}{n}\sum_{t=1}^{n}(Y_t - \overline{Y_t})^2 \tag{8}$$

Here, M_{loss} = mean square error, n = sample size, Y_t = actual value at time t, $\overline{Y_t}$ = forecast value at time t.

4   Results and Validation

Two different datasets have been used for implementing the attack method. The qualitative as well as quantitative approaches are used to evaluate the performance of attack data. This section introduces the datasets and the performance evaluation matrices used. Moreover, we present an exploratory analysis of all the results.

4.1   Dataset Description

For evaluation, we conduct experiments using two different datasets with different event signatures. We consider simulated data from the IEEE-14 bus and 4-Machine Kundur systems. The parameters considered in this dataset are frequency, voltage magnitude, voltage angle, current magnitude, and current phase angle of transmission lines and buses, respectively. We consider manipulating measurements communicated from some of the PMUs in the grid.

4.2   Performance Evaluation Metrics

Here, we discuss the metrics we use for evaluating the similarity of the generated attack data with the real time-series data. We consider the *maximum mean discrepancy* (MMD), *normalized cross correlation* (NCC), and *peak signal to noise ratio* (PSNR) metrics.

Maximum Mean Discrepancy (MMD): The MMD [17] measures the distance between the probability distributions by drawing samples. Given N samples from the first distribution, P_x, and M samples from the second distribution P_y, Eq. 9 gives the estimate of MMD.

$$MMD = \frac{1}{N^2}\sum_{i=1}^{N}\sum_{j=1}^{N}K(x_i,x_j) - \frac{2}{MN}\sum_{i=1}^{N}\sum_{j=1}^{M}K(x_i,y_j) + \frac{1}{M^2}\sum_{i=1}^{M}\sum_{j=1}^{M}K(y_i,y_j) \tag{9}$$

Here $K(x,y) = \exp\left(\frac{-\|x-y\|^2}{2\sigma^2}\right)$ is the radial basis function (RBF) kernel.

Normalized Cross Correlation (NCC): NCC is a method to calculate the incidences of a pattern or vector in another. The NCC of two signals x and $\overline{x}$ of dimension $(M \times N)$ can be defined as in Eq. 10.

$$NC = \frac{\frac{1}{MN}\sum_{m=1}^{M}\sum_{n=1}^{N}\overline{x}(m,n) \times x(m,n)}{\sqrt{var(\overline{x}) \times var(x)}} \tag{10}$$

Peak Signal to Noise Ratio (PSNR): PSNR is the ratio between the maximum possible power of a signal and the power of corrupting noise. PSNR is expressed as a logarithmic quantity using a decibel (dB) scale. Usually, the PSNR is used to quantify the reconstruction quality and defined via mean square error (MSE). Equation 11 represents the PSNR between synthetic and real signals.

$$PSNR_i = 20 \log_{10} \left(\frac{MAX}{\sqrt{\frac{1}{MN} \sum_{m=1}^{M} \sum_{n=1}^{N} [x_i(m,n) - \overline{x_i}(m,n)]^2}} \right) \quad (11)$$

M and N are the length and width of both the real and generated attack data. MAX is the maximum possible value in the corresponding signal. i is the index of the signal. x is the normal data, and $\overline{x}$ is the generated attack data constructed using DTCGAN.

4.3   Result Analysis

1. *Attack Vector Generation:* To generate the attack data, a sample of 10 seconds undergoes manipulation through DTCGAN as shown in Fig. 3. The PSNR of the attack sample falls within the range of $37.6 - 39.2$, and NCC is 0.98, which indicates an effective attack vector generation. we have computed the MMD between the output of the attack and the real data during the training of DTCGAN, which shows a significant improvement of the similarity progressively during the epochs. Figure 4 presents the similarity indexes of real and attack data.
2. *Sample Statistics After Attack:* We implemented the attack on 400 test samples. Due to the PSNR range, the attack is not easy to detect, as described in [11]. Further, we use time series clustering for attack detection, where the detection rate is 2.3% of the attack sample.
3. *Attack Effect Analysis:* To inspect the impact of the attack on frequency prediction, the absolute deviation of predicted values from the original values is computed. The deviation exceeds 10% for 80% of the sample. Hence, the attack can seriously affect stability management due to frequency. The prediction error is mainly concentrated in the $(0.0, 0.3)$ interval. The prediction results show that the attack can have a greater impact on the frequency prediction strategy.

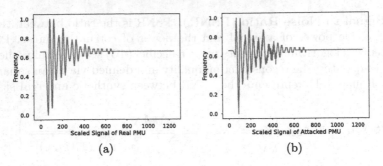

Fig. 3. (a) Real PMU Signal (b) Attacked PMU Signal

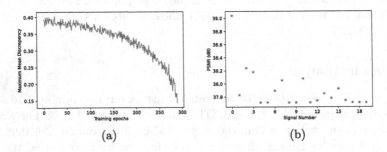

Fig. 4. (a) Maximum Mean Discrepancy (b) Peak Signal Noise Ratio

4.4 Comparison of Attack Methods

As per the literature, Liu et al. in [11] have given an efficient method of using GAN to inject an attack into the grid. Hence, We compare our results with their work to exhibit the advantage of our model. Our system has the configuration: Intel core i9, 64G RAM, NVDIA P100 GPU. We run the code using *TensorFlow, Python.*

For generating the attack vector upon reaching the Nash equilibrium, the average computation time per sample of our model is 0.19 ms, whereas the model in [11] takes 0.26 ms. We used interpolation [6] to merge the generated attack data to the real PMU data to smoothen the change, which takes negligible time. The average computation time of our LSTM-based prediction model is 0.03 ms which can be considered as a faster and more reliable model to implement in real time.

The detection rate of our attack is 2.3%, which is significantly smaller as compared to the attack in [11] i.e., 5.3%. The prediction error due to the attack we injected spreads over more samples than the attack modeled in [11]. Figure 5 shows a comparison of the prediction errors of both models.

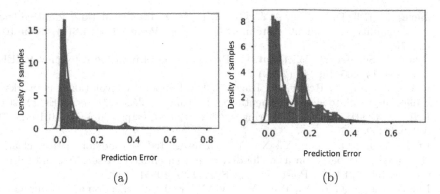

Fig. 5. (a) Prediction Deviation due to [11] (b) Prediction Deviation due to our model

5 Conclusion

This work proposes a false data injection attack on PMU data of a smart grid using a GAN that generates time series data. The attack strategy is testified against the attack detection strategies of the smart grid. The idea has been implemented on two different datasets with different event signatures. Though the proposed attack injects abnormal data of sufficient duration, it is not recognized easily. Also, the injected attack is capable of disturbing the normal operations in the grid. Using some similar architectures of GAN, there is a possibility of creating more types of cyber attacks considering different signatures of events that we plan to work on in the future.

Acknowledgements. We are thankful to the Ministry of Education (Govt. of India) and CPRI-funded project: EE/PB/CPRI/2022/8.85 for supporting the work.

References

1. Alohali, B., Kifayat, K., Shi, Q., Hurst, W.: Replay attack impact on advanced metering infrastructure (AMI). In: Hu, J., Leung, V.C.M., Yang, K., Zhang, Y., Gao, J., Yang, S. (eds.) Smart Grid Inspired Future Technologies. LNICST, vol. 175, pp. 52–59. Springer, Cham (2017). https://doi.org/10.1007/978-3-319-47729-9_6
2. Cook, A.A., Mısırlı, G., Fan, Z.: Anomaly detection for IoT time-series data: a survey. IEEE Internet Things J. **7**(7), 6481–6494 (2019)
3. Cubuk, E.D., Zoph, B., Schoenholz, S.S., Le, Q.V.: Intriguing properties of adversarial examples. arXiv preprint arXiv:1711.02846 (2017)
4. Deng, R., Xiao, G., Lu, R., Liang, H., Vasilakos, A.V.: False data injection on state estimation in power systems-attacks, impacts, and defense: a survey. IEEE Trans. Industr. Inf. **13**(2), 411–423 (2016)
5. Gotti, D., Amaris, H., Larrea, P.L.: A deep neural network approach for online topology identification in state estimation. IEEE Trans. Power Syst. **36**(6), 5824–5833 (2021)
6. Griffiths, D.V., Smith, I.M.: Numerical Methods for Engineers. CRC Press, Boca Raton (2006)

7. James, J., Hill, D.J., Lam, A.Y., Gu, J., Li, V.O.: Intelligent time-adaptive transient stability assessment system. IEEE Trans. Power Syst. **33**(1), 1049–1058 (2017)
8. Kruse, J., Schäfer, B., Witthaut, D.: Predictability of power grid frequency. IEEE Access **8**, 149435–149446 (2020)
9. Lea, C., Vidal, R., Reiter, A., Hager, G.D.: Temporal convolutional networks: a unified approach to action segmentation. In: Hua, G., Jégou, H. (eds.) ECCV 2016. LNCS, vol. 9915, pp. 47–54. Springer, Cham (2016). https://doi.org/10.1007/978-3-319-49409-8_7
10. Li, F., Wang, Q., Tang, Y., Xu, Y.: An integrated method for critical clearing time prediction based on a model-driven and ensemble cost-sensitive data-driven scheme. Int. J. Electr. Power Energy Syst. **125**, 106513 (2021)
11. Liu, Z., Wang, Q., Ye, Y., Tang, Y.: A GAN based data injection attack method on data-driven strategies in power systems. IEEE Trans. Smart Grid **13**, 3203–3213 (2022)
12. Mengis, M.R., Tajer, A.: Data injection attacks on electricity markets by limited adversaries: worst-case robustness. IEEE Trans. Smart Grid **9**(6), 5710–5720 (2017)
13. Mestav, K.R., Luengo-Rozas, J., Tong, L.: Bayesian state estimation for unobservable distribution systems via deep learning. IEEE Trans. Power Syst. **34**(6), 4910–4920 (2019)
14. Petitjean, F., Ketterlin, A., Gançarski, P.: A global averaging method for dynamic time warping, with applications to clustering. Pattern Recogn. **44**(3), 678–693 (2011)
15. Song, Q., Tan, R., Ren, C., Xu, Y.: Understanding credibility of adversarial examples against smart grid: a case study for voltage stability assessment. In: Proceedings of the Twelfth ACM International Conference on Future Energy Systems, pp. 95–106 (2021)
16. Su, J., Vargas, D.V., Sakurai, K.: One pixel attack for fooling deep neural networks. IEEE Trans. Evol. Comput. **23**(5), 828–841 (2019)
17. Sutherland, D.J., et al.: Generative models and model criticism via optimized maximum mean discrepancy. arXiv preprint arXiv:1611.04488 (2016)
18. Szegedy, C., et al.: Intriguing properties of neural networks. arXiv preprint arXiv:1312.6199 (2013)
19. Tan, B., Yang, J., Pan, X., Li, J., Xie, P., Zeng, C.: Representational learning approach for power system transient stability assessment based on convolutional neural network. J. Eng. **2017**(13), 1847–1850 (2017)
20. Tang, J., Sui, H.: Power system transient stability assessment based on stacked autoencoders and support vector machine. In: IOP Conference Series: Materials Science and Engineering, vol. 452, p. 042117. IOP Publishing (2018)
21. Tong, X., Qi, W.: False data injection attack on power system data-driven methods based on generative adversarial networks. In: 2021 IEEE Sustainable Power and Energy Conference (iSPEC), pp. 4250–4254. IEEE (2021)
22. Wu, S., Zheng, L., Hu, W., Yu, R., Liu, B.: Improved deep belief network and model interpretation method for power system transient stability assessment. J. Mod. Power Syst. Clean Energy **8**(1), 27–37 (2019)
23. Zhang, J.E., Wu, D., Boulet, B.: Time series anomaly detection for smart grids: a survey. In: 2021 IEEE Electrical Power and Energy Conference (EPEC), pp. 125–130. IEEE (2021)
24. Zhong, X., Jayawardene, I., Venayagamoorthy, G.K., Brooks, R.: Denial of service attack on tie-line bias control in a power system with PV plant. IEEE Trans. Emerg. Top. Comput. Intell. **1**(5), 375–390 (2017)

Detecting Web-Based Attacks: A Comparative Analysis of Machine Learning and BERT Transformer Approaches

Razaq Jinad, Khushi Gupta[✉], Chukwuemeka Ihekweazu, Qingzhong Liu, and Bing Zhou

Sam Houston State University, Huntsville, TX, USA
{raj032,kxg095,cei004,qxl005,bxz003}@shsu.edu

Abstract. As web attacks continue to evolve, web applications are increasingly vulnerable to various security threats and network attacks. Malicious actors can inject harmful code in an HTTP request to launch attacks like SQL injection, XSS, buffer overflow, and others. Detecting and classifying unknown web attacks is essential for enhancing the reliability and security of web applications. In this study, we employ a Transformer called Bidirectional Encoder Representations (BERT) and several machine learning techniques (CNN, SVM, Random Forest, Naive Bayes, etc.) to categorize HTTP requests based on their attack type. We then compare the results obtained from all the techniques and observe that BERT achieves the highest accuracy of 99% compared to all other classification methods used.

Keywords: Web attack detection · Machine Learning · Cybersecurity

1 Introduction

With the rapid advancements in global networking and communication technologies, many of our daily activities, such as social networking, electronic banking, e-commerce, etc., have migrated to cyberspace. However, the open, anonymous, and uncontrolled infrastructure of the internet also provides a fertile ground for cyberattacks, making it a serious vulnerability. Among the most commonly targeted attack vectors are web servers and web-based applications, with businesses experiencing over 200 million web attacks monthly, including SQL injection attacks, XSS code execution, and other types of attacks. Typically, web servers and web-based applications receive and transmit information using queries in the form of HTTP traffic, which contains strings of parameters with assigned values. Attackers are able to manipulate these queries and perform web attacks simply by embedding executable code or malicious code in URL requests. Therefore, it is crucial to identify the attack types as this knowledge allows us to take appropriate and effective countermeasures against potential threats.

© The Author(s), under exclusive license to Springer Nature Switzerland AG 2023
H. Fujita et al. (Eds.): IEA/AIE 2023, LNAI 13926, pp. 325–332, 2023.
https://doi.org/10.1007/978-3-031-36822-6_28

Conventional threat detection techniques rely on rule matching to examine known attack characteristics. Unfortunately, this approach fails to identify unknown vulnerabilities or attack methods. Therefore, there is a pressing need to swiftly and precisely detect unfamiliar threat attacks and accurately categorize various attacks to enhance the ability to detect web attacks. In this research, we propose a detection method that scrutinizes HTTP request packets to identify web-based attacks.

Our research aims to detect and categorize unknown web attacks using various machine learning models. This research uses a dataset of HTTP requests of six different unknown web attacks. To accomplish this, we evaluate the effectiveness of different machine learning techniques such as Decision Tree, Support Vector Machine (SVM), K-Nearest Neighbor (KNN), Naive Bayes, Logistic Regression, Random Forest, and Convolutional Neural Networks (CNN). Additionally, we apply a pre-trained transformer model called BERT [2] to classify web attacks and compare their performance with traditional machine learning algorithms. The objectives of this paper are as follows:

- To identify the most effective machine learning model for detecting and classifying unknown web attacks.
- To compare the performance of a transformer model with traditional machine learning algorithms for web attack detection and classification.
- To explore the strengths and weaknesses of different machine learning models for web attack detection and classification.

The structure of this paper is as follows. Section 2 describes the work related to similar efforts. Section 3 describes the methodology used in the research, expounding on feature extraction, selection, and classification methods. Experimental results and discussion are provided in Sect. 4. Finally, the paper is summarized in Sect. 5 and draws some conclusions.

2 Related Work

In this section, we review and summarize some of the commonly explored areas with regard to web attack detection and classification.

Choi et al. [1] propose a method using machine learning to detect malicious URLs of all the popular attack types and identify the nature of the attack a malicious URL attempts to launch. Their approach uses various discriminative features, including textual properties, link structures, webpage contents, DNS information, and network traffic. The experimental analysis was carried out with 40,000 benign URLs and 32,000 malicious URLs extracted from real-world data. The results of the presented approach exhibited excellent performance with a detection accuracy of over 98% for malicious URLs and over 93% for identifying attack types.

The study [5] aimed to propose an anomaly-based Web attack detection architecture using CNN deep learning methods in a Web application. The proposed architecture is implemented in the HTTP CSIC-2010v2 dataset with CNN algorithms. In the presented study, CNN-based detection architecture was developed to automatically extract patterns in HTTP data, part of which included using a bag of words for preprocessing. Normal and anomaly HTTP data classification was then performed, which yielded the most optimal CNN architecture accuracy rate, which was higher than 96%.

Additionally, Vartouni et al. [7] propose a web application firewall based on anomaly detection using machine learning algorithms. Their approach analyzes the HTTP traffic, and to construct features from HTTP data, an n-gram model that is based on the character is applied. To reduce the dimensionality of the problem, a stacked auto-encoder with different configurations is implemented to extract relevant features from data. Deep neural networks are used as feature learning methods, whereas isolation forest is used as a classifier.

The work [8] proposes an anomaly detection method based on multi-models to detect Web attacks. The technique is designed by inspecting the HTTP request messages to identify attacks. Three machine learning models, namely the probability distribution model, the hidden Markov model, and the one-class SVM model are employed to inspect different fields of the HTTP request messages to detect anomalies. Every HTTP request message is partitioned into seven fields: method, Web resource, attribute sequence, attribute value, HTTP version, header, and header input value. The detection mechanism of each model and the corresponding feature extraction algorithm are presented. The experimental results show that the multi-model-based detection method has an apparent advantage in detecting Web attacks.

Lastly, [4] proposed a methodology to detect web attacks. This involves using the BERT tokenizer to get the to obtain the vectors corresponding to the URLs in the HTTP requests. The word vectors then obtained are used as input to the MLP model. The experimental results reveal that the proposed approach achieves a success rate of 99% in the classification of anomalous and normal requests.

To the best of our knowledge, no research has tackled the detection of different types of unknown web attacks using HTTP request features. Additionally, we use a transformer model called BERT, which outperforms all the machine-learning models tested in our research and all the other research methodologies performed for web attack detection giving an accuracy of 99.2%.

3   Methodology

The methodology we propose consists of two primary sections: manual analysis and transformer analysis. The manual analysis involves various techniques for data cleaning and manipulation, as well as the use of eight machine-learning models for classification. However, the transformer analysis section employs the Bidirectional Encoder Representations from Transformers (BERT) encoder for preprocessing and a deep learning model called BERT and a Convolutional Neural Network model. Figure 1 provides a visual representation of our proposed methodology.

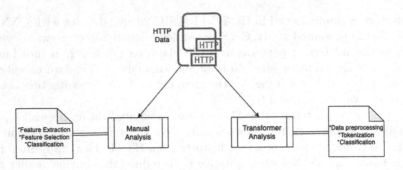

Fig. 1. Proposed Methodology.

3.1 Dataset

To carry out this analysis, we use six individual datasets, each containing records of HTTP requests for a specific type of web attack that was unknown. These datasets consist of a total of 33,000 HTTP requests and are divided into six columns, which represent the different fields of a request, and a column for the class label that depicts the type of web attack we aim to classify. The columns in the dataset are Method, User-agent, URL, Referer, and Body.

3.2 Manual Analysis

In the manual analysis approach, two feature extraction approaches, namely Lexical analysis and Bag of Words, were employed to extract features from the fields of HTTP requests.

Lexical Features. Lexical features pertain to statistical properties derived from HTTP request fields, such as the length of the field, the number of digits, the number of parameters present in the query section of the URL, and whether the URL is encoded. The following lexical features were extracted URL scheme, URL path length, URL host length, number of parameters, number of sub-directories, number of special characters, URL entropy, number of digits, number of letters and each alphabet in the URL, length of the HTTP field, and Has keywords. Due to their low computational requirements and high accuracy in classification, lexical features have become a prevalent source of machine learning.

The following lexical features were extracted in this experiment, as shown in Table 1.

- **URL Scheme:** The URL's scheme indicates what level of security has been configured on the webpage (HTTP/HTTPS).
- **URL path length:** The URL path is often modified to conduct web attacks, by embedding malicious code or the insertion and modification of SQL-like statements.

- **URL host length:** The average length of a legitimate URL is 25 characters [6].
- **Number of parameters:** A query string consists of an ordered list of n pairs of parameters with their corresponding values [3].
- **Number of sub-directories and single-character directories:** This feature can be useful, for example, in the case of directory traversal attacks. The count of the sub-directories in the HTTP field will be high.
- **Number of special characters:** These features can be useful in detecting many web attacks, for example, during directory traversal attacks. To gain unauthorized access to files in a server the directory is traversed using ".." and "/" escapes. In this case, the count of the special characters would be very high.
- **URL entropy:** English text has fairly low entropy, i.e., it is predictable. By inserting characters in the URL, the entropy changes more than usual. For identifying the randomly generated malicious URLs, alphabet entropy is used.
- **Number of digits:** Malicious URLs often contain more than the usual amount of digits. Thus, this can be a useful feature to extract.
- **Number of letters and each alphabet in the URL:** In the case of normal HTTP request fields, they mostly have a regular character distribution. In the case of attacks such as buffer overflow attacks, a completely different character distribution can be served.
- **Length of the HTTP field:** HTTP request fields do not vary greatly in length. Malicious input, however, violates this assumption, such as in the case of a buffer overflow attack, which is executed by passing a string containing shell code that is long.
- **Has keywords:** We check the HTTP fields for the presence of sensitive keywords that may be indicators of web attacks. During SQL injection attacks, malicious users execute SQL-like statements thus, the count of keywords such as SELECT, INSERT, UPDATE, etc. will be high.

Bag of Words. The BoW is a simple and flexible machine learning modeling method used to extract features from the text [5]. In the experiment, we implemented the BoG technique only on the URL field. We broke down the URL into smaller words by substituting special punctuation characters with a space. The URL is then split based on the space, which creates a list of keywords extracted from the URLs. Keywords whose length is less than three characters are discarded, while the rest are stored in a list. The unique words are then counted based on how many times they appear. Due to the large number of unique words extracted, to get the final set of features, we picked the words that have appeared 50 times or more. This approach was taken keeping in mind the fact that the higher the frequency of words, the more likely it is the attack type. We then used Chi-square feature selection to select the best 1500 features out of the 1698 features produced by BoW.

Classification. Before the classification stage, we combined the lexical features (350) and the BoW features (1500) for a total of 1850 features. For the classification of our data, we employ seven machine-learning models in order to compare the performances of the models. The utilized models are decision tree, Support Vector Machine (SVM), K-Nearest Neighbors (KNN), Naive Bayes, Logistic Regression, and Random Forest.

3.3   Transformer Analysis

Transformers are deep learning models that adopt the self-attention mechanism. That is, they differentially weigh the significance of each part of the input data. They are primarily used for Natural Language Processing (NLP) and computer vision problems. BERT is a type of pre-trained transformer. Generally, transformers have encoders and decoders that read input bidirectionally. Encoders read the text input, and decoders produce predictions for the task. There are different BERT models. The analysis and classification of the dataset involve three stages: data preprocessing, tokenization, and classification.

Data Preprocessing. The preprocessing of data is done as the first step in this phase. The first process is to remove all the HTML tags from the dataset. Then, punctuation signs and numbers were eliminated. Finally, single characters and multiple spaces are removed. After all of these processes, we then concatenate all of the relevant features into one feature.

Tokenization. The result of the concatenation from the processing stage is the input of this stage. Tokenization is a mechanism used in NLP to convert texts to individual words(tokens) before changing to number vectors. There are different types of tokenization algorithms. In this research, we use the BERT tokenizer to tokenize our input.

Classification. The classification of the input is done using the traditional BERT and 1D convolutional neural network classifiers.

1. BERT Classifier: The BERT classifier uses the original BERT model called "bert_en_uncased_L-12_H-768_A-12". The model uses 12 hidden layers, a hidden size of 768, and 12 attention heads. It takes input text as a sequence of wordpiece tokens, which it then converts into token embeddings. These embeddings are then processed by the transformer layers and extract high-level features from the input text.
2. Convolutional Neural Network Classifier: After the tokenization, the sentences are set as input for the BERT classification model. First, we pad sentences within each batch to make it of equal length. After the input sentence is padded and shuffled, the final vector space representation is generated. This is the input to the model. The model consists of three CNN initialized with

filter values of 2, 3, and 4, respectively. Global max pooling is applied to the output of each CNN layer. Finally, the three CNN layers are concatenated together, and their output is fed to the first densely connected neural network. The second densely connected neural network is used to predict the output classes of the model. The neural network uses the Adam optimizer with a batch size of 32 and a learning rate value of 0.1.

4   Results

This section discusses the experimental results of the web attack analysis. In this paper, we aim to compare and contrast different encoding techniques and machine learning models' efficacy in the classification of web attacks.

Table 1 lists the different encoding types and various machine learning techniques used and their respective accuracy value.

Table 1. Accuracy values of the machine learning techniques used

Encoding Techniques	ML Technique	Accuracy Value
Manual Encoding	Decision Tree	78.38%
Manual Encoding	Convolutional Neural Network	42.52%
Manual Encoding	Support Vector Machine	98.77%
Manual Encoding	K nearest neighbor	93.32%
Manual Encoding	Naive Bayes	49.81%
Manual Encoding	Logistic Regression	77.08%
Manual Encoding	Random Forest	83.41%
BERT Encoding	BERT Model	77.53%
BERT Encoding	**Convolutional Neural Network**	**99.31%**

For the manual encoding technique, the highest accuracy value was achieved by SVM with 98.77%. However, for the BERT encoding technique, the CNN achieved the highest accuracy value of 99.31%, while the BERT model itself achieved an accuracy of 77.53%. The high accuracy of the BERT encoding and Convolutional Network model may be due to the fact that BERT is a powerful model which is trained on a large corpus of text data and can capture complex language features and relationships between words and phrases, which can lead to better performance on tasks such as text classification. Furthermore, it could be attributed to the CNN model, which can effectively capture spatial features in data.

5   Conclusion

In this research, we examine various web attack types. We then detect and classify the web attacks with different machine-learning methods. Our analysis involved two different stages. First, we manually analyze the data and classify it using traditional models. The other analysis used BERT transformers which automatically analyze the web attack. The results of our analysis and classification showed that the BERT analysis performed relatively well and is suitable for processing these kinds of problems.

With the exceptional performance of the BERT performance, a future direction of this research is to analyze and classify the dataset with several types of transformers.

References

1. Choi, H., Zhu, B.B., Lee, H.: Detecting malicious web links and identifying their attack types. In: 2nd USENIX Conference on Web Application Development (WebApps 11) (2011)
2. Devlin, J., Chang, M.W., Lee, K., Toutanova, K.: BERT: pre-training of deep bidirectional transformers for language understanding. arXiv preprint arXiv:1810.04805 (2018)
3. Kruegel, C., Vigna, G., Robertson, W.: A multi-model approach to the detection of web-based attacks. Comput. Netw. **48**(5), 717–738 (2005)
4. Seyyar, Y.E., Yavuz, A.G., Ünver, H.M.: An attack detection framework based on BERT and deep learning. IEEE Access **10**, 68633–68644 (2022)
5. Tekerek, A.: A novel architecture for web-based attack detection using convolutional neural network. Comput. Secur. **100**, 102096 (2021)
6. Vara, K.D., Dimble, V.S., Yadav, M.M., Thorat, A.A.: Based on URL feature extraction identify malicious website using machine learning techniques. Int. Res. J. Innov. Eng. Technol. **6**(3), 144 (2022)
7. Vartouni, A.M., Kashi, S.S., Teshnehlab, M.: An anomaly detection method to detect web attacks using stacked auto-encoder. In: 2018 6th Iranian Joint Congress on Fuzzy and Intelligent Systems (CFIS), pp. 131–134. IEEE (2018)
8. Zhang, M., Lu, S., Xu, B.: An anomaly detection method based on multi-models to detect web attacks. In: 2017 10th International Symposium on Computational Intelligence and Design (ISCID), vol. 2, pp. 404–409. IEEE (2017)

Dynamic Resampling Based Boosting Random Forest for Network Anomaly Traffic Detection

Huajuan Ren, Ruimin Wang, Weiyu Dong$^{(\boxtimes)}$, Junhao Li, and Yonghe Tang

State Key Laboratory of Mathematical Engineering and Advanced Computing,
Zhengzhou, China
dongxinbaoer@163.com

Abstract. Network anomaly traffic detection is an important technique for detecting intrusion activities and maintaining cyberspace security. Random forest is widely used in network anomalous traffic detection due to its good detection performance. However, Random Forest suffers from the insufficient ability to handle difficult samples and poor performance in dealing with imbalanced network traffic distribution. To address these two problems, a boosting random forest for network anomaly detection, called BRF, is proposed. The proposed method embeds the random forest model into Boosting training mechanism to enhance its classification ability for difficult samples. In the iterations, Random Forest is provided with relatively balanced and diverse training sets by dynamic resampling to alleviate the traffic imbalance problem. The effectiveness of BRF is demonstrated by multi-classification experiments on the NSL-KDD and UNSW-NB15 datasets. Compared with some shallow machine learning, deep learning, and ensemble learning methods, BRF has advantages in accuracy and time efficiency, which is a promising method for network anomaly detection.

Keywords: Network Traffic · Anomaly Detection · Random Forest ·
Class Imbalance · Dynamic Resampling

1 Introduction

In recent years, cybersecurity incidents have increased rapidly, and people are facing more and more serious security threats from computer network systems. From November 2021 to October 2022, Kaspersky Lab detected 505,879,385 attacks launched from online resources across the globe, and 15.37% of internet user computers worldwide experienced at least one Malware-class attack [1]. Information transmission and interaction in cyberspace are carried by network traffic. For example, attackers often launch attacks with the help of network connections. Network traffic data contains critical information, and thus using it to discover attacks in the network has great potential. Network traffic anomaly detection provides the basis for identifying network intrusions, which is an important technique for maintaining network security [2].

H. Fujita et al. (Eds.): IEA/AIE 2023, LNAI 13926, pp. 333–344, 2023.
https://doi.org/10.1007/978-3-031-36822-6_29

Machine learning techniques have been widely adopted in network anomaly traffic detection studies, which do not rely on expert knowledge and can adapt to increasingly complex network traffic distributions [3]. In most solutions, network traffic anomaly detection is abstracted as a classification problem in machine learning, where labeled traffic samples are used to train an anomaly detector, in turn identifying unlabeled traffic sample types.

The main classification algorithms used to build anomaly detection models are shallow machine learning, deep learning, and ensemble learning. Ensemble learning combines multiple complementary and diverse shallow machine learning models and typically outperforms individual models [4]. Deep learning methods have an overwhelming advantage on unstructured and domain-relational data (e.g., images, text, speech, etc.) but underperform on structured tabular data with uncertainty in inter-feature correlation. In fact, the traffic data after parsing is exactly tabular data. Comparatively, the integrated weak learner is a more common and effective solution [5,6]. The literature [6] indicates that decision tree-based models, especially Random Forest (RF) combining multiple trees, should be preferred when dealing with security problems that require computational speed and interpretation of inputs leading to specific outputs. RF is less prone to overfitting, insensitive to noise and outliers, and fast in processing high-dimensional data. However, the random integration process often leads to an overgeneralized RF model that is less capable of handling difficult samples. In addition, the network traffic distribution tends to be imbalanced, i.e., benign samples and frequent attack samples tend to be in the majority, while rare attack samples are in the minority. Affected by the imbalanced data distribution, RF has low accuracy in identifying minority class attacks.

In light of this, we propose a boosting random forest based on dynamic resampling named BRF. The proposed method trains the RF with a Boosting mechanism and provides the training set for RF by dynamic resampling in each iteration. The Boosting integration framework improves the current model based on feedback from the previous training results, enhancing the ability of RF to classify difficult samples. Dynamic resampling exploits the error distribution to undersample the majority class traffic samples, providing relatively balanced and diverse training sets for RF, which facilitates classification ability improvement.

In summary, the main contributions of this paper are as follows.

· The Boosting integration framework is employed to combine multiple RF models to improve the ability of RF to handle difficult samples.
· In the iterations, dynamic resampling is introduced to provide relatively balanced and diverse training subsets for the base RF models, alleviating the network traffic distribution imbalance problem.
· The experimental results demonstrate that the proposed method has higher detection accuracy compared to the baseline methods.

The rest of this paper is organized as follows. Section 2 presents some historical work and random forest methods relevant to this study. Section 3 describes our proposed method in detail. Section 4 shows experiments and analysis. Section 5 concludes this paper.

2   Related Works

In the existing studies, the main classification algorithms used to build anomaly detection models are shallow machine learning, deep learning, and ensemble learning. To date, some classical machine learning algorithms are still used for network anomaly detection, such as Support Vector Machines (SVM) [2,7,8], Decision Trees (DT) [9–11], and K-Nearest Neighbor (KNN) [12]. These shallow machine-learning approaches are rarely applied alone to build anomaly detection models and are mostly combined with feature selection algorithms or other classification methods to improve detection accuracy.

The great success of deep learning in computer vision and natural language processing has motivated researchers to apply deep learning in network anomaly detection. Deep Neural Networks (DNN) [13], Convolutional Neural Networks (CNN) [14], Recurrent Neural Networks (RNN) [15], and their variants [16–18] have been applied to network anomaly detection. Deep learning has powerful characterization capabilities that improve the model accuracy to some extent, but designing the network structure, tuning the parameters, and training the model often take a long time. Deep learning-based models are unsuitable for deployment in real-world network anomaly detection environments.

Ensemble learning combines multiple weaker classifiers to form a strong classifier to improve classification performance. The idea of ensemble learning has been used not only for combining shallow machine learning [19–21] but also for deep learning [4,18]. Even though integrating deep learning can improve accuracy, it will further increase computational complexity. RF integrates multiple decision tree models with high detection accuracy and time efficiency, with widespread applications in network anomaly detection [22,23].

RF randomly selects data subsets to train multiple decision trees and integrates the classification results in a voting manner, which is a classical Bagging type of ensemble learning algorithm trained in parallel. In RF, Classification And Regression Tree (CART) is used as the base classifier, and the training subsets are randomly selected from the original samples by replacement technique. In addition to random sampling, RF also implements random feature selection. Due to random sampling and feature selection, RF has sufficient generalization capability to resist overfitting. However, overgeneralizing the model leads to an insufficient ability to handle difficult samples. Although RF performs well for balanced data, it is ineffective for skewed network traffic distribution.

3   Methodology

Aiming at the insufficient ability of RF to handle difficult samples and imbalanced network traffic distribution, the Boosting training mechanism and dynamic resampling strategy are adopted, presenting a boosting random forest model based on dynamic resampling, i.e., BRF. First, we outline the model framework. Then, dynamic resampling is described in detail. Finally, the boosting process of model training is introduced.

3.1   Overview

BRF iteratively trains the RF model through the Boosting mechanism. Dynamic resampling provides relatively balanced training subsets for RF. The framework is shown in Fig. 1, where Random undersampling (RUS) randomly selects the same number of samples as the minority class from the majority class samples and merges them with the minority class samples to get the training subset.

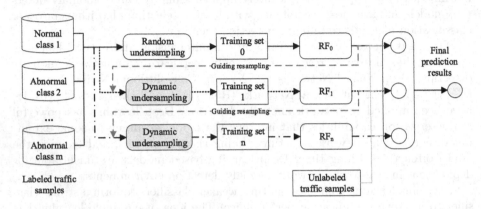

Fig. 1. The framework of BRF.

The Boosting mechanism sequentially trains the base classifiers, and the misclassified samples will receive relatively more attention in the next training. This approach can improve the ability of the model to handle difficult samples. The dynamic resampling approach uses the error distribution of the iterative model to undersample the majority class traffic samples, providing relatively balanced and diverse training sets for RF base models, which is beneficial for improving classification performance.

3.2   Dynamic Resampling

To balance the distribution of the network traffic dataset and to provide more diverse training subsets for RF, dynamic resampling is implemented before each iteration. This dynamic resampling relies on the Boosting mechanism, where a subset from the majority class is selected and combined with the minority class samples to create the training subset for the current iteration. The implementation of dynamic resampling can be summarized into three key steps, i.e., determining the number of samples, the sampling range, and the sampling weights within the sampling range.

First, for the determination of the sampling number N, the sample number N_{min} of the most minority class is used as a starting value to explore the optimal sampling number in fixed steps. If the sample number of a class is higher than N, then undersampling is performed. Compared with the RUS, which directly sets N_{min} as the sampling number, the proposed method can provide a relatively well-distributed dataset and avoid overfitting caused by small training samples.

Second, the training samples to be sampled are divided into multiple sampling zones and sampled in a targeted manner to achieve sample diversity in each sampling round. The samples in each sampling zone have similar characteristics, and the samples in the sampling zone are updated with iterative training. In the proposed method, the sampled samples are partitioned by an absolute classification error distribution that is updated with the Boosting iteration mechanism.

The absolute classification error describes how difficult it is for a sample to be classified correctly. Based on this concept, the samples to be sampled are divided into l sampling areas, and the error distribution of the jth sampling area is in the range $\left[\frac{j-1}{l}, \frac{j}{l}\right]$. The distribution of the classification error changes with iterative training, and therefore the samples in the sampling area change dynamically.

Third, the non-normalized sampling weight (as shown in Eq. 1) is calculated utilizing the average classification error $\bar{E}_j$ for each sample area. $\bar{E}_j$ is given in Eq. 2, where L_j denotes the set of sample contained in the jth sampling area and e_s is the absolute classification error of the sample s.

$$w_j = \frac{1}{\bar{E}_j} \tag{1}$$

$$\bar{E}_j = \frac{\sum_{s \in L_j} e_s}{|L_j|} \tag{2}$$

The normalized sampling weight for j^{th} sample area is calculated as shown in Eq. 3, and the sampling number of jth sample area is calculated as shown in Eq. 4.

$$w_j^{nor} = \frac{w_j}{\sum_{u=1}^{l} w_u} \tag{3}$$

$$N_j = w_j^{nor} \times N \tag{4}$$

The above sampling process changes dynamically with Boosting iterations, providing relatively balanced and diverse training subsets for RF.

3.3   Boosting Procedure

Let D denotes the set of all training samples, D_c represents the set of all training samples with class c. There are m classes in the training set, and let the value of c be an integer in the interval $[1, m]$. The training process of BRF is described in Algorithm 1.

Algorithm 1: Boosting Random Forest (BRF).

Input: Training set D, Iterations n, Number of sample areas l, Sampling number N

Output: Final ensemble $F(x) = \frac{1}{n+1}\sum_{u=0}^{n} RF_u(x)$

1 Train classifier RF_0 on the training subset obtained by RUS

2 **for** $i=1$ *to* n **do**

3   sampled subset $D' \leftarrow \oslash$

4      $F_i(x) = \frac{1}{i}\sum_{u=0}^{i-1} RF_u(x)$

5   **for** $r=1$ *to* m **do**

6   **if** $|D_c| > N$ **then**

7   Divid all samples in D_c into l areas by the absolute error distribution based on $F_i(x)$

8   Calculate the average classification error for the jth sample area as in Eq. 2

9   Calculate the non-normalized sampling weight of the jth sample area as in Eq. 1

10   Normalize the sampling weights as in Eq. 3

11   Resample N_j samples from the jth sample area (as in Eq. 4) to create the sampled dataset D_c'

12             $D' \leftarrow D' \cup D_c'$

13   **else**

14             $D' \leftarrow D' \cup D_c$

15   **end**

16   **end**

17   Train RF_i using D'

18 **end**

Boosting is used as the fundamental integration framework for the BRF model. In each iteration, a training subset is provided for the base classifier using dynamic resampling (i.e., lines 5–15), and then the new training subset is used to train the classifier. At the end of the iteration, all the obtained RF classifiers are accumulated and averaged to get the final ensemble classifier.

4 Experiments and Analysis

In this section, we show the experimental results of BRF in network anomaly traffic detection and discuss the effects of Boosting and dynamic resampling on model performance.

4.1 Dataset Description

NSL-KDD [24] and UNSW-NB15 [25] datasets were adopted to evaluate the performance of BRF, and the related descriptions are shown in Table 1. These two datasets are widely used benchmark datasets in network anomaly detection research works [19, 26].

Table 1. Description of two datasets.

Dataset	Class	Training set	Test set	Features
NSL-KDD	Normal	67343	9711	41
	DoS	45927	7458	
	Probe	11656	2421	
	U2R	52	200	
	R2L	995	2754	
	Total	125973	22544	
UNSW-NB15	Normal	56000	37000	47
	Fuzzers	18184	6062	
	Analysis	2000	677	
	Backdoors	1746	583	
	Dos	12264	4089	
	Exploits	33393	11132	
	Generic	40000	18871	
	Reconnaissance	10491	3496	
	Shellcode	1133	378	
	Worm	130	44	
	Total	175341	82332	

The dataset preprocessing includes one-hot encoding of categorical attributes and standardization of numerical attributes. The normalization was performed using the Z-Score approach as shown in Eq. 5, where x is the original sample, σ is the standard deviation, μ is the mean, and x^* is the result of the standardization.

$$x^* = \frac{x - \mu}{\sigma} \tag{5}$$

4.2   Experimental Setup

NSL-KDD[1] and UNSW-NB15[2] specify the datasets used for training and testing. The predefined datasets were used for training and testing. The experiments were run on Microsoft Windows 10 64-bit operating system with Intel(R) Core(TM) i7-8750H CPU and 32GB memory, and with Python 3.7.11 as the programming language.

The overall performance of the model was evaluated using Accuracy (ACC), Macro Average F1-score (Macro.F1), and Macro Area Under Curve (Macro.AUC) metrics. For the classification performance evaluation on each class, F1-Score (F1) was employed. To evaluate the efficiency of the model, the training time (TT) was calculated in seconds (abbreviated as s) as a measurement unit.

---

[1] https://www.unb.ca/cic/datasets/nsl.html.
[2] https://research.unsw.edu.au/projects/unsw-nb15-dataset.

The performance of the proposed BRF was compared with the anomaly detection models based on some classical machine learning methods, and the baseline methods involved in the comparison were the following three categories.

- Shallow Machine Learning: CART, KNN, SVM.
- Deep Learning: DNN, CNN, RNN.
- Ensemble Learning: RF, Adaptive Boosting (AdaBoost), Light Gradient Boosting Machine (LightGBM).

In BRF, the iterations and the number of sample areas were set to 50 and 5, and the sampling number was set to 52 for the NSL-KDD dataset and 2000 for the UNSW-NB15 dataset. CART, KNN, SVM, RF, and AdaBoost were implemented using scikit-learn[3], a third-party module for Python, where the iterations for RF and AdaBoost were set to 50 and all other parameters were set to default. LightGBM was executed by lightgbm module[4], with the iteration number of 50 and other parameters as default. The deep learning models were implemented by Keras framework with references [13–15]. Specifically, for DNN, five groups of "Fully connected+Dropout(0.01)" layers were set. For CNN, two groups of "Convolution1D+Convolution1D+MaxPooling1D(2)" and one group of "Fully connected+Dropout(0.01)" layers were designed. For RNN, four groups of "Fully connected RNN+Dropout(0.1)" layers were used.

4.3 Experimental Results and Analysis

The overall performance results of all tested methods on two datasets are shown in Table 2, where the best classification results are marked in bold black font.

Table 2. The results of the tested methods on NSL-KDD and UNSW-NB15.

Method	NSL-KDD				UNSW-NB15			
	ACC	Macro. F1	Macro. AUC	TT(s)	ACC	Macro. F1	Macro. AUC	TT(s)
CART	0.755	0.517	0.712	2.229	0.723	0.478	0.820	2.552
KNN	0.745	0.508	0.737	0.149	0.728	0.438	0.803	0.250
SVM	0.767	0.543	0.886	2790.173	0.695	0.334	0.937	13001.178
DNN	0.748	0.494	0.902	1242.278	0.729	0.447	0.896	3076.982
CNN	0.729	0.490	0.890	4604.452	0.746	0.454	0.914	8927.582
RNN	0.780	0.557	0.915	751.199	0.742	0.456	0.927	652.651
RF	0.759	0.489	0.855	10.784	**0.754**	0.468	0.931	31.859
AdaBoost	0.661	0.402	0.815	18.904	0.558	0.249	0.639	39.847
LightGBM	0.741	0.513	0.779	3.369	0.720	0.402	0.825	9.604
BRF(ours)	**0.838**	**0.675**	**0.935**	79.349	0.734	**0.498**	**0.939**	367.445

---

[3] https://scikit-learn.org/stable/index.html.
[4] https://pypi.org/project/lightgbm/.

As shown in Table 2, for the NSL-KDD dataset, BRF outperforms other tested methods in ACC, Macro.F1, and Macro.AUC, which indicates that BRF has better classification ability and achieves higher detection accuracy. The proposed method improves the classification effectiveness of RF by 10.4%, 38.0%, and 9.36% on the above three metrics, respectively. It is shown from Table 2 that BRF performs better than the other tested methods on the UNSW-NB15 dataset in terms of Macro.F1 and Macro.AUC metrics. Compared to RF, BRF improves by 2.14% and 0.86% on these two metrics. The training time of BRF is increased compared to some machine learning methods but is much less than that of deep learning models.

To evaluate the detection ability of the models for each traffic class, the models with better performance among the three baseline methods are selected to demonstrate F1 for each class. For the NSL-KDD dataset, SVM, RNN, and RF perform better in classification accuracy. For the UNSW-NB15 dataset, CART, RNN, and RF perform better. The detailed classifications of these representative methods for multiple classes on both datasets are shown in Fig. 2 and Fig. 3.

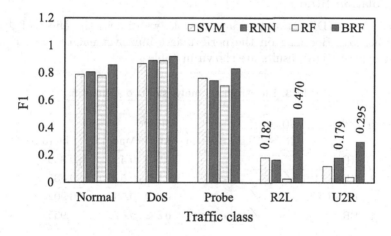

Fig. 2. F1 of representative methods on the NSL-KDD dataset.

In Fig. 2, the F1 of BRF is higher than other models for each class. F1 is the harmonic mean of Precision and Recall, which indicates that the proposed model has better comprehensive classification ability for each traffic class. In particular, for the R2L and U2R classes, BRF improves 158% and 64.8% on F1 compared to the suboptimal model.

From Fig. 3, for the most minority class Worm, BRF improves 5.94% on F1 compared to the suboptimal model. For the UNSW-NB15 dataset, BRF has better overall classification ability than other methods (see Table 2), but the performance on each class is not outstanding, which is attributed to the more complex feature space and traffic category distribution in the UNSW-NB15 dataset.

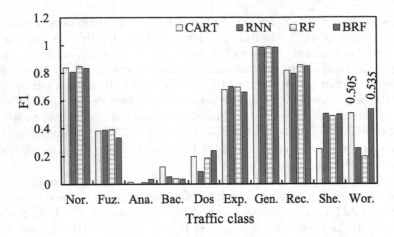

Fig. 3. F1 of representative methods on the UNSW-NB15 dataset.

4.4   Ablation Study

With the NSL-KDD dataset as an example, we discuss the effect of dynamic resampling and Boosting on the performance improvement of the RF model, and the experimental results are shown in Table 3.

Table 3. Effectiveness analysis of two strategies.

Method	strategy			Metric		
	RUS	DUS	Boosting	ACC	Macro.F1	Macro.AUC
(1) RF	-	-	-	0.759	0.489	0.855
(2) RF+ RUS	✓	-	-	0.734	0.520	0.885
(3) RF+DUS	-	✓	-	0.789	0.589	0.902
(4) BRF	-	✓	✓	0.838	0.675	0.935

Model (2) combines random undersampling with RF, using random undersampling to provide a balanced training subset for RF. Compared with RF, its Macro.F1 and Macro.AUC are improved to some extent. Model (3) combines dynamic resampling with RF, and each evaluation metric is improved compared to model (2), indicating that dynamic resampling is more beneficial to model performance improvement than random undersampling. Model (4), the proposed model, introduces the Boosting mechanism based on model (3), and the experimental comparison illustrates the effectiveness of the Boosting mechanism.

5   Conclusion

In this paper, we propose a dynamic resampling-based boosting random forest method, i.e., BRF, which trains the random forest models with the Boosting mechanism and provides the training subset for the random forest by dynamic resampling in each iteration. The Boosting ensemble framework enhances the classification ability of the random forest for difficult samples. The dynamic resampling method utilizes the error distribution to undersample the majority class traffic samples, providing relatively balanced and diverse training subsets for the base random forest models. The experimental evaluation results show that BRF improves the classification ability of random forests and outperforms baseline methods. In future works, we will validate the effectiveness and generality of the method in broader network traffic scenarios and develop anomaly detection models for more complex traffic distribution.

Acknowledgment. This research was supported by Key R&D projects in Henan Province of China under grant number 221111210300.

References

1. Kaspersky Lab: Kaspersky security bulletin 2022 (2022). https://securelist.com/ksb-2022-statistics/108129/. Accessed 6 Feb 2023
2. Ma, Q., Sun, C., Cui, B., Jin, X.: A novel model for anomaly detection in network traffic based on kernel support vector machine. Comput. Secur. **104**, 102215 (2021)
3. Yang, J., Chen, X., Chen, S., Jiang, X., Tan, X.: Conditional variational autoencoder and extreme value theory aided two-stage learning approach for intelligent fine-grained known/unknown intrusion detection. IEEE Trans. Inf. Forensics Secur. **16**, 3538–3553 (2021)
4. Zhong, Y., et al.: HELAD: a novel network anomaly detection model based on heterogeneous ensemble learning. Comput. Netw. **169**, 107049 (2020)
5. Liu, Z., Wei, P., Jiang, J., Cao, W., Bian, J., Chang, Y.: MESA: boost ensemble imbalanced learning with meta-sampler. Adv. Neural. Inf. Process. Syst. **33**, 14463–14474 (2020)
6. Casas, P., Marín, G., Capdehourat, G., Korczynski, M.: MLSEC-benchmarking shallow and deep machine learning models for network security. In: 2019 IEEE Security and Privacy Workshops (SPW), pp. 230–235. IEEE (2019). https://doi.org/10.1109/SPW.2019.00050
7. Kuang, F., Xu, W., Zhang, S.: A novel hybrid KPCA and SVM with GA model for intrusion detection. Appl. Soft Comput. **18**, 178–184 (2014)
8. Gu, J., Lu, S.: An effective intrusion detection approach using SVM with naïve Bayes feature embedding. Comput. Secur. **103**, 102158 (2021)
9. Tian, Q., Han, D., Hsieh, M.Y., Li, K.C., Castiglione, A.: A two-stage intrusion detection approach for software-defined IoT networks. Soft. Comput. **25**, 10935–10951 (2021)
10. Mohammadi, S., Mirvaziri, H., Ghazizadeh-Ahsaee, M., Karimipour, H.: Cyber intrusion detection by combined feature selection algorithm. J. Inf. Secur. Appl. **44**, 80–88 (2019)
11. Zhao, X., Huang, G., Jiang, J., Gao, L., Li, M.: Research on lightweight anomaly detection of multimedia traffic in edge computing. Comput. Secur. **111**, 102463 (2021)
12. Li, W., Yi, P., Wu, Y., Pan, L., Li, J.: A new intrusion detection system based on KNN classification algorithm in wireless sensor network. J. Electr. Comput. Eng. **2014** (2014)

13. Vinayakumar, R., Alazab, M., Soman, K., Poornachandran, P., Al-Nemrat, A., Venkatraman, S.: Deep learning approach for intelligent intrusion detection system. IEEE Access **7**, 41525–41550 (2019)
14. Vinayakumar, R., Soman, K., Poornachandran, P.: Applying convolutional neural network for network intrusion detection. In: 2017 International Conference on Advances in Computing, Communications and Informatics (ICACCI), pp. 1222–1228. IEEE (2017). https://doi.org/10.1109/ICACCI.2017.8126009
15. Vinayakumar, R., Soman, K., Poornachandran, P.: Evaluation of recurrent neural network and its variants for intrusion detection system (IDS). Int. J. Inf. Syst. Model. Des. (IJISMD) **8**(3), 43–63 (2017)
16. Wang, W., et al.: HAST-IDS: learning hierarchical spatial-temporal features using deep neural networks to improve intrusion detection. IEEE Access **6**, 1792–1806 (2017)
17. Imrana, Y., Xiang, Y., Ali, L., Abdul-Rauf, Z.: A bidirectional LSTM deep learning approach for intrusion detection. Expert Syst. Appl. **185**, 115524 (2021)
18. Bedi, P., Gupta, N., Jindal, V.: I-SiamIDS: an improved Siam-IDS for handling class imbalance in network-based intrusion detection systems. Appl. Intell. **51**, 1133–1151 (2021). https://doi.org/10.1007/s10489-020-01886-y
19. Tama, B.A., Lim, S.: Ensemble learning for intrusion detection systems: a systematic mapping study and cross-benchmark evaluation. Comput. Sci. Rev. **39**, 100357 (2021)
20. Çavuşoğlu, Ü.: A new hybrid approach for intrusion detection using machine learning methods. Appl. Intell. **49**(7), 2735–2761 (2019). https://doi.org/10.1007/s10489-018-01408-x
21. Rajadurai, H., Gandhi, U.D.: A stacked ensemble learning model for intrusion detection in wireless network. Neural Comput. Appl. **34**, 1–9 (2020). https://doi.org/10.1007/s00521-020-04986-5
22. Boahen, E.K., Bouya-Moko, B.E., Wang, C.: Network anomaly detection in a controlled environment based on an enhanced PSOGSARFC. Comput. Secur. **104**, 102225 (2021)
23. Nazir, A., Khan, R.A.: A novel combinatorial optimization based feature selection method for network intrusion detection. Comput. Secur. **102**, 102164 (2021)
24. Tavallaee, M., Bagheri, E., Lu, W., Ghorbani, A.A.: A detailed analysis of the KDD cup 99 data set. In: 2009 IEEE Symposium on Computational Intelligence for Security and Defense Applications, pp. 1–6. IEEE (2009). https://doi.org/10.1109/CISDA.2009.5356528
25. Moustafa, N., Slay, J.: UNSW-NB15: a comprehensive data set for network intrusion detection systems (UNSW-NB15 network data set). In: 2015 Military Communications and Information Systems Conference (MilCIS), pp. 1–6. IEEE (2015). https://doi.org/10.1109/MilCIS.2015.7348942
26. Ring, M., Wunderlich, S., Scheuring, D., Landes, D., Hotho, A.: A survey of network-based intrusion detection data sets. Comput. Secur. **86**, 147–167 (2019)

Various Applications

A Data Propagation Method of Internet of Vehicles Based on Sharding Blockchain

Chen Chen[1] and Quan Shi[2](✉)

[1] School of Information Science and Technology, Informatization Center, Nantong University, Nantong, China
[2] School of Transportation and Civil Engineering, Nantong University, Nantong, China
sq@ntu.edu.cn

Abstract. Blockchain technology has been successfully applied to finance and medical treatment recently. It is the prototype of the next generation of cloud computing, which is expected to reconstruct human social activities. IoV is an essential part of human social activities. Traditional centralized management and data storage are not suitable for IoV, which satisfies large-scale and low latency. Therefore, decentralization, distributed management, and distributed storage may become the future technology trends of IoV. However, when we take decentralized techniques, the data and communication must have high-security requirements. According to the characteristics of IoV, this paper discussed the sharding design of Blockchain and proposed an IoV model-based sharding Blockchain. Based on this model, we designed a Sharding algorithm for the RSU Blockchain layer (RSU-SA) to elect full nodes and sharding with good scalability and stability. Secondly, by introducing the correlation degree of light nodes, we adopted the light node evaluation matrix, established the data propagation subtree, and implemented a tree-based data propagation algorithm (TDPA). Finally, we simulated the above two algorithms. Simulation results showed that the Sharding algorithm for the RSU Blockchain layer (RSU-SA) is more effective with a stable network life cycle. The experimental results verified the effect of tree depth on data block propagation. It revealed that the tree-based partition data propagation algorithm effectively reduced the block data transmission delay.

Keywords: Blockchain · Internet of Vehicles (IoV) · Sharding Algorithm · Road Side Unit (RSU) · Data Propagation Algorithm

1 Introduction

Based on 5G and Internet of Things (IoT) technologies, traditional Vehicular AD-hoc Networks (VANET) and Vehicular to Everything (V2X) will be integrated into the Internet of Vehicles (IoV) [1]. However, a hungry number of nodes in IoV need to access this vast network, and the traffic to be processed is substantial. At the same time, traditional centralized management and data storage will face significant challenges as the traffic load on the centralized system increases. Therefore, decentralization, distributed management, and distributed storage may be the future technology trends of IoV. However, if

H. Fujita et al. (Eds.): IEA/AIE 2023, LNAI 13926, pp. 347–359, 2023.
https://doi.org/10.1007/978-3-031-36822-6_30

we adopt decentralized techniques, the data and communication must have high-security requirements.

Blockchain aims to solve the problems of high cost, inefficiency, and insecure data storage shared in centralized organizations. Generalized Blockchain technology has many benefits and proposes a new distributed infrastructure and distributed computing paradigm for the Internet. Therefore, integrating Blockchain technology can significantly improve the security, intelligence, ample data storage, and efficient management of IoV. However, the high efficiency and low latency requirements of IoV pose new challenges for integrating Blockchain technology. The Transmission delay, consensus efficiency, and TPS of Blockchain are all problems that need to be solved urgently. The contributions of this paper are as follows:

  i. This paper designed a sharding double-chain structure BIoV model;
 ii. We designed the Sharding algorithm for the RSU Blockchain layer (RSU-SA) to realize the election and sharding of all nodes in the RSU blockchain layer. Simulation results showed that the Sharding algorithm for the RSU Blockchain layer (RSU-SA) is more effective with a stable network life cycle and data translation;
iii. We proposed a tree-based data propagation algorithm (TDPA). Compared with the existing data propagation algorithms, the proposed algorithm can reduce the data propagation transmission delay and improve transmission efficiency.

The rest of this paper is structured as follows: Sect. 2 reviews shared Blockchain research and related literature on data transfer. Section 3 discusses the sharding Blockchain-based IoV system model. Section 4 designs the sharding algorithm for the RSU Blockchain layer (RSU-SA) and a tree-based data propagation algorithm (TDPA) to reduce the data transmission delay of BIoV. In Sect. 5 we have simulated the above two algorithms and compared them with the existing algorithms. Finally, Sect. 6 concludes with a summary of the current research and future research directions.

2   Related Work

2.1   Sharding Blockchain

Sharding technology was first proposed and applied in databases [2]. All participating nodes in the network are divided into multiple shards, and each shard is only responsible for maintaining its corresponding data. In this way, it achieves scalability of the network processing power. As the network scale increases, we add more shards to enhance the processing power. Sharding Blockchain was first proposed by ELASTICO [3], combining sharding and Blockchain technologies to increase transaction throughput, which is the number of transactions processed per second. Since then, many researchers have been on shared Blockchains, such as Zilliqa [4] and Ethereum-2 [5].

In general, sharding Blockchain has the following three characteristics. The first is sharding communication. The participating nodes are divided into different shards, where the nodes in each shard need only internal communication most of the time. The second is sharding computation, which means that each shard is only responsible for processing its corresponding transaction. When the number of nodes in the network increases, more fragments can be added to achieve scalability. The third is sharding storage. Storing shards means that nodes of different shards only need to store the data of their corresponding shard. This paper mainly discusses the important role of communication in sharding Blockchain systems.

2.2 Data Propagation Algorithm for Blockchain

Blockchain is a decentralized distributed system, and one of the most challenging problems to solve is data synchronization between multiple nodes. The Gossip protocol used by traditional blockchain systems such as Bitcoin and Ethereum. Although increasing the connectivity of peers can reduce latency, it also leads to intolerable bandwidth waste.

Researchers believe that bandwidth utilization can be improved by optimizing the network structure. For example, Paper [6] proposes a topology optimization scheme where nodes score each peer using link information such as transmission delay, while adaptively deciding which neighbors to connect to reduce block propagation delay. In this paper, Wang X et al. [7] proposes Swift, a new broadcast mechanism for blockchain systems. Based on unsupervised learning and greedy algorithm, the P2P topology and broadcast algorithm in the structured network are optimized, which effectively reduces the propagation delay of the blockchain P2P network and avoids the waste of redundant bandwidth. A stability-aware consensus protocol [8] is proposed to solve the unstable topology problem in Blockchain-based IoV. Hu, W et al. [9] proposed using time series and gossip protocols to build consensus in the Internet of Vehicles (IoV). However, in integrating IoV and Blockchain, we need to improve the performance of Blockchain to meet the low-latency requirements of IoV.

3 Problem Model

3.1 The System Mode of BIoV

According to the idea of fragmentation, we proposed a BIoV model with a sharding double-chain structure, whose system model is shown in Fig. 1. The BIoV model with the hierarchical double-chain structure includes three nodes: vehicles, RSUs, and cloud services. We divide the above network model into three layers:

i. BIoV-devices layer: consists of vehicles with onboard units (OBU), and each cluster of vehicles is controlled by an RSU within its communication range. Vehicles in different clusters according to their driving directions and geographical locations. RSUs control and complete vehicle safety authentication. They also control vehicles creating, joining, and leaving clusters;

ii. RSU-Blockchain layer: we design the Sharding algorithm for the RSU Blockchain layer (RSU-SA) to select the full nodes and sharding. The full nodes of this layer are responsible for the network routing function in sharding and provide the trust management function of vehicles. The light nodes generate transaction data and regional consensus and allow devices to use regional Blockchain services, and provide the function of storing blocks. The RSUs in a sharding constitute sharing the same distributed ledger.

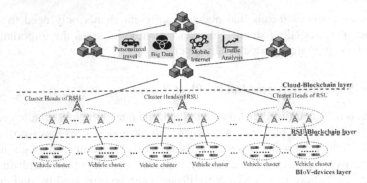

Fig. 1. A sharding double-chain model of BIoV

iii. Cloud-Blockchain service layer: Composed of cloud service nodes, it mainly realizes cross-partition consensus, data transaction management, block management, and trust management. In addition, this layer also provides mobile interconnection, personalized travel, traffic travel, mass data analysis, and other services for relevant vehicles or terminals through data offloading.

In our proposed model, only full nodes perform mining. Therefore, the proposed solution can significantly reduce the storage and computing resource consumption of the BIoV system.

3.2 The Sharding Model of the RSU-Blockchain Layer

In the model (see Fig. 2), light nodes only need to perform intra-slice communication most of the time and send critical information to the full nodes of the shard. Full nodes are typically responsible for cross-shard communication, and each shard has at least one full node. So full nodes need to have stronger communication capabilities than other on-chip light nodes.

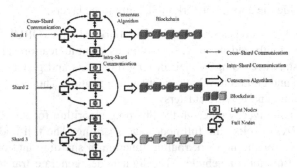

Fig. 2. The sharding model of the RSU Blockchain layer

In order to describe the partition-based mathematical model more intuitively, we use the parameter definition in Table 1. If the m-th full node sharding contains two light nodes as n_1, n_2, we denote as $s_m=\{n_1, n_2\}$.

Table 1. Description of parameters based on the sharding model

Symbol	Definition
sum	the number of full nodes
num	the number of light nodes
$H = sum + num$	the number of nodes
l_{ik}	the distance from the i-th light node to the k-th light node
L_{ij}	the distance from the i-th full node to the j-th full node
$Nodes = \{N_1, N_2, \cdots, N_{sum+num}\}$	the set of all RSU nodes
$NF = \{s_1, s_2, \cdots, s_{sum}\}$	the set of full nodes
$NF = \{s_1, s_2, \cdots, s_{sum}\}$	the set of light nodes

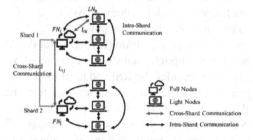

Fig. 3. The Sharding model of nodes

Definition 1: The distance between all nodes is shown in Fig. 3, that is, the distance loss matrix E_{FF}:

$$E_{FF} = \begin{pmatrix} 0 & \cdots & l_{isum} \\ \vdots & \ddots & \vdots \\ l_{sum1} & \cdots & 0 \end{pmatrix} \tag{1}$$

where sum represents the number of full nodes and l_{ik} represents the distance from the i-th light node to the k-th light node.

Definition 2: Distance energy loss matrix from full node to light node E_{FL}:

$$E_{FL} = \begin{pmatrix} l_{11} & \cdots & l_{1num} \\ \vdots & \ddots & \vdots \\ l_{sum1} & \cdots & l_{sumnum} \end{pmatrix} \tag{2}$$

where *num* denotes the number of light nodes, L_{ij} denotes the distance from the i-th full node to the j-th full node, and $L_{ij}=0$ when i = j.

Definition 3: A set of shards of the RSU blockchain layer is defined as a 0–1 matrix X of sum*num dimension:

$$x_{ik} = \begin{cases} 1 & n_k \in s_i \\ 0 & else \end{cases} \tag{3}$$

where $x_{ik}=1$ denotes that the k-th light node belongs to the shard of the i-th full node

Through the above definitions of the three functions (1), (2), and (3), we establish the mathematical model of sharding in the RSU Blockchain layer.

4 Solution Algorithm

4.1 A Sharding Algorithm for the RSU-Blockchain Layer (RSU-SA)

The traditional blockchain increases the data transmission delay by increasing the number of nodes, but it causes a waste of network bandwidth. We design the partitioning algorithm to divide the RSU nodes in the IoV into multiple shards, and each shard is only responsible for maintaining its corresponding data. In this way, the scalability of the processing power of the BIoV network is achieved. As the size of the network increases, we add more shards to enhance the processing power.

This section presents a sharding algorithm (RSU-SA) for the RSU Blockchain layer. First, we define s_i denotes the computational storage capacity of N_i, c_i means the storage capacity of N_i. This algorithm divides the RSU nodes into the full edge node of the set NF and the light edge node of the set NL. Then, we need to consider the distance loss between light and full nodes for RSU Blockchain layer sharding.

The process of RSU-SA (see Fig. 4.) is described as follows: First, we initialize the RSU Blockchain layer and generate nodes in a specific area through a random network generation function. Second, the nodes were divided into full nodes and light nodes c_i and s_i. Finally, E_{FL} is calculated according to formula (2), and the smallest value is obtained by comparing the matrix rows. The smallest value is assigned to 1 and the others to 0, so the piecewise matrix X can be obtained.

In the RSU Blockchain layer sharding model, each shard still relies on PoW, PoS, or other methods to confirm transactions. As the number of shard nodes increases, the transaction processing power may decrease sharply, so we consider the internal shards transport model, which will be discussed in detail in the next section.

4.2 Tree-Based Data Propagation Algorithm (TDPA)

In large-scale IoV applications, most service tasks have low latency time constraints. However, the traditional consensus mechanism in Blockchain is very time-consuming. We need to design tree structures with high connectivity and small broadcast depth to reduce data transmission delay. Therefore, according to the conclusion in the paper [10], this paper proposes a tree-based data propagation algorithm (TDPA) to reduce the block propagation time.

Algorithm1: the sharding algorithm of the RSU Blockchain layer（RSU-SA）
Input: $Nodes = \{n_1, n_2, \cdots, n_{sum}\}$
Output: X
1: Initialize 100*100 randomly produces 100 nodes H=100 NF=NL=∅, minimum space required for storing Blockchain: s_{min}, minimum computation: c_{min}.

2: Nodes Node classification
     for $n_i \in$ Nodes
         if $s_i \geqslant s_{min}$ and $c_i \geqslant c_{min}$ then
             $n_i \rightarrow$ NF;
         else
             $n_i \rightarrow$ NL;
         end if
     end for

3: Calculate the matrix E_{FL} according to equation (2)
4: Matrix row comparisons are taken to be minimal, assigning the minimum to be 1 and the others to be 0
5: if $S_m = \emptyset$ calculate the matrix E_{FF} according to equation (1)   define S_m as the light node with minimum E_{FF}

Fig. 4. Pseudo-code of the sharding algorithm of the RSU Blockchain layer

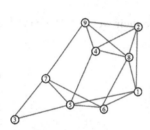

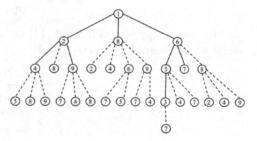

Fig. 5. Randomly generated network

Fig. 6. The propagation process of traditional Blockchain

To explain propagation trees more vividly, we take the small-scale randomly generated network topology shown in Fig. 5 as an example. In this topology, there are nine RSU nodes and sixteen edges. We assume that node 1 is a full node and can generate blocks. From Fig. 6, we can see that some light nodes repeatedly propagate during propagation, such as node 8, which is located on layer 2 and gets the block from node 1 during propagation during actual blocking. When node 8 appears on layer 3, it will not receive the block from node 2 since it has been received and verified. Each dashed line in Fig. 6 implies the verification process of repeated blocks. We turn the block propagation time problem into a propagation tree depth problem. Therefore, for a tree structure with a certain number of nodes, it is necessary to compress the propagation tree in depth to reduce the time of block propagation.

Definition 6: Light node association degree, which represents the ability of light nodes to receive and propagate information.

$$M_i = \sum_{j \in N_{(i)}} M(i,j) = \sum_{j \in N_{(i)}} (logF(i) - logF(j)) \tag{4}$$

$$F(i) = \frac{D(i)^{-1}}{\sum_{j \in N_{(i)}} D(j)^{-1}} \tag{5}$$

where D(i) denotes the degree of the i-th light node, and N(i) notes the set of neighbors of the light node n_i. F(i) denotes the linking coefficient of the light node n_i.

Definition 7: We consider the three indicators as the correlation degree of light nodes M_i, computing power C_i, and average transmission distance L_i between light nodes to construct the evaluation matrix:

$$E_{3num} = \begin{pmatrix} C_1 & C_2 \cdots & C_{num} \\ M_1 & M_2 \cdots & M_{num} \\ L_1 & L_2 \cdots & L_{num} \end{pmatrix} \tag{6}$$

$$L_i = \frac{\sum_{j \in N_{(i)}} L(i,j)}{D(i)} \tag{7}$$

We use the entropy weight method [11] to determine their weights. We can obtain the weights of the three indices $r(i)$, $i = 3$

$$r_j = \frac{1 - H_j}{m - \sum_{i=1}^{m} H_j} \tag{8}$$

$$H_j = -k * \sum_{t=1}^{num} f_{jt} ln f_{jt} \tag{9}$$

$$f_{jt} = \frac{e_{jt}}{\sum_{t=1}^{num} e_{jt}} \tag{10}$$

$$k = \frac{1}{ln num} \tag{11}$$

$$\omega(i) = r_1 * \widehat{C_i} + r_{21} * \widehat{M_i} + r_3 * \widehat{L_i} \tag{12}$$

$$\widehat{C_i} = \frac{C_i - C_{min}}{C_{max} - C_{min}}, \widehat{M_i} = \frac{M_i - M_{min}}{M_{max} - M_{min}}, \widehat{L_i} = \frac{L_i - L_{min}}{L_{max} - L_{min}} \tag{13}$$

Here, C_{min} and C_{max} represent the minimum and maximum computing power of light nodes. M_{min} and M_{max} denote the minimum and maximum light node association degree, and L_{min} and L_{max} mean the minimum and maximum average distance of light nodes.

We divide the light nodes within the partition into M transmission subtrees. The data transmission delay t_m of block data in each subtree is the sum of the verification delay $V = \{V_1, \ldots, V_M\}$ and data transmission delay $d_{i,j}$ of all nodes in the subtree.

$$t_m = \sum_{N'} v_i + \sum_{N'} d_{i,j} \tag{14}$$

where N' means the set of all paths from the full node to the plot point.

The total delay of block data propagation T_t is the maximum delay of block data propagation in all subtrees:

$$T_t = \max\{t_1, t_2, \cdots, t_M\} \tag{15}$$

In Algorithm 2 (see Fig. 7), the lowest level of the subtree is obtained by comparing w_i. Then we use the same method to determine the upper level until the root node of all subtrees is found. Finally, we obtain the block data transmission delay of the whole partition according to multiple subtrees' block data propagation time.

Algorithm 2: Tree-based data propagation algorithm (TDPA)
Input: $m, L, C, N(j)$
1、 calculate M_i according to Equations (4) and (5);
2、 calculate L_i according to Equations (7) ;
3、 construct the light node evaluation matrix according to (4)-(7); Obtain the weight w_i of each light node by calculating r_j
4、 construct the propagation subtree process
4.1 traverse the light nodes to find out n_j =max $\{w_j\}$. The n_j is the cluster head of the T-subtree, n_j is the leaf node of $Tree_j$;
4.2 if n_i in the is the set of $N(j)$, n_i is the cluster head of subtree-N, Delete n_i from the set of cluster heads in the T-subtree; else n_j =max $\{w_j\}$, Delete n_i;
4.3 $n_i \rightarrow Tree_{j1}$, $Tree_{i1} \rightarrow Tree_{j2}, \ldots, n_i \rightarrow Tree_{jroot}$;
5、 Output subtree-N and the cluster head; Obtain the T_t according to (14) and (16);

Fig. 7. The block propagation process of the traditional Blockchain

5 Simulation and Evaluation

5.1 Analysis of Simulation Results of the RSU-SA

For Algorithm 1, we conducted experiments in three aspects to test the algorithm results and performance. The operating system used in the experiment is Windows 11. Performed on a single computer equipped with an Intel(R) Core (TM) i7-12700K CPU, 3.60 GHz, and 64-GB RAM processor.

First, we used python programming language to implement Algorithm 1 to complete the election and fragmentation of all nodes. We compared the re-execution time (see Fig. 8) of the RSU-SA in the paper with Low-Energy Adaptive Clustering Hierarchy (LEACH) [12], Distributed Energy-efficient Clustering (DEEC) [13], and improved-LEACH (I-LEACH) [14] algorithms. The RSU-SA proposed in this paper only takes 10ms to form a shard when there are 500 nodes, which greatly improves the performance of RSU-SA.

Second, we carried out comparison experiments in the network lifetime and data transmission. We assumed a randomly generated network of 500 RSUs, conducted 5000

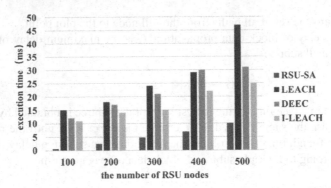

Fig. 8. Comparison of the running time of the LEACH, DEEC, I-LEACH, RSU-SA

rounds, and sent 4000 bits of data to get the final experimental data. In Fig. 9(a), the RSU-SA algorithm improves the network lifetime of nodes by 10%. RSU-SA performs more effectively in network lifetime than the other three algorithms. In Fig. 9(b), the RSU-SA algorithm proposed in this paper reaches the maximum after 2500 rounds. The latter is nearly three times higher than the former. It indicates that RSU-SA is superior to the other three in data transmission.

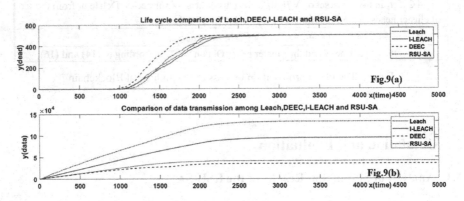

Fig. 9. The comparison of the four algorithms when the number of nodes = 500. (a) means the comparison of the four algorithms on life cycle, (b) means the comparison of the four algorithms on data transmission

5.2 Analysis of Simulation Results of TDPA

In this section, we designed two sets of experiments for simulation. First, we investigated the impact of tree-based depth on partitioned data propagation algorithms (see Fig. 10). When the number of nodes is below 3000, the growth of data transmission delay is not apparent with the increase of nodes. However, when the number of nodes exceeds 3000 and continues to increase, the block data transmission delay increases faster. In the case of the same number of nodes, the deeper the tree is, the more significant the data transmission delay will be serious. So our method to improve the efficiency of block data transmission by compressing the propagation tree in-depth and increasing the number of nodes in each layer is feasible.

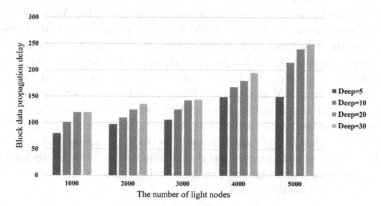

Fig. 10. Effect of tree depth on block data propagation delay

In order to verify the advantage of TDPA in data transmission delay, this paper designed the second set of experiments, that is, the comparison experiment of data transmission delay methods. The experiment simulated TDPA and compared it with the traditional Blockchain and LayerChain [10]. The tree-based cluster data propagation algorithm (TDPA) significantly reduces block data transmission delay compared to traditional Blockchain. Compared with LayerChain, the block data transmission delay is reduced by nearly 10% (see Fig. 11).

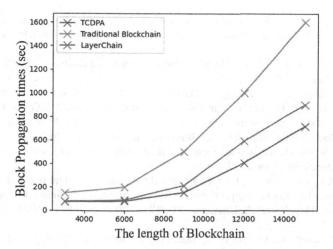

Fig. 11. Comparison of block data propagation latency

6 Summary and Scope

This paper proposes a blockchain-based partition model for IoV. We designed two algorithms. The Sharding algorithm for the RSU Blockchain layer (RSU-SA) is used to partition the blockchain-based IoV, control the scale of the Blockchain, and improve the performance of consensus, storage, and transaction processing. We propose the tree-based data propagation algorithm (TDPA) to alleviate the long delay problem. The algorithm describes the block propagation process as multiple propagation subtrees and reduces the propagation time by depth compression of the depth of each propagation tree. Our proposed solution can improve the operational efficiency of Blockchain in large-scale low-latency IoV applications. Finally, the algorithm's feasibility is verified by simulation experiments, and the block transmission delay is greatly improved. In the later stage, we consider implementing and improving the algorithm in Hyperledger. In addition, we will consider lightweight identity and message authentication protocols to ensure the security of node identity and data dissemination in BIoV. We hope to solve the existing security and scalability problems of IoV through the smart contract and incentive mechanism of Blockchain.

Funding Acknowledgment. This is a part research accomplishment of the following projects:

    1) "Postgraduate Research & Practice Innovation Program of Jiangsu Province (KYCX21_3087)", which is supported by Education Department of Jiangsu Province, China.

    2) "The National Natural Science Foundation of China (61771265)", which is supported by National Natural Science Foundation of China.

    3) "The Key Science and Technology Foundation of Nantong (MS22021034)," which is supported by The Science and Technology Bureau of Nantong.

References

1. Huang, S.Y., Chen, S.S., Chen, M.X., Chang, Y.C., Chao, H.C.: The efficient mobile management based on metaheuristic algorithm for internet of vehicle. Sensors, **22**(3), 1140(2022)
2. Corbett, J.C., et al.: Spanner: Google's globally distributed database. ACM Trans. Comput. Syst. **31**(3), 8:1–8:22 (2013)
3. Luu, L., Narayanan, V., Zheng, C., Baweja, K., Gilbert, S., Saxena, P.: A secure sharding protocol for open blockchains. In: Proceedings of the 2016 ACM SIGSAC Conference on Computer and Communications Security, October 24–28, pp. 17–30, Vienna, Austria (2016)
4. Zilliqa Team. Zilliqa. https://www.zilliqa.com/. Accessed 25 Jan 2022
5. Wang, J., Wang, H.: Monoxide Ethereum. Shard Chains. https://ethereum.org/en/eth2/shard-chains/. Accessed 25 Jan 2022
6. Ozisik, A.P., Andresen, G., Levine, B.N., et al.: Graphene: efficient interactive set reconciliation applied to blockchain propagation. In Proc. ACM Special Interest Group Data Communication, New York, NY, USA, pp. 303–317 (2019). https://doi.org/10.1145/3341302.334 2082
7. Wang, X., Jiang, X., Liu, Y., et al.: Data propagation for low latency blockchain systems. IEEE J. Sel. Areas Commun. **40**(12), 3631–3644 (2022)
8. Kim, S.: Impacts of mobility on performance of blockchain in VANET. IEEE Access **7**, 68646–68655 (2019)

9. Hu, W., Hu, Y., Yao, W., Li, H.: A blockchain-based byzantine consensus algorithm for information authentication of the Internet of vehicles. IEEE Access 7, 139703–139711 (2019)
10. Yu, Y., Liu, S., Yeoh, P.L., Vucetic, B., Li, Y.: LayerChain: a hierarchical edge-cloud blockchain for large-scale low-delay industrial Internet of Things applications. IEEE Trans. Industr. Inf. 17(7), 5077–5086 (2020)
11. Fu, Y., He, Z.: Entropy-based weighted decision combining for collaborative spectrum sensing over byzantine attack. IEEE Wirel. Commun. Lett. 8(6), 1528–1532 (2019)
12. Heinzelman, W.B., Chandrakasan, A.P., Balakrishnan, H.: An application-specific protocol architecture for wireless microsensor networks. IEEE Trans. Wirel. Commun. 1(4), 660–670 (2020)
13. Nehra, V., Sharma, A.K., Tripathi, R.K.: I-DEEC: improved DEEC for blanket coverage in heterogeneous wireless sensor networks. J. Ambient. Intell. Humaniz. Comput. 11(9), 3687–3698 (2020)
14. Chen, C., Quan, S.: RSU cluster deployment and collaboration storage of IoV based blockchain. Sustainability 14, 16152 (2022)

Air Pollution Forecasting Using Multimodal Data

Minh-Anh Ton-Thien[1,2,3], Chuong Thi Nguyen[1,2,3], Quang M. Le[1,2,3],
Dat Q. Duong[1,2,3], Minh-Son Dao[4], and Binh T. Nguyen[1,2,3(✉)]

[1] University of Science, Ho Chi Minh City, Vietnam
ngtbinh@hcmus.edu.vn
[2] Vietnam National University, Ho Chi Minh City, Vietnam
[3] AISIA Research Lab, Ho Chi Minh City, Vietnam
[4] National Institute of Information and Communications Technology (NICT),
Tokyo, Japan

Abstract. Air pollution is one of the most concerning problems worldwide. It leads to the necessary time series forecasting of particulate matter (PM) concentrations. In this study, we propose an effective way to improve the results of PM10 and PM25 forecasting tasks by combining meteorological features and timestamp information using datasets from Hanoi, Vietnam. We apply the data processing step to remove outliers and impute missing data issues. By conducting five deep learning models, MLP, 1D-CNN, LSTM, Bi-LSTM, and Stacked LSTM, the experimental results show that adding more timestamps information helped improve the results in 68% of cases compared to other methods. Furthermore, the Vanilla LSTM model with combined features will give better results in the long-term forecast than the other. We plan to extend our approach by combining more features from multiple sources and applying more robust models for the main problem.

Keywords: PM10 forecast · PM25 forecast · Deep learning model

1 Introduction

In recent decades, the rapid development of industry in many countries has significantly impacted the environment worldwide, especially air pollution. Investigating fitting forecasting models can help urban managers take suitable actions to improve air quality. In many developing countries in Southeast Asia, people in big cities face air pollution from transportation, e.g., cars, motorbikes, buses, and factories. It is worth noting that, in the long-term, air pollution can affect human health, induce asthma, harm the cardiovascular, and lead to potential cancer [8]. Therefore, if we can predict air pollution in the future (hourly or daily), we can plan and hold appropriate activities to protect our health.

Particulate matter in the atmosphere is formed based on chemical reactions from exhaust gasses from vehicles and factory production activities. It includes particles with diameters smaller than $10\,\mu m$ (PM10) and fine particles having diameters smaller than 2.5 μm (PM25). There have been many studies focused on forecasting PM values. Van Donkelaar et al. developed a technique for estimating surface PM25 concentrations from satellite observations [2]. Zhao and colleagues provide a new solution for predicting PM25 pollution with atmospheric sensing data [11]. Satvik Garg and collaborators adopt different models like ARIMA, FBProphet, LSTM, and 1D-CNN to estimate the concentration of PM25 in the environment [5]. However, those studies focus on improving the results by using and developing better models. According to our knowledge, there is a lack of research using feature data related to timestamp information.

This paper aims to combine different types of data, including meteorological data from monitoring stations (PM10, PM25, temperature, humidity, wind speed, etc.) and timestamp information. We extract timestamp information from the datasets and employ different deep-learning models to predict PM10 and PM25 values. We compare cases when we only used data from monitoring stations (Approach 1) and when we combined meteorological and timestamp information (Approach 2). Using data collected in two districts of Hanoi (the capital of Vietnam), the experiments show that combining both pieces of information increases results in most cases.

The contribution of our work can be described as follows: (i) we research how to improve multivariate time series forecast PM10 and PM25 task results by combining meteorological features and timestamps information using simple deep learning models; (ii) from there, people can extend our work further by applying more deep learning models and combining data from multiple sources to achieve better performance in the time series forecasting of PM concentrations tasks.

2   Related Work

Forecasting the PM10 and PM25 values is a new problem that has developed recently, attracting the attention of many research groups. Up to now, several methods have been studied as follows. Van Donkelaar and co-workers [2] have shown that Satellite-derived total-column AOD (aerosol optical depth), when combined with a chemical transport model, can provide an appropriate estimation of global long-term average PM25 concentrations. In [3], Dat et al. proposed a method to predict AQI values and ranks of a specific location in Ho Chi Minh City in Vietnam and Fukuoka in Japan. They used machine learning classifiers (e.g., Random Forest, Support Vector Machine, etc.) and various features, such as timestamp, location, and public weather to construct proper models for the main problem. The experimental results show that, using Random Forest with a combination of all types of features mentioned above, the overall performance can be the highest in many cases. Another extension in [4] is a development of the former, in which they used stacking methods [10] to combine the strength of available models to boost the overall performance.

Zhao et al. [11] introduced a deep learning model convolutional recurrent neural network (CRNN) to predict PM25 with atmospheric sensing data from the transboundary air pollution data. They collected these data from 33 coastal cities in China and Fukuoka's environmental monitoring data. In 2021, Satvik Garg and collaborators [5] compared ARIMA, FBProphet, and deep learning models such as LSTM, 1D-CNN to estimate the concentration of PM25 using data from 12 stations in Beijing. Their results convey that all methods give comparative result outcomes in average root mean squared error. However, LSTM outperforms all other models regarding mean absolute percentage error.

3   Methodology

This section will present the feature extraction procedure and how to construct suitable models for the problem.

3.1   Timestamp Feature Extraction

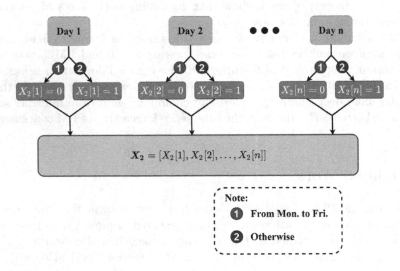

Fig. 1. The construction of the feature vector *weekend* X_2 in Fig. 5

Predicting air quality is complex due to the dynamic nature, volatility, and high variability in the time and space of pollutants and particulates.

There is no denying that vehicle pollution is a major contributor to air pollution, especially in urban cities. When cars, motorbikes, buses, trucks, and trains burn gasoline, it emits pollutants into the air, such as carbon monoxide, hydrocarbons, nitrogen oxide, and particulate matter. The global transport sector accounts for almost 25% of energy-related carbon dioxide emissions, which is rising. As such, traffic density directly affects air pollution.

Working hours also affect air quality because manufacturing, construction, and living activities are taking place and emitting pollutants into the air. Our

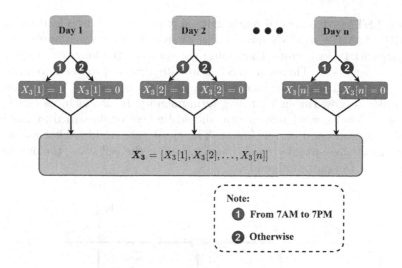

Fig. 2. The construction of the feature vector *working hour* X_3 in Fig. 5

idea is that high-density traffic and emissions increase air pollution during weekends and working hours. From the "Date Time" information, we extract two new features that are *weekend* and *working hour*. This idea is implemented by encoding the time into a vector of 0, 1 to include two new variables, *weekend* and *working_hour*.

As shown in Fig. 1, with the variable *weekend*, the time vector of the time from Monday to Friday is encoded as 0. However, during Saturday and Sunday weekends, the time vector is 1.

Similarly, in Fig. 2, with *working hour*, the time vector is 1 in the range 7 AM to 7 PM, whereas this is 0. The time steps of the two new variables *weekend* and *working hour* are synchronized with other weather and air quality variables, as depicted in Fig. 5, and used for the Approach 2.

3.2 Model Selection

In our experiments, we conduct five deep learning models, including two baseline models, multilayer perceptron (MLP) and one-dimensional convolutional neural network (1D-CNN), and three variants of long short-term memory (LSTM) models (Vanilla LSTM, bi-directional LSTM (Bi-LSTM), and Stacked LSTM).

MLP: An MLP is characterized by several hidden layers of input nodes connected as a directed graph between the input and output layers. For example, our multivariate time series forecast tasks use a one-hidden layer MLP model with 200 nodes.

1D-CNN: A standard CNN model has four layers: input, convolutional, pooling and output layers. In our problems, we apply the 1D-CNN model with filters = 64, kernel size = 2, and pool size = 2.

Vanilla LSTM: Traditional mathematical statistics and deep learning models like ARIMA, MLP, or CNN have shown its disadvantage when applied to time series forecast tasks because they could not consider the long-term dependence of time series data. Therefore, LSTM architecture is proposed to solve that problem. An LSTM cell, as shown in Fig. 3, has a cell state C that allows the information to flow through for long-term memory. It also includes three gates: forget gate decides what information should be kept or discarded by looking at the previous state and current input. The input gate decides what information is essential at the current step and how to add to the cell state; the output gate decides what the output should be.

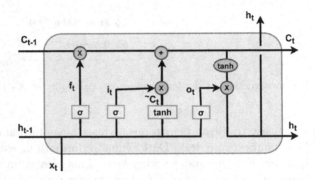

Fig. 3. The architecture of a LSTM cell

Bi-LSTM: Bi-LSTM model, initially developed from Bidirectional Recurrent Network (Bi-RNN) [9], consists of two LSTM layers: one taking the input in a forward direction and the other in a backward direction. The architecture of an unfolded Bi-LSTM, as depicted in Fig. 4, helps the network go through the input simultaneously to recognize the pattern of our data better. However, it is worth noticing that LSTM cells calculate the hidden layer weights iteratively, so the more LSTM layers we use, the slower the model will be.

Stacked LSTM: Stacked LSTM is a model that includes multiple LSTM layers. Remarkably, making the model deeper has proved its effect in sequence data in some cases. In our study, we used 2-layers stacked LSTM architecture.

4   Experiments

This section will present the dataset, evaluation metrics, experimental settings, results, and further related discussion.

4.1   Datasets

We experiment on two datasets collected at various monitoring stations in Hanoi, the capital of Vietnam, namely, Cau Giay and Minh Khai. Each data point was collected hourly and included features about meteorological information as given

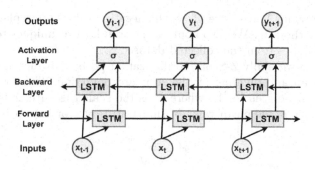

Fig. 4. The architecture of an unfolded Bi-LSTM

in Table 1. For example, the Cau Giay dataset was collected from January 03, 2019, to December 11, 2020. Meanwhile, the Minh Khai dataset was collected from January 01, 2019, to December 11, 2020.

Table 1. Features list in both datasets

Feature Name	Unit
Date Time	YYYY-MM-DD HH
PM10	$\mu g/m^3$
PM25	$\mu g/m^3$
NO2	$\mu g/m^3$
NO	$\mu g/m^3$
NOx	$\mu g/m^3$
CO	$\mu g/m^3$
SO2	$\mu g/m^3$
O3	$\mu g/m^3$
Temperature	$^\circ C$
Humidity	%
Wind Speed	m/s
Rain	mm
Wind Direction	$^\circ$
Atmospheric Pressure	hPa
Solar Radiation	W/m^2

4.2 Data Preprocessing

Due to errors in the data collection process, one can observe that the "NO" feature has some negative values on both datasets. However, as the datasets mentioned above were collected hourly and due to the nature of time-series data, the value from a particular hour is expected to correlate with its corresponding value from previous hours. Therefore, the negative values are replaced using the forward fill method [6]. We also apply some standard techniques to impute the missing data issues from the collected dataset.

In addition, we apply Z-Score normalization [1] by subtracting each feature from their mean and dividing by the standard deviation. The formula of standardization can be seen in [1], where x' is the scaled feature, x is the original feature vector, $\hat{x}$ is the mean value of that feature vector, and σ is its standard deviation.

$$x' = \frac{x - \hat{x}}{\sigma} \tag{1}$$

4.3   Evaluation Metrics

For evaluating the models' performance in forecasting PM10 and PM25 tasks, we use root mean square error (RMSE) and mean absolute error (MAE). RMSE is the square root of the average magnitude of the error. It gives a relatively high weight to significant errors. MAE is the average over absolute values of the differences between predicted and ground truth values, and all the individual differences are weighted equally in the average. The formula of metrics is defined as follows:

$$RMSE = \sqrt{\frac{\sum_{i=1}^{N} (y_i - \hat{y}_i)^2}{N}} \tag{2}$$

$$MAE = \frac{1}{N} \sum_{i=1}^{N} |y_i - \hat{y}_i|, \tag{3}$$

where N is the number of data points, y_i is the i-th measurement from the models, and $\hat{y}_i$ is its ground truth.

4.4   Experiment Settings

We divide each dataset into three groups (ordering by timestamp): the first 70% of the data for training, the next 15% for validation, and the last 15% of the data for testing. First, we run experiments using the information of the previous seven days (168 data points), 14 days (336 data points), and 30 days (720 data points) to predict the PM10 and PM25 values of the upcoming 1, 3, and 7 days (24, 72 and 168 data points) to extract the most relevant features for the main problem.

The Adam optimizer [7] with a learning rate of 0.0001 is employed for model training, and the number of epochs used during training is 20 with a batch size of 128, and the number of nodes is 200. To avoid overfitting, for the 3 LSTM models, we also add Dropout layers with a rate of 0.2.

4.5   Results and Analysis

We conduct experiments using five different deep learning models to measure the effects of two approaches. More detailed, "Approach 1" is when we only use meteorological features, and "Approach 2", as shown in Fig. 5, is the combination of meteorological features and timestamp features (*weekend* and *working hour*). The results are shown in Tables 2, 3, and 4.

Table 2. The experimental results of using the previous seven days to predict.

Approach	Model	1 day		3 days		7 days	
		RMSE	MAE	RMSE	MAE	RMSE	MAE
1 CauGiayPM10	Vanilla LSTM	**0.6583**	**0.4837**	**0.7473**	**0.5876**	0.8107	0.6580
	Bi-LSTM	0.6905	0.5145	0.7821	0.6216	0.8828	0.7144
	Stacked LSTM	0.6604	0.4841	0.7907	0.6156	0.8054	**0.6542**
	MLP	1.0407	0.8078	1.1352	0.8829	1.1198	0.8867
	CNN	0.6916	0.5206	0.8056	0.6720	**0.7963**	0.6704
2 CauGiayPM10	Vanilla LSTM	0.6359	**0.4735**	**0.7267**	**0.5761**	**0.7667**	**0.6287**
	Bi-LSTM	**0.6333**	0.4751	0.7987	0.6263	0.8452	0.6858
	Stacked LSTM	0.6349	0.4744	0.7406	0.5807	0.8117	0.6586
	MLP	1.0340	0.8051	1.1234	0.8753	1.1100	0.8796
	CNN	0.6830	0.5145	0.8036	0.6780	0.7921	0.6712
1 CauGiayPM25	Vanilla LSTM	0.5999	0.4358	0.7073	0.5527	0.7698	**0.6257**
	Bi-LSTM	0.6631	0.4965	0.7788	0.6145	0.8295	0.6631
	Stacked LSTM	0.6390	0.4602	0.7420	0.5730	0.7942	0.6394
	MLP	1.0378	0.8024	1.1327	0.8795	1.1326	0.8923
	CNN	0.6790	0.5164	0.7641	0.6458	**0.7450**	0.6279
2 CauGiayPM25	Vanilla LSTM	**0.6051**	**0.4443**	**0.6937**	**0.5433**	**0.7439**	**0.6084**
	Bi-LSTM	0.6347	0.4741	0.8236	0.6369	0.8244	0.6637
	Stacked LSTM	0.6294	0.4516	0.7222	0.5619	0.7790	0.6318
	MLP	1.0350	0.8024	1.1160	0.8691	1.1352	0.8954
	CNN	0.6726	0.5101	0.7628	0.6314	0.7499	0.6340
1 MinhKhaiPM10	Vanilla LSTM	**0.7053**	**0.5367**	1.0130	0.7584	0.9425	0.7681
	Bi-LSTM	0.7475	0.5729	1.0156	0.7944	1.0470	0.8245
	Stacked LSTM	0.7892	0.6041	1.1289	0.8372	1.0297	0.8200
	MLP	1.5880	1.2230	1.6642	1.2944	1.5696	1.2345
	CNN	0.8181	0.6579	**0.8411**	**0.7061**	**0.8214**	**0.6916**
2 MinhKhaiPM10	Vanilla LSTM	**0.7169**	**0.5471**	1.0267	0.7726	0.9539	0.7812
	Bi-LSTM	0.7567	0.5860	0.9253	0.7261	0.9932	0.8011
	Stacked LSTM	0.7718	0.5860	1.0605	0.7883	1.0296	0.8203
	MLP	1.5432	1.1892	1.6359	1.2740	1.5561	1.2252
	CNN	0.8089	0.6408	**0.8564**	**0.7185**	**0.8199**	**0.6901**
1 MinhKhaiPM25	Vanilla LSTM	**0.6838**	**0.5236**	0.9712	0.7451	0.9003	0.7414
	Bi-LSTM	0.7176	0.5545	1.0353	0.8166	1.1702	0.9279
	Stacked LSTM	0.7721	0.5885	1.0763	0.8007	1.0082	0.8139
	MLP	1.6434	1.2643	1.6745	1.2989	1.6383	1.2801
	CNN	0.7699	0.6112	**0.8628**	**0.7342**	**0.8137**	**0.6975**
2 MinhKhaiPM25	Vanilla LSTM	**0.6759**	**0.5207**	1.0889	0.8377	0.9607	0.7794
	Bi-LSTM	0.7373	0.5692	1.0434	0.8201	1.1045	0.8824
	Stacked LSTM	0.7395	0.5624	1.1060	0.8252	1.0337	0.8280
	MLP	1.6329	1.2544	1.6341	1.2703	1.6180	1.2685
	CNN	0.7864	0.6327	**0.8494**	**0.7290**	**0.8171**	**0.7002**

Table 3. The experimental results of using the previous 14 days to predict.

Approach	Model	1 day		3 days		7 days	
		RMSE	MAE	RMSE	MAE	RMSE	MAE
1 CauGiayPM10	Vanilla LSTM	0.6308	0.4674	0.7318	0.5762	**0.7701**	0.6334
	Bi-LSTM	**0.6166**	**0.4518**	**0.7253**	**0.5378**	0.7965	**0.6260**
	Stacked LSTM	0.6775	0.5014	0.7427	0.5799	0.8175	0.6602
	MLP	1.4914	1.1713	1.6687	1.3173	1.5109	1.1962
	CNN	0.7760	0.6338	0.7938	0.6756	0.7855	0.6669
2 CauGiayPM10	Vanilla LSTM	0.6144	0.4591	**0.7359**	0.5732	0.7695	0.6264
	Bi-LSTM	**0.5972**	**0.4395**	0.7486	**0.5492**	**0.7529**	**0.5910**
	Stacked LSTM	0.6350	0.4718	0.743	0.5831	0.8220	0.6661
	MLP	1.5218	1.1936	1.5769	1.2420	1.4344	1.1354
	CNN	0.7761	0.6472	0.7982	0.6738	0.7909	0.6711
1 CauGiayPM25	Vanilla LSTM	0.5905	0.4289	**0.6787**	0.5297	**0.7406**	**0.6082**
	Bi-LSTM	**0.5775**	**0.4277**	0.7121	**0.5207**	0.8204	0.6480
	Stacked LSTM	0.6042	0.4487	0.6974	0.5356	0.7702	0.6242
	MLP	1.6834	1.3210	1.6667	1.3142	1.4377	1.1360
	CNN	0.7584	0.6509	0.7667	0.6528	0.7454	0.6314
2 CauGiayPM25	Vanilla LSTM	0.5889	0.4325	**0.6837**	0.5321	**0.7403**	**0.6036**
	Bi-LSTM	**0.5662**	**0.4151**	0.6997	**0.5102**	0.7834	0.6124
	Stacked LSTM	0.6060	0.4469	0.7007	0.5465	0.7706	0.6238
	MLP	1.4332	1.1234	1.6256	1.2813	1.4928	1.1794
	CNN	0.7282	0.6039	0.7473	0.6360	0.7450	0.6314
1 MinhKhaiPM10	Vanilla LSTM	0.6945	0.5290	1.0214	0.7811	0.8842	0.7256
	Bi-LSTM	**0.6868**	**0.5170**	**0.9673**	**0.6774**	0.9347	0.7357
	Stacked LSTM	0.7582	0.5820	1.1172	0.8366	1.0229	0.8191
	MLP	2.6347	2.0431	2.4134	1.8859	2.0829	1.6403
	CNN	0.8112	0.6648	0.8312	0.6979	**0.8263**	**0.6945**
2 MinhKhaiPM10	Vanilla LSTM	**0.6292**	**0.4828**	**0.7494**	**0.6037**	**0.8077**	**0.6695**
	Bi-LSTM	0.6573	0.5008	0.8197	0.6597	0.8310	0.6835
	Stacked LSTM	0.6602	0.5023	0.7696	0.6225	0.8169	0.6796
	MLP	2.7803	2.1196	2.3890	1.8714	2.0711	1.6312
	CNN	0.8232	0.6760	0.8393	0.7053	0.8215	0.6906
1 MinhKhaiPM25	Vanilla LSTM	**0.6617**	0.5080	0.9349	0.7230	0.9477	0.7836
	Bi-LSTM	0.6680	**0.5064**	0.8613	**0.6452**	0.8984	0.7018
	Stacked LSTM	0.7586	0.5790	1.1194	0.8391	1.0097	0.8171
	MLP	3.0822	2.3633	2.5106	1.9746	2.1234	1.6753
	CNN	0.8289	0.6980	**0.8255**	0.7056	**0.8174**	**0.6997**
2 MinhKhaiPM25	Vanilla LSTM	**0.6156**	**0.4742**	**0.7631**	**0.6188**	**0.8068**	**0.6774**
	Bi-LSTM	0.6662	0.5115	0.8287	0.6584	0.8250	0.6791
	Stacked LSTM	0.6321	0.4819	0.8085	0.6557	0.8419	0.7075
	MLP	3.0731	2.3597	2.4919	1.9528	2.0928	1.6558
	CNN	0.8367	0.7093	0.8080	0.6912	0.8134	0.6961

From the results shown in Tables 2, 3, and 4, by comparing productions of Approach 1 of each model with its outcomes on Approach 2, one can see that in 68% of cases, the combination of both meteorological and timestamp features can

Table 4. The experimental results of using the previous 30 days to predict.

Approach	Model	1 day		3 days		7 days	
		RMSE	MAE	RMSE	MAE	RMSE	MAE
1 CauGiayPM10	Vanilla LSTM	0.6283	0.4709	0.7327	0.5714	0.7739	0.6270
	Bi-LSTM	**0.5965**	**0.4547**	**0.6869**	**0.5406**	**0.7699**	**0.6104**
	Stacked LSTM	0.6585	0.4833	0.7519	0.5765	0.7994	0.6394
	MLP	2.6261	2.0398	2.5313	1.9937	2.1105	1.6739
	CNN	0.7709	0.6565	0.7658	0.6516	0.7756	0.6589
2 CauGiayPM10	Vanilla LSTM	**0.6154**	**0.4595**	0.6986	0.5502	**0.7603**	0.6191
	Bi-LSTM	0.6170	0.4711	**0.6809**	**0.5387**	0.7632	**0.6087**
	Stacked LSTM	0.6372	0.4720	0.7479	0.5833	0.7764	0.6290
	MLP	2.4619	1.8893	2.5393	1.9849	2.1116	1.6665
	CNN	0.7673	0.6511	0.7652	0.6511	0.7758	0.6591
1 CauGiayPM25	Vanilla LSTM	0.5915	0.4357	0.6719	0.5269	0.7585	0.6129
	Bi-LSTM	**0.5525**	**0.4120**	**0.6410**	**0.4959**	**0.7054**	**0.5569**
	Stacked LSTM	0.6195	0.4538	0.7238	0.5580	0.7954	0.6373
	MLP	3.0671	2.3732	2.4877	1.9514	2.1519	1.7079
	CNN	0.7136	0.6099	0.7178	0.6126	0.7327	0.6219
2 CauGiayPM25	Vanilla LSTM	**0.5714**	**0.4195**	0.6770	0.5282	0.7436	0.6040
	Bi-LSTM	0.5819	0.4402	**0.6344**	**0.4944**	0.7560	**0.5926**
	Stacked LSTM	0.5953	0.4380	0.7029	0.5467	0.7908	0.6324
	MLP	3.0851	2.3669	2.5311	1.9897	2.1484	1.7039
	CNN	0.7240	0.6201	0.7193	0.6138	**0.7326**	0.6218
1 MinhKhaiPM10	Vanilla LSTM	**0.6974**	**0.5330**	0.8967	0.7100	0.8890	0.7282
	Bi-LSTM	0.7056	0.5341	**0.8115**	**0.6400**	0.8276	**0.6636**
	Stacked LSTM	0.7775	0.5981	1.0409	0.8022	1.0209	0.8134
	MLP	4.6312	3.5391	3.9739	3.0887	2.7875	2.1854
	CNN	0.8249	0.6797	0.8232	0.6874	**0.8236**	0.6886
2 MinhKhaiPM10	Vanilla LSTM	**0.6603**	**0.5098**	**0.7713**	0.6184	0.8095	0.6638
	Bi-LSTM	0.6857	0.5265	0.7720	**0.6114**	**0.7976**	**0.6468**
	Stacked LSTM	0.6851	0.5292	0.7931	0.6410	0.8176	0.6733
	MLP	4.8715	3.7111	4.0904	3.1939	2.7163	2.1361
	CNN	0.8366	0.6805	0.8232	0.6874	0.8236	0.6885
1 MinhKhaiPM25	Vanilla LSTM	**0.6676**	**0.5116**	1.0517	0.8118	0.9508	0.7784
	Bi-LSTM	0.7174	0.5445	0.8643	**0.6749**	0.9090	0.7335
	Stacked LSTM	0.7307	0.5634	1.1035	0.8337	1.0391	0.8289
	MLP	5.0384	3.9296	3.7998	2.9607	2.6621	2.1024
	CNN	0.8232	0.6886	**0.8165**	0.6942	**0.8170**	**0.6952**
2 MinhKhaiPM25	Vanilla LSTM	**0.6430**	**0.4982**	0.8324	0.6674	**0.8089**	**0.6696**
	Bi-LSTM	0.6825	0.5244	**0.7941**	**0.6369**	0.8353	0.6870
	Stacked LSTM	0.6609	0.5090	0.8146	0.6573	0.8310	0.6897
	MLP	5.2779	4.1381	3.9799	3.0975	2.7681	2.1744
	CNN	0.8243	0.6996	0.8166	0.6944	0.8168	0.6950

achieve better performance in forecasting PM concentrations. Specifically, in the experiments using the previous seven days (168 data points), Vanilla LSTM and 1D-CNN show better results than other models in both approaches. Interestingly,

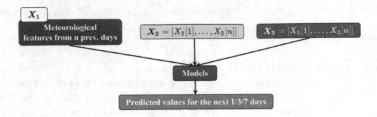

Fig. 5. The overview of the proposed method "Approach 2".

when forecasting using the previous 14 days (336 data points) to predict PM10 and PM25 on one following day in the Cau Giay dataset, the Bi-LSTM model of Approach 2 gives the best results with RMSE respectively 0.5972 and 0.5662. Otherwise, in the Minh Khai dataset, Vanilla LSTM in Approach 2 outperforms every model in all the cases. Moreover, when using the previous 30 days (720 data points) to predict, Vanilla LSTM in Approach 2 still achieved the best results on both datasets in most cases. It is worth noticing that when using the previous 30 days (720 data points) to forecast, two baseline models MLP and CNN, in Approach 2, show worse results than in Approach 1. One can explain this as follows. Using more features increases the length of input sequences. The two models above have shown their disadvantages as they seem not to consider the long-term dependence of time series data.

In summary, our proposed method, Approach 2, when combined with Vanilla LSTM, can help improve the performance of the forecasting PM concentrations tasks. Remarkably, using the additional timestamp information *weekend* and *working hour* can help improve the model's efficiency.

5   Conclusion

This work aims to study the effects of forecasting PM concentrations by combining meteorological features and timestamp information. We have conducted experiments with five deep learning models, MLP, 1D-CNN, Vanilla LSTM Bi-LSTM, and Stacked LSTM, using two datasets from Hanoi, Vietnam. From the experiments, the Vanilla LSTM model yields more promising results for long-term forecasting of the PM concentrations when combined with all features. In the future, we will extend this research by combining more features from multiple sources and applying more deep-learning models.

Acknowledgments. We want to thank the University of Science, Vietnam National University Ho Chi Minh City, and AISIA Research Lab in Vietnam for supporting us throughout this paper. This research is funded by Vietnam National University Ho Chi Minh City (VNU-HCM) in Vietnam under the grant number DS2023-18-01.

References

1. Cousineau, D., Chartier, S.: Outlier detection and treatment: a review. Int. J. Psychol. Res. **3**(1), 58–67 (2010). ISSN 2011–7922
2. van Donkelaar, A., et al.: Global estimates of ambient fine particulate matter concentrations from satellite-based aerosol optical depth: development and application. Environ. Health Perspect. **118**(6), 847–855 (2010)
3. Duong, D.Q., et al.: Multi-source machine learning for AQI estimation. In: 2020 IEEE International Conference on Big Data (Big Data). IEEE, December 2020. https://doi.org/10.1109/bigdata50022.2020.9378322
4. Duong, D.Q., Le, Q.M., Nguyen-Tai, T.L., Nguyen, H.D., Dao, M.S., Nguyen, B.T.: An effective AQI estimation using sensor data and stacking mechanism. In: Frontiers in Artificial Intelligence and Applications. IOS Press, September 2021. https://doi.org/10.3233/faia210040
5. Garg, S., Jindal, H.: Evaluation of time series forecasting models for estimation of PM2.5 levels in air. In: 2021 6th International Conference for Convergence in Technology (I2CT), pp. 1–8 (2021). https://doi.org/10.1109/I2CT51068.2021.9418215
6. Kamalov, F., Sulieman, H.: Time series signal recovery methods: comparative study. In: 2021 International Symposium on Networks, Computers and Communications (ISNCC). IEEE, October 2021. https://doi.org/10.1109/isncc52172.2021.9615669
7. Kingma, D.P., Ba, J.: Adam: a method for stochastic optimization (2014). https://doi.org/10.48550/ARXIV.1412.6980, https://arxiv.org/abs/1412.6980
8. Manisalidis, I., Stavropoulou, E., Stavropoulos, A., Bezirtzoglou, E.: Environmental and health impacts of air pollution: a review. Front. Public Health **8** (2020). https://doi.org/10.3389/fpubh.2020.00014, https://www.frontiersin.org/article/10.3389/fpubh.2020.00014
9. Schuster, M., Paliwal, K.: Bidirectional recurrent neural networks. IEEE Trans. Signal Process. **45**(11), 2673–2681 (1997). https://doi.org/10.1109/78.650093
10. Wolpert, D.H.: Stacked generalization. Neural Netw. **5**(2), 241–259 (1992). https://doi.org/10.1016/s0893-6080(05)80023-1
11. Zhao, P., Zettsu, K.: Convolution recurrent neural networks for short-term prediction of atmospheric sensing data. In: 2018 IEEE International Conference on Internet of Things (iThings) and IEEE Green Computing and Communications (GreenCom) and IEEE Cyber, Physical and Social Computing (CPSCom) and IEEE Smart Data (SmartData), pp. 815–821 (2018). https://doi.org/10.1109/Cybermatics_2018.2018.00159

Adjacent-DBSCAN Enhanced Time-Varying Multi-graph Convolution Network for Traffic Flow Prediction

Yinxin Bao[1] and Quan Shi[1,2](✉)

[1] School of Information Science and Technology, Nantong University, Nantong, China
sq@ntu.edu.cn
[2] School of Transportation and Civil Engineering, Nantong University, Nantong, China

Abstract. Accurately predicting traffic flow is very challenging since the traffic flow is collected from hundreds of sensor nodes, which are affected by multiple factors. The existing methods based on graph convolution focus on unified spatial-temporal feature extraction for all nodes, while ignoring the differences between nodes and the correlation between internal and external features. To overcome these shortcomings, we propose an adjacent-DBSCAN enhanced time-varying multi-graph convolution network (ADETMCN) for traffic flow prediction. First, we use the adjacency matrix to optimize the DBSCAN clustering algorithm and divide the raw traffic nodes into multiple highly correlated node clusters. Then, the multi-graph spatial feature, composed of the adjacency graph feature, the correlation graph feature, and the travel intention graph feature, automatically explores the internal and external spatial features of nodes. Next, the time-variant feature, composed of the minute periodic feature, the hour periodic feature, and the daily periodic feature, automatically extracts short-term and long-term spatial-temporal correlation by fusing the multi-graph spatial features. Extensive experiments on five real-world datasets show that the performance of the proposed model is superior to the most advanced methods.

Keywords: Traffic Flow Prediction · Spatial-Temporal Correlation · Graph Convolution · Machine Learning · Clustering Algorithm

1 Introduction

Accurate and real-time traffic flow prediction is crucial in intelligent transportation systems (ITS) [1], which has potential benefits for improving traffic efficiency, reducing traffic accidents, enhancing traffic safety, and assisting traffic management. Therefore, it is crucial to improve the accuracy of traffic flow prediction models [2].

The evolution of traffic flow is affected by historical data and various complex factors, such as special events (COVID-19), bad weather, and holidays. Because of the above nonlinear factors, using existing prediction methods to accurately and real-time predict traffic flow is very challenging. In the existing literature, a wide range of prediction methods are roughly divided into model-driven and data-driven methods [3]. The

H. Fujita et al. (Eds.): IEA/AIE 2023, LNAI 13926, pp. 372–384, 2023.
https://doi.org/10.1007/978-3-031-36822-6_32

former methods are widely used in small sample traffic flow prediction due to their high computational efficiency and solid explanatory ability. However, the model-driven methods ignore the spatial-temporal correlation of traffic flow in the road network, resulting in unsatisfactory results in large-scale nonlinear traffic flow prediction. The graph convolutional network (GCN) in data-driven methods can effectively map the traffic structure of the real world to the deep neural network architecture, enhancing the extraction of spatial-temporal features [4]. Compared with classical methods, traffic flow prediction methods based on graph convolution can provide better prediction results [5].

The existing improved GCN prediction model focuses on enhancing the extraction of spatial-temporal features by using fixed period input historical data and improved adjacency matrix. However, there are still several areas that need improvement in practical model applications. On the one hand, due to not considering the impact of weather, it is difficult for the model to effectively learn the difference between traffic flow on sunny and rainy days. On the other hand, there are hundreds of sensor nodes in a real road network, so it is difficult to establish a model to learn the feature changes of all nodes [6]. Based on the above reasons, to improve the prediction performance, it is necessary to deal with the following two critical issues: (1) How to design a practical clustering algorithm to classify the highly correlated nodes into the same node cluster? (2) How to build a unified architecture GCN network for different node clusters and consider multi-cycle temporal, data correlation, and external features?

To overcome the above issues, a novel adjacent-DBSCAN enhanced time-varying multi-graph convolution network (ADETMCN) is proposed to better extract the spatial-temporal correlation of traffic flow. The main contributions of this work are summarized as follows:

(1) Adjacent DBSCAN Clustering. Considering that the traditional clustering algorithm ignores the connectivity between nodes, based on DBSCAN clustering, the adjacency matrix is used to filter the unconnected nodes.
(2) Time-Varying Multi-Graph Convolution Network. The adjacent graph feature, the correlation graph feature, and the travel intention graph feature extraction module are constructed and fused into multi-graph spatial features. The minute periodic feature, the hour periodic feature, and the daily periodic feature extraction module are constructed and fused into time-varying features.
(3) Experiments with Real-world Datasets. Extensive experiments are carried out on five real-world datasets, and the proposed graph framework is superior to the most advanced prediction methods in terms of accuracy and robustness.

2 Related Works

Due to its excellent spatial feature extraction ability for non-Euclidean road structures, GCN is widely used for traffic flow prediction in real road networks As an essential variant of GNN, GCN performs well in processing non-Euclidean data [7]. Inspired by this, Zhao et al. used GCN and GRU to analyze urban road networks' spatial and temporal correlation, and used an adjacency matrix to express the node relationship [8]. Li et al. proposed a diffusion convolution recurrent neural network (DCRNN), which used two-way random walks and an Encoder-Decoder architecture on traffic maps [9]. Yu et al. proposed a spatial-temporal graph convolution network (STGCN) and constructed a graph based on distance relationships to measure node correlation [10]. However, STGCN ignored that historical observations at different locations will affect the traffic status at different times in the future. Based on STGCN, Guo et al. proposed attention-based spatial-temporal graph convolution network (ASTGCN), which modeled the three temporal attributes, and improved the capture of dynamic spatial-temporal features [11]. In order to improve the synchronous capture ability of spatial-temporal correlation in ASTGCN, Song et al. proposed the spatial-temporal synchronous graph convolution network (STSGCN), which improved the capture of traffic flow heterogeneity [12]. To better integrate spatial-temporal feature graphs, Li et al. proposed a spatial-temporal fusion graph neural network (STFGNN) to learn the complex spatial correlations and dynamic trends of temporal patterns between different roads [13]. Jin et al. proposed an automated dilated spatial-temporal synchronous graph module to capture short-term and long-term spatiotemporal correlations at a deeper level [14]. Ali et al. used a fully connected neural network to extract interference contributions from external factors in their prediction model [5]. Unlike the above model, the ADETMCN model not only achieves clustering of road network nodes, but also achieves joint extraction of multi graph spatial features and time-varying features of node clusters, effectively extracting dynamic spatial-temporal features.

3 Preliminaries

3.1 Problem Definition

Given the traffic sensor set of N nodes, the graph $G = (V, E, A)$ is used to describe the correlation of traffic features (flow, speed and density). $V = \{v_1, v_2, \ldots, v_N\}$ represents different nodes, E represents the set of edges, and the adjacency matrix $A \in \mathbb{R}^{N \times N}$ is usually used to describe E. The traffic features recorded by node V at time T are $H = \{h_{n,1}, h_{n,2}, h_{n,3}, \ldots, h_{n,t}, \ldots, h_{n,T}\}$, $t \in T$. $h_{n,t}$ represents the traffic features of the n-th sensor at time t. The time interval is the sensor recording interval. The obtained feature graph G is as follows:

$$G = \begin{bmatrix} h_{1,1} & h_{1,2} & \cdots & h_{1,T} \\ h_{2,1} & h_{2,2} & \cdots & h_{2,T} \\ \vdots & \vdots & \ddots & \vdots \\ h_{N,1} & h_{N,2} & \cdots & h_{N,T} \end{bmatrix} \tag{1}$$

The traffic flow prediction problem is defined as the given historical graph $G(T)$, the predicted graph $G(T + \Delta t)$ at a certain time in the future, and Δt is the predicted time interval.

3.2 Analysis of Complex Features Affecting Traffic Flow

Traffic flow is affected by spatial-temporal features and external features, as shown in Fig. 1. Let's take Node A as an example, Fig. 1 (a) shows that Node A is not only affected

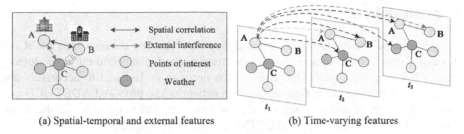

(a) Spatial-temporal and external features   (b) Time-varying features

Fig. 1. Analysis of complex features affecting traffic flow

by the spatial correlation between Node B, but also by the external interference of weather factors. Figure 1 (b) shows that Node A has significant time-varying features in different periods. Node A at t_1 will not only affect Node A at t_2 and t_3, but also affect other nodes at t_2. Therefore, it is crucial to effectively excavate the complex spatial-temporal features of traffic flow.

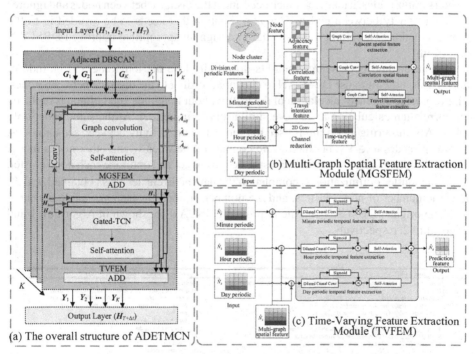

Fig. 2. (a) The overall structure of ADETMCN. (b) Multi-Graph Spatial Feature Extraction Module (MGSFEM). (c) Time-Varying Feature Extraction Module (TVFEM)

4   Methodology

To overcome the shortcomings of existing methods, based on the improved DBSCAN clustering algorithm, this paper first divides road network nodes into multiple clusters. Then a time-varying multi-graph convolution network is designed to accurately and efficiently predict the traffic flow of the road network. The proposed ADETMCN will explore the internal and external spatial-temporal correlation of nodes in the traffic network. The overall structure of ADETMCN is shown in Fig. 2(a).

4.1   Adjacent DBSCAN Clustering Algorithm

DBSCAN clustering algorithm is a traditional density-based clustering algorithm. Input sensor longitude and latitude data $D_{lon}(i)$ and $D_{lat}(i)$, $i \in N$, N is the number of sensors. The process of DBSCAN is shown in Algorithm 1. After DBSCAN clustering operation, the sensor nodes $V = \{v_1, v_2, ..., v_i, ..., v_N\}$ are divided into K node clusters, and V_k represents the node set contained in the k-th node cluster. When the DBSCAN algorithm clusters traffic nodes, it takes too much account of the distance between nodes and ignores the connectivity between nodes. This is a situation that needs to be avoided in traffic flow prediction. Therefore, it is essential to design an appropriate improved DBSCAN algorithm.

Because some open-source datasets do not disclose the longitude and latitude of nodes, it is difficult to use DBSCAN to cluster according to the distance between nodes. Therefore, the distance calculation of datasets without longitude and latitude is replaced by correlation calculation to achieve similar clustering effect. At the same time, only DBSCAN clustering algorithm is used to ignore the connectivity between sensor nodes. There are nodes $v_i \in V_k$, but there is no connection between v_i and other nodes in V_k. Therefore, the adjacency matrix is constructed to cluster and optimize each node cluster. After the cluster optimization is completed, the new node cluster $\widehat{V}_k$ is obtained, $k \in K$, K is the number of node clusters, and the number of nodes in each new node cluster is $\widehat{N}_k$. The original DBSCAN and the improved DBSCAN are shown in Algorithm 1 and Algorithm 2, respectively.

Algorithm 1 DBSCAN

Input: $D_{traffic}$ c is the dataset, R is the radius, and P_{Min} is the minimum number of points
Output: K node clusters
1: $C = 0$ // Initialize the cluster counter
2: for each unvisited point P in dataset $D_{traffic}$ do
3:     mark P as visited
4:     N = getNeighbors(P, R) // Find adjacent nodes based on distance
5:     if $|M| < P_{Min}$ then // $|M|$ represents the size of the set N
6:         mark P as Noise // Mark P as a noise point
7:     else
8:         $C = C+1$ // Create a new cluster
9:         add P to cluster C // Add P to cluster C
10:        for each point P' in N do
11:            if P' is not visited then
12:                mark P' as visited
13:                N' = getNeighbors(P', R)
14:                if $|N'| >= P_{Min}$ then
15:                    add N' to N // Add the points in N' to N
16:                end if
17:            end if
18:            if P' is not yet a member of any cluster then
19:                add P' to cluster C // Add P' to cluster C
20:            end if
21:        end for
22:    end if
23: end for
24: **return** V_k // Represents the node set contained in the k-th node cluster

---

Algorithm 2 Adjacent DBSCAN

Input: K node clusters after DBSCAN clustering
Output: The nodes in each node cluster have connectivity
1: **for** each unvisited cluster V_k in node clusters V_K **do**
2:     $N_k = |V_k|$ // The number of nodes in the k-th node cluster
3:     sum $= 0$
4:     **for** $i = 1 \rightarrow N_k$ **do**
5:         **for** $j = 1 \rightarrow N_k$ **do**
6:             sum $=$ sum$+A_k(i,j)$
7:         **end for**
8:         if sum $= 0$ then
9:             mark i as v_s
10:            for v_s in other node clusters do
11:                A_{sm} // Construct adjacency matrix with other node clusters
12:                if $A_{sm} > 0$ then
13:                    $s \in V_m$
14:                end if
15:            end for
16:        else
17:            Traverse the next node cluster
18:        end if
19:    end for
20: end for
21: **return** $\hat{V}$ // Ensure that nodes in all node clusters are connected

4.2 Multi-graph Spatial Feature Extraction Module

The function of the multi-graph spatial feature extraction module is to extract the dynamic spatial features of the multi-period traffic flow. The specific structure is shown in Fig. 2 (b). The input of the node cluster is divided into minute periodic feature $H_{min} \in [\widehat{N}_k, L]$, hour periodic feature $H_{hour} \in [\widehat{N}_k, L]$ and daily periodic features $H_{day} \in [\widehat{N}_k, L]$. The extraction of spatial features requires channel superposition and fusion of three periodic features. The superposition and fusion operations are as follows:

$$H_F = f_{conv}(H_{min} \| H_{hour} \| H_{day}) \in \left[\widehat{N}_k, 1, L\right] \tag{2}$$

where $\|$ represents splicing operation, which is used for channel stacking. f_{conv} is a 2D convolution operation for channel fusion. H_F Represents the fusion feature input, $\widehat{N}_k$ represents the number of nodes contained in the k-th node cluster, and L represents the length of the input sequence.

The adjacency matrix in the node cluster is defined as $\widehat{A}_{adj}(k)$ indicates whether there is a direct connection between nodes. In order to better describe the data association within the node cluster. The graph convolution network is used for feature extraction. The operation is as follows:

$$H_{adj}^{l+1} = f_A\left(H_F^l, \widehat{A}_{adj}\right) = f_A(\widehat{A}_{adj} H_F^l W_{adj}^l) \tag{3}$$

where H_{adj}^{l+1} is the adjacency graph feature output of the $l+1$ layer, W_{adj}^l is the weight in the adjacency graph feature extraction module, f_A is the activation function. The final output of the adjacency graph feature extraction module is defined as H_{adj}.

There is not only physical connection but also data correlation between nodes in the node cluster. Pearson correlation coefficient method is used to calculate the correlation between different nodes and form the association matrix $\widehat{A}_{cor}(k)$, the Pearson correlation coefficient method is defined as:

$$corr_{k,i,j} = \left[\sum_{t=1}^{T}\left(h_{i,t}(k) - \text{Mean}(h_i(k))\right)\left(h_{j,t}(k) - \text{Mean}(h_j(k))\right)\right] / (\text{Std}(h_i(k))\text{Std}(h_j(k))) \tag{4}$$

where $h_{i,t}(k)$ and $h_{j,t}(k)$ are the features of sensor i and j in the k-th node cluster at time t, respectively, $\text{Std}(h_i(k))$ and $\text{Std}(h_j(k))$ are the standard deviations of the selected nodes, and $\text{Mean}(h_i(k))$ and $\text{Mean}(h_j(k))$ are the mean values of the selected nodes. Traverse the calculation to obtain the incidence matrix $\widehat{A}_{cor}(k)$ of all node clusters. The graph convolution network is used for feature extraction, and the operation is defined as:

$$H_{cor}^{l+1} = f_A\left(H_F^l, \widehat{A}_{cor}\right) = f_A(\widehat{A}_{cor} H_F^l W_{cor}^l) \tag{5}$$

where H_{cor}^{l+1} is the feature output of the correlation graph of the $l+1$ layer, W_{cor}^l is the weight in the correlation graph feature extraction module. The final output of the correlation graph feature extraction module is defined as H_{cor}.

External factors such as weather and accidents can affect people's willingness to travel. This paper establishes an external factor matrix $\widehat{A}_{int}(k)$ to reflect the impact of external factors on people's willingness to travel. $\widehat{A}_{int}(i,j)$ is constructed to represent the travel intention of node i to node j. This paper does not consider the travel direction. By default, the travel intention from i to j is equivalent to the travel intention from j to i. The graph convolution network is used for feature extraction, and the operation is defined as:

$$H_{int}^{l+1} = f_A\left(H_F^l, \widehat{A}_{int}\right) = f_A\left(\widehat{A}_{int}H_F^l W_{int}^l\right) \tag{6}$$

where H_{int}^{l+1} is the feature output of the travel intention graph on the $l+1$ layer, W_{int}^l is the weight in the adjacency graph feature extraction module. The final output of the travel intention graph feature extraction module is defined as H_{int}.

The self-attention module is constructed to fuse the output of adjacency graph, correlation graph and travel intention graph features, and the operation is defined as:

$$H_S = f_A(f_{Att}(H_{adj}) + f_{Att}(H_{cor}) + f_{Att}(H_{int})) \tag{7}$$

where f_{Att} is the forward calculation of the self-attention module, which is defined as:

$$f_{Att}(H) = (H)^{Tr} \bullet Atten(H) \tag{8}$$

$$Atten(H) = \frac{e^{(H \bullet (H)^{Tr})}}{\sum_1^T e^{(H \bullet (H)^{Tr})}} \tag{9}$$

where Tr is a transpose operation. Finally, the output of the multi-image spatial feature extraction module is H_S.

4.3 Time-Varying Feature Extraction Module

The structure of time-varying feature extraction module is shown in Fig. 2 (c). Unlike the fusion of multi graph spatial features, the output of the time-varying feature extraction module needs to consider not only the contributions of multi graph spatial features, but also the contributions of different periods. Therefore, it is necessary to construct three cyclic inputs.

The input of minute periodic feature or hour periodic feature or daily periodic feature extraction module is:

$$H_{MI/HI/DI} = f_{conv}(H_{min/hour/day}||H_S) \in [\widehat{N}_k, 1, L] \tag{10}$$

A gated dilated causal convolution module is established to avoid the disappearance of 1D CNN gradient. First, by expanding causal convolution, input $H_{MI/HI/DI} \in [\widehat{N}_k, L]$ is mapped to $H_{I1}||H_{I2} \in [\widehat{N}_k, 2c_{out}]$, and the operation is defined as:

$$H_{I1}||H_{I2} = f(W_{Dila}H_{MI/HI/DI} + b_{Dila}) \tag{11}$$

the channel is split into $H_{I1} \in [\widehat{N}_k, c_{out}]$ and $H_{I2} \in [\widehat{N}_k, c_{out}]$, W_{Dila} and b_{Dila} is the weight and bias term of the dilated causal convolution, c_{out} is the sequence length of the prediction output. Through GLU gated unit,

$$Y_{M/H/D} = H_{I1} \odot \sigma(H_{I2}) \in \left[\widehat{N}_k, c_{out}\right] \tag{12}$$

minute periodic feature Y_M, hour periodic feature Y_H and daily periodic feature Y_D are obtained. $\odot$ is Hadamard product, σ is sigmoid function.

Self-attention module is constructed to fuse periodic features, and the operation is defined as:

$$Y_T(k) = f_A\left(f_{Att1}(Y_M) + f_{Att2}(Y_H) + f_{Att3}(Y_D)\right) \in [\widehat{N}_k, c_{out}] \qquad (13)$$

where $Y_T(k)$ is the final predicted value of the k-th node cluster. After integrating multiple node clusters, the predicted output of all nodes is $\widehat{Y}_T \in [N, c_{out}]$.

Table 1. Information for datasets

Datasets	PEMS03	PEMS04	PEMS07	PEMS08	SZ-taxi
Location	In California, USA	In California, USA	In California, USA	In California, USA	In Shenzhen, China
Date	9/1–11/30/2018	1/1–2/28/2018	5/1–8/31/2017	7/1–8/31/2016	1/1–1/31/2015
Time interval	5 min	5 min	5 min	5 min	15 min
Data type	flow	flow	flow	flow	speed
Nodes	358	307	883	170	156
Intervals	26208	16992	28224	17856	2976

5 Experiments

5.1 Real-World Datasets

Five real-world datasets were used to verify the proposed model's prediction performance, including PEMS03, PEMS04, PEMS07, PEMS08 and SZ-taxi. Four PeMS datasets were proposed by the California Transportation Agency Performance Measurement System (PeMS). The SZ-taxi dataset was collected in Luohu District, Shenzhen, China. We only use the traffic flow as the experimental data, and the data collection interval is 5 min. To generate the travel intention matrix corresponding to the five datasets, the weather data is collected from https://www.almanac.com/weather/history/CA. The specific information of the dataset is shown in Table 1.

5.2 Experimental Settings

Hyperparameter. This paper was based on the Intel I7–12700 CPU and Nvidia 3080 GPU as the experimental environment to train and test the proposed model. The experiment was developed based on the Pytorch-GPU framework, and the Adam optimizer was used to optimize the model parameters. The initial learning rate was set to 0.0001 and the attenuation rate was set to 0.2. The maximum number of iterations was set to 900, the batch size was set to 30, the division ratio of training set and test set was set to 7:3, and the test set results are repeated for 15 rounds.

Comparison Models. To verify the superiority of the proposed model, this paper selected eight comparison models. The eight models were LSTM, CNN, DCRNN [9], STGCN [10], ASTGCN [11], STSGCN [12], STFGCN [13] and Auto-DSTSGN [14]. The eight comparative models and the proposed model were trained and tested using the same experimental environment.

Evaluating Indicator. Three evaluation indexes, including root mean square error (RMSE), mean absolute error (MAE), and mean absolute percentage error (MAPE), were used to evaluate the prediction performance.

$$RMSE = \sqrt{\frac{1}{p} \sum_{i=1}^{p} (Y_{Real}(i) - Y_{Pred}(i))^2} \tag{14}$$

$$MAE = \frac{1}{p} \sum_{i=1}^{p} |Y_{Real}(i) - Y_{Pred}(i)| \tag{15}$$

$$MAPE = \frac{100\%}{p} \sum_{i=1}^{p} |\frac{Y_{Real}(i) - Y_{Pred}(i)}{Y_{Real}(i)}| \tag{16}$$

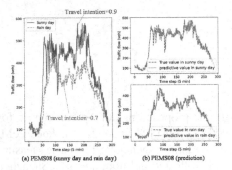

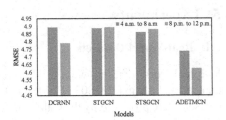

Fig. 3. Fitting performance of ADETMCN on PEMS datasets

Fig. 4. Comparison of prediction performance in different periods

5.3 Experimental Results

Prediction Performance of ADETMCN. The ADETMCN model considers the impact of different weather on travel intention. Figure 3 shows the traffic flow under two weather conditions and different travel intentions, intuitively showing the impact of weather. It can be found that the traffic flow on sunny days is significantly greater than that on rainy days. This experiment proves that different weather does have different effects on traffic

Table 2. Comparison with the average results of comparison models

Classical models		LSTM	CNN	DCRNN	STGCN	ASTGCN	STSGCN	STFGNN	Auto-DSTSGN	ADETMCN
Datasets	Metrics									
PeMS03	RMSE	35.233	32.987	30.427	30.314	29.676	28.873	28.342	25.170	**24.977**
	MAE	21.132	20.725	18.239	17.485	17.693	17.379	16.773	14.592	**14.083**
	MAPE(%)	21.561	20.773	18.924	17.472	19.289	16.882	16.309	14.226	**14.097**
PeMS04	RMSE	41.732	39.076	38.383	35.423	35.222	34.136	31.891	30.488	**30.322**
	MAE	27.162	27.078	24.926	22.721	22.933	21.014	19.836	18.854	**18.765**
	MAPE(%)	18.598	17.623	17.482	14.688	16.577	13.905	**13.021**	13.213	13.123
PeMS07	RMSE	45.927	40.794	38.856	38.758	42.571	38.894	35.878	33.024	**32.981**
	MAE	30.021	32.141	25.764	25.382	28.352	24.768	22.087	20.089	**20.025**
	MAPE(%)	13.532	12.361	11.693	11.087	13.889	10.663	9.253	8.571	**8.499**
PeMS08	RMSE	34.074	29.528	27.837	27.829	28.380	27.555	26.231	23.772	**23.684**
	MAE	22.373	21.858	17.861	18.035	18.591	17.883	16.642	14.749	**14.711**
	MAPE(%)	14.682	13.790	11.458	11.427	13.246	11.709	10.608	9.451	**9.420**

flow. Figure 3 shows that the proposed model can fit the traffic flow well under different weather conditions.

Performance Comparison with Comparative Models. To verify the advantages of the proposed model, this paper used eight models for comparison. Four datasets of PEMS were used to test the prediction performance. Table 2 shows the average numerical results of the nine models on the four datasets. With RMSE as the evaluation index, the prediction accuracy of ADETMCN was 0.4529% higher than that of the best model in the comparison models.

To verify the sensitivity of different models to the traffic peak, we selected the SZ-taxi test set from 4 a.m. to 8 a.m. and 8 p.m. to 12 p.m. to show the prediction performance of each model. Figure 4 shows that the proposed model has the best prediction results for both periods.

The long-term prediction ability of the model is essential. This paper proposes a time-varying feature extraction module to extract long-term and dynamic time features. The PEMS03 dataset was used to test the multi-step prediction ability of various models. The time steps were set to 5 min, 15 min, 30 min and 60 min, respectively. It can be seen from Fig. 5 that the prediction performance of all models decreases with the increase of time step, but the proposed model still maintains good prediction performance.

Ablation Experiments. To verify the advantages of the proposed model structure, this paper carried out ablation experiments on different components, and respectively designed ADETMCN-A with only adjacency spatial feature extraction module, ADETMCN-C with only correlation spatial feature extraction module, ADETMCN-T with only travel intention spatial feature extraction module and ADETMCN-NT without time-varying feature extraction module. PEMS03 was used as a test set, the prediction accuracy of RMSE for different variants and the time consumed per 30 batches are shown in Table 3. Ignoring the influence of multi-image spatial features, the training time of the model can be reduced by 10.585%, but the accuracy decreased by 3.071%. Params correspond to the space complexity and represent the size of the memory occupied.

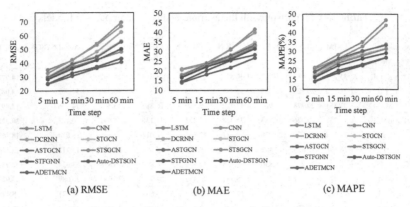

(a) RMSE   (b) MAE   (c) MAPE

Fig. 5. Comparison of long-term prediction performance

Meanwhile, FLOP corresponds to the time complexity, which can be used to measure the computational complexity and determine the computational time of the algorithm. The smaller the FLOPs, the smaller the computational complexity required. Compared with STSGCN, the Params and FLOPs of the proposed model increased by 33.425% and 46.661%, respectively, and the prediction accuracy increased by 13.494%.

Table 3. Experimental results of ablation of different components

Model	Train cost of each epoch(s), batch size = 30	Params (M)	FLOPs (G)	RMSE
STSGCN	**166.942**	**1.095**	**13.210**	28.873
ADETMCN-A	282.192	1.406	17.613	25.813
ADETMCN-C	283.817	1.428	17.852	25.744
ADETMCN-T	284.778	1.439	17.978	25.656
ADETMCN-NT	267.391	1.335	16.301	25.184
ADETMCN	313.615	1.461	19.374	**24.977**

5.4 Discussion

In Sect. 5.3, multiple experiments were conducted to verify the predictive performance of ADETMCN. Section 5.3 shows the results of the proposed model and the comparison models on five datasets. To verify the advantages of ADETMCN, this paper selected LSTM, CNN, DCRNN, STGCN, ASTGCN, STSGCN, STFGNN, and Auto-DSTSGN as the comparison models. According to the test results on the PEMS datasets, with RMSE as the evaluation index, the prediction accuracy of ADETMCN was 0.4529% higher than that of the comparison model with the best performance. LSTM has been used to extract temporal features, but lacks the ability to extract spatial features. CNN has been used to extract the spatial features of Euclidean structure, but the real-world road network is generally non-Euclidean structure, which is difficult to mine the spatial features of the road network effectively. DCRNN, STGCN and ASTGCN have all tried to extract spatial-temporal features, but these three models used convolution modules in temporal features, which is difficult to capture long-term time features effectively. STFGNN and STSGCN adopted spatial-temporal synchronization graph to extract long-term temporal features, but it is difficult to flexibly capture short-term and long-term spatial-temporal correlations. Auto-DSTSGN proposed an extended spatial-temporal synchronous graph convolution framework based on the spatial-temporal synchronous graph to balance short-term and long-term dependent learning. However, like the above methods, Auto-DSTSGN established a unified model for all nodes in the road network to learn features, ignoring the clustering of nodes with high correlation, which can easily lead to low universality of the model. Through the experiments in Sect. 5.3, this paper verified the long-term prediction ability of the proposed model, and verified the rationality of the model structure through ablation experiments. The experimental results show that the proposed model exhibits excellent prediction performance in traffic flow prediction tasks.

6 Conclusion

This paper proposed an adjacent-DBSCAN enhanced time-varying multi-graph convolution network for traffic flow prediction. The design of the multi-graph spatial feature extraction module and the time-varying feature extraction module effectively enhanced the extraction of long-term and short-term spatiotemporal features. Experiments on five real-world datasets showed that the proposed model was superior to the most advanced methods. Of course, the ADETMCN model still has problems of high computational cost and low explanatory power. In the future, our work will focus on the mathematical interpretation of the model, the mathematical derivation of convergence and the optimization of the structure.

References

1. Li, L., Jiang, R., He, Z., Chen, X., Zhou, X.: Trajectory data-based traffic flow studies: a revisit. Transp. Res. Part C: Emerg. Technol. **114**, 225–240 (2020)
2. Hou, Q., Leng, J., Ma, G., Liu, W., Cheng, Y.: An adaptive hybrid model for short-term urban traffic flow prediction. Physica A **527**, 1–10 (2019)
3. Pan, Y.A., Guo, J., Chen, Y., Li, S., Li, W.: Incorporating traffic flow model into a deep learning method for traffic state estimation: a hybrid stepwise modeling framework. J. Adv. Transp. **2022**, 1–17 (2022)
4. Zhang, Y., Lu, Z., Wang, J., Chen, L.: FCM-GCN-based upstream and downstream dependence model for air traffic flow networks. Knowl.-Based Syst. **260**, 1–11 (2023)
5. Ali, A., Zhu, Y., Zakarya, M.: Exploiting dynamic spatio-temporal graph convolutional neural networks for citywide traffic flows prediction. Neural Netw. **145**, 233–247 (2022)
6. Guo, C., Chen, C.H., Hwang, F.J., Chang, C.C., Chang, C.C.: Fast spatiotemporal learning framework for traffic flow forecasting. IEEE Trans. Intell. Transp. Syst. 1–11 (2022)

7. Han, S.Y., Zhao, Q., Sun, Q.W., Zhou, J., Chen, Y.H.: EnGS-DGR: traffic flow forecasting with in-definite forecasting interval by ensemble GCN, Seq2Seq, and dynamic graph reconfiguration. Appl. Sci. **12**(6), 1–14 (2022)

8. Zhao, L., Song, Y., Zhang, C.: T-GCN: a temporal graph convolutional network for traffic prediction. IEEE Trans. Intell. Transp. Syst. **21**(9), 3848–3858 (2020)

9. Li, Y., Yu, R., Shahabi, C., Liu, Y.: Diffusion convolutional recurrent neural network: data-driven traffic forecasting. In: ICLR 2018, Vancouver, Canada, pp. 1–16 (2018)

10. Yu, B., Yin, H., Zhu, Z.: Spatio-temporal graph convolutional networks: a deep learning frame-work for traffic forecasting. In: IJCAI 2018, pp. 3634–3640. IJCAI, Stockholm, Sweden (2018)

11. Guo, S., Lin, Y., Feng, N., Song, C., Wan, H.: Attention based spatial-temporal graph convolutional networks for traffic flow forecasting. In: AAAI 2019, vol. 2019, pp. 922–929. AAAI, Hawaii (2019)

12. Song, C., Lin, Y., Guo, S., Wan, H.: Spatial-temporal synchronous graph convolutional networks: a new framework for spatial-temporal network data forecasting. In: AAAI 2020, vol. 2020, pp. 914–921. AAAI, Palo Alto (2020)

13. Li, M., Zhu, Z.: Spatial-temporal fusion graph neural networks for traffic flow forecasting. In: AAAI 2021, vol. 35, pp. 4189–4196. AAAI (2021)

14. Jin, G., Li, F., Zhang, J., Wang, M., Huang, J.: Automated dilated spatio-temporal synchronous graph modeling for traffic prediction. IEEE Trans. Intell. Transp. Syst., 1–11 (2022)

A Survey on Automated Code Evaluation Systems and Their Resources for Code Analysis

Md. Mostafizer Rahman[1,2]([✉])(iD), Yutaka Watanobe[2](iD),
and Mohamed Hamada[2](iD)

[1] Dhaka University of Engineering & Technology, Gazipur, Bangladesh
mostafiz26@gmail.com, mostafiz@duet.ac.bd
[2] The University of Aizu, Aizuwakamatsu, Japan
{yutaka,hamada}@u-aizu.ac.jp

Abstract. The automated code evaluation system is designed to reliably evaluate user-submitted code. Code is first compiled and then tested on a homogeneous surface using defined input and output test cases. Automated code evaluation systems are gaining popularity due to their wide range of applications and valuable accumulated resources. The success of machine learning techniques emboldens researchers to use them for source code analysis tasks, and a large number of real-life solution codes from automated evaluation systems adds significant value. In this paper, we review the state-of-the-art of automated code evaluation systems and their resources for code analysis tasks using machine learning. We classify these code evaluation systems into several categories, including programming contests, programming learning, recruitment, online compilers, and additional modules of other systems. We research the datasets available in these systems for code analysis. Moreover, we summarize the machine learning-based code assessment tasks, including error detection, code comprehension, review, search and representation, refactoring, and repair using these datasets.

Keywords: Automated Evaluation System · Online Judge · Code Assessment · Coding Analysis · Machine Learning

1 Introduction

Over the past three decades, we have witnessed the growing popularity of programming computing events such as the International Collegiate Programming Contest (ICPC), which is considered the largest, oldest, and most competitive programming competition for students from universities around the world. ICPC provides an opportunity for students to interact with each other, improve their programming skills, algorithmic thinking, teamwork, and problem solving process. In 1970, the first edition of ICPC was held at Texas A&M University [61], and today ICPC is one of the most prestigious programming competitions in the

H. Fujita et al. (Eds.): IEA/AIE 2023, LNAI 13926, pp. 385–396, 2023.
https://doi.org/10.1007/978-3-031-36822-6_33

world. After the first ICPC final, many other algorithmic competitions adopted similar automated evaluation system (AES). The International Olympiad in Informatics (IOI) is one of them, which started using AES in 1989. Cormack et al. [13] described the basic rules, evaluation procedure, and scoring functions used by the most popular programming contests such as ICPC and IOI.

The key component of this competitive programming environment is a system that automatically verifies the correctness of submitted solutions based on the results obtained on predefined input/output test datasets. It also evaluates the resource usage limits (e.g., memory and time) for each solution. This type of system is called an *automated evaluation system*[1] (AES) or *online judge* (OJ) system. The idea of OJ system was first introduced by Kurnia and collaborators [29] in 2001, which supports automated and real-time evaluation of submitted solution codes. However, the development, implementation, and maintenance of an AES is not a trivial task, as many important and crucial factors must be considered for its safety and smooth operation. In general, the AES evaluates submitted codes on local or cloud-based infrastructures and should be prepared to tackle a wide range of threats during the evaluation process. For example, submitted codes may be executable files or source codes that modify the test environment, force a longer compilation time, force the use of restricted resources (e.g., memory and time), and so on. A detailed description of possible threat types and countermeasures for a programming competition is presented in a research paper [15].

Apart from competitive programming, AESs have various supporting functions that are commonly used in different application domains, including programming learning, online compilers, data mining, recruitment, and development. In addition, the resources such as evaluation results, solution codes, and logs of AESs are treated as valuable treasures for educational and industrial research. Meanwhile, many academic research have produced significant results based on the resources of AESs, as these systems are used for programming tutoring in various academic institutions [42,43]. In addition, the collected data resources of AES are considered one of the largest real-world code repositories, which lead to software engineering researches such as software code analysis, vulnerability prediction, source code search, suggesting class and method names, and software refactoring [6,34,35,44,62].

In recent years, advances in artificial intelligence (AI), particularly in machine learning (ML) and deep learning (DL), have made significant progress in the areas of text [2,31], image [28,54], and speech [17] processing. These advances in ML and DL are deeply rooted in the acceleration of many open source codes and computational hardware, which encourages practitioners and researchers to tackle source code and software engineering problems [30,58]. In the context of source code analysis, researchers and practitioners have employed ML and DL models for code-related tasks, such as code representation [4,21], testing, code synthesis, refactoring, code completion, code summarization, and code repair.

---

[1] The terms automated evaluation system, automated assessment system, and online judge are used synonymously.

The use of ML and DL for code analysis is increasing, and at the same time, the available methods, techniques, resources, tools, and datasets are also increasing. This poses a challenge for researchers to understand the landscape of available resources and research directions. However, there are a large number of attempts to summarize specific application-oriented research in the form of surveys.

In the last few years, AES resources have become potential datasets for various code analysis tasks. The CodeNet [40] is a large-scale dataset consisting of 14 million real-world solution codes and about 500 million lines of code in about 55 programming languages. These codes are collected from the Aizu [63] and AtCoder [1] online judge systems. CodeNet is a curated dataset and ready for applying code analysis tasks such as code classification and code similarity. POJ-104 [8] and GCJ [56] are widely used benchmark datasets derived from pedagogical AES and Google Code Jam (2008-2020) competition, respectively. GCJ-297 is another benchmark dataset consisting of 297 problems and approximately 208K solution codes. A detailed discussion of the code analysis tasks and the corresponding benchmark datasets can be found in CodeXGLUE [33].

The scope of this paper is as follows: To the best of our knowledge, there is no survey of automated code evaluation systems and their resources for code analysis tasks, we therefore decided to fill this gap. First, we present a survey of existing AESs and their potential application domains. This is because the diversity of these systems is large, so the application-based classification is of great importance to researchers and practitioners. Next, we summarize the datasets generated by the AESs and other platforms for the coding tasks. These summarized datasets can be useful to practitioners and researchers for further coding analysis tasks.

2   Automated Evaluation Systems

The Automated Evaluation System (AES) is a reliable, secure, and continuous online evaluation system for algorithms submitted by users distributed around the world. For better understanding, the AES evaluation method can be defined as follows:

Definition 1. *(Evaluation Method). The evaluation method consists of three main steps. (i) code submission, (ii) code evaluation with test datasets, and (iii) evaluation score.*

In the code submission phase, the submitted code is compiled and verified whether the code is executable in a homogeneous evaluation environment or not. If the verification is successful, each solution code is reliably evaluated on a coherent evaluation infrastructure using problem-specific test cases. The evaluation of the test cases determines for each submission: (i) the code executes without errors, (ii) the resource constraints (time and memory) have not been exceeded for a given problem, (iii) the obtained result satisfies problem definitions. Finally, the evaluation score is calculated considering all test case results. There are few literature reviews on the classification of contests organized using

Table 1. OJ systems used for the competitive programming contests

Name	In-use	Language	# Problems	# Users	Founded
UVa Online Judge	Yes	Eng	4,300	300,000	1995
Aizu Online Judge	Yes	Eng, Jap	3,000	120,000	2004
National Tsing Hua University Online Judge	Yes	Eng	10,000	–	2015
National Taiwan University Online Judge	Yes	Chi	2600	600	2016
Sphere Online Judge (SPOJ)	Yes	Eng, Pol, Por, Viet	20,000	315,000	2004
Codeforces	Yes	Eng, Rus	3,000	600,000	2010
Google Code Jam	Yes	Eng	450	670,000	2003
Facebook Hacker Cup	Yes	Eng	–	80,000	2011
Peking University Online Judge	Yes	Eng, Chi	3,000	250,000	2003
HUSTOJ	Yes	Eng, Chi	650	26,000	2014
TopCoder Competitive Programming	Yes	Eng	5,200	4,000	2001
Timus Online Judge	Yes	Eng	1,000	110,000	2000
IEEEXtreme	Yes	Eng	–	–	2006

AES. Pohl [37] was the first to propose a classification of programming contests based on criteria such as contest style, duration, submission and evaluation methods, scoring, and entrance. In addition, classifications based on programming contests, types of programming exercises, and characteristics of the AES have also been discussed in studies [12]. However, most of these classifications are limited to single applications such as education or programming contests. There is no clear classification of AESs based on their potential applications that can be useful for users. Therefore, we decided to classify AESs based on their applications.

2.1 Competitive Programming Contest

OJ systems have a wide range of applications for competitive programming. Many educational institutions use this platform to prepare their students to participate in competitive programming contests. Competitive programming contests are also held by organizations and have gained popularity. The first OJ is UVa [48], which gained great popularity worldwide. It was founded in 1995 at the University of Valladolid in Spain. Based on the collected UVa dataset, Skiena and Revilla [51] wrote the book "Programming Challenges: The Programming Contest Training Manual" to help programmers in programming contests. A partial list of OJ systems is given in Table 1.

2.2 Academic Tool

Recently, OJ systems have emerged as academic tools for programming learning, programming assignments, and assessment. Teachers/instructors at many educational institutions automatically grade students' assignments using OJ. The benefits of using OJ system in education are innumerable. For example, the submitted solution codes are checked with higher accuracy, no wrong solutions are accepted, students can get their result immediately, and the teacher can take

Table 2. OJ systems used for the Education

Name	In-use	Language	# Problems	Founded
UVa Online Judge	Yes	Eng	4,300	1995
Aizu Online Judge	Yes	Eng, Jap	3,000	2004
Jutge.org	Yes	Eng, Esp, Fre, Cat, Dut	4,843	2006
CodeChef	Yes	Eng	3,000	2009
CodeHunt	Yes	Eng	8,300	2014
Codecademy	Yes	Eng	–	2011
CodeWars	Yes	Eng	1,200	2012
URI Online Judge	Yes	Eng, Spa, Por	1,100	2011

action to improve students' programming skills based on the result. A successful application of the OJ system for algorithms and data structures and analytical investigation based on the collected data is presented in studies [11, 42, 43]. Ala-Mutka [3] gave a detailed review of the application of OJ systems in education. A review [25] presented the available software for automatic assessment of programming tasks that may increase interest in learning programming. In contrast, Fonte et al. [14] presented the advanced version of OJ system that can be used to provide valuable feedback to programmers to help them understand where the problem lies and how to improve the solution code. A partial list of OJ systems for education is shown in Table 2.

2.3   Recruitment

There are numerous platforms that use OJ systems to support the hiring process. These platforms are mainly commercial and automatically evaluate the submitted codes and rank the programmers. We present some OJ systems that are used for recruitment. For example, *HackerEarth, HackerRank, Qualified, CodeEval, Codility*, and so on. *HackerEarth* is an online platform dedicated to hiring talented developers, hosting crowdsourcing-based ideas and organizing hackathons. *Codility* helps hiring managers find the best developers from a large pool of skilled programmers in the shortest possible time.

2.4   Online Compilers and Development Platforms

Another category of OJ systems are online compilers, where the codes developed in different languages by user solutions can be compiled and executed remotely through a browser. *Codeanywhere* is one of the most feature-rich online compilers that offers a dedicated custom development environment and real-time collaboration. It allows users to automatically connect to GitHub, Amazon Cloud, FTP servers and Bitbucket. *Coding Ground* offers a full-featured IDE that allows users to edit, compile and run their projects in the cloud. In addition to online

Table 3. OJ systems used for the online compilers and development platforms

Name	In-use	Founded	Compiler	Development Platform
Codeanywhere	Yes	2013	✓	✗
Coding Ground	Yes	2006	✓	✗
DOMJudge	Yes	2004	✗	✓
Mooshak	2015	2005	✗	✓
SIO2	Yes	2012	✗	✓
Ideone	Yes	2009	✓	✗
Codio	Yes	2013	✓	✗
TestMyCode	Yes	2013	✗	✓
Programiz	Yes	–	✓	✗
CodeSkulptor	Yes	2012	✓	✗
CloudCoder	Yes	2012	✗	✓
Tsinghua Online Judge	Yes	2012	✗	✓

compilers, many OJ development platforms are available to host programming competitions or educational activities in local infrastructure. *DOMjudge* is a well-known OJ development platform that can be easily installed to host programming contests. It allows users to prepare and run programming contests according to ACM ICPC rules. A partial list of OJ systems for online compilers and development platforms can be found in Table 3.

3   Resources of Automated Evaluation Systems

The numerous applications of OJ systems in various domains regularly generate diverse data resources (e.g., solution codes, assessment results, and submission logs). These real-world and rich data resources have become attractive for coding, educational, learning analytic, and data mining research [43, 45]. In a study [42], a comprehensive data-driven analysis based on OJ data was conducted. The experimental results show the shortcomings of students' programming and the scope of possible improvements. Hsiao et al. [22] leveraged an educational learning analysis tool called "Web Programming Grading Assistant (WPGA)" to study the effectiveness of students' programming learning. Rahman et al. [43] conducted educational data mining using OJ data to support programming learning. However, benchmark datasets have had a significant impact on the growth of coding-related research using ML. In this section, we focus on the benchmark datasets for code intelligence research. Code search [18, 39] is important when programmers want to use other codes. This system automatically finds semantically similar codes based on a natural language query. The code completion system [34, 47] can help programmers automatically complete their code. Also, the code-to-code translation system [49] assists programmers translate their code from one language to another (e.g., Python to Java and Java to

Table 4. A list of benchmark datasets and their application in coding analysis

Sl.	Dataset Name	Coding Tasks	Size
1	CodeNet [40]	code classification, code similarity	14 million
2	Aizu [63]	code classification, code-to-code translation, code completion, refactoring, summarization	7.5 million
3	AtCoder [1]	code classification, code-to-code translation, code completion, refactoring, summarization	7.5 million
4	BigCloneBench [52]	code clone	6 million
5	POJ-104 [8]	code classification, code similarity, code clone	1 million
6	PY150 [46]	code completion	150,000
7	Devign [65]	fault detection	27,318
8	Bugs2Fix [55]	code repair	122,000
9	CodeSearchNet [24]	code summarization	1.1 million
10	CodeXGLUE [33]	Clone detection, defect detection, cloze test, code completion, code translation, code search, code repair, code summarization, text-to-code generation	–

Python). As the use of real datasets for coding-related research increases, therefore, we present a list of available datasets from platforms such as OJ, contest platforms, and GitHub in Table 4.

4   Code Analysis Using Machine Learning

According to Evans Data Corporation[2], there were approximately 23.9 million professional developers in 2019, and that number is expected to reach approximately 28.7 million by the end of 2024 [33]. The ML-based code intelligence can be used to improve the productivity of a growing number of professional programmers. At the same time, benchmark datasets have a significant impact on the growth of applied ML research. Recently, researchers have begun to utilize statistical models such as neural networks for code analysis tasks. In addition, the application of pre-trained models that learn from large programming data such as BERT, GPT, CodeBERT, and IntelliCode Compose, have achieved great success in a wide range of coding tasks. With the growth of resources, datasets, tools, and methods, code analysis research is also expanding. Therefore, Table 5 summarizes recent attempts of code analysis tasks using ML.

Also, a brief description of the coding tasks with ML is as follows. The purpose of the task *defect detection* is to identify errors/defects within the body of the source code. Classification of codes as buggy or not is based on the identification of errors in the code. *Clone detection* is used to identify semantically

---

[2] https://evansdata.com/press/viewRelease.php?pressID=278.

Table 5. Machine learning approaches for coding analysis tasks

Sl.	Code Analysis Task	Article
1	Defect Detection	[9,38,41,65]
2	Clone Detection	[10,36,52,59]
3	Code Completion	[32,34,47,53]
4	Code Repair	[7,16,20,35]
5	Code Search	[18,50,57,60]
6	Code Summarization	[5,23,27,64]
7	Text-to-Code Generation	[19,26]
8	Code Classification	[34,35,44,62]

similar code. It has two subtasks: searching for similar codes and classification. *Code completion* is another task that helps programmer complete code correctly. Programmers sometimes get confused what to write next, and in such cases, code completion helps them to complete the code. Code completion can be done in two ways (*i*) token-level completion and (*ii*) line-level completion. *Code repair* task identifies bugs and automatically fix them. Typically, they identify bugs in the code and fix them according to the context of the code. *Code search* is a task that measures the semantic relevance between the code and natural language. This is the activity of searching the code based on a natural language query. *Code summarization* provides an aggregated summary comment of the code. *Text-to-code* task is used to generate codes based on the input of the natural language description. *Code classification* can be done in many ways, such as classifying source code based on programming language, application, and error.

5   Conclusion

The widespread applications of automated evaluation systems (AESs) are undeniable, and the scope of this system continues to grow. Therefore, the categorization of AESs based on their application is of great importance to users. Moreover, the data resources generated by AESs can be useful for various research and development activities. In this survey paper, we have provided a comprehensive yet concise overview of AESs and their data resources. First, we focused on the categorization of AESs based on their application areas. Next, we present the available datasets of AESs that enable users to perform their research and development work. We also present various coding analysis tasks using machine learning to solve programming problems.

Acknowledgment. This research was financially supported by the Japan Society for the Promotion of Science (JSPS) KAKENHI. Grant Number: 23H03508.

References

1. Atcoder. https://atcoder.jp/
2. Abdeljaber, O., Avci, O., Kiranyaz, S., Gabbouj, M., Inman, D.J.: Real-time vibration-based structural damage detection using one-dimensional convolutional neural networks. J. Sound Vib. **388**, 154–170 (2017). https://doi.org/10.1016/j.jsv.2016.10.043
3. Ala-Mutka, K.M.: A survey of automated assessment approaches for programming assignments. Comput. Sci. Educ. **15**(2), 83–102 (2005)
4. Allamanis, M., Barr, E.T., Devanbu, P., Sutton, C.: A survey of machine learning for big code and naturalness. ACM Comput. Surv. **51**(4) (2018). https://doi.org/10.1145/3212695
5. Allamanis, M., Peng, H., Sutton, C.: A convolutional attention network for extreme summarization of source code. In: International Conference on Machine Learning, pp. 2091–2100. PMLR (2016)
6. Allamanis, M., Sutton, C.: Mining source code repositories at massive scale using language modeling. In: Proceedings of the 10th Working Conference on Mining Software Repositories, pp. 207–216. MSR '13, IEEE Press (2013)
7. Amorim, L.A., Freitas, M.F., Dantas, A., de Souza, E.F., Camilo-Junior, C.G., Martins, W.S.: A new word embedding approach to evaluate potential fixes for automated program repair. In: 2018 International Joint Conference on Neural Networks (IJCNN), pp. 1–8 (2018). https://doi.org/10.1109/IJCNN.2018.8489079
8. Ben-Nun, T., Jakobovits, A.S., Hoefler, T.: Neural code comprehension: a learnable representation of code semantics. In: Proceedings of the 32nd International Conference on Neural Information Processing Systems, pp. 3589–3601. NIPS'18, Curran Associates Inc., Red Hook, NY, USA (2018)
9. Butgereit, L.: Using machine learning to prioritize automated testing in an agile environment. In: 2019 Conference on Information Communications Technology and Society (ICTAS), pp. 1–6 (2019). https://doi.org/10.1109/ICTAS.2019.8703639
10. Büch, L., Andrzejak, A.: Learning-based recursive aggregation of abstract syntax trees for code clone detection. In: 2019 IEEE 26th International Conference on Software Analysis, Evolution and Reengineering (SANER), pp. 95–104 (2019). https://doi.org/10.1109/SANER.2019.8668039
11. Cheang, B., Kurnia, A., Lim, A., Oon, W.C.: On automated grading of programming assignments in an academic institution. Comput. Educ. **41**(2), 121–131 (2003). https://doi.org/10.1016/S0360-1315(03)00030-7
12. Combéfis, S., Wautelet, J.: Programming trainings and informatics teaching through online contests. Olymp. Inform. **8**, 21–34 (2014)
13. Cormack, G., Munro, I., Vasiga, T., Kemkes, G.: Structure, scoring and purpose of computing competitions. Inform. Educ. **5**(1), 15–36 (2006)
14. Fonte, D., Cruz, D.d., Gançarski, A.L., Henriques, P.R.: A flexible dynamic system for automatic grading of programming exercises (2013)
15. Forisek, M.: Security of programming contest systems (2007)
16. Goues, C.L., Pradel, M., Roychoudhury, A.: Automated program repair. Commun. ACM **62**(12), 56–65 (2019)
17. Graves, A., Jaitly, N., Mohamed, A.R.: Hybrid speech recognition with deep bidirectional LSTM. In: 2013 IEEE Workshop on Automatic Speech Recognition and Understanding, pp. 273–278 (2013). https://doi.org/10.1109/ASRU.2013.6707742
18. Gu, X., Zhang, H., Kim, S.: Deep code search. In: 2018 IEEE/ACM 40th International Conference on Software Engineering (ICSE), pp. 933–944 (2018). https://doi.org/10.1145/3180155.3180167

19. Guo, D., Tang, D., Duan, N., Zhou, M., Yin, J.: Coupling retrieval and meta-learning for context-dependent semantic parsing. arXiv preprint arXiv:1906.07108 (2019)
20. Gupta, R., Pal, S., Kanade, A., Shevade, S.: DeepFix: fixing common c language errors by deep learning. In: Proceedings of the Thirty-First AAAI Conference on Artificial Intelligence, pp. 1345–1351. AAAI'17, AAAI Press (2017)
21. Hellendoorn, V.J., Devanbu, P.: Are deep neural networks the best choice for modeling source code? In: Proceedings of the 2017 11th Joint Meeting on Foundations of Software Engineering, pp. 763–773. ESEC/FSE 2017, Association for Computing Machinery, New York, NY, USA (2017). https://doi.org/10.1145/3106237.3106290
22. Hsiao, I.H., Huang, P.K., Murphy, H.: Integrating programming learning analytics across physical and digital space. IEEE Trans. Emerg. Top. Comput. 8(1), 206–217 (2020). https://doi.org/10.1109/TETC.2017.2701201
23. Hu, X., Li, G., Xia, X., Lo, D., Lu, S., Jin, Z.: Summarizing source code with transferred API knowledge. In: Proceedings of the 27th International Joint Conference on Artificial Intelligence, pp. 2269–2275. IJCAI'18, AAAI Press (2018)
24. Husain, H., Wu, H.H., Gazit, T., Allamanis, M., Brockschmidt, M.: Codesearch-net challenge: evaluating the state of semantic code search. arXiv preprint arXiv:1909.09436 (2019)
25. Ihantola, P., Ahoniemi, T., Karavirta, V., Seppälä, O.: Review of recent systems for automatic assessment of programming assignments. In: Proceedings of the 10th Koli Calling International Conference on Computing Education Research, pp. 86–93. Koli Calling '10, Association for Computing Machinery, New York, NY, USA (2010). https://doi.org/10.1145/1930464.1930480
26. Iyer, S., Cheung, A., Zettlemoyer, L.: Learning programmatic idioms for scalable semantic parsing. arXiv preprint arXiv:1904.09086 (2019)
27. Iyer, S., Konstas, I., Cheung, A., Zettlemoyer, L.: Summarizing source code using a neural attention model. In: Proceedings of the 54th Annual Meeting of the Association for Computational Linguistics (Volume 1: Long Papers), pp. 2073–2083 (2016)
28. Krizhevsky, A., Sutskever, I., Hinton, G.E.: Imagenet classification with deep convolutional neural networks. Commun. ACM 60(6), 84–90 (2017)
29. Kurnia, A., Lim, A., Cheang, B.: Online judge. Comput. Educ. 36(4), 299–315 (2001). https://doi.org/10.1016/S0360-1315(01)00018-5
30. Le, T.H.M., Chen, H., Babar, M.A.: Deep learning for source code modeling and generation: models, applications, and challenges. ACM Comput. Surv. 53(3) (2020). https://doi.org/10.1145/3383458
31. Lee, S.M., Yoon, S.M., Cho, H.: Human activity recognition from accelerometer data using convolutional neural network. In: 2017 IEEE International Conference on Big Data and Smart Computing (BigComp), pp. 131–134 (2017). https://doi.org/10.1109/BIGCOMP.2017.7881728
32. Liu, F., Li, G., Zhao, Y., Jin, Z.: Multi-task learning based pre-trained language model for code completion. In: Proceedings of the 35th IEEE/ACM International Conference on Automated Software Engineering, pp. 473–485. ASE '20, Association for Computing Machinery, New York, NY, USA (2021). https://doi.org/10.1145/3324884.3416591
33. Lu, S., et al.: CodeXGLUE: a machine learning benchmark dataset for code understanding and generation. arXiv preprint arXiv:2102.04664 (2021)
34. M. Mostafizer, R., Watanobe, Y., Nakamura, K.: A neural network based intelligent support model for program code completion. Sci. Program. 2020 (2020). https://doi.org/10.1155/2020/7426461

35. M. Mostafizer, R., Watanobe, Y., Nakamura, K.: A bidirectional LSTM language model for code evaluation and repair. Symmetry **13**(2) (2021). https://doi.org/10.3390/sym13020247
36. Mostaeen, G., Roy, B., Roy, C.K., Schneider, K., Svajlenko, J.: A machine learning based framework for code clone validation. J. Syst. Softw. **169**, 110686 (2020)
37. Pohl, W.: Computer science contests for secondary school students: approaches to classification. Inform. Educ. **5**(1), 125–132 (2006)
38. Pradel, M., Sen, K.: Deepbugs: a learning approach to name-based bug detection. Proc. ACM Program. Lang. **2**(OOPSLA) (2018). https://doi.org/10.1145/3276517
39. Premtoon, V., Koppel, J., Solar-Lezama, A.: Semantic code search via equational reasoning. In: Proceedings of the 41st ACM SIGPLAN Conference on Programming Language Design and Implementation, pp. 1066–1082. PLDI 2020, Association for Computing Machinery, New York, NY, USA (2020). https://doi.org/10.1145/3385412.3386001
40. Puri, R., et al.: Project CodeNet: a large-scale AI for code dataset for learning a diversity of coding tasks. arXiv preprint arXiv:2105.12655 1035 (2021)
41. Qasem, O.A., Akour, M., Alenezi, M.: The influence of deep learning algorithms factors in software fault prediction. IEEE Access **8**, 63945–63960 (2020). https://doi.org/10.1109/ACCESS.2020.2985290
42. Rahman, M.M., Watanobe, Y., Kiran, R.U., Thang, T.C., Paik, I.: Impact of practical skills on academic performance: a data-driven analysis. IEEE Access **9**, 139975–139993 (2021). https://doi.org/10.1109/ACCESS.2021.3119145
43. Rahman, M.M., Watanobe, Y., Matsumoto, T., Kiran, R.U., Nakamura, K.: Educational data mining to support programming learning using problem-solving data. IEEE Access **10**, 26186–26202 (2022)
44. Rahman, M.M., Watanobe, Y., Nakamura, K.: Source code assessment and classification based on estimated error probability using attentive LSTM language model and its application in programming education. Appl. Sci. **10**(8), 2973 (2020)
45. Rahman, M.M., Watanobe, Y., Rage, U.K., Nakamura, K.: A novel rule-based online judge recommender system to promote computer programming education. In: Fujita, H., Selamat, A., Lin, J.C.-W., Ali, M. (eds.) IEA/AIE 2021. LNCS (LNAI), vol. 12799, pp. 15–27. Springer, Cham (2021). https://doi.org/10.1007/978-3-030-79463-7_2
46. Raychev, V., Bielik, P., Vechev, M.: Probabilistic model for code with decision trees. SIGPLAN Not. **51**(10), 731–747 (2016)
47. Raychev, V., Vechev, M., Yahav, E.: Code completion with statistical language models. In: Proceedings of the 35th ACM SIGPLAN Conference on Programming Language Design and Implementation, pp. 419–428. PLDI '14, Association for Computing Machinery, New York, NY, USA (2014)
48. Revilla, M.A., Manzoor, S., Liu, R.: Competitive learning in informatics: the UVA online judge experience. Olymp. Inform. **2**(10), 131–148 (2008)
49. Roziere, B., Lachaux, M.A., Chanussot, L., Lample, G.: Unsupervised translation of programming languages. In: Proceedings of the 34th International Conference on Neural Information Processing Systems. NIPS'20, Curran Associates Inc., Red Hook, NY, USA (2020)
50. Sachdev, S., Li, H., Luan, S., Kim, S., Sen, K., Chandra, S.: Retrieval on source code: a neural code search. In: Proceedings of the 2nd ACM SIGPLAN International Workshop on Machine Learning and Programming Languages, pp. 31–41. MAPL 2018, Association for Computing Machinery, New York, NY, USA (2018)
51. Skiena, S.S., Revilla, M.A.: Programming challenges: the programming contest training manual. ACM SIGACT News **34**(3), 68–74 (2003)

52. Svajlenko, J., Islam, J.F., Keivanloo, I., Roy, C.K., Mia, M.M.: Towards a big data curated benchmark of inter-project code clones. In: 2014 IEEE International Conference on Software Maintenance and Evolution, pp. 476–480 (2014)
53. Svyatkovskiy, A., Deng, S.K., Fu, S., Sundaresan, N.: Intellicode compose: code generation using transformer. In: Proceedings of the 28th ACM Joint Meeting on European Software Engineering Conference and Symposium on the Foundations of Software Engineering, pp. 1433–1443. ESEC/FSE 2020, Association for Computing Machinery, New York, NY, USA (2020). https://doi.org/10.1145/3368089.3417058
54. Szegedy, C., et al.: Going deeper with convolutions. In: 2015 IEEE Conference on Computer Vision and Pattern Recognition (CVPR), pp. 1–9 (2015)
55. Tufano, M., Watson, C., Bavota, G., Penta, M.D., White, M., Poshyvanyk, D.: An empirical study on learning bug-fixing patches in the wild via neural machine translation. ACM Trans. Softw. Eng. Methodol. 28(4), 1–29 (2019)
56. Ullah, F., et al.: Cyber security threats detection in internet of things using deep learning approach. IEEE Access 7, 124379–124389 (2019). https://doi.org/10.1109/ACCESS.2019.2937347
57. Wan, Y., Shu, J., Sui, Y., Xu, G., Zhao, Z., Wu, J., Yu, P.S.: Multi-modal attention network learning for semantic source code retrieval. In: Proceedings of the 34th IEEE/ACM International Conference on Automated Software Engineering, pp. 13–25. ASE '19, IEEE Press (2020). https://doi.org/10.1109/ASE.2019.00012
58. Wan, Z., Xia, X., Lo, D., Murphy, G.C.: How does machine learning change software development practices? IEEE Trans. Softw. Eng. 47(9), 1857–1871 (2021). https://doi.org/10.1109/TSE.2019.2937083
59. Wang, W., Li, G., Ma, B., Xia, X., Jin, Z.: Detecting code clones with graph neural network and flow-augmented abstract syntax tree. In: 2020 IEEE 27th International Conference on Software Analysis, Evolution and Reengineering (SANER), pp. 261–271. IEEE (2020)
60. Wang, W., Zhang, Y., Zeng, Z., Xu, G.: Trans ˆ3: a transformer-based framework for unifying code summarization and code search. corr abs/2003.03238 (2020). arXiv preprint arXiv:2003.03238 (2020)
61. Wasik, S., Antczak, M., Badura, J., Laskowski, A., Sternal, T.: A survey on online judge systems and their applications. ACM Comput. Surv. 51(1) (2018). https://doi.org/10.1145/3143560
62. Watanobe, Y., Rahman, M.M., Kabir, R., Amin, M.F.I.: Identifying algorithm in program code based on structural features using cnn classification model. Appl. Intell. 53, 12210–12236 (2022)
63. Watanobe, Y.: Aizu online judge (2018). https://onlinejudge.u-aizu.ac.jp/
64. Wei, B., Li, G., Xia, X., Fu, Z., Jin, Z.: Code Generation as a Dual Task of Code Summarization. Curran Associates Inc., Red Hook, NY, USA (2019)
65. Zhou, Y., Liu, S., Siow, J., Du, X., Liu, Y.: Devign: Effective Vulnerability Identification by Learning Comprehensive Program Semantics via Graph Neural Networks. Curran Associates Inc., Red Hook, NY, USA (2019)

Respiratory Disease Classification Using Chest Movement Patterns Measured by Non-contact Sensor

Suphachok Buarukⓘ, Chayud Srisumarnkⓘ, Sivakorn Seinglekⓘ,
Warisa Thaweekulⓘ, and Somrudee Deepaisarn(✉)ⓘ

Sirindhorn International Institute of Technology, Thammasat University,
Bangkok 12120, Pathum Thani, Thailand
somrudee@siit.tu.ac.th

Abstract. The demand for health monitoring devices is continuously increasing, particularly to measure vital signs, which are crucial to early detection and further diagnosis of diseases. This research uses a non-contact mm-wave sensor to measure signals of respiratory patterns from a programmed patient simulator, including four diseased patterns and normal control patterns. The study compares and contrasts the performance of deep learning and machine learning approaches in respiratory disease classification. The number of peaks and valleys, short-term energy, and instantaneous frequency were extracted from the sensor records into the features for training machine learning models. A simple deep-learning architecture with a one-dimension convolutional layer was also applied for classification without the need for feature extraction. The performance of machine learning and deep learning models for respiratory disease classification are evaluated using the F1-score. The results of machine learning models with varied window size, sliding size, and number of samples yield similar performance, attaining the F1-score values of up to 1.000. In contrast, deep learning model performance improves with the increasing number of samples regardless of the window and sliding sizes, without the need to perform feature extraction.

Keywords: Respiratory Diseases · Non-contact Sensor · mm-wave Sensor · Artificial Intelligence · Classification

1 Introduction

There are several types of abnormal respiratory patterns, such as Apnea, Tachypnea, Kussmaul respiration, Cheyne-Stokes respiration, Biot's respiration, and Apneustic breathing [23]. These respiratory disease affects billions of people worldwide, as reported by the Global Burden of Disease [18]. Monitoring abnormal patterns can support the diagnosis of the physiological conditions of a patient

Supported by Graduate Scholarship Program for Excellent Thai Students (ETS), Sirindhorn International Institute of Technology, Thammasat University.

H. Fujita et al. (Eds.): IEA/AIE 2023, LNAI 13926, pp. 397–409, 2023.
https://doi.org/10.1007/978-3-031-36822-6_34

[17]. Sleep Apnea is one of the most dangerous respiratory diseases characterized by repeated behavior of shallow or interrupted breathing during sleep, leading to poor sleep quality and life-threatening conditions [9]. The global statistics indicate that middle-aged and elderly people have a higher chance of sleep apnea disorder [14]. Despite its high prevalence, many cases remain undiagnosed due to the lack of accessible diagnostic technologies [15]. The current standard monitoring system to track the vital signs for a diagnostic or personal health check still requires physical contact with persons [4]. There have been several studies that demonstrate the potential of non-contact measurement to acquire respiratory rate using various methods, aiming to replace the traditional physically-contact measurement. For example, the application of computer vision and radar system technologies [10,16,19].

Vital signs are the most fundamental indicators of the body's conditions, including respiratory rate (RR), heart rate (HR), blood pressure, and body temperature [6]. The vital sign measurements are seen as an early examination of a patient's health status and diagnosis of diseases. The previous work emphasizes RR measurement to the object on a millimeter scale for tract movement of the chest; for instance, the movement of the chest relates to RR that the range is 4–12 mm [3], with the frequency of 12–20 breaths per minute (bpm) [12]. Iyer et al. (2022) recently reported that three radar systems, including ultra wide band (UWB), continuous wave (CW), and frequency modulated continuous wave (FMCW), have been suggested as potential chest movement measurements. The FMCW radar is the most suitable sensor to employ the wave mechanism in measuring chest movement patterns compared to the other radar system, enabling the RR as well as HR detection [8], achieving the accuracy of 93% [21]. A similar setup was proposed by Sun et al. where microwave radar was used as a non-contact tool to detect HR and RR. Additionally, Q. Wang et al. used FMCW radar to classify respiratory patterns. The measurement of RR can be used to analyze patterns and diagnose normal and abnormal patterns of Biot's respiration, Tachypnea, Bradypnea, and Cheyne-stokes respiration [20].

This research aims to enable the non-contact measurement of RR using the application of a mm-wave sensor. The patient simulator was used to mimic a patient subject for data collection with ground truth labels of respiratory patterns. The breathing waveform dataset measured using the mm-wave collected from the patient simulator was used to classify respiratory patterns. The signal feature extraction was performed to obtain the input for classification using machine learning (ML). No feature extraction was performed for the simple Deep Learning (DL) approach. The paper is organized as follows: Sect. 2 presents the methods of data acquisition, data pre-processing, feature extraction, and classification models. The classification results for all experiments are presented and discussed in Sect. 3. Finally, the findings are concluded in Sect. 4.

2 Methods

2.1 Data Acquisition

The overview framework of the experimental setup used in this research is demonstrated in Fig. 1. A mm-wave sensor (IWR1642BOOST model, Texas Instruments), which transmits continuous waves of frequency 77 GHz and receives its reflection, was used in this research. The collected signal data points from the sensor were recorded in equal interval timestamps to ease the data processing and analyzing procedure. The respiratory waveform reflects the periodic motion of the breathing with direction between $-\pi$ to π [8].

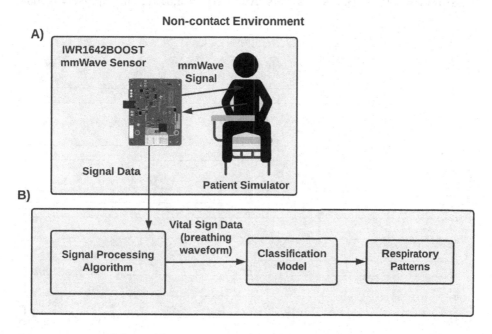

Fig. 1. Experiment setup with patient simulator

The patient simulator (SUSIE S2000 model, Gaumard Scientific Company, USA) was used as a subject. It provides ground truths with controllable parameters, patterns, and environment. The adjustable rate and depth of respiration are the main features for identifying respiratory patterns, which were investigated in this work. The patient simulator can configure symptoms of different respiratory diseases showing abnormal vital signs. For the apparatus set-up, the sensor was placed at a distance of 25 cm from the middle of the chest of the patient simulator sitting on the hospital bed. The front of the chest faced the direction of the wave transmission.

In this work, multiple types of respiratory patterns were collected as the dataset for the analysis. The patient simulator is programmed to simulate five respiratory patterns: normal, Biot's, Apnea, Apneustic, and Kussmaul. The HR is set constant at 75 beats per minute. The RR is set at 13 breaths per minute for the normal control case. For the diseased cases, the respiratory signals were varied automatically according to the simulated software. Each pattern of respiration is described as follows: Kussmaul is rapid breathing with a sudden change in respiratory depth [1]. Biot's breathing appears as a period of rapid respiration followed by a pause in breathing [24]. Apneustic respiration is a breathing pattern in which a man takes one deep breath and then pauses for a few seconds [13]. Finally, Apnea refers to no inspiratory circulation for at least 10 s [9]. The waveform of all these respiratory patterns is shown in Fig. 2. The total length of signals acquired for each respiratory pattern was as follows: Normal = 2,985 s, Kussmaul = 2,977 s, Biot's = 2,036 s, Apneustic = 3,519 s, and Apnea = 3,265 s.

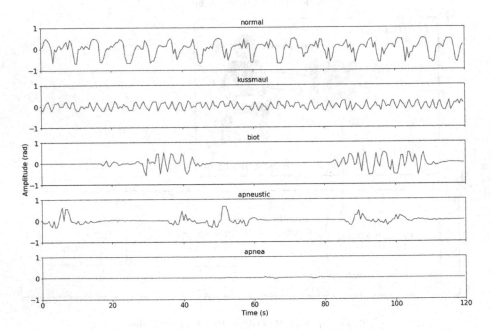

Fig. 2. Examples of 2-min waveforms of different respiratory patterns, including Normal, Kussmual, Biot's, Apneustic, and Apnea, measured from the patient simulator using the IWR1642BOOST mm-wave sensor.

2.2   Data Pre-processing

The raw respiratory signals underwent pre-processing prior to classification. The reduced resolution signals 2 Hz were used for the analysis. The values that were outside the phase difference range between $-\pi$ to π were determined as unwanted noise, specified as undefined (not a number; NaN) values in the calculation. The 3rd-order spline interpolation was applied to fill up the data points with NaN values. These methods give the appropriate signal waveform for further data augmentation. Finally, the pre-processed data were augmented using a window sliding approach with varied window lengths of 120, 180, and 240 s and sliding sizes of 30, 60, and 90 s. The augmented respiratory data were utilized as direct inputs for classification using the simple deep-learning models but underwent further feature extraction for classification using the machine-learning models.

2.3 Feature Extraction

Processing of signal data often involves the extraction of physical features or relevant information from the signals, such as frequency, amplitude, and phase. Moreover, feature extraction helps reduce the dimensionality of the data, which can make it easier to visualize and understand. The extracted features from signal data can be split into three groups for carrying out classification tasks [20], as described below.

Peak and Valley Points: Identifying peaks (local maxima) and valleys (local minima) in signal data is common in signal processing. The Valley-Peak Detection (VPD) algorithm in which the biomedical signal is focused was studied extensively by Kuntamalla *et al.* [11]. This algorithm was developed with a particular target relating to the data from the cardiovascular system. Finding the number of peaks, valleys, and the differences between them includes the steps as follows:

1. The initial signal data are processed with a three-point moving average (MA) smoothing filter to reduce noise. Forward and backward filters were used to handle the phase shift that is eliminated by MA filtering.
2. All peaks and valleys are identified according to their ordinal index in the raw signal $S = \{s_n\}_{n=1}^{N} := \{s_1, s_2, s_3, \ldots, s_N\}$, where N is a positive integer, resulting in an increasing sequence of all peaks $P = \{p_i = s_k : s_k \text{ is a peak}\}$ and all valleys $V = \{v_i = s_k : s_k \text{ is a valley}\}$.
3. The series of peaks and valleys are first decided by comparing the positions of their first point. The VPD processing, as described in Eq. 1, has to start with the valley point.

$$\text{VPD}(k) = p_k - v_k, \qquad k = 1, 2, 3, \ldots, m \qquad (1)$$

4. The final candidate of peak and valley are calculated by searching with the condition in the VPD sequence, as described in Eq. 2. The peak points for instances that satisfy this condition are removed from the candidate sequence of peaks. This modified VPD algorithm is repeated until the number of peak points stays the same for two iterations.

$$\text{VPD}(k) < 0.7 \cdot \frac{\text{VPD}(k-1) + \text{VPD}(k) + \text{VPD}(k+1)}{3} \qquad (2)$$

where $k = 2, \ldots, m - 1$.

Normalized Short-Term Energy: The time-varying energy can be used to differentiate between weak and strong respiratory patterns. A weak respiratory pattern is characterized by a lower energy signal, while a higher energy signal characterizes a strong respiratory pattern. Normalized short-term energy allows more accurate comparisons between different respiratory patterns and reduces the impact of noise on the signal. The process for obtaining an average and standard deviation (SD) of the normalized short-term energy is summarized as follows:

1. The raw signal S is first normalized using the maximum absolute amplitude:

$$s_n^{(1)} = \frac{s_n}{\max_{s \in S}\{|s|\}} \tag{3}$$

Let $S^{(1)} = \{s_n^{(1)}\}_{n=1}^N := \{s_1^{(1)}, s_2^{(1)}, s_3^{(1)}, \ldots, s_N^{(1)}\}$
2. The normalized signal $s_n^{(1)}$ is then transformed as follows:

$$s_n^{(2)} = -1 + \frac{s_n^{(1)} - \min_{s \in S^{(1)}}\{s\}}{\max_{s \in S^{(1)}}\{s\} - \min_{s \in S^{(1)}}\{s\}} \tag{4}$$

3. The normalized short-term energy can be calculated by taking a square of the amplitude of the signal at each point over a period of time length:

$$E_n = \sum_{i=n-(L-1)}^{n} (s_i^{(2)})^2, \quad n \geq L \tag{5}$$

where L is the length of the rectangular window function. In this work, $L = 8$ was applied to calculate the normalized short-term energy.
4. The average and SD of short-term energy is then calculated to be used as the represent features.

Instantaneous Frequency: This signal feature can be used to characterize the signal and enable the detection of changes in the signal data that change over time. The breathing rate can be determined from a respiratory signal using the instantaneous frequency [7]. This is especially useful in applications such as monitoring respiratory patterns.

1. The analytical signal $s_a(t)$ with the terms of the Hilbert transform $\mathcal{H}$ [5], can be used to represent the raw signal, $s(t) = a(t)\cos\phi(t)$, as follows:

$$s_a(t) = s(t) + iy(t) = a(t)e^{i\phi(t)}, \quad y(t) = \mathcal{H}[s(t)] \tag{6}$$

where $a(t) = \sqrt{s^2(t) + y^2(t)}$ is the instantaneous amplitude of the signal at time t. $\phi(t)$ is the instantaneous phase which can be expressed as:

$$\phi(t) = \arctan\left(\frac{y(t)}{s(t)}\right) \tag{7}$$

2. The instantaneous frequency can be derived directly from the derivative of phase:

$$f(t) = \frac{1}{2\pi}\frac{d}{dt}\phi(t) \tag{8}$$

3. The average, SD, and the minimum of instantaneous frequency are then calculated to be used as the represent features.

2.4   Classification Models

In this work, two mainstream classification methods that are widely applicable for data classification were utilized, including machine learning (ML) and simple deep learning (DL) methods. Each classification method has its own distinctive point and training procedure. On the one hand, the ML method is the statistical-based approach where the models can find the correlation between the data features. However, the data feature for ML models is recommended to undergo appropriate pre-processing and feature extraction to achieve optimal classification performance. On the other hand, the simple DL methods perform the feature extraction within the simple DL structure itself as a black box procedure as well as the classification of feature characteristics. This paper compares the performance of the simple DL classification model on the raw data with the application of ML models with some recommended feature extraction techniques for respiratory signals.

Machine Learning Approach. This work performed the ML classification task by using the PyCaret framework [2] which showed the capability to classify extracted features in time series data. Eight features selected from the respiratory data were used as input features in the support vector machine (SVM), k-nearest neighbors (KNN), extra tree (ET), random forest (RF), and decision tree (DT) models along with the class label on each particular respiratory pattern. The extracted features consisted of the number of peaks, the number of valleys, the difference between peaks and valleys, and the average and SD of normalized short-term energy. The average, SD, and the minimum of instantaneous frequency were also considered to be the features of the ML models. Fifty iterations of random hyper-parameter tuning were performed on the ML model training. Each training model was optimized using a 10-fold cross-validation. Each model is then evaluated, compared, and discussed in the result and discussion section.

Deep Learning Approach. In this work, a simple one-dimension convolutional layer was also performed to observe the predictability of the data using a deep learning (DL) model compared with the ML models. The pre-processed dataset was fed to the model without any feature extraction step. The layers of the model consisted of a 240×1 input layer followed by a one-dimensional *Convolution* layer along with a *Dropout*, and a *Maxpooling* layer. The outputs from those three layers are flattened and fed to the fully-connected layer which then classifies the data into five unique classes of respiratory patterns.

2.5   Training and Test Data

For the collected dataset, the data representing each respiratory pattern are not of equal size and length in order to mimic the natural behavior of real-world incidents. Therefore, the proportion of the training dataset to the test dataset is set to be equal for all respiratory patterns to ensure a fair introduction of all patterns into the training and testing data. In this study on the ML and DL approaches, 80% of the data for each respiration pattern was used as the training dataset, with the remaining 20% reserved as the testing dataset.

3   Results and Discussion

In this work, respiratory disease classification using chest movement patterns measured by the non-contact mm-wave sensor was performed using the ML models with an application of the feature extraction technique compared to the DL approach. The study evaluated the trade-off between including and omitting feature extraction in the case of using ML and DL models, respectively, using the F1-score. Where ground truth labels of respiratory disease exist, experimental results are presented and discussed in this section. The dataset used in this study was with imbalanced classes, which is often present in health data. This means that the numbers of samples in the observed respiratory patterns were different, which may lead to biased classification results. The use of F1-score aggregated metrics is a well-established approach to the imbalanced-data classification task [22]. The F1-scores indicating classification performance on experiments varying the window size of the signal, sliding size of the signals, number of samples, and classification techniques, are shown in Table 1. Discussion in terms of optimal model parameter selection and interpretation of results are provided as follows.

Table 1. F1-score of respiratory patterns classification using each feature extraction method with varying window size, sliding size, number of samples, and classification models.

Parameters		Samples	Classification algorithms					
Window size (s)	Sliding size (s)		SVM	KNN	ET	RF	DT	DL
120	30	894	0.989	0.947	0.977	0.994	0.972	0.994
	60	454	0.945	0.955	0.944	0.978	0.912	0.897
	90	306	0.984	1.000	1.000	1.000	0.967	0.864
180	30	842	0.982	0.988	0.994	1.000	0.976	0.964
	60	428	0.965	0.988	0.977	0.977	0.927	0.830
	90	288	0.965	0.949	0.966	0.966	0.949	0.891
240	30	790	0.987	0.994	1.000	1.000	0.994	0.981
	60	402	0.949	0.975	0.963	0.988	0.963	0.896
	90	274	0.945	0.982	1.000	0.964	0.964	0.829

There are differences in the computational requirements of ML and DL approaches. The ML approach extensively requires appropriate data pre-processing and involves an additional step of feature extraction prior to the respiratory signal classification. The feature extraction requires further computation to retrieve the meaningful piece of information. The use of different window lengths and window sizes for each ML model with the application of feature extraction makes no significant difference in classification performance. This is because the statistical features are preserved regardless of the window size of data samples. Specifically, the normalized short-term energy of a wave signal at each data point is proportional to its amplitude square. As long as the amplitudes of the signals show consistent characteristics throughout the signals, varying the window size does not significantly change the average or standard deviation of the normalized short-term energy. Similarly, the instantaneous frequency of a wave is related to its variations over time; therefore, observing its statistical properties is supposed to be unaffected by the length of the signals. Even though the number of peaks and valleys depends on the selected signal window size, they are supposed to be consistent among the same breathing class. As a result, these extracted features can be used to classify the pattern of breathing signals with more or less the same performance.

The feature importance order of the extracted statistical features is illustrated in Fig. 3. High classification performance occurs because breathing patterns are obviously different as seen by the waveform patterns from the non-contact mm-wave sensor. The average energy as the most important feature can be calculated from the square of the amplitude. The pattern in each disease has a different physical representation in high peak, low peak, and no peak which directly influences the energy, as presented in Fig. 2, which is consistent with Kunczik et al. [10] who apply the respiratory belt sensors and camera to classify normal and abnormal respiratory patterns, including Kussmaul, Biot's, Apnea, etc. As opposed to the ML approach, the DL approach eliminated the need for feature extraction, resulting in a more convenient computational protocol.

Another important finding was that the variation in window length and sliding size affected differently on the ML and DL approaches. According to Table 1, the DL approach could achieve a high level of efficiency if the appropriate window and sliding size are applied. The DL approach shows its trend to achieve higher classification performance when the sliding size of the window is smaller. That is the smaller size of sliding thus gives the larger dataset for the DL model, allowing for an improved F1-score, as shown in the results. The higher number of samples as a result of smaller sliding sizes yields higher classification performance regardless of the window size. In the experiment with a window size of 120 s and a sliding size of 30 s, the performance of the DL approach is optimal and is comparable to that of the ML approach. The confusion matrix in Fig. 4 from DL with the above conditions of the window and sliding size presents the result of five classified respiratory patterns, including Apnea, Apneustic, Biot's, Kussmaul, and Normal respiration. It shows that the classification of a case is confused between Biot's and Apneustic. Classification algorithms can struggle to classify between the two patterns of respiration because they have very similar characteristics as illustrated in Fig. 2. A deep learning model with optimized model architecture and parameter tuning can satisfy this high level of precision and accuracy. Whereas, in the case of using ML models, appropriate feature selection must be carefully performed on the training data in order to ensure the model performance that generalizes well.

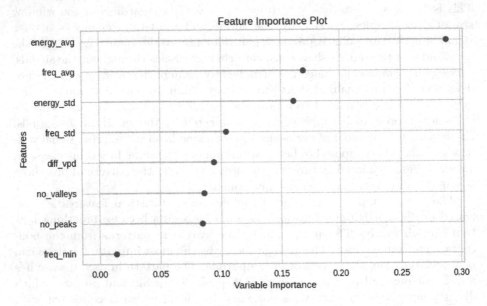

Fig. 3. Feature importance for Random Forest Classifier model training. From top to bottom, statistical features are ordered by importance level, including average normalized short-term energy, average instantaneous frequency, standard deviation of the normalized short-term energy, standard deviation of instantaneous frequency, difference between the number of peaks and number of valleys, number of valleys, number of peaks, and minimum instantaneous frequency. The window length and window sliding size are 240 and 30 s, respectively.

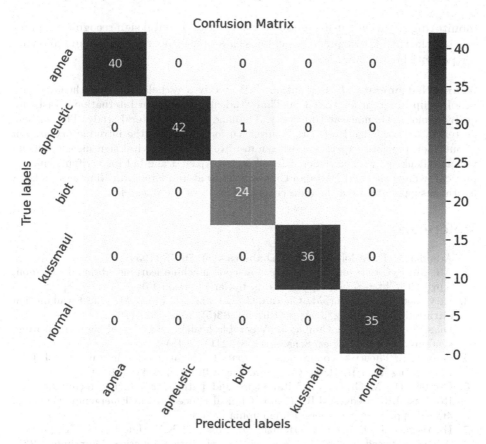

Fig. 4. Confusion Matrix resulting from applying the simple deep learning model with 1D convolutional layer on a test dataset with the window size and sliding size of 120 and 30 s, respectively.

4 Conclusion

Patterns of respiration can be identified by the physical breathing waveform. This research utilized a non-contact mm-wave sensor for measuring the chest movements and turning them into signal waveforms characterizing the breathing patterns. The extracted features from the raw signal enable the ML models to recognize the relationship between the signal features, leading to high-performance classification. The DL model can achieve a comparable classification performance with ML without performing the feature extraction. DL requires a large number of training data, while the window size can be relatively small. The ML approach can reach an F1-score of 1.000 with the application of the feature extraction technique. Moreover, the analysis of statistical feature extraction provides an understanding of short-term energy, instantaneous frequency, peak, and valley that can represent signals in the classification of respiratory disease patterns. This work also emphasizes the great importance of the remote monitoring of patients using a non-contact sensor for vital sign recognition, eliminating the need for frequent in-person visits to healthcare facilities and allowing for potential early diagnosis.

Acknowledgement. The first author (S.B.) receives a scholarship from the Graduate Scholarship Program for Excellent Thai Students, Sirindhorn International Institute of Technology, Thammasat University, Thailand, for his doctoral study. The authors gratefully acknowledge Prof. Dr. Wenwei Yu for organizing the introductory session about their previous experience using mm-wave sensors for vital sign measurements. Special thanks go to Tharit Sereekiatdilok and Apisit Dang-Iad for verifying mathematical expressions; and Nattapol Chiewnawintawat and Krongkan Nimmanwatthana for their support through the data collection phase of the research.

References

1. Adlersberg, D.: Adolf kussmaul. Diabetes **4**(1), 76–78 (1955)
2. Ali, M.: PyCaret: an open source, low-code machine learning library in Python, April 2020. https://www.pycaret.org, pyCaret version 1.0
3. De Groote, A., Wantier, M., Chéron, G., Estenne, M., Paiva, M.: Chest wall motion during tidal breathing. J. Appl. Physiol. **83**(5), 1531–1537 (1997)
4. Dias, D., Paulo Silva Cunha, J.: Wearable health devices-vital sign monitoring, systems and technologies. Sensors **18**(8), 2414 (2018)
5. Gabor, D.: Theory of communication. part 1: The analysis of information. J. Inst. Electr. Eng.-Part III Radio Commun. Eng. **93**(26), 429–441 (1946)
6. Gorgas, D., McGrath, J.: Vital signs and patient monitoring techniques. In: Roberts, J.R., Hedges, J.R., (eds.), Clinical Procedures in Emergency Medicine: 4th ed., pp. 3–28. Saunders, Philadelphia (2004)
7. Harrison, S.J., Bianchi, S., Heinzle, J., Stephan, K.E., Iglesias, S., Kasper, L.: A Hilbert-based method for processing respiratory timeseries. Neuroimage **230**, 117787 (2021)
8. Iyer, S., et al.: mm-wave radar-based vital signs monitoring and arrhythmia detection using machine learning. Sensors **22**(9), 3106 (2022)
9. Javaheri, S., et al.: Sleep apnea: types, mechanisms, and clinical cardiovascular consequences. J. Am. Coll. Cardiol. **69**(7), 841–858 (2017)
10. Kunczik, J., Hubbermann, K., Mösch, L., Follmann, A., Czaplik, M., Barbosa Pereira, C.: Breathing pattern monitoring by using remote sensors. Sensors **22**(22), 8854 (2022)
11. Kuntamalla, S., Reddy, L.R.G.: An efficient and automatic systolic peak detection algorithm for photoplethysmographic signals. Int. J. Comput. Appl. **97**(19) (2014)
12. Lindh, W.Q., Pooler, M., Tamparo, C.D., Dahl, B.M., Morris, J.: Delmar's Comprehensive Medical Assisting: Administrative and Clinical Competencies. Cengage Learning, Boston (2013)
13. Lumsden, T.: Observations on the respiratory centres in the cat. J. Physiol. **57**(3–4), 153–160 (1923)
14. Lyons, M.M., Bhatt, N.Y., Pack, A.I., Magalang, U.J.: Global burden of sleep-disordered breathing and its implications. Respirology **25**(7), 690–702 (2020)
15. Organization, W.H., et al.: WHO compendium of innovative health technologies for low resource settings, 2011–2014: assistive devices, eHealth solutions, medical devices, other technologies, technologies for outbreaks. World Health Organization (2015)

16. Singh, A., Rehman, S.U., Yongchareon, S., Chong, P.H.J.: Multi-resident non-contact vital sign monitoring using radar: a review. IEEE Sens. J. **21**(4), 4061–4084 (2020)
17. Somers, V., Arzt, M., Bradley, T.D., Randerath, W., Tamisier, R., Won, C.: Servo-ventilation therapy for sleep-disordered breathing. Chest **153**(6), 1501–1502 (2018)
18. Soriano, J.B., et al.: Prevalence and attributable health burden of chronic respiratory diseases, 1990–2017: a systematic analysis for the global burden of disease study 2017. Lancet Respir. Med. **8**(6), 585–596 (2020)
19. Villarroel, M., Jorge, J., Pugh, C., Tarassenko, L.: Non-contact vital sign monitoring in the clinic. In: 2017 12th IEEE International Conference on Automatic Face & Gesture Recognition (FG 2017), pp. 278–285. IEEE (2017)
20. Wang, Q., et al.: Frequency-modulated continuous wave radar respiratory pattern detection technology based on multifeature. J. Healthc. Eng. **2021** (2021)
21. Wang, Y., Wang, W., Zhou, M., Ren, A., Tian, Z.: Remote monitoring of human vital signs based on 77-GHZ mm-wave FMCW radar. Sensors **20**(10), 2999 (2020)
22. Wegier, W., Ksieniewicz, P.: Application of imbalanced data classification quality metrics as weighting methods of the ensemble data stream classification algorithms. Entropy **22**(8), 849 (2020)
23. Whited, L., Graham, D.D.: Abnormal respirations. In: StatPearls [internet]. StatPearls Publishing (2022)
24. Wijdicks, E.F.M.: Biot's breathing. J. Neurol. Neurosurg. Psychiatry **78**(5), 512–513 (2007)

Author Index

Printed in the United States
by Baker & Taylor Publisher Services